Canadian
Book
of the Road

Canadian
Book
of the Road

Published by
the Canadian Automobile Association,
in conjunction with
The Reader's Digest Association (Canada) Ltd.

Acknowledgments

The publishers acknowledge with thanks the assistance of the following organizations and individuals:

Department of Economic Development, Northwest Territories
Department of Tourism, Province of Newfoundland
Department of Tourism, Province of Nova Scotia
Department of Tourism, Parks and Conservation, Province of
    Prince Edward Island
Department of Travel and Information, Yukon Territory
Manitoba Department of Tourism, Recreation and Cultural Affairs
Ministère du Tourisme, de la Chasse et de la Pêche du Québec
Ontario Ministry of Industry and Tourism
Saskatchewan Department of Tourism and Renewable Resources
Tourism British Columbia
Tourism New Brunswick
Travel Alberta

Department of Energy, Mines and Resources

Alberta Automobile Association
British Columbia Automobile Association
Manitoba Motor League
Ontario Motor League
Saskatchewan Motor Club

J. A. Carman and the Canadian Government Office of Tourism
F. Gerald Brander and the Travel Industry Association of Canada

A. A. Bailey	Elaine Johnston	Elinor Miller
Pierre Beaupré	Michael Joy	Gina Mrklas
Robert Benn	Angela Kelly	Wendy Nordvik-Carr
Richard Boileau	Rob Kensel	R. Barry Redfern
John Bugden	Jack Kerr	Mary Richaud
Bruce Garrity	Irvin Kroeker	Harvey Sawler
Hazen T. Gorman	Prof. E. H. Lange	Matthew Scott
Russ D. Graham	Sheila K. Larmer	Bruce Sutherland
G. David Hall	Daryll McCallum	Brian Thompson
Jill Hames	John MacCormack	Keltie Voutier
Marc Hardy	Grant McCrae	Peter Walls
Barbara Hladysh	Wyn McIntyre	Doug Wheeler
Harold Hollett	Rhea MacLaughlan	Douglas White
John Howse	Sharon Martin	Don Wickett
Derek R. Johnston	Nolan Matthies	

Thanks is expressed also to provincial highways departments, provincial parks departments, regional tourist associations and tourist bureaus, city and municipal offices across Canada, McGill University Libraries and the Westmount Library.

EDITOR: A. R. Byers
ART DIRECTOR AND DESIGNER: Lucie Martineau
ART DIRECTOR (maps): Pierre Léveillé
ASSISTANT EDITORS: David L. Dunbar, Douglas R. Long, Peter Madely,
    Philomena Rutherford, Ian Walker, Ken Winchester
ASSISTANT DESIGNERS: Johanne Martel, Diane Mitrofanow, Michel Rousseau,
    Odette Sévigny, Lyne Young
ASSISTANT DESIGNERS (maps): Mary Ashley, Hélène Caza, Céline Larivière,
    Alex Wallach
EDITORIAL RESEARCHERS: Patricia Derrick, Horst D. Dornbusch, Barbara Peck,
    and Alice Farnsworth, Marie-Claire Lachapelle, Deena A. Soicher
MAP RESEARCHER: Richard Copeland
PICTURE RESEARCHERS: Guylaine Mongeau, and Rachel Irwin, Susan Wong
ADMINISTRATOR: Denise Hyde-Clarke
COORDINATOR: Nicole Samson-Cholette
INDEXER: Carolyn McConnell
COPY PREPARATION: Lynne Abell, Diane McClenaghan
PRODUCTION: Holger Lorenzen
CARTOGRAPHY: Aéro Photo Inc., Quebec City

ISBN 0-88850-080-7
Printed in Canada 79 80 81 / 6 5 4 3 2 1

Foreword

As President of the Canadian Automobile Association, I am delighted to introduce *Canadian Book of the Road*. This all-inclusive motoring guide leads you along an endless variety of fascinating roads—some of which are famous, and some virtually unknown except to local residents. It records the infinite variety of the Canadian roadside . . . the marvelous sights you will see and the exciting things you can do.

CAA is proud to be associated with the Reader's Digest in the publication of this truly remarkable guide. Similar books have been produced for countries in Europe but this is the first such volume to appear in Canada, a country vaster than all of Europe.

Canadian Book of the Road provides detailed full-color maps of highways, byways and major cities. This unique, informative guide shows where fun and adventure are waiting. In addition, it gives a panoramic view of Canada.

Since 1913, CAA has been deeply involved in all aspects of tourism and has been helping its members with their travel plans. The organization's one and a half million members have come to expect the best in travel information and maps. For this reason, I recommend this book not only to our own members, but to all Canadians who enjoy traveling across this great land.

Cyril Shaw
President
Canadian Automobile Association

How to Use the Book

Canadian Book of the Road is a complete motoring guide to virtually every part of Canada you can reach by car. This 408-page book takes you along more than 48,000 kilometres (30,000 miles) of highways and byways across Canada. It leads you to great recreational locations, awesome scenic wonders, secluded beauty spots, sites where history was made, quaint villages where traditional customs and crafts survive, and bustling, dynamic cities.

Canadian Book of the Road presents all these attractions in 180 road units. There are 168 units that trace routes through country regions, and 12 that describe major cities. The road units, numbered from 1 to 180, fill 368 pages. There are 176 double-page road units; those for Vancouver, Toronto, Ottawa and Montreal have four pages each. (The book has no page numbers.)

Preceding the road units is a 14-page atlas section showing where the various road units are located. By referring to the atlas maps, you can select road units in areas that interest you.

Road unit number.

Endpoints of the road unit.

Distance in kilometres between the endpoints, including the return distance of side trips off the main route.

Name of the region dealt with in the road unit.

An inset map, taken from the atlas section, showing the road unit in relation to its surrounding area. By turning back to the atlas map, you can locate adjacent road units.

A detailed strip map of the road unit. The route is marked in red. Route lengths range from 50 to more than 500 kilometres.

A compass sign.

A miles/kilometres conversion scale.

Symbols identify all the attractions on each road unit. Symbols for various attractions in a specific area are grouped under the name of the nearest city, town or park. There are 45 symbols in all. They are explained in one common legend (see box below, right).

Black figures between two black dots indicate point-to-point distances.

Red figures between two red dots indicate accumulated distances.

City Road Unit

Descriptions of major attractions.

An introductory description of the region.

Road unit number.

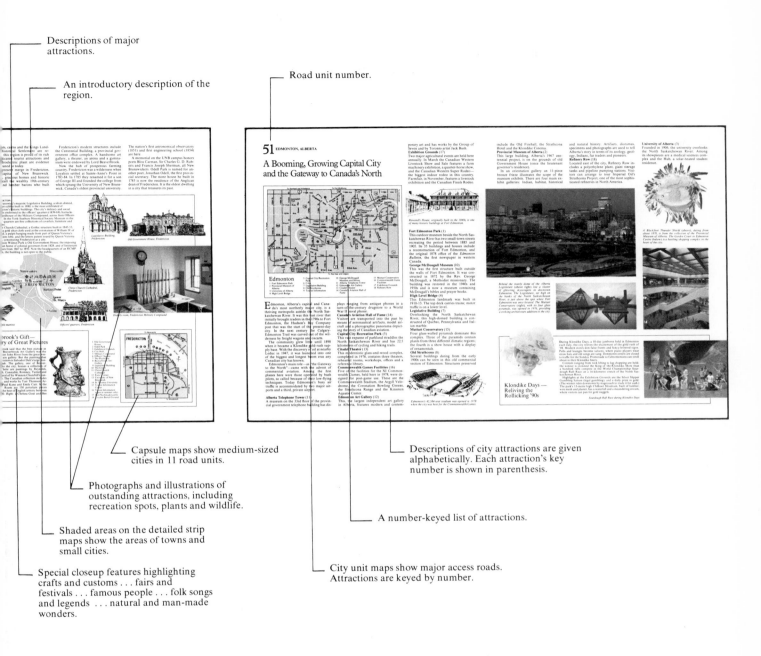

Capsule maps show medium-sized cities in 11 road units.

Photographs and illustrations of outstanding attractions, including recreation spots, plants and wildlife.

Shaded areas on the detailed strip maps show the areas of towns and small cities.

Special closeup features highlighting crafts and customs . . . fairs and festivals . . . famous people . . . folk songs and legends . . . natural and man-made wonders.

Descriptions of city attractions are given alphabetically. Each attraction's key number is shown in parenthesis.

A number-keyed list of attractions.

City unit maps show major access roads. Attractions are keyed by number.

Map Features and Symbols

The legend explaining the features and symbols on the detailed strip maps is on the foldout page at the back of the book. By leaving this page unfolded, you can refer easily from any road unit to the legend.

Road Unit Atlas

This atlas has seven index maps of Canada. Map I shows the entire country and identifies six major areas which appear in more detail in maps II-VII. These area maps pinpoint the book's 180 road units, and identify them by number, within boxes. Below is a list of the road units, grouped by area, with the endpoints for all units, except those in the North.

I. GENERAL MAP OF CANADA

II. THE WEST

1. Port Renfrew/Victoria, B.C.
2. Victoria, B.C.
3. Victoria/Swartz Bay/Victoria, B.C.
4. Goldstream Provincial Park/ Nanaimo, B.C.
5. Port Alberni/Rathtrevor Beach Provincial Park, B.C.
6. Tofino/Port Alberni, B.C.
7. Cumberland/Kelsey Bay, B.C.
8. Campbell River/Gold River, B.C.
9. Langdale/Lund, B.C.
10. Horseshoe Bay/Mount Currie, B.C.
11. Vancouver, B.C.
12. Haney/Harrison Hot Springs, B.C.
13. White Rock/Bridal Veil Falls Provincial Park, B.C.
14. Hope/Kamloops, B.C.
15. Tashme/Osoyoos, B.C.
16. Enderby/Penticton, B.C.
17. Greenwood/Kimberley, B.C.
18. Nakusp/Howser, B.C.
19. Invermere/Crowsnest Pass, B.C.
20. Squilax/Mount Revelstoke National Park, B.C.
21. Glacier National Park/Yoho National Park, B.C.
22. Vermilion Pass/Fairmount Hot Springs, B.C.
23. Masset/Sandspit, B.C.
24. Prince Rupert/Hazelton, B.C.
25. Moricetown/Prince George, B.C.
26. Williams Lake/Bella Coola, B.C.
27. Williams Lake/Bowron Lake Provincial Park, B.C.
28. Lillooet/Williams Lake, B.C.
29. Kamloops/Yellowhead Pass, B.C.
30. Yellowhead Pass/Roche a Perdrix, Alta.
31. Willmore Wilderness Park/ Edson, Alta.
32. Jasper/Sunwapta Pass, Alta.
33. Saskatchewan River Crossing/ Moraine Lake, Alta.
34. Lake Louise/Banff, Alta.
35. Canmore/Calgary, Alta.
36. Calgary, Alta.
37. Coleman/Okotoks, Alta.
38. Crowsnest, B.C./Pincher Creek, Alta.
39. Waterton Lakes National Park/ Saint Mary River Dam, Alta.
40. Fort Macleod/Keho Lake, Alta.
41. Drumheller/Brooks, Alta.
42. (See III. The Prairies)
43. Banff National Park/Rocky Mountain House, Alta.
44. Mission Beach/Sundre, Alta.
45. Red Deer/Dry Island Buffalo Jump Provincial Park, Alta.
46. Devon/Ponoka, Alta.
47. Stettler/Castor, Alta.
48. Vermilion Provincial Park/ Coronation, Alta.
49. High Prairie/Slave Lake, Alta.
50. Evansburg/St. Albert, Alta.
51. Edmonton, Alta.
52. Fort Saskatchewan/Cooking Lake, Alta.
53. Pakan/Mundare, Alta.
54. Athabasca/Owl River, Alta.
55. St. Paul/Wolf Lake, Alta.

III. THE PRAIRIES

42. Medicine Hat/Cypress Hills Provincial Park, Alta.
56. The Battlefords/Meadow Lake Provincial Park, Sask.
57. Saskatoon/Fort Carlton Historic Park, Sask.
58. Prince Albert/Otter Rapids, Sask.
59. Hudson Bay, Sask./Flin Flon, Man./Hudson Bay, Sask.
60. Maple Creek/Swift Current, Sask.
61. Wood Mountain Historic Park/ Minton, Sask.
62. Cutbank/Moose Jaw, Sask.
63. Manitou Beach/Regina, Sask.
64. Cannington Manor Historic Park/ Oxbow, Sask.
65. Echo Valley Provincial Park/ Esterhazy, Sask.
66. Greenwater Lake Provincial Park/Yorkton, Sask.
67. Asessippi Provincial Park/ Gladstone, Man.
68. Virden/Manitou, Man.
69. Shilo/St. François Xavier, Man.
70. Carman/Ste. Anne, Man.
71. Winnipeg, Man.
72. Lower Fort Garry/Hecla Provincial Park, Man.
73. St. Andrews/Grand Beach Provincial Park, Man.
74. Ste. Anne/Seven Sisters Falls, Man.

IV. THE CANADIAN SHIELD/ THE GREAT LAKES

75. Kenora/Kakabeka Falls, Ont.
76. Thunder Bay/Rainbow Falls Provincial Park, Ont.
77. Hawk Junction/Thessalon, Ont.
78. Espanola/South Baymouth/ Little Current, Ont.
79. Sudbury/Parry Sound, Ont.
80. Penetanguishene/Owen Sound, Ont.
81. Tobermory/Wiarton, Ont.
82. Kapuskasing/Kirkland Lake, Ont.
83. Englehart/North Bay, Ont.
84. North Bay/Renfrew, Ont.
85. Grand Bend/Rondeau Provincial Park, Ont.
86. Windsor/Wheatley, Ont.
87. Hawk Cliff/Shakespeare, Ont.
88. Doon/Guelph, Ont.

89. Long Point Provincial Park/Blair, Ont.
90. Hamilton/St. Catharines, Ont.
91. Niagara-on-the-Lake/Thorold, Ont.
92. Dundas/Black Creek Conservation Area, Ont.
93. Toronto, Ont.
94. Barrie/Dwight, Ont.
95. Dorset/Burleigh Falls, Ont.
96. Haliburton/Lakefield, Ont.
97. Warsaw Caves/Trenton, Ont.
98. Belleville/Amherstview, Ont.
99. Kingston/Smiths Falls, Ont.

V. THE ST. LAWRENCE VALLEY/ THE MARITIMES

100. Mill of Kintail/Manotick, Ont.
101. Ottawa, Ont.
102. Aylmer/La Pêche, Que.
103. Gananoque/Johnstown, Ont.
104. Iroquois/South Lancaster, Ont.
105. Williamstown/L'Orignal, Ont.
106. Coteau-du-Lac/Lachine, Que.
107. Papineauville/Saint-Eustache, Que.
108. Montreal, Que.
109. Sainte-Rose/Parc du Mont-Tremblant, Que.
110. Terrebonne/Pointe-aux-Trembles, Que.
111. La Prairie/Hemmingford, Que.
112. Lacolle/Saint-Ours, Que.
113. Rougemont/Stanbridge East, Que.
114. Magog/Georgeville, Que.
115. Sherbrooke/Victoriaville, Que.
116. Sainte-Marie/Lac-Mégantic, Que.
117. Boucherville/Sainte-Croix, Que.
118. Trois-Rivières/Saint-Tite, Que.
119. Cap-de-la-Madeleine/Neuville, Que.
120. Quebec City, Que.
121. Bois de Coulonge/Cartier-Brébeuf National Historic Park, Que.
122. Sainte-Pétronille/Saint-François/ Sainte-Pétronille, Que.
123. Beauport/Cap-Tourmente, Que.
124. Baie-Saint-Paul/Baie-Sainte-Catherine, Que.
125. Lévis/Rimouski, Que.
126. Hébertville/Alma, Que.
127. Larouche/Petit-Saguenay, Que.
128. Tadoussac/Moisie, Que.
129. Sainte-Flavie/Saint-Joachim-de-Tourelle, Que.
130. Anse-Pleureuse/Penouille, Que.

131. Matapédia/Gaspé, Que.
132. Mount Carleton Provincial Park/ New Mills, N.B.
133. Jacquet River/Burnt Church, N.B.
134. Saint-François-de-Madawaska/ Grand Falls, N.B.
135. Drummond/Woodstock, N.B.
136. Medutic/Fredericton, N.B.
137. Marysville/Nelson-Miramichi, N.B.
138. Baie-Sainte-Anne/Moncton, N.B.
139. St. Stephen/Letete, N.B.
140. St. George/Chance Harbour, N.B.
141. Saint John, N.B.
142. Oromocto/Saint John, N.B.
143. Kingston/Hillsborough, N.B.
144. Alberton/Bloomfield Provincial Park, P.E.I.
145. Summerside/Portage/Summerside, P.E.I.
146. Kensington/Parkdale, P.E.I.
147. Scales Pond Provincial Park/ Charlottetown, P.E.I.
148. Southport/Georgetown, P.E.I.
149. Mount Stewart/Cardigan, P.E.I.
150. Yarmouth/Digby, N.S.
151. Deep Brook/Bridgetown, N.S.
152. Bridgetown/New Ross, N.S.
153. Port William/Mount Uniacke, N.S.
154. East Medway/Pubnico Beach, N.S.
155. Voglers Cove/Prospect, N.S.
156. Halifax, N.S.
157. Advocate Harbour/Bible Hill, N.S.
158. Joggins/Balmoral Mills, N.S.
159. Pictou/Port Hastings, N.S.
160. Minasville/Eastern Passage, N.S.
161. Lawrencetown/Auld Cove, N.S.
162. Margaree Valley/Englishtown, N.S.
163. Port Hastings/North Sydney/Port Hastings, N.S.
164. Sydney/Louisbourg/Sydney, N.S.

VI. NEWFOUNDLAND

165. Channel-Port aux Basques/Deer Lake, Nfld.
166. Wiltondale/L'Anse aux Meadows, Nfld.
167. Badger/Gambo, Nfld.
168. Glovertown/Bonavista, Nfld.
169. Goobies/Heart's Content, Nfld.
170. Bay de Verde/Outer Cove, Nfld.
171. St. John's, Nfld.
172. Donovans/Petty Harbour, Nfld.

VII. THE NORTH

173 to 180 (Information about the northern road units precedes area map VII.)

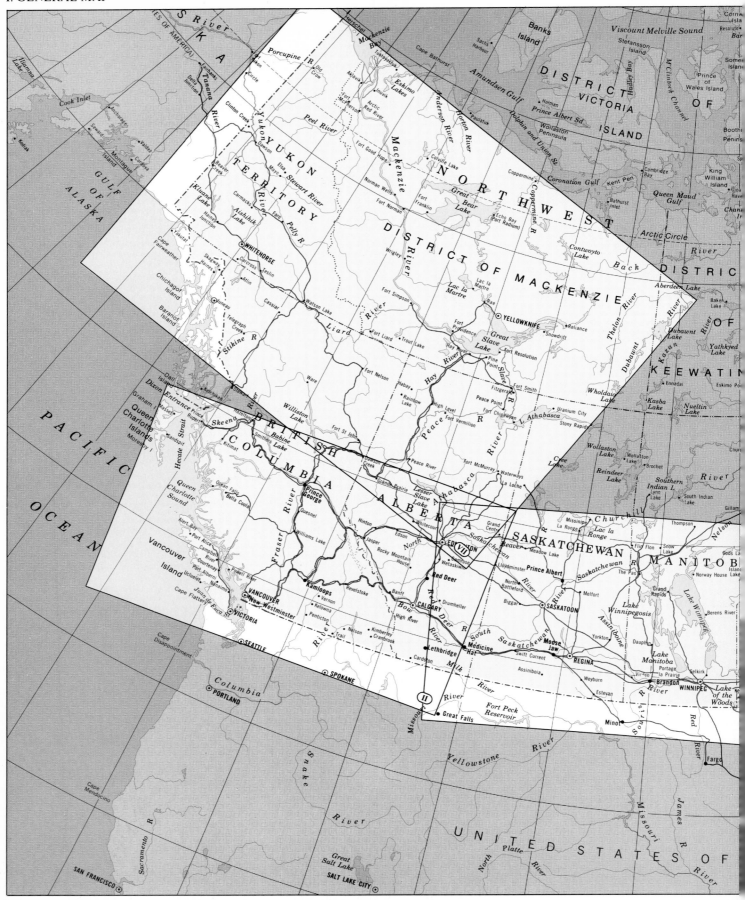

on Island

In Lancaster Sd

BAFFIN BAY

Arctic Bay
Borden Peninsula
Bylot Island
Pond Inlet
rodeur eninsula

FRANKLIN

othia

Clyde

Igloolik
Hall Beach

Committee Bay
Melville Peninsula

TERRITORIES

BAFFIN ISLAND

Foxe Basin

Cape Henry Kater

Cumberland Peninsula
Pangnirtung
Nettilling Lake
Cumberland Sd

DAVIS STRAIT

Disko Island

GOTHAAB

Cape Dyer

Cape Farewell

Repulse Bay
Vansittart Island
Cape Dorchester
Foxe Peninsula
Cape Dorset

Amadjuak Lake

Lemieux Islands

Frobisher Bay
Lake Harbour

Wager Bay
Southampton Island
Roes Welcome Sd
Coral Harbour
Salisbury Island
Nottingham Island

Big Island
Resolution Island

Cape Chidley

LABRADOR SEA

Chesterfield Inlet
Coats Island
Mansel Island

Ivujivik
Sugluk
Deception
Maricourt (Wakeham)
Koartac
Akpatok Island

Port Burwell
Nouveau-Québec (George River)
Hebron
Nutak

NEWFOUNDLAND

ATLANTIC

Cape Smith
Povungnituk R
Povungnituk

Bellin (Payne)

Ungava Bay

George River

Hopedale
Makkovik
Groswater Bay
Cartwright

HUDSON

Ottawa Islands

BAY

Cape Tatnam

Feuilles River (Leaf River)
Mélèzes River
Fort-Chimo
Kokso R
Caniapiscau R

Baleine River (Whale River)

North West River
Goose Bay
Hamilton In
Lake Melville

Battle Harbour
St Anthony

ISLAND OF NEWFOUNDLAND

Fort Severn
River
Winisk

Inoucdjouac (Port Harrison)
Lake Minto

Eau Claire Lake

Bienville Lake

Poste-de-la-Baleine

Schefferville
Smallwood Reservoir
Churchill Falls
Churchill

Little Mecatina R

Ashuanipi Lake
Labrador City

Romaine R

Blanc-Sablon
Notre Dame Bay
Funk I
Gander
Bonavista

Grand Falls

ST JOHN'S

Cape Race

VI

Belcher Islands

Severn River
Winisk
Pickle Lake
Lac Seul

ONTARIO

Armstrong
Sioux Lookout
Nipigon

Lake Nipigon
Atikokan

THUNDER BAY

Lake Superior

Caniapiscau Lake

La Grande River (Fort George River)
Fort George

Nitchequon
Labrador City

Gagnon

Manicouagan Reservoir

GREENLAND

Port au Choix
Port aux Basques
Channel
Stephenville
Marystown
Miquelon Islands (France)
St-Pierre (France)

Placentia B

V

James Bay
Akimiski Island
Eastmain River
Eastmain
Fort Rupert
Fort Albany
Moosonee

Lake Mistassini

Moisie River

Manicouagan

Sept-Iles
Port-Cartier

Anticosti Island

Gulf of St Lawrence

Madeleine Islands

Sydney
Cape Breton Island
Canso

Sable Island

OCEAN

Albany River
Nakina
Geraldton
Hearst
Kapuskasing
Cochrane
Ames
Senneterre

QUEBEC

Chibougamau
Matagami

Lake St-Jean
Roberval

Desmaraisville
Gouin Reservoir

Chicoutimi
Alma
Arvida
Port-Alfred
La Tuque

Baie-Comeau
Matane
Ste-Anne-des-Monts
Gaspé
Chandler

Rimouski
Campbellton
Bathurst
Chatham

Chaleur Bay
Tracadie

PRINCE EDWARD ISLAND
CHARLOTTETOWN
Summerside
New Glasgow
Truro

NOVA SCOTIA

HALIFAX
Bridgewater
Shelburne
Cape Sable
Yarmouth

Nipigon
Marathon
Wawa

Timmins
Kirkland Lake
Noranda
Rouyn
Val-d'Or

St-Maurice R

Maniwaki
Mont-Laurier

Shawinigan
Trois-Rivières
QUEBEC
Lévis
Thetford Mines

Drummondville
Sorel
St-Hyacinthe
Sherbrooke

Edmundston
Rivière-du-Loup

Woodstock
FREDERICTON
St Stephen

Newcastle
NEW BRUNSWICK

Moncton
SAINT JOHN

Amherst
Kentville

Bay of Fundy

Sault Ste Marie
Blind River

SUDBURY
North Bay
Deep River
Pembroke
Renfrew
Petawawa

Ottawa River

Hull
OTTAWA
Cornwall

St-Jérôme
MONTREAL
St-Jean
Granby

Lake Champlain

Connecticut R

Nipissing
Lake Nipissing
Parry Sound

Smiths Falls
Brockville
Kingston

Belleville
Trenton
Peterborough

Georgian Bay

Manitoulin Island

Owen Sound
Barrie
Oshawa

Lake Huron

Goderich
TORONTO
Lake Ontario
St CATHARINES
Niagara Falls
BUFFALO

KITCHENER
Guelph
Brantford
HAMILTON
LONDON
St Thomas
Sarnia
Chatham

Lake Erie

Hudson R

SYRACUSE
ALBANY
BOSTON

Cape Cod

Nantucket Island

IV

EAPOLIS
PAUL
Mississippi R

MILWAUKEE
Lake Michigan

GRAND RAPIDS

DETROIT
WINDSOR

CLEVELAND
TOLEDO
CHICAGO

NEW YORK
Long Island

PROVIDENCE

ERICA

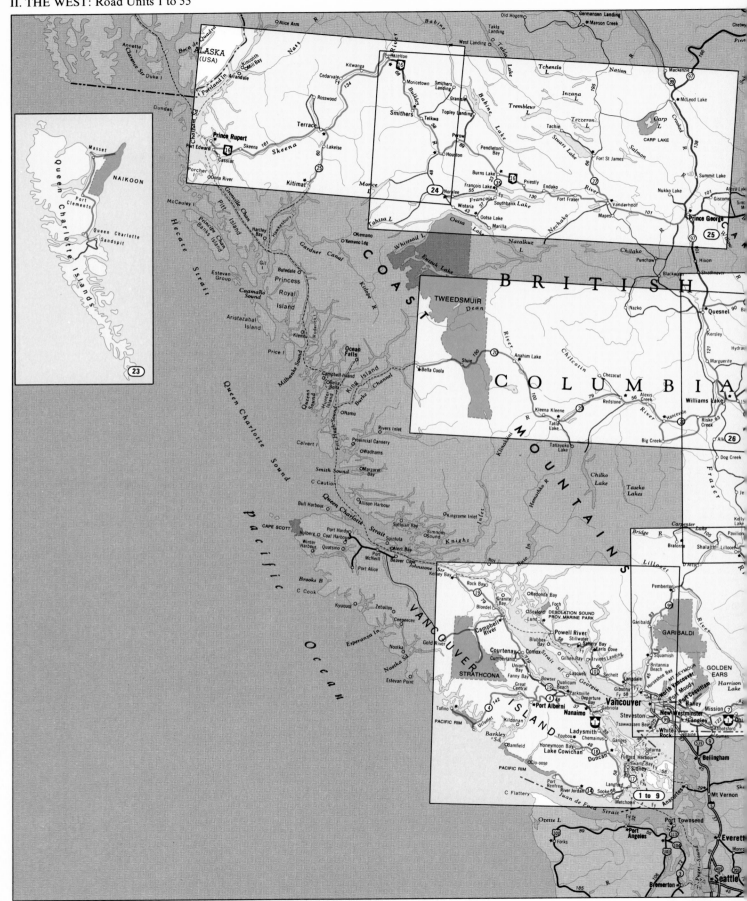

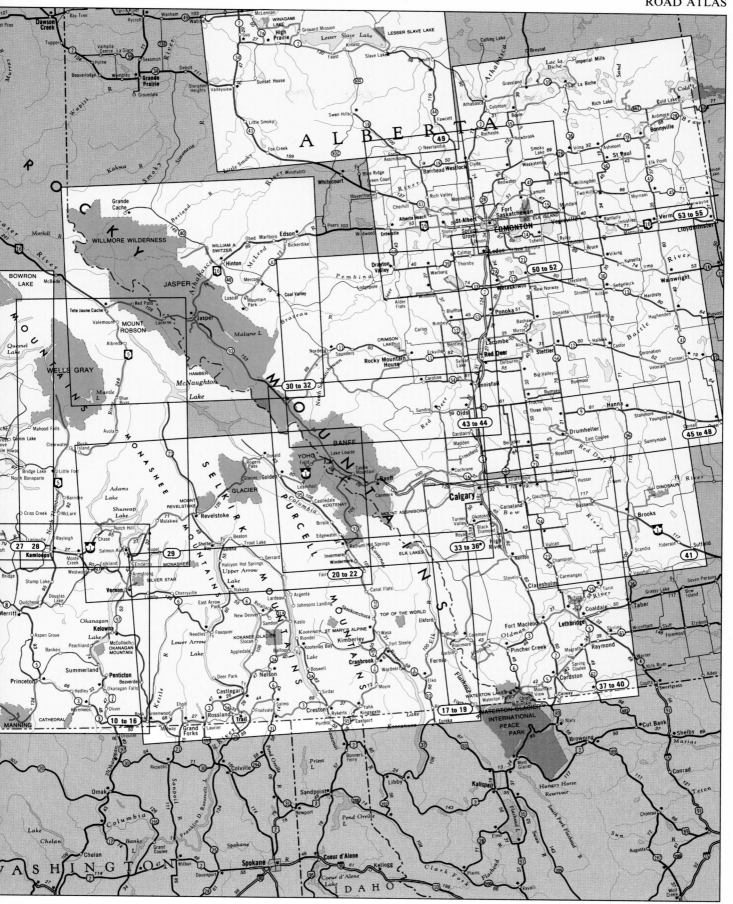

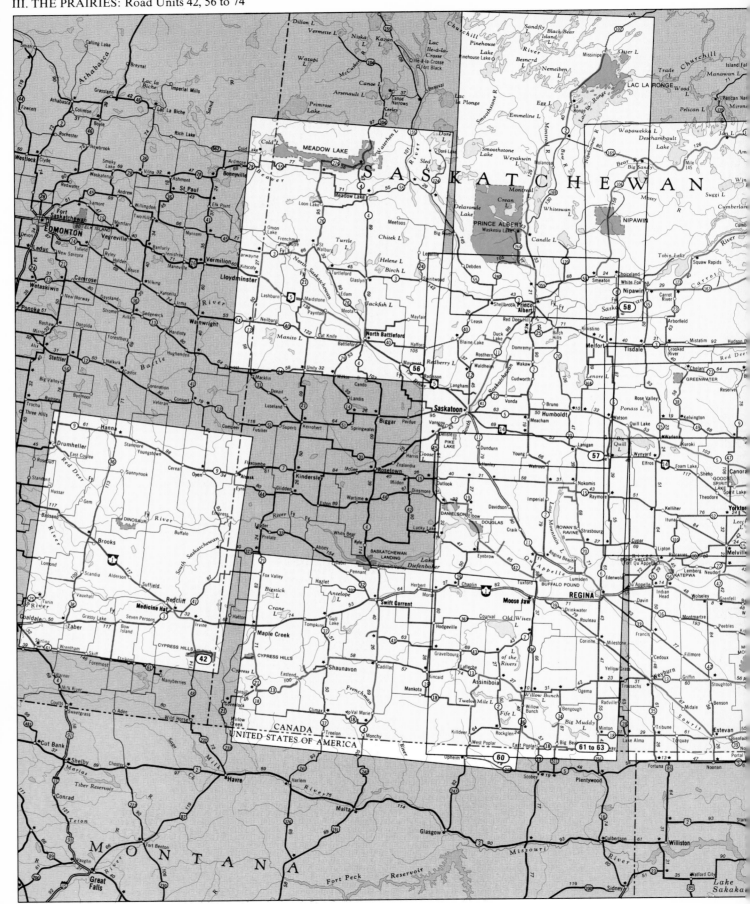

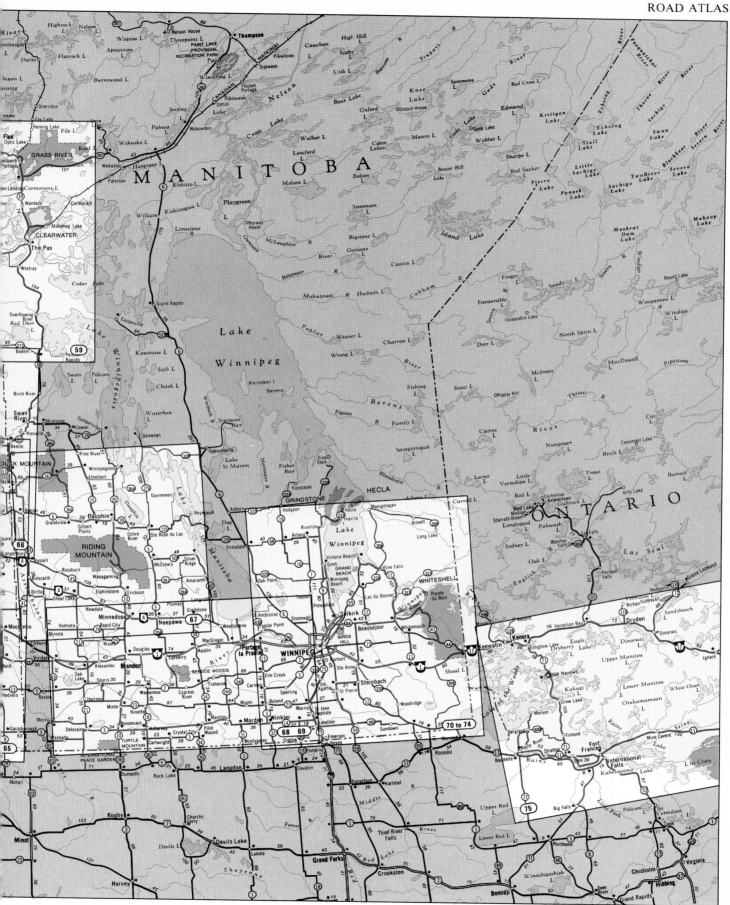

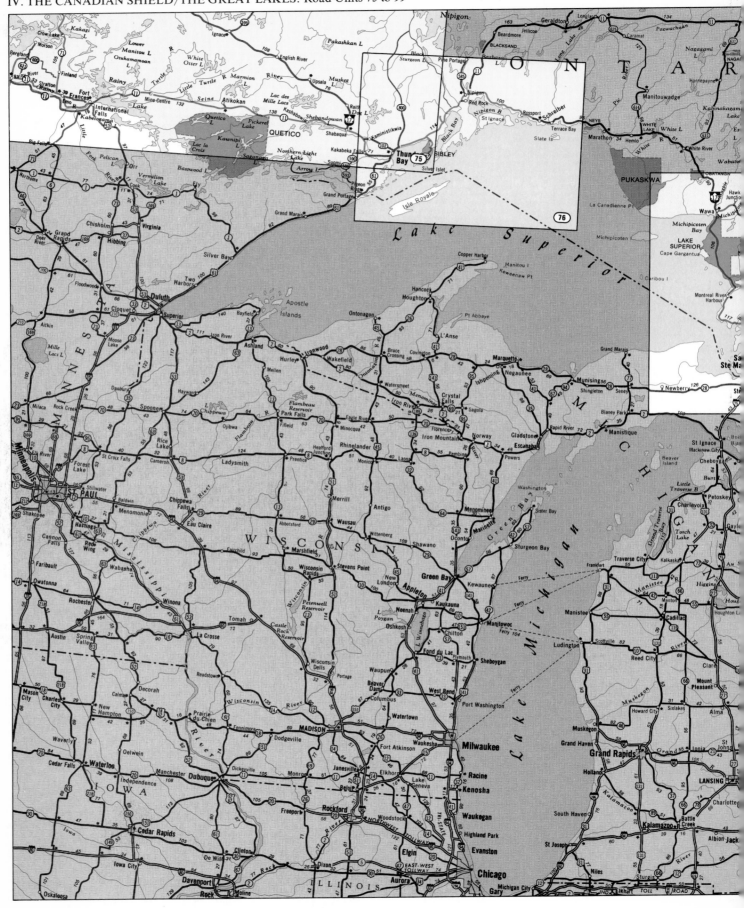

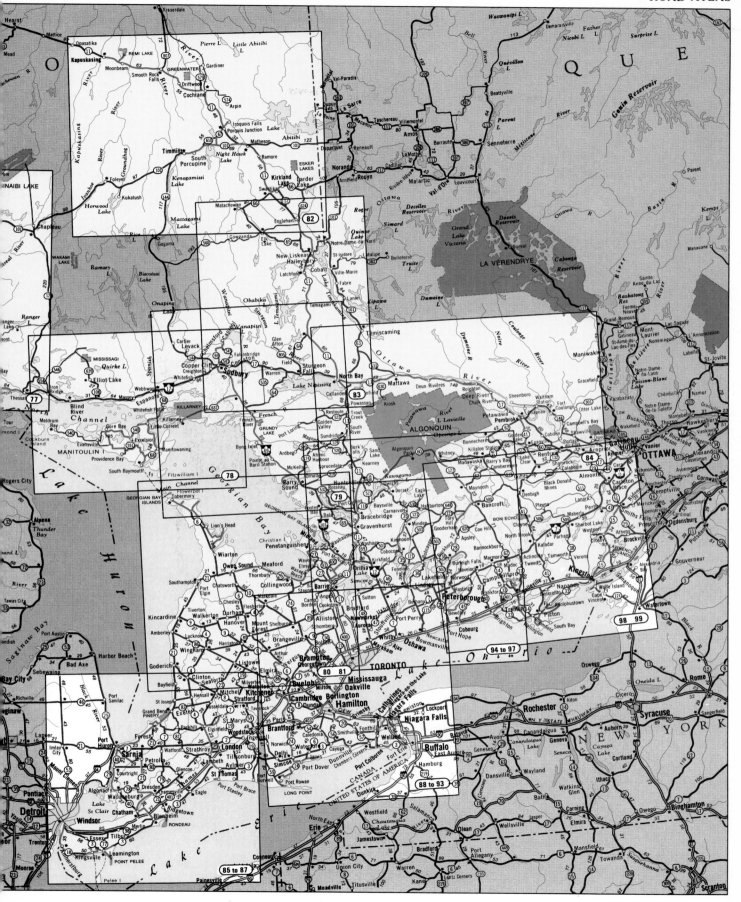

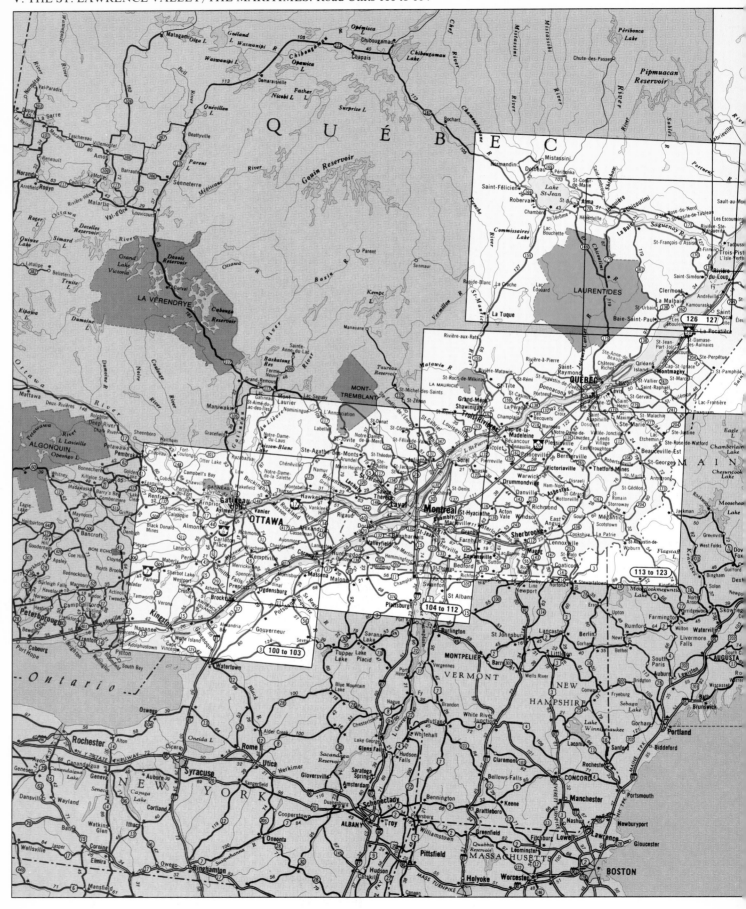

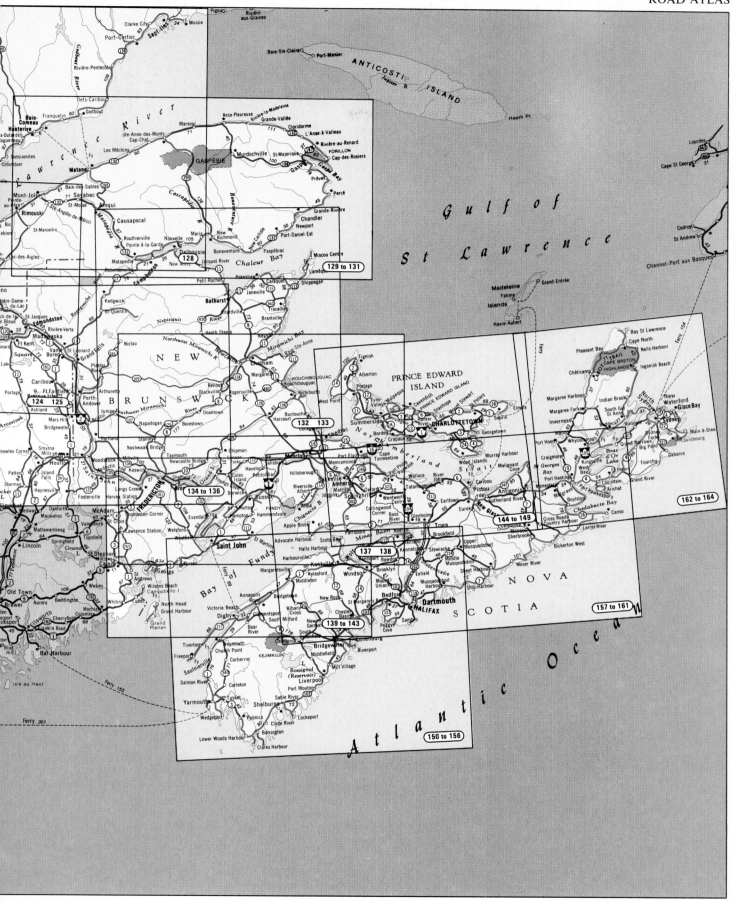

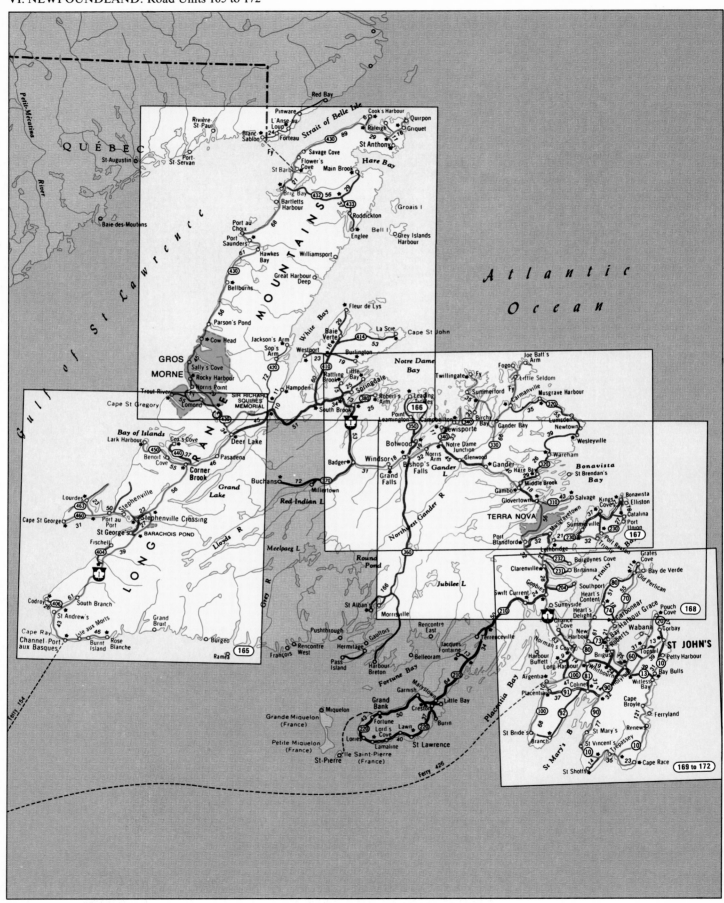

Northern Adventure Roads

The northern road units cover a
wild and beautiful country—once
impossibly remote but now open for
adventure. They take you along all-
weather roads that include some of
Canada's most famous highways:
the Alaska, the Klondike and the
Mackenzie. Map VII on the following two pages of the atlas section
pinpoints these road units in the
North.

Driving North

The unpaved highways stretching across Canada's Northwest are often described as hazardous. In fact, they are well engineered and well maintained. With planning and care, the traveler can minimize the problems they present.

There are long distances between northern garages and accommodations. You can check the location of the services along your route at tourist information bureaus. Make reservations well in advance because accommodations are limited. (If you intend to drive north in winter, contact the territorial or provincial tourism departments about road conditions.)

The main difference between summer driving in the north and elsewhere in Canada is the need for protection against gravel and dust. A northern garage will prepare your car before you set out. Headlights should be fitted with clear plastic covers. A wire-mesh screen across the grille will shield it and the radiator.

Flying gravel can easily damage the gas tank: inserting heavy rubber matting between the gas tank and its securing straps provides adequate protection. Substituting metal fuel lines for rubber underneath the car helps ensure against ruptures.

Dust is worst in construction areas and where heavy rain has disturbed road surfaces. (After a prolonged downpour, highways may be impassable; check with the nearest RCMP detachment, road maintenance office or tourist information bureau.) To help keep dust out of the car, close the windows and turn on the fan. Filters in the heating and air-conditioning systems keep out some dust. Mosquito netting placed over the air intake keeps out more.

Do not drive fast on gravel roads. A speeding car throws gravel and a cloud of dust, creating a hazard for other vehicles. At high speeds you can easily lose control of your car if you hit a pothole or begin to slide over the small, loose stones. Speeding on gravel will also wear down tires quickly and lead to a blowout. Do not be tempted to drive in the middle of the road, where the surface may be smoother. An oncoming vehicle, also in the middle of the road, may appear unexpectedly.

It is advisable to carry an extra tire, a tow rope or chain, tools and spare parts, a first-aid kit, and extra food. If you have a breakdown, stay with your car and flag down a passing driver for assistance. Do not venture more than 100 metres from the road; you can easily become disoriented and lost.

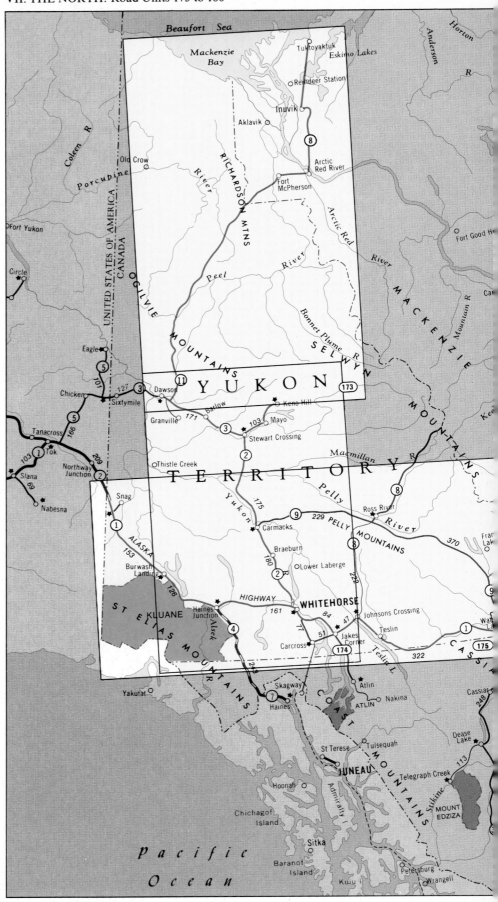

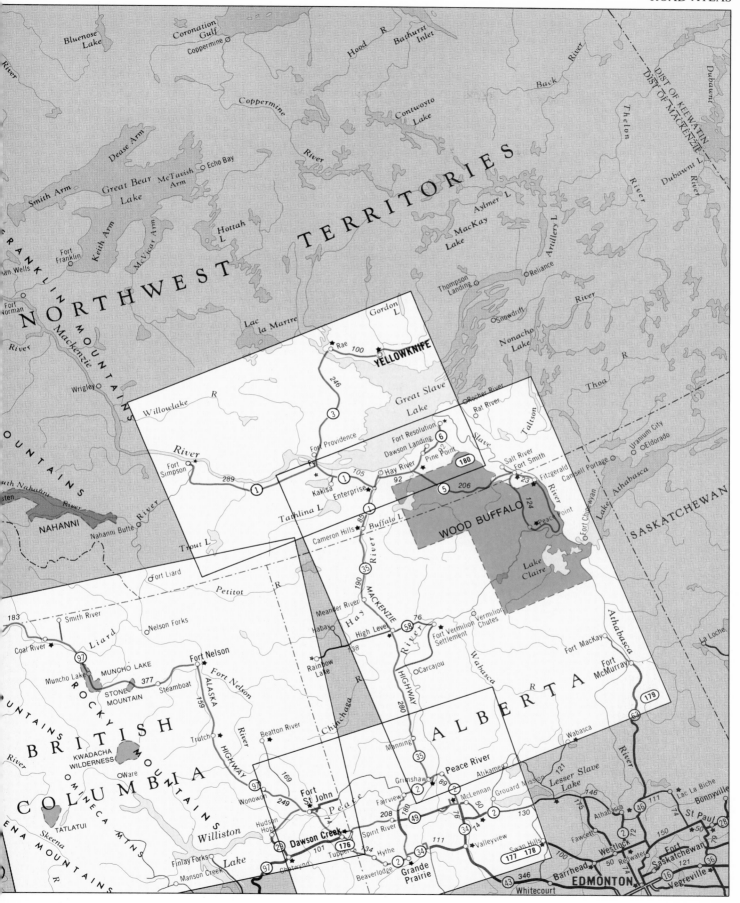

Restless Tides and Dense Forests Along a Mist-Shrouded Coast

Vancouver Island

Winding along the coast of southern Vancouver Island, Highway 14 is one of Canada's most breathtaking drives. Echoes of the past are everywhere: old coach inns, forts, lighthouses, churches and monuments. The scenery varies from the pastoral to the spectacular: beaches and headlands, neat fields and wild forests, the mountains of the Olympic Peninsula high and hazy across the Juan de Fuca Strait. Fog and mist often envelop this landscape, bestowing a quality of deep mystery.

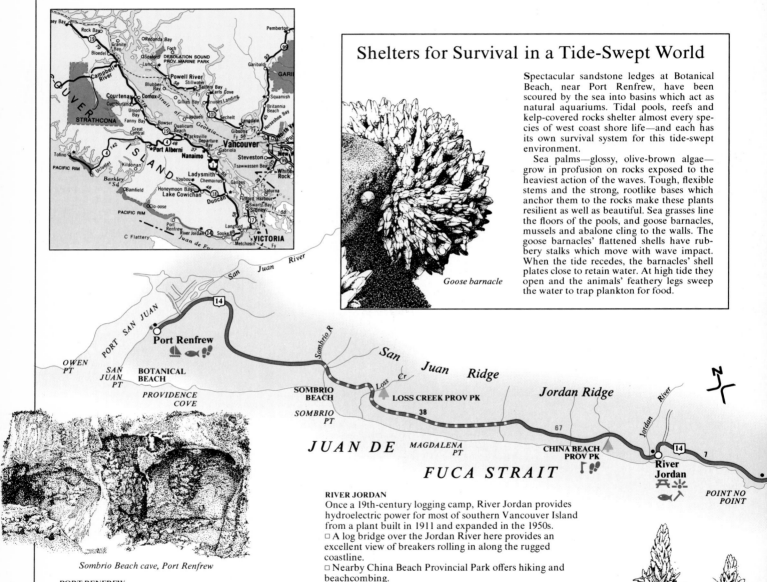

Shelters for Survival in a Tide-Swept World

Spectacular sandstone ledges at Botanical Beach, near Port Renfrew, have been scoured by the sea into basins which act as natural aquariums. Tidal pools, reefs and kelp-covered rocks shelter almost every species of west coast shore life—and each has its own survival system for this tide-swept environment.

Sea palms—glossy, olive-brown algae—grow in profusion on rocks exposed to the heaviest action of the waves. Tough, flexible stems and the strong, rootlike bases which anchor them to the rocks make these plants resilient as well as beautiful. Sea grasses line the floors of the pools, and goose barnacles, mussels and abalone cling to the walls. The goose barnacles' flattened shells have rubbery stalks which move with wave impact. When the tide recedes, the barnacles' shell plates close to retain water. At high tide they open and the animals' feathery legs sweep the water to trap plankton for food.

Goose barnacle

Sombrio Beach cave, Port Renfrew

PORT RENFREW
The British Columbia Forest Products Company holds timber rights in this area. Port Renfrew is the company town.
□ At Sombrio Beach are deep, surf-carved caves, a waterfall, and a sandstone shelf pitted with tidal pools.
□ Port Renfrew is the southern terminus of the West Coast Trail, a former lifesaving path. Hikers must be ferried across the Gordon River to the trail head, now part of Pacific Rim National Park. From there it is a rugged, week-long trek north to Bamfield.

RIVER JORDAN
Once a 19th-century logging camp, River Jordan provides hydroelectric power for most of southern Vancouver Island from a plant built in 1911 and expanded in the 1950s.
□ A log bridge over the Jordan River here provides an excellent view of breakers rolling in along the rugged coastline.
□ Nearby China Beach Provincial Park offers hiking and beachcombing.

POINT NO POINT
From one survey point, this section of coastline appeared to early navigators to be a prominent headland. Sightings from a different angle showed no point at all. An 1895 survey designated the area as "Glacier Point," but local residents preferred the more whimsical "Point No Point." In 1957, their appeal was upheld by the Canadian Geographical Place Names Board. "Point No Point" became official.

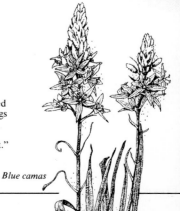

Blue camas

0 1 2 3 4 5 Miles
0 2 4 6 8 Kilometres

The intricate coastline was well known to 18th-century Spanish explorers, who anchored their ships here in search of gold. Later, homesteaders fought the dense bush, but eventually they drifted away, abandoning their hard-won clearings to the forest. When Highway 14 was completed in 1957, the riches lay not in gold or farming, but in lumber and fishing.

Some 200 species of birds and 20 types of mammals inhabit the sea and shore—some seldom seen because they are nocturnal or attuned to the dense, often impenetrable forest. At Botanical Beach, near Port Renfrew, receding tides reveal a rich variety of marine life in tidal pools.

The coastline here is a winding and a twisting of waterways, a confusion of islands and bays, inlets and cliffs whose flanks slip sharply into the sea. In places, the forest opens up to sweeping views of the Juan de Fuca Strait, a hint of the broad Pacific beyond.

Sooke harbor

ROYAL ROADS MILITARY COLLEGE
James Dunsmuir, a premier and later a lieutenant governor of British Columbia, invested much of his personal profits from coal, lumber and shipping in the most opulent estate in western Canada. Sandstone and granite parapets crown the stone Hatley Castle (1908). Promenades pass Italian, French and Japanese gardens, game courts, stables and guest cottages. Following Dunsmuir's death in 1920, the property was purchased by the federal government, which established Royal Roads Military College. The estate's botanical gardens are open to the public.

*Hatley Castle,
Royal Roads Military College*

SOOKE
This important logging, farming and fishing center has Canada's southernmost harbor.
□ The area's first settler was Capt. Walter Grant, who established a farm here in 1849 under contract to the Hudson's Bay Company. No dedicated farmer, Grant and several of his tenants were soon lured to the goldfields of California. But Grant did leave a lasting mark on Vancouver Island. During a winter trip to Hawaii, he was given several broom seeds by the British consul. Planted on Grant's farm, the hardy broom eventually spread throughout the island.
□ All Sooke Day, held in July, features logging competitions such as high rigging, sawing, birling (log rolling), and ax throwing. Food is prepared at the fairground the way prospectors cooked during the 1864 gold rush at nearby Leech River: beef is roasted in a pit of alder coals, and salmon is grilled over open fires.

METCHOSIN
St. Mary the Virgin Church, a simple black and white frame building (1879), is the "Easter Lily Church." In spring, masses of dogtooth violets spread a white mantle among the headstones of pioneers buried near this church that they helped to build.

Black oyster catcher

Columbian black-tailed deer

Fisgard Lighthouse, Fort Rodd Hill National Historic Park

FORT RODD HILL NATIONAL HISTORIC PARK
Fortified in 1895, Fort Rodd Hill was an important coastal defense battery for many years. A battery of six-inch cannon protected Victoria Harbour and the Royal Navy yards at Esquimalt until the fort was declared obsolete in 1956. The cannon are gone, but their bunkers remain—huge cement horseshoes on a grassy knoll overlooking the ocean. Visitors can inspect the fort's command post, the warrant officers' quarters, the smith's shop and forge, the canteen and the guardhouse.
□ Adjacent to the fort is Fisgard Lighthouse, a 14-metre column that has guided ships through the Juan de Fuca Strait since 1860. Its light is visible for 16 kilometres in clear weather. (The lighthouse is not open to the public.)
□ A herd of tame Columbian black-tailed deer roams the 18-hectare park surrounding the fort and lighthouse.

A Gentle City That Preserves Its Totems and High Tea

In the beginning it was a fur-trade post, then a booming gold-rush town. Now it is Canada's gentlest city, a civilized place of unhurried streets and enchanting gardens where flowers bloom year round.

Victoria, capital of British Columbia, is also Victorian, a bit of England consciously preserved amid the primitive beauty of the Pacific coast. Some of this is to please the tourists—the double-decker buses and tallyho carriages—but most of it is natural. The people and the city are mostly British in origin; this is reflected in fine shops selling tweeds and bone china, white-clad lawn bowlers behind the Crystal Garden, high tea in the Empress Hotel, and the crack of a cricket bat in Beacon Hill Park.

Victoria is elegant and modern, but its past is well preserved in museums, art galleries, pioneer homes and great mansions. In Thunderbird Park, near the dignified Parliament Buildings, is a forest of totem poles that evokes the highly developed Indian cultures of the Pacific coast.

The city moves at a quiet but steady pace, its inner harbor dotted with pleasure craft and its streets bustling with strollers.

Art Gallery of Greater Victoria (20)
Canadian artists represented include A.Y. Jackson, David Milne, Homer Watson

and Emily Carr. Also displayed are Auguste Rodin's bronze statue, *Mercury Emerging from a Cloud*, and Pier Fiorentino's painting, *Madonna and Child with Saint John*. In an outstanding Oriental collection are por-

Among Victoria's attractions are tree-shaded Beacon Hill Park (right) and its 38-metre totem pole (detail below), and the Provincial Museum and Archives (below right).

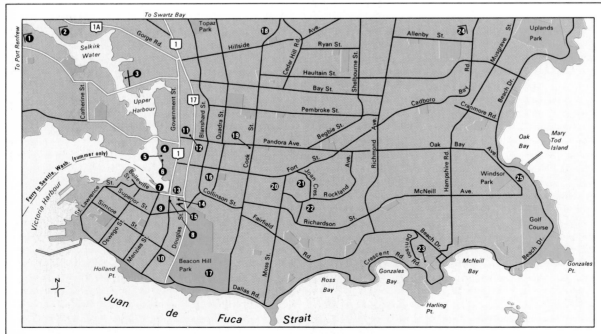

Victoria

1 Craigflower Schoolhouse Museum
2 Craigflower Manor
3 Point Ellice House Museum
4 Bastion Square
5 Maritime Museum of British Columbia
6 Tourist Information
7 Pacific Undersea Gardens, Limited
8 British Columbia Provincial Archives/ British Columbia Provincial Museum
9 Parliament Buildings
10 Emily Carr House
11 Centennial Square
12 McPherson Playhouse
13 Empress Hotel
14 Thunderbird Park
15 Helmcken House Historical Museum
16 Christ Church Cathedral
17 Beacon Hill Park
18 Spencer Castle
19 CAA
20 Art Gallery of Greater Victoria
21 Craigdarroch Castle
22 Government House
23 Walbran Park
24 University of Victoria
25 Sealand of the Pacific, Limited

The Parliament Building (above) was built of native stone and slate in 1898. A weathered, 19th-century totem (right) is preserved in Thunderbird Park.

celain figures and intricate jade carvings.

Bastion Square (4)
Restorations in this downtown neighborhood, once a muddy hangout for prospectors and drifters, include the city's first jail and courthouse (1889).

Beacon Hill Park (17)
Expansive lawns, rose gardens, an aviary, a cricket field and an outdoor theater grace this park, a gift to the city from the Hudson's Bay Company in 1882. Here are a Chinese bell cast in 1627, a 38-metre totem pole, and a plaque marking Kilometre Zero of the Trans-Canada Highway.

Centennial Square (11)
Surrounding the square are the renovated Old City Hall (1878), the McPherson Playhouse (1912), and an attractive shopping arcade.

Craigdarroch Castle (21)
Robert Dunsmuir, "coal king of Vancouver Island," built this great mass of stone and stained glass for his wife. It was completed only after his death in 1889.

Craigflower Manor (2)
This estate was originally a farm established in 1853 by HBC bailiff Kenneth McKenzie. Now a museum, the restored manor displays 19th-century furniture and artifacts.

Craigflower School (1)
Western Canada's oldest standing schoolhouse (1855) is now a pioneer museum.

Empress Hotel (13)
With its vine-covered walls and formal gardens, this impressive waterfront edifice is a historic site as well as an opulent hotel. Long the city's social center, the hotel was built by the CPR in 1905.

Helmcken House (15)
Built in 1852 by J. S. Helmcken, who helped negotiate British Columbia's entry into Confederation, this house is now a provincial museum.

Maritime Museum (5)
Displays tracing Victoria's maritime history include ship models, figureheads, ships' tools, bells, naval uniforms and a cat-o'-nine-tails. The 11-metre *Tilikum* (1860), a dugout canoe modified to a three-masted schooner, sailed from Victoria to England in 1901-04.

Pacific Undersea Gardens (7)
A giant octopus, sharks, sea cucumbers and other sea life are viewed through windows below the surface of the inner harbor.

Parliament Buildings (9)
These imposing buildings house the British Columbia government. Crowning the copper-covered dome of the main building (1898) is a statue of Capt. George Vancouver.

Across the street from the Parliament Buildings are the Provincial Museum and Archives (8) and the 62-bell Netherlands Centennial Carillon, a gift from Canadians of Dutch origin. A great dugout canoe with

Imposing Craigdarroch Castle, completed in 1898, now houses the Victoria Conservatory of Music.

eight carved wooden figures of Nootka Indian whalers dominates the first floor of the museum. There are Emily Carr paintings, wildlife dioramas, and a replica of Captain Cook's HMS *Discovery*.

Point Ellice House Museum (3)
Victorian furnishings are displayed in the ancestral home of Peter O'Reilly, one of the founders of British Columbia.

Sealand of the Pacific (25)
A glassed-in observation gallery provides underwater views of seals, sea lions, eels and sea plumes; in another pool are two killer whales.

Spencer Castle (18)
This Tudor-style mansion, built early in the 1900s, is crowned by a four-story turret.

Thunderbird Park (14)
A collection of totem poles, most carved between 1850 and 1890, represents the styles of several Pacific coast tribes. The park has cedar dugout canoes and a replica of a 19th-century Kwakiutl house.

Klee Wyck —Victoria's 'Crazy Old Millie Carr'

1871-1945   EMILY CARR   painter peintre
Canada /6

To the Indians of Vancouver Island she was *Klee Wyck*—the Laughing One. To the stolid citizens of her native Victoria she was "Crazy Old Millie Carr"—an eccentric painter who wheeled her pet monkey around in a baby carriage.

Influenced by the Impressionists and Canada's Group of Seven, Emily Carr evolved a bold style that captured the haunting mystery of deserted Indian villages and the wild grandeur of British Columbia's coast. Her paintings are characterized by sculptural forests and skies bursting with light and energy.

Despite early criticism of her work, Emily Carr produced about 1,000 major paintings and drawings before her death in 1945. Her book *Klee Wyck* won the 1941 Governor-General's Award for literature. Her painting *Big Raven* (*left*) adorns a stamp commemorating the centennial of her birth (1971). The restored Emily Carr House (10) is now a museum and art gallery.

Coach Roads and Hedges, and the Skylarks of England

Vancouver Island

Low tide at Patricia Bay

PATRICIA BAY

The sandy sweep of Patricia Bay abounds in marine life. Each receding tide reveals goose barnacles clinging to drifting logs, shrimps digging in the sand, and a teeming multitude of other creatures—swimmers, drifters, crawlers and burrowers. Beachcombing enthusiasts watch for telltale squirts of water in the sand, then dig down on the seaward side to harvest littleneck and butter clams. Great numbers of shorebirds congregate on the beach and headlands in winter.

Secluded Islands in the Strait of Georgia

Gulf Islands car ferry

The tranquil Gulf Islands, lying north of the Saanich Peninsula in the Strait of Georgia, can be reached by car ferry from Swartz Bay. They consist of 15 relatively large islands and several dozen smaller ones, some of which are islets scarcely above water at high tide. Their rugged coastlines are molded by wind and sea; their hollows and caves are created by undercutting waters.

Saltspring Island was settled in the 1850s by California blacks—many of them former slaves—who built successful farming and lumbering operations. Later, lured by the Fraser River gold rush, other settlers arrived in the area. Many remained to establish fruit farms. Today there is no commercial fruit production, but the old fruit trees still stand.

Saltspring lamb, raised on the island's salty marshes and served as a traditional English roast with mint sauce, is a local delicacy. On sand and gravel beaches visitors can find butter and horse clams, rock and Dungeness crabs, and oysters.

BUTCHART GARDENS

In a vast bowl amphitheater of solid rock—a former quarry—thousands of flowering plants, trees and shrubs create a wonderland of color. Footpaths lead across emerald lawns past towering arborvitae trees to a lake banked with marigolds. From the far rim of the bowl, hung with ivy, a waterfall cascades into a fountained pool. The gardens, with several distinctive sections, are planned to bloom year round. The Italian topiary garden has trees and shrubs trimmed in ornamental shapes, Florentine arches and statuary, and a star-shaped lily pond flanked by beds of seasonal flowers. In the Japanese garden are bonsai (dwarf trees), rhododendrons, a secluded waterfall, lacquered bridges and lantern-lit summerhouses on stilts. Arched walkways wind through the English rose garden. The road to the gardens has been planted with more than 500 Japanese cherry trees. At night, the soft glow of hidden lamps illuminates the paths and gardens.

Butchart Gardens

```
0    5    1    1.5   2    2.5 Miles
0    1    2    3    4 Kilometres
```

Vancouver Island's Saanich Peninsula is a gentle place. Nothing dramatic, no great mountains or wild rivers, just the quiet pleasures of country life. There are beaches for clam digging and bird-watching, countless little meandering lanes, weathered churches and welcoming inns, fresh produce and old-fashioned hospitality.

Many of the peninsula's roads trace old stagecoach routes, now paved but still for the most part narrow, sinuous and hemmed in by thick hedges. Roadside gardens are bright with fragrant English violets, and here and there are gabled Tudor cottages. Beyond the old cemetery of Holy Trinity Church (1885), in the fields around Victoria Airport, short-eared owls and English skylarks soar. Though the skylark, buffy brown and little bigger than a sparrow, is difficult to see, its tireless torrent of melody is unmistakable.

Butchart Gardens, at the end of a winding road lined with flowering cherry trees, is a onetime limestone quarry transformed into a fabulous huge flower bowl. High on a rocky bluff nearby, the dome of the Dominion Astrophysical Observatory looms above gnarled Garry oaks like something from science fiction.

Scattered in the Strait of Georgia off the northern tip of the Saanich Peninsula is the archipelago of the Gulf Islands. Accessible by sea and air, they have a slow-paced existence of field, forest and seascape, happily oblivious to the world outside.

SIDNEY
Saanich Peninsula history is highlighted in the Sidney Historical Society Museum, housed in a former customs building (1912). Displays include an early edition of Capt. George Vancouver's Journals (1801), farm tools, Indian artifacts and a dugout cedar canoe.
□ Sidney Spit Marine Provincial Park, on Sidney Island, is five kilometres by ship from town. There are several campsites and picnic areas.

A quiet road on the Saanich Peninsula

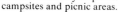

Christmas holly

Garry oak

SAANICHTON
Western Canada's oldest agricultural fair has been held here each September since 1871. On the fairground are two museums of local history. The Pioneer Museum, in a log building (1932), displays pioneer artifacts from the Saanich Peninsula. The Centennial Museum has a collection of early farm machinery.

DOMINION ASTROPHYSICAL OBSERVATORY
Maintained by the National Research Council, the observatory is equipped with a 182-centimetre reflecting telescope, in operation since 1918. On display is the original mirror, used until 1974—a two-tonne piece of ordinary glass polished to within a tolerance of .000001 centimetre. On Saturday evenings visitors can watch the observatory in action as the dome roof slides back and the giant telescope swings around to focus on a particular star.

ROYAL OAK
The University of Victoria's Maltwood Memorial Museum of Historic Art has an important collection of period furniture, arts and crafts, and Oriental artifacts. There are Sung and Ming dynasty vases and paintings on silk, a Wei third-century unglazed horse head, and a 40-centimetre Ming sculpture of the *God of Longevity*. The museum is housed in a Tudor-style mansion (1939), originally a restaurant.

Erythroniums

Skylarks and Holly, Only in the Saanich

The song of the skylark is heard in the Saanich Peninsula—the only place in North America where these birds are found. Homesick English settlers brought more than 100 pairs of skylarks to the peninsula in the early 1900s. The field-dwelling birds thrived throughout the farming country of the peninsula, whose mild climate is similar to that of England.

The name Saanich comes from an Indian word meaning "fertile soil." Japanese cherry trees and plum trees blossom here in February and daffodils—13 million a year are shipped from Saanichton alone—bloom in April. Loganberries are the major crop on the peninsula's many berry farms. The area also supports an industry unique in Canada—the growing of Christmas holly.

Wildflowers such as erythroniums and the rarer trillium grow along roadsides and among groves of elm, cedar, arbutus and fir.

English skylark

CORDOVA CHANNEL

17

20

6

ELK BEAVER LAKE PK

Elk Lake

DOMINION ASTROPHYSICAL OBSERVATORY

Prospect Lake

Prospect Lake

Beaver Lake

14

3.5

Royal Oak

SAANICH

17

CORDOVA BAY

Lake Hill

Sevenoaks

1

Trans-Canada Highway

1

VICTORIA
(see Road Unit 2)

Esquimalt

Oak Bay

CADBORO BAY

CATTLE PT

PLUMPER PASSAGE

5

In Dairy and Logging Country, the Famous Cowichan Sweaters

Vancouver Island

This part of Vancouver Island is known for its hand-knit sweaters, fine dairy herds and scenic logging roads.

Sweaters from Cowichan River valley sheep are renowned for their durability and distinctive patterns. Designs are derived from those on cedar bark and wild goat wool blankets once worn by Coast Salish Indians. Cowichan sweaters are made from undyed wool heavy with lanolin, a grease which makes them rain-resistant.

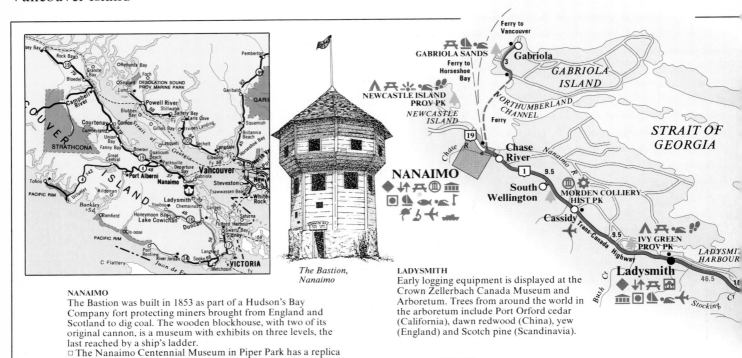

The Bastion, Nanaimo

NANAIMO

The Bastion was built in 1853 as part of a Hudson's Bay Company fort protecting miners brought from England and Scotland to dig coal. The wooden blockhouse, with two of its original cannon, is a museum with exhibits on three levels, the last reached by a ship's ladder.

□ The Nanaimo Centennial Museum in Piper Park has a replica of a coal mine, showing equipment and methods used from 1853 to 1968; a reproduction of a Victorian living room; Indian and Chinese collections; and relics from the city's HBC period (1852-62).

□ Prehistoric rock carvings in Petroglyph Provincial Park represent humans, birds, wolves, lizards and sea monsters.

□ Nanaimo claims the title of "Bathtub Capital of the World." Powered bathtubs and other outlandish craft are navigated across the Strait of Georgia from Nanaimo to Vancouver in the Great International Bathtub Race each July.

LADYSMITH

Early logging equipment is displayed at the Crown Zellerbach Canada Museum and Arboretum. Trees from around the world in the arboretum include Port Orford cedar (California), dawn redwood (China), yew (England) and Scotch pine (Scandinavia).

DUNCAN

At the British Columbia Forest Museum, between May and September, a steam engine rumbles along 2.5 kilometres of narrow-gauge track through 16 hectares of forest, over a 92-metre trestle, and past donkey engines, a sawmill, a waterwheel and a cedar log three metres in diameter. Other exhibits at the museum include Little Jakey, a steam log-hauler (c. 1890), hand-pump cars, two gasoline-powered locomotives, and a slice from the base of a Douglas fir which dates from about A.D. 640. Along Forester's Walk are 25 species of trees, including 300-year-old Douglas firs 55 metres high.

□ Whippletree Junction, a recreated turn-of-the-century town, has a livery stable, a fire hall, a general store, a barber shop, a blacksmith-gunsmith shop and an ice-cream parlor.

Great International Bathtub Race, Nanaimo to Vancouver

LAKE COWICHAN

This community is at the eastern end of Cowichan Lake, a year-round source of giant cutthroat and rainbow trout. Roads girdling the 45-kilometre-long lake take visitors deep into fragrant mossy forests. The densest stands of fir on Vancouver Island are in Gordon Bay Provincial Park, west of Honeymoon Bay—a sawmill settlement named for a settler who left to bring a bride from England. He never returned, but the name stuck.

0 1 2 3 4 5 Miles
0 2 4 6 8 Kilometres

In the gentle climate of the Cowichan Valley (*Cowichan* is an Indian word meaning warmed by the sun), the small farms the pioneers wrested from the forests yielded abundant forage. It was ideal for raising cattle, so dairying thrived. Today the Holstein herds in the Cowichan Valley produce much of British Columbia's milk.

Dairy exhibits are featured at the annual post-Labor Day Cowichan Exhibition in Duncan. Special events include sheepdog trials and logger sports. For lumbering, too, is an important industry in this area. Logging roads weave through forests where camp and picnic sites have been developed by the lumber industry and the B.C. Forest Service. Because some logging roads are closed during working hours, visitors should check with the Forest Service before setting out to explore these backwoods. Travelers must yield to logging trucks, which travel at high speeds and often in convoys.

Galiano Galleries, Gabriola Island

GABRIOLA ISLAND.
With one of the best climates in North America, Gabriola Island is green in winter, a garden of wildflowers in spring. This 50-square-kilometre haven, a short ferry ride from Nanaimo, is a fine place for beachcombing, clam digging and oyster gathering. The island is also known for its rock formations. Most famous are the 90-metre-long, 4-metre-high Galiano Galleries, which wind and waves have carved in sandstone at Malaspina Point in Gabriola Sands Provincial Park.
□ South of the galleries are stalactites which hang from a 30-metre-high cliff.

COWICHAN BAY
A missionary priest, the Rev. Peter Rondeault, kept cows and sold butter, using the proceeds to build the "Butter Church" in 1870. Sandstone for the structure was quarried from nearby Comiaken Hill. The church, on a Cowichan Indian reserve, was restored in 1958.
□ Cowichan Bay is a favorite with coho salmon anglers.
□ Deep-sea ships load lumber at the harbor, which has five marinas.

The "Butter Church," Cowichan Bay

MILL BAY
This community at the north end of the Malahat Drive, the coast road built in 1911, is said to enjoy the most temperate climate in Canada. There are ocean and lake fishing, hunting, boating, a golf course, tennis clubs, marinas, and a ferry service to Brentwood Bay, southwest on the Saanich Peninsula.
□ In the Mill Bay United Church cemetery are headstones dating from the mid-1800s.

GOLDSTREAM PROVINCIAL PARK
Gold was discovered here in 1855 and old mining shafts and tunnels are still to be seen. Throughout the park are Douglas firs, some almost 600 years old. Arbutus, Canada's only broad-leafed evergreen, grows alongside flowering dogwood on the three-kilometre Arbutus Ridge Trail. Oregon grape, red huckleberry, salmonberry and thimbleberry are abundant. A variety of wildflowers includes trilliums, calypso bulbosa orchids and twinflowers.
□ Thousands of chum and coho salmon head up the shallow Goldstream River each November, bound for spawning grounds.

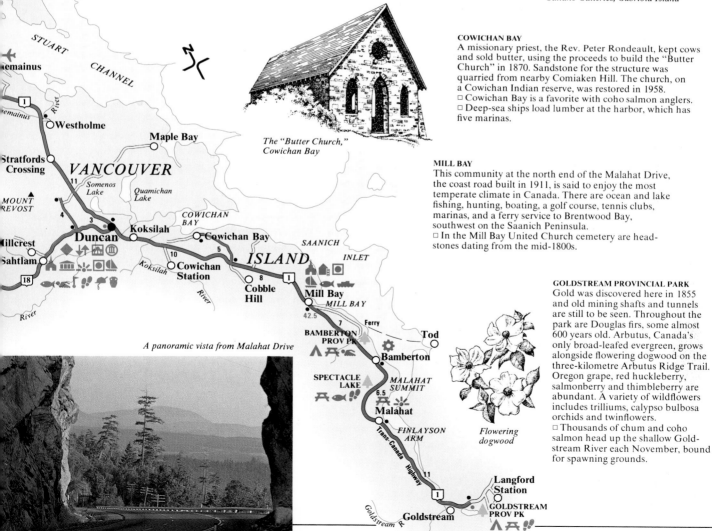

A panoramic vista from Malahat Drive

Flowering dogwood

Fine Fishing and Towering Firs in the Shadow of Mount Arrowsmith

Vancouver Island

Reaching halfway into Vancouver Island, Alberni Inlet is one of the major waterways of Canada's west coast. From this channel the island's forest products are shipped to countries around the rim of the Pacific. The inlet is also a fertile fishing ground where salmon are intercepted as they head for spawning rivers.

At the end of the inlet is Port Alberni, a community of about 20,000. The highway between here and Parksville lies in the shadow of Mount Arrowsmith and climbs

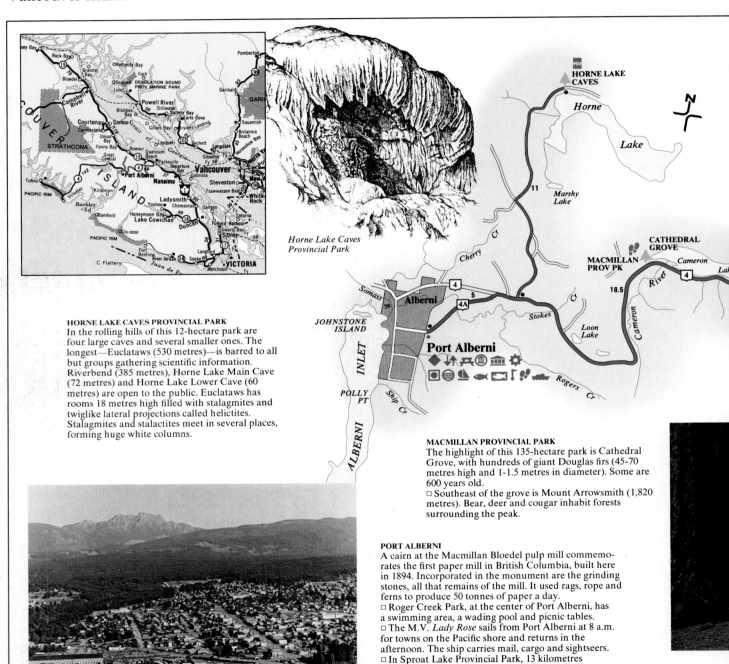

Horne Lake Caves
Provincial Park

HORNE LAKE CAVES PROVINCIAL PARK
In the rolling hills of this 12-hectare park are four large caves and several smaller ones. The longest—Euclataws (530 metres)—is barred to all but groups gathering scientific information. Riverbend (385 metres), Horne Lake Main Cave (72 metres) and Horne Lake Lower Cave (60 metres) are open to the public. Euclataws has rooms 18 metres high filled with stalagmites and twiglike lateral projections called helictites. Stalagmites and stalactites meet in several places, forming huge white columns.

MACMILLAN PROVINCIAL PARK
The highlight of this 135-hectare park is Cathedral Grove, with hundreds of giant Douglas firs (45-70 metres high and 1-1.5 metres in diameter). Some are 600 years old.
□ Southeast of the grove is Mount Arrowsmith (1,820 metres). Bear, deer and cougar inhabit forests surrounding the peak.

PORT ALBERNI
A cairn at the Macmillan Bloedel pulp mill commemorates the first paper mill in British Columbia, built here in 1894. Incorporated in the monument are the grinding stones, all that remains of the mill. It used rags, rope and ferns to produce 50 tonnes of paper a day.
□ Roger Creek Park, at the center of Port Alberni, has a swimming area, a wading pool and picnic tables.
□ The M.V. *Lady Rose* sails from Port Alberni at 8 a.m. for towns on the Pacific shore and returns in the afternoon. The ship carries mail, cargo and sightseers.
□ In Sproat Lake Provincial Park, 13 kilometres northwest, are Indian rock carvings of mythological beasts. Visitors to this 40-hectare park can fish for cutthroat trout.
□ A Chinook salmon hatchery at Robertson Creek, 22 kilometres northwest of Port Alberni, has facilities for incubating three million eggs.

Port Alberni

0	1	2	3	4	5 Miles

0	2	4	6	8 Kilometres

Little Qualicum Falls

through Vancouver Island's highest road pass (370 metres). Much of the forested terrain along this route was scarred by a fire in 1967; the effects are still visible.

At Cathedral Grove in Macmillan Provincial Park are towering stands of Douglas fir, trees that were seedlings when Cabot sailed to North America in 1497. Nearby forests have abundant wildlife, including deer, bear, wolf and cougar. (Vancouver Island's concentration of cougar is believed the greatest in North America.)

Parksville is a popular vacation headquarters for visitors to this region. Situated on a beautiful bay on the east coast of the island, the town is noted for its fine beaches, excellent fishing and lovely parks. Annual events include a horse show in May, a pageant in July, and a salmon derby and barbecue in mid-August.

PARKSVILLE

A 1.5-kilometre beach on the Strait of Georgia, good salmon and trout fishing, and two nearby parks—on the Englishman River and the Little Qualicum River—make Parksville a popular resort.
□ The Canadiana Museum, on Highway 19, displays Indian and Inuit artifacts, firearms, early photographs and music boxes.
□ At nearby French Creek is St. Ann's Church, a stone structure built in the early 1900s. Its rectory dates from 1912.

St. Ann's Church, French Creek

LITTLE QUALICUM FALLS PROVINCIAL PARK

Picturesque Little Qualicum Falls, plunging 60 metres down three giant steps, is at the end of a 1.5-kilometre trail that starts at the park entrance. The park covers four square kilometres and has 100 campsites and scores of picnic tables. There are several places for swimming, and the river area just above and below the park provides good trout fishing. Scenic trails lead to nearby Mount Arrowsmith.

RATHTREVOR BEACH PROVINCIAL PARK

A 1.5-kilometre sand beach, the longest on Vancouver Island, skirts the park's eastern edge. At low tide almost 200 hectares of flats are exposed. Among 42 species of birds found here is the black brant, an endangered member of the Canada goose family. This park covers some 350 hectares—mostly flatland—and has several nature trails.

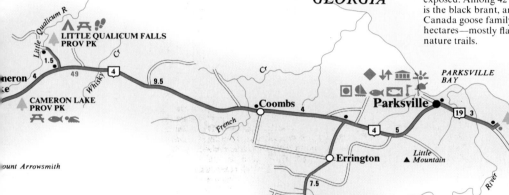

STRAIT OF GEORGIA

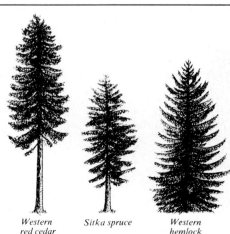

Black brant

Cathedral Grove, Macmillan Provincial Park

ENGLISHMAN RIVER FALLS PROVINCIAL PARK

This 100-hectare park, one of the most popular on Vancouver Island, has 100 individual campsites and 37 picnic sites. The Englishman River descends from snowfields high in the Beaufort Range and carries with it Kamloops, steelhead, cutthroat and rainbow trout. A wooden footbridge offers visitors a dramatic view of 40-metre Englishman River Falls.

A Grove of Giant Trees

The world's biggest trees grow in the ancient rain forests of the Pacific coast. As in every forest, these trees compete to reach sunlight essential for growth. But in the rain forest, abundant water and a long growing season—and the long life of Pacific coast conifers—enable trees to soar to heights impossible in other forests.

In most parts of the world trees are tall at 30 metres. In mature Pacific rain forests they average 60 metres, and giants grow to more than 90 metres.

Logging has destroyed most rain forests, but the best and most accessible in British Columbia is Cathedral Grove in Macmillan Provincial Park. Here, huge Douglas firs, with some red cedars and Sitka spruce, grow in dense stands on thick, wet moss cushions. Ferns, mosses and lichens often grow high up the trees, whose upper branches sometimes interlock. In the dense undergrowth, grow only shade-tolerant western hemlocks, which will replace the firs centuries from now.

Western red cedar   *Sitka spruce*   *Western hemlock*

Whales and Sea Lions Off a Surf-Swept Shoreline

Vancouver Island

Pacific Rim National Park clings to Vancouver Island's rugged west coast where surf-swept beaches, rocky headlands and craggy islands are bathed by the Pacific—and battered by its fury.

The sea provides for every visitor: surfers ride waves off Long Beach, fishermen cast for lingcod in the sea pounding, clam diggers probe white sands for geoduck and razor clams, beachcombers search for the ocean's exotic castoffs.

Pacific Rim's Broken Islands Group—

Tufted puffin

TOFINO
A salmon, herring and shrimp fleet docks at this harbor, named in 1792 for Vincente Tofino, a Spanish admiral. The town is also a mining and logging center.
□ Eight kilometres north are the remains of Fort Defiance, established in 1791 by fur trader Robert Gray. He later discovered the Columbia River and named it for his ship.
□ The Maritime Museum here displays cannonballs, harpoons and the remains of sunken ships.

CLELAND ISLAND
Tufted puffins nest in rocky hollows on this treeless island. The puffin uses short wings and webbed feet to "fly" under water. It can carry as many as 10 fish in its red, blue and yellow beak. Rhinoceros auklets and more than 10,000 storm petrels are also found here.

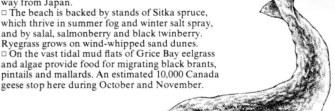

LONG BEACH
This 11-kilometre crescent of hard-packed, nearly white sand in Pacific Rim National Park is often shrouded in fog. As the mists lift, strollers and clam diggers explore the steaming sands. Beachcombers browse for refuse cast up by the sea—weirdly twisted driftwood, colorful shells and glass fishing floats that winds and currents have pushed all the way from Japan.
□ The beach is backed by stands of Sitka spruce, which thrive in summer fog and winter salt spray, and by salal, salmonberry and black twinberry. Ryegrass grows on wind-whipped sand dunes.
□ On the vast tidal mud flats of Grice Bay eelgrass and algae provide food for migrating black brants, pintails and mallards. An estimated 10,000 Canada geese stop here during October and November.

Pacific gray whale

Long Beach, Pacific Rim National Park

PACIFIC RIM NATIONAL PARK
This park has three sections—Long Beach, the Broken Islands Group and the West Coast Trail. The dense rain forests of Long Beach are backed by the 1,200-metre Mackenzie Range. Tidal mud flats attract thousands of migrating waterfowl. A boat tour from Long Beach takes visitors to the Sea Lion Rocks where Steller's sea lions often sun. Radar Hill, near Highway 4 at the north end of Long Beach, affords a splendid view of Vancouver Island. The Broken Islands Group—100 islands in Barkley Sound—offer fine fishing for coho and Chinook salmon. The West Coast Trail is a coastal wilderness area between Bamfield and Port Renfrew. The trail itself skirts the shore and passes through stands of Sitka spruce and lush stream-eroded ravines.

Steller's sea lions, Sea Lion Rocks

0 1 2 3 4 5 Miles
0 2 4 6 8 Kilometres

known as the "graveyard of the Pacific"—has claimed 50 vessels in the last 100 years. Scuba divers explore barnacle-encrusted wrecks.

A trail in the park once helped shipwrecked sailors reach safety. Other paths lead to sea caves, weathered rock arches, water-blasted blowholes, and tidal pools inhabited by barnacles, mussels, limpets and hermit crabs.

At Tofino and Ucluelet, bustling ports adjacent to the park, restaurants serve fresh- and saltwater fish, crabs, oysters and shrimps.

Sproat Lake and its tributary, the Taylor River, teem with trout and salmon during the spawning season. Giant Douglas fir and western red cedar flourish in dense stands on the blue-tinted Mackenzie Range.

Fishing boats, Tofino

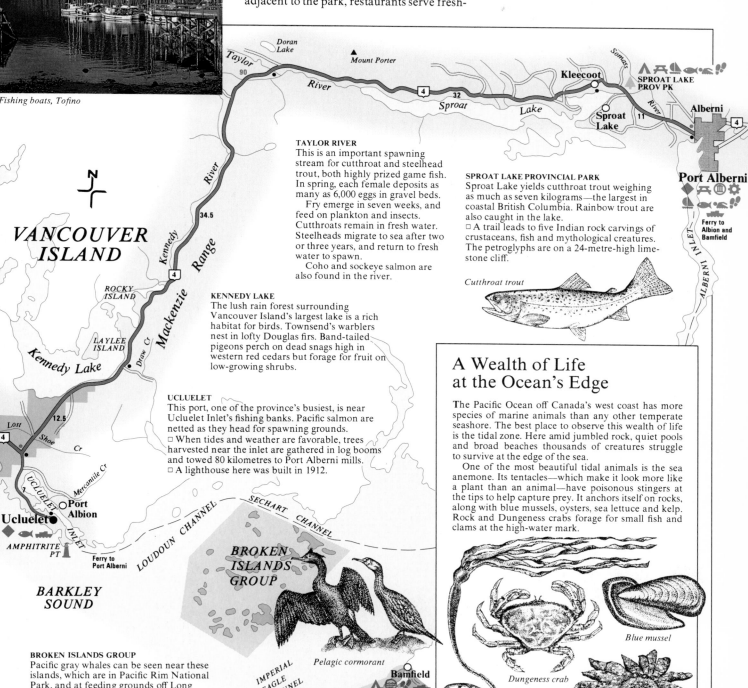

VANCOUVER ISLAND

TAYLOR RIVER
This is an important spawning stream for cutthroat and steelhead trout, both highly prized game fish. In spring, each female deposits as many as 6,000 eggs in gravel beds.
Fry emerge in seven weeks, and feed on plankton and insects. Cutthroats remain in fresh water. Steelheads migrate to sea after two or three years, and return to fresh water to spawn.
Coho and sockeye salmon are also found in the river.

KENNEDY LAKE
The lush rain forest surrounding Vancouver Island's largest lake is a rich habitat for birds. Townsend's warblers nest in lofty Douglas firs. Band-tailed pigeons perch on dead snags high in western red cedars but forage for fruit on low-growing shrubs.

UCLUELET
This port, one of the province's busiest, is near Ucluelet Inlet's fishing banks. Pacific salmon are netted as they head for spawning grounds.
□ When tides and weather are favorable, trees harvested near the inlet are gathered in log booms and towed 80 kilometres to Port Alberni mills.
□ A lighthouse here was built in 1912.

SPROAT LAKE PROVINCIAL PARK
Sproat Lake yields cutthroat trout weighing as much as seven kilograms—the largest in coastal British Columbia. Rainbow trout are also caught in the lake.
□ A trail leads to five Indian rock carvings of crustaceans, fish and mythological creatures. The petroglyphs are on a 24-metre-high limestone cliff.

Cutthroat trout

A Wealth of Life at the Ocean's Edge

The Pacific Ocean off Canada's west coast has more species of marine animals than any other temperate seashore. The best place to observe this wealth of life is the tidal zone. Here amid jumbled rock, quiet pools and broad beaches thousands of creatures struggle to survive at the edge of the sea.

One of the most beautiful tidal animals is the sea anemone. Its tentacles—which make it look more like a plant than an animal—have poisonous stingers at the tips to help capture prey. It anchors itself on rocks, along with blue mussels, oysters, sea lettuce and kelp. Rock and Dungeness crabs forage for small fish and clams at the high-water mark.

Blue mussel

Dungeness crab

Kelp

Sea anemone

Pelagic cormorant

BROKEN ISLANDS GROUP
Pacific gray whales can be seen near these islands, which are in Pacific Rim National Park, and at feeding grounds off Long Beach. Harbor seals inhabit the islands' sheltered lagoons. Pelagic cormorants and more than 170 pairs of bald eagles nest here.

Port Alberni

Sproat Lake

Alberni

Port Albion

Ucluelet

AMPHITRITE PT.

BARKLEY SOUND

BROKEN ISLANDS GROUP

LOUDOUN CHANNEL

SECHART CHANNEL

IMPERIAL EAGLE CHANNEL

Bamfield

WEST COAST TRAIL

CAPE BEALE

Kichha Lake

KEEHA BAY

PACHENA BAY

Rich Farmland, Fighting Salmon and Indian Rock Carvings

Vancouver Island

Until the 1890s, only a trail led northward from the Comox Valley. Although a rough wagon road was built by 1904, the first paved road north to Kelsey Bay was built during the Second World War.

Today, Highway 19 leads from the flourishing farmland of the Comox Valley, where fresh fruits, vegetables and honey can be bought at roadside stands, to Campbell River and the forestry community of Kelsey Bay. Courtenay, on Vancouver Island's east coast, is at the southeast corner

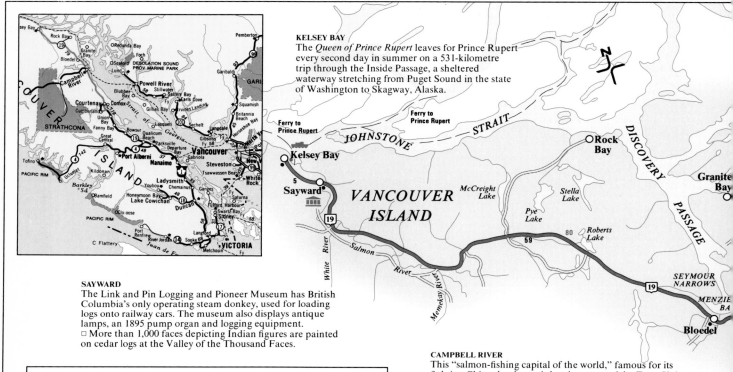

KELSEY BAY
The *Queen of Prince Rupert* leaves for Prince Rupert every second day in summer on a 531-kilometre trip through the Inside Passage, a sheltered waterway stretching from Puget Sound in the state of Washington to Skagway, Alaska.

SAYWARD
The Link and Pin Logging and Pioneer Museum has British Columbia's only operating steam donkey, used for loading logs onto railway cars. The museum also displays antique lamps, an 1895 pump organ and logging equipment.
□ More than 1,000 faces depicting Indian figures are painted on cedar logs at the Valley of the Thousand Faces.

CAMPBELL RIVER
This "salmon-fishing capital of the world," famous for its fighting Chinook salmon, is headquarters of the Tyee Club. Membership is awarded to fishermen who land trophy-sized Chinooks (more than 14 kilograms), called tyee.
□ A July salmon festival includes a parade, fishing derby, and war canoe races.
□ The town is a lumber and commercial fishing center. There are guided tours of a pulp and paper mill five kilometres north at Duncan Bay.
□ A five-metre-tall totem pole with bear designs stands outside Campbell River Centennial Museum. In the rotunda is a huge thunderbird. The museum's Indian artifacts are principally from the Kwakiutl and Nootka tribes, a few are Salishan. There are also collections of guns, logging and mining equipment and pioneer household articles.

Campbell River harbor

Colorful Castoffs of the Pacific Coast

Purple shore crab

Red rock crab

Hairy horse crab

Pacific beaches are littered with colorful shells of crabs that thrive by the shore. A crab shell splits when it gets too tight—sometimes twice or three times a year. The animal climbs out with a soft, new shell. The crab fills its body with water until the shell expands to a comfortable size, then hardens. The kelp crab, which frequents beds of eel grass, covers its shell with a camouflage of seaweed and barnacles. It transfers its disguise to a new shell with each moult. Hermit crabs, with soft, shell-less abdomens, live in empty snail shells, and move into bigger homes as they grow. Pea crabs live inside the mantle cavity of horse clams, existing on some of the clam's food.

The two best-known species are purple and green shore crabs, which are found under rocks on most beaches. Red rock crabs, which live on gravel beaches, are brick red with black pincers. The edible crab, which usually burrows in sand, is larger than the red rock crab, and uniformly colored from light buff to reddish brown. The hairy horse crab has a yellow-orange shell and is covered with stiff, rusty-brown hairs.

0 2 4 6 8 10 Miles
0 4 8 12 16 Kilometres

of the valley. The hiking and skiing area of Forbidden Plateau can be reached from a lodge 24 kilometres northwest of the town. A year-round car ferry links nearby Comox with Powell River on the mainland across the Strait of Georgia.

Miracle Beach Provincial Park, on the coast, has abundant marine life and a spectacular view of the Coast Mountains.

Where the Campbell River flows into the narrow, turbulent channel of Discovery Passage is the town of Campbell River, famous for towering trees in surrounding forests and trophy-sized fighting salmon in nearby waters. Visitors can enjoy fishing, camping and hiking here, and cross by ferry to Quadra Island, with its centuries-old Indian rock carvings.

From Campbell River, Highway 19 passes the small logging and farming community of Sayward. This town is the southernmost port of call of the *Queen of Prince Rupert*, which cruises the Inside Passage to and from Prince Rupert.

Quadra Island

QUADRA ISLAND

Quadra Island, nearly 24 kilometres long, is the largest island in the Discovery Passage.

□ Accessible by ferry from Campbell River, Quadra has an Indian village and authentic totem poles. Cape Mudge has the most important Indian rock carvings on the Pacific coast. Petroglyphs on 26 boulders include masks and mythological creatures.

□ A lighthouse was built on the cape in 1898 to guide ships through the narrow entrance of Discovery Passage.

□ Rebecca Spit Provincial Park has campsites, picnic sites and boat facilities. Gravel roads at the island's northern end lead to freshwater lakes, the old Finnish settlement site at Granite Bay, and the "Lucky Jim" gold and copper mine, discovered when workmen were laying a logging railway.

□ Visitors can hike, fish and beachcomb, and gather oysters and clams.

SEYMOUR NARROWS

Vertical rock walls, in places more than 60 metres high, line the deep, blue waters of Seymour Narrows. The cliffs on the west side of the narrows are part of Vancouver Island.

□ Until the late 1950s Ripple Rock was the graveyard of ships negotiating the treacherous currents and eddies of the narrows. In 1958 this navigational hazard was eliminated in Canada's biggest controlled explosion.

Glaucous-winged gull

MIRACLE BEACH PROVINCIAL PARK

Porpoises and hair seals can be seen near the mouth of Black Creek. Killer whales are often spotted in the Strait of Georgia. Several types of crabs and seabirds inhabit the shorelines and 195 plant species have been identified. Mammals in the park include black-tailed deer, raccoons and black bears.

□ A nature house has a herbarium and a saltwater aquarium showing the area's tidal pool life.

□ Self-guiding and conducted nature walks skirt the shore and wander through forests of hemlock and Douglas fir.

Indian rock carvings, Cape Mudge, Quadra Island

MITLENATCH ISLAND PROVINCIAL NATURE PARK

Mitlenatch is a Salish Indian word meaning "calm water all around." Harbor seals are common and sea lions are sometimes spotted off this small, craggy island. Colonies of red sea urchins blanket rocky shores, and garter snakes frequent tidal pools to feed on blennies, sculpins and clingfish. Purple and orange sea stars abound in rock crevices. Thousands of seabirds, including black oyster catchers, glaucous-winged gulls and pelagic cormorants, nest on rocky ledges. The prickly pear cactus, the only cactus found on the British Columbia coast, blooms here during hot, dry days in June.

COURTENAY

The Courtenay and District Historical Society Museum features artifacts from Cumberland's Chinatown, a pioneer kitchen and dairy, and a blacksmith shop and forge. Indian displays include baskets and fish traps. A fossil collection features a 70-million-year-old impression of a fern found in a Cumberland coal mine.

"1-Spot," a locomotive brought here in 1909 by the Comox Logging and Railway Company, is displayed outside the museum, along with a Haida totem pole.

CUMBERLAND

Swayback buildings of an almost deserted Chinatown are reminders of Cumberland's days as a booming coal-mining center. During the 1890s, Cumberland's Chinatown was reputedly bigger than San Francisco's. When coal mining ended in 1966, the Chinese community all but disappeared. Cumberland is now a quiet resort village. Old buildings still in use include a hospital (1894) and a post office (1907).

Map labels:
QUADRA ISLAND
Heriot Bay REBECCA SPIT
REBECCA SPIT PROV PK
Duncan Bay
Campbell River
LK FALLS PROV PK (see Road Unit 8)
CAPE MUDGE
19
23
MITLENATCH ISLAND PROV NATURE PK
MITLENATCH ISLAND
VANCOUVER ISLAND
STRAIT OF GEORGIA
OYSTER BAY
Oyster River
MIRACLE BEACH PROV PK
Black Creek
58
Merville
11.5
KITTY COLEMAN BEACH
Tsolum River
12
KIN BEACH
Comox
Ferry to Powell River
COMOX HARBOUR
Courtenay
5.5
Royston
19
Cumberland
Trent R

The Pacific Wilderness That Awed Captain Cook

Vancouver Island

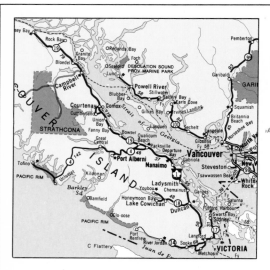

Life-jacketed canoeists and kayakers preparing to run the Campbell River

Coast deer

GOLD RIVER

Canada's first all-electric town, Gold River was built in six months in 1965 to house employees of a pulp mill. It is in the Gold River valley at the junction of the Gold and Heber rivers, 14 kilometres from the Tahsis Company mill. □ *Uchuck III*, a converted Second World War minesweeper, runs 56 kilometres between Gold River and Zeballos farther north, three times a week, stopping at coastal settlements with supplies and passengers. One stop is Friendly Cove, where Capt. James Cook landed in 1778.

An Island Named for Rival Sea Captains

George Vancouver was a 20-year-old midshipman on the 1778 James Cook expedition when he first saw the island he later named.

In 1789, after the Spanish seized British trading vessels and a small battery in Nootka Sound, Britain threatened war. Spain capitulated, and Vancouver (now a commander) was sent to secure the territory. In 1792, he met with Capt. Juan Bodega y Quadra, sent by Spain to negotiate the transfer. They became friends and the Englishman named the island "Vancouver's and Quadra's Island." Quadra's name was eventually dropped and given to a smaller island in the Strait of Georgia. A stained-glass window (*left*) commemorating the first meeting between the rival sea captains is in Friendly Cove Catholic Church.

Gold River

Inlet

Muchalat

NOOTKA ISLAND

Friendly Cove

NOOTKA SOUND

PACIFIC OCEAN

Salmon River

Crown Mountain ▲

BIG DEN NATURE CONSERV AREA

Big Den Mountain ▲

Elkhorn Mountain ▲

Heber River

Elk River

Gold River

Ucona River

NOOTKA SOUND

Capt. James Cook, the first European to stand on Canada's west coast, named his 1778 anchorage King George's Sound, but later changed it to Nootka, under the mistaken impression that this was its Indian name. Eleven years later, Spain seized control of the sound. This act almost led to war between Spain and England. In 1792 a British naval expedition under the command of George Vancouver met the Spaniards at Friendly Cove to take possession of the Nootka Sound territory.

Mariner Mountain

Hikers in Strathcona Provincial Park

0 1 2 3 4 5 Miles
0 2 4 6 8 Kilometres

The fog-shrouded landscape of Vancouver Island has changed little since Capt. James Cook anchored off Friendly Cove in 1778. Nowadays, visitors can call on Friendly Cove aboard *Uchuck III*, a converted minesweeper that supplies coastal settlements with everything from logging machinery to livestock.

Strathcona Provincial Park preserves a vast tract of the wilderness admired by Cook. Halfway between Campbell River and Gold River, a road skirts the eastern shore of Buttle Lake and provides access to the 2,240-square-kilometre park. Western red cedar and Douglas fir dominate the valleys, giving way to myriad wildflowers on higher slopes. To the west of Buttle Lake is 2,200-metre Golden Hinde, the highest peak on Vancouver Island. Wolverine, coast deer and the last remaining elk on Vancouver Island inhabit the park. From Great Central Lake, a 16-kilometre trail leads to Della Falls, a 440-metre ribbon of cascading water.

Fishermen marvel at the size and gameness of the Chinook salmon in the Campbell River. Salmon of 36 kilograms and more have been recorded here, and fishing is as much a way of life in this area as it was for the original Indian inhabitants.

Visitors here can comb wide beaches for clams, climb rugged mountain trails, and marvel—as did Captain Cook—at the spectacular scenery of Vancouver Island.

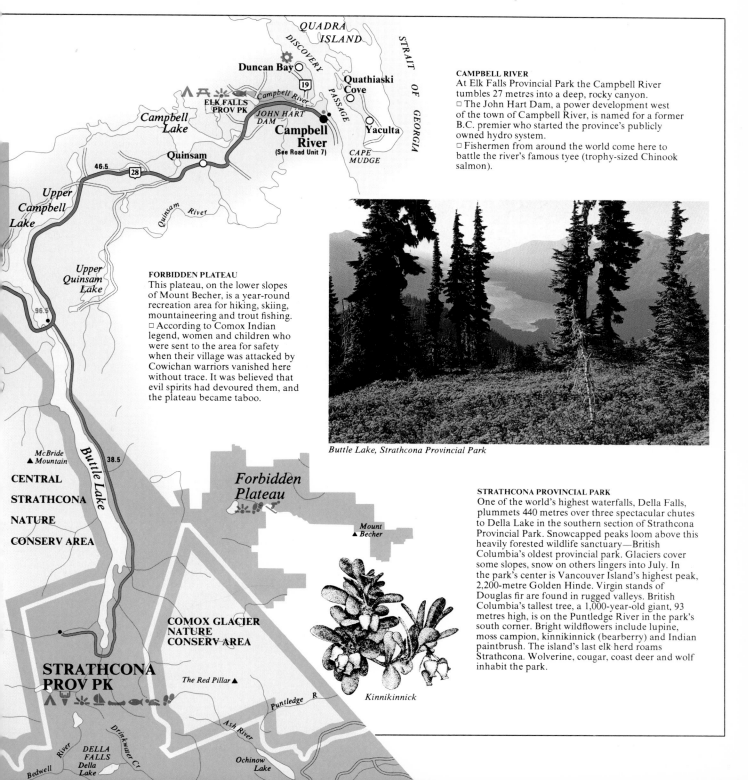

CAMPBELL RIVER
At Elk Falls Provincial Park the Campbell River tumbles 27 metres into a deep, rocky canyon.
□ The John Hart Dam, a power development west of the town of Campbell River, is named for a former B.C. premier who started the province's publicly owned hydro system.
□ Fishermen from around the world come here to battle the river's famous tyee (trophy-sized Chinook salmon).

FORBIDDEN PLATEAU
This plateau, on the lower slopes of Mount Becher, is a year-round recreation area for hiking, skiing, mountaineering and trout fishing.
□ According to Comox Indian legend, women and children who were sent to the area for safety when their village was attacked by Cowichan warriors vanished here without trace. It was believed that evil spirits had devoured them, and the plateau became taboo.

Buttle Lake, Strathcona Provincial Park

Kinnikinnick

STRATHCONA PROVINCIAL PARK
One of the world's highest waterfalls, Della Falls, plummets 440 metres over three spectacular chutes to Della Lake in the southern section of Strathcona Provincial Park. Snowcapped peaks loom above this heavily forested wildlife sanctuary—British Columbia's oldest provincial park. Glaciers cover some slopes, snow on others lingers into July. In the park's center is Vancouver Island's highest peak, 2,200-metre Golden Hinde. Virgin stands of Douglas fir are found in rugged valleys. British Columbia's tallest tree, a 1,000-year-old giant, 93 metres high, is on the Puntledge River in the park's south corner. Bright wildflowers include lupine, moss campion, kinnikinnick (bearberry) and Indian paintbrush. The island's last elk herd roams Strathcona. Wolverine, cougar, coast deer and wolf inhabit the park.

A Place in the Sun
on a Mountainous Coast

Sunshine Coast

Highway 101 between Langdale and Lund follows British Columbia's Sunshine Coast, aptly named for its mild climate of warm summers and balmy winters. Annual precipitation is about 900 millimetres, some 170 millimetres less than rainy Vancouver.

Although the Sunshine Coast is on the mainland, it has no road connection with the rest of British Columbia. Access is by ferry only—across Howe Sound between Horseshoe Bay and Langdale, and across

POWELL RIVER
The MacMillan Bloedel pulp and paper plant is one of the world's largest and produces mainly newsprint. A breakwater of ten ships, anchored in place and chained together, creates a storage pond for logs. The plant may be toured between May and August.
□ An abandoned logging road south of Powell River is now a 24-kilometre hiking trail with picnic tables and campsites. It leads through stands of Douglas fir and hemlock and a 160,000-hectare tree farm.

LUND
This small fishing village is the northern terminus of Highway 101, one of North America's longest roads. The highway parallels the Pacific Coast between here and San Ysidro, Calif.
□ The Lund Hotel was built in 1905 by the village's first settlers, two Swedish brothers, who arrived in December 1899 and named the site after their hometown.

Carved Masks, Lavish Ceremonies

More than any other native Canadians, the Indians of Canada's west coast were blessed with natural wealth: salmon from the sea; game, roots and berries from the forests, and cedar wood for frame houses and dugout canoes. Among the native peoples who still live along this coast are the Haida (on the Queen Charlotte Islands), the Gitksan (in the Skeena River valley), and the Coast Salish (along the Strait of Georgia). Freed from the pressing needs of survival in the past,

these Indians developed rich, regional cultures. They expressed their art in totem poles, carved masks, and brightly colored weavings. Wealth determined social status. At a lavish potlatch ceremony a host would destroy his possessions and shower guests with gifts. Modern versions of this ceremony (*below*) are still part of west coast Indian life. There has also been a renewal of traditional arts and skills, such as mask carving among the Coast Salish Indians at Sechelt.

Killer whale

PENDER HARBOUR
Pender Harbour is one of the main sources of killer whales (properly known as *orcas*) for the world's aquariums. Traveling in packs of up to 100, their triangular dorsal fins cutting through the waves, killer whales feed on salmon which frequent the harbor's shallow waters year-round.

The largest of the porpoises, the killer whale grows up to nine metres long and can weigh up to eight tonnes. For centuries the killer whale has been maligned in tales and legends as a ravenous monster which attacks other porpoises, whales and even man. But it feeds mainly on fish and only occasionally on a weakened porpoise or whale. The killer whale is at the top of the ocean food chain and has no natural enemies. It is highly intelligent, curious, and has a great need for companionship. When encountering man it is friendly, even in the wild.

0	2	4	6	8	10 Miles
0	4	8	12	16 Kilometres	

the Strait of Georgia between Comox on Vancouver Island and Powell River.

The Sunshine Coast has broad beaches, rugged headlands, quiet lagoons and lakes backed by heavily forested uplands—all set against the backdrop of the Coast Mountains to the east. The serene beauty of the land and the unhurried life-style of its people make this area an ideal outdoor retreat. Sportfishing for salmon and cod is a year-round activity. There is excellent swimming in the warm waters of Howe Sound and Sechelt Inlet. Four provincial parks offer facilities for boaters and campers.

From Langdale, Highway 101 runs through Gibsons, the film location of CBC-TV's *The Beachcombers*. It continues north to Sechelt, located on a narrow strip of land between Sechelt Inlet and the Strait of Georgia, then winds past the sheltered bay of Pender Harbour. Along the upper Sunshine Coast near Powell River, hikers can take to the woods on abandoned logging roads.

Breakwater of anchored ships, Powell River

EGMONT
Skookumchuck Narrows, four kilometres southeast of Egmont, is a 400-metre-wide, rock-strewn tidal bore between Jervis and Sechelt inlets. Skookumchuck is Chinook (a Coast Salish dialect) for "turbulent water." Four times daily—twice during flood tide and twice during ebb tide—the waters of the Pacific Ocean rush through the narrow passage creating boiling rapids, eddies and whirlpools. Extreme tides, mostly in spring, may reach five metres in height and a speed of 20 kilometres per hour. The roar of churning waters can be heard for many kilometres. The tidal spectacle can be viewed from Roland and Narrows points, two lookouts within a provincial park along the western edge of the Narrows.

SECHELT
Coast Salish Indian craftsmen on a reserve about 1.5 kilometres east of Sechelt have kept alive the traditional weaving and carving skills of their ancestors. Examples of their work are on display in the reserve's administrative center. Exhibits include woven cedar bark baskets, wooden masks, a brightly colored carved desk, and jewelry made of shells and jade.

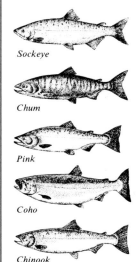

Coast Salish mask, Sechelt

Five Superb Salmon of the Pacific Coast

Five indigenous salmon species have made the tidal waters of the Sunshine Coast a fisherman's paradise. The fish are most abundant between June and August.

Chinook are the largest Pacific salmon, weighing up to 55 kilograms. They can be identified by a lightly spotted blue-green back and a black lower jaw.

Coho salmon weigh up to 10 kilograms. They are distinguished by a bright, silvery body with a metallic-blue stripe, and have a white lower jaw.

Sockeye salmon are the slimmest and most streamlined of the species. They weigh up to 3.5 kilograms and are a silvery blue.

Chum salmon resemble sockeye, but have faint, gridlike bars and black specks on their silvery sides. They weigh up to 5 kilograms.

Pink salmon are the smallest of the species, with a maximum weight of 2.5 kilograms. They have heavily spotted backs.

Sockeye
Chum
Pink
Coho
Chinook

GIBSONS
Salmon Rock, near the entrance of Gibsons' harbor, is one of British Columbia's finest fishing areas. Chinook and coho salmon are present throughout the year. The Elphinstone Pioneer Museum documents the evolutionary development of mollusks and crustaceans in a 25,000-shell collection.

□ A cairn at Gower Point, some four kilometres southwest, marks where George Vancouver stopped in June 1792 while mapping the Pacific Coast of North America. Nearby is a campground.

Gibsons

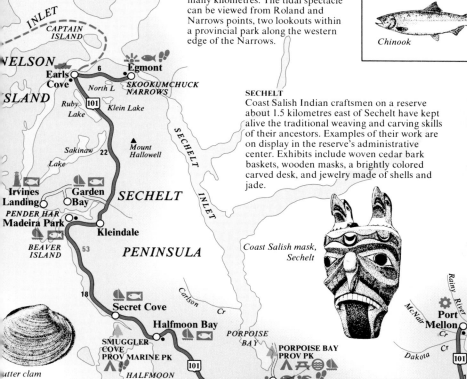

Butter clam

Moon snail

Horse clam

A View of Howe Sound From a Cliff-Hugging Highway

Howe Sound/Garibaldi Provincial Park

North of Vancouver the Seaview Highway (Highway 99) weaves through some of the most spectacular coastal scenery in British Columbia. Blasted through granite on the east side of Howe Sound, the highway in places hugs near-vertical mountain slopes. Far below the steam-driven *Royal Hudson* chuffs along a twisting ribbon of track between Vancouver and Squamish. Marbled murrelets, seabirds whose nesting site is unknown, are seen bobbing in the waters of Howe Sound.

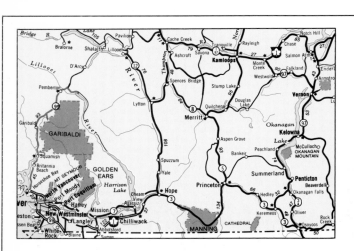

Alpine skiing, Whistler Mountain

MOUNT CURRIE
Hand-hewn log houses line the main street of this Indian reservation and Roman Catholic mission. Native craftsmen here weave split cedar roots into intricate basket designs.
□ Bronco busting, calf roping and chuckwagon races are featured in one of the largest rodeos in British Columbia, held here in May.

WHISTLER MOUNTAIN
With abundant snow from November to May, Whistler is one of Canada's finest ski areas. All runs are more than a kilometre in length; the longest is some 11 kilometres. Whistler is also a base for helicopter expeditions onto nearby glaciers. There, experienced skiers can enjoy icy fields of unbroken powder snow.

SQUAMISH
Squamish is a lumber center where huge log booms are assembled for towing to southern mills. Overlooking the village is Stawamus Chief, a 762-metre mountain resembling the head of an Indian. Three kilometres south is 198-metre-high Shannon Falls.
□ The *Royal Hudson*, a restored steam locomotive (1940), pulls a sight-seeing excursion train between Vancouver and Squamish during the summer.
□ Squamish Day, the first Saturday in August, features log-rolling and tree-climbing contests.

Fjords and Hanging Valleys on an Ice-Carved Coast

Some of Canada's most beautiful scenery is found among the tangle of islands, fjords and towering mountains of the Pacific coast. This dramatic landscape was created during the last ice age, when the coastline sagged under an immense burden of ice, and glaciers carved cliffs and riverbeds. Some 11,000 years ago the ice sheet began to melt. The ocean rose and flooded inland. Some river valleys, widened and deepened by glaciers, became fjords—arms of the sea (such as Howe Sound). Tributary valleys that had not been deepened by glacial erosion were stranded atop the fjords' steep walls. Waters that drain these "hanging valleys" often cascade hundreds of metres down the sides of fjords.

When the weight of the ice lifted, the land began to rise. For a time surf pounded on shores that are now mountainsides 300 metres above sea level.

The Royal Hudson

BRITANNIA BEACH
At the British Columbia Museum of Mining, visitors are given a hard hat, a raincoat, and a seat on a covered mining train which enters the murky depths of the Britannia copper mine (no longer in operation). Here, early mining techniques are demonstrated. In 1930-35, this and several neighboring mines were the British Empire's largest producers of copper. The History House building has beams from the mine's early machine shop.

Highway 99 by Howe Sound

0 2 4 6 8 10 Miles

0 4 8 12 16 Kilometres

The lumber town of Squamish, where Highway 99 turns inland, is in an alpine setting of forest and mountains. Gazing down on the town is the granite visage of the 762-metre-high Stawamus Chief. Beyond, in a cloud of spray and mist, Shannon Falls cascades nearly 200 metres.

An all-weather gravel road north of Squamish is the main access to Garibaldi Provincial Park. The primitive character of the park endures in a rugged landscape of canyons, gulleys and glaciated peaks.

Snowcapped mountains surround the Indian village of Mount Currie and present a tranquil backdrop for square-timbered barns with moss roofs.

It was through this harsh but beautiful wilderness that fortune-seekers trekked to the goldfields of the Cariboo in 1862-66. The Lillooet Shortcut, a rough logging road between Mount Currie and Lillooet, follows part of their trail, past abandoned cabins, forests and icy lakes.

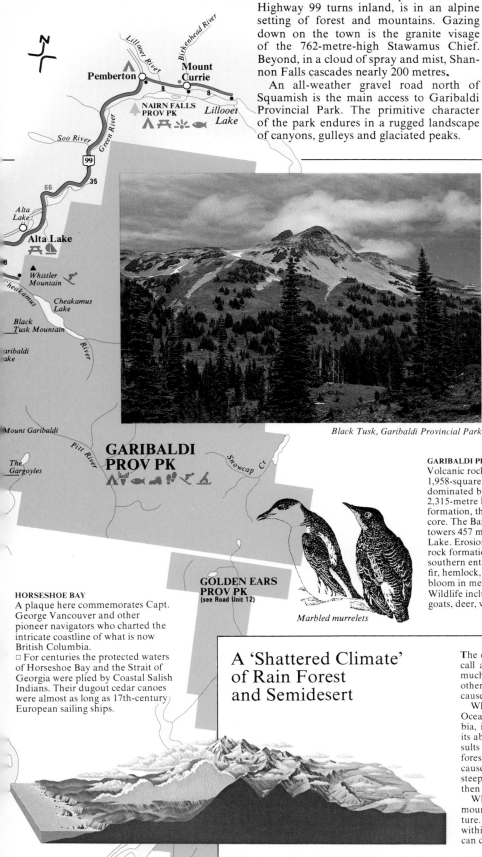

Black Tusk, Garibaldi Provincial Park

LILLOOET SHORTCUT

Tracing an ancient Indian trail through the mountains, the Lillooet Shortcut winds for 96 kilometres between Mount Currie and Lillooet. From sandbars along the Birkenhead River, anglers can cast for Chinook and coho salmon, Dolly Varden, and rainbow and steelhead trout. A decrepit log building in a forest clearing is all that remains of Port Douglas, once a mining boom town. During the Cariboo Gold Rush, the town boasted several stores, restaurants, hotels and saloons (and witnessed British Columbia's first legal hanging). Between Mount Currie and Lillooet Lake the road follows part of the original gold rush trail. It was here, in 1862, that 21 Asian camels were imported to pack equipment and supplies into the interior. (The animals proved unmanageable, however, and were released to fend for themselves in the bush.)

GARIBALDI PROVINCIAL PARK

Volcanic rock formations are found throughout this 1,958-square-kilometre wilderness park, which is dominated by 2,678-metre Mount Garibaldi. Atop 2,315-metre Black Tusk Mountain is a basalt formation, the eroded remains of an ancient volcanic core. The Barrier, a lava flow 1.5 kilometres long, towers 457 metres above the west side of Garibaldi Lake. Erosion has sculpted The Gargoyles—strange rock formations reached by a trail from the park's southern entrance. Garibaldi Park is forested with fir, hemlock, balsam and red cedar, and alpine flowers bloom in meadows beneath sharp, glaciated peaks. Wildlife includes grizzly and black bears, mountain goats, deer, wolverines and martens.

Marbled murrelets

HORSESHOE BAY

A plaque here commemorates Capt. George Vancouver and other pioneer navigators who charted the intricate coastline of what is now British Columbia.

□ For centuries the protected waters of Horseshoe Bay and the Strait of Georgia were plied by Coastal Salish Indians. Their dugout cedar canoes were almost as long as 17th-century European sailing ships.

A 'Shattered Climate' of Rain Forest and Semidesert

The coast of British Columbia has what meteorologists call a shattered climate. While some parts receive as much as 800 centimetres of rain and snow in a year, others get barely 50 centimetres. These extremes are caused by the rugged, intricate topography of the coast.

When warm, moisture-laden air from the Pacific Ocean reaches the coastal mountains of British Columbia, it is forced upward. The air cools as it rises, and its ability to retain moisture is greatly reduced. This results in heavy rainfall, which feeds lush coastal rain forests on the mountains' western slopes. Some fjords cause even greater precipitation in limited areas: their steep sides act as a funnel, compressing rain clouds, then driving them upward at the end of the fjord.

When air masses descend the eastern slopes of the mountains, they become warmer and retain more moisture. The result is often a dramatic reduction in rainfall within a few kilometres—a "rain shadow" effect that can create barren, semidesert conditions.

11 VANCOUVER, B.C.

The Pacific for a Doorstep, Coastal Peaks for a Backyard

No single image can portray Vancouver. Cosmopolitan and small-townish, always changing, the city has grown from a mill town to a metropolis in less than a century.

The shantytown that sprang up around a Burrard Inlet sawmill in 1862 was incorporated as the City of Vancouver in April 1886. In June of that year a forest fire raced toward the waterfront and the ramshackle frame buildings. An hour later the town was a smoking ruin.

Within weeks, a fire engine was purchased, new streets were laid out, and brick and stone buildings were erected. By the end of 1886 Vancouver was a city of 5,000 looking confidently to the future.

Immigrants poured into the young city after the Second World War, among them thousands of Europeans who added a continental flavor to traditionally British Vancouver. Between 1951 and 1978 the population of Greater Vancouver swelled from 530,000 to more than one million, and the city sprawled into Burnaby, Port Coquitlam, New Westminster, Delta and Surrey.

Part of Vancouver's appeal is the sheer beauty of its setting. Behind the sweep of its beaches soar high-rise buildings, symbols of dynamic urban growth. The city's harbors and inlets are freckled with pleasure craft and oceangoing vessels from around the world. To the north of Vancouver are the mountain parks of Hollyburn, Grouse and Seymour; to the south and east are the fertile farmlands of the Fraser River valley.

Burnaby Mountain Park (20)
A lookout atop Burnaby Mountain has sweeping views of Indian Arm Inlet, the Strait of Georgia, the Fraser River Delta and the distant mountains of Vancouver Island.
Capilano Canyon Park (5)
Swaying 69 metres above the Capilano River, the 135-metre-long Capilano Suspension Bridge (the world's longest foot-

Vancouver is a major financial, commercial, industrial and transportation center—in a magnificent setting between the sea and the Coast Mountains. Strung precariously across Capilano Canyon, the world's longest footbridge (above) has thrilled visitors since 1899. Papier-mâché dragon (left) in North America's second largest Chinatown is a reminder of Vancouver's rich ethnic mix.

bridge) has thrilled visitors since it was erected in 1899.

Centennial Fountain (33)
British Columbia's rugged coast is symbolized by water flowing over black marble sculptures representing sea-washed rocks.

Centennial Lacrosse Hall of Fame (22)
The sport of lacrosse is honored with displays dating back to an 1878 photograph of a St. Catharines, Ont. team. The museum is crowded with cups, autographed balls and pictures of lacrosse's great players.

Centennial Museum (27)
Displays trace local history from the rowdy fur-trade days to the genteel Victorian era. Among the exhibits is a CPR car from Canada's first transcontinental train to Vancouver (1887).

Chinatown (36)
Even the telephone booths wear pagoda-style roofs in this three-block neighborhood of Oriental restaurants, shops, teahouses and social clubs. Vancouver's Chinatown is the second largest in North America (after San Francisco's).

Christ Church Cathedral (32)
Built in 1894-95 and enlarged in 1909, this impressive stone Anglican church is now surrounded by downtown high rises.

Exhibition Park (17)
Sport goes on year round at this 70-hectare playground: horse racing at the five-furlong track, lacrosse and hockey at the Pacific Coliseum, and track and field at Empire Stadium. The Pacific National Exhibition, western Canada's largest fair, is held here in August. In the B.C. Pavilion are the provincial Sports Hall of Fame and the Challenger Relief Map of British Columbia. This 22-by-24-metre topographical map, which took seven years to construct, is built of 968,842 pieces of plywood. Visitors can view the map from an overhead gallery or a moving platform.

Grouse Mountain (6)
Canada's largest aerial tramway carries visitors to and from the top of 1,192-metre Grouse Mountain and provides a panoramic view of Vancouver, its harbor and surrounding mountains.

Heritage Village (19)
Burnaby's B.C. Centennial project is a living museum of turn-of-the-century west coast life. Smoke curls from a blacksmith shop, a 1903 linotype machine clatters in a newspaper office, and music drifts from a Victrola phonograph. Among several re-created buildings are a general store, an ice-cream parlor, an apothecary shop and a one-room schoolhouse.

Irving House (23)
Built in 1862-64 for Capt. William Irving, this two-story home in New Westminster is now a museum of B.C. history. The frame building has the original wallpaper, Wilton carpets imported from England in the 1860s, period furniture and a coach built for the visit Governor-General Dufferin made to the Cariboo goldfields in 1876.

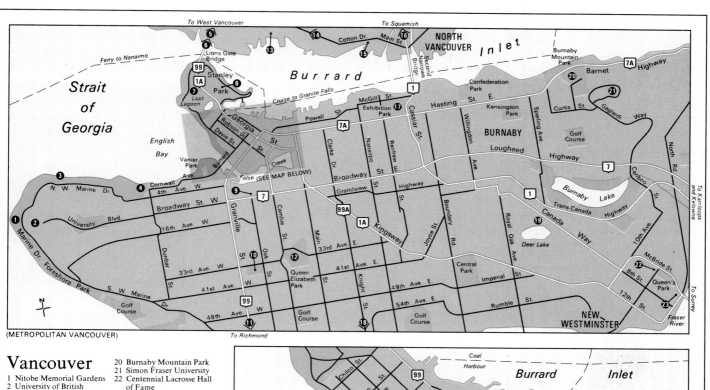

(METROPOLITAN VANCOUVER)

Vancouver
1 Nitobe Memorial Gardens
2 University of British Columbia
3 Spanish Banks
4 Old Hastings Mill Store Museum
5 Capilano Canyon Park
6 Grouse Mountain
7 Stanley Park
8 Vancouver Public Aquarium
9 CAA
10 Vandusen Botanical Display Garden
11 Richmond Arts Center
12 Queen Elizabeth Park
13 Royal Hudson
14 Lighthouse Park
15 Park and Tilford Gardens
16 Lynn Canyon Park
17 Exhibition Park
18 Reifel Waterfowl Refuge
19 Heritage Village
20 Burnaby Mountain Park
21 Simon Fraser University
22 Centennial Lacrosse Hall of Fame
23 Irving House
24 Kitsilano Beach
25 Maritime Museum
26 H.R. MacMillan Planetarium
27 Centennial Museum
28 Vancouver Art Gallery
29 Robsonstrasse
30 Orpheum Theater
31 Tourist Information
32 Christ Church Cathedral
33 Centennial Fountain
34 Gastown
35 Queen Elizabeth Theater
36 Chinatown

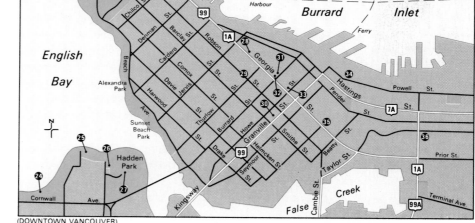

(DOWNTOWN VANCOUVER)

Kitsilano Beach (24)
Engine 373, the locomotive that pulled the first passenger train from Montreal to Vancouver (1887), is in a park here.

Lighthouse Park (14)
Nature trails lead past giant Douglas fir and cedar trees, eagles' nests and rocky coves to Point Atkinson Lighthouse (1874).

Lynn Canyon Park (16)
An 80-metre-high suspension footbridge, smaller than Capilano's but just as thrilling, spans Lynn Creek.

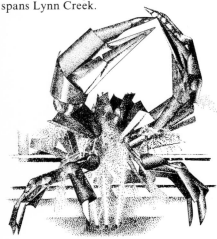

The Crab *sculpture outside MacMillan Planetarium*

MacMillan Planetarium (26)
Projection and sound systems simulate the night sky on a 19-metre dome.

Maritime Museum (25)
The city's B.C. Centennial project houses ship models, maps, photographs and artifacts illustrating the province's maritime history. The prize exhibit is the 30-metre RCMP schooner *St. Roch* (1928) which, in 1940-42, battled Arctic ice to become the first ship to navigate the Northwest Passage from west to east. Two years later it made an 11,672-kilometre return voyage to Vancouver in 86 days.

Nitobe Memorial Gardens (1)
This traditional Japanese garden has an artificial mountain, a miniature stream and a pond filled with golden carp and spanned by five bridges.

Old Hastings Mill Store Museum (4)
Built in 1865 by Capt. Edward Stamp, the store is Vancouver's oldest building, one of the few not destroyed in the 1886 fire.

Orpheum Theater (30)
Saved from the wrecker's ball in 1972, the ornate theater (1927) is now the home of the Vancouver Symphony Orchestra.

Park and Tilford Gardens (15)
Flowers are displayed year round in rhododendron, rose, colonnade, nature woods, Oriental and flower gardens.

Queen Elizabeth Park (12)
Rolling lawns are interspersed with paths leading to a rose garden, sunken garden, arboretum and the colorful Quarry Gardens. A tiny church, an old mill with working waterwheel and a miniature pineapple grove are enclosed beneath the 42-metre

Vancouver's 144 parks range from pocket-size patches to 400-hectare Stanley Park (above), an escape from the big-city din mere minutes away. Polar bears frolic in the park's zoo (right). Its beauty doubled by a luminous reflection, MacMillan Planetarium (below right) is a showpiece of modern architecture.

triodetic dome of the Bloedel Conservatory.

Queen Elizabeth Theater (35)
The 2,800-seat theater is set in a landscaped plaza. A smaller adjoining theater is the home of the Playhouse Theater Company.

Reifel Waterfowl Refuge (18)
Some 220 bird species have been recorded in this marshy estuary of Westham Island. The refuge supports Canada's largest wintering waterfowl population and is a resting place for more than 12,000 snow geese flying between Siberia and California.

Richmond Arts Center (11)
In this museum and art gallery in Minoru Park are military and aeronautical artifacts and exhibits tracing local history.

Robsonstrasse (29)
Officially, it's Robson Street, but the concentration of ethnic shops and restaurants—particularly German—has earned this two-block area its popular name.

Royal Hudson (13)
The steam-driven *Royal Hudson* makes a six-hour return trip along Howe Sound between Vancouver and Squamish. An open observation car, a bar car and several passenger cars, all authentically refurnished, enhance the nostalgic journey.

Simon Fraser University (21)
Crowning 360-metre Burnaby Mountain and commanding breathtaking views of the city, Burrard Inlet and Indian Arm, the university is noted for its striking modern architecture.

Spanish Banks (3)

Off this long, sandy beach on June 22, 1792, Capt. George Vancouver met the captains Galiano and Valdez and accepted Spain's surrender of the northwest coast. "It was dawn for Britain," reads a plaque on the cliffs, "but twilight for Spain."

Stanley Park (7)

Dedicated in 1899, this forest park on Vancouver's doorstep was named for Lord Stanley, governor-general of Canada in 1888-93 and presenter of the Stanley Cup. Some 35 kilometres of trails skirt Lost Lagoon, Beaver Lake, and stands of huge Douglas fir, hemlock and cedar. A seawall footpath passes Second and Third beaches and Siwash Rock—a young Indian turned to stone, according to the legend told by E. Pauline Johnson.

A lookout at Prospect Point gives fine views of the North Shore mountains and Lions Gate Bridge, which spans the harbor

entrance. A replica of the dragon figurehead of the liner *Empress of Japan* that plied the Pacific from 1891 to 1922 is on the seawall path near Brockton Point Lighthouse. Nearby is a collection of Indian totem poles. At Hallelujah Point, named in honor of the Salvation Army, the Nine O'Clock Gun has boomed out its signal each evening since 1894.

The Stanley Park Zoo houses more than 570 species. Among them are polar bears, otters, monkeys and seals, and one of the world's finest collections of king penguins.

University of British Columbia (2)

The wooded Endowment Lands, surrounding mountains and the sea form a striking setting for the UBC campus at Point Grey. Its 300 buildings include the UBC Health Sciences Center—a modern teaching and research hospital—and the stone Main Library, which houses more than 1.5 million books. At the Geological Sciences Center

Vancouver's Gastown Hums With New Life

Vancouver was founded as Gastown (34), a cluster of waterfront shanties near a lumber mill. The nearest drinking spot was in New Westminster until John "Gassy Jack" Deighton arrived in 1867 and set up his saloon. Deighton was a Yorkshireman who came to Canada in the 1860s and tried his hand at odd jobs before turning to pubkeeping. To build his saloon, he enlisted volunteer lumberjacks and fortified them with spirits. In just 24 hours, the Deighton House was open for business. As the settlement prospered, it became known as Gastown. Over the decades it declined into a slum but now hums with new life as buildings are restored and refurbished as boutiques, antique shops, pubs, cafés and art galleries.

While saner folk watch, some 200 bathers brave the chill waters of English Bay during the New Year's Day Polar Bear Swim (left), *staying in anywhere from two seconds to two hours. Centerpiece of Queen Elizabeth Park is this former quarry* (below) *transformed into a lush sunken garden.*

is the M.Y. Williams Museum of Geology and its extensive collection of fossils, minerals and gemstones. Also open to the public are the Frederic Wood Theater, the animal barns of the university's farm and the floral displays of the UBC Botanical Gardens. The ultramodern Museum of Anthropology houses a major collection of massive Indian carvings and totem poles.

Vancouver Art Gallery (28)

Modern Canadian artists are represented in the gallery's permanent collection that includes works of the Group of Seven, and major paintings of British Columbia artist Emily Carr.

Vancouver Public Aquarium (8)

Killer and beluga whales, dolphins, Atlantic harp seals and rare sea otters are among more than 8,500 specimens and 650 species on view here. The two-million-litre whale pool has underwater viewing areas and outdoor terraces.

Vandusen Botanical Display Garden (10)

Created from a former golf course, this park has three small lakes, a hedge maze and more than a dozen gardens.

A Landscape Like Holland ...
and the Legend of the Sasquatch

North Shore, Lower Fraser River Valley

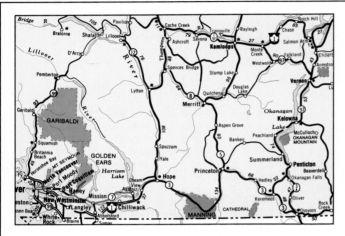

Golden Ears Mountain

GOLDEN EARS PROVINCIAL PARK

The snow-crested twin peaks of 1,706-metre Golden Ears Mountain dominate 55,000-hectare Golden Ears Provincial Park, wedged between Pitt Lake to the west and the Mount Judge Howay Recreation Area to the east. At Alouette Lake are two campgrounds with swimming and boating facilities. Hiking trails lead through forests of Douglas fir, western red cedar, hemlock and balsam in the park's lower regions. Stands of alpine fir, yellow cedar and mountain hemlock thrive at higher elevations.

PITT LAKE

This lake, a widening of the Pitt River, stretches some 25 kilometres between the steep, forested slopes and glacier-capped peaks of the Coast Mountains at its northern reaches and bogs of sphagnum moss at its southern end. Near the lake's outlet are tangles of swamp laurel and huckleberry, where rare sandhill cranes nest each spring. The waters of Pitt Lake rise and fall with the tides of the Pacific Ocean.

□ In the 1880s, a Salish Indian named Slumach claimed to have found a gold-rich creek gushing from a cavern north of the lake. Slumach was hanged for murder in 1891, without having revealed the creek's location. Since then, 16 persons have perished while searching for Slumach's "El Dorado."

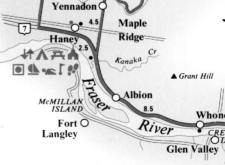

A Dutch Polder in the Mountains

In Pitt Polder, on the east bank of the Pitt River and in the shadows of the Coast Mountains to the north and east, herds of Holstein and Guernsey dairy cattle browse in lush meadows. (Polder is Dutch for a tract of low-lying land reclaimed from a river or the sea.) Sheltered behind dikes and neatly segmented by a web of drainage channels, these pastures were once impassable marshes regularly flooded by the Pitt River. In 1948, Dutch immigrants acquired the area and used their native dike-building skills to turn it into a polder. Over paths on top of the dikes, hikers and bicyclists can explore this man-made farmland.

Meadows in the Pitt Polder

HANEY

The Anglican Church of St. John the Divine is British Columbia's oldest church. It was built by the Royal Engineers in 1858 at Derby, on the south shore of the Fraser River three kilometres upstream. In 1882, the building was floated across the river and moved to its present site.

□ In Dyck's Dinosaur Park are life-sized models of prehistoric animals and a collection of fossils.

The drive between Haney and Harrison Hot Springs passes through the flat, verdant Fraser Valley, flanked by the Fraser River to the south and the Coast Mountains to the north. Across this low-lying plain flow dozens of creeks, rivers and narrow lakes, carrying the mountains' runoff into the silty waters of the Fraser, which here flows sedately to the Pacific.

Dairy farming is one of the valley's main forms of agriculture. Along the Pitt River, one of the Fraser's tributaries, Dutch immigrants have diked and drained marshy flood plains and landscaped the reclaimed area to resemble the countryside of their native Holland.

In contrast with the valley's fertile pastures, the slopes of the Coast Mountains are densely forested with fir, cedar and hemlock. Some basalt peaks are almost 1,800 metres high; many are covered with snowfields and glaciers.

The legendary Sasquatch is believed by some to roam the wooded slopes of the Coast Mountains. Sasquatch Provincial Park is named after the apelike giant.

At Harrison Hot Springs are mineral springs said to have been discovered one chilly day in 1859, when a gold miner fell from his canoe into Harrison Lake and found the water unusually warm. The lake is today a popular vacation spot.

The Sasquatch: Man, Ape or Legend?

The mountain slopes around Harrison Lake are Sasquatch country. Reportedly seen dozens of times in British Columbia and the northwestern United States, the Sasquatch is usually described as an apelike creature, up to twice the size of a man, with a flattened nose, sloping forehead and long, swinging arms. Its footprint is said to be almost 45 centimetres long.

The strongest evidence that Sasquatches exist is a short color film, taken by an amateur photographer near Yakima, Wash., in the mid-1960s, that shows a large apelike creature loping across a clearing. Scientists disagree as to the film's authenticity.

Visitors to Sasquatch Provincial Park, 6.5 kilometres north of Harrison Hot Springs, are more likely to sight bald eagles, great blue herons and mallards than they are to spot the legendary monster.

Harrison Lake

HARRISON MILLS
The Kilby Museum in Harrison Mills was built as a general store and post office in 1904. It is now a provincial historic site, where merchandise from the early 1900s—the lifetime collections of Acton Kilby, the store's original proprietor—is on display in antique showcases and on shelves.

MISSION CITY
The town's name is taken from the St. Mary's Indian Mission, founded here by Oblate Fathers in 1861.
□ On Mount Mary Ann, overlooking the Fraser Valley, is the Benedictine monastery of Westminster Abbey with its impressive 51-metre Pfitzer bell tower.
□ Among the town's attractions are Mission Raceways, a 400-metre-long drag strip, and Derby Downs, a three-lane paved track where the Western Canada Soap Box Derby championships are held every Canada Day weekend.

Pfitzer bell tower, Mission City

HARRISON HOT SPRINGS
Two mineral hot springs are the main attractions of this small vacation resort at the southern end of 65-kilometre-long Harrison Lake. Up to 20 litres per minute of the springs' sulphur- and potash-rich waters are cooled to 37°C (from their original 68°C and 72°C) and piped into one outdoor and two indoor public swimming pools and into the baths of a health spa.
□ The town has a sand beach dredged from the bed of Harrison Lake. Boaters can explore the lake's remote coves, beaches and islets.

AGASSIZ
On Mount Agassiz, north of this town, is a lookout over the Fraser Valley. A plaque tells that, during the past 50 million years, the Fraser River has built up a 1.5-kilometre-thick layer of silt on top of the valley's ancient floor.
□ On gravel bars upstream, rock hounds find agates deposited by the Fraser River.

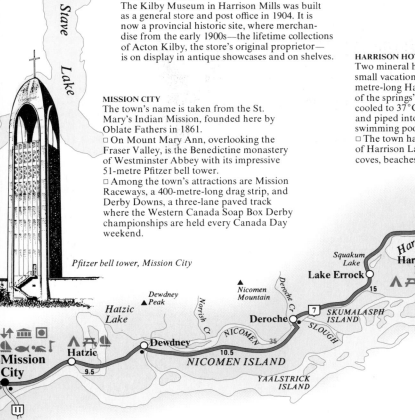

Stave Lake

Harrison Lake

SASQUATCH PROV PK

ECHO ISLAND

Harrison Hot Springs

Bear Mountain

Mount Agassiz

7.5

22   14.5   Agassiz

7

Harrison River

Harrison Mills   2

Squakum Lake

Lake Errock   15

Fraser River

Nicomen Mountain

Deroche Cr.

Deroche   7   SKUMALASPH ISLAND   SLOUGH

Dewdney Peak

Norrish Cr.

Hatzic Lake

NICOMEN   35

Mission City

Hatzic   9.5   Dewdney   10.5   NICOMEN ISLAND

YAALSTRICK ISLAND

11

Where the Fraser Turns Tame, a Garden for Vancouver

South Shore, Lower Fraser River Valley

Fort Langley

FORT LANGLEY

At Fort Langley, a palisaded Hudson's Bay Company trading post on the banks of the Fraser River, the Crown Colony of British Columbia was inaugurated on Nov. 19, 1858. The ceremony took place in the Big House, which contained officers' quarters, guest rooms and a community hall. Furnished in 1850s style, the house is now reconstructed as the centerpiece of an eight-hectare national historic park. The original fort was completed in 1841 and abandoned 45 years later. Other structures include an artisans' building, where craftsmen in period costumes make barrels like those used to export salted salmon, and a bastion, which served as a lookout for armed sentries. In a warehouse (1840), the fort's only original structure, are furs, traps, a balance scale, trade goods, provisions and a press used to bale furs into 50-kilogram packs.

Sentry in period costume
at Fort Langley

SURREY

Surrey is British Columbia's largest municipality by area, an amalgamation of the towns of Sunnyside, Cloverdale, Newton, Guildford and Whalley, covering 342 square kilometres.
□ The Surrey Zoo is a showcase of the province's wild animals. There are black bears, red foxes, bobcats, cougars, hawks and falcons and a rare black timber wolf.
□ The Serpentine Fen, a marshy area at the mouth of the Serpentine River, is an outdoor laboratory for New Westminster's Douglas College. Part farm and part wildlife refuge, it is shared by cattle, 35 species of wild animals, more than 100 species of birds, lush wetland flora and an orchard. Pheasants and wood ducks are raised for release in the wild. Visitors can hike through the fen on marked trails.

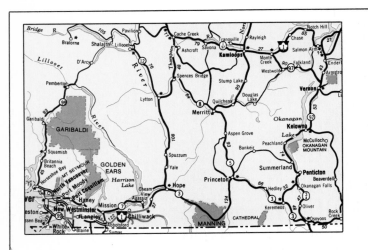

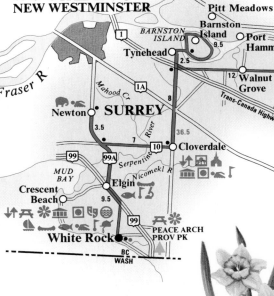

WHITE ROCK

This is the southwesternmost community on the Canadian mainland. A giant boulder lies on a sand beach at Semiahmoo Bay. Sailors used to paint it white as a navigation mark; hence the community's name.
□ The International Peace Arch straddles the Canadian-American border in a 20-hectare park jointly maintained by British Columbia and the state of Washington. It commemorates the peaceful relations that have existed between the United States and Canada since 1814.

Daffodil

ABBOTSFORD

Each August almost 1,000 aircraft, ranging from vintage biplanes to modern jets, soar over this quiet farming community during the Abbotsford International Air Show. This is North America's largest aviation and aerospace trade fair, with demonstrations of the industry's latest products, formation flights, parachuting and stunt-flying performances.
□ From the Abbotsford area come 80 percent of British Columbia's eggs and 90 percent of Canada's raspberries. At nearby Bradner, some 400 varieties of daffodils are grown. The Bradner Flower Show is held each Easter.

Rufous hummingbird

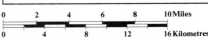

| 0 | 2 | 4 | 6 | 8 | 10 Miles |
| 0 | 4 | 8 | 12 | 16 Kilometres |

By the time the Fraser River reaches the broad flood plain stretching about 100 kilometres between Chilliwack and the Pacific Ocean, it is no longer the torrent that cut the Fraser Canyon into British Columbia's interior plateau. Instead it meanders sluggishly here, toward its wide delta at the sea. The Fraser Valley's 1,500-metre-thick layer of rich soil is silt which the river has gathered on the wild journey from its headwaters near 3,954-metre Mount Robson—the highest peak in the Canadian Rockies.

This 50-million-year accumulation, interrupted only by glaciation and mountain formation, has made the Fraser Valley British Columbia's most fertile farmland.

Dairy farms and market gardens support prosperous rural communities in the valley. Milk-processing plants, cheese factories, canneries, frozen-food plants, cattle- and poultry-feed industries and farm machinery sales and service outlets are the mainstays of Chilliwack, Abbotsford and Surrey, the valley's principal communities. Agricul-

tural fairs such as the Chilliwack Fall Exhibition and the Bradner Flower Show are showcases of the region's farm products. The Fraser Valley is the main source of food for the nearly 1.5 million people who live in Greater Vancouver.

CHILLIWACK
British Columbia and Alberta livestock, Fraser Valley crops and flowers, modern farm machinery and a horse show are major attractions of the Chilliwack Fall Exhibition, held in mid-August.
□ At the Salish Weavers' Headquarters, Indian artisans make woolen belts, bags, blankets, rugs and tapestries using traditional techniques and designs.
□ The Royal Canadian Engineers Military Museum, on the grounds of CFB Chilliwack, features a diorama of the Battle of Waterloo with 1,500 lead soldiers, military artifacts and memorabilia of Col. Richard C. Moody, the Engineers' first commander in British Columbia (1856-63).

BRIDAL VEIL FALLS PROVINCIAL PARK
Bridal Veil Falls is a 25-metre-high curtain of water descending over a sheer cliff. A 10-minute walk up a steep trail leads from a picnic site to a lookout below the falls, which provides a fine view of the misty veil. Experienced climbers can reach the base of the falls, above the lookout, via a rocky incline.

Chilliwack Lake

CHILLIWACK LAKE
At the northern tip of Chilliwack Lake are a youth hostel, a campground, picnic sites, a beach and a boat-launching ramp. A narrow logging road along the lake's eastern shore leads to Sapper Park, a picnic site at the lake's southern end. The park was built by the Royal Canadian Engineers on the site where a party of sappers (military engineers) camped in the 1850s while surveying the International Boundary.

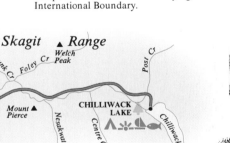
Narrow-capped morel

Cultus Lake Indian Festival

CULTUS LAKE
The lake's name comes from the Salish Indian *kul* meaning bad or worthless. But its setting among the foothills of the Cascade Mountains belies its uninviting name. Cultus Lake Provincial Park, with four campgrounds, swimming beaches and boat-launching ramps, lines most of the lake's shore.
□ During the annual Cultus Lake Indian Festival in June, Indians from British Columbia and the state of Washington stage an 11-kilometre war-canoe race across the lake.

Grand, Wild and Beautiful: Hells Gate and the Raging Fraser

Fraser and Thompson River Valleys

Two of Canada's most famous rivers, the Fraser and the Thompson, push through central British Columbia. At Lytton, where they converge, visitors can see the blue-green waters of the Thompson swallowed in the murky torrent of the Fraser—within less than 50 metres.

North of Lytton, along the banks of the Thompson, the terrain is hilly, bare of almost everything except sagebrush. Herds of beef cattle, tended by cowboys on horseback, graze on the expansive rangeland.

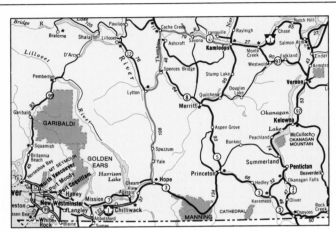

Hells Gate Airtram

LYTTON
This town was founded during the gold rush of 1858 as a staging point on the Cariboo Road. It was named for Sir Edward Bulwer-Lytton, the British Colonial Secretary at the time.
□ Jackass Mountain, to the south, was named for the mules that carried miners' and ranchers' supplies. Because of its difficult terrain, the mountain was originally known as the Hill of Despair.
□ Rock hounds in this region seek not only what gold remains but also fine jade.
□ Anglers can fish for steelhead trout in the Fraser River here.

Johnson Peak landslide, near Hope

HELLS GATE
The Fraser Canyon is at its narrowest here, barely 30 metres across. The gorge is 180 metres deep and the Fraser River thunders through it at more than 7 metres a second.
□ A rockslide at Hells Gate in 1914 drastically constricted the channel, hindering the progress of salmon to their spawning grounds and causing huge losses to the fishing industry during the next 30 years. Fish ladders built since 1945 bypass the turbulent waters. The fish ladders can be seen from a suspension bridge.
□ The Hells Gate Airtram takes visitors across the gorge for a close-up look at the Fraser River.

ALEXANDRA BRIDGE
Three bridges have spanned the Fraser River here. The site was chosen by a Royal Engineers sergeant in 1861. The first bridge built in that year was named for Alexandra, Princess of Wales, who was later Edward VII's queen. The second bridge, of similar design and in the same place, still exists—upstream from a $14 million Trans-Canada Highway bridge erected in 1962. On this latest bridge a cairn commemorates the work of the Royal Engineers in constructing the Cariboo Wagon Road.

HOPE
Some 15 kilometres east of the town, huge boulders are strewn over a wide area and a plaque at a lookout tells how, in January 1965, the side of Johnson Peak plunged into the valley below, burying the highway to a depth of 45 metres.
□ The 130-kilometre Hope-Princeton Highway was opened in 1949, making vast Manning Provincial Park accessible to the public. The highway climbs from near sea level at Hope to the 1,370-metre summit of Allison Pass.

Phacelia

YALE
The Anglican Church of St. John the Divine, the oldest house of worship in British Columbia on its original site, dates from 1859-60. It was built by miners who flocked here when gold was discovered in 1858 at nearby Hill's Bar. Once the richest of some 25 sandbars in a 50-kilometre stretch of the Fraser, Hill's Bar yielded gold worth $2 million.
□ A plaque commemorates Yale's founding in 1848 as a fur-trading post. Fifteen years later it became the southern terminus of the Cariboo Wagon Road. Later it was important during construction of the CPR

Thompson River, near Lytton

South of Lytton is Hells Gate. The raging Fraser River and the grandeur of the surrounding mountains make this rugged gorge a photographer's delight. In 1808, when explorer Simon Fraser became the first white man to pass this way, he wrote: "I . . . have never seen anything like this country. We had to pass where no human should venture . . . ."

Today, travelers on Highway 1 venture here—just to see the wildness and beauty. The spectacular Fraser Canyon remains much as it was when the explorer first journeyed down the river that now bears his name. Lookouts have been built on the route. Airtrams at Hells Gate and Boston Bar whisk sightseers across deep gorges of the Fraser.

This region was the domain of Indians and fur traders until 1858, when thousands of prospectors arrived in search of gold. Although this wealth was quickly depleted, many of the early settlements, such as Hope, Yale and Lytton, survived.

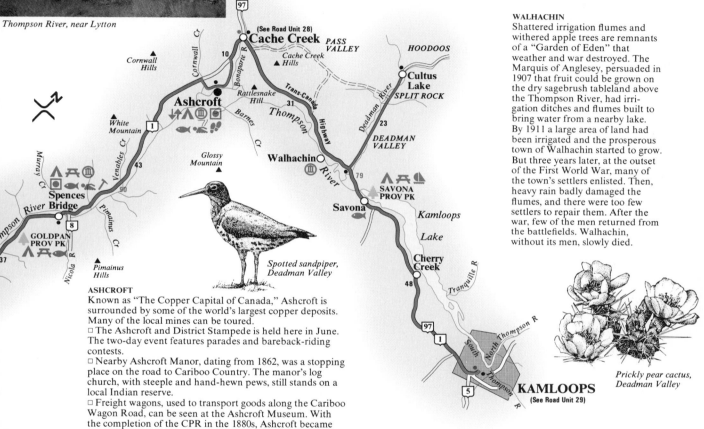

Spotted sandpiper, Deadman Valley

WALHACHIN

Shattered irrigation flumes and withered apple trees are remnants of a "Garden of Eden" that weather and war destroyed. The Marquis of Anglesey, persuaded in 1907 that fruit could be grown on the dry sagebrush tableland above the Thompson River, had irrigation ditches and flumes built to bring water from a nearby lake. By 1911 a large area of land had been irrigated and the prosperous town of Walhachin started to grow. But three years later, at the outset of the First World War, many of the town's settlers enlisted. Then, heavy rain badly damaged the flumes, and there were too few settlers to repair them. After the war, few of the men returned from the battlefields. Walhachin, without its men, slowly died.

Prickly pear cactus, Deadman Valley

ASHCROFT

Known as "The Copper Capital of Canada," Ashcroft is surrounded by some of the world's largest copper deposits. Many of the local mines can be toured.
□ The Ashcroft and District Stampede is held here in June. The two-day event features parades and bareback-riding contests.
□ Nearby Ashcroft Manor, dating from 1862, was a stopping place on the road to Cariboo Country. The manor's log church, with steeple and hand-hewn pews, still stands on a local Indian reserve.
□ Freight wagons, used to transport goods along the Cariboo Wagon Road, can be seen at the Ashcroft Museum. With the completion of the CPR in the 1880s, Ashcroft became the gateway to Cariboo Country, farther north.

St. John the Divine, Yale

High Cliffs and Hoodoos

Deadman Valley, one of the hottest and driest areas of British Columbia, was named about 1815 after a North West Company employee who was murdered here by his Indian companion. Much of the area is desert, dotted with hardy scrub, sagebrush and prickly pear cactus. Other parts are surprisingly fertile.

A road leads north from the Trans-Canada Highway, through the Deadman Valley, to the town of Cultus Lake. Along this road a multicolored cliff formation called Split Rock rises 60 metres from the Deadman River. Volcanic in origin, Split Rock is fretted with caves and fissures. Beyond Split Rock are five hoodoos, almost 12 metres high, that stand like sentinels near the northern end of the valley. These eroded pinnacles of rock and clay, each topped by an overhanging capstone, resemble giant mushrooms.

There are several lakes in the valley, and fishing for rainbow trout and kokanee salmon is good.

Hoodoos, Deadman Valley

Red Cedars in the Rain Forest, Prickly Pear Cactus in the Desert

Southwestern British Columbia

Few roads in Canada pass through a greater variety of vegetation, within such a short distance, than Highway 3 between Tashme and Osoyoos. At the western end there are dense rain forests; to the east is a desert where prickly pear cactus thrives.

In Manning Provincial Park, the highway climbs 1,350-metre Allison Pass through clumps of stunted alpine fir with an undergrowth of wild rhododendron. The eastern slope of the pass is covered by a thick blanket of Engelmann spruce which grad-

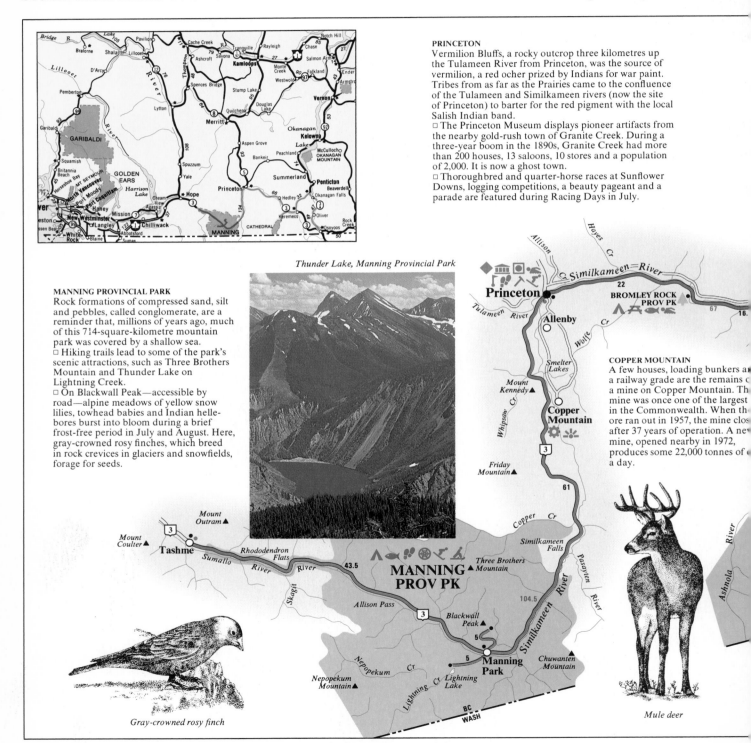

PRINCETON
Vermilion Bluffs, a rocky outcrop three kilometres up the Tulameen River from Princeton, was the source of vermilion, a red ocher prized by Indians for war paint. Tribes came from as far as the Prairies to the confluence of the Tulameen and Similkameen rivers (now the site of Princeton) to barter for the red pigment with the local Salish Indian band.
□ The Princeton Museum displays pioneer artifacts from the nearby gold-rush town of Granite Creek. During a three-year boom in the 1890s, Granite Creek had more than 200 houses, 13 saloons, 10 stores and a population of 2,000. It is now a ghost town.
□ Thoroughbred and quarter-horse races at Sunflower Downs, logging competitions, a beauty pageant and a parade are featured during Racing Days in July.

Thunder Lake, Manning Provincial Park

MANNING PROVINCIAL PARK
Rock formations of compressed sand, silt and pebbles, called conglomerate, are a reminder that, millions of years ago, much of this 714-square-kilometre mountain park was covered by a shallow sea.
□ Hiking trails lead to some of the park's scenic attractions, such as Three Brothers Mountain and Thunder Lake on Lightning Creek.
□ On Blackwall Peak—accessible by road—alpine meadows of yellow snow lilies, towhead babies and Indian hellebores burst into bloom during a brief frost-free period in July and August. Here, gray-crowned rosy finches, which breed in rock crevices in glaciers and snowfields, forage for seeds.

COPPER MOUNTAIN
A few houses, loading bunkers and a railway grade are the remains of a mine on Copper Mountain. The mine was once one of the largest in the Commonwealth. When the ore ran out in 1957, the mine closed after 37 years of operation. A new mine, opened nearby in 1972, produces some 22,000 tonnes of ore a day.

Gray-crowned rosy finch

Mule deer

Mountain road to Mascot and Nickel Plate mines, near Hedley

ually gives way to aspen, juniper, lodgepole pine and red cedar. Between Princeton and Keremeos, the scenery changes to rolling hills with sagebrush cover, where Herefords roam expansive ranges in search of nourishment, which is sparse. In the desert surrounding Osoyoos, irrigation has created lush orchards which produce some of Canada's earliest fruits each season.

Between Tashme and Manning Provincial Park, and between Princeton and Keremeos, the road follows the route of the old Dewdney Trail. This 468-kilometre former mule track, blazed by British engineer Edward Dewdney in the 1860s, connected Hope, on the Fraser River, with the goldfields of the Kootenay region.

HEDLEY

The ruins of two mineheads, the Nickel Place and Mascot, are perched on Nickel Plate Mountain overlooking the town of Hedley. A precipitous switchback road, three kilometres east of Hedley, leads to the mines. For almost half a century, until they closed in 1955, the mines produced almost $1 million worth of gold, silver, copper and arsenic each year. The path of an aerial tramway, which cut through the forest and carried the ore to a mill at the base of the mountain, can still be seen.

VASEUX LAKE PROVINCIAL PARK

This park, on the shore of Vaseux Lake, is in one of Canada's few deserts. Annual precipitation here seldom exceeds 20 centimetres (less than one-fifth that of Vancouver). Bighorn sheep and mule and white-tailed deer graze among patches of antelope bush, mariposa lily, Oregon grape and prickly pear cactus. Rattlesnakes, painted turtles and jumping mice are common. On the lake, rare trumpeter swans stop during spring and fall migrations and Canada geese live here year round.

Kaleden's Observatory Listens to the Stars

Astronomers at the Dominion Radio Astrophysical Observatory near Kaleden listen to radio waves emitted by celestial bodies. Their "ears" are two types of radio telescopes: giant dish-shaped metal reflectors and large field arrays of antennas. These instruments receive radio waves of different lengths from space. For example, a small reflector at the Kaleden Observatory records the 11-centimetre radio waves from the sun. The 26-metre reflector (*above*) collects the 21-centimetre-long emissions from more distant sources. In a field near the Kaleden Observatory 624 antennas arranged in a giant T form a receiver that picks up waves 13.5 metres long. Radio telescopes have led to the discovery of remote galaxies too far away to be photographed by the largest optical telescopes. (The observatory may be visited on Sunday afternoons in summer.)

SPOTTED LAKE

This lake, some eight kilometres west of Osoyoos, has a higher concentration of minerals than almost any body of water in the world. The minerals include magnesium sulfate (Epsom salts), sodium sulfate, calcium sulfate, sodium chloride and sodium carbonate. Except in spring and after heavy rains, the lake is almost dry. Evaporation reduces it to mud pools covered by a few centimetres of water. The pools shimmer in hues of green and blue as sunlight is reflected by the dissolved minerals. At a nearby health spa, arthritic and rheumatic ailments are treated with warm packs of mud from the lake, and baths in heated lake water.

KEREMEOS COLUMNS PARK

The only access to this 20-hectare park is by a steep eight-kilometre logging road, which branches off Highway 3 about three kilometres north of Keremeos. The park is named for a 90-metre wide jumble of hexagonal rocks which rises 30 metres from the base of a lava escarpment outside the park boundary.

CATHEDRAL PROVINCIAL PARK

Six lakes with trout (rainbow and cutthroat), five glacier-topped peaks about 2,500 metres high, and a campground on the Ashnola River are the focal points of 73-square-kilometre Cathedral Provincial Park. Hiking trails lead to eroded quartzite rocks resembling a cluster of buildings and to a towering granite cliff, 2,545 metres above sea level, which gives sweeping views of the park.

OSOYOOS

A narrow sand spit almost cuts Osoyoos Lake in two. It projects from the lake's west shore, creating a shallow ford—a *sooyoos* in Okanagan Indian dialect. Osoyoos, a version of the Indian word, became the name of the settlement which sprang up here in the mid-1800s. Indian, fur-trade and gold-miners' trails between the Fraser Valley and the Kootenays once ran across the sand spit; now it is part of Highway 3.
□ A log building (1892), once used as jail, church and schoolhouse, is now the Osoyoos Museum.

Spotted Lake

(Map labels)

Skaha Lake
Kaleden
6
Okanagan Falls
24
VASEUX LAKE PROV PK
80
Apex Mountain
3A
Vaseux Lake
Nickel Plate Mountain
edley
3
21
Vaseux Cr
19.5
Keremeos
Olalla
KEREMEOS COLUMNS PK
INKANEEP PROV PK
8
Tugulnuit Lake
Similkameen
9
3
Fairview
Oliver
Keremeos
3A
River
97
14
Mount Kobau
Okanagan R
Crater Mountain
21
Osoyoos Lake
3
Spotted Lake
HAYNES POINT PROV PK
Osoyoos
Ewart Cr
CATHEDRAL PROV PK
akeview ountain
BC WASH

Bathtub Races, Torchlight Parades and Lush Orchards

Okanagan Valley

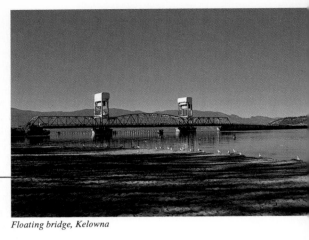

Floating bridge, Kelowna

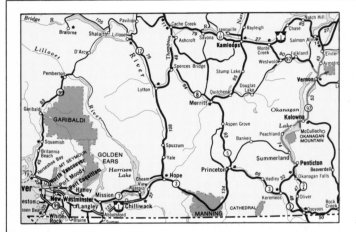

KELOWNA

A third of all apples harvested in Canada are shipped from Kelowna.

□ The first white settlement in the Okanagan was a mission, established in 1859 by the Rev. Charles Pandosy and members of his order. They planted fruit trees, and their farm and ranch (their brand was OM for Oblates of Mary) attracted other settlers.

□ A 1,400-metre-long floating bridge, built in 1958, links Kelowna with Westbank and is the longest of its kind in Canada.

□ The Kelowna International Regatta early in August is the city's biggest annual event. The 150 competitions and exhibitions include a water ballet, waterskiing and hydroplane tournaments.

□ The winter highlight of the year in Kelowna is the annual Snowfest. Events include a parade, casino, dances, and a snowmobile race.

Kelowna International Regatta

Ogopogo— the Monster of Okanagan Lake

Long before white men came to the Okanagan Valley, Indians told of a lake monster they called *N'ha-a-tik*. The creature lived in a cave near present-day Kelowna at a place called Squally Point. Indians rarely canoed near here; when they did, they would throw an animal overboard as a sacrifice.

N'ha-a-tik received its modern name in 1924 when it was dubbed "Ogopogo." A small stone statue of Ogopogo (*below*) in a Kelowna park is all most people see of the monster, but there are occasional reports from persons who claim to have seen the real thing. Ogopogo is said to be between 9 and 21 metres long, a fast swimmer with a head shaped like that of a sheep, goat or horse.

SUMMERLAND

A Canada Department of Agriculture Research Station is located at the southern entrance to this town. Established in 1914, the station covers some 325 hectares of choice land. Part of it is an ornamental garden displaying a rich assortment of flowers and trees. The garden is an excellent spot for a picnic.

□ Visitors can tour the Summerland Trout Hatchery. The fish raised here are used to stock many B.C. lakes.

PENTICTON

To the nomadic Salish Indians, *Pen-Tak-Tin* was a "place to stay forever." And so it was to Thomas Ellis, who arrived here from Ireland in 1866 and planted the first orchard in the Okanagan Valley. A plaque seven kilometres south honors Ellis, and a scale model of his homestead and some of his farm equipment are displayed at the Penticton Museum and Archives.

□ *Sicamous*, the last CPR stern-wheeler on Okanagan Lake (launched in 1914 and retired in 1951) is moored here. On board is a stage where the Penticton Theatre Club performs daily.

□ Lions, tigers, giraffes, zebras and camels are among more than 350 animals at the Okanagan Game Farm, eight kilometres south. The farm covers some 225 hectares.

□ Penticton holds a peach festival and the British Columbia Square Dance Jubilee in August. In autumn the town holds an Oktoberfest.

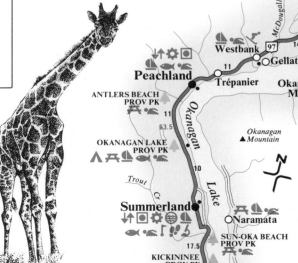

Giraffe, Okanagan Game Farm

0 2 4 6 8 10 Miles
0 4 8 12 16 Kilometres

The Okanagan Valley abounds in spectacular mountain scenery, lush orchards and quiet roads lined with fruit stands. Its northern end is dotted with dairy farms and is famed for its cheese industry. More than three million tonnes of cheddar are produced here annually.

Most years the Okanagan has more than 2,000 hours of sunshine. The Penticton area claims 10 hours of sunshine a day in July and August—more, say locals, than Hawaii.

Summer fairs and festivals include the Interior Provincial Exhibition, one of the biggest agricultural festivals in British Columbia. Begun in 1899, the four-day event is held in early September at Armstrong.

Another popular event is the Kelowna Regatta, held on Okanagan Lake (home of the legendary lake monster, Ogopogo). The regatta, held in early August, features bathtub races, and swimming and diving competitions. Other attractions in the valley are the Okanagan Game Farm, south of Penticton, annually visited by more than 100,000 people, and the historic O'Keefe Ranch, which reflects the pioneer life-style of a century ago.

Winters in the Okanagan Valley are crisp. The climate encourages outdoor activities such as skiing and snowmobiling. Western Canada's biggest winter carnival is held at Vernon in February. The celebration includes torchlight parades, dogsled races and sleighrides.

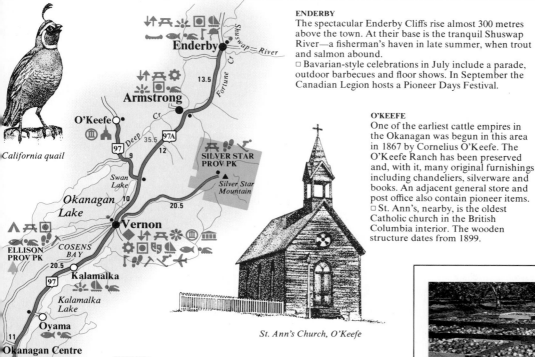

California quail

ENDERBY
The spectacular Enderby Cliffs rise almost 300 metres above the town. At their base is the tranquil Shuswap River—a fisherman's haven in late summer, when trout and salmon abound.
□ Bavarian-style celebrations in July include a parade, outdoor barbecues and floor shows. In September the Canadian Legion hosts a Pioneer Days Festival.

O'KEEFE
One of the earliest cattle empires in the Okanagan was begun in this area in 1867 by Cornelius O'Keefe. The O'Keefe Ranch has been preserved and, with it, many original furnishings including chandeliers, silverware and books. An adjacent general store and post office also contain pioneer items.
□ St. Ann's, nearby, is the oldest Catholic church in the British Columbia interior. The wooden structure dates from 1899.

ARMSTRONG
This small, proudly western town began as a ranching community. Today it is the trading center for a productive agricultural district—the Spallumcheen Valley—and has important vegetable- and fruit-packing industries.
□ A railway runs down the middle of Armstrong's main street. The street is lined with false-front stores and has raised wooden sidewalks. Inside the Armstrong hotel is a dining room with an old, hand-carved piano and a snuff dispenser still in daily use. Visitors can sample Armstrong's famous cheddar cheese.

St. Ann's Church, O'Keefe

VERNON
Exhibits in the Vernon Museum and Archives include an Indian dugout canoe and a 1908 Metz automobile. There are Salish Indian artifacts, pioneer implements and such turn-of-the-century relics as a livery stable coach and a double cutter (sleigh). The museum is part of the Vernon Civic Center.
□ Polson Park has a Chinese teahouse, a Japanese garden and a nine-metre floral clock made of 3,500 plants. The clock is the only one of its kind in western Canada.
□ Vernon's recreation complex, built in 1965-66, has a 25-metre pool, an auditorium, a gymnasium, an eight-sheet curling rink and outdoor tennis courts.

Apple harvest in the Okanagan Valley

A Cornucopia of Fruit From a Lush, Lovely Valley

Once only cactus and sagebrush grew on the dry slopes of the Okanagan Valley. Today, after irrigation, the valley is the "fruit basket of Canada," where orchards and vineyards flourish in fertile soil and mild temperatures. Fruit ripens earlier here than anywhere else in the country.

A third of the apples eaten in Canada are grown in the Okanagan. Visitors to Kelowna can tour the Sun-Rype plant and see fruit turned into juices, concentrates, nectars and pie fillings. Wineries in Kelowna and Penticton, which use locally grown grapes combined with imported varieties, can also be toured.

Roadside fruit stands—there are more than 100 between Enderby and Penticton—open with the ripening of cherries in June. The following months bring a cornucopia of fruit—apricots, peaches, pears, plums, nectarines, melons and apples.

Japenese garden, Polson Park, Vernon

Long Lakes; Flocks of Birds; Berries, Peaches and Plums

Kootenay Region

Paulson Bridge on Highway 3, north of Christina Lake

CASTLEGAR

Mining-camp relics are displayed in the Castlegar Museum along with an ornate printing press (1893), a wooden camera and various weapons.

□ A communal village in Ootischenia was built in 1971-72 to show the Doukhobor way of life in the west Kootenay country. Borscht and Russian bread and noodles are sold Saturday mornings in the summer at a market in the village.

□ In Brilliant is the tomb of Peter Verigin, who led Doukhobors to British Columbia from Saskatchewan in 1912. The tomb has been damaged by bombs several times, apparently by extremist members of the sect, and is now fenced.

KOOTENAY SKYWAY

This 70-kilometre highway, Canada's highest major road, reaches 1,600 metres in Stagleap Provincial Park and is the highest all-weather pass in the country. It connects Salmo and Creston and has spectacular views of the Selkirk Mountains and Kootenay Lake.

GREENWOOD

A former British Columbia Supreme Court building now houses the Greenwood Museum. Displays include early mining and logging equipment, and Japanese artifacts. (About 2,500 Japanese-Canadians were moved here from the west coast after Canada went to war with Japan in 1941.)

□ Bell-shaped slag formations—dumped in the early 1900s by the British Columbia Copper Company—are on the outskirts of town.

Fire engine, Grand Forks

GRAND FORKS

Located at the confluence of the Granby and Kettle rivers, Grand Forks is the unofficial capital of the Boundary country, a 200-kilometre-long chain of valleys along the U.S. border.

□ The Boundary Museum displays articles as varied as hearse lamps, a Russian samovar and a Doukhobor spinning wheel. Outside exhibits include a stagecoach and an early fire engine (c.1897).

□ Christina Lake is one of the warmest and clearest lakes in British Columbia. The lake abounds in bass and rainbow trout.

TRAIL

Trail International Days in late May are five days of art and handicraft exhibitions, and festivities involving ethnic groups. A rodeo, track-and-field competitions and a 140-kilometre bicycle race are Trail's main contributions to the British Columbia Festival of Sports on weekends in late May and early June.

□ Much of Canada's silver is produced at Cominco's lead-zinc smelter—as a byproduct of lead and zinc concentrate. *City of Lead and Zinc*, a frieze by Victoria artist George Norris, decorates a window at city hall. Cominco's 480,000-horsepower hydroelectric plant at Waneta may be visited in summer.

□ A cairn at the site of Fort Shepherd (1856-70), a Hudson's Bay Company post at the junction of the Columbia and Pend d'Oreille rivers, was built from the fort's rubble.

□ Tourist information is available at the Trail Memorial Center, which contains a public library, meeting rooms, and curling and skating areas.

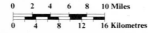

Towering mountains and gentle valleys, sparkling lakes and inviting beaches—this is British Columbia's Kootenay region.

One of the most popular areas for tourists—particularly canoeists—is the Arrow lakes. Flanked by the Selkirk and Monashee mountains, the Upper and Lower Arrow lakes stretch for 185 kilometres but are seldom wider than 3 kilometres. Beaches and campgrounds line their shores.

The Kootenay River links the Arrow lakes with Kootenay Lake and the Creston Valley. Lush and lovely, nestled between the 2,000-metre peaks of the Selkirk and Purcell mountains, the valley is a cluster of neat towns, a patchwork of grainfields and orchards, an expanse of lakes and marshes—and a bird-watcher's delight. Thousands of geese, swans and ducks pass this way regularly.

Strawberries, raspberries, pears, cherries, peaches, plums and apples are cultivated here in abundance, and in July the town of Creston celebrates with a blossom festival. Another July festival, Bavarian-style, is held at nearby Kimberley. The event attracts thousands of visitors.

Much of the Kootenay country was shaped by gold-seekers who flocked here in the 1890s. Their presence can still be felt in museums, ghost towns and abandoned mine workings scattered throughout the region.

Happy Hans, symbol of Kimberley's Beerfest

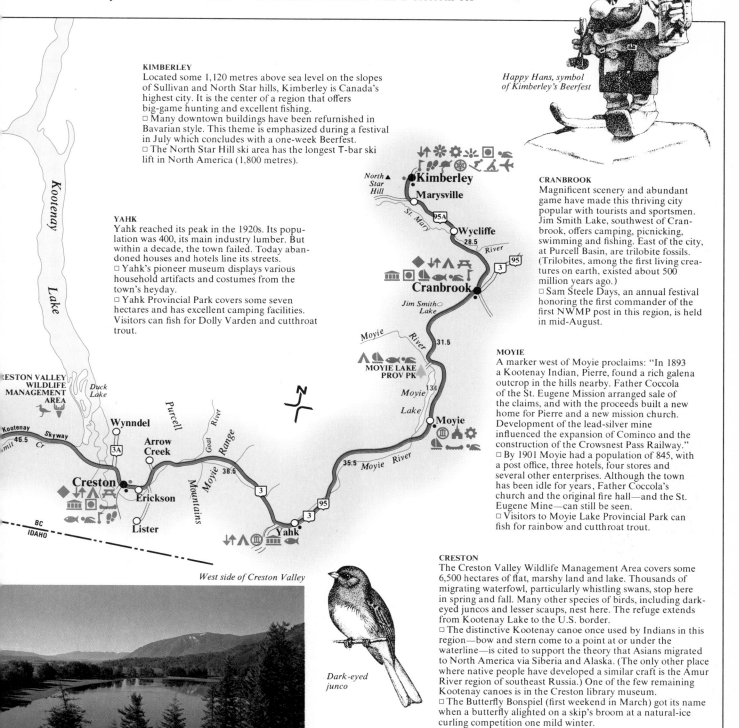

KIMBERLEY
Located some 1,120 metres above sea level on the slopes of Sullivan and North Star hills, Kimberley is Canada's highest city. It is the center of a region that offers big-game hunting and excellent fishing.
□ Many downtown buildings have been refurnished in Bavarian style. This theme is emphasized during a festival in July which concludes with a one-week Beerfest.
□ The North Star Hill ski area has the longest T-bar ski lift in North America (1,800 metres).

YAHK
Yahk reached its peak in the 1920s. Its population was 400, its main industry lumber. But within a decade, the town failed. Today abandoned houses and hotels line its streets.
□ Yahk's pioneer museum displays various household artifacts and costumes from the town's heyday.
□ Yahk Provincial Park covers some seven hectares and has excellent camping facilities. Visitors can fish for Dolly Varden and cutthroat trout.

CRANBROOK
Magnificent scenery and abundant game have made this thriving city popular with tourists and sportsmen. Jim Smith Lake, southwest of Cranbrook, offers camping, picnicking, swimming and fishing. East of the city, at Purcell Basin, are trilobite fossils. (Trilobites, among the first living creatures on earth, existed about 500 million years ago.)
□ Sam Steele Days, an annual festival honoring the first commander of the first NWMP post in this region, is held in mid-August.

MOYIE
A marker west of Moyie proclaims: "In 1893 a Kootenay Indian, Pierre, found a rich galena outcrop in the hills nearby. Father Coccola of the St. Eugene Mission arranged sale of the claims, and with the proceeds built a new home for Pierre and a new mission church. Development of the lead-silver mine influenced the expansion of Cominco and the construction of the Crowsnest Pass Railway."
□ By 1901 Moyie had a population of 845, with a post office, three hotels, four stores and several other enterprises. Although the town has been idle for years, Father Coccola's church and the original fire hall—and the St. Eugene Mine—can still be seen.
□ Visitors to Moyie Lake Provincial Park can fish for rainbow and cutthroat trout.

CRESTON
The Creston Valley Wildlife Management Area covers some 6,500 hectares of flat, marshy land and lake. Thousands of migrating waterfowl, particularly whistling swans, stop here in spring and fall. Many other species of birds, including dark-eyed juncos and lesser scaups, nest here. The refuge extends from Kootenay Lake to the U.S. border.
□ The distinctive Kootenay canoe once used by Indians in this region—bow and stern come to a point at or under the waterline—is cited to support the theory that Asians migrated to North America via Siberia and Alaska. (The only other place where native people have developed a similar craft is the Amur River region of southeast Russia.) One of the few remaining Kootenay canoes is in the Creston library museum.
□ The Butterfly Bonspiel (first weekend in March) got its name when a butterfly alighted on a skip's broom at a natural-ice curling competition one mild winter.

West side of Creston Valley

Dark-eyed junco

Where a Steep Trail Traces Slocan Valley's 'Silver Past'

Kootenay Region

Sight-seeing, photography and fishing are the major objectives of most summer visitors to the West Kootenay region—and few are disappointed. Much of the route between Nakusp and Howser is fringed with snow-mantled mountains, and lakes where fish abound. Rainbow trout—some of the world's biggest—are caught here, as well as Dolly Varden and kokanee salmon. Game includes deer and bear.

At New Denver a steep hiking trail leads to the top of 2,280-metre Idaho Peak. The

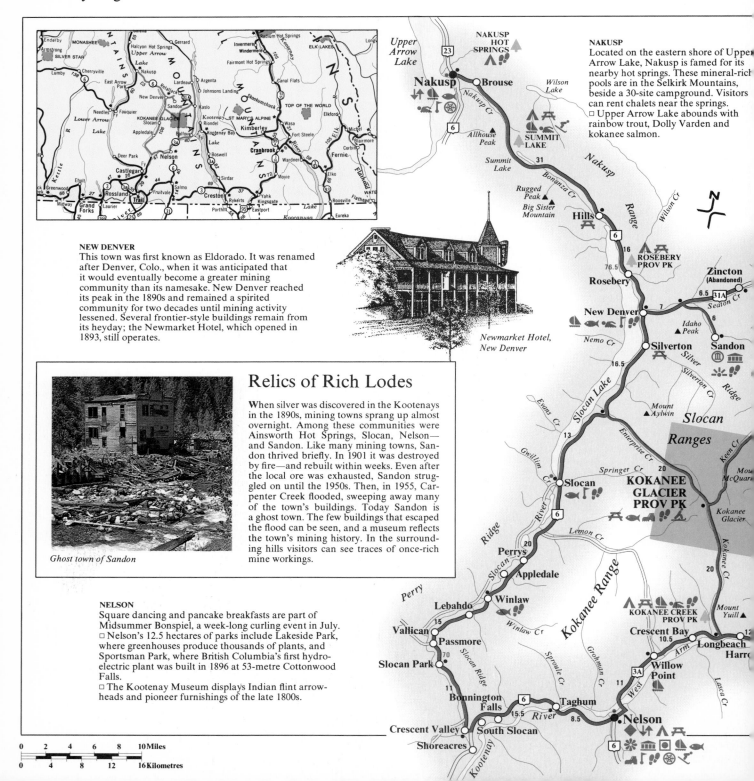

NAKUSP

Located on the eastern shore of Upper Arrow Lake, Nakusp is famed for its nearby hot springs. These mineral-rich pools are in the Selkirk Mountains, beside a 30-site campground. Visitors can rent chalets near the springs.
□ Upper Arrow Lake abounds with rainbow trout, Dolly Varden and kokanee salmon.

Newmarket Hotel, New Denver

NEW DENVER

This town was first known as Eldorado. It was renamed after Denver, Colo., when it was anticipated that it would eventually become a greater mining community than its namesake. New Denver reached its peak in the 1890s and remained a spirited community for two decades until mining activity lessened. Several frontier-style buildings remain from its heyday; the Newmarket Hotel, which opened in 1893, still operates.

Relics of Rich Lodes

When silver was discovered in the Kootenays in the 1890s, mining towns sprang up almost overnight. Among these communities were Ainsworth Hot Springs, Slocan, Nelson—and Sandon. Like many mining towns, Sandon thrived briefly. In 1901 it was destroyed by fire—and rebuilt within weeks. Even after the local ore was exhausted, Sandon struggled on until the 1950s. Then, in 1955, Carpenter Creek flooded, sweeping away many of the town's buildings. Today Sandon is a ghost town. The few buildings that escaped the flood can be seen, and a museum reflects the town's mining history. In the surrounding hills visitors can see traces of once-rich mine workings.

Ghost town of Sandon

NELSON

Square dancing and pancake breakfasts are part of Midsummer Bonspiel, a week-long curling event in July.
□ Nelson's 12.5 hectares of parks include Lakeside Park, where greenhouses produce thousands of plants, and Sportsman Park, where British Columbia's first hydro-electric plant was built in 1896 at 53-metre Cottonwood Falls.
□ The Kootenay Museum displays Indian flint arrowheads and pioneer furnishings of the late 1800s.

| 0 | 2 | 4 | 6 | 8 | 10 Miles |
| 0 | 4 | 8 | 12 | 16 Kilometres |

way is lined with abandoned tunnels and mine dumps, ghosts of the 1890s when rich silver, lead and zinc deposits made the Slocan Valley famous. Near the summit of Idaho Peak is Sandon, once a silver boom town. The Idaho Lookout, a provincial fire tower, provides a spectacular panorama of the region.

At Nelson, jagged peaks tower to 2,750 metres above ice cliffs and alpine lakes in nearby Kokanee Glacier Provincial Park. The 20-metre Bonnington Falls and rapids boil on the Kootenay River below some magnificent mountain scenery. Rocks in the area bear Indian paintings of undetermined age and origin.

At Ainsworth Hot Springs visitors can bathe in mineral-rich waters or explore the dark passageways of the Cody Caves. Farther north, at Kaslo, is the drydocked sternwheeler *Moyie*, now a museum. South of Howser visitors can see the mammoth Duncan Dam, part of the multimillion-dollar Columbia River project.

Meadow Creek spawning channel, Howser

Kokanee salmon

KASLO
S.S. *Moyie*, last of the Kootenay Lake sternwheelers, is now both a museum and a monument to Kaslo's pioneers. The 50-metre vessel, built in 1896, was used for 60 years.
□ Big silver strikes in 1893 made Kaslo a thriving city. It is now a village again, a popular resort and distribution center for the Lardeau Valley.
□ The town's annual May Day festival includes a parade, craft displays and log-rolling and hang-gliding competitions.

HOWSER
A swimming area and boat-launching ramp have been created here as part of the Duncan Dam reservoir. Although the dam cannot be toured, a viewpoint overlooks the structure.
□ At nearby Meadow Creek is a three-kilometre-long spawning channel for kokanee salmon. In the first seven years of operation, more than two and a half million kokanee passed through the channel. The kokanee begin spawning in mid-August.

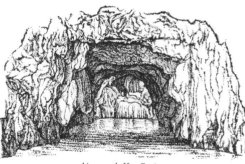

Ainsworth Hot Springs

AINSWORTH HOT SPRINGS
Discovered in the 1880s by Henry Cody, a prospector searching for gold, the Cody Caves near Ainsworth Hot Springs received little publicity until 1966, when they were designated a provincial park. The biggest chamber is the Throne Room, a 38-square-metre limestone gallery of "soda straws" (hollow fingers of calcium), stalactites and stalagmites. Other chambers include an echo room, and a room with an underground creek that drops 11 metres over upper and lower Cody Falls.
□ Not far from the caves visitors can relax and bathe in the invigorating waters of the Ainsworth Hot Springs.

Days of the Stern-Wheelers

Boat travel on Kootenay Lake peaked with the arrival of prospectors seeking silver, zinc and lead—and by the 1890s a fleet of stern-wheelers plied the lake. These steamships carried supplies for the mines, and passengers to lakeside settlements. But with the coming of the railway in the early 1900s, the need for water transportation was greatly reduced (although stern-wheelers continued to be made until the 1920s). The last stern-wheeler on the lake, the S.S. *Moyie*, was retired in 1957.

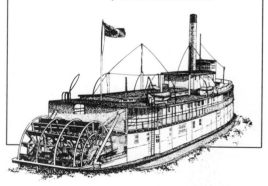

BALFOUR
This tiny community at the junction of the north, south and west arms of Kootenay Lake is the western terminus of the longest free ferry ride in North America. The 45-minute trip takes visitors across Kootenay Lake to Kootenay Bay.
□ Swimming, year-round fishing, boating, houseboating, and miniature golf are available in Balfour.

Kootenay Lake near Ainsworth Hot Springs

Duncan
Lake

Howser

Glacier

Meadow
Creek

Marblehead

Hamill Cr

Cooper Creek

Argenta

Lardeau

Davis Cr

48.5

Johnsons
Landing

Fry Cr
FRY CREEK
CANYON
REC AREA

28.5

Mount
Schroeder

Schroeder Cr

Mount
Buchanan

Kaslo

Mirror Lake

Woodbury Cr 20

Ainsworth
Hot Springs

CODY
CAVES

Kootenay
Bay

15

Ferry To Procter

Queens Bay

PILOT
BAY

Balfour

Kootenay
Lake

Lardeau River

Duncan River

Kootenay Lake

Kaslo River

31

20

31A

31

2

Gold in the Wild Horse River, Coal From the Rockies

Kootenay Region

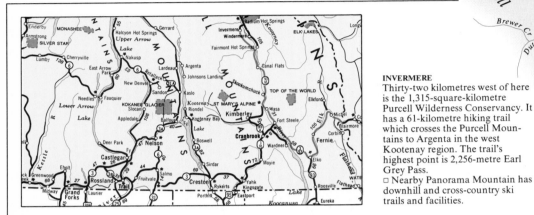

Looking for River Gold— With a Pan and a Little Luck

Visitors to Fort Steele Provincial Historic Park can pan for gold in nearby Wild Horse River, scene of a gold rush in the mid-1860s. The only equipment needed to recover nuggets or flakes is a traditional shallow steel or plastic pan (15 to 40 centimetres in diameter) and a little luck.

Fill the pan three-quarters full with sand and gravel from the riverbed or from rock crevices flooded during spring run-off. Fill the rest of the pan with water and knead (1) to remove stones and pebbles. Now shake the pan from side to side so that heavy material (gold is the heaviest) sinks to the bottom. The lighter sands are then washed away by tilting the pan and rotating it gently in the river's current (2) until a coarse dark layer, called concentrate, remains. Gold nuggets and flakes show up against the concentrate and can be picked out.

Extracting gold dust from the concentrate is more complicated. Many early prospectors used a method called mercury amalgamation. A small amount of mercury (about 12 grams per kilogram of concentrate) was kneaded into the wet mixture. It absorbed the gold and worked its way to the top, where it was collected and squeezed through a cloth (to be reused)—leaving a paste which was mostly gold. The remaining mercury was evaporated by heating the paste over fire, leaving pure gold.

Commercial mines have adapted the mercury amalgamation method on a large scale. But it is not recommended for amateur prospectors because mercury fumes are extremely poisonous.

INVERMERE
Thirty-two kilometres west of here is the 1,315-square-kilometre Purcell Wilderness Conservancy. It has a 61-kilometre hiking trail which crosses the Purcell Mountains to Argenta in the west Kootenay region. The trail's highest point is 2,256-metre Earl Grey Pass.
□ Nearby Panorama Mountain has downhill and cross-country ski trails and facilities.

PREMIER LAKE PROVINCIAL PARK
This 67-hectare park is at the south end of Premier Lake, some 15 kilometres east of Skookumchuck. A campground has swimming beaches and boat-launching facilities. In the lake are rainbow and brook trout. White-tailed and mule deer and wapiti come to its shores to drink.

WASA LAKE PROVINCIAL PARK
The sharp nasal call of the common nighthawk can be heard at dusk, as it hunts insects in this park at the northern corner of 2.3-kilometre-long Wasa Lake. A campground with sandy beaches and a boat-launching ramp is backed by a mixed forest of ponderosa and lodgepole pine, Douglas fir and trembling aspen. Western chipmunks and Columbian ground squirrels are the park's most common mammals.

Common nighthawk

Bull thistle

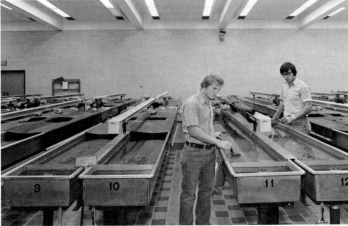

Kootenay Trout Hatchery, Wardner

The road between Invermere and Crowsnest Pass leads through the east Kootenay region. The Kootenays comprise the area between the Rocky and Selkirk mountains and are divided into an eastern and a western region by the Purcell Mountains.

Near Invermere is skiing on the groomed slopes and trails of Panorama Mountain and hiking through the silent majesty of the Purcell Mountains.

South of Invermere, past Windermere, Columbia, Premier and Wasa lakes—all excellent for fishing, boating and swimming—is the historic town of Fort Steele. Originally named Galbraith's Ferry, Fort Steele sprang up in the 1860s, when gold was discovered in nearby Wild Horse River. In the 1880s the settlement became the major town of the east Kootenay region, but declined around the turn of the century after it failed to get a railway connection. As the gold ran out, coal was discovered near Fernie in the 1870s and became the region's mainstay. The CPR relied on Kootenay coal for its steam locomotives after the opening of the transcontinental line in 1885. Today the area between Fernie and Crowsnest Pass is one of the world's major soft coal strip-mining districts, which fuels industries in North America and the Orient.

Fort Steele Provincial Historic Park

Waterwheel, Fort Steele Provincial Historic Park

SPARWOOD
Sparwood is one of British Columbia's newest towns, created in 1960 atop the largest soft coal deposits in North America. Here five million tonnes of coal are strip-mined annually by Kaiser Resources from the largest mine of its kind in Canada. The coal is shipped directly to industries in western North America and Japan, or turned into coke for smelters in Canada and the United States. Kaiser conducts regular tours of its mining complex.

FORT STEELE PROVINCIAL HISTORIC PARK
The Kootenay Gold Rush of 1864 is commemorated in restored Fort Steele, named after the Mounties' legendary Sam Steele, who established a police post here in 1887. Visitors can ride a stagecoach, pan for gold, and tour some 40 buildings including the police barracks, a ferry office (1864), three churches, a schoolhouse and a nine-metre waterwheel.
□ The town originated as a ferry terminal on the Kootenay River in 1864. Within two decades it had become the administrative center of the east Kootenay region. But the town began to decline in 1898, when it was bypassed by the CPR.

FERNIE
As the sun sets on 2,506-metre Mount Hosmer, some 15 kilometres northeast of Fernie, the shadow of a man on a galloping horse appears on the mountain wall. According to legend, the ghostly figure, cast by the jagged surface of the mountain, reminds the town that it was once cursed by a Kootenay Indian chief. In the 1880s, William Fernie, the town's founder, angered the Indians when he broke his engagement to the chief's daughter. The Indians lifted the curse in 1964.

RDNER
he Kootenay Trout Hatchery, eight kilo-
res north of Wardner, some eight million
bow, brook, lake and cutthroat trout are
ed each year from eggs collected in the
l. A constant flow of fresh, cool water
ugh giant troughs and ponds simulates
fishes' natural environment. The
chery's water consumption equals that
town of 50,000. Visitors are welcome
ear.

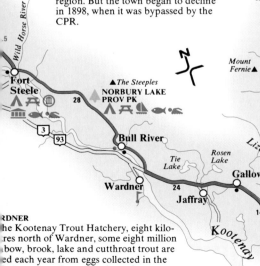

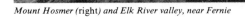
Mount Hosmer (right) and Elk River valley, near Fernie

Canada's Houseboat Capital... and Swarms of Sockeyes

South-Central British Columbia

The fur trade, a short-lived gold rush and the transcontinental railway, all lured fortune-seekers to "the Shuswap." In their wake, thousands of vacationers now throng to this gentle wilderness.

Protected anchorages, warm water and safe, sandy beaches have made Shuswap Lake a boater's paradise. Sicamous, one of several bustling towns ringing the lake, proudly bills itself as the "Houseboat Capital of Canada."

From Sicamous boaters have access to

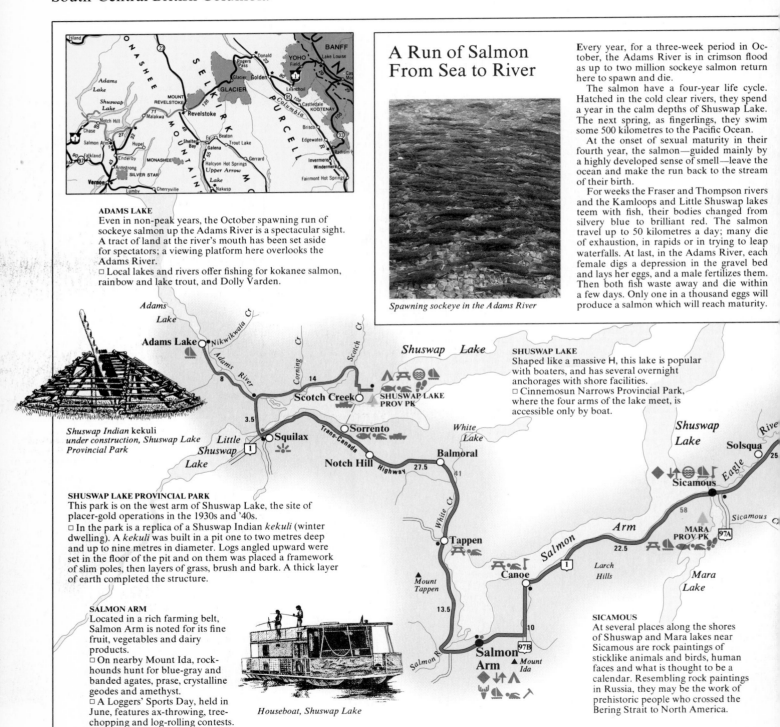

A Run of Salmon From Sea to River

Every year, for a three-week period in October, the Adams River is in crimson flood as up to two million sockeye salmon return here to spawn and die.

The salmon have a four-year life cycle. Hatched in the cold clear rivers, they spend a year in the calm depths of Shuswap Lake. The next spring, as fingerlings, they swim some 500 kilometres to the Pacific Ocean.

At the onset of sexual maturity in their fourth year, the salmon—guided mainly by a highly developed sense of smell—leave the ocean and make the run back to the stream of their birth.

For weeks the Fraser and Thompson rivers and the Kamloops and Little Shuswap lakes teem with fish, their bodies changed from silvery blue to brilliant red. The salmon travel up to 50 kilometres a day; many die of exhaustion, in rapids or in trying to leap waterfalls. At last, in the Adams River, each female digs a depression in the gravel bed and lays her eggs, and a male fertilizes them. Then both fish waste away and die within a few days. Only one in a thousand eggs will produce a salmon which will reach maturity.

Spawning sockeye in the Adams River

ADAMS LAKE
Even in non-peak years, the October spawning run of sockeye salmon up the Adams River is a spectacular sight. A tract of land at the river's mouth has been set aside for spectators; a viewing platform here overlooks the Adams River.
□ Local lakes and rivers offer fishing for kokanee salmon, rainbow and lake trout, and Dolly Varden.

Shuswap Indian kekuli under construction, Shuswap Lake Provincial Park

SHUSWAP LAKE
Shaped like a massive H, this lake is popular with boaters, and has several overnight anchorages with shore facilities.
□ Cinnemousun Narrows Provincial Park, where the four arms of the lake meet, is accessible only by boat.

SHUSWAP LAKE PROVINCIAL PARK
This park is on the west arm of Shuswap Lake, the site of placer-gold operations in the 1930s and '40s.
□ In the park is a replica of a Shuswap Indian *kekuli* (winter dwelling). A *kekuli* was built in a pit one to two metres deep and up to nine metres in diameter. Logs angled upward were set in the floor of the pit and on them was placed a framework of slim poles, then layers of grass, brush and bark. A thick layer of earth completed the structure.

SALMON ARM
Located in a rich farming belt, Salmon Arm is noted for its fine fruit, vegetables and dairy products.
□ On nearby Mount Ida, rockhounds hunt for blue-gray and banded agates, prase, crystalline geodes and amethyst.
□ A Loggers' Sports Day, held in June, features ax-throwing, tree-chopping and log-rolling contests.

Houseboat, Shuswap Lake

SICAMOUS
At several places along the shores of Shuswap and Mara lakes near Sicamous are rock paintings of sticklike animals and birds, human faces and what is thought to be a calendar. Resembling rock paintings in Russia, they may be the work of prehistoric people who crossed the Bering Strait to North America.

0 1 2 3 4 5 Miles
0 2 4 6 8 Kilometres

two lakeside provincial parks and almost 1,600 kilometres of attractive shoreline dotted with marinas, campgrounds and fine swimming spots.

One of many natural attractions in the Shuswap is the sockeye salmon run in the Adams River. During a three-week period in October, as many as two million salmon in crimson spawning colors gather to bury their eggs in a short stretch of riverbed.

In contrast with placid Shuswap Lake is the high, rocky spine of Mount Revelstoke National Park. Erosion and glaciers have relentlessly chipped and carved its landscape. Abundant rainfall in the park supports thick forests of giant cedar and hemlock in the valleys, and a kaleidoscope of alpine flowers on the peaks. Rising to the very top of 1,938-metre Mount Revelstoke, Summit Road presents a spectacular transition from the park's dense lowland forest to alpine meadows.

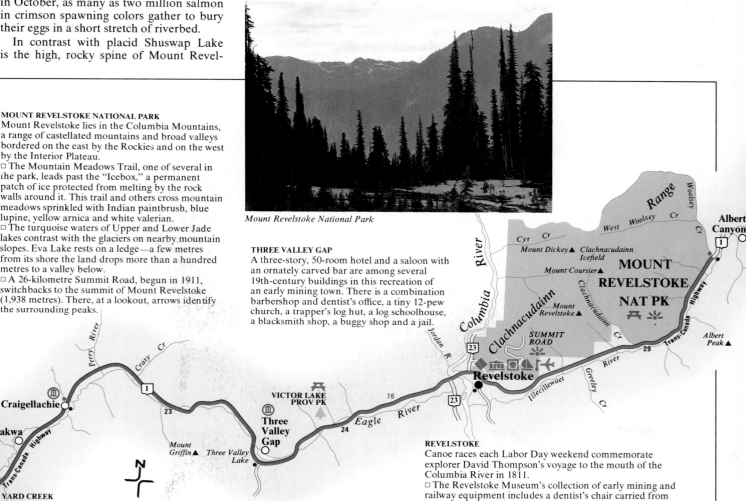

Mount Revelstoke National Park

MOUNT REVELSTOKE NATIONAL PARK

Mount Revelstoke lies in the Columbia Mountains, a range of castellated mountains and broad valleys bordered on the east by the Rockies and on the west by the Interior Plateau.
□ The Mountain Meadows Trail, one of several in the park, leads past the "Icebox," a permanent patch of ice protected from melting by the rock walls around it. This trail and others cross mountain meadows sprinkled with Indian paintbrush, blue lupine, yellow arnica and white valerian.
□ The turquoise waters of Upper and Lower Jade lakes contrast with the glaciers on nearby mountain slopes. Eva Lake rests on a ledge—a few metres from its shore the land drops more than a hundred metres to a valley below.
□ A 26-kilometre Summit Road, begun in 1911, switchbacks to the summit of Mount Revelstoke (1,938 metres). There, at a lookout, arrows identify the surrounding peaks.

THREE VALLEY GAP

A three-story, 50-room hotel and a saloon with an ornately carved bar are among several 19th-century buildings in this recreation of an early mining town. There is a combination barbershop and dentist's office, a tiny 12-pew church, a trapper's log hut, a log schoolhouse, a blacksmith shop, a buggy shop and a jail.

REVELSTOKE

Canoe races each Labor Day weekend commemorate explorer David Thompson's voyage to the mouth of the Columbia River in 1811.
□ The Revelstoke Museum's collection of early mining and railway equipment includes a dentist's chair carried from mine to mine during a gold rush here in the early 1900s.

Where the Last Spike Was Hammered Home

Canada's most famous photograph (*left*) shows Donald Smith, a director of the CPR, driving the last spike in Canada's first transcontinental railway. The date was Nov. 7, 1885; the site, a siding named Craigellachie, in Eagle Pass. Smith hammered home an ordinary iron spike. There was a moment of silence, and then a cheer went up among the men who were gathered around. "All I can say is that the work has been well done in every way," summed up William Cornelius Van Horne, the stubborn, hard-driving CPR vice-president who had completed the railway in four years when everybody said it couldn't be done in ten. Today a cairn marks the spot where the last spike was driven. A plaque beside the nearby Trans-Canada Highway reads: "A nebulous dream was a reality: an iron ribbon crossed Canada from sea to sea. Often following the footsteps of early explorers, nearly 3,000 miles of steel rail pushed across vast prairies, cleft lofty mountain passes, twisted through canyons, and bridged a thousand streams."

Revelstoke

Snow-Mantled Peaks in a Mountain Playground

Kootenay Region

The 8,000-kilometre Trans-Canada Highway encounters few regions as spectacular as the hot springs, ice fields and glaciers of the Purcell, Selkirk and Rocky mountains. Between Glacier and Yoho national parks, the Trans-Canada follows the Illecillewaet, Columbia and Kicking Horse rivers through a mountain playground resplendent with awe-inspiring beauty. For those who seek nature's solitude, the region has a vast network of trails along rocky slopes and through evergreen forests.

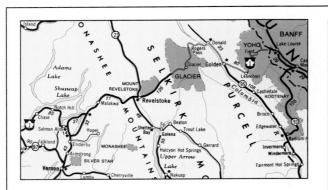

In Glacier National Park, one of the world's heaviest snowfalls creates huge avalanches that can strip mountains of trees and bury sections of road. Concrete snow sheds, one more than half a kilometre long, cover the Trans-Canada Highway at danger spots. Earth dams and barriers of rubble divert less severe slides. When scientists notice avalanche buildups, parts of the highway are closed and an artillery crew fires howitzer shells into unstable snow. This triggers an avalanche, but under controlled conditions, and prevents dangerous accumulations of snow.

Fighting Avalanches With Artillery

GLACIER NATIONAL PARK
The ancient mountains of the Selkirk Range, formed millions of years before the Rockies, cradle more than 100 glaciers in this 1,350-square-kilometre park. The Illecillewaet and Asulkan glaciers near the slopes of Mount Sir Donald are reached by hiking trails from the Illecillewaet campground. More than 250 square kilometres of glaciers and *névé* (granular snow) provide superb skiing in the Asulkan Valley. The park's slow-moving rivers of ice spawn a glistening network of alpine lakes, rivers and waterfalls. Thick forests of western red cedar and western hemlock are home to ravens and Steller's jays. Grasses and mountain flowers such as alpine anemones and glacier lilies thrive in meadows above the tree line.
□ The park was established in 1886 and for more than 70 years was accessible only by railroad. Now it is traversed by 43 kilometres of the 147-kilometre Rogers Pass section of the Trans-Canada Highway.

Alpine anemone

Glacier National Park

ROGERS PASS
One of the world's most beautiful mountain roads is the Rogers Pass section of the Trans-Canada Highway (between Golden and Revelstoke). It winds past rugged peaks, emerald lakes and immense ice fields, threads deep ravines and clings to precipitous cliffs. A 1.5-kilometre hiking trail at the summit of 1,320-metre Rogers Pass wanders east through the Selkirk Range.

Clark's nutcracker

| 0 | 2 | 4 | 6 | 8 | 10 Miles |
| 0 | 4 | 8 | 12 | 16 Kilometres |

More than 100 glaciers mantle the peaks of the Purcell Mountains and Selkirk Range in Glacier National Park. Meltwater from the glaciers spawns hundreds of alpine lakes, rivers and waterfalls. Thick forests and meadows covered with lush grasses and vivid wildflowers are also part of the stunning scenery.

The glacier-fed Kicking Horse River (named for an ornery packhorse) courses through Yoho National Park. Yoho's peaks—30 of which are more than 3,000 metres—are interlaced with spectacular alpine waters.

Blue-green Emerald Lake and its collar of evergreens are surrounded by gargantuan ice-topped peaks. The Yoho River, milky gray with silt from Yoho Glacier, crashes into the clear Kicking Horse River at the Meeting of the Waters. The misty plume of Laughing Falls, and 381-metre Takakkaw Falls, Canada's highest waterfall, are in the Yoho River valley.

Takakkaw Falls, Yoho National Park

EMERALD LAKE
Lovely Emerald Lake in Yoho National Park, named for its deep green color, is surrounded by a dozen snowcapped peaks. Hiking trails lead to 2,180-metre Burgess Pass to the east, Hamilton Falls and Hamilton Lake to the west, and Wapta Icefield to the north. A trail skirts Emerald Lake and passes a picnic area and a horse rental stable.

TAKAKKAW FALLS
Canada's highest uninterrupted cascade plunges 381 metres into the Yoho River. The stream that feeds this waterfall in Yoho National Park originates in Daly Glacier and courses through a U-shaped hanging valley. Nearby is the Meeting of the Waters, where the Yoho River, laden with silt from Yoho Glacier, merges with the clear Kicking Horse River.

Steller's jay

YOHO NATIONAL PARK
This 536-square-kilometre wonderland on the west slope of the Rockies richly deserves its Indian name of Yoho—an exclamation of awe and astonishment. West of Field, the Kicking Horse River has carved a hole in a wall of sedimentary rock, leaving a 15-metre-long natural bridge. To the southwest, at Wapta Falls, the river is a 60-metre-wide sheet of water. Some 400 kilometres of trails lead to other geological features. In Hoodoo Valley are 15-metre-high pillars of glacial till capped by precariously balanced boulders. Wildlife includes wapiti, bear, moose, deer, mountain goat and 180 species of birds. Valleys are clothed with evergreens—lodgepole pine, Douglas fir and white spruce—and above the 2,133-metre tree line are colorful alpine flowers and bushes. The Trans-Canada Highway, which passes through the park, offers superb views of Yoho's peaks—30 of which are higher than 3,000 metres.

Skiers in Yoho National Park

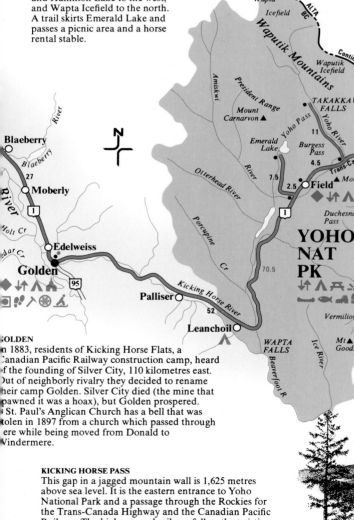

GOLDEN
In 1883, residents of Kicking Horse Flats, a Canadian Pacific Railway construction camp, heard of the founding of Silver City, 110 kilometres east. Out of neighborly rivalry they decided to rename their camp Golden. Silver City died (the mine that spawned it was a hoax), but Golden prospered. St. Paul's Anglican Church has a bell that was stolen in 1897 from a church which passed through here while being moved from Donald to Windermere.

KICKING HORSE PASS
This gap in a jagged mountain wall is 1,625 metres above sea level. It is the eastern entrance to Yoho National Park and a passage through the Rockies for the Trans-Canada Highway and the Canadian Pacific Railway. The highway and railway follow the twisting Kicking Horse River across the park. The pass straddles the Continental Divide, a height of land which separates rivers and streams flowing to the Pacific, Arctic and Atlantic oceans.

Boulder-capped hoodoo,
Yoho National Park

Primroses and Mountain Goats in a Park of Hanging Glaciers

Kootenay National Park

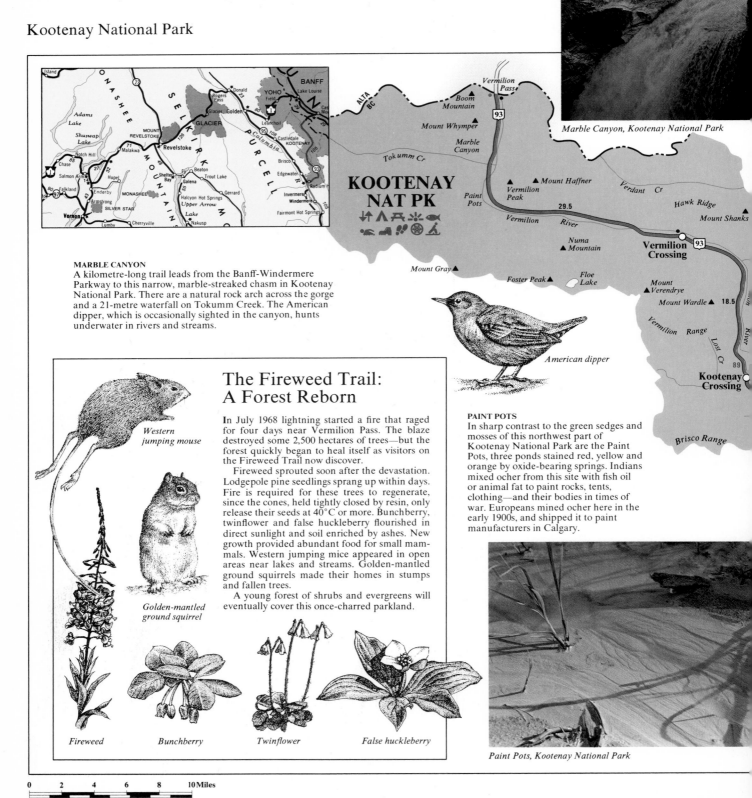

Marble Canyon, Kootenay National Park

KOOTENAY NAT PK

MARBLE CANYON
A kilometre-long trail leads from the Banff-Windermere Parkway to this narrow, marble-streaked chasm in Kootenay National Park. There are a natural rock arch across the gorge and a 21-metre waterfall on Tokumm Creek. The American dipper, which is occasionally sighted in the canyon, hunts underwater in rivers and streams.

American dipper

Western jumping mouse

Golden-mantled ground squirrel

The Fireweed Trail: A Forest Reborn

In July 1968 lightning started a fire that raged for four days near Vermilion Pass. The blaze destroyed some 2,500 hectares of trees—but the forest quickly began to heal itself as visitors on the Fireweed Trail now discover.

Fireweed sprouted soon after the devastation. Lodgepole pine seedlings sprang up within days. Fire is required for these trees to regenerate, since the cones, held tightly closed by resin, only release their seeds at 40°C or more. Bunchberry, twinflower and false huckleberry flourished in direct sunlight and soil enriched by ashes. New growth provided abundant food for small mammals. Western jumping mice appeared in open areas near lakes and streams. Golden-mantled ground squirrels made their homes in stumps and fallen trees.

A young forest of shrubs and evergreens will eventually cover this once-charred parkland.

PAINT POTS
In sharp contrast to the green sedges and mosses of this northwest part of Kootenay National Park are the Paint Pots, three ponds stained red, yellow and orange by oxide-bearing springs. Indians mixed ocher from this site with fish oil or animal fat to paint rocks, tents, clothing—and their bodies in times of war. Europeans mined ocher here in the early 1900s, and shipped it to paint manufacturers in Calgary.

Fireweed

Bunchberry

Twinflower

False huckleberry

Paint Pots, Kootenay National Park

| 0 | 2 | 4 | 6 | 8 | 10 Miles |
| 0 | 4 | 8 | | 12 | 16 Kilometres |

Blessed with magnificent mountain scenery, Kootenay National Park is a striking blend of hot springs and cold lakes, of deep canyons and of glaciers twisting down lofty summits. This 1,406-square-kilometre park lies on the western slopes of the Rocky Mountains, and borders Banff and Yoho national parks.

In summer, streams draining glaciers rush down mountain slopes and empty into the Vermilion, Kootenay and Columbia rivers. Some lakes nestle among mountains with steep rocky walls which plunge to the water's edge. Hundreds of pools, marshes and small lakes lie in glacial depressions called kettles. Wildflowers—mariposa lilies, dwarf Canadian primroses and butterworts—cover meadows near hanging glaciers and snowfields.

Western tanagers, pine siskins and Audubon's warblers are found in the forests. Mountain goats, grizzly bears and wapiti inhabit the park. Moose and deer are frequently seen at creekside "licks"—clay banks rich in minerals that animals find pleasant-tasting.

Landmarks along the Banff-Windermere Parkway (Highway 93) dividing the park are Radium Hot Springs, the Sinclair and Marble canyons, the Paint Pots and, at the northern entrance, 1,650-metre Vermilion Pass—the boundary between Alberta and British Columbia, and the summit of the Continental Divide. Rivers east of here drain to the Arctic Ocean or Hudson Bay. Waters to the west flow toward the Pacific.

KOOTENAY NATIONAL PARK

This park was established in 1920 to preserve canyons, mineral hot springs and waterfalls along the Banff-Windermere Parkway. The 105-kilometre highway provides dramatic views of snowcapped mountains. It passes through Sinclair Canyon, whose sheer walls rise some 61 metres above the road, over 1,485-metre Sinclair Pass, and skirts the Rock Wall, a vertical face of the Vermilion Valley.
□ The self-guiding Fireweed, Marble Canyon and Paint Pots trails begin along the parkway. The Fireweed Trail, near Vermilion Pass, loops through meadows of fireweed, harebell, yellow columbine, Labrador tea, and lodgepole pine.
□ Kootenay National Park is actually an ancient ocean floor that, some 75 million years ago, was compressed, folded and sculpted into the Rocky Mountains. Marble Canyon follows a fault in the limestone and marble bedrock, which has been eroded to depths of 37 metres by Tokumm Creek. A 21-metre waterfall at the head of the canyon is milky white from glacial meltwaters that feed it.
□ Two park-operated mineral pools at Radium Hot Springs are open year round, and night swimming is permitted in summer.

Spring-Fed Pools— Rich in Minerals, Bathwater Warm

Hot springs originate as surface water (1)—rain or melted snow—which seeps through cracks or faults until it is heated by molten rock (2) some five kilometres underground. Temperatures as high as 1,000°C turn the water to steam, which rises through cracks in the rocks, condenses into water as it cools, and bubbles from the ground (3) as warm as bathwater. Some two million litres of water gush from the ground each day at Radium Hot Springs.

Health spas and bathing pools are often built near hot springs because the mineral-rich water is reputed to relieve arthritis and other ailments. A trace of dissolved radium gives Radium Hot Springs its name—but the radioactivity is less than that of a watch's illuminated dial.

RADIUM HOT SPRINGS

This year-round resort at the foot of Redstreak Mountain developed where hot, odor-free mineral water gushes from the ground at as much as 45°C. Around these springs that Indians called kootemik (places of hot water) are two outdoor pools, steam rooms, plunge baths and dressing rooms. A self-guiding nature trail offers a 30-minute hike east to Sinclair Canyon.
□ Stations of the Cross on a steep hill behind Queen of Peace Roman Catholic Church overlook the Columbia River valley and Kootenay National Park.
□ This is a departure point for Columbia River cruises. Sightseers frequently see bighorn sheep, deer, bears, ospreys, and golden and bald eagles on the river's shores.

Mountain goats, Kootenay National Park

WINDERMERE

St. Peter's Anglican Church, sometimes called St. Peter's the Stolen, was originally built in Donald, some 160 kilometres north. When the CPR abandoned Donald in 1897, the bishop granted the church to a neighboring congregation. But St. Peter's parishioners who moved to Windermere dismantled their church and took it with them by rail and Columbia River barge.
□ A monument commemorates Kootenae House, established in 1807 by David Thompson as the first trading post on the Columbia River.

FAIRMONT HOT SPRINGS

...dorless mineral springs are at the ...rthern end of Columbia Lake, ...e source of the Columbia River. ...nternational hang-gliding ...mpetitions are held at nearby ...vansea Mountain in August. ...he nearby Dutch Creek ...odoos are the most impressive ...their kind west of Alberta.

A Sense of Mystery,
Traces of a Haida Past

Queen Charlotte Islands

The rugged mountains and lush forests of the Queen Charlotte Islands are often shrouded in mist and rain, heightening a sense of mystery in the remote land that was once the domain of Haida Indians. Here and there in the silent forests are the remains of ancient Haida totem poles and dugout canoes. Along the coast are a number of abandoned whaling stations.

The Queen Charlottes are poised on the brink of the continental shelf. The islands'

McIntyre Bay

Robert Davidson's totem pole, Haida

DIXON ENTRANCE

McINTYRE BAY

ENTRY PT

MASSET HAR

Haida

Masset

DELKATLA INLET

GRAHAM ISLAND

Drizzle Lake

MASSET SOUND

Pure Lake

KUMDIS ISLAND

Port Clements

MASSET INLET

HAIDA

The first new totem pole in this Indian village in almost a century was erected in 1969. It was carved by artist Robert Davidson in honor of his grandfather, a Haida chief.
□ Two more new totems are at a museum displaying Haida artifacts.

MASSET

This is the largest settlement on Graham Island. Most residents work in the town's fishing industry—a crab cannery and a fish-freezing plant. Tiny Delkatla Inlet provides a harbor for the local fishing fleet. Huge Sitka spruce, their lower branches thick with mosses, grow in the dense forests here. Canada geese, sandhill cranes, trumpeter swans and other waterfowl stop during migration at nearby Delkatla Wildlife Sanctuary.

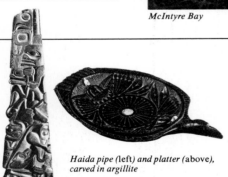

Haida pipe (left) and platter (above), carved in argillite

Beauty in Carved Stone

The Haida, whose domain was the lush Queen Charlotte Islands, were expert hunters and fishermen, fearless warriors, and skilled wood-carvers. From cedar logs they built longhouses and seagoing dugout canoes, and carved totem poles.

After Europeans arrived in 1774, the Haida traded for goods and liquor. Sea otters and seals were slaughtered almost to extinction in only 40 years. The Haida, nearly annihilated by the white man's diseases, abandoned ancestral homes and settled in villages now called Skidegate Mission and Haida.

In the 1820s, with the discovery of argillite, a soft, slatelike stone found only at Slatechuck Mountain on Graham Island, the Haida used their wood-carving skills to make stone sculptures with designs based on their mythology. Beautiful argillite ornaments (*above*) made by modern craftsmen at Haida and Skidegate Mission attest to the survival of this unique art form.

The Golden Spruce, near Port Clements

PORT CLEMENTS

Port Clements, an early settlement on Masset Inlet, is a logging and fishing community. On the Yakoun River, south of Port Clements, a trail leads into a rain forest. One tall tree of gold looms from the dark green woods. The Golden Spruce, more than 300 years old and 50 metres tall, is a mystery to foresters. It produces only green-boughed seedlings.
□ Farther southwest another trail leads to an uncompleted Haida dugout canoe, dating from at least 1900. Other uncompleted canoes have been found in the bush, but this site (cleared by logging operations) is the only accessible one on the Queen Charlotte Islands. Signs mark the trail, and the canoe is protected by a shelter.

0 2 4 6 8 10 Miles
0 4 8 12 16 Kilometres

west coasts plummet almost 3,050 metres to the floor of the Pacific Ocean. But the seabed of Hecate Strait, which separates the islands from the British Columbia mainland, is part of the continental shelf and in some places only 15 metres deep.

Although the islands are at the latitude of James Bay, winters are mild. The seasons are moderated to an annual average of 8°C by the great Kuroshio (Japan) Current, a warm ocean stream.

The two main islands, separated by Skidegate Channel, are Graham Island to the north and Moresby Island to the south. Most visitors arrive in the Charlottes at Sandspit Airport on Moresby (from Vancouver or Prince Rupert), then travel by bus to Alliford Bay, where a ferry crosses Skidegate Inlet to Skidegate on Graham Island. Cars can be rented at Sandspit, and on Graham Island at Masset, Queen Charlotte and Port Clements.

Logging roads lead off the main road into the interior. They are open to the public after working hours and on weekends.

Naikoon Provincial Park

NAIKOON PROVINCIAL PARK

Naikoon, the Haida name for the jutting northeast corner of Graham Island, means "long nose." Here, some 707 square kilometres of wilderness have been preserved in Naikoon Provincial Park.

The park has nearly 97 kilometres of beaches, where creatures such as burrowing razor clams are found. At a picnic site on McIntyre Bay, a footpath leads to the top of 109-metre Tow Hill. To the north across Dixon Entrance are Alaska's Dall and Prince of Wales islands. At the end of a hard-packed sand beach is Rose Point, the northeastern tip of the Charlottes. Beyond the breakers of Dixon Entrance and Hecate Strait, fishermen trap Dungeness crabs.

High-Flying Eagles and Ancient Murrelets

The streamlined, powerful peregrine falcon (one of the fastest of all birds) is more abundant in the Queen Charlotte Islands than anywhere else in the world. Easily overtaking flying prey, this bird often kills in the air with a single blow from its large, taloned feet.

Bald eagles (*left*) nest in tall trees all over the islands. The adults' white heads and tail plumage contrast sharply with their brown, almost black bodies. The young are brown, mottled with white, until their fourth year. In late summer and early fall, bald eagles can be seen flocking to salmon-spawning streams.

Subspecies of the saw-whet owl, hairy woodpecker and Steller's jay are restricted to these islands, as are ancient murrelets (the Queen Charlottes are their only Canadian breeding ground).

SKIDEGATE MISSION

A single weathered totem pole, about a hundred years old, stands at the Haida village of Skidegate Mission. A new totem, carved by Haida artist Bill Reid, forms part of the front of the Skidegate Haida band council house, which is built in the style of a traditional Haida longhouse.
□ Here Haida craftsmen fashion gold and silver rings, bracelets, brooches and earrings in traditional designs. Others produce argillite ornaments and miniature totems.
□ Haida artifacts at the Queen Charlotte Islands Museum include bone and antler tools and a traditional bentwood carved box (with sides made of a single piece of wood, steamed and bent into shape).
□ On the shore north of Skidegate Mission is Balance Rock, a four-metre-high boulder which balances on a narrow base.

Balance Rock, north of Skidegate Mission

QUEEN CHARLOTTE ISLANDS

HECATE STRAIT

Oeanda River

Cape Ball R

CAPE BALL

NAIKOON PROV PK

River

Mayer River

ayer ake

22

Tlell

18.5

Tlell River

LAWN PT

Lawnhill O—— HALIBUT BIGHT

DEAD TREE PT

51.5

18.5

BALANCE ROCK

SKIDEGATE INLET

O Sandspit

Skidegate Mission

Skidegate

14.5 MORESBY ISLAND

Queen Charlotte O—— 5

O Alliford Bay
Ferry

LINA ISLAND

MAUDE ISLAND

KAGAN BAY

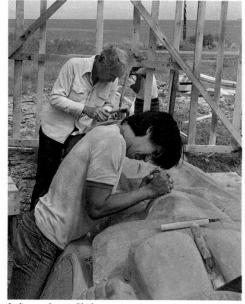

Indian sculptors, Skidegate

The 'River of Mists' in a Land of Totem Poles

Skeena River Valley

Called by Indians "the river of mists," the Skeena surges through rock-ribbed canyons and past sculpted mountains on its journey to the Pacific Ocean. Along the Yellowhead Highway, travelers can witness the river's final flourishes.

Its headwaters are icy, emerald pools in the Gunanoot Mountains. From there, the Skeena flows in a broad valley flanked by 1,800-metre peaks, then is joined by the muddy Bulkley River at Hazelton.

High above the junction of the rivers is

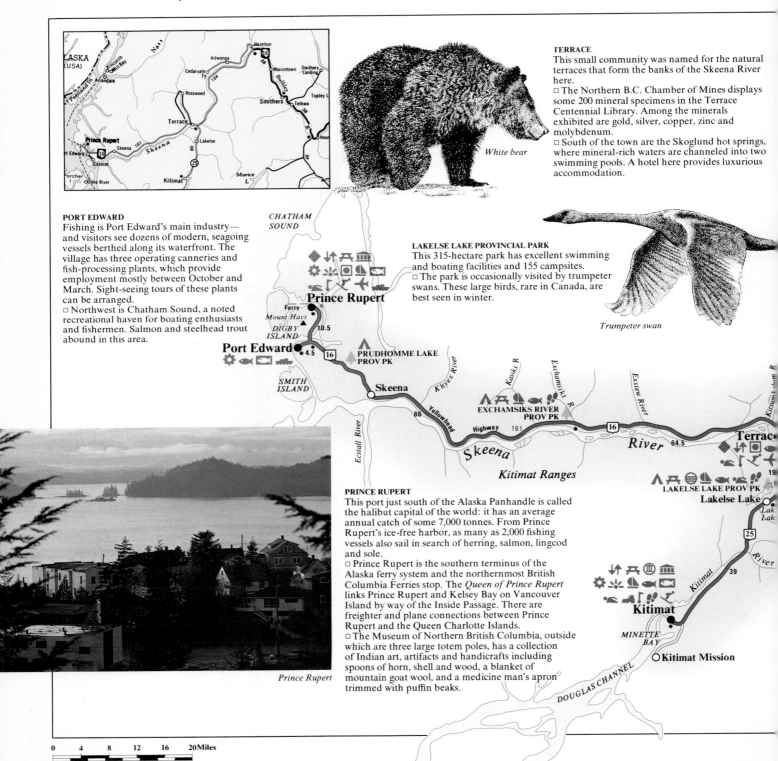

White bear

Trumpeter swan

Prince Rupert

TERRACE
This small community was named for the natural terraces that form the banks of the Skeena River here.
□ The Northern B.C. Chamber of Mines displays some 200 mineral specimens in the Terrace Centennial Library. Among the minerals exhibited are gold, silver, copper, zinc and molybdenum.
□ South of the town are the Skoglund hot springs, where mineral-rich waters are channeled into two swimming pools. A hotel here provides luxurious accommodation.

PORT EDWARD
Fishing is Port Edward's main industry—and visitors see dozens of modern, seagoing vessels berthed along its waterfront. The village has three operating canneries and fish-processing plants, which provide employment mostly between October and March. Sight-seeing tours of these plants can be arranged.
□ Northwest is Chatham Sound, a noted recreational haven for boating enthusiasts and fishermen. Salmon and steelhead trout abound in this area.

LAKELSE LAKE PROVINCIAL PARK
This 315-hectare park has excellent swimming and boating facilities and 155 campsites.
□ The park is occasionally visited by trumpeter swans. These large birds, rare in Canada, are best seen in winter.

PRINCE RUPERT
This port just south of the Alaska Panhandle is called the halibut capital of the world: it has an average annual catch of some 7,000 tonnes. From Prince Rupert's ice-free harbor, as many as 2,000 fishing vessels also sail in search of herring, salmon, lingcod and sole.
□ Prince Rupert is the southern terminus of the Alaska ferry system and the northernmost British Columbia Ferries stop. The *Queen of Prince Rupert* links Prince Rupert and Kelsey Bay on Vancouver Island by way of the Inside Passage. There are freighter and plane connections between Prince Rupert and the Queen Charlotte Islands.
□ The Museum of Northern British Columbia, outside which are three large totem poles, has a collection of Indian art, artifacts and handicrafts including spoons of horn, shell and wood, a blanket of mountain goat wool, and a medicine man's apron trimmed with puffin beaks.

Rocher Déboulé Mountain, a 2,438-metre peak furrowed by meltwater channels. Within 65 kilometres of the confluence are communities such as Kispiox, Kitwanga and Kitseguecla—and the greatest concentration of totem poles in Canada.

The Skeena bursts through the Coast Mountains at Kitselas, then empties into the Pacific at Prince Rupert, the province's second most important port (after Vancouver). Its harbor is a colorful mixture of fishing fleets and pleasure craft. Waterfront canneries process halibut, the port's main catch. Founded on Kaien Island at the turn of the century, Prince Rupert is the Canadian National Railway's western terminus. A huge grain elevator at the railhead stores prairie wheat for shipment overseas. Farther south, Kitimat is a haven for sport fishermen, who troll for salmon in the sheltered waters of Douglas Channel.

Longhouses, 'Ksan Indian Village

SKEENA RIVER
The Skeena by day is beautiful and changeable—shrouded in mist one moment, bright in sunshine the next. It rises in northern British Columbia and winds through narrow canyons and broad valleys to the Pacific. The mouth of the Skeena is near Prince Rupert, a port city where pleasure craft, fishing boats, cruise ships and ferries dock. Tides push up the Skeena almost to the town of Terrace. North of Terrace the river separates the Nass and Bulkley ranges of the Hazelton Mountains; west of Terrace it enters the Coast Mountains. There are few permanent settlements north of Kispiox, except logging and trapping camps.

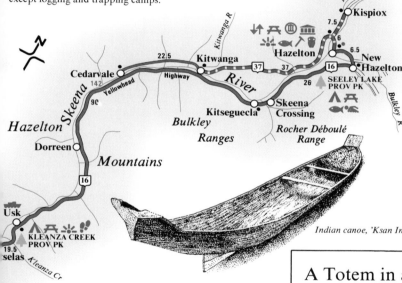

Indian canoe, 'Ksan Indian Village

HAZELTON
'Ksan, near Hazelton, is a reconstruction of a Gitksan Indian village that stood at the junction of the Bulkley and Skeena rivers in 1872, when the first white men arrived. The village's six cedar longhouses, its totem poles, fish traps, smokehouses and dugout canoes make it the showplace of a region rich in Indian culture, a heavily forested land the Gitksan considered sacred.

Two of the longhouses have designs painted over the doorways and most have carved interior poles. In the Stone Age House are some 50 mannequins of Indians making clothes and utensils from cedar bark. The Feast House shows the life of the Gitksan people after traders brought muskets, iron kettles and blankets. The Treasure House is a museum of costumes, handicrafts and carvings. Gitksan crafts are offered for sale in one longhouse. In two others, Indian students are taught carving, and experienced carvers can be seen at work.

KITIMAT
This town was built in the wilderness in the early 1950s by the Aluminum Company of Canada, on a site chosen because of its deep-sea harbor, the proximity of hydroelectric power at Kemano (southeast of Kitimat) and its level land for building.
□ Alcan's aluminum smelter, one of the world's biggest, with an annual capacity of almost 300,000 tonnes, is eight kilometres from Kitimat's center; beyond is the harbor where alumina from Jamaica and Australia is unloaded and from which Kitimat aluminum ingots are shipped to dozens of countries. Illustrated lectures, films and bus tours of the smelter and dock areas are provided in summer.
□ The Kitimat Museum has art exhibits and natural history displays.
□ There is year-round saltwater fishing in Douglas Channel (lingcod, salmon and halibut) and during most seasons there is good fishing in the Kitimat River and its tributaries (salmon, trout and Dolly Varden).

A Totem in a Top Hat
The Gitksan Indians were hunters and fishermen who prospered in the mild Skeena River valley with its plentiful fish and wildlife. In their leisure time the Gitksan developed elaborate art forms—songs, dances, and totem poles carved in red cedar.

By the mid-19th century, with the arrival of white traders, metal tools replaced stone implements. Gitksan totem-pole carving enjoyed a brief "golden age." When the Gitksan were forced to work for European employers to obtain the white man's coveted trade goods, they lost the free time for their arts. Missionaries and government officials tore down totem poles, and banned rituals, ceremonies and dances as pagan observances.

Fears that the few remaining Gitksan treasures would be lost or destroyed led to the construction in 1970 of the 'Ksan Village. New artifacts were produced by local carvers, and ceremonial dancing and singing were revived. Of the five totem poles in the village, one with a top-hatted figure (*right*) was erected to mark the help of non-Indians in restoring the Gitksan way of life.

Steelhead Trout, Salmon and Stands of White Spruce

North-Central British Columbia

Highway 16 leads across a gently rolling plateau, bordered by the Coast Mountains to the west and by the high spine of the Rockies to the east. This region is freckled with lakes—from icy trout ponds to huge reservoirs teeming with arctic char.

In the clear waters of Tchesinkut Lake, trout are tantalizingly visible at depths of seven metres. Babine Lake, north of Topley, is an important spawning ground for sockeye salmon. Its shoreline is indented with secluded bays and inlets.

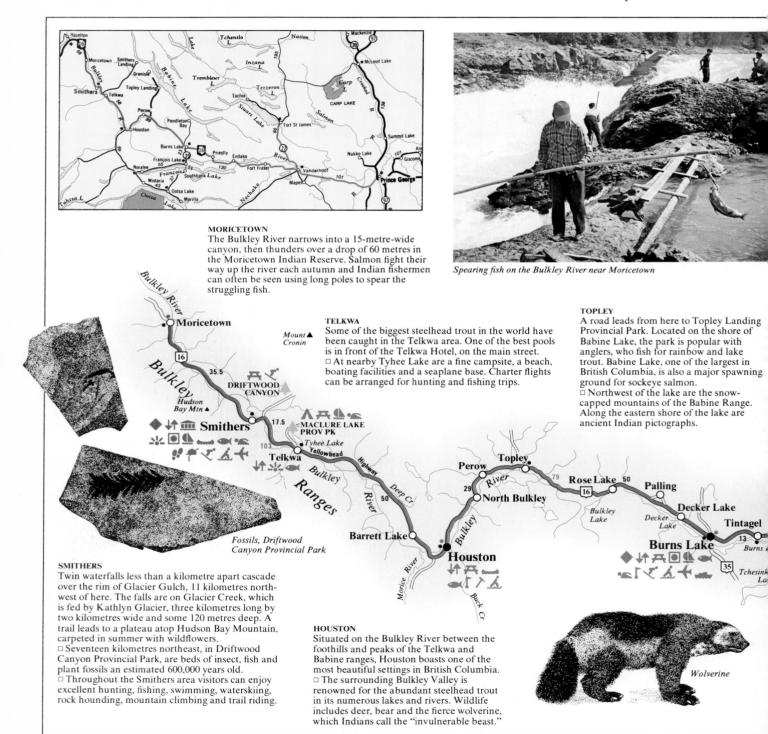

Spearing fish on the Bulkley River near Moricetown

MORICETOWN
The Bulkley River narrows into a 15-metre-wide canyon, then thunders over a drop of 60 metres in the Moricetown Indian Reserve. Salmon fight their way up the river each autumn and Indian fishermen can often be seen using long poles to spear the struggling fish.

TELKWA
Some of the biggest steelhead trout in the world have been caught in the Telkwa area. One of the best pools is in front of the Telkwa Hotel, on the main street.
□ At nearby Tyhee Lake are a fine campsite, a beach, boating facilities and a seaplane base. Charter flights can be arranged for hunting and fishing trips.

TOPLEY
A road leads from here to Topley Landing Provincial Park. Located on the shore of Babine Lake, the park is popular with anglers, who fish for rainbow and lake trout. Babine Lake, one of the largest in British Columbia, is also a major spawning ground for sockeye salmon.
□ Northwest of the lake are the snow-capped mountains of the Babine Range. Along the eastern shore of the lake are ancient Indian pictographs.

Fossils, Driftwood Canyon Provincial Park

Wolverine

SMITHERS
Twin waterfalls less than a kilometre apart cascade over the rim of Glacier Gulch, 11 kilometres northwest of here. The falls are on Glacier Creek, which is fed by Kathlyn Glacier, three kilometres long by two kilometres wide and some 120 metres deep. A trail leads to a plateau atop Hudson Bay Mountain, carpeted in summer with wildflowers.
□ Seventeen kilometres northeast, in Driftwood Canyon Provincial Park, are beds of insect, fish and plant fossils an estimated 600,000 years old.
□ Throughout the Smithers area visitors can enjoy excellent hunting, fishing, swimming, waterskiing, rock hounding, mountain climbing and trail riding.

HOUSTON
Situated on the Bulkley River between the foothills and peaks of the Telkwa and Babine ranges, Houston boasts one of the most beautiful settings in British Columbia.
□ The surrounding Bulkley Valley is renowned for the abundant steelhead trout in its numerous lakes and rivers. Wildlife includes deer, bear and the fierce wolverine, which Indians call the "invulnerable beast."

| 0 | 4 | 8 | 12 | 16 | 20 Miles |
| 0 | 8 | 16 | 24 | | 32 Kilometres |

Anglers can land steelhead trout where the Bulkley River passes the town of Telkwa. Nearby the river flows through a reserve where Indians spear salmon struggling upstream to spawn.

Farther north along the Bulkley River, the town of Smithers lies at the base of Hudson Bay Mountain. This 2,438-metre peak, with its three-kilometre-long icy blue Kathlyn Glacier, affords excellent downhill skiing. In summer its meadows are ablaze with alpine flowers.

Rivers lined with cottonwoods meander through farms and ranches in the Vanderhoof district. The horizon is broken by serrated peaks with summits wreathed in mist.

In 1807, Simon Fraser's men felled stands of white spruce near the junction of the Nechako and Fraser rivers to build Fort George (present-day Prince George). Pulp-and-paper-processing plants and sawmills have made this community the commercial capital of north-central British Columbia.

Sinkut Falls, near Vanderhoof

Fraser's Fort in New Caledonia

Fort St. James dates from 1806, when Simon Fraser and John Stuart built a North West Company fort here. When the company merged with the Hudson's Bay Company in 1821, the HBC made Fort St. James its chief post in New Caledonia, a vast area between the Rockies and the Coast Mountains. One of the old fur warehouses (*left*), a clerk's house (c. 1880) and a fish cache remain on the site, now a national historic park.

A Roman Catholic mission was founded here in 1843 and Our Lady of Good Hope Church (1870) is still used for services.

A Carrier Indian village—"Carrier" because widows once carried around their dead husbands' ashes—adjoins Fort St. James. In the village is the grave of Kwah, a Carrier chief who saved the life of James Douglas (governor of British Columbia between 1858 and 1864) in an Indian uprising. Douglas was an HBC assistant factor at Fort St. James in the late 1820s.

VANDERHOOF
This town is the geographical center of British Columbia. It was named after Herbert Vanderhoof, a Chicago publicity agent hired in 1908 by the Canadian government to launch a campaign to attract settlers to western Canada.
□ The town, in the Nechako Valley, is on a major Canada goose flyway. To the west is Fraser Lake, where Simon Fraser built a North West Company fort in 1806. There is a monument to the explorer.

FORT FRASER
A plaque near the spot where the last spike of the Grand Trunk Pacific Railway was driven (April 7, 1914) is less than two kilometres east of this village.
□ Just west of Fort Fraser is Fraser Lake, a settlement beside the lake of the same name. The town has boat-launching facilities and a small landing strip. There are tours of the area's mining complex. A winter carnival is held in February, and a fishing derby lasts from May to October.

BURNS LAKE
This community began as a tent town, founded in 1914 by a trapper named Barney Mulvaney. In 1917 Mulvaney had the townsite surveyed and sold in lots. A cabin which he operated as a gambling hall—nicknamed "The Bucket of Blood"—can still be seen. Next to it once stood Mulvaney's hotel.
Near Burns Lake, on the road to Tadako, a white picket fence surrounds the grave of "Bulldog" Kelly, shot and killed in a poker game argument in 1913. The grave is all that remains of the railway camp of Freeport.

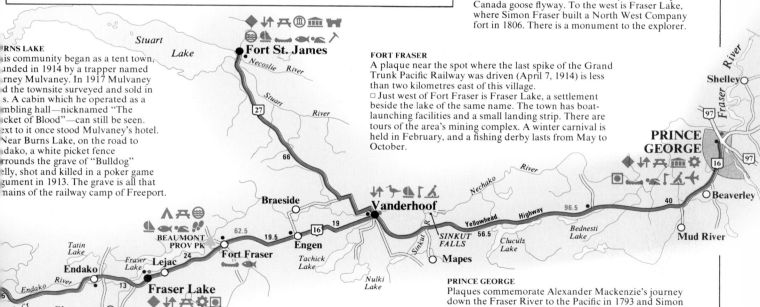

Prince George

PRINCE GEORGE
Plaques commemorate Alexander Mackenzie's journey down the Fraser River to the Pacific in 1793 and Simon Fraser's founding of Fort George 14 years later.
□ The city rebuilt Fraser's North West Company fort on its original site in 1958—in 36-hectare Fort George Park. Within the palisade is a museum. Mounted birds and animals reflect the area's natural history; the façades of pioneer buildings—a hotel, a surveyor's office and a general store—serve as backgrounds for exhibits of pioneer furnishings.
□ The 445-kilometre Cariboo Highway from Cache Creek joins the John Hart Highway at Prince George. The Hart Highway leads 410 kilometres northeast to Dawson Creek, the southern terminus of the Alaska Highway.
□ Logging sports, scuba diving and dogsled and car races on the Tabor Lake ice are features of the week-long Prince George Winter Carnival in January.

Open Rangelands, Steep Canyons and Coastal Rain Forests

Central British Columbia

West of Williams Lake Highway 20 winds through open rangelands, wild sedge and grass meadows and clumps of lodgepole pine. This is the expansive Chilcotin country, a section of British Columbia's interior plateau that lies between the Fraser River and the Coast Mountains. It is one of the province's main ranching

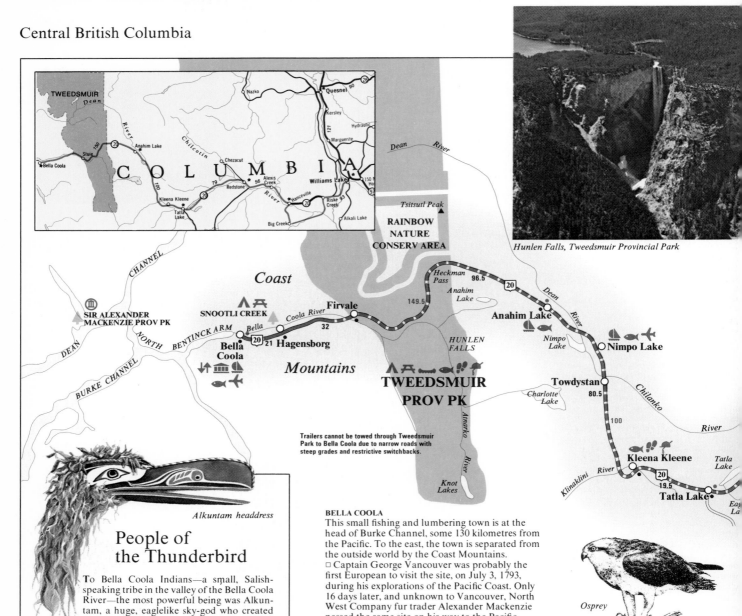

Hunlen Falls, Tweedsmuir Provincial Park

Trailers cannot be towed through Tweedsmuir Park to Bella Coola due to narrow roads with steep grades and restrictive switchbacks.

Alkuntam headdress

People of the Thunderbird

To Bella Coola Indians—a small, Salish-speaking tribe in the valley of the Bella Coola River—the most powerful being was Alkuntam, a huge, eaglelike sky-god who created the world. His beating wings caused thunder, his snapping eyes lightning. The god lived high in the Coast Mountains, where supernatural beings staged dances and dramas for his entertainment. His worshipers believed that after death the soul of a Bella Coola ascended to the benevolent Alkuntam.

The Bella Coola once numbered about 3,000. But diseases brought by traders decimated their numbers. Today there are about 600 living in the town of Bella Coola. Their ancient tribal dances still are reenacted at special private ceremonies in the winter.

BELLA COOLA
This small fishing and lumbering town is at the head of Burke Channel, some 130 kilometres from the Pacific. To the east, the town is separated from the outside world by the Coast Mountains.
□ Captain George Vancouver was probably the first European to visit the site, on July 3, 1793, during his explorations of the Pacific Coast. Only 16 days later, and unknown to Vancouver, North West Company fur trader Alexander Mackenzie passed the same site on his way to the Pacific Ocean. On a rock in Dean Channel, some 40 kilometres west of here, Mackenzie inscribed these words: "Alex Mackenzie from Canada by land 22ᵈ July 1793." Sir Alexander Mackenzie Provincial Park has been established around what is believed to be Mackenzie's Rock. The park is accessible only by boat.
□ Bella Coola was founded in 1894, by about 90 Norwegian-Americans escaping an economic depression in the United States. The Bella Coola Museum exhibits household articles, tools and fishing implements used by these pioneers.

Osprey

ANAHIM LAKE
A stampede is held at Anahim Lake during the second weekend of July.
□ At nearby Ulkatcho Indian Village are smokehouses where Indians dry salmon caught in the Atnarko River in Tweedsmuir Provincial Park.
□ There is fly-fishing for rainbow trout in the quiet waters of Anahim Lake.

0 4 8 12 16 20 Miles

0 8 16 24 32 Kilometres

areas, where cattle roam freely, often grazing alongside the highway or ambling across it. (On Chilcotin roads cattle have the right-of-way!)

Between Hanceville and Redstone the drive is along the Chilcotin River, which flows through steep canyons—some more than 300 metres deep—marked by sandstone pillars and lava escarpments.

Leaving the river, the road meanders past quiet lakes such as Puntzi, Tatla, Nimpo and Anahim, where fly-fishing for rainbow trout is excellent. Nights in this area can be cold, even in summer. The village of Kleena Kleene, for instance, at 880 metres elevation, has only 30 frost-free days per year.

At Anahim Lake the road leaves the Chilcotin plateau and climbs over 1,500-metre Heckman Pass through the mountains of Tweedsmuir Provincial Park. (Because the narrow road has steep grades and precarious switchbacks, trailers cannot be used in the park and must be left at Anahim Lake.)

Beyond the park the highway twists for 20 breathtaking kilometres into the Bella Coola Valley, a region of coastal rain forests some 1,000 metres below, with tangles of salmonberry, thimbleberry, bearberry, maple and cedar. The road ends at Bella Coola on the tidal flats of North Bentinck Arm, an extension of Burke Channel, a fjord of the Pacific Coast.

TWEEDSMUIR PROVINCIAL PARK
Imposing snowcapped mountains, grassy basins, alpine meadows, glaciers, fast rivers, deep canyons, peaceful lakes, and thundering waterfalls make Tweedsmuir Provincial Park one of Canada's most varied wilderness areas.
□ This 9,600-square-kilometre park is bounded on the north by Ootsa and Whitesail lakes, on the west by the Coast Mountains, and on the east by British Columbia's interior plateau. Highway 20 cuts through the southern tip of the park; the northern portion has no road access.
□ A 16-kilometre hiking trail leads south between Atnarko River Campground and Hunlen Falls, whose 366-metre drop is the third highest in Canada. Nearby Lonesome Lake is the winter home for about 400 trumpeter swans, an estimated 20 percent of the world's population of this endangered species.
□ The Atnarko and Talchako rivers and their tributaries provide fishing for cutthroat, steelhead and rainbow trout, and coho and chinook salmon. In fall local Indians meet at pools on the rivers, as they have done for centuries, to spear and net fish to be smoked for winter use.

Williams Lake Stampede, Williams Lake

WILLIAMS LAKE
Williams Lake is the gateway to Chilcotin country, a cattle-grazing area to the west. Dubbed the "cowboy capital" of British Columbia, the town is the province's main livestock center. Its stockyards handle about 40,000 head of cattle annually.
□ Traditional cowboy skills are displayed at the Williams Lake Stampede, a four-day event held each July. Rodeo performers from Canada and the United States compete for prizes in bronc riding, steer wrestling, calf roping, bull riding, wild-cow milking, and wild-horse racing. Between competitions, there are cowboy breakfasts, barbecues and square dances.

RISKE CREEK
Almost 400 California bighorn sheep live in this triangular, 450-hectare provincial game preserve at the confluence of the Chilcotin and Fraser rivers, some 20 kilometres south of Riske Creek. California bighorns are one of only six species of wild sheep in the world. These stocky animals can be seen climbing the steep river banks.

Farwell Canyon, Chilcotin River

California bighorn sheep

Cowboy Country

The Chilcotin region is a 5,000-square-kilometre plateau of rangeland, where tens of thousands of beef cattle roam expanses of unfenced grassland. The herds are mostly Herefords, efficient grazers who are hardy and fast-maturing. Cowboys ride out in all weather to tend their animals. They round up the herds for sales or winter feeding, keep them from straying, and rope and brand young animals.

Ranching has been the mainstay of the Chilcotin since settlement began here in the 1860s. The grasslands attracted stockmen who found a ready market for their beef in the gold camps of the Cariboo, east of the Fraser River. Now the cattle are sold at the Williams Lake stockyards.

Gold-Rush Relics, Roadhouses and an El Dorado named Barkerville

Central British Columbia

The Williams Lake-Quesnel-Barkerville stretch of the modern Cariboo Highway follows parts of a wagon road, built in stages during the Gold Rush of the 1860s. Between Williams Lake and Kersley, Highway 97 leads through Cariboo country, a vast rolling plateau with scattered groves of aspen and lodgepole pine, and with sloughs and small, shallow lakes.

Near Soda Creek the road passes the northern entrance of the 435-kilometre-long Fraser Canyon. North of Kersley the high-

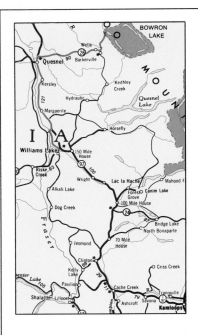

QUESNEL

Until the mid-1800s a Hudson's Bay Company store (now restored on Front Street) was the only building on the site of what is now Quesnel. But the Cariboo Gold Rush of the 1860s led to the development of a town here, where miners from the goldfields farther east bought supplies. Now the town is the largest in the Cariboo with more than 7,000 persons.
□ A Cornish waterwheel from the gold rush days is preserved on the east bank of the Fraser River. It was used to pump out mine shafts. The Quesnel Museum in Le Bourdais Park displays gold-mining equipment, including a sluice box and a pan and rockers.
□ During Billy Barker Days, a four-day celebration in July, Quesnel commemorates its gold rush origins. Gold-pan-throwing contests, dances, raft races, and a lottery for a chunk of Cariboo gold are among the highlights of the festivities.

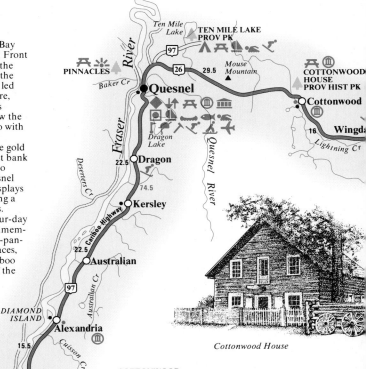

Cottonwood House

COTTONWOOD

Here, in a 10-hectare provincial historic park, is Cottonwood House, the only complete surviving roadhouse from the 610-kilometre Cariboo Wagon Road between Yale and Barkerville. The building dates from 1864. It still contains its old furnishings brought to the Cariboo during the gold rush of the 1860s. Among the period pieces are desks, chests, a table, two reclining chairs, a barrel stove and a kitchen stove with two ovens.

SODA CREEK

This community is at the head of the perilous 435-kilometre Fraser Canyon (between here and Yale). From here north the Fraser River is navigable for 650 kilometres. During the Cariboo Gold Rush, steam engines, boilers and other ship parts were brought here and assembled into stern-wheelers. The first vessel was built in 1863. Eventually a fleet of nine steamers ferried miners and their supplies along the 90-kilometre stretch of Fraser River between here and Quesnel. From there the only route to the goldfields was by land.
□ In 1921 the era of steam navigation on the upper Fraser ended when the last of the stern-wheelers was wrecked near Prince George. A plaque, 18 kilometres north, commemorates the contribution the stern-wheelers made to the development of the Cariboo.

Basalt columns, Alexandria

ALEXANDRIA

A cairn marks the approximate site of Fort Alexandria, a North West Company fur-trading post, built in 1821 and named for Alexander Mackenzie, the first man to cross the northern part of North America by land from coast to coast.
□ The McInnis House, believed to have been one of the fort's farm buildings, is three kilometres south. During the 1860s it served as a stopping place for miners en route to the goldfields.
□ The modern Cariboo Highway passes west of a formation of basalt columns, known as the "devil's palisades."

way crosses an area thick with Engelmann spruce and alpine fir. A maze of creeks and streams draining the Cariboo Mountains has cut gullies and canyons into the land. Precipitation is high, usually more than 120 centimetres annually (about 20 centimetres more than Vancouver).

Here nature has placed one of the strongest lures known to man: gold. Among cracks in the rocks of the Cariboo Mountains are threaded thick veins of it. Erosion and ice age glaciers wore away much of the metal.

It was deposited in the form of powder, flakes or nuggets in the sand and gravel beds of Cariboo rivers and streams.

In the early 1800s, Indians sold chunks of gold to the Hudson's Bay Company. When the company exchanged the metal for money at the San Francisco mint, in February 1858, the rumors of untold riches in the Cariboo flew out and a gold rush began.

Almost all settlements along the Cariboo Highway owe their origins to the influx of

gold-seekers during the following decade. These men built stopping places along their transportation routes, supply centers and mining towns. When the gold ran out, in the 1870s and '80s, many fortune seekers drifted away, but others stayed. They had discovered the Cariboo's other treasures: its timber, its ranchland and its great outdoors.

WELLS
The Cariboo Gold Quartz Mine, opened in 1933 and abandoned in 1967, is a relic of a relatively unknown, second Cariboo Gold Rush. In the 1920s, a prospector named Fred Wells discovered a rich gold vein in the hard quartz rock of Cow Mountain, south of here. The gold was the same kind that had started the rush of the 1860s. Mining of the gold led to the founding of Wells.

Great horned owl

BOWRON LAKE PROVINCIAL PARK
Set against the backdrop of the snow-capped 2,100-metre peaks of the Cariboo Mountains, this 1,216-square-kilometre park has six major lakes and connecting waterways that form a 116-kilometre-long circular canoe route. Moose and deer feed in marshes along the Bowron River. Caribou, mountain goats and grizzly bears frequent higher elevations. The lakes and streams abound with steelhead trout, Dolly Varden, and kokanee salmon. A campground with a canoe-launching facility is on the north shore of Bowron Lake.

BARKERVILLE
Some 75 buildings have been restored or reconstructed in what was, in the 1860s, a boom town in the wilderness—and the gold capital of the Cariboo. Barkerville is now a 65-hectare provincial historic park. There are Kelly's and Denny's saloons, where lucky miners drank and gambled away their riches, where unlucky ones drowned their disappointments, and where a lonesome miner could have a dance with a barmaid for $10. Entertainment of the kind popular in Barkerville's heyday is presented in the Théâtre Royal. Sourdough bread and stew are still served at the "Wake-Up Jake" Coffee Saloon and Lunch House. In St. Saviour's Anglican Church it was the custom never to put less than $2 in the collection plate. In the Barkerville Cemetery, picket-fenced graves mark the end of the trail for many participants of the Cariboo Gold Rush.

St. Saviour's Anglican Church, Barkerville

Vaudeville show, Theatre Royal, Barkerville

Billy Barker— Rich Man, Poor Man

Billy Barker's Shaft (now restored), at the south end of Barkerville, is where it all started on Aug. 21, 1862. Barker (*above*), a 42-year-old Cornish sailor, reached Williams Creek in the summer of 1862, four years after the first gold strike in the Cariboo. On Aug. 13, Billy and six companions staked a claim in one of the few easily accessible spots still available. Others had panned and sluiced there before and found nothing. To the jibes of old-timers the seven men began digging down into the gravel. Eight days later, at a depth of 16 metres, they hit pay dirt: 30 centimetres yielded $1,000; within four years the claim would relinquish over $600,000 in gold. The jokes about crazy Billy stopped and other prospectors rushed to stake claims near his. In his honor the collection of stores, cabins and saloons that grew up around his shaft was named Barkerville. In 1863 Billy married a widow from Victoria with a taste for high living. She helped him spend his gold as fast as it came out of the ground and then left him. Poor Billy died penniless in a Victoria old men's home, on July 11, 1894, and was laid to rest in a pauper's grave.

Steep Canyons and Sagebrush on the Road to Caribou Country

Central British Columbia

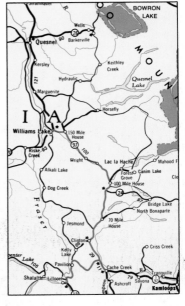

100 MILE HOUSE

A stopping place on the Cariboo Wagon Road since 1861, 100 Mile House is now a thriving lumber and ranching community of more than 1,200 persons. (Fire destroyed the original wooden roadhouse in 1937.) A red stagecoach from the gold-rush period is preserved in front of the Red Coach Inn. A carpenter's shop from the town's pioneer days serves as a chapel for the Emissaries of Divine Light.
□ In the Jens Antique Car Museum are some 20 vintage cars, including a 1907 Cadillac and a staff car used by Reichsmarshall Hermann Göring during the Second World War.
□ The 42-kilometre Cariboo Cross-Country Ski Marathon, run from Lac la Hache, is held each January. The finish line is at 100 Mile House.

Stagecoach, 100 Mile House

Balsam root

An Arduous Expedition Down the Fraser

Where Highway 12 now permits easy travel through the Fraser Canyon between Lillooet and Pavilion, two dozen adventurers spent several days in early June 1808, covering the same distance, moving slowly along narrow ledges and slippery rocks over the churning waters.

Led by North West Company fur trader Simon Fraser, the men were on their way from Fort George (now Prince George) to the Pacific Ocean. They were the first Europeans to travel the river—which they believed to be the Columbia and a trade route to the sea. Their goal was to secure it for British North America against rival claims from the United States.

After 35 days the expedition reached the river's delta, near present-day New Westminster. Fraser concluded this was neither the Columbia nor a trade route. Though he considered his journey a commercial failure, he had saved one of the major rivers west of the Rockies from the American grasp. The river and canyon now bear his name.

Simon Fraser in the Canyon, a painting by John Innis

Fraser Canyon between Lillooet and Pavilion

LILLOOET

Lillooet's wide main street dates from the 1860s. It was laid out so that two 10-tonne freight wagons, two hitched together and hauled by up to 10 spans of oxen, mules or horses, could turn in it. In 1863-64, during Lillooet's brief boom period as the southern terminus of the Cariboo Wagon Road, these large wagons left here with supplies for the Cariboo goldfields. The town declined after 1865, when it was bypassed by a new branch of the Wagon Road which started farther south at Yale.
□ The Lillooet and District Museum exhibits memorabilia from the town's pioneer and gold-rush past. Opposite the museum is a stone cairn marking "Mile 0" of the original Cariboo Wagon Road. The road's construction is commemorated by a plaque on the east bank of the Fraser River, facing the town.

0	3	6	9	12	15 Miles
0	6	12	18	24 Kilometres	

The road between Lillooet and Williams Lake leads through parts of British Columbia's interior plateau, a region scoured by glaciers during the last ice age and broken up by deposits of rock and gravel, and by gorges formed by meltwater.

North of Lillooet the road hugs the east wall of the steep Fraser Canyon for almost 60 kilometres. Then it skirts 1,665-metre Mount Pavilion and turns northeast passing through level sagebrush country. At Clinton it joins the Cariboo Highway, which leads north past stands of lodgepole pine and expansive ranches.

The drive between Lillooet and 150 Mile House is over part of British Columbia's oldest mainland road, the Cariboo Wagon Road. Built in 1861-63, between Lillooet and Soda Creek (47 kilometres north of 150 Mile House), it was the main supply route to the goldfields of the Cariboo. Roadside stations, usually 25 kilometres apart, were built to serve construction crews and, later, travelers. Called "Mile Houses" they were named for their distances from Lillooet, "Mile 0." At milepost 100, for instance, was 100 Mile House, from which sprang the present town of the same name.

Within a decade the wagon road was extended by a southern branch between Yale and Clinton, and by a northern addition between Soda Creek and Barkerville in the heart of the gold country. For more than a century the road and its successors have served those who followed the original gold miners—ranchers, loggers and tourists.

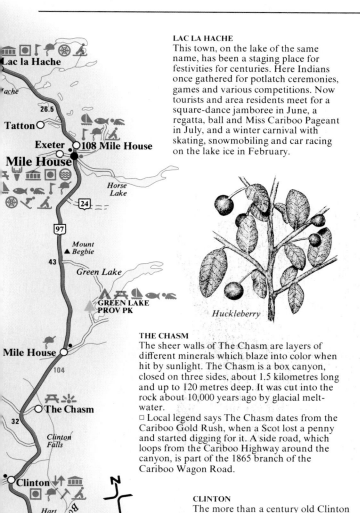

LAC LA HACHE
This town, on the lake of the same name, has been a staging place for festivities for centuries. Here Indians once gathered for potlatch ceremonies, games and various competitions. Now tourists and area residents meet for a square-dance jamboree in June, a regatta, ball and Miss Cariboo Pageant in July, and a winter carnival with skating, snowmobiling and car racing on the lake ice in February.

Huckleberry

THE CHASM
The sheer walls of The Chasm are layers of different minerals which blaze into color when hit by sunlight. The Chasm is a box canyon, closed on three sides, about 1.5 kilometres long and up to 120 metres deep. It was cut into the rock about 10,000 years ago by glacial meltwater.
□ Local legend says The Chasm dates from the Cariboo Gold Rush, when a Scot lost a penny and started digging for it. A side road, which loops from the Cariboo Highway around the canyon, is part of the 1865 branch of the Cariboo Wagon Road.

CLINTON
The more than a century old Clinton Ball, a two-day celebration in May, is believed the oldest annual event in British Columbia. It recalls the town's beginnings at the junction of two branches of the Cariboo Wagon Road.

By the late 1860s the ball was already a tradition. It then lasted up to a week and was the social event of the year in the Cariboo. People in their finest evening clothes, from as far as 300 kilometres away, came to the Clinton Hotel—formerly the 47 Mile House—to dance, drink, and gamble.

The hotel burned down in 1958, but in the South Cariboo Historical Society Museum is a pair of red glass wine decanters from its bar.

Fences by the Roadside—
the Snake Rail and the Russell

Log fences line much of the Cariboo Highway as it winds through the rangeland of British Columbia's interior. The fences are practical and cheap. They require no post holes, which would be difficult to dig into the rocky Cariboo soil. Nor do they need nails or wire. They are made entirely of lodgepole pine, the most abundant timber in the Cariboo.

Fence styles vary depending on terrain. The two most popular designs are the snake rail and the Russell. The snake rail is a wide-angled zigzag fence of equally long sections. It is four to five logs high and the logs are notched where they join. The Russell fence (*above*) is straight and held upright by teepee-like structures at the section joints.

On the road to the summit of Mount Pavilion

CACHE CREEK
The town had its beginnings in the 1860s as a stopping place on the Yale-Clinton branch of the Cariboo Wagon Road. In 1874 the British Columbia government chose Cache Creek as the site for the first boarding school in the interior of the province. The school, which provided instruction to about 50 youngsters from the Cariboo region, no longer exists.
□ On an Indian reserve is Bonaparte Church, built in 1894 and named after the nearby Bonaparte River. Its original log walls are now covered with boards.

Bonaparte Church, Cache Creek

Silent Volcanoes, Echoing Waterfalls and the Rockies' Highest Peak

Wells Gray and Mount Robson Provincial Parks

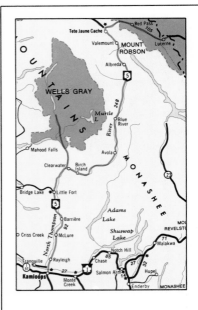

Helmcken Falls, Wells Gray Provincial Park

WELLS GRAY PROVINCIAL PARK

Among a dozen large waterfalls in the park are 135-metre-high Helmcken Falls and Dawson Falls, 90 metres wide and 18 metres high. In the Murtle River is the Mush Bowl, a series of riverbed craters carved by raging waters. A 240-metre-high extinct volcano rises from the north shore of Kostal Lake. On the rim of its cone, 1,500 metres above sea level, is a stand of Douglas fir, a tree which normally grows at lower elevations. A round-trip canoe route winds for 102 kilometres between the Clearwater Lake campground and Azure Lake. Canoeists can fish for rainbow trout downstream from 14-metre-high Rainbow Falls. There are more than 100 icy mineral springs in the park. Golden eagles and rufous hummingbirds are occasionally sighted—particularly at abandoned Ray Farm. The 19-kilometre Battle Mountain Trail leads through subalpine forest to Caribou Meadows, a grassy expanse laced with streams and marshes and dotted with colorful wildflowers.

SPAHATS CREEK PROVINCIAL PARK

Spahats Creek has carved a 120-metre-deep gorge through an ancient lava flow in the park. The canyon ends at Spahats Creek Falls, where the creek cascades 60 metres into the Clearwater River. An observation deck overlooks the falls.

CLEARWATER

In early July, Clearwater celebrates Overlander Days with a raft race down the runoff-swollen North Thompson River from Clearwater to Kamloops. The log rafts are realistic reproductions of those used by pioneers, and crews dress in period costume during the two-day, 130-kilometre race. Canoeists paddling this scenic stretch of the North Thompson will encounter a fast current and mild rapids.

Fort Kamloops

KAMLOOPS

A Hudson's Bay Company trading post, built of logs in 1821, has been reassembled on the grounds of the Kamloops Museum. On display in the museum are Salish Indian basketry and carvings, a furnished Victorian drawing room, medical equipment used in an early Kamloops hospital and, from the Kamloops jail, an invitation to a hanging in 1899.
□ The Kamloops Ranch Museum in Riverside Park has a recreated HBC factor's cabin and displays early stagecoaches and farm machinery.
□ A plaque 22 kilometres east of Kamloops commemorates the steamboats that plied the Thompson River in the 1880s, aiding exploration and settlement of the British Columbia interior.
□ Tod Mountain has 18 square kilometres of ski slopes and a 2,786-metre-long double chair lift, North America's longest.

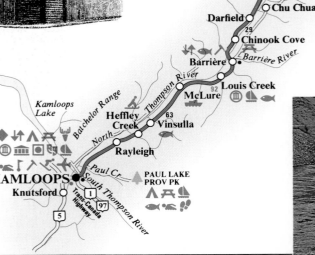

0   4   8   12   16   20 Miles
0   8   16   24   32 Kilometres

Lava and water have shaped the broad valley of the North Thompson River. In the not-too-distant geological past, volcanoes created and changed the landscape with each eruption. Penned in or diverted, rivers widened into lakes, scoured deep gorges and funneled into plummeting waterfalls.

At Spahats Creek Provincial Park, the volcanic origins of the area are still visible. Here, Spahats Creek crashes through a steep-walled gorge whose exposed rock layers represent past volcanic upheavals.

Near the entrance to Wells Gray Provincial Park, Helmcken Falls roars its welcome as it plunges 135 metres over the brink of a lava-layered precipice. The vast wilderness park echoes everywhere with the rumbling of falling water, but there is more: silent volcanoes, mineral springs, serene mountain-edged lakes and vast ice fields.

Farther east, in Mount Robson Provincial Park, are the highest peak in the Canadian Rockies and the deepest cave in Canada. Clear, cold lakes teem with kokanee salmon and brook, rainbow, steelhead and Kamloops trout.

The breathtaking Yellowhead Highway winds past these parks and the small towns strewn along the North Thompson. The highway traces the route of the Overlanders of 1862, fortune-seekers who risked their lives to reach Cariboo gold. Many of these pioneers remained, cleared homesteads, and built rough-hewn log homes, snake fences and wagon bridges that still stand.

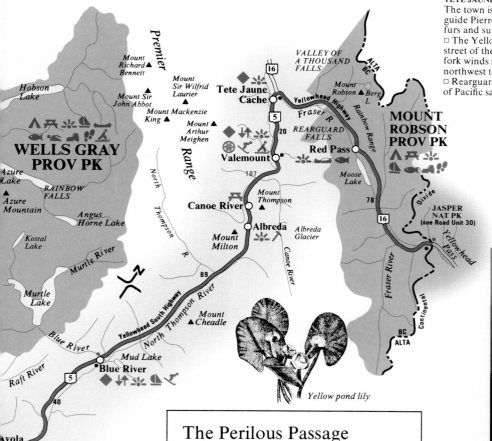

Yellow pond lily

Overlander Days Raft Race, North Thompson River

The Perilous Passage of the Overlanders

The "speediest, safest and most economical route to the gold diggings," promised the British Columbia Overland Transit Company in 1862. More than 200 men and one pregnant woman with three children bought tickets and set out in May from Quebec and Ontario to seek gold in the Cariboo Country.

They expected a leisurely trip. Instead the "Overlanders" creaked across the Prairies in Red River carts, then struggled on foot through the Rockies.

At the turbulent Fraser River, most built dugout canoes and log rafts and ran the river; several were drowned. By Sept. 10 this group reached Fort George (present-day Prince George).

Thirty-six others struggled down the North Thompson River and, half-starved, reached Fort Kamloops on Sept. 13 with one casualty. The next day Mrs. August Schubert gave birth to the first white child born in the interior of British Columbia. The goldfields, however, proved barren for all but one Overlander.

TETE JAUNE CACHE
The town is named for fair-haired Indian trapper and guide Pierre Hatsinaton ("Tête Jaune"), who stored his furs and supplies here in the early 1800s.
□ The Yellowhead Highway—the 2,976-kilometre "main street of the North"—splits at Tete Jaune Cache. One fork winds southwest to Kamloops, the other angles northwest to Prince Rupert.
□ Rearguard Falls marks the farthest inland migration of Pacific salmon.

VALEMOUNT
This town, formerly a logging camp known as "Swift Creek Spur 2," now serves as a base for helicopter skiing expeditions into the Premier Range.
□ Margaret McKirdy's clay sculptures, displayed in her Valemount home, include a trapper on snowshoes, a farmer leaning on his shovel to talk, and loggers, storekeepers and cooks.
□ Dogsled races highlight the Winter Carnival, held in February.

Mount Robson

MOUNT ROBSON PROVINCIAL PARK
Bordered on the east by the Continental Divide and Jasper National Park, Mount Robson preserves more than 200,000 hectares of snowcapped mountains, forested valleys, precipitous canyons, glacier-fed lakes and wild rivers. The 22-kilometre Berg Lake Trail runs from the Yellowhead Highway through the Valley of a Thousand Falls to Berg Lake at the base of 3,953-metre Mount Robson. Some 15 glaciers are seen along the trail, among them Berg Glacier, 1,800 metres thick and nearly a kilometre wide. Berg Lake is often dotted with ice slabs that have broken away from the glacier. At the southern tip of the park are the headwaters of the Fraser River. Arctomys Cave, surveyed to a depth of 522 metres, lies in a valley east of Mount Robson. The 2,400-metre-long passage to the bottom is difficult even for experienced cavers.

An Alpine Wilderness Filled with Wildlife

Jasper National Park

Gray jay

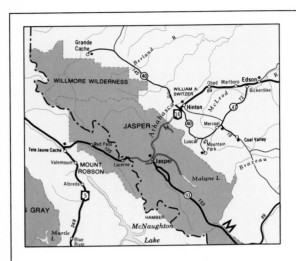

JASPER

In the last century Jasper was a way station for wilderness travelers—trappers, missionaries, geologists, surveyors, naturalists and prospectors. The first facility for park visitors was established in 1915 in the form of a tent camp on Lac Beauvert. Today the town is a year-round recreation center with facilities ranging from the primitive to the plush.

□ Located near the confluence of the Athabasca and Miette rivers, Old Fort Point is the site of Henry's House (1811), an early fur-trade post. Nearby grassy slopes are a grazing area for mule deer.

□ Pyramid Lake Drive winds for eight kilometres north to 2,722-metre Pyramid Mountain and a pair of sparkling glacial lakes.

□ The totem pole outside the railway station was carved by Haida Indians of the Queen Charlotte Islands.

□ A cairn near the mouth of the Rocky River commemorates Jasper House, built by the North West Company in 1813 and run by Jasper Hawes.

Black bear

A view of Jasper from The Whistlers

YELLOWHEAD HIGHWAY

The 2,987-kilometre highway is named for Tête Jaune (Yellow Head), a fair-haired Indian trapper and guide whose real name was Pierre Hatsinaton. It extends from Portage la Prairie, Man., into British Columbia, splitting at Tête Jaune Cache. One branch leads southwest to Kamloops, the other west and north to Prince Rupert.

Entering Jasper National Park from the east, the highway follows the Athabasca River through a low, arid valley. West of Jasper townsite the scenery changes dramatically as the highway climbs through the narrow, densely forested Miette Valley—the route of 19th-century fur brigades traveling west to New Caledonia (central British Columbia).

Yellowhead Pass, 1,131 metres above sea level, is one of the lowest gaps along the entire Continental Divide. Waters east of the divide flow to the Arctic Ocean via the Miette, Athabasca and Mackenzie rivers. West of the divide, runoff feeds the Fraser River flowing into the Pacific.

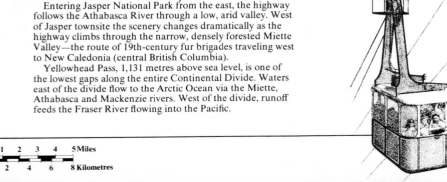

THE WHISTLERS

The long, shrill whistle of the hoary marmot, a member of the woodchuck family, gives the mountain its name.

□ From an altitude of 1,267 metres, skytrams whisk passengers at 420 metres a minute to the 2,250-metre level, providing spectacular views of Jasper townsite and the ring of mountains that surrounds it. Some 40 lakes dot the broad valley of the Athabasca River—remnants of one large lake which once covered the area. Across the valley are the reddish quartzite cliffs of Pyramid Mountain.

Skytram, The Whistlers

| 0 | 1 | 2 | 3 | 4 | 5 Miles |
| 0 | 2 | 4 | 6 | 8 Kilometres |

Jasper National Park is a sweeping expanse of scenic beauty—of awesome mountain peaks and centuries-old glacial ice, of flower-carpeted meadows and mirrorlike lakes.

In the early 1800s the need for a fur-trade route across the Continental Divide brought the first white men to this alpine wilderness. Three log buildings were built for weary voyageurs traveling over the Yellowhead and Athabasca passes. The ramshackle settlement was named Jasper House after North West Company clerk Jasper Hawes. In 1907 the coming of the railway through Yellowhead Pass prompted the federal government to preserve the area as a national park.

Today, Jasper covers more than 10,800 square kilometres, of which only 800 square kilometres are flat valley bottoms. Grassy meadows carpet the lower slopes, where rainfall is scant. Higher up, a moister climate has produced bands of forest on the mountain flanks. Above the timberline—about 2,100 metres—a subarctic climate stunts even tenacious alpine vegetation.

Mule deer graze among the poplar and jack pine stands of the Miette and Athabasca valleys. Bighorn sheep share their lofty range with mountain goats, but are left far behind when the goats climb to narrow ledges shared only with eagles. Rarest of all sights in the park is the mountain caribou herd that ranges by the headwaters of Maligne Lake.

*Roche
a Perdrix*

PUNCHBOWL FALLS
The falls, where Mountain Creek plummets over a limestone cliff, have cut a narrow cleft into the stone. Below, the falls have eroded a picturesque pool. The pebbly bedrock was formed in the bed of a fast-moving stream about 130 million years ago.
□ A dark seam of low-grade coal, 30 centimetres thick, is visible nearby.

**Miette
Hot Springs**

Miette Hot Springs

Lofty Peaks From a Primeval Sea

A vast sea covered the land where the Rockies now tower. For 500 million years, the seafloor was pressed downward by heavy layers of sediment (sand, silt and remains of marine life). Since new layers built up as fast as the seafloor sank, the sea remained shallow. Eventually, pressure turned the sediment to rock.

Great geological forces beneath the earth's crust pushed the rock layers eastward, causing them to fold and buckle. In places the layers cracked along fault lines, and some of the oldest rocks were thrust upward to overlap younger rock. Erosion continued to shape the land; rivers carried debris east from the highlands and deposited it on broad plains and swamps.

The great plains continued to rise, and as river gradients became steeper the effects of erosion were more pronounced. Water carved broad valleys and left behind jutting peaks of resistant rock. Ice-age glaciers helped sculpt the ridges and glacial meltwater later formed deep mountain lakes. Millions of years from now further erosion will have reduced the Rockies to rolling plains.

150 MILLION YEARS AGO

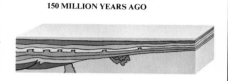

50 MILLION YEARS AGO

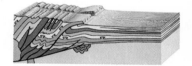

2 MILLION YEARS AGO

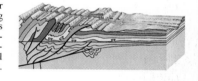

MIETTE HOT SPRINGS
The hottest spring water in the Canadian Rockies—54°C—is piped into a swimming pool here and cooled to 39°. The waters are believed to originate as rain and melted snow which have seeped into bedrock fissures. This runoff is heated at depths of several thousand metres, then percolates back to the surface at the rate of a million litres a day.

MEDICINE LAKE
For most of the year Medicine Lake is a dry gravel bed. In summer, runoff and glacial meltwater transform it into a lake eight kilometres long and up to 18 metres deep. The lake has no apparent outlet except in times of high water. It drains into subsurface channels, emerging in the Maligne River farther downstream.

Medicine Lake

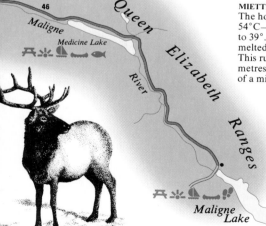

Mountain caribou

SKYLINE TRAIL
This hiking trail parallels the Maligne River for 43 kilometres—more than 25 of them above the timberline. The trail passes the Snowbowl, a lovely subalpine meadow sprinkled with wildflowers, and Wabasso Lake—a stark, rocky pond set in a steep-walled cirque. From The Notch can be seen a panorama of summits including distant Mount Robson (3,954 metres), the highest peak in the Canadian Rockies.

*SAMSON
NARROWS*

*Maligne
Mtn ▲*

MALIGNE LAKE
Emerald-green Maligne Lake is set among the snow-mantled peaks of the Front Range and stretches for nearly 22 kilometres. Some 11,000 years ago, a massive tongue of ice advanced down the valley, gouging out the deep basin that today contains Maligne Lake.
□ At the Samson Narrows, a brook flowing from Maligne Mountain has deposited debris and sediment that nearly cut the lake in half.

Big Game and Abandoned Mines in the Faraway Foothills

West-Central Alberta

This foothills region is ideal vacation country for anglers, nature lovers, big-game hunters, and those who would explore the wilderness.

In 4,597-square-kilometre Willmore Wilderness Park—Alberta's largest wilderness area—visitors can hike or canoe for a few days (or a few weeks) without meeting or seeing another person. There are no permanent residents and, except for a few Forest Service cabins and some fire lookouts, no buildings in this wilderness. Automobiles

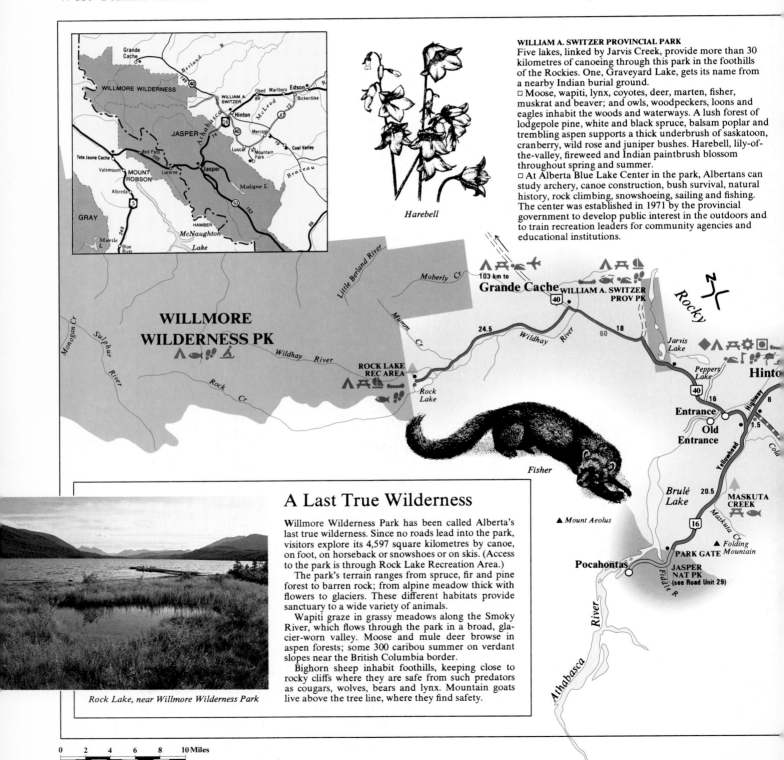

Harebell

Fisher

Rock Lake, near Willmore Wilderness Park

WILLIAM A. SWITZER PROVINCIAL PARK

Five lakes, linked by Jarvis Creek, provide more than 30 kilometres of canoeing through this park in the foothills of the Rockies. One, Graveyard Lake, gets its name from a nearby Indian burial ground.

□ Moose, wapiti, lynx, coyotes, deer, marten, fisher, muskrat and beaver; and owls, woodpeckers, loons and eagles inhabit the woods and waterways. A lush forest of lodgepole pine, white and black spruce, balsam poplar and trembling aspen supports a thick underbrush of saskatoon, cranberry, wild rose and juniper bushes. Harebell, lily-of-the-valley, fireweed and Indian paintbrush blossom throughout spring and summer.

□ At Alberta Blue Lake Center in the park, Albertans can study archery, canoe construction, bush survival, natural history, rock climbing, snowshoeing, sailing and fishing. The center was established in 1971 by the provincial government to develop public interest in the outdoors and to train recreation leaders for community agencies and educational institutions.

A Last True Wilderness

Willmore Wilderness Park has been called Alberta's last true wilderness. Since no roads lead into the park, visitors explore its 4,597 square kilometres by canoe, on foot, on horseback or snowshoes or on skis. (Access to the park is through Rock Lake Recreation Area.)

The park's terrain ranges from spruce, fir and pine forest to barren rock; from alpine meadow thick with flowers to glaciers. These different habitats provide sanctuary to a wide variety of animals.

Wapiti graze in grassy meadows along the Smoky River, which flows through the park in a broad, glacier-worn valley. Moose and mule deer browse in aspen forests; some 300 caribou summer on verdant slopes near the British Columbia border.

Bighorn sheep inhabit foothills, keeping close to rocky cliffs where they are safe from such predators as cougars, wolves, bears and lynx. Mountain goats live above the tree line, where they find safety.

are prohibited. Local commercial outfitters take families horseback riding along trails in summer, and guide hunters in the fall.

Bear, deer, moose, mountain sheep and wapiti, abundant in the park, are found throughout the region. Hunters regard this as one of the finest big-game areas in the world, and flock to Edson and Hinton in the autumn.

Within easy reach of these towns are abandoned mines—ghostly reminders of the heyday of the "Coal Branch." This once thriving area of coal-mining towns prospered from 1910 to the 1930s, revived during the Second World War, but slumped again in the late '40s, when the railways introduced diesel-powered engines.

Tourism is now the area's most important industry—but old ties are strong. Among the thousands camping and fishing here on weekends there are usually some former residents of these once-thriving, close-knit communities.

Sailing at the Alberta Blue Lake Center, William A. Switzer Provincial Park

HINTON
Visitors here may tour North Western Pulp and Power Ltd., Alberta's only pulp mill.
□ Hikers and horseback riders can explore a 20-kilometre restored section of the Bighorn Trail, an early pack trail that extended some 140 kilometres along the Bighorn Ridge between Hinton and Nordegg. There are two wilderness campsites on the trail.
□ About 1,000 wild horses, descendants of once-enormous herds, roam near Hinton in the wooded foothills of the Rockies. Relentlessly rounded up, first by cowboys, then by hunters to supply pet-food manufacturers, wild horses have all but disappeared from the Canadian West.

FOLDING MOUNTAIN
This mountain, typical of the eastern ranges of the Rockies, is clearly visible from Highway 16, about 18 kilometres west of Hinton.
Its layers of rock, once horizontal, folded when the Rocky Mountains were formed. The layer of gray rock (mainly limestone) was deposited by a warm shallow sea which covered North America more than 300 million years ago. Above it is brown siltstone laid down by another sea 100 million years later.

McLEOD RIVER
Fed by melting snow and rain, this clear, cold river abounds in Rocky Mountain whitefish, Dolly Varden, eastern brook trout, walleye, northern pike and arctic grayling.

Rocky Mountain whitefish

EDSON
The Grand Trunk Pacific Railway (a forerunner of the CNR) created this town in 1910 when it built a branch line from here into the coal-rich area to the south. In its heyday Edson was promoted as "Gateway to the Last Great West." Today, although most of the branch installations are gone, Edson is still an important stop on the CN line.
□ Summer events here include a rodeo, and a two-day sidewalk jamboree featuring street dancing, bands, auctions, and art and craft displays.

'Coal Branch' Boom Times

Coal-burning locomotives crossing the Prairies in the early 1900s required huge amounts of fuel. To meet this demand, the Grand Trunk Pacific Railway (later part of the CNR) established small mining towns, such as McLeod River, Erith, Robb, Mercoal and Cadomin, in the Alberta foothills south of Edson. This string of communities, linked only by rail, became known as the "Coal Branch."

Isolation created a fervent community spirit. Hockey and baseball teams from the Coal Branch won provincial championships; moonshine kept local parties going all weekend.

By the 1940s, 10,000 people lived along the Coal Branch. But when trains switched to diesel engines after the Second World War, the mines closed down and the miners moved away—though many still return to camp and fish.

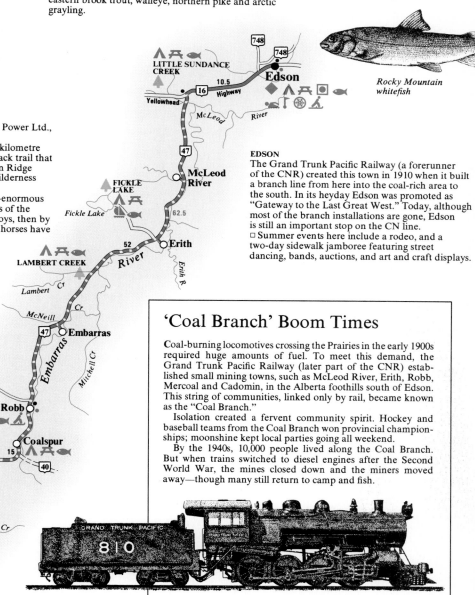

Coal-burning locomotive of the Grand Trunk Pacific Railway (c.1914)

A Land of Glaciers
Along the Continental Divide

Jasper National Park

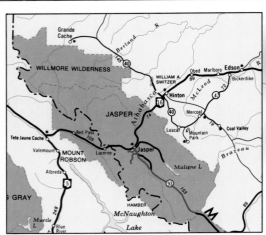

Athabasca Falls

ATHABASCA FALLS

In a cloud of spray and mist, the Athabasca River plu[n]
22 metres over a ragged cliff of Precambrian quartzite
at Athabasca Falls. Below the falls the river roars thro[ugh]
a narrow gorge and emerges at a line of cliffs a few
hundred metres beyond. Near the falls, old channels [and]
potholes indicate that the river has changed its course
several times in the past. A fine sediment gives the riv[er]
a milky appearance.

Crawling Glaciers
That Break into a Gallop

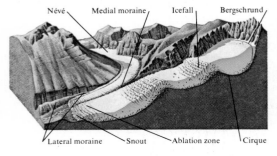

Névé Medial moraine Icefall Bergschrund

Lateral moraine Snout Ablation zone Cirque

High in the Rocky Mountains lie vast permanent ice fields
that spawn glaciers—rivers of ice. Unlike the frozen water
of a lake or pond, glacial ice forms from snow that remains
from winter to winter. The granular snow that survives each
year is called *névé* or *firn*. It accumulates in a firn field, often
a sheltered mountain slope which weathering and ice erode
into giant steep-walled depressions called *cirques*.

After many years, pressure changes the ice crystals (which
were once snow crystals) into glacier ice. This mass begins
to flow under the pressure of its own weight, usually a few
centimetres a day, but sometimes "galloping" at 10 to 100
times its normal rate.

A *bergschrund* is the deep crevasse that appears when
the flowing ice breaks away from a mountain wall. *Icefalls*,
massive blocks of jagged ice, form when brittle surface ice
cracks as it moves down a steep descent. Debris deposited
by the glacier creates *lateral moraines* (visible as dark strips
at a glacier's edges); when two glaciers flow together the
lateral moraines merge to become a *medial moraine* (a dark
strip down the center). The lower part of the glacier is in
the *ablation zone* (area of melting).

MOUNT EDITH CAVELL

This majestic peak (3,365 metres) is
named for a British nurse executed by a German
firing squad during the First World War.
□ Angel Glacier lies in a saddle on the flank of the
mountain and a tongue of the glacier licks into
the valley.
□ Glacier-fed Cavell Lake nestles in a rock-walled
amphitheater. Reflected in the lake's turquoise water
is the sheer northeastern face of Mount Edith Cavell.
□ A trail into the valley bottom opposite Angel Glacier
passes over a mass of boulders, cobbles, sand and rock
flour ground and scattered by glacial action.

COLUMBIA ICEFIELD

Once part of the vast ice sheet that
covered most of Canada for more
than a million years, the Columbia
Icefield is the largest accumulation
of ice in the Rocky Mountains. It
blankets an area of nearly 300
square kilometres to depths of
900 metres.
□ The most accessible of the many
glaciers that jut from the main
body of the icefield is the Athabasca
Glacier, which can be reached from
the Icefields Parkway. Snowmobile
tours on the glacier give visitors
a close look at mill holes (deep,
circular depressions) and crevasses
(long, nearly vertical fissures).
Athabasca Glacier, receding at
about seven metres a year, may
begin to advance by 1990.

Athabasca Glacier, Columbia Icefield

Adjoining Banff National Park at the Columbia Icefield, Jasper National Park sweeps northwest along the Continental Divide. It is a ragged rectangle some 200 kilometres long and close to 90 kilometres across at its widest.

From east to west, gradually loftier ranges rear up from the foothills of Alberta. These mountains once formed a prehistoric ocean floor. Geologic forces created the present landscape of ice-capped peaks.

Each of three entrances to the park is guarded by sentinel mountains. The most spectacular gateway is Sunwapta Pass on the Icefields Parkway. At the summit, a flower-carpeted meadow provides a view of 3,435-metre Mount Athabasca.

Leaving the Icefields Chalet at 2,100 metres, the parkway winds down to the valley of the Sunwapta River 450 metres below. At Summit Viewpoint, forested ridges frame the hanging glaciers of Mount Kitchener (3,450 metres) and the Stutfield Glacier. The breathtaking scenery is often enhanced by the sight of a black bear or a bighorn ram foraging beside the road. Jasper's abundant wildlife is a main park attraction, to be seen and photographed but not fed.

Hikers and trail riders take to the backcountry for days or weeks at a time on more than 900 kilometres of trails traversing this wilderness of mountains, glaciers, lakes and wild rivers.

ICEFIELDS PARKWAY

The 230-kilometre Icefields Parkway ranks among the great highroads of the world and commands some of the most majestic scenery in the Canadian Rockies. It runs between Lake Louise and Jasper townsite, following in turn the Bow, Mistaya, North Saskatchewan, Sunwapta and Athabasca rivers, crossing the Bow and Sunwapta passes and presenting a panorama of peaks, glaciers, waterfalls and canyons. Some landmarks bear the names of early guides and explorers—Wilcox, Stanley, Nigel; others have descriptive names such as Tangle Ridge and Whirlpool River, or Indian names such as Sunwapta (turbulent river).

SUNWAPTA RIVER

From its headwaters at the foot of the Athabasca Glacier, the Sunwapta courses through a deep valley carved by eons of erosion. In places the river flows in several intertwining channels across a broad riverbed choked with silt and gravel—a braided pattern typical of glacier-fed rivers.
□ Some 56 kilometres south of Jasper, the green Sunwapta is divided by a small, pine-clad island. Swiftly the arms are reunited in a headlong plunge through the two canyons of Sunwapta Falls. A kilometre downstream the river adds its volume to the mighty Athabasca and 30 kilometres farther the combined waters hurtle over Athabasca Falls.

Sunwapta River

POBOKTAN CREEK

Quartzite boulders litter both sides of the Icefields Parkway where rockslides have swept down here from the mountain slopes to the east. Above the boulder field, near the top of the ridge, is a distinct pink scar where part of the rock sheared away. The Sunwapta River now breaks in rapids over the foot of the slide area. The rock itself has been used extensively as building stone in Jasper National Park.
□ To the southeast of Poboktan Creek loom Tangle Ridge and 3,315-metre Sunwapta Peak. In the opposite direction Endless Chain Ridge stretches to the northwest.

Audubon's warbler

Bighorn ram

TANGLE RIDGE

Carved and scoured by glacial action, the mass of Tangle Ridge (2,953 metres) rises dramatically to the east of the Icefields Parkway. Boulders and rock faces bear striations—lines and furrows gouged by glacial debris.
□ Beauty Creek is a fast-flowing mountain stream which rises behind Tangle Ridge, then cascades to the Sunwapta River through a deep canyon and over a series of limestone cliffs.

NIGEL PEAK

Named for 19th-century guide Nigel Vavasour, the 3,160-metre peak rises like a giant layer cake from the valley floor. The mountain's alternating layers of limestone and shaly rock are bent into a U-shaped fold called a syncline.
□ A trail winds from the highway to 2,167-metre Nigel Pass with sweeping views of the surrounding mountains.

Rocky Mountain goats

SUNWAPTA PASS

Jasper and Banff national parks border one another here, along the divide between the headwaters of the Sunwapta and North Saskatchewan rivers. Waters flowing north from this divide eventually reach the Arctic Ocean via the Mackenzie River, while those flowing south cross the Prairies via the Saskatchewan River to Hudson Bay.
□ The Icefields Parkway crosses the divide at 2,035 metres above sea level. At this elevation snowbanks remain in sheltered areas throughout the summer. Like many high valleys near timberline, the bottomland near Sunwapta Pass is virtually treeless.

Iridescent Lake Louise... and Trails Alive with Color

Banff National Park

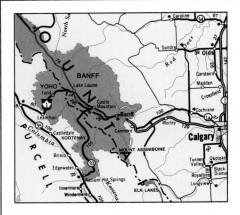

SASKATCHEWAN RIVER CROSSING

The crossing is part of the historic route to Howse Pass followed by explorer David Thompson in 1807.
□ To the south, Mount Murchison (3,333 metres) rises more than a thousand metres from the valley floor. Indians believed the mountain to be the highest in the Rockies.
□ The North Saskatchewan River is born in the gravel-strewn tongue of the Saskatchewan Glacier, just off the Icefields Parkway.

HOWSE RIVER

In 1807, the North West Company sent David Thompson up the North Saskatchewan River from Rocky Mountain House to establish a trading post west of the Rockies. Traveling by horse and canoe, Thompson crossed Howse Pass (southwest of Howse Peak) in June, blazing the earliest trade route across the Rockies. The pass, peak and river were later named for Joseph Howse, a trader with the rival Hudson's Bay Company who followed Thompson's trail in 1810.

WATERFOWL LAKES

Upper and Lower Waterfowl Lakes are two in a series of lakes through which the Mistaya River flows on its 32-kilometre journey to the North Saskatchewan River. The low, marshy lakes attract a variety of wildlife, including moose.
□ Here, as in few points along its length, the Continental Divide appears as a sheer barrier of rock. So wall-like is the divide here that it is difficult to distinguish where one mountain ends and the next begins. Two peaks that dominate the scene are ice-covered Howse Peak (3,291 metres) and the leaning, pyramid-shaped Mount Chephren (3,266 metres).
□ From the Waterfowl Lakes Campground, a trail leads to the rock amphitheaters containing Cirque and Chephren lakes.

Lower Waterfowl Lake

Mistaya Canyon

MISTAYA RIVER

Gathering its waters from glaciers and streams along the Continental Divide, the Mistaya River snakes past majestic, snow-mantled peaks. Ice-age glaciers gouged the wide Mistaya Valley.
□ A short nature trail drops down from a roadside pull-off to Mistaya Canyon. Here the rushing waters of the river have cut deeply into the limestone bedrock to form a narrow, twisting gorge with vertical walls. Swirling rocks and boulders have ground rounded potholes into the base of the canyon walls.
□ A footbridge spans the gorge, and trails lead to Sarbach Lookout (five kilometres) and Howse Pass (27 kilometres).

BARBETTE GLACIER

This alpine glacier is set within a deep cirque on the southwest flank of Mount Patterson (3,197 metres). The glacier's meltwaters drop 300 metres into Mistaya Lake. Although the three-kilometre-long lake is one of the largest in the Mistaya River Valley, it is so well hidden by the surrounding forest that few visitors have ever seen it. Only a kilometre from the highway, the lake can be reached by a steep trail.

PEYTO LAKE

Between Lake Louise and Saskatchewan Crossing, the Icefields Parkway passes a series of large lakes formed by glacier-fed streams. Off the highway at Bow Pass, a viewpoint overlooks Peyto Lake, named for Bill Peyto, a turn-of-the-century mountain man and respected guide who later became a park warden at Banff. The lake is fed by the meltwaters of Peyto Glacier, a tongue of the extensive Wapta Icefield.

0 1 2 3 4 5 Miles
0 2 4 6 8 Kilometres

Banff National Park was created by an Act of Parliament in 1887, but the real story of the park begins much earlier.

Once covered by a vast inland sea, the area underwent dramatic geologic changes some 70 million years ago. Like folds in a crinkling blanket, mountains emerged from the ancient sea floor. Over the centuries the erosive forces of wind, water and ice carved them to their present shapes.

The mountains of Banff are a geologist's delight. Layer upon layer of sedimentary rock can be distinguished in the peaks that flank the road, and geological oddities range from potholes to hanging valleys.

The most visible—and striking—of the forces that have shaped Banff are the glaciers that cling to the mountains and poke their icy tongues into the valleys. Emerald-green Lake Louise, like many of the park's lakes, owes its iridescent color to glacial sediment.

Although the park is dominated by rock and ice, nature enlivens even the harshest scene. Mountain roads and trails are alive with color—magenta fireweed, blue clematis and yellow columbine.

Banff's fauna is no less diverse than its flora. Sixty species of mammals and 225 species of birds make their homes in the park. Banff's most formidable resident, the grizzly, is rarely encountered, but black bears frequent campgrounds and garbage dumps in search of food. A sharp eye will sight moose, elk, deer, beavers, marmots, pikas and, perhaps, Rocky Mountain sheep.

BOW PASS
This summit serves as the watershed for the North and South Saskatchewan River systems. Waters that drain from this divide meet again in central Saskatchewan. There, the two branches join and flow to Hudson Bay.
□ A trail from the Bow Pass Viewpoint follows a fire road to the Bow Fire Lookout some two kilometres away. In late summer the meadows are colored with heather, mountain avens, globeflowers, western anemones and alpine forget-me-nots. Hoary marmots are often seen lumbering across the alpine tundra or sunbathing on rocks. The elusive pika, another high-country resident, is recognized by its sharp, clipped cry of warning.

HECTOR LAKE
Blue-green Hector Lake is named for Dr. James Hector, geologist with the Palliser Expedition and the first white man to pass through this valley, in the autumn of 1858. Surrounding the lake is the Waputik ("white goat") Range.
□ Rising above the south end of the lake is Pulpit Peak (2,724 metres). On its slopes grow some of the most northerly stands of alpine larch in the Rockies. In the fall, their needles turn from pale green to gold, splashing the slopes with color.
□ Avalanche scars can be seen fingering down from the upper ridges of Pulpit Peak into the forest below. A hanging valley on the northwest slope contains tiny Turquoise Lake.

KICKING HORSE PASS
The pass straddles the Continental Divide at an elevation of 1,624 metres. While exploring the pass in 1858, geologist James Hector was kicked by a packhorse and, while unconscious, was almost buried by his grieving Stoney Indian guides.
□ Early locomotives traveled so slowly up Kicking Horse Pass that seats were attached to the front of the engines so that passengers could savor the scenery.

Hector Lake

Western anemone

Pika

LAKE LOUISE
The scene first surveyed in 1882 by a CPR workman named Tom Wilson is today one of the most familiar mountain vistas in the world.
□ The impressive Chateau Lake Louise stands atop a giant glacial moraine that dams the lake, whose waters are a milky green color due to suspended sediments.
□ The 6.5-kilometre Plain-of-the-Six-Glaciers Trail leads to a spectacular view of the Victoria Glacier. Almost 150 metres thick in places, the glacier covers more than two square kilometres.
□ The Whitehorn Gondola, Canada's longest (3.2 kilometres), carries visitors to a vantage point 500 metres above Lake Louise.

MORAINE LAKE
Emerald-green Moraine Lake, somewhat smaller than Lake Louise, is set before the spectacular backdrop of the Wenkchemna Peaks. Great cones of glacial debris, pried loose by the freezing and thawing of ice, flank the lake's southeast shore. The gigantic rock pile that dams the lake is believed by geologists to be the remains of two massive rock slides from the 2,314-metre Tower of Babel above.
□ A lodge at the lake offers accommodation and meals throughout the summer. Canoe rentals are also available.

VALLEY OF THE TEN PEAKS
Cradling Moraine Lake are the sharp, glaciated Wenkchemna (an Indian word for ten) Peaks. Quartzites lend a reddish-orange hue to the mountains' lower slopes. Steep gray limestone cliffs comprise the summits.
□ A trail from Moraine Lake Lodge climbs steadily for 2.4 kilometres to open, subalpine meadows at the foot of Sentinel Pass (2,610 metres). The meadows are laced with stands of stunted Engelmann spruce, alpine fir and alpine larch, and dotted with several small lakes.

Map labels: Icefields Parkway, Rocky Mountains, 93, 24, MOSQUITO CREEK, Bow Peak, St. Nicholas Pk, Hector Lake, Crowfoot Glacier, Mt Balfour, Waputik Range, Waputik Pk, Continental Divide, Mount Hector, Bow River, Pipestone River, Bath Cr, Kicking Horse Pass, Stephen, 7.5, 93, 17, Lake Louise, 1, 5, Mount St. Piran, Lake Louise, The Beehive, Mount Whyte, Fairview Mountain, Mt Aberdeen, Paradise Cr, 2, 1A, 18, 13, Trans-Canada Highway, 1, 93, Mount Temple, Sentinel Pass, Eiffel Peak, Pinnacle Mtn, Tower of Babel, Moraine Cr, Valley of the Ten Peaks, Moraine L, Mount Babel, Allen Mount, ALTA BC, 76, Crow Lake, N

High Peaks and Hot Springs in Canada's First Park

Banff National Park

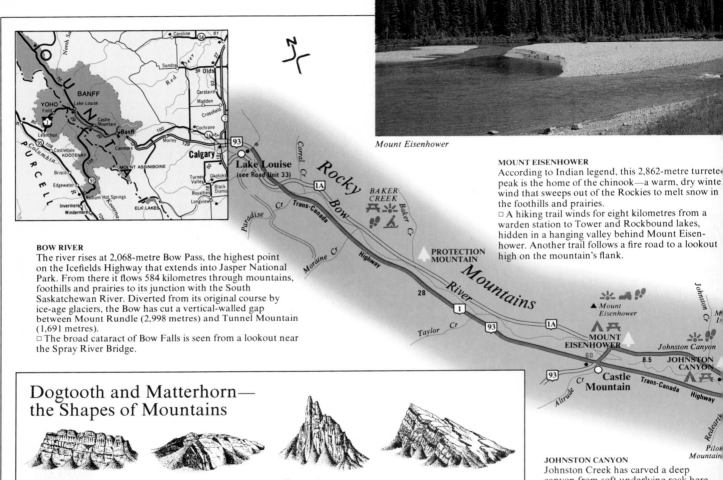

Mount Eisenhower

BOW RIVER

The river rises at 2,068-metre Bow Pass, the highest point on the Icefields Highway that extends into Jasper National Park. From there it flows 584 kilometres through mountains, foothills and prairies to its junction with the South Saskatchewan River. Diverted from its original course by ice-age glaciers, the Bow has cut a vertical-walled gap between Mount Rundle (2,998 metres) and Tunnel Mountain (1,691 metres).
□ The broad cataract of Bow Falls is seen from a lookout near the Spray River Bridge.

MOUNT EISENHOWER

According to Indian legend, this 2,862-metre turreted peak is the home of the chinook—a warm, dry winter wind that sweeps out of the Rockies to melt snow in the foothills and prairies.
□ A hiking trail winds for eight kilometres from a warden station to Tower and Rockbound lakes, hidden in a hanging valley behind Mount Eisenhower. Another trail follows a fire road to a lookout high on the mountain's flank.

JOHNSTON CANYON

Johnston Creek has carved a deep canyon from soft underlying rock here, and plummets over Upper and Lower Falls farther downstream.
□ Among the canyon's wildlife is the dipper or water ouzel, a bird which lives at the very edge of turbulent mountain streams. In feeding, the dipper will wade, swim, dive, even walk underwater on the streambed.
□ The Ink Pots are a group of seven springs located in a meadow beyond the canyon. Two of the pools are noted for their murky, blue-green color—a hue created by suspended sediments.
□ To the west, open meadows mark the site of Silver City, a mining boom town. During its heyday (1883-85), the town boasted a population of 2,000, four general stores and several hotels. The mines failed to meet expectations, however, and a disputed claim helped to speed the town's demise.

Dogtooth and Matterhorn— the Shapes of Mountains

Castellate mountain

Anticlinal mountain

Dogtooth mountain

Dipping layered mountain

Synclinal mountain

Sawtooth mountains

Matterhorn mountain

Complex mountain

Visitors to Banff have long noted the distinctive shapes of individual mountains.

Castellate mountains (such as Mount Eisenhower) are made from alternating layers of sedimentary rock. As softer layers erode, the harder rock is undermined and breaks off, forming steep slopes and cliffs.

One side of a *dipping layered* mountain (Mount Rundle) is usually a smooth slope from peak to base, following the angle of a single layer of rock.

A jagged *dogtooth* mountain (Mount Louis) results when erosion leaves behind a near-vertical core of resistant rock. Long ridges of such peaks are called *sawtooth* mountains (Sawback Range).

The folding of sedimentary rock layers creates arched *anticlinal* mountains (Fairholme Range) and trough-shaped *synclinal* mountains (Cirrus Mountain). A mountain with both anticlines and synclines is said to be *complex* (Palliser Range). A *matterhorn* mountain is formed when glaciers carve depressions in the sides of a peak creating a pyramidal summit.

| 0 | 1 | 2 | 3 | 4 | 5 Miles |

| 0 | 2 | 4 | 6 | 8 Kilometres |

The first and most famous of Canada's national parks is an incomparable combination of towering peaks and high meadows, emerald lakes and keen mountain air. These—and sulphur hot springs—have made Banff National Park one of North America's most spectacular scenic and recreation areas.

In the winter of 1883, CPR workmen noticed wisps of steam rising from a fissure on the south side of the Bow Valley. A candle lowered down the hole on a string revealed a cavern with a pool of steaming, sulphurous water. The upshot, in June 1887, was an Act of Parliament designating 673 square kilometres around the springs as "Rocky Mountains Park."

As befits Canada's oldest park—now 6,640 square kilometres and spanning the Continental Divide for 240 kilometres—Banff offers a wide variety of ways to enjoy its natural splendors. One starting point is Banff townsite, a bright and bustling community of some 3,200 permanent residents who, thanks to a skiing boom, serve a year-round tourist population. Split by the Bow River, the town is surrounded by a stunning mountain landscape crisscrossed by more than 1,000 kilometres of hiking trails.

Near the Bow River bridge stands the Banff Springs Hotel. Far below, the glinting blue of the river winds through a green valley past the limestone walls of Tunnel Mountain (1,691 metres) and Mount Rundle (2,998 metres).

MOUNT NORQUAY
From Banff townsite, a 5.7-kilometre road climbs to a lookout 300 metres above the valley floor with expansive views of the major mountains and valleys to the south and east. Dominating the peaks is the sloping, layer-cake summit of Mount Rundle (2,998 metres).
□ Known locally as the Green Spot, an open meadow adjacent to the viewpoint is fringed with huge Douglas fir trees.
□ From Mount Norquay Lodge, cable cars and open chair lifts rise 390 metres in ten minutes to the 2,100-metre level.

LAKE MINNEWANKA
Sightseeing launches ply this 19-kilometre-long lake near Banff. It is the largest in the park and the only lake on which motors are permitted. The mountains along the north shore comprise the southern terminus of the Palliser Range. The massive cliffs of Mount Inglismaldie (2,964 metres) contain the lake to the south.
□ The foundations of the small resort town of Minnewanka lie beneath the cold waters of the lake. The resort flourished during the early 1900s but was abandoned with construction of a dam in 1912. The lake's level was raised 4 metres in 1912 and another 19 metres in 1941.

Banff townsite

VERMILION LAKES
A nine-kilometre drive skirts the shores of the three Vermilion Lakes. The surrounding wetland, a marshy area of the Bow River, is rich in plant and animal life. Sedges, rushes and swamp horsetail provide a habitat for beaver and muskrat. On slightly drier ground grow willows, black currants and bracted honeysuckle. Beyond the wetland are groves of white spruce sprinkled with poplars. Ringing the lakes are Sulphur Mountain, Mount Rundle and the peaks of the Sundance Range.

(map labels)
Lake Minnewanka
Mount Inglismaldie ▲
Cascade Mountain 5.5
Cascade River
TWO JACK LAKE
Forty Mile Cr.
Stony Squaw Mountain ▲ 4.5
Highway 1
Mount Louis ▲
Mount Norquay
Mount Edith ▲
Mount Cory
Vermilion Lakes 2
Trans-Canada
Tunnel Mountain ▲
Banff
Hole in the Wall
Cave and Basin Hot Springs
BOW FALLS
Sulphur Mountain
Mount Rundle
River
Massive Mountain ▲
Healy Cr.
Sundance Cr.
Sundance Canyon
1A
30
1

BANFF
The townsite of Banff is the park's headquarters and a year-round recreation center for tourists, horseback riders, skiers, hikers and mountain climbers.
□ The Archives of the Canadian Rockies house a community library and research center for the history of the region.
□ Specimens of wildlife native to Banff National Park are displayed in the Banff Natural History Museum.
□ Indian lore and customs are shown in dioramas at the Luxton Museum, built to resemble a 19th-century fur-trade post.
□ The Banff Center is one of North America's foremost schools of visual and performing arts. The center's program of concerts, drama and ballet is highlighted by the week-long Festival of the Arts in late summer.
□ Parades, dances and traditional ceremonies are featured during Banff Indian Days, a three-day gathering of Alberta Indians.

SULPHUR MOUNTAIN
One of Banff's most popular attractions is the Sulphur Mountain lift. Four-passenger gondolas rise 690 metres in eight minutes to the summit ridge (2,348 metres) and a sweeping panorama of mountains and valleys.
□ At Upper Hot Springs, an outdoor swimming pool (47°C) is open year-round. Rich in minerals, the spring water is also slightly radioactive.

CAVE AND BASIN HOT SPRINGS
This is the birthplace of Banff National Park. In the early days, bathers descended into the cave by means of a ladder through a hole in the cavern ceiling. Since then a tunnel has been burrowed into the chamber so that visitors can view the historic site. Inside the grotto, jagged rock walls arch above steaming Cave Pool, fed by sulphur springs flowing at 675 litres a minute.

Mount Rundle

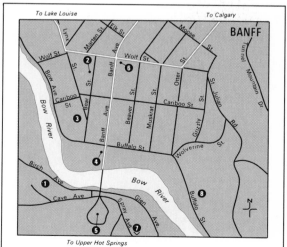

(Banff inset map labels)
To Lake Louise
To Calgary
BANFF
Elk St.
Lynx St.
Marten St.
Moose St.
Wolf St.
Banff Ave.
Otter St.
Bow Ave.
Cariboo St.
Bear St.
Muskrat St.
Cariboo St.
Grizzly St.
Squirrel St.
Tunnel Mountain Dr.
Bow River
Beaver St.
Buffalo St.
Wolverine St.
Birch Ave.
Cave Ave.
Bow River
Spray Ave.
Glen Ave.
Buffalo St.
To Upper Hot Springs

1 Luxton Museum
2 CAA
3 Archives of the Canadian Rockies
4 Banff Natural History Museum
5 Banff Park Administration Building
6 Tourist Information
7 Banff Springs Hotel
8 Banff Center

Cobalt-Blue Lakes and Cutthroats in the Wild Kananaskis Valley

Southwestern Alberta

Horse packing in the Stoney Wilderness Centre

Stoney Indian emblem

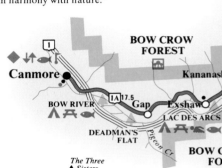

STONEY WILDERNESS CENTRE
In a unique outdoor education program sponsored by the Stoney Indians, teenagers from across Canada spend two weeks of their summer holiday sleeping in tepees, baking bannock over a campfire and riding horseback through the foothills near Morley. The students are taught camping and traditional Indian skills by native instructors and learn to "tread the delicate face of this land in harmony with nature."

CANMORE
The triple peaks of The Three Sisters near Canmore are made of molten rock, solidified beneath the earth's surface, then thrust up among older peaks.
□ Ski runs up to 1,200 metres long are at Pigeon Mountain, a popular winter resort.

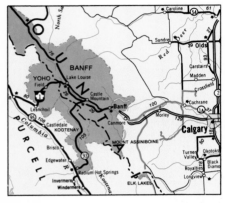

The Three Sisters, near Canmore

BOW VALLEY PROVINCIAL PARK
When the last glacier receded from the eastern foothills some 10,000 years ago, it left behind a number of glacial remnants that are visible in this park. Eskers (serpentine ridges) and moraines are landforms composed of glacial debris. Where blocks of trapped glacial ice melted and the ground above sank, kettles and potholes were formed.
□ The meeting of three major vegetation zones—mountain, forest and grassland—is responsible for the diverse flora of the Bow Valley.
□ Nearby Wildlife Unlimited is a 140-hectare park with some 50 species, many normally seen only in remote areas of Canada. Bears, wolves, wapati, foxes and a variety of birds of prey are kept in large enclosures.

KANANASKIS FOREST EXPERIMENT STATION
Established in 1934, the station serves as a living laboratory for forest management. Also located at the station is the University of Calgary's Environmental Sciences Center.
□ An early administration building called the Colonel's Cabin (1936) is made of lodgepole pine logs.
□ The 2.5-kilometre self-guiding Resource Management Trail winds through a portion of the 6,070-hectare experimental forest. The first loop leads to an observation deck and shows forest vegetation, the role of fire in forest ecology, wildlife habitat and climate. A second loop focuses on forest management techniques including logging and reforestation.

Hoary marmot

KANANASKIS PROVINCIAL PARK
The rugged wilderness of Alberta's first and largest mountain provincial park has been a camping area for at least 5,000 years. Several ancient campsites have been unearthed here, and early Indians may have hunted mammoths as well as bison in this area. Outstanding scenery includes six large lakes, ice caps, remnant valley glaciers, alpine tundra, waterfalls and canyons. The lowest elevation in the park is 1,737 metres.

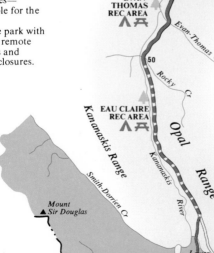

0 1 2 3 4 5 Miles
0 2 4 6 8 Kilometres

The Kananaskis Valley has changed little since explorer John Palliser came here in 1858. It remains a land of cobalt-blue lakes, lush meadows, thundering cataracts, and sheer mountain flanks.

Because it embraces both prairie and mountain, the Kananaskis region is alive with fascinating plants and animals. In summer the lowlands are sprinkled with pasqueflowers, wild roses, moss phlox and geraniums of brilliant pinks and purples.

White-tailed deer, wary of cougars and coyotes, move stealthily across open meadows. Higher up, the grasses give way to a dense carpet of lichens and mosses, and the lodgepole pine forests to Engelmann spruce, alpine fir and larch. Above the timberline, marmots, pikas and mountain goats forage among hardy perennials and stunted alpine shrubs.

Many rivers have their chill births here as glacial trickles threading down the slopes of the Kananaskis and Opal ranges. Cutthroat, rainbow, brook and brown trout rise and strike fiercely in these translucent streams.

A pattern of trunk roads winds through the Kananaskis bush, affording access for fire fighters and foresters protecting a vital watershed area. These roads also enable campers and fishermen to explore a great wilderness.

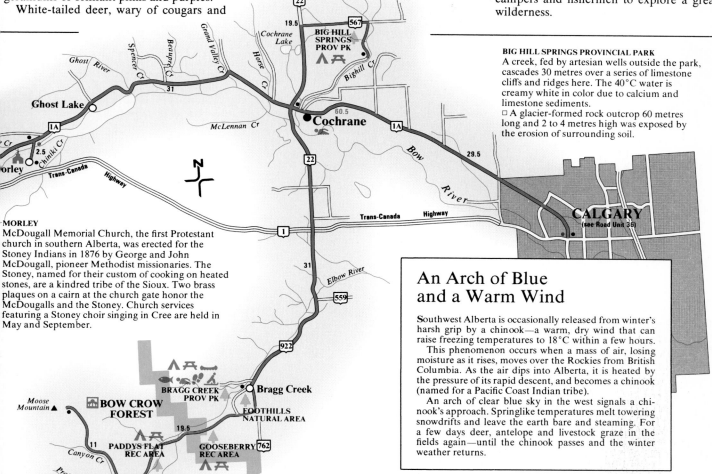

BIG HILL SPRINGS PROVINCIAL PARK
A creek, fed by artesian wells outside the park, cascades 30 metres over a series of limestone cliffs and ridges here. The 40°C water is creamy white in color due to calcium and limestone sediments.
□ A glacier-formed rock outcrop 60 metres long and 2 to 4 metres high was exposed by the erosion of surrounding soil.

An Arch of Blue and a Warm Wind

Southwest Alberta is occasionally released from winter's harsh grip by a chinook—a warm, dry wind that can raise freezing temperatures to 18°C within a few hours.

This phenomenon occurs when a mass of air, losing moisture as it rises, moves over the Rockies from British Columbia. As the air dips into Alberta, it is heated by the pressure of its rapid descent, and becomes a chinook (named for a Pacific Coast Indian tribe).

An arch of clear blue sky in the west signals a chinook's approach. Springlike temperatures melt towering snowdrifts and leave the earth bare and steaming. For a few days deer, antelope and livestock graze in the fields again—until the chinook passes and the winter weather returns.

MORLEY
McDougall Memorial Church, the first Protestant church in southern Alberta, was erected for the Stoney Indians in 1876 by George and John McDougall, pioneer Methodist missionaries. The Stoney, named for their custom of cooking on heated stones, are a kindred tribe of the Sioux. Two brass plaques on a cairn at the church gate honor the McDougalls and the Stoney. Church services featuring a Stoney choir singing in Cree are held in May and September.

MOOSE MOUNTAIN
The Ice Cave is an extensive system of chambers, corridors, tunnels and fissures that riddles Moose Mountain. Large stalactites (formations hanging from the ceiling) and stalagmites (formations growing up from the floor) line the cave. These icelike deposits are created by the evaporation of dripping water rich in lime. Some meet in midair, forming a glistening column stretching six metres from floor to ceiling. Ice crystals scattered on the cave floor sparkle like diamonds, and a subterranean lake is frozen most of the year. The cave entrance, 210 metres above the valley floor, is reached by a 3.2-kilometre trail.

COCHRANE
The Cochrane Ranch, established in 1881, was the earliest major ranching enterprise in Alberta. Leaseholders originally paid one cent per acre per year. In 1906, almost the entire block was sold to the Mormon Church for $6 million—the largest land deal in Alberta to that time.
□ Colorful hang gliders soar and wheel above Cochrane Hill. Air currents and thermals (rising columns of warm air) along the ridge enable skilled pilots to keep their manned kites aloft. Novice hang-glider pilots must receive 15 hours of instruction before they are permitted to fly here.

Hang glider, Cochrane

ELBOW FALLS
After a series of rapids, the Elbow River drops 10 metres over a limestone cliff in Elbow Falls. Part of the water then flows into an underground cavern, and reappears some 30 metres downstream. Small fissures and potholes flank the falls.

BRAGG CREEK PROVINCIAL PARK
Winding through this small park is the fast-flowing Elbow River, its shale-littered banks rising 10 metres in places. When water levels are high, experienced canoeists and kayakers challenge the river's powerful current and numerous rapids.
□ A small wildlife museum in Bragg Creek displays mounted specimens of local wildlife.

Cowboys, Oil and Skyscrapers in Alberta's 'Sandstone City'

Oil, discovered at nearby Turner Valley in 1914, transformed the former cow town. Today more than 400 companies in Calgary are directly involved in the oil industry. While Edmonton serves the front lines of the oil industry, Calgary hosts its front offices and does its banking.

Burns Memorial Gardens (5)
Sandstone from the dismantled home of pioneer cattleman Patrick Burns is used in the walls and walkways of this hillside beauty spot.

Calgary Tower (9)
The top levels of this 190-metre tower include an observation deck and a revolving restaurant with a panorama of prairie, foothills and mountains.

Centennial Planetarium (7)
Images of planets and stars are projected onto a 20-metre-wide, domed screen in a 255-seat theater. Films, plays, lectures and concerts are presented in a 265-seat auditorium. A Lancaster Bomber, a Vampire jet, a Hawker Hurricane and a Sikorsky helicopter are among restored aircraft in the Transportation Technology and Science Museum.

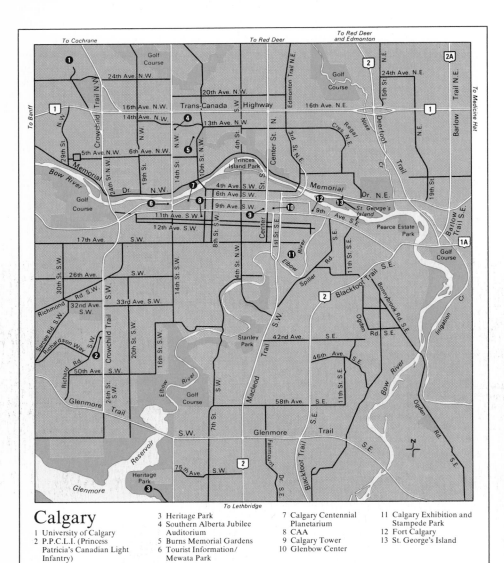

Calgary

1 University of Calgary
2 P.P.C.L.I. (Princess Patricia's Canadian Light Infantry)
3 Heritage Park
4 Southern Alberta Jubilee Auditorium
5 Burns Memorial Gardens
6 Tourist Information/ Mewata Park
7 Calgary Centennial Planetarium
8 CAA
9 Calgary Tower
10 Glenbow Center
11 Calgary Exhibition and Stampede Park
12 Fort Calgary
13 St. George's Island

Calgary's burgeoning skyline houses more than 400 oil-industry firms, and boasts such striking modern buildings as the Centennial Planetarium (right).

Fort Calgary (12)
In Central Park are the wooden foundations of Fort Calgary (1875), the sandstone foundations of later buildings, and a shingled one-room log cabin (c.1880), which is Calgary's oldest building on its original site. Exhibits in an interpretive center include a shaving brush with carved bone handle, an 1853 coin, and patent medicine bottles excavated at the site of the North West Mounted Police post here.

Soaring symbol of oil-fueled progress, Calgary's skyline continually climbs against the horizon, rimmed 100 kilometres to the west by the Rocky Mountains. Blessed with a dry, bracing climate and warmed by winter chinook winds, Calgary has grown from a muddy garrison to a major center in less than a century. But the white-collar city reverts to jeans each summer during its famous Calgary Stampede, when cowboys—real and drugstore—join in street dances, rodeos and parades.

The city started as Fort Calgary, a North West Mounted Police post built in 1875. The settlement that grew around the fort became a trading center. With the completion of the Canadian Pacific Railway in 1885 came a flood of homesteaders and ranchers. (Today, thousands of cattle are auctioned daily in public stockyards near the city center.)

Log construction was prohibited in Calgary after fire gutted 14 wooden houses in 1886. Yellow sandstone from area quarries was used instead. Many fine buildings such as the six-story Grain Exchange, the turreted Bank of Montreal, the Alberta Hotel and the old City Hall were constructed with this material, making Calgary known as "The Sandstone City."

Glenbow Center (10)

The library and archives in this eight-story building contain documents, tape record-

Calgary remembers its rural, small-town past at Heritage Park (below).

ings, movies, diaries, microfilm copies of western newspapers, 100,000 photographs, and 30,000 books and pamphlets.

The museum depicts the Plains Indian as hunter, nomad and trader. There are Inuit artifacts, a rare collection of Midewiwin (Indian Grand Medicine Society) scrolls, letters by and a gun that belonged to Métis leader Louis Riel.

Indian, Inuit and western artists are represented in the art gallery. *Aurora Borealis,* a four-story, acrylic sculpture by James Houston, dominates the stairwell.

Heritage Park (3)

A pioneer community has been recreated on a peninsula in the Glenmore Reservoir. Buildings include a hotel (1906) with a two-story outhouse, a general store (c.1905), a ranch house (1904), a working elevator (1909), and an opera house built of logs in 1896. There are a 200-passenger sternwheeler and a train pulled by a steam locomotive. Visitors may buy bread made from stone-ground flour.

Jubilee Auditorium (4)

The Southern Alberta Jubilee Auditorium, with seating for 2,750, is the twin of an auditorium in Edmonton. Both were built in 1955 to commemorate Alberta's 50th anniversary as a province.

Mewata Park (6)

One of the steam locomotives known as the Selkirks is in Mewata Park. Between 1929 and the early 1950s, the CPR used 35 of these giants on its main line between Calgary and Revelstoke, B.C.

P.P.C.L.I. Museum (2)

The original flag of the Princess Patricia's Canadian Light Infantry, designed and sewn by the princess, is in the regiment's museum.

St. George's Island (13)

Dinny, a 10-metre-high dinosaur in Dinosaur Park, is one of 46 life-size concrete statues of creatures that roamed Alberta millions of years ago. The adjoining Calgary Zoo has a Himalayan snow leopard, Canada's only breeding pair of South American spectacled bears, a tropical aviary and a conservatory.

University of Calgary (1)

Once the University of Alberta at Calgary, it was granted autonomy in 1964, and renamed in 1966.

Ceremonial headdress (left) once worn by Sioux chief Sitting Eagle is displayed at Glenbow Center. Family of Man by Mario Armengol (above), seen at Expo 67, is at Calgary's Education Centre.

Calgary's Wild and Woolly Stampede Days

Wranglers calm a feisty bronco.

Dancing in the streets, Indians in colorful regalia, the thunder of hooves, the creak of harness and chuck wagon . . . for 10 days in July it's the Calgary Stampede (11), one of the biggest and most famous shows in the world.

There's saddle and bareback broncobusting, Brahma bull and buffalo riding, a wild-horse race, calf wrestling and wild-cow milking as cowboys scramble for more than $200,000 in prizes. The most hair-raising event was invented in Alberta—races in which four chuck wagons, 20 riders and 32 horses all dash for a single point on the track.

There are fireworks, grandstand shows, a midway, a frontier casino, livestock exhibits, thoroughbred horse racing and a village with Sarcee, Stony, Peigan, Blood and Blackfoot tepees. Fancy livestock are brought to town and prettied up like beauty contestants to compete for blue ribbons and money. The fun includes a parade of cowboys, Indians and Mounties—and flapjacks at curbside.

Foothills, Ranches, and Rumors of Gold

Southwestern Alberta

This is part of Alberta's renowned foothills country, the land of the chinook where the flat of the prairie gives way to the gentle roll of the Porcupine Hills and their upward march to the Rocky Mountains. Here is some of the finest grazing land in Canada. Grasses cure on the stalk, producing a natural hay, and in winter the chinook—a warm, dry wind from the west—sweeps down from the Rockies and melts the snow, enabling livestock to feed freely on the exposed vegetation.

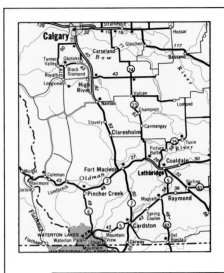

THE HUMP

Men still search these parts for a lost gold mine—and settle, not unhappily, for views such as seen (right) from The Hump, a 1,996-metre elevation off the Forestry Trunk Road. Prospectors named Blackjack and Lemon are said to have found gold near here in the 1880s, but they quarreled and Lemon killed Blackjack with an ax. Two Indians witnessed the slaying and (so the legend goes) their chief put a curse on the place and removed all evidence of gold. When Lemon returned he went insane. Nearly a century later there are those who insist there is—somewhere—a Lost Lemon Gold Mine.

View from The Hump

Lodgepole Pine, a Tree Born of Fire

The lodgepole pine is the commonest tree in the Alberta foothills. It grows to 30 metres and has thin, scaly, yellow-brown bark and bright yellow-green needles. Indians used the straight, strong trunks as tepee poles; they boiled the soft inner bark for food. Today the lodgepole pine's moderately hard wood is used for railway ties, mine props and pulp.

This tree's cones release seeds only at 40°C or higher—temperatures that occur in the forest only during a fire. The seeds germinate within days and the seedlings develop rapidly on the mineral-rich, fire-prepared ground. Lodgepole pines frequently form dense stands of timber, sometimes merging with jack pine.

The lodgepole pine is also common on the west coast. The coastal variety is often scrubby and cracked and has thick, furrowed reddish brown bark. It is used locally for firewood.

MOUNT LIVINGSTONE

The white-crowned sparrow, common in the Mount Livingstone area and throughout this part of Alberta, is found from low valleys to mountain meadows. Larger than most sparrows (17 to 19 centimetres long), it has a gray, black-and-white-striped head, a gray, brown-streaked back, a white throat patch and two white bars on each wing. Its underside is gray, its tail, dark brown.

LIVINGSTONE FALLS
REC AREA

LIVINGSTONE
FALLS

Savanna Cr

Spears Cr

Deep Cr

19.5

940

White Cr

BOW-CROW

OLDMAN RIVER
REC AREA

Dutch Cr

6.5

DUTCH CREEK
REC AREA

65.5

FOREST

Racehorse Cr

9.5

517

RACE HORSE CREEK
REC AREA

Daisy Cr

Vicary Cr

Trunk Road

30

Forestry

Blairmore Cr

3

Crowsnest R

Coleman

White-crowned sparrow

Cattle grazing near Mount Livingstone

| 0 | 2 | 4 | 6 | 8 | 10 Miles |
| 0 | 4 | 8 | 12 | 16 Kilometres |

Ranching began soon after the arrival of the North West Mounted Police in 1874. The Mounties introduced law and order to the region. Before long the ranchers began to prosper as the demand for beef cattle and sheep grew. One of the first herds of cattle was brought across the mountains from British Columbia where ranching had flourished since the gold rush days of the 1860s. Subsequent herds were brought from Montana and eastern Canada.

Many pioneer ranchers were ex-Mounties who developed a society here reminiscent of their former way of life but with a distinctive western flavor. It was a sports-oriented society where cricket, polo, horse racing and hunting were popular. Balls were held in conjunction with sports gatherings, and musical evenings and theatrical events were common.

The life of the foothills ranching community remained relatively unchanged until 1914, when many men went to war. The area remained ranch country—and some of its institutions such as race meets survived—but it never recaptured the old-world gentility of its past.

BIG ROCK

This giant boulder, 40 metres by 18 metres by 9 metres and estimated to weigh 16,330 tonnes, is the biggest among thousands in a 644-kilometre chain called the Foothills Erratics Train. One theory is that the train was created by a rock slide onto a moving glacier; as the glacier melted, the rocks dropped in its wake. Although this train is at least 10,000 years old, it is slowly losing its distinctive identity. Weathering and erosion have split Big Rock.

Big Rock near Okotoks

OLD WOMAN'S BUFFALO JUMP

A flash flood here in 1952 exposed a blanket of bones and a buffalo kill apparently 1,500 years old. Sandstone cliffs over which Indians stampeded the animals were presumably much higher than now (seven metres). There are traces of ritual cairns and medicine wheels (boulders placed in circles). Blackfoot ceramics 300 years old have been unearthed.

HIGH RIVER

Replicas of a barbershop and a blacksmith shop of the sort the homesteaders knew are in the Museum of the Highwood. Settlers' and ranchers' tools and effects and prehistoric Indian artifacts are exhibited. There is also a collection of lamps. One display records the geological history of this area with rocks, fossils, petrified wood, the tooth of a mammoth and parts of a dinosaur skeleton arranged in time sequence. The art of saddle making can be seen at two harness shops in town.

Brand marks on the wall of the blacksmith shop, Museum of the Highwood, High River

NANTON

"The Tap" at nearby Mosquito Creek Crossing is a spring where pre-railway travelers rested on the dusty trail between Calgary and Fort Macleod in the 1800s. In Centennial Park is a Second World War Lancaster; a plaque tells the history of this famous class of four-engined bombers. There are provincial campgrounds at Mosquito Creek and at Willow Creek, 24 kilometres south.

Western saddle, High River

CHAIN LAKES PROVINCIAL PARK

This four-square-kilometre park is noted for outstanding scenery and excellent fishing. Rimmed by the Rocky Mountains and the Porcupine Hills, it contains one of Alberta's most heavily stocked trout lakes, the 11-kilometre-long Chain Lakes Reservoir. This reservoir was formed in the early 1960s out of three small lakes. It links up with Willow Creek and the Oldman River. A pleasant canoe route follows these rivers through the foothills where deer, elk, moose, black bear and coyote roam. Chain Lakes Provincial Park has 140 campsites.

Bar-U and Lazy-S... Brands of the West

Branding—the marking of livestock to denote ownership—may have originated some 4,000 years ago in Egypt. The practice was brought to the Americas by the Spanish and was adopted in western Canada in the late 1870s. Initially brands were simple, often a single letter. But as more brands were registered, variations were introduced. (An important consideration was to choose a brand that could not easily be altered by rustlers.) Cattle were sometimes branded on the ribs or hip, occasionally on the shoulder, jaw or neck.

U̅	Brands are read from the left, from the top down or the outside in. This brand is the Bar-U.
MP	Letters joined together were called "running." The running MP was the brand of the North West Mounted Police.
∾	Any letter lying on its side was called lazy—in this case the Lazy-S.
P‿	Any letter with a curved line below was called "rocking": the Rocking-P.
⊍	A letter with its upper ends extending outward was called "flying." This is the Flying-U.

Map labels
Sheep River
7
Spring
6.5
Okotoks
SHEEP CREEK
20.5
Aldersyde
2A
Tongue Cr
Highwood R
High River
9.5
540
Little Bow River
49.5
OLD WOMAN'S BUFFALO JUMP HIST. SITE 1.5
2
2A
19.5
Cayley
Mosquito Cr
Connemara
Silver Lake
2
Nanton
Stimson Cr
INDIAN GRAVE AREA
24
Chain Lakes Reservoir
922
Cross Cr
CHAIN LAKES PROV PK
533
38.5
Springhill Cr
Nanton Cr
90.5
Willow Cr
Mott Cr

Fair Winds and a Great Slide on a Famous Mountain Route

Southwestern Alberta

Scenery is excitingly varied in southwestern Alberta. From this stretch of road are to be seen rolling ranch country, the foothills, the towering majesty of the Rockies—and the scars of long-ago calamities, chief among them the great Frank Slide of 1903. Seventy lives were lost in that disaster when a landslide on Turtle Mountain all but obliterated the town of Frank. Today the site is a classified historical site and is one of the most photographed landmarks in the Crowsnest region.

The Town That Awoke to a Nightmare

Scattered rocks perhaps 30 metres deep cover three square kilometres of the valley of the Oldman River in gruesome testimony to the Frank Slide of April 29, 1903. That day at 4:10 a.m. a wedge of limestone 915 metres wide, 640 metres high and 150 metres thick hurtled down the side of Turtle Mountain toward the sleeping town of Frank. After only 100 seconds some 82 million tonnes of rock were strewn across the valley floor, 70 persons were dead, and part of the town—including a mine plant and a railway siding—had disappeared.

Geologists believe the slide was due to a mild earthquake that had passed through the area in 1901, and to the opening of a huge chamber in a mine at the base of Turtle Mountain.

After the slide a new town was begun nearby. Today a plaque marks the site of the old town; a highway runs through the debris left by the slide.

The Frank Slide

CROWSNEST PASS

Magnificent Crowsnest Mountain guards the north side of this famous pass. The mountain—originally the Cree *kah-ka-ioo-wut-tshis-tun*—was so named because of the number of crows that nest below its peak.
□ Discovered in 1873, the Crowsnest Pass is one of the lowest routes through the Rockies (1,357 metres above sea level) Highway 3 follows the floor of the Crowsnest between some of the Rockies' most magnificent peaks, linking Alberta's oldest and richest ranching area with the spectacular lakes and mountains of the Kootenay region of British Columbia.

Crowsnest Mountain

COLEMAN

"Ten Ton Toots," a retired train engine that residents hail as "the biggest piggy bank in the world," is here. The locomotive is used as a receptacle for charitable donations. Another locomotive—complete with boxcars and caboose—lies at the bottom of Crowsnest Lake where it came to rest in the early 1900s. The train was carrying illicit whiskey during prohibition; it left the track after the driver had sampled his cargo. The whiskey was never recovered.

COLEMAN VOLCANIC DEPOSITS

A plaque just west of Coleman records that rocks here are an estimated 100 million years old—older than the Rocky Mountains—and the only significant occurrence of volcanic materials in Alberta. They consist of ash and cinders; many large blocks are similar to the pumice bombs ejected by some modern volcanoes. Because there is little lava, geologists believe volcanoes here were violent and explosive.

BLAIRMORE

A crow nesting in a tree is the symbol of this first settlement in the Crowsnest Pass. The missionary Jean de Smet discovered coal in the pass in the mid-1800s; after the CPR pushed a branch line through here in 1898, Blairmore became an important bituminous coal-mining center. In the town is a life-size statue of a coal miner, sculpted (with an ax) from a 350-year-old tree. Behind it is a 1914 locomotive that was used in the Hillcrest Collieries, about seven kilometres east of the town.
□ Hillcrest was the site of one of Canada's worst mining disasters, a gas and dust explosion that killed 189 men on June 19, 1914. Near the spot is their mass grave, unmarked but for a picket fence.

Statue of a coal miner, Blairmore

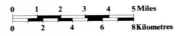

But there is plenty more to photograph: rivers and coulees, lovely Lundbreck Falls, Bow-Crow Forest reserve, Beaver Mines Lake, with a superb view of 2,163-metre-high Whistler Mountain to the south, and such lush routes as the Adanac Road—between Lynx Creek and Hillcrest Mines—a road through a spectacular forest of lodgepole pine.

On this route there are several former townsites. Some reached their peak supplying railways ties as the CPR pushed through the Crowsnest in 1897-98. Others such as Passburg, near Bellevue, were planned as coal-mining centers. But they were abandoned when schemes to transform local coal into coke for industrial purposes failed. Some coal is still dug in the pass, and oil and gas have been discovered.

The wind in the Crowsnest Pass sometimes reaches 160 kilometres an hour and has been known to push boxcars as much as 24 kilometres. Old-timers tell of a wind-measuring device that was made up of a steel ball suspended by a chain from a high pole. When the ball and chain pointed straight out, residents figured there was a "fair wind."

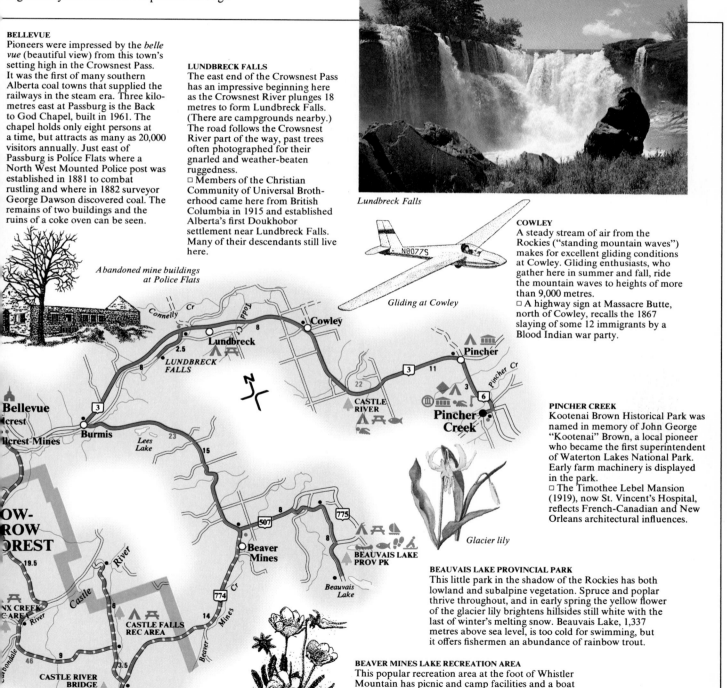

Lundbreck Falls

BELLEVUE
Pioneers were impressed by the *belle vue* (beautiful view) from this town's setting high in the Crowsnest Pass. It was the first of many southern Alberta coal towns that supplied the railways in the steam era. Three kilometres east at Passburg is the Back to God Chapel, built in 1961. The chapel holds only eight persons at a time, but attracts as many as 20,000 visitors annually. Just east of Passburg is Police Flats where a North West Mounted Police post was established in 1881 to combat rustling and where in 1882 surveyor George Dawson discovered coal. The remains of two buildings and the ruins of a coke oven can be seen.

Abandoned mine buildings at Police Flats

LUNDBRECK FALLS
The east end of the Crowsnest Pass has an impressive beginning here as the Crowsnest River plunges 18 metres to form Lundbreck Falls. (There are campgrounds nearby.) The road follows the Crowsnest River part of the way, past trees often photographed for their gnarled and weather-beaten ruggedness.
□ Members of the Christian Community of Universal Brotherhood came here from British Columbia in 1915 and established Alberta's first Doukhobor settlement near Lundbreck Falls. Many of their descendants still live here.

Gliding at Cowley

COWLEY
A steady stream of air from the Rockies ("standing mountain waves") makes for excellent gliding conditions at Cowley. Gliding enthusiasts, who gather here in summer and fall, ride the mountain waves to heights of more than 9,000 metres.
□ A highway sign at Massacre Butte, north of Cowley, recalls the 1867 slaying of some 12 immigrants by a Blood Indian war party.

PINCHER CREEK
Kootenai Brown Historical Park was named in memory of John George "Kootenai" Brown, a local pioneer who became the first superintendent of Waterton Lakes National Park. Early farm machinery is displayed in the park.
□ The Timothee Lebel Mansion (1919), now St. Vincent's Hospital, reflects French-Canadian and New Orleans architectural influences.

Glacier lily

BEAUVAIS LAKE PROVINCIAL PARK
This little park in the shadow of the Rockies has both lowland and subalpine vegetation. Spruce and poplar thrive throughout, and in early spring the yellow flower of the glacier lily brightens hillsides still white with the last of winter's melting snow. Beauvais Lake, 1,337 metres above sea level, is too cold for swimming, but it offers fishermen an abundance of rainbow trout.

BEAVER MINES LAKE RECREATION AREA
This popular recreation area at the foot of Whistler Mountain has picnic and camp facilities and a boat launch. In spring the landscape is ablaze with flowers. One of the commonest is the western spring beauty, a white or pink flower that grows at the edge of woodlands. The flower, its leaves and stem make a delicious salad.

Western spring beauty

Where Shining Peaks Rise Sheer from the Prairies

Southwestern Alberta

Few places in Canada can equal the dramatic contrast of landscapes in Waterton Lakes National Park. Snowcapped peaks rise abruptly from low, rolling grasslands. The proximity of prairie and mountain gives the park its unique character, and offers visitors a stunning variety of scenery.

A narrow strip of foothills parallels the Rockies in the northeast corner of the park, and supports luxuriant grasslands carpeted with prickly rose, many-flowered aster and wild geranium.

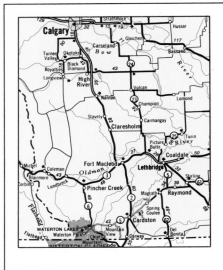

WATERTON LAKES NATIONAL PARK
In 1932 Waterton Lakes National Park was linked with Glacier National Park in Montana to form the world's first international peace park.
□ The three Waterton lakes, connected by Bosporus and Dardanelles straits, separate the Lewis and Clark mountain ranges. The lakes lie in a valley that was formed by a river but was deepened and sculpted by glaciation. The park is noted for its geological formations—U-shaped valleys, hanging valleys and canyons.
□ More than 160 kilometres of hiking trails meander through the park, linking such features as Red Rock Canyon and Cameron Falls. The cruise ship *International* travels the length of Upper Waterton Lake. A herd of 20 bison grazes in a paddock near the northern entrance to the park.

RED ROCK CANYON
A self-guiding hiking trail in Waterton Lakes National Park follows the brightly colored canyon of Blakiston Creek. The 20-metre-high canyon walls were streaked red, purple, green and yellow by chemical changes of minerals in the rocks. Ripples in cliffs and fossils of algae are evidence that an ancient sea once covered this area.

In recent geological time (about a million years ago), glaciers carried boulders here from surrounding mountains.

Looming above the canyon is Mount Blakiston (2,926 metres), the highest peak in the park.

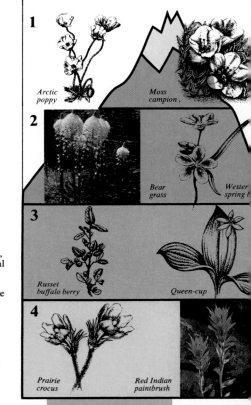

1. Arctic poppy — Moss campion
2. Bear grass — Western spring t[...]
3. Russet buffalo berry — Queen-cup
4. Prairie crocus — Red Indian paintbrush

Waterton Lakes National Park

CAMERON LAKE
A hiking trail in the southwest corner of Waterton Lakes National Park passes waterfalls, canyons and towering cliffs, then crosses a steep rise. Below is Cameron Lake, a blue gem set in a bowl-shaped valley at the foot of Mount Custer.

DISCOVERY WELL
The site of western Canada's first oil well is marked by a cairn in Waterton Lakes National Park. For centuries Kutenai Indians had used oil from seepage pools along Cameron Creek to help heal wounds. Settlers had used it to lubricate wagons. In 1902, a prosperous rancher named John Lineham sank a well that produced up to 300 barrels of oil a day. Four years later the flow ebbed and the well was shut down.

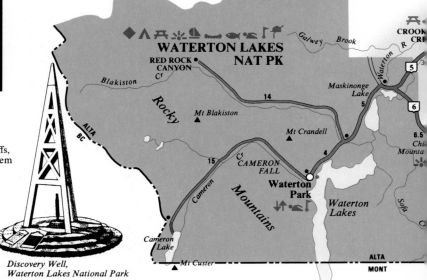

Discovery Well, Waterton Lakes National Park

0	1	2	3	4	5 Miles
0	2	4	6		8 Kilometres

Towering above the prairie is a "land of shining mountains," once the floor of an immense inland sea. Movements of the earth's crust uplifted layers of sediment, and subsequent glaciation sculpted the landscape.

Mount Blakiston (2,926 metres) is the highest peak in the park, but many others soar to 2,500 metres. Some mountains are streaked red, green, gray and purple by chemicals. Others, such as Chief Mountain, are isolated and castlelike.

One of the oldest geological formations in the Rockies—more than a billion years old—is along Cameron Creek near the town of Waterton Park. Cameron Lake, like many others in the park, is in a cirque, a steep-walled basin carved by glaciers. The clear lake waters are fed by snowfields high in the mountains.

Life Zones of a Park

From icy peaks to dry prairie, Waterton Lakes National Park abounds with plant life. Botanists have classified vegetation in zones according to elevation.

1 Arctic/Alpine Zone (2,225-2,375 metres to peaks): Above the tree line is tundra. Arctic poppy and moss campion huddle close to the ground, out of the wind.

2 Hudsonian Zone (1,830 to 2,225-2,375 metres): Evergreens flourish in the cold, dry air, though often stunted by high winds. Flowers such as western spring beauty and bear grass also grow at this elevation.

3 Canadian Zone (1,370 to 1,830 metres): Douglas maple, white spruce and lodgepole pine comprise this heavily forested region. Russet buffalo berry, silvery lupine and queen-cup are also found here.

4 Prairie and Parkland zones (1,280 to 1,370 metres): Rough fescue and blue grama grasses predominate. Prairie crocus and Red Indian paintbrush thrive amid aspen groves.

Rough fescue

St. Mary River Dam

ST. MARY RIVER DAM
This earth-fill dam and its 27-kilometre-long St. Mary Reservoir have transformed the surrounding semiarid prairie—once considered unsuitable for agriculture—into a prosperous farming region.

Irrigation makes possible the cultivation of sugar beets, potatoes, peas, beans, corn, carrots and other vegetables.

In 1897 Mormons from Utah dug more than 100 kilometres of canals and tapped the St. Mary River for Canada's first major irrigation project. But the canals usually ran dry in midsummer when water was most needed. In 1946, the St. Mary River was dammed to create a reservoir that would provide a reliable source of water for irrigation.

CHIEF MOUNTAIN
This castle-shaped mountain in Waterton Lakes National Park is a prominent landmark. It is a klippe—a peak separated from its mountain range by erosion.

Chief Mountain is "upside down." Old rocks overrode younger rocks when this peak was being formed.

A Temple on the Plains

Canada's only Mormon temple is in Cardston. A white granite edifice, it was built in 1913-23 by Mormons who had come to Alberta from Utah. The granite was quarried in British Columbia's Kootenay Valley; each stone was hand shaped. Visitors may tour the grounds.

Cardston was named for Charles Ora Card, a son-in-law of Brigham Young and leader of 40 Mormon families who immigrated here in 1887. He was the town's first mayor, and built a gristmill, a sawmill and a cheese factory. His restored and refurnished log cabin (1887) is now a museum. The Card family Bible is displayed along with hand-carved furniture.

Sunshine, Sugar Beets and Old Whiskey Forts

Southwestern Alberta

Whiskey forts—riotous trading posts where liquor was sold illegally to Indians—flourished in the late 19th century in this region of southern Alberta. The liquor contained anything from red peppers to red ink. Yet a cupful was worth a fine buffalo robe; a quart, a fast horse.

A letter from one of these posts reflects

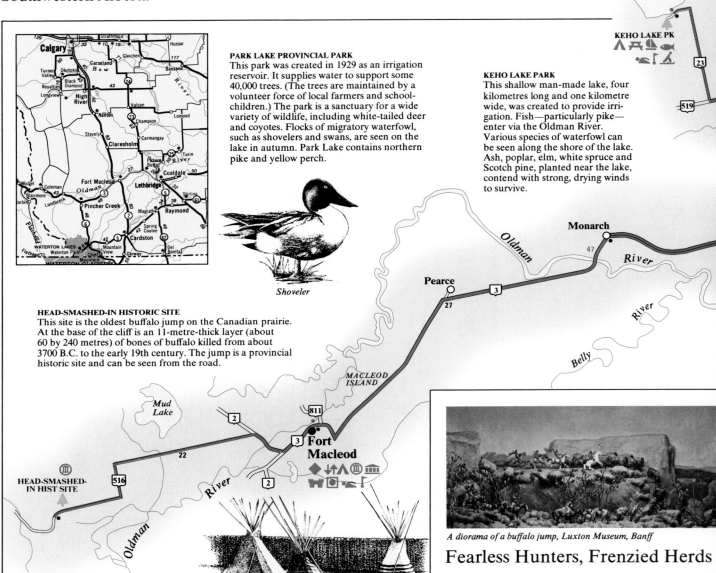

PARK LAKE PROVINCIAL PARK
This park was created in 1929 as an irrigation reservoir. It supplies water to support some 40,000 trees. (The trees are maintained by a volunteer force of local farmers and schoolchildren.) The park is a sanctuary for a wide variety of wildlife, including white-tailed deer and coyotes. Flocks of migratory waterfowl, such as shovelers and swans, are seen on the lake in autumn. Park Lake contains northern pike and yellow perch.

KEHO LAKE PARK
This shallow man-made lake, four kilometres long and one kilometre wide, was created to provide irrigation. Fish—particularly pike—enter via the Oldman River. Various species of waterfowl can be seen along the shore of the lake. Ash, poplar, elm, white spruce and Scotch pine, planted near the lake, contend with strong, drying winds to survive.

Shoveler

HEAD-SMASHED-IN HISTORIC SITE
This site is the oldest buffalo jump on the Canadian prairie. At the base of the cliff is an 11-metre-thick layer (about 60 by 240 metres) of bones of buffalo killed from about 3700 B.C. to the early 19th century. The jump is a provincial historic site and can be seen from the road.

A diorama of a buffalo jump, Luxton Museum, Banff

Fearless Hunters, Frenzied Herds

Before the advent of firearms, Indians killed bison by driving thundering herds over steep cliffs known as buffalo jumps. The oldest site of this kind in Canada is at Head-Smashed-In.

In preparation for the kill, the Indians built drive lines—two rows of piled stones that converged at the buffalo jump. (The drive lines at Head-Smashed-In start about 11 kilometres from the cliff edge.) Hunters stampeded the bison between the drive lines, and the frenzied animals rushed over the cliff edge.

Bison provided the Indians with most of their necessities. Introduction of firearms to Alberta (c.1850) led to thoughtless slaughter of the bison by Indians and whites. Within 30 years, the huge herds had disappeared from the plains—and the simple economy of the Indians collapsed.

Tepees, Fort Macleod

FORT MACLEOD
A replica of the first North West Mounted Police fort stands at the edge of town. The original fort, built in 1874, was on a nearby island in the Oldman River. Buildings in the reconstructed fort include a museum with early NWMP weapons and uniforms, and artifacts from the original fort. There are a law office, blacksmith shop, chapel and medical-dental center. Displays in the center include a foot-pedal drill and a primitive X-ray machine (c.1910). Within the fort's palisade are Indian tepees and covered wagons.

the lawlessness that prevailed: "My partner Will Geary got to putting on airs and I shot him and he is dead. The potatoes is looking good . . ."

Law and order finally came in the 1870s when the North West Mounted Police arrived—led by legendary scout Jerry Potts, a bandy-legged half-breed who drank excessively and trimmed mustaches with his six-shooter. (Potts's grave is near Fort Macleod.)

Today some of Alberta's finest grain farms are found on this now tranquil prairie. Sugar beets are an important crop. The landscape undulates, giving unexpected, often spectacular views of deep-cut coulees and eroded banks along the Oldman River. Trees are few, planted mainly as windbreaks by farmers. Solitary grain elevators stand like sentinels, guarding the rich patchwork of gold, beige and brown fields.

Lethbridge, Alberta's third largest city, is a major meat-packing and grain-distribu-tion center. Originally called Coalbanks, Lethbridge was built on coal in the 1870s. But coal now is secondary to livestock, grain and sugar beets, and the oil and gas that spring from the surrounding land. The city boasts that it receives more hours of sun-shine annually than any other place in Canada. But the semiarid climate makes irrigation essential. Some 400,000 hectares of land surrounding the city are watered by reservoirs, canals and sprinkler systems.

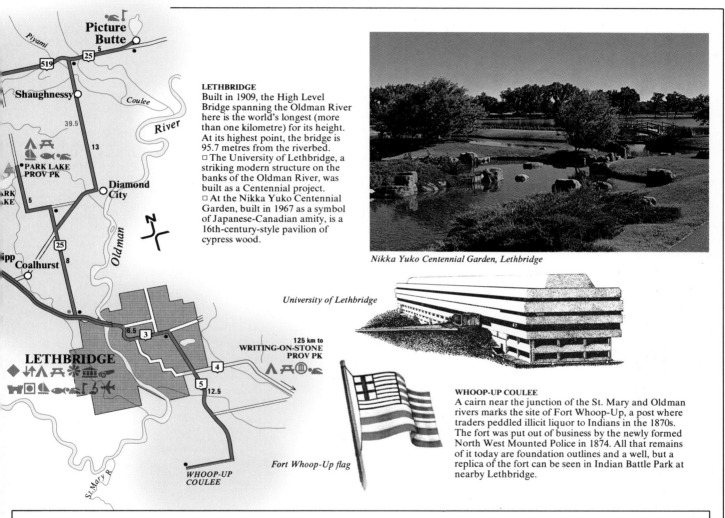

LETHBRIDGE
Built in 1909, the High Level Bridge spanning the Oldman River here is the world's longest (more than one kilometre) for its height. At its highest point, the bridge is 95.7 metres from the riverbed.
□ The University of Lethbridge, a striking modern structure on the banks of the Oldman River, was built as a Centennial project.
□ At the Nikka Yuko Centennial Garden, built in 1967 as a symbol of Japanese-Canadian amity, is a 16th-century-style pavilion of cypress wood.

Nikka Yuko Centennial Garden, Lethbridge

University of Lethbridge

Fort Whoop-Up flag

WHOOP-UP COULEE
A cairn near the junction of the St. Mary and Oldman rivers marks the site of Fort Whoop-Up, a post where traders peddled illicit liquor to Indians in the 1870s. The fort was put out of business by the newly formed North West Mounted Police in 1874. All that remains of it today are foundation outlines and a well, but a replica of the fort can be seen in Indian Battle Park at nearby Lethbridge.

'Writings' on Sandstone

An Indian drawing of a battle between dozens of armed mounted warriors (*right*) is carved on the sandstone cliffs of Writing-on-Stone Provincial Park (125 kilometres south-east of Lethbridge). Other "writings" depict a buffalo hunt, mountain goats, wapiti and deer. The petroglyphs were carved over a 300-year period.

The park's sandstone has been shaped by wind and water: bizarre rock towers (hoodoos) line the Milk River, and once led Indians to believe spirits lived in this valley.

In 1899 a North West Mounted Police outpost was established here to curb whiskey smuggling. Some of the post's buildings have been reconstructed.

Writing-on-Stone Provincial Park

Weird Hoodoos, Ancient Bones and Strange Mechanical Scarecrows

East-Central Alberta

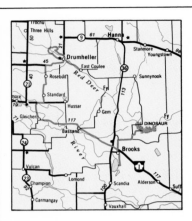

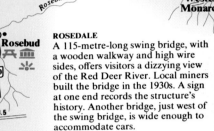

HORSESHOE CANYON

Horseshoe Canyon covers almost 200 hectares of badlands and is more than 1.5 kilometres at its widest. On the canyon floor are petrified shells and wood, and dinosaur bones. Visitors may also come across ancient Indian artifacts such as arrowheads. Vegetation includes sagebrush, saskatoon and chokecherry.

DRUMHELLER

The Drumheller Exhibition and Stampede, in July, features arts and crafts displays, parades, rodeo events, canoe races, dances and barbecues.
□ Just outside the town is the Homestead Antique Museum. Its collections include farm tractors (1915-25) restored and in running condition, a barbershop (c.1915), and dolls and toys from the 1890s.

DINOSAUR TRAIL

The Dinosaur Trail leads west from Drumheller to a 1.6 kilometre-wide valley nearly 120 metres deep—a vast prehistoric graveyard where whole skeletons of dinosaurs have been found. This "Valley of the Dinosaurs" is part of Alberta's Badlands, a long, dry stretch of terrain dotted with cacti and mushroom-shaped columns of clay and rocks called hoodoos.
□ Along this 48-kilometre drive is the "Biggest Little Church in the World," a tiny pink and white structure with a bright brass bell shining in its belfry. The church seats 20,000 people a year—six at a time.
□ The trail climbs to a lookout at the edge of Horse Thief Canyon, drops again, then skirts oil and wheat country before winding back toward Drumheller. The Munson Ferry transports cars to the west side of the Red Deer River.
□ Near the end of the Dinosaur Trail is Prehistoric Park, where life-size dinosaur models are displayed.

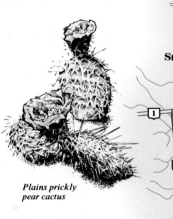

Plains prickly pear cactus

ROSEDALE

A 115-metre-long swing bridge, with a wooden walkway and high wire sides, offers visitors a dizzying view of the Red Deer River. Local miners built the bridge in the 1930s. A sign at one end records the structure's history. Another bridge, just west of the swing bridge, is wide enough to accommodate cars.

EAST COULEE

The first coal mine was opened here in 1924, by J. N. Murray. Four years later the railway arrived, facilitating transportation and encouraging industrial growth. East Coulee experienced its greatest expansion between 1928 and 1955, when the population reached some 3,500 (mostly mining families) and coal output peaked. During one period six coal mines operated full time in the area. Only the Atlas Mine still operates today. Plant tours are available to visitors in summer.

A Fossil Repository Older than the Rockies

The sunbaked, multilayered walls of the Red Deer River valley are a record of eons of land building. Silts and sands were carried here millions of years ago by streams flowing into the Mowry Sea, which once covered the North American plains. Each layer of sediment became a storehouse for the dead plant, animal and marine life of its age. In time this primordial mud turned to rock, and fossils were formed.

Some 70 million years ago enormous underground pressures began to thrust the Rocky Mountains out of the plains. The Red Deer River and its tributaries were shifted eastward, cutting a deep valley and exposing ancient rock layers and fossil remains. Furrowed gullies and strangely shaped hoodoos (rock pillars) are evidence of continuing erosion by the elements.

Hoodoos, Red Deer Valley

CLUNY

A metal cross near here marks the grave of Crowfoot, chief of the Blackfoot. A simple inscription on the cross reads: "Father of His People." Raised as a warrior—he was only 13 when he took part in his first raid—he fought in 19 battles and was wounded six times. But he realized the futility of intertribal warfare and became a man of peace. In 1877, at Blackfoot Crossing, five kilometres south of Cluny, he signed Treaty Seven with the British Crown, surrendering almost 130,000 square kilometres of Indian land.
□ A century later, on July 6, 1977, His Royal Highness Prince Charles and seven Blackfoot chiefs took part in a reenactment of the signing of the historic treaty at Blackfoot Crossing.
□ Near the treaty site is a boulder effigy of Young Medicine Man, a Blood Indian killed in 1872 by a Blackfoot avenging the death of a fellow tribesman at the hands of Young Medicine Man's band.

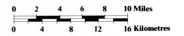

0	2	4	6	8	10 Miles
0	4	8	12	16 Kilometres

Alberta's Red Deer Badlands, millions of years ago the domain of the dinosaur, is a wild and windswept expanse of eroded hoodoos, weathered bluffs and steep-sided gullies. Awed by its rough magnificence, artist A. Y. Jackson described this area as "the most paintable valley in western Canada."

The best-preserved badlands are in Dinosaur Provincial Park. From a vantage point near the park entrance, visitors can look out over some 9,000 hectares of this eerie, sandstone landscape—and see, perhaps, the ghosts of Tyrannosaurus Rex and other prehistoric giants.

Near Drumheller, the scenery changes. Wheat grows waist-high on gently rolling prairie, and here and there oil pumps dot the fields like strange mechanical scarecrows. Antelope, deer, duck, partridge and pheasant in abundance make this area popular with sportsmen. Fish caught here include pike, walleye and trout.

Drumheller—named after Sam Drumheller who, in 1911, began the first coalmining operation here—is a popular base for tourists exploring the Red Deer Badlands. The 50-kilometre Dinosaur Trail gives travelers a fascinating tour through an area rich in fossils.

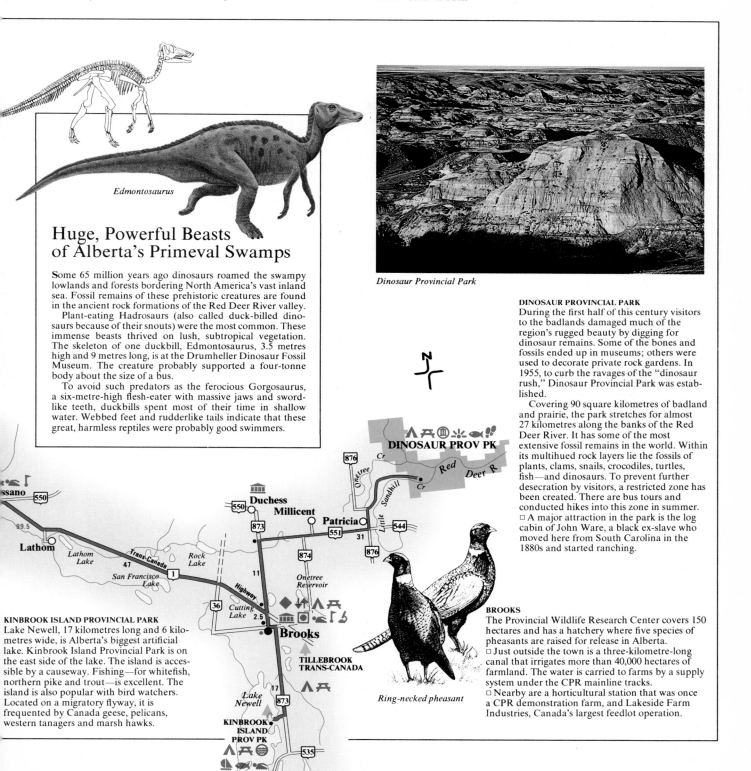

Dinosaur Provincial Park

Huge, Powerful Beasts of Alberta's Primeval Swamps

Some 65 million years ago dinosaurs roamed the swampy lowlands and forests bordering North America's vast inland sea. Fossil remains of these prehistoric creatures are found in the ancient rock formations of the Red Deer River valley.

Plant-eating Hadrosaurs (also called duck-billed dinosaurs because of their snouts) were the most common. These immense beasts thrived on lush, subtropical vegetation. The skeleton of one duckbill, Edmontosaurus, 3.5 metres high and 9 metres long, is at the Drumheller Dinosaur Fossil Museum. The creature probably supported a four-tonne body about the size of a bus.

To avoid such predators as the ferocious Gorgosaurus, a six-metre-high flesh-eater with massive jaws and sword-like teeth, duckbills spent most of their time in shallow water. Webbed feet and rudderlike tails indicate that these great, harmless reptiles were probably good swimmers.

Edmontosaurus

DINOSAUR PROVINCIAL PARK
During the first half of this century visitors to the badlands damaged much of the region's rugged beauty by digging for dinosaur remains. Some of the bones and fossils ended up in museums; others were used to decorate private rock gardens. In 1955, to curb the ravages of the "dinosaur rush," Dinosaur Provincial Park was established.

Covering 90 square kilometres of badland and prairie, the park stretches for almost 27 kilometres along the banks of the Red Deer River. It has some of the most extensive fossil remains in the world. Within its multihued rock layers lie the fossils of plants, clams, snails, crocodiles, turtles, fish—and dinosaurs. To prevent further desecration by visitors, a restricted zone has been created. There are bus tours and conducted hikes into this zone in summer.
□ A major attraction in the park is the log cabin of John Ware, a black ex-slave who moved here from South Carolina in the 1880s and started ranching.

KINBROOK ISLAND PROVINCIAL PARK
Lake Newell, 17 kilometres long and 6 kilometres wide, is Alberta's biggest artificial lake. Kinbrook Island Provincial Park is on the east side of the lake. The island is accessible by a causeway. Fishing—for whitefish, northern pike and trout—is excellent. The island is also popular with bird watchers. Located on a migratory flyway, it is frequented by Canada geese, pelicans, western tanagers and marsh hawks.

Ring-necked pheasant

BROOKS
The Provincial Wildlife Research Center covers 150 hectares and has a hatchery where five species of pheasants are raised for release in Alberta.
□ Just outside the town is a three-kilometre-long canal that irrigates more than 40,000 hectares of farmland. The water is carried to farms by a supply system under the CPR mainline tracks.
□ Nearby are a horticultural station that was once a CPR demonstration farm, and Lakeside Farm Industries, Canada's largest feedlot operation.

Climbing Above the Prairies...
'The Hills That Shouldn't Be'

Southeastern Alberta

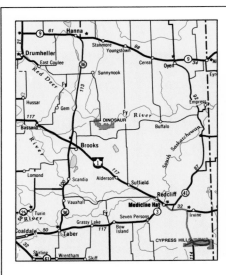

Gentle valleys, forested hillsides, grassy meadows, a rolling belt of brilliant green that breaks a treeless prairie—these are Alberta's Cypress Hills.

High elevation (1,372 metres above sea level) spared the western part of the hills from glaciation that scoured the surrounding prairie some 10,000 years ago. The hills were the only part of western Canada left uncovered by a kilometre-thick sheet of ice between the Rockies and the Laurentians. Centuries ago the hills were a natural

Glass blower at the Altaglass plant, Medicine Hat

The Day the Medicine Man Lost His Hat

The citizens of Medicine Hat are often asked to explain the origin of their town's unusual name. Stories abound, but perhaps the most popular is of a fierce battle between Cree and Blackfoot warriors beside a southern Alberta river. The Cree fought bravely until their medicine man fled across the river. In midstream he lost his headdress, which the Cree believed to be a bad omen. They lost heart and were slaughtered. The battle site was called *Saamis* (Blackfoot for "medicine man's hat"). The name was given to the settlement that sprang up nearby in 1882.

MEDICINE HAT
The three-day Medicine Hat Exhibition and Stampede in July attracts circuit cowboys from all over North America and crowds of more than 40,000. Activities include parades, flapjack breakfasts, chuckwagon races, an agricultural exhibition and livestock and horse shows.
□ Skeletons of saber-toothed tigers, camels and dinosaurs unearthed along the South Saskatchewan River are displayed in the Medicine Hat Historical Museum, along with prehistoric arrowheads and pottery.
□ At the Altaglass plant visitors may tour 16 greenhouses and watch craftsmen shape glass ornaments.
□ Beneath the city is an aquifer—a buried, preglacial river—which provides Medicine Hat with unlimited cool water.
□ In nearby Redcliff visitors are welcome to Medalta Potteries, Canada's only manufacturer of stoneware crocks.

Looking south to the Sweetgrass Hills of Montana, from Head of the Mountain, Cypress Hills Provincial Park

HEAD OF THE MOUNTAIN
This is the highest elevation (1,500 metres) between the Rocky Mountains and Labrador. Unlike the rest of western Canada, this summit was never covered by ice-age glaciers. From here visitors can see as far south as the Sweetgrass Hills of Montana. To the south and east Head of the Mountain slopes gently to the prairie, but to the north and west are nearly vertical cliffs. The high Cypress Hills are moister and cooler than the surrounding prairie. Lodgepole pine, common to the Rockies, grows on upper reaches. Forests of white spruce and trembling aspen thrive at lower elevations.

barrier separating Cree and Blackfoot Indians. Both tribes battled for possession of this hunting ground, rich in grizzly bear, wapiti and bison.

In 1859 John Palliser led a British survey team into the region, then owned by the Hudson's Bay Company. He recorded that much of the land was desert or semidesert, unsuitable for settlement. But he called the hills "an island in a sea of grass."

Settlers came in the next decade—attracted by the hills fertility and bountiful wildlife. But construction of roads and dams, and cattle grazing and the clearing of land for farms destroyed much of the region's natural beauty.

Today the most attractive area of Alberta's Cypress Hills (the range extends into Saskatchewan) has been preserved in 200-square-kilometre Cypress Hills Provincial Park. Here, visitors can still enjoy the scenic wilderness that Blackfoot Indians called *Ketewius Netumoo*—"the hills that shouldn't be."

In contrast to this tranquil park is the busy city of Medicine Hat. Vast natural gas reserves here—today more than 20 billion cubic metres—prompted Rudyard Kipling, in 1907, to describe this as a place with "all hell for a basement."

Wild Orchids and Coyotes in the Cool, Moist Hills

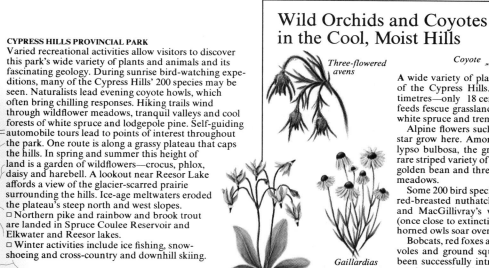

Three-flowered avens

Coyote

Gaillardias

Shooting stars

CYPRESS HILLS PROVINCIAL PARK
Varied recreational activities allow visitors to discover this park's wide variety of plants and animals and its fascinating geology. During sunrise bird-watching expeditions, many of the Cypress Hills' 200 species may be seen. Naturalists lead evening coyote howls, which often bring chilling responses. Hiking trails wind through wildflower meadows, tranquil valleys and cool forests of white spruce and lodgepole pine. Self-guiding automobile tours lead to points of interest throughout the park. One route is along a grassy plateau that caps the hills. In spring and summer this height of land is a garden of wildflowers—crocus, phlox, daisy and harebell. A lookout near Reesor Lake affords a view of the glacier-scarred prairie surrounding the hills. Ice-age meltwaters eroded the plateau's steep north and west slopes.
□ Northern pike and rainbow and brook trout are landed in Spruce Coulee Reservoir and Elkwater and Reesor lakes.
□ Winter activities include ice fishing, snowshoeing and cross-country and downhill skiing.

A wide variety of plants thrives in the cool, moist air of the Cypress Hills. An annual rainfall of 46 centimetres—only 18 centimetres fall on the plains—feeds fescue grasslands and stands of lodgepole pine, white spruce and trembling aspen.

Alpine flowers such as silvery lupine and shooting star grow here. Among 14 orchid species are the calypso bulbosa, the green-flowered bog orchid and a rare striped variety of round-leafed orchid. Gaillardia, golden bean and three-flowered aven brighten grassy meadows.

Some 200 bird species have been sighted in the hills: red-breasted nuthatches, mourning doves, Audubon and MacGillivray's warblers, and trumpeter swans (once close to extinction). Red-tailed hawks and great horned owls soar over grasslands.

Bobcats, red foxes and coyotes prey on shrews, mice, voles and ground squirrels. Wapiti and moose have been successfully introduced to the area. Pronghorn antelope and white-tailed and mule deer also roam the hills.

BATTLE CREEK
The broad shelf of rock that caps the Cypress Hills is best seen at the headwaters of this creek. Forty million years ago this plateau was the bed of a stream that carried quartz pebbles and stones east from the Rocky Mountains. The gravel hardened into a concretelike conglomerate that protects the hills from erosion.

ELKWATER LAKE
On this spring-fed lake, noted for its cool, clear water, is one of Alberta's oldest resorts. A park established in 1929 on the lake's southern shore is now part of Cypress Hills Provincial Park. A swallow colony nests in cliffs along the north shore. Wild turkeys can be seen near the Elkwater campground. This large brown bird, an ancestor of the domestic turkey, was introduced into the hills in 1962, and is now found throughout the park.

Elkwater Lake, Cypress Hills Provincial Park

REESOR LAKE
Great blue herons, kingfishers, cormorants and red-necked grebes fish in this tranquil lake. Stands of trembling aspen and white spruce south of the lake are home to wapiti and white-tailed and mule deer. Ruffed and sharp-tailed grouse forage in grasslands and aspen groves to the north.

Mourning dove

Elkwater Lake

Elkwater

Spruce Coulee Reservoir

Reesor Lake

Battle

The Bench

CYPRESS HILLS PROV PK

Graburn

Nine Mile Cr

4.5

9.5

48

40.5

Cr

A Rugged Region
Where Wild Horses Roam

West-Central Alberta

This vast scenic wilderness was explored in the early 1800s by David Thompson, who earned a reputation as one of the finest geographers in history. Thompson's records and maps were so accurate that many of them are used today. He charted the Great Lakes, the 49th parallel, and the Saskatchewan, Athabasca and Columbia river basins.

This rugged, spectacular region is steeped in the history of the fur trade. Thompson's North West Company headquarters, Rocky

Abraham Lake

NORDEGG
This abandoned town was named after Martin Nordegg, a German immigrant who came to Canada in 1906. He helped establish the Canadian Northern Western Railway and the Brazeau Collieries here. Development of the mine was carried on as the railway was being constructed, and in 1914 some 544 tonnes of coal were being mined daily. Disaster struck the mine in 1941 when an explosion took the lives of 29 men. In 1955 the mine closed down, and with it the town.

CRESCENT FALLS
These spectacular falls on the Bighorn River are near the David Thompson Highway. A scenic hike leads to a lookout onto the Bighorn Canyon.

BIG HORN DAM
Visitors to this 91-metre-high dam, begun in 1969 by Calgary Power Ltd. and completed in 1972, will see Alberta's longest man-made lake—a 48-kilometre-long reservoir named Abraham Lake. Water from the dam is channeled through a 335-metre tunnel to a hydro-electric plant which houses two generators with a total capacity of 120,000 kilowatts. The powerhouse may be toured by appointment. Abraham Lake, named after a family of Stoney Indians who lived in the area for many years, is stocked with Dolly Varden and brook trout.

KOOTENAY PLAINS
A version of the Indian sun dance is enacted here. Traditionally, the sun dance was the most important religious ceremony for about 20 Plains Indian tribes. It occurred every summer before the annual buffalo hunt. The ceremony was held within a circle (symbolizing the sun) and the sun-dance lodge was the focal point. The lodge was never dismantled, but was left to deteriorate naturally. Several recently constructed lodges can be seen in this area.
□ Kootenay Plains is one of the few mountain areas in this region that is natural grassland. The climate is moderate and snow, rare.

FORESTRY TRUNK ROAD
This 998-kilometre gravel road is the only continuous north-south route through Alberta's western forests. Linking Grande Prairie in the north with the Crowsnest Pass in the south, it was built over 15 years, beginning in 1948. Service stations, grocery stores and lunch counters are at points along the road, and campgrounds are located at regular intervals. In the adjacent Clearwater-Rocky Forest Reserve are mountain sheep and goats, and wapiti, moose, deer and bears. Travelers should check the road and weather conditions before setting off.
□ One of the highlights of the Forestry Trunk Road is Ram River Falls, where white water plunges spectacularly into a deep, dark ravine. The falls can best be viewed from a nearby lookout. A recreation area here has picnicking and camping facilities.

SIFFLEUR WILDERNESS AREA
Valleys, streams and rugged mountain terrain characterize the 412-square-kilometre Siffleur Wilderness Area, a remote sanctuary where visitors may travel only on foot. Wapiti and mountain goats are common here, and grizzly bears are occasionally seen.

Siffleur Canyon, Siffleur Wilderness Area

Mountain House, was at the heart of the richest fur-producing area in northwestern Canada. Annually it shipped great bales of otter, sable, cross fox and other furs. During its stormy history the fort was burned to the ground by Indians three times. But it was rebuilt by dogged traders each time until the decline of furs forced abandonment of the post in 1869. Upriver from Rocky Mountain House is a cliff over which Indians stampeded thousands of bison to their deaths.

Hunting has been greatly curbed since the days of the fur trade and many fur-bearing animals can be seen in their natural habitat in wilderness areas set aside by the Alberta government. Here, too, small herds of wild horses may be glimpsed.

Trail trips into the Rockies are increasingly popular as visitors discover the thrill of exploring by horseback. Some of the best fishing in western Canada is found in this region. Trout, perch, pike, goldeye and Dolly Varden are common. Splendid

waterfalls—such as those on the Ram River—also attract visitors.

Still only moderately populated, this area was first settled about 1900. The newcomers established industries that took advantage of the wealth of local timber—producing mine props, railway ties, fence posts and telegraph poles. Oil, mining and mixed farming also contribute to the area's economy.

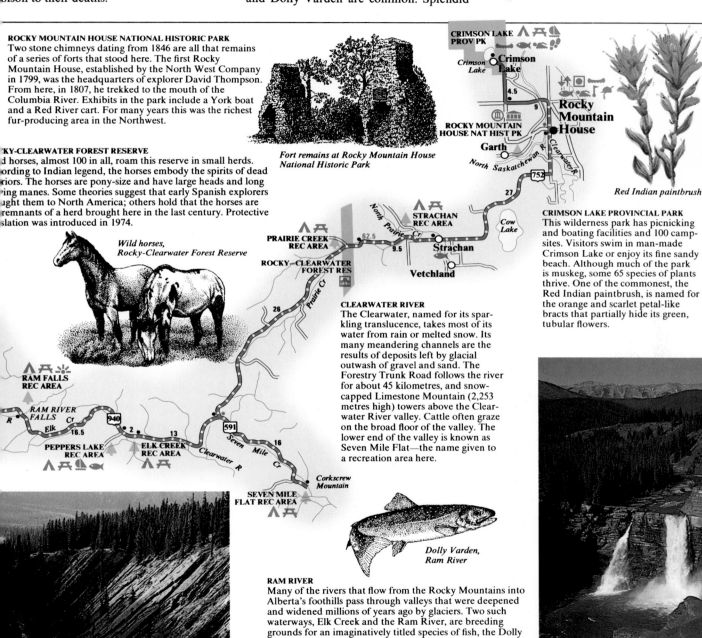

ROCKY MOUNTAIN HOUSE NATIONAL HISTORIC PARK
Two stone chimneys dating from 1846 are all that remains of a series of forts that stood here. The first Rocky Mountain House, established by the North West Company in 1799, was the headquarters of explorer David Thompson. From here, in 1807, he trekked to the mouth of the Columbia River. Exhibits in the park include a York boat and a Red River cart. For many years this was the richest fur-producing area in the Northwest.

ᴷY-CLEARWATER FOREST RESERVE
d horses, almost 100 in all, roam this reserve in small herds. ᵒrding to Indian legend, the horses embody the spirits of dead ᵣiors. The horses are pony-size and have large heads and long ᵛing manes. Some theories suggest that early Spanish explorers ᵘght them to North America; others hold that the horses are ᵉremnants of a herd brought here in the last century. Protective ˢlation was introduced in 1974.

Fort remains at Rocky Mountain House National Historic Park

Wild horses, Rocky-Clearwater Forest Reserve

Red Indian paintbrush

CRIMSON LAKE PROVINCIAL PARK
This wilderness park has picnicking and boating facilities and 100 campsites. Visitors swim in man-made Crimson Lake or enjoy its fine sandy beach. Although much of the park is muskeg, some 65 species of plants thrive. One of the commonest, the Red Indian paintbrush, is named for the orange and scarlet petal-like bracts that partially hide its green, tubular flowers.

CLEARWATER RIVER
The Clearwater, named for its sparkling translucence, takes most of its water from rain or melted snow. Its many meandering channels are the results of deposits left by glacial outwash of gravel and sand. The Forestry Trunk Road follows the river for about 45 kilometres, and snow-capped Limestone Mountain (2,253 metres high) towers above the Clearwater River valley. Cattle often graze on the broad floor of the valley. The lower end of the valley is known as Seven Mile Flat—the name given to a recreation area here.

Dolly Varden, Ram River

RAM RIVER
Many of the rivers that flow from the Rocky Mountains into Alberta's foothills pass through valleys that were deepened and widened millions of years ago by glaciers. Two such waterways, Elk Creek and the Ram River, are breeding grounds for an imaginatively titled species of fish, the Dolly Varden—named after Miss Dolly Varden, a character in Charles Dickens's *Barnaby Rudge* who wore a pink polka-dot dress. This orange- or red-spotted char weighs as much as 14 kilograms. It matures at six years and can live to 18 or more. A fall spawner, it favors cold, clear, gravel-bottomed streams, which it enters between September and November. It usually winters in lakes.

Ram River Falls

Wild Roses by the Roadside, White Sand by a Prairie Lake

Central Alberta

Between Pigeon and Buck lakes, Highway 13 passes through rolling parkland. At each crest of the road, there are sweeping views of gentle hills and scattered groves of trembling aspen. In fields west of Buck Lake, donkey-head pumps nodding with a hypnotic rhythm tap the Pembina Oil Field, one of the world's largest.

The landscape changes as the traveler turns south on Highway 12. The road parallels the Blindman River and cuts through the lush, green farmland of its valley. This

MISSION BEACH
The Rev. Robert T. Rundle, the first resident missionary (1840) in what is now Alberta, founded a Methodist agricultural mission here in 1847. Near a two-story log and stone retreat house is a stone altar on a concrete platform. Flanking the altar are two 10-metre-high stylized arms with symbols of Indian culture, Christianity and agriculture carved in relief.

*Log church,
Pas-Ka-Poo Historical Park,
Rimbey*

RIMBEY
In Pas-Ka-Poo Historical Park, a restored church (1908) contains an 1873 Bible and the original pews and altar. A restored log schoolhouse (1903) has original blackboards and desks. Other buildings include the former Rimbey town office, a general store and a trapper's cabin. Also on the grounds are a threshing machine (1915) and a steam engine (1910). Flower gardens border a pond in the park.
□ Chuck-wagon racing is the main attraction in a June rodeo.

MEDICINE LODGE HILLS
These hills, 22 kilometres south of Rimbey, were once the site of Indian rituals celebrating the arrival of spring. Today, downhill ski runs and snowmobile trails wind through the hills' forests of trembling aspen and white spruce—forests frequented by mule and white-tailed deer.
□ Aspen Beach Provincial Park, east of the hills, has a broad beach on warm, shallow Gull Lake.

SUNDRE
In a campground alongside the Red Deer River is a reconstructed log cabin (1913) furnished with pioneer artifacts. On the second floor is a display of stuffed animals.
□ A 60-kilometre stretch of the Red Deer River between Mountain Aire Lodge and Sundre is dotted with rapids and falls. Only experienced white-water canoeists should attempt this route.

Below Rich Farmland, 'Pools' of Oil in Spongelike Rock

Although oil men speak of pools or fields, oil does not lie underground in vast liquid-filled caverns. Instead, deposits are held—like water in a sponge—in porous rock such as limestone and sandstone.

One of the world's largest oil fields—the 3,200-square-kilometre Pembina field west of Buck Lake in central Alberta—lies below rich farmland. Reserves may total 7.5 billion barrels of oil, but less than two billion barrels can be extracted. Some wells are more than 1.5 kilometres deep.

Pembina oil is in a stratigraphic trap: a porous oil-bearing layer of rock below nonporous rock. Some deposits in the Alberta foothills are in fault traps: rock layers that have cracked and shifted out of alignment, sealing off porous oil reservoirs.

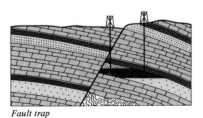
Fault trap

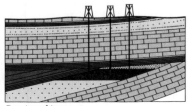
Stratigraphic trap

0 2 4 6 8 10 Miles
0 4 8 12 16 Kilometres

region produces most of Alberta's oats and barley, and half of its cattle. Wheat and rapeseed thrive in its rich, black soil. The roadside in summer is ablaze with wild roses, bluebells and fireweed.

Along this route the faint outline of the Rockies—illusive as a mirage—can be glimpsed. The first unmistakable view of the mountains is at Sundre, where Highway 27 dips down into the Red Deer River valley. From this point, travelers may venture westward to the vacation playgrounds of the Rocky Mountain Forest Reserve and Banff National Park.

But recreation is as attractive in this area as it is farther west. Four provincial parks—Aspen Beach, Ma-Me-O-Beach, Pigeon Lake and Red Lodge—offer water sports in the "dry" central Alberta plain. Sailing competitions are held at Jarvis Bay Provincial Park on Sylvan Lake, noted for its beaches of fine, white sand. At Buck Lake, pike, yellow perch and walleye can be landed in a June fishing derby.

Interior of "The Spruces," Innisfail Historical Village

INNISFAIL

In a historical park are 10 buildings transported from the surrounding countryside to recreate a typical pioneer village. In summer, tea is served each Friday in the dining room of "The Spruces," a log roadhouse built in 1886 on the Calgary-Edmonton wagon trail. Other buildings include a railway station (1904) and a blacksmith shop (1915).
□ A plaque in a campground commemorates Anthony Henday of the Hudson's Bay Company, the first European in this area. In 1754 he explored the Prairies to persuade Indians to trade furs at Hudson Bay.

Icelandic Legacies: Alberta's First Library and a Leading Poet

In 1888-89, a hundred almost penniless Icelanders took homesteads along Alberta's Medicine River, after an unsuccessful attempt to settle in North Dakota. Their first years in Canada were difficult: the Icelanders knew little about farming, and the heavy soil was hard to work. They lived in sod huts and ate fish, game and berries. Markerville became the center of their close-knit community—with a post office and, in 1891, probably the first library in Alberta. A butter and cheese factory provided steady incomes.

One of these early pioneers, Stephen G. Stephansson, has been called Canada's leading poet. But few Canadians have read his work: all his poems are in Icelandic. Stephansson died in 1927 and was buried near his home in Markerville. The poet's house (*left*) is now a historic site.

BOWDEN

The Royal Canadian Mounted Police training kennels, five kilometres north of Bowden, are open to the public during the week. In 1929 Sgt. John N. Cawsey of the provincial police purchased a German shepherd named Dale to help him patrol central Alberta. The dog proved invaluable in tracking suspects. Sergeant Cawsey and Dale joined the Mounties in 1932. Five years later the force established a training school for men and dogs. The canine corps originally included Riesenschnauzers, Doberman pinschers—even mongrels. The force finally selected German shepherds, a strong, courageous and hardy breed. Today, about 15 dogs teamed with masters undergo 14 weeks of training. The animals learn basic obedience, then progress to agility courses and search-and-rescue training.

German shepherd

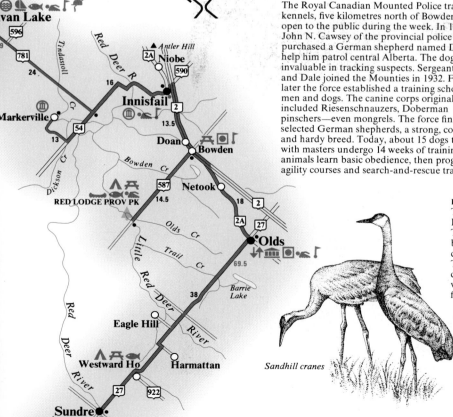

RED LODGE PROVINCIAL PARK

This park's abundant beaver live in burrows along the Little Red Deer River (most beaver inhabit lodges). Their dams form quiet pools where northern pike and brook trout may be landed. Several pairs of sandhill cranes that nest nearby are occasionally sighted here. These tall, brown birds, noted for their buglelike mating call, feed on insects, berries and grain. Moose and white-tailed deer winter in the park's white spruce forests.

Sandhill cranes

OLDS

Olds College, founded in 1913, is an agricultural school with 750 full-time students. It emphasizes business aspects of farming.
□ Mountain View Museum has turn-of-the-century photographs that tell of the area's pioneers and early history.

Map labels:
Sylvan Cr
1
Sylvan Lake
596
781
24
9
Tindastoll
Red Deer R
Antler Hill
2A
Niobe
590
16
Markerville
54
13
Innisfail
2
13.5
Dickson Cr
Bowden Cr
Doan
Bowden
587
Netook
RED LODGE PROV PK
14.5
18
2
Olds Cr
Trail Cr
2A
27
Olds
69.5
Little Red Deer
38
Barrie Lake
Red Deer River
Eagle Hill
Westward Ho
Harmattan
27
922
Sundre
760
584

A Moonscape of Fluted Bluffs and Stark Spires

Central Alberta

Eerie but exquisite are the ravines and rock formations of the Red Deer Badlands. West of the city of Red Deer, this two-kilometre-wide, deep-cut section of the Red Deer River winds 320 kilometres southeast to Brooks. This great, eroded gash is perhaps most dramatic when approached from the west near Dry Island Buffalo Jump Provincial Park.

Fields of rapeseed and wheat grow right to the canyon rim. Then greens and golds of crops give way to gorges devoid of vege-

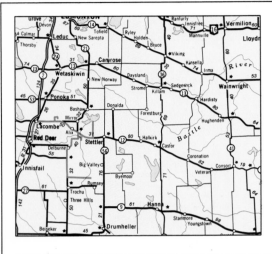

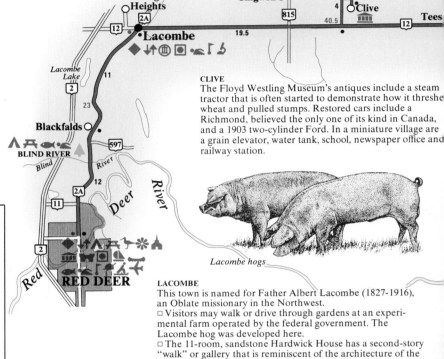

A Swirling Structure

"I don't design boxes," said Edmonton architect Douglas Cardinal, an Indian born and raised in Red Deer. The swirling brick structure of St. Mary's Church in Red Deer, completed in 1968, was his first major project after he graduated from the University of Texas.

The exterior of this award-winning church curves shell-like around a semicircular interior. The altar is the focus: aisles radiate from it like spokes. Natural light from an immense concrete tube suspended from the ceiling illuminates the altar.

For the Métis community of Grouard in northern Alberta, Cardinal designed simple log houses that can be built by the families who will live in them.

St. Mary's Church, Red Deer

CLIVE
The Floyd Westling Museum's antiques include a steam tractor that is often started to demonstrate how it threshed wheat and pulled stumps. Restored cars include a Richmond, believed the only one of its kind in Canada, and a 1903 two-cylinder Ford. In a miniature village are a grain elevator, water tank, school, newspaper office and railway station.

Lacombe hogs

LACOMBE
This town is named for Father Albert Lacombe (1827-1916), an Oblate missionary in the Northwest.
□ Visitors may walk or drive through gardens at an experimental farm operated by the federal government. The Lacombe hog was developed here.
□ The 11-room, sandstone Hardwick House has a second-story "walk" or gallery that is reminiscent of the architecture of the Maritimes. Built about 1910, this private residence has ornate woodwork and leaded windows.

RED DEER
Chinese painting, Scottish glass cutting, and Ukrainian silversmithing are among crafts demonstrated by some 15 ethnic groups at an International Folk Festival in July. Other annual events include five rodeos (one at the six-day Red Deer Exhibition in mid-July) and the Highland Games in June.
□ The city hall, a massive structure of exposed concrete columns and beams, was the winning entry in a Canada-wide design competition in 1961. The building is in a large park containing some 40,000 plants.
□ A 1902 Holsman Autobuggy, a 1918 Kissel Kar Speedster and a 1922 Ford Firewagon (a Model T used as fire engine) are among 21 vehicles in the C. R. Parker collection.
□ Fort Normandeau, built in 1885 during the Northwest Rebellion, was a North West Mounted Police post in 1886-93. It has been restored near its original site.

Ukrainian dancers at the International Folk Festival, Red Deer

0 1 2 3 4 5 Miles
0 2 4 6 8 Kilometres

tation save for stubborn cactus and lichen. Roads twist to the valley floor some 122 metres below. At the bottom is the muddy Red Deer River, contrasting with the pinks, yellows and greens of rock walls layered like a giant cake.

These layers record eons of land building. Once this was a swampy delta at the edge of an inland sea. Rivers and streams flowing east from the still-forming Rockies dumped billions of tonnes of sediment into this marshy region. The primordial mud even-

tually turned to rock, then was eroded by glaciers, wind and water into a stark moon-scape of steep, isolated hills called buttes, and pillars of erosion-resistant clay, sand and gravel called hoodoos.

The multicolored valley walls contain not only dinosaur remains but also the fossils of crocodiles, turtles, fish, oyster shells and of trees that once flourished here—red-wood, swamp cypress, plane tree and sub-tropical gingko.

Scoured by ancient glaciers, Buffalo Lake

is the largest in the Badlands. According to Indian legend, the 19-kilometre-long lake was formed by water pouring from a young bull killed by two Sarcee warriors. The legend tells that many of the hunters' tribe drowned here the following spring when the lake ice broke beneath them. The barking of dogs and the laughter of children are said to come from the bottom of the lake.

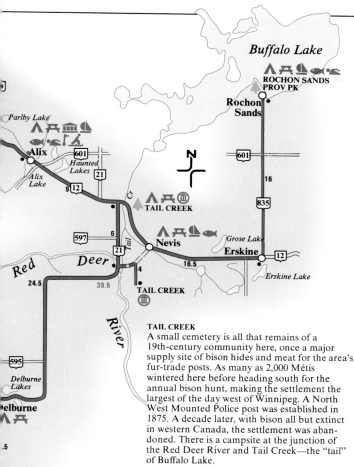

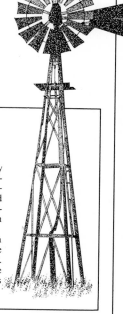

ROCHON SANDS PROVINCIAL PARK
Several sandy beaches on Buffalo Lake are in Rochon Sands Provincial Park, a small area with aspen groves and saskatoon and chokecherry shrubs. Baltimore orioles inhabit the park and great blue herons are seen in the vicinity. This is a favorite spot for fishermen (yellow perch and northern pike), swimmers, and water-skiers. Many campers and picnickers use this sheltered park.

Power and Water From Prairie Windmills

Most Alberta farmers used oil lamps as recently as the mid-1950s, when only a fifth of the province's farms had electricity. A few farmers generated small amounts of electricity with "wind chargers"—windmills connected to storage batteries. Old wooden windmills can still be seen in some areas.

Many farmers in central Alberta still rely on the wind. Modern windmills on steel towers drive pumps that supply water for homes and livestock. The windmills are a cheap and practical source of power in Alberta's parkland, where winds average 15 kilometres an hour.

TAIL CREEK
A small cemetery is all that remains of a 19th-century community here, once a major supply site of bison hides and meat for the area's fur-trade posts. As many as 2,000 Métis wintered here before heading south for the annual bison hunt, making the settlement the largest of the day west of Winnipeg. A North West Mounted Police post was established in 1875. A decade later, with bison all but extinct in western Canada, the settlement was abandoned. There is a campsite at the junction of the Red Deer River and Tail Creek—the "tail" of Buffalo Lake.

DRY ISLAND BUFFALO JUMP PROVINCIAL PARK
Turkey vultures soar above a 140-metre-deep valley in this scenic park beside the Red Deer River. Plants and animals characteristic of the prairies, badlands and northern forest regions, and a tremendous variety of landforms are among the park's diverse natural features.

The park is named for a mesa, or island of isolated, water-eroded rock. Gullies, round-topped hills called buttes, and pillars of rock called hoodoos are typical of badlands. Yellow umbrella plant, salt sage, winter fat, prickly pear cactus, thorny buffalo berry, sagebrush and long-leafed sage not found in the surrounding uplands grow here.

Trees in a massive landslide area include aspen, paper birch and balsam poplar. Juniper, saskatoon, pin cherry, chokecherry and wild rose shrubs form a thick ground cover.

Bones near the base of a cliff mark the site of a buffalo jump. Indians once stampeded the animals over this precipice.

Dry Island Buffalo Jump Provincial Park

'Donkey Heads' Bob Quietly Where 'Black Gold' Gushed

Central Alberta

In the rippling grain fields near Leduc, pumps, known as "donkey heads," bob up and down to a slow, steady rhythm. From the earth beneath rich farmland, the pumps draw oil that has been stored there for millions of years.

The Leduc field has been yielding oil since the late 1940s. Until that time, Canada's oil sources (notably the Turner Valley, south of Calgary) provided less than 10 percent of the nation's needs. Years of exploration yielded no significant new supplies.

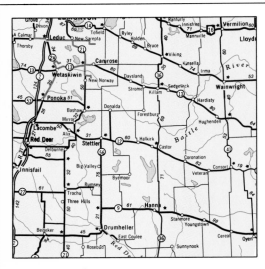

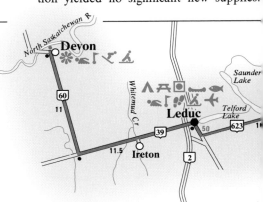

DEVON
Cacti, yucca plants, gladioli and peonies grow amid sand dunes and ponds at the University of Alberta Devonian Botanic Garden—North America's most northerly botanic garden. Every known Alberta plant is among some 26,000 species exhibited. A plaque at the entrance notes that part of the Leduc oil field lies 1.5 kilometres underground.

"Donkey head" oil pump near Leduc

LEDUC
The site of Imperial Leduc No. 1—the well that on Feb. 13, 1947, tapped the 300-million-barrel Leduc oil field—is marked by a plaque 17 kilometres northwest. Imperial Oil had drilled 133 dry holes before striking oil at 1,771 metres here. Nearby is the site of Atlantic No. 3, a well that went wild in March 1947, spewing oil for almost six months before catching fire.

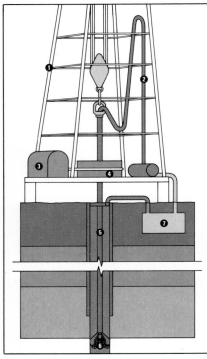

Roughnecks and Rock Cuttings

Oil exploration in the late 1800s was simple, and usually successful: prospectors drilled wherever they found oil or gas seeping out of the ground. Today, as oil becomes scarce, companies looking for new sources use more sophisticated methods. Scientists study the land for clues to what lies underground. Oil is usually found in porous sedimentary rock (such as sandstone) covered by dense, nonporous rock. Seismologists locate such structures by setting off small explosions and analyzing the shock waves that rebound to the surface. Other clues to underground oil deposits are provided by aerial photographs, and by gravimeters and magnetometers, which measure differences in the earth's gravity and magnetism.

Once a promising spot has been discovered, the drilling crew (called "roughnecks") set up the derrick (1) that supports the drill pipe (2). An engine (3) powers the rotary table (4) that drives the drill pipe downward. Inside the pipe is the stem (5) which has a hard-toothed bit (6) at the end. As the stem turns, the bit cuts through rock layers. Specially formulated mud (7) is pumped through the stem to lubricate the bit and bring rock cuttings to the surface. The mud also fills the hole to prevent gushers, which occur when oil under high pressure rushes out of the ground.

Provincial building, Ponoka

PONOKA
A midsummer stampede features calf roping, steer wrestling, and saddle and bareback riding.
□ A four-story, enclosed atrium with a year-round tropical garden is part of Ponoka's modern provincial building which houses eight government departments and a courthouse. The curvilinear brick structure was built in 1977 as part of a government decentralization program.
□ Books, documents and photographs in a museum at the Alberta Hospital trace the province's history of mental health care. The brick and sandstone hospital, opened in 1911, was the first in Alberta for the treatment of mental illness.

All that changed on Feb. 13, 1947, the day "black gold" gushed from the Imperial Leduc No.1 well.

Within a year, 61 derricks—some as high as 15-story buildings—were drilling on the prairies near Leduc. But the discovery brought its dangers. Atlantic No. 3, a little to the northwest of the discovery well, went out of control in March 1947. After spewing oil over the prairie for six months, the rogue well burst into flames. (To seal the well, oilmen used 20,000 bags of cement, 16,000 bags of sawdust, 1,000 sacks of cottonwood hulls, eight railway carloads of wood fiber, and two carloads of turkey feathers.)

The awesome fire made the public aware that Alberta was a major oil-producing area. There was further investment, and intensive exploration of other gas and oil fields. As the oil poured out, new wealth flooded in. By the 1970s, Alberta had 11,592 oil wells and 10,806 gas wells in some 30 major fields.

The derricks have long since gone from Leduc, as oilmen seek new sources underground or in oil-rich tar sands. (The high steel tower which was used to drill the discovery well has been moved to a site on the southern outskirts of Edmonton.) Pumping and storing oil is the business of Leduc today, with farming a second source of wealth.

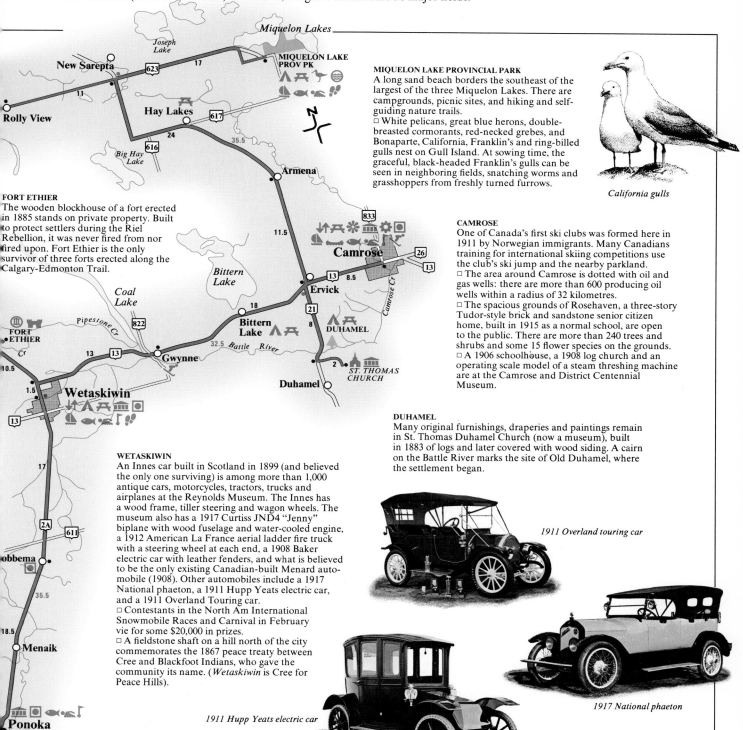

MIQUELON LAKE PROVINCIAL PARK
A long sand beach borders the southeast of the largest of the three Miquelon Lakes. There are campgrounds, picnic sites, and hiking and self-guiding nature trails.
□ White pelicans, great blue herons, double-breasted cormorants, red-necked grebes, and Bonaparte, California, Franklin's and ring-billed gulls nest on Gull Island. At sowing time, the graceful, black-headed Franklin's gulls can be seen in neighboring fields, snatching worms and grasshoppers from freshly turned furrows.

California gulls

FORT ETHIER
The wooden blockhouse of a fort erected in 1885 stands on private property. Built to protect settlers during the Riel Rebellion, it was never fired from nor fired upon. Fort Ethier is the only survivor of three forts erected along the Calgary-Edmonton Trail.

CAMROSE
One of Canada's first ski clubs was formed here in 1911 by Norwegian immigrants. Many Canadians training for international skiing competitions use the club's ski jump and the nearby parkland.
□ The area around Camrose is dotted with oil and gas wells: there are more than 600 producing oil wells within a radius of 32 kilometres.
□ The spacious grounds of Rosehaven, a three-story Tudor-style brick and sandstone senior citizen home, built in 1915 as a normal school, are open to the public. There are more than 240 trees and shrubs and some 15 flower species on the grounds.
□ A 1906 schoolhouse, a 1908 log church and an operating scale model of a steam threshing machine are at the Camrose and District Centennial Museum.

DUHAMEL
Many original furnishings, draperies and paintings remain in St. Thomas Duhamel Church (now a museum), built in 1883 of logs and later covered with wood siding. A cairn on the Battle River marks the site of Old Duhamel, where the settlement began.

WETASKIWIN
An Innes car built in Scotland in 1899 (and believed the only one surviving) is among more than 1,000 antique cars, motorcycles, tractors, trucks and airplanes at the Reynolds Museum. The Innes has a wood frame, tiller steering and wagon wheels. The museum also has a 1917 Curtiss JND4 "Jenny" biplane with wood fuselage and water-cooled engine, a 1912 American La France aerial ladder fire truck with a steering wheel at each end, a 1908 Baker electric car with leather fenders, and what is believed to be the only existing Canadian-built Menard automobile (1908). Other automobiles include a 1917 National phaeton, a 1911 Hupp Yeats electric car, and a 1911 Overland Touring car.
□ Contestants in the North Am International Snowmobile Races and Carnival in February vie for some $20,000 in prizes.
□ A fieldstone shaft on a hill north of the city commemorates the 1867 peace treaty between Cree and Blackfoot Indians, who gave the community its name. (*Wetaskiwin* is Cree for Peace Hills).

1911 Overland touring car

1917 National phaeton

1911 Hupp Yeats electric car

A Pastoral Refuge for a Pacifist People

Central Alberta

A Hutterite family of Alberta

Coal-oil lamps, Donalda

Buffalo Lake

DONALDA

Lamps that burned whale oil, lard and tallow are among some 500 in the privately owned Lawson Lamp Collection. On display are 200 miniature kerosene lamps, peg lamps (so called because they fitted in candle holders) and sparking lamps, the timepieces of old-time courtships. These lamps, containing only enough oil to last about an hour, were lit by fathers when boyfriends called on the girls in the family. When the light went out, the suitors had to leave.

Antiques displayed with the lamp collection include an Edison Gem Gramophone with cylinder records, and a mouseproof kitchen cabinet brought to Donalda in a covered wagon in 1903.
□ In scenic Meeting Creek valley east of town are some of Alberta's most fascinating badlands. Hills and coulees here are a natural playground for skiers, tobogganers and snowmobilers. A snowmobile rally here is held in February.

Where Salt Grass Grows by Prairie Lakes

Barren, salt-crusted shores characterize the thousands of alkaline lakes, marshes and sloughs throughout the parkland of central Alberta. Natural salts, concentrated by evaporation, make these waters deadly to fish and most aquatic plants. Only salt-loving plants known as halophytes, such as sea blite, salt grass (*above*), and samphire, grow near these shores.

At the end of the last ice age, receding glaciers left shallow depressions in this region. Runoff, containing dissolved salts from surrounding alkali soils, has filled the depressions creating alkaline (often lifeless) bodies of water.

The numerous freshwater lakes and ponds in central Alberta, however, teem with plants and animals. Willows and aspens commonly grow to lake edges here. Pintails, mallards and other ducks nest in the dense bulrushes and cattails that surround prairie sloughs. Insects and grain from nearby fields provide a reliable food supply for these birds.

STETTLER

Some 20 different makes of churns are in a butter-making display in the Stettler Town and Country Museum.
□ This town has a 25-metre-long, indoor, heated swimming pool, a nine-hole golf course, paved tennis courts and pari-mutuel horse racing. Within a short driving distance are good hunting and fishing, provincial parks, prehistoric sites and ski hills.

Century-old barrel churn, Stettler

| 0 | 1 | 2 | 3 | 4 | 5 Miles |
| 0 | | 2 | 4 | 6 | 8 Kilometres |

Much of this region is farmed by the Hutterites, members of a religious sect founded in Europe in the 16th century. Persecuted for rejecting infant baptism and refusing to bear arms, Hutterites migrated frequently before settling in western Canada during the First World War. Some 6,000 are in central Alberta.

The Hutterites hold property in common and perform work collectively. Each communal settlement has about 100 residents —some 10 families. Offshoot colonies are formed when the population nears 150. Jobs are rotated frequently by the elected *wirt*, or household boss. The head of the colony is an elected lay preacher.

Families occupy simple, almost identical apartments. Meals are eaten in a communal dining hall, where men and women, grouped according to age, sit at separate tables. The Hutterites reject old age pensions, unemployment insurance, welfare, the rights to vote and to hold public office. Infants, from 18 weeks, are cared for in nurseries. From age two, they spend six hours a day in *klein-schul* or nursery school.

The Hutterites speak a German dialect, and German is the language of their church services. Most trace their families back to the 1500s—and wear clothes reminiscent of that era. The men wear dark suits, broad-brimmed hats and, if married, beards. Women wear ankle-length dresses in plaids and prints and polka-dot kerchiefs.

FORESTBURG

Guided tours are available weekdays at Forestburg Collieries Ltd., which operates one of the world's largest power shovels. The 30-metre-high giant, on four crawler tracks, can move more than 900 cubic metres of earth an hour. It took 38 railway cars to transport the machine here in 1949, when strip mining replaced the underground techniques in use since 1907.
□ Coal mining is a major industry in this part of Alberta, a province with more than half Canada's coal reserves and the nation's second largest coal producer (after Nova Scotia). When the coal is extracted, the mined area is reclaimed by replacing topsoil and reseeding the area with grass and trees.
□ This area has good cross-country skiing and pike fishing.

Animal Life of Alberta's Parkland Belt

White-tailed deer

Meadowlark

Varying hare

The area around Stettler and Castor is part of the Alberta parkland. This broad belt of aspen groves and grasslands between northern forest and open prairie is home to a wide variety of animals.

Varying hare (named for their coats: gray brown in summer, white in winter) and white-tailed deer feed on the bark of young aspens in winter, often killing the trees. In summer deer venture into grasslands to browse on twigs and plants.

Burrowing rodents common in the grasslands are badgers, Richardson's ground squirrels (or gophers) and 13-lined ground squirrels. Earth moved by their burrowing helps to spread shrubs and aspens: seeds germinate easily in the loose soil.

Insects attract many birds to aspen groves; downy and hairy woodpeckers, least flycatchers and yellow warblers nest here. Other birds, such as horned larks and meadowlarks, live only in the grasslands. Birds of prey, such as red-tailed hawks, nest in aspen groves and hunt over the grasslands.

BIG KNIFE PROVINCIAL PARK

This park is on a reservoir upstream from a major power plant on the Battle River. In the heart of a farming district, it is one of the few sites in this area of Alberta where recreation lands are reserved for public use. The park, a mixture of forest and grassland, contains dense stands of poplar, birch and white spruce. There are facilities for camping, picnicking, canoeing and boat launching, and there is good fishing for northern pike.

The park commemorates two Cree warriors, Big Man and Knife, who fought and killed each other beside Big Knife Creek more than 200 years ago. A plaque marks the site.

Battle River near Big Knife Provincial Park

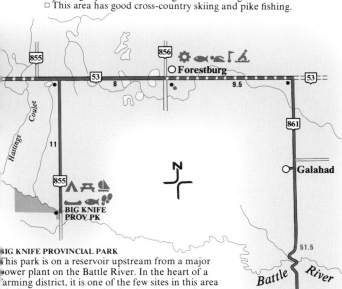

CASTOR

The center for some of the finest duck, geese and deer hunting in Alberta, this community has two airstrips, a stock car track, golf course and heated swimming pool. There are boating, swimming and free camping on Castor Creek, fishing at the Huber Dam (rainbow trout) and the Canadian Utilities Dam (pike and pickerel), and waterskiing on the Tarr Reservoir.
□ At the edge of town is the John Filipenko collection of yard ornaments—weathervanes and windmills fashioned from automobile shock absorbers, bicycle wheels and bleach bottles.

Weathervane, John Filipenko collection, Castor

Golden Fields, Salty Sloughs and Silver-Green Valleys

East-Central Alberta

Hillsides veined with gullies and dotted with groves of trees; fields golden with ripening rapeseed; sloughs rimmed with salt; valleys silver green with wolf willow—such are the vistas of this undulating countryside.

At the turn of the century, colorful government posters portrayed the Prairies as "Canada West—The Last Best West," and told of its ranching and farming potential. A quarter-section (160 acres) could be bought for $10. Farmers' sons from Ontario

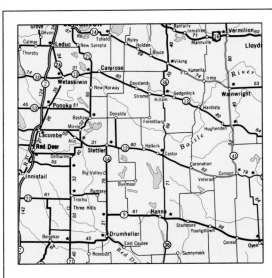

Ribstones

VERMILION
Recreational facilities in this tree-lined town include a heated outdoor swimming pool, a nine-hole golf course and a kilometre-long snowmobile track. Annual events include the week-long Vermilion Red Hat Mardi Gras in February, rodeos in April and October, and an agricultural fair in Ju

Golden bean

VERMILION PROVINCIAL PARK
Plants seldom found this far north—puccoon, bladderpod, purple prairie clover, buffalo bean and the poisonous golden bean—grow here. White-tailed deer and coyotes roam through aspen groves. Canada geese, herons and swans feed in marshes.

The park has camping, picnicking, fishing (walleye, yellow perch and northern pike), boating and a sandy beach.

RIBSTONES HISTORICAL SITE
Two quartzite rocks important in Cree Indian hunting rituals are here. On each rock is a centimetre-deep relief of a bison's backbone and ribs, painstakingly engraved with pebbles and sand some 1,000 years ago. One rock (about 130 by 90 centimetres) represents a bull bison; the other (130 by 40 centimetres), a cow.

Indians could survey their hunting grounds from this site and watch the bison migrate. Bison were sacrificed on the stones to ensure a successful hunt. When settlers arrived here in the early 1900s, Indians were still leaving beads, tobacco and meat at the stones.

Peregrine falcon

A Swift and Graceful Bird Saved From Extinction

All birds of prey—hawks, falcons, eagles, owls—are in danger of extinction. They are at the end of a food chain that progresses from plant-eaters to insect-eaters to flesh-eaters. Pesticides, which become more concentrated at each link in the chain, accumulate at dangerously high levels in birds of prey.

Only two wild peregrine falcons were known to exist in Alberta in 1970. The peregrine, one of the swiftest birds of prey, can dive faster than 320 kilometres an hour. But its speed and power—distinct advantages in nature—do not protect it from man's poisons.

In 1970 the Canadian Wildlife Service established a center at Camp Wainwright to breed peregrines in captivity, and introduce them to the wild. There are now about 100 peregrines at the center. Naturalists use closed-circuit television to monitor the birds.

0 2 4 6 8 10 Miles

0 4 8 12 16 Kilometres

and the Maritimes, adventuresome Britons, oppressed Mennonites and Ukrainians and Americans whose own West was filling up flocked here. They planted crops and built homes—and endured droughts, dust storms, hailstorms, grass fires, grasshopper plagues, and frosts that blighted a season's hopes.

Many a homesteader kept body and soul together by gathering bison bones in the wedge-shaped Nose Hills north of Veteran. The bones were piled in the hills from the days when Indians stampeded bison over bluffs. For years a major export to the United States, where they were used in fertilizer and for refining sugar, the bones netted $10 to $16 a ton.

Homesteaders unsuited to the harsh life soon left. Those who measured up to the land and the climate remained, and found a good and prosperous life. Some of the giant tractors with which they broke the prairie sod still throb to life at Wraight's Tractor Museum near Veteran. Other links with these hardy pioneers are a reconstructed kitchen and parlor at the Wainwright Pioneer Museum, and exhibits in the Pioneer Panorama Museum at Czar.

Alberta wheat harvest

WAINWRIGHT

A reconstructed post office with furniture and equipment from the early 1900s, when this district was settled, old milking equipment and a wooden cradle churn are part of the Wainwright Museum.
□ Oil and gas, discovered here in 1921, are piped from some 400 wells. An early rig is among oil-drilling exhibits in Petroleum Park.
□ British army units train at CFB Camp Wainwright, formerly Buffalo National Park. Bison, wapiti and deer roamed these grounds in 1908-41. A fiberglass statue of a bison, the town symbol, stands at one of the entrances to Wainwright.

War memorial, Wainwright

CZAR

Despite its Russian name, this area was settled mainly by Scandinavians. The Prairie Panorama Museum has pioneer household items, books, costumes and toys, and displays that illustrate the natural and archaeological history of the Prairies. Prized exhibits are some 1,100 pairs of salt and pepper shakers, in designs ranging from mallard ducks to praying hands.
□ On Shorncliffe Lake are municipally operated camping and picnic grounds, and beach and boating facilities.

NEUTRAL HILLS

For centuries Plains Indians kept the Neutral Hills as a hunting preserve where no fighting or raiding was allowed. Their folklore tells how the hills were raised by the Great Spirit to keep two warring tribes apart. The Indians then held a great council and made peace.

A cairn of stones at the highest point in the hills marks what is said to have been the meeting spot.

Archaeologists have discovered many Indian ceremonial sites in the hills, including tepee rings, and boulder outlines of bison and turtles.

Silverberry

GOOSEBERRY LAKE PROVINCIAL PARK

Because of its high alkaline content Gooseberry Lake has no fish. But it provides the only swimming spot in the area. The park has camping, picnicking and boat-launching facilities and a golf course.

Aspen, lance-leaf, poplar, silverberry, wild rose and willow grow in moist areas of the park and on the lakeshore. Windbreaks of pine, spruce and caragana have been planted but require a great deal of care to survive in the dry, sandy soil. Coyotes, Richardson's ground squirrels and meadowlarks are among the park's fauna.

VETERAN

Wraight's Tractor Museum displays an oil-cooled 1910 Rumely with a 15-horsepower motor, a 1928 Hart-Parr, and a 1929 John Deere. All the museum's 46 tractors, used in Alberta and Saskatchewan in the early 1900s, are in working order. Other exhibits are threshing machines and stationary engines used to power feed grinders and washing machines.

Rumely tractor (1910), Veteran

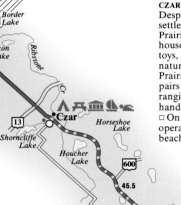

CORONATION

[Thi]s community, settled in 1897, was [na]med for the coronation of George [V i]n 1911. Streets and avenues are [na]med Windsor, Mary, Queen, King, [Ro]yal and George.
[On] the migration route of the large [Ca]nada goose, the Coronation district [off]ers some of the best goose hunting [in] Alberta.
[A]nnual events include a rodeo in [Ju]ne and an agricultural fair and exhi[bit]ion in August.

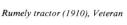

Border Lake
Dixon Lake
Ribstone
13 Czar
Horseshoe Lake
Shorncliffe Lake
Houcher Lake
600
45.5
56.5
Neutral Hills
41
Gooseberry Lake
GOOSEBERRY LAKE PROV PK
11
Consort
Loyalist Cr
12
24
Loyalist
NOSE HILL
884
48
Veteran
Ribstone Cr
24
Throne
Coronation
12 Federal
872

Where the Sun Sets Late on Farmland, Lake and Forest

Lesser Slave Lake

The summer sun sets late in this region of farmland, lake and forest. (At eleven o'clock, it is still light enough to fish, golf, or pitch a tent.) The area was once the preserve of the Slavey Indians, for whom many of its sites are named. (It was the warlike Cree who, contemptuous of their peaceful kin, called them slaves, or Slavey.)

Northern Alberta's Indians surrendered vast tracts of land to the Canadian government in 1899. The treaty was signed near Grouard, the oldest settlement (1872) in

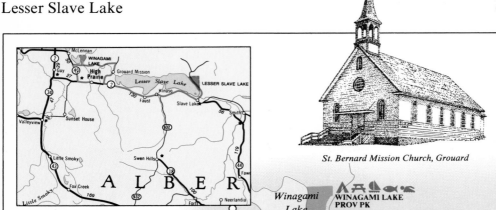

St. Bernard Mission Church, Grouard

GROUARD
This hamlet, once a bustling town on the overland route to the Klondike from Edmonton, is named for Bishop Emile Jean Baptiste Grouard (1840-1931), an Oblate missionary to the Indians, and translator and publisher of hymnals and prayer books in the languages of various tribes. A painting behind the altar in the 1½-story, wood frame St. Bernard Mission Church is by Bishop Grouard. He is buried in the adjoining cemetery.

WINAGAMI LAKE PROVINCIAL PARK
A woodland setting (aspen, balsam and poplar) and a long sandy beach have made the park popular with campers, picnickers and swimmers. There is good fishing (northern pike, walleye, and yellow perch) and boating.
□ Bald eagles, greater yellowlegs, rusty blackbirds, Franklin's gulls, and 15 species of woodpeckers are among some 150 bird species sighted here. Black bears, moose, deer and red foxes roam through an underbrush of cranberries and wild roses. Northern green orchids and marsh cinquefoil are abundant in swampy areas.

A Great Man of Prayer

In 1863 a young Roman Catholic missionary, Father Emile Jean Baptiste Grouard, arrived in the remote Peace River district of northern Alberta. For 68 years—until his death at age 91—he worked with the Cree and Beaver Indians of the Northwest.

Many Indians blamed missionaries for sickness and famine; but Father Grouard, who learned to speak eight Indian dialects, became their trusted friend. *Kitchi-Aya-miheiviyiniw* (Great Man of Prayer), they called him. He set up the first press in the Peace River district, and translated and printed hymns and prayer books. He was an accomplished artist; one of his paintings still hangs in the St. Bernard Mission Church in Grouard—the town named after him.

Grouard, who was named archbishop in 1930, died in 1931. His grave can be seen in the mission cemetery in Grouard.

HIGH PRAIRIE
A sword and a 3,000-year-old adze (an ancient cutting tool) are among curiosities in the High Prairie and District Museum. The sword, possibly made in the early 1800s, was plowed up about a mile from here in 1923. How it got there is a mystery. The adze, made of metamorphic stone of a type not native to this area, was found near where the sword was unearthed. An extensive collection of pioneer furniture includes washing machines made of wood by pioneers about 1900, and a brass bed with posts some 10 centimetres in diameter.
□ There are an outdoor swimming pool, a golf course and, just east of town, a campground. A stampede is held in August.

Myrtle warbler

FAUST
A piece of stained glass, salvaged during the Second World War from the bombed St. Paul's Cathedral in London, has been placed in a window at St. Paul's Anglican Church here. The glass has a rosette pattern.
□ This hamlet on Giroux Bay of Lesser Slave Lake is a center for commercial fishing, lumbering and mink ranching. The Swan Hills oil fields are to the south.

Map labels: McLennan, WINAGAMI LAKE, Grouard Mission, High Prairie, Guy, Lesser Slave Lake, LESSER SLAVE LAKE, Kinuso, Faust, Slave Lake, Valleyview, Sunset House, Smith, Little Smoky, Swan Hills, Little Smoky, Fox Creek, Neerlandia, Faw, ALBER[TA]

Kathleen, Winagami Lake, WINAGAMI LAKE PROV PK, Prairie Echo, BUFFALO BAY, Grouard Mission, Grouard, South Heart River, East Prairie River, West Prairie River, Maurice Lake, Iroquois Lakes, High Prairie, Noon Cr, Triangle, Enilda, Mud Cr, Sucker Cr, Joussard, Arcadia Cr, Mission Cr, Driftpile, Driftpile, Salt Cr

this area. At the turn of the century, Grouard boasted banks, restaurants, a hotel, a newspaper and 4,000 souls. (In 1905 it vied with the smaller and less busy Edmonton to become the provincial capital.)

Grouard's growth began when gold was discovered in the Klondike in 1896. The town was on the overland, all-Canadian route from Edmonton to the Yukon. The town grew as long as settlers ventured northward. Supplies to the fast-growing northern communities were hauled across frozen Lesser Slave Lake by horse-drawn sleds in winter, by steamboats in summer.

The eastern terminus of the lake traffic was the town of Slave Lake, known then as Sawridge. The community was settled in 1898 by would-be prospectors who decided to stay rather than face the arduous journey to the Yukon. With five boats in regular service, Sawridge proudly called itself the steamboat capital of Canada. The boats were withdrawn when the railway came through in 1914. Both Grouard and Sawridge sank into obscurity.

Fifty years later the town of Slave Lake enjoyed a new importance when oil was discovered in the area. From some 500 persons in the 1960s, the population has grown to about 4,000 today.

Lesser Slave Lake

LESSER SLAVE LAKE
Dunes up to six metres high are in a five-kilometre-long belt at the southern tip of 1,195-square-kilometre Lesser Slave Lake, one of the largest bodies of water in Alberta. (The term "Lesser" was added to the name of the lake to distinguish it from Great Slave Lake in the N.W.T.)
□ Bald eagles and ospreys inhabit Lesser Slave Lake Provincial Park. Moose, deer, wolves and bears, including some grizzlies, roam the poplar-, spruce- and birch-clad hills.
□ Swimming, fishing (walleye and northern pike), boating and canoeing are excellent in the park. There are boat-launching facilities on Lesser Slave Lake and three large campgrounds—North Shore, Lily Creek and Marten Creek. Hikers have a panoramic view of the lake and rolling countryside from the top of 915-metre Marten Mountain.

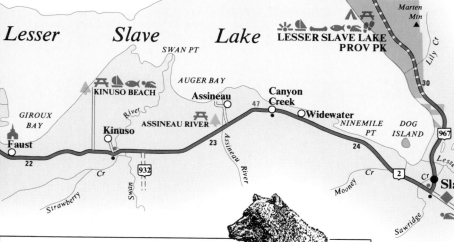

Bay-breasted warbler

The Magnificent Grizzly

The grizzly bear ranks with the shark as an object of terror for man. But in fact the grizzly avoids man, and an attack is usually the result of a sudden meeting at close range.

These magnificent bears once roamed as far east as the Red River. Because of man's encroachment, grizzlies are found only in parts of the Yukon and Northwest Territories, the Rocky Mountains, and the Swan Hills, south of Lesser Slave Lake.

The grizzly is a massive, heavy-limbed animal ranging from creamy yellow to black. In spite of its reputation as a cattle killer, it usually eats fish, rodents, insects, roots and berries.

SLAVE LAKE
The area around this town was once an Indian hunting ground and was a stopping place on a land and water route used by war parties, early explorers, traders, Klondike prospectors and Peace River pioneers. The Hudson's Bay Company had two trading posts here when frustrated gold-seekers settled the district in 1898. By the 1900s the area was a transportation and trading center for settlers moving northward. Four cargo ships and one passenger boat made regular stops here at the height of riverboat traffic. This fell off in 1914 when the railway arrived.

The town was first known as Sawridge for its saw-edged sand ridges. The name was changed to Slave Lake in 1923.

Water rose to more than a metre's depth on main street during a 1935 flood. The following year the town's buildings were loaded on sleds and moved over the ice to high ground some four kilometres from the original site.
□ Fireworks, logging contests and a fastball tournament are featured at a July and August carnival called Riverboat Daze.

In Fertile Farming Country, Echoes of a Missionary Past

Central Alberta

The Cree Indians called the Rev. Albert Lacombe, "the man with a good heart." The Oblate priest came west in 1852 and built the first school in Alberta. Ten years later, using hand-hewn timbers, ropes, horses, and every able-bodied man in the parish, Father Lacombe erected the first bridge in western Canada, at a mission called St. Albert.

The school and the bridge no longer stand, but the region's churches, missions and schools reflect the devotion of La-

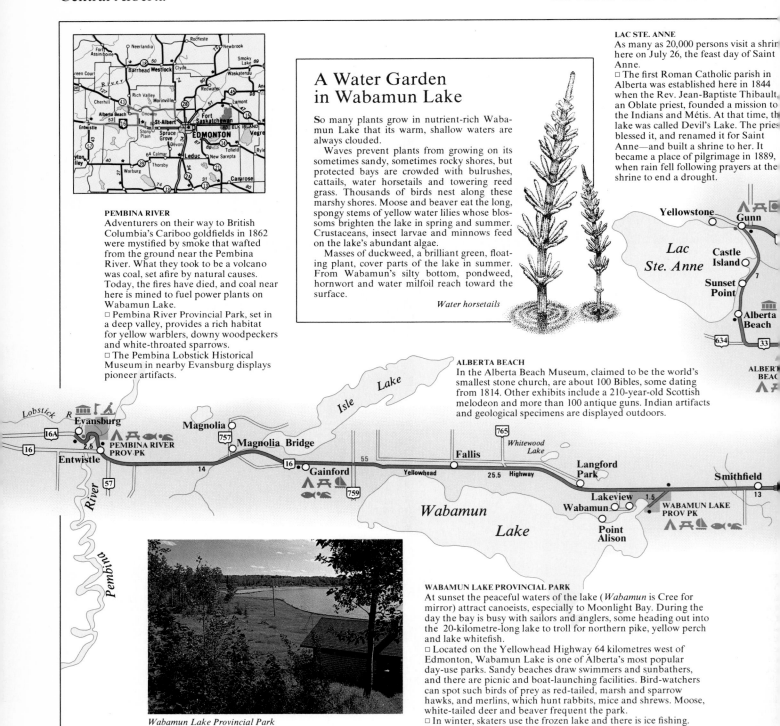

PEMBINA RIVER

Adventurers on their way to British Columbia's Cariboo goldfields in 1862 were mystified by smoke that wafted from the ground near the Pembina River. What they took to be a volcano was coal, set afire by natural causes. Today, the fires have died, and coal near here is mined to fuel power plants on Wabamun Lake.
□ Pembina River Provincial Park, set in a deep valley, provides a rich habitat for yellow warblers, downy woodpeckers and white-throated sparrows.
□ The Pembina Lobstick Historical Museum in nearby Evansburg displays pioneer artifacts.

A Water Garden in Wabamun Lake

So many plants grow in nutrient-rich Wabamun Lake that its warm, shallow waters are always clouded.

Waves prevent plants from growing on its sometimes sandy, sometimes rocky shores, but protected bays are crowded with bulrushes, cattails, water horsetails and towering reed grass. Thousands of birds nest along these marshy shores. Moose and beaver eat the long, spongy stems of yellow water lilies whose blossoms brighten the lake in spring and summer. Crustaceans, insect larvae and minnows feed on the lake's abundant algae.

Masses of duckweed, a brilliant green, floating plant, cover parts of the lake in summer. From Wabamun's silty bottom, pondweed, hornwort and water milfoil reach toward the surface.

Water horsetails

LAC STE. ANNE

As many as 20,000 persons visit a shrine here on July 26, the feast day of Saint Anne.
□ The first Roman Catholic parish in Alberta was established here in 1844 when the Rev. Jean-Baptiste Thibault, an Oblate priest, founded a mission to the Indians and Métis. At that time, the lake was called Devil's Lake. The priest blessed it, and renamed it for Saint Anne—and built a shrine to her. It became a place of pilgrimage in 1889, when rain fell following prayers at the shrine to end a drought.

ALBERTA BEACH

In the Alberta Beach Museum, claimed to be the world's smallest stone church, are about 100 Bibles, some dating from 1814. Other exhibits include a 210-year-old Scottish melodeon and more than 100 antique guns. Indian artifacts and geological specimens are displayed outdoors.

Wabamun Lake Provincial Park

WABAMUN LAKE PROVINCIAL PARK

At sunset the peaceful waters of the lake (*Wabamun* is Cree for mirror) attract canoeists, especially to Moonlight Bay. During the day the bay is busy with sailors and anglers, some heading out into the 20-kilometre-long lake to troll for northern pike, yellow perch and lake whitefish.
□ Located on the Yellowhead Highway 64 kilometres west of Edmonton, Wabamun Lake is one of Alberta's most popular day-use parks. Sandy beaches draw swimmers and sunbathers, and there are picnic and boat-launching facilities. Bird-watchers can spot such birds of prey as red-tailed, marsh and sparrow hawks, and merlins, which hunt rabbits, mice and shrews. Moose, white-tailed deer and beaver frequent the park.
□ In winter, skaters use the frozen lake and there is ice fishing.

0   1   2   3   4   5 Miles
0   2   4   6   8 Kilometres

combe and other early missionaries, who brought their religion to Indians weakened by the white man's alcohol and illnesses.

A model of the mission bridge, carved from one of its beams, is displayed in the Father Lacombe Museum in St. Albert. Also shown are some of the missionary's books in Cree and Blackfoot, and his snowshoes, presumably worn on his long winter treks to remote Indian camps. Father Lacombe's grave is behind the St. Albert Church.

Morinville was founded by the Rev. Jean-Baptiste Morin, like Lacombe Quebec-born. The CPR, completed in 1885, brought immigrants from Europe to farm this fertile area.

Visitors to a Saturday market in Stony Plain, a major grain and livestock center, find a cornucopia of local produce: crisp vegetables, new cheese, eggs and honey, and home-baked bread and pies. Handicraft booths display quilts, weaving and apple head dolls.

Farmers' market, Stony Plain

MORINVILLE
Ornate St. Jean-Baptiste Roman Catholic Church was built in 1907 and restored in 1973. Triple spires, arched doorways and circular windows reflect traditional Quebec church design. Murals depicting biblical scenes embellish the walls and ceiling above the altar. The church, part of which was built of logs in 1895, is a provincial historic site.

GLORY HILLS
North of Stony Plain the road dips and climbs through the rugged Glory Hills. Each summit offers a panoramic view of the countryside. Clear blue lakes bordered by tall spruce trees provide cool, secluded picnic areas.

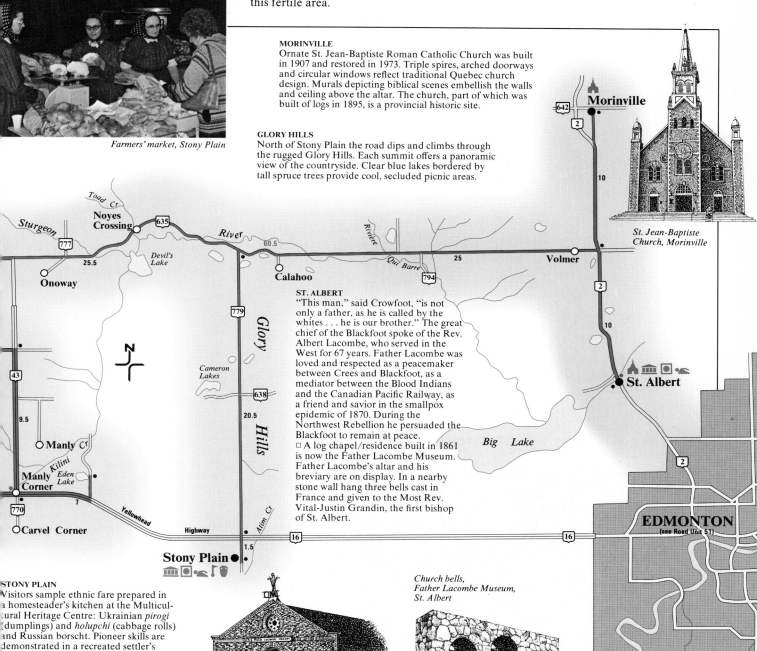

St. Jean-Baptiste Church, Morinville

ST. ALBERT
"This man," said Crowfoot, "is not only a father, as he is called by the whites . . . he is our brother." The great chief of the Blackfoot spoke of the Rev. Albert Lacombe, who served in the West for 67 years. Father Lacombe was loved and respected as a peacemaker between Crees and Blackfoot, as a mediator between the Blood Indians and the Canadian Pacific Railway, as a friend and savior in the smallpox epidemic of 1870. During the Northwest Rebellion he persuaded the Blackfoot to remain at peace.
□ A log chapel/residence built in 1861 is now the Father Lacombe Museum. Father Lacombe's altar and his breviary are on display. In a nearby stone wall hang three bells cast in France and given to the Most Rev. Vital-Justin Grandin, the first bishop of St. Albert.

Church bells, Father Lacombe Museum, St. Albert

Father Lacombe Museum, St. Albert

STONY PLAIN
Visitors sample ethnic fare prepared in a homesteader's kitchen at the Multicultural Heritage Centre: Ukrainian *pirogi* (dumplings) and *holupchi* (cabbage rolls) and Russian borscht. Pioneer skills are demonstrated in a recreated settler's cabin. Townsfolk make soap, butter and ice cream, and card and weave wool. Old books and photographs in a library tell the history of Stony Plain.
□ A statue of a horse and rider by Don Bednar was erected in 1974 to commemorate the centennial of the North West Mounted Police in Alberta.

A Booming, Growing Capital City and the Gateway to Canada's North

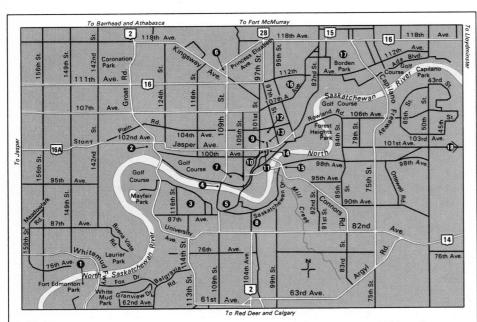

Edmonton

1 Fort Edmonton Park
2 Provincial Museum of Alberta
3 University of Alberta
4 High Level Bridge
5 Capital City Recreation Park
6 CAA
7 Legislative Building
8 Old Strathcona
9 Tourist Information
10 George McDougall Museum and Shrine
11 Alberta Telephone Tower
12 Edmonton Art Gallery
13 Citadel Theater
14 Canada's Aviation Hall of Fame
15 Muttart Conservatory
16 Commonwealth Game Facilities
17 Exhibition Grounds
18 Refinery Row

Edmonton, Alberta's capital and Canada's most northerly major city, is a thriving metropolis astride the North Saskatchewan River. It was this vast river that initially brought traders in the 1790s to Fort Edmonton, the Hudson's Bay Company post that was the start of the present-day city. In the next century the Calgary-Edmonton Trail was carved out of the wilderness by freight wagons and oxcarts.

The community grew little until 1898 when it became a Klondike gold-rush supply base. With the discovery of oil at nearby Leduc in 1947, it was launched into one of the biggest and longest boom eras any Canadian city has known.

Edmonton's main role—as "the Gateway to the North"—came with the advent of commercial aviation. Among the first planes here were those operated by bush pilots, so called because of their low-flying techniques. Today Edmonton's busy air traffic is accommodated by two major airports and a third, private airport.

Alberta Telephone Tower (11)

A museum on the 33rd floor of the provincial government telephone building has displays ranging from antique phones in a turn-of-the-century drugstore to a World War II naval phone.

Canada's Aviation Hall of Fame (14)

Visitors are transported into the past by means of aeronautical artifacts, model aircraft and a photographic panorama depicting the story of Canadian aviation.

Capital City Recreation Park (5)

This vast expanse of parkland straddles the North Saskatchewan River and has 22.5 kilometres of cycling and hiking trails.

Citadel Theater (13)

This modernistic glass-and-wood complex, completed in 1976, contains three theaters, rehearsal rooms, workshops, offices and a reference library.

Commonwealth Games Facilities (16)

Five of the facilities for the XI Commonwealth Games, held here in 1978, were designed for post-game use. These are the Commonwealth Stadium, the Argyll Velodrome, the Coronation Bowling Greens, the Strathcona Range and the Kinsmen Aquatic Center.

Edmonton Art Gallery (12)

This, the largest independent art gallery in Alberta, features modern and contemporary art and has works by the Group of Seven and by Toronto artist Jack Bush.

Exhibition Grounds (17)

Two major agricultural events are held here annually. In March the Canadian Western Livestock Show and Sale features a farm machinery exhibition, a quarter-horse show, and the Canadian Western Super Rodeo— the biggest indoor rodeo in this country. Farmfair, in November, features a livestock exhibition and the Canadian Finals Rodeo.

Rowand's House, originally built in the 1840s, is one of many historic buildings at Fort Edmonton.

Fort Edmonton Park (1)

This outdoor museum beside the North Saskatchewan River has two small-town streets recreating the period between 1885 and 1905. Its 35 buildings and houses include a reconstruction of Fort Edmonton, and the original 1878 office of the *Edmonton Bulletin*, the first newspaper in western Canada.

George McDougall Museum (10)

This was the first structure built outside the walls of Fort Edmonton. It was constructed in 1872 by the Rev. George McDougall, a Methodist missionary. The building was restored in the 1940s and 1950s and is now a museum containing McDougall's bibles and prayer books.

High Level Bridge (4)

This Edmonton landmark was built in 1910-13. The top deck carries trains; motor traffic is on a lower level.

Legislative Building (7)

Overlooking the North Saskatchewan River, this high-domed building is constructed of Quebec, Pennsylvania and Italian marble.

Muttart Conservatory (15)

Four glass-walled pyramids dominate this complex. Three of the pyramids contain plants from three different climatic regions; the fourth is a show house with a display of ornamentals.

Old Strathcona (8)

Several buildings dating from the early 1900s can be seen in this old commercial section of Edmonton. Structures preserved

Edmonton's 42,584-seat stadium was opened in 1978 when the city was host for the Commonwealth Games.

include the Old Firehall, the Strathcona Hotel and the Klondike Cinema.

Provincial Museum of Alberta (2)

This large building, Alberta's 1967 centennial project, is on the grounds of old Government House (once the lieutenant governor's residence).

In an orientation gallery an 11-piece bronze frieze illustrates the scope of the museum exhibits. There are four main exhibit galleries: Indian, habitat, historical and natural history. Artifacts, dioramas, specimens and photographs are used to tell Alberta's story in terms of its zoology, geology, Indians, fur traders and pioneers.

Refinery Row (18)

Located east of the city, Refinery Row includes a polyethylene plant, giant storage tanks and pipeline pumping stations. Visitors can arrange to tour Imperial Oil's Strathcona Project, one of the most sophisticated refineries in North America.

University of Alberta (3)

Founded in 1906, the university overlooks the North Saskatchewan River. Among its showpieces are a medical sciences complex and the Hub, a solar-heated student residence.

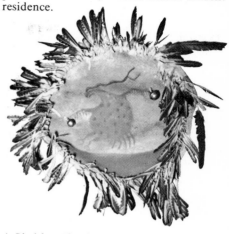

A Blackfoot Thunder Shield (above), dating from about 1870, is from the collection of the Provincial Museum of Alberta. The Garden Court in Edmonton Centre (below) is a bustling shopping complex in the heart of the city.

Behind the stately dome of the Alberta Legislature (above right) rise a cluster of glittering skyscrapers in downtown Edmonton. The Legislature, set high on the banks of the North Saskatchewan River, is just above the spot where Fort Edmonton was once located. The Muttart Conservatory (right), with its four glass pyramids, was opened in 1976, providing a striking architecture addition to the city.

Klondike Days — Reliving the Rollicking '90s

During Klondike Days, a 10-day jamboree held in Edmonton each July, the city relives the excitement of the gold rush of '98. Modern stores don false fronts and fancy-lettered signs. Pubs and lounges become saloons, where piano players wear straw hats and old songs are sung. Downtown streets are closed to traffic for the Sunday Promenade so Edmontonians can stroll about in their Klondike finery.

Contests ranging from rock lifting to log chopping are held; the winner is crowned the King of the Klondike. More than a hundred rafts compete in the World Championship Sourdough Raft Race on a 16-kilometre stretch of the North Saskatchewan River.

Highlights at the Exhibition Grounds are the Silver Slipper Gambling Saloon (legal gambling), and a daily prize in gold. (The winner rides downtown by stagecoach to trade it for cash.) The park's 13-metre high Chilkoot Mountain, built of lumber, wire mesh and plaster, has a waterfall and a meandering stream, where visitors can pan for gold nuggets.

Sourdough Raft Race during Klondike Days

Bottles for Baby Grizzlies, Sanctuary for Huge Buffalo

Central Alberta

This region's two major attractions, the Alberta Game Farm and Elk Island National Park, are only 32 kilometres east of Edmonton.

The Alberta Game Farm has been described as a zoo in reverse—where the visitors are "fenced in" and the animals roam free. The areas where some 4,000 animals wander are immense. The founder-director, Al Oeming, believes wild creatures need a sense of freedom to thrive.

Oeming, a zoologist, financed the game

FORT SASKATCHEWAN
A three-by-two-metre mural in the Fort Saskatchewan Museum tells the town's story from the days of Anthony Henday, the first white man to explore this part of Alberta. A Hudson's Bay Company trader-explorer, Henday traveled into Blackfoot country south of here in 1754-55.

The museum has collections of photographs and Indian and pioneer relics. One artifact is a copying machine (c.1908) in which wet linen and sheets of tin were used for duplicating. A two-story, red brick courthouse (1909), a two-story log farmhouse (c.1900), the Soda Lake Anglican Church (c.1911), and a schoolhouse (c.1905) are among restored buildings in a small park. Horse-drawn harvesting machinery and steam-engine threshing machines are displayed. A cairn is formed of stones from the original RCMP fort (1875).

Log schoolhouse, Fort Saskatchewan Museum

UKRAINIAN CULTURAL HERITAGE VILLAGE
Domed churches and other pioneer buildings are in the Ukrainian Cultural Heritage Village, just outside the east gate of Elk Island National Park. The buildings were relocated here from original sites in surrounding communities. □ A farmers' market is held on weekends and there is a harvest festival in September.

ALBERTA GAME FARM
On this 627-hectare farm, wild creatures from the tropics have adapted to the Alberta climate. Arabian camels, Malay tapirs, Sahara Desert addaxes and African waterbuck winter on the same snow-blanketed plains and muskeg as grizzly bears, musk-oxen, arctic foxes and caribou. Two Peary caribou, the first ever taken into captivity, were brought here from the Arctic in 1970. North America's only Chinese water deer, rare, pure-bred vicunas from Chile, and the world's only captive breeding herd of Rocky Mountain goats are among some 4,000 mammals here. Others include Tibetan yaks, Père David's deer, wallabies, white rhinoceros, and Przewalski horses—rare animals that closely resemble their prehistoric ancestors. The Alberta Game Farm also has some 3,500 birds spanning 95 different species. Exotic flamingos from South America, red-breasted geese and Bewick's swans from the U.S.S.R. are found on two-kilometre-long Lost Lake.

Malay tapirs

Mandarin duck, Alberta Game Farm

Wallabies

0 1 2 3 4 5 Miles
0 2 4 6 8 Kilometres

farm—and his early studies—by working as a professional wrestler and wrestling promoter. He started the farm with 250 animals in the late 1950s. Today the game farm is also a research center and supplies animals to zoos.

Feeding times at the game farm are popular with thousands of visitors, who come and watch while grizzly bear cubs are bottle-fed, or llamas and giant moose munch hand-held snacks.

Set in the northern section of the 30-to-60-metre-high Beaver Hills, Elk Island National Park is named for the large wapiti (elk) herds which once roamed the area. Trapping, hunting and settlement had all but wiped out the wapiti in 1906, when the federal government set aside this sanctuary.

A national park since 1930, Elk Island is enclosed by a two-metre-high fence to keep the wildlife population intact. It has North America's smallest and largest mammals—the pygmy shrew and the plains bison. Moose, mule deer and beaver are also found here.

Trees of the park include aspen, birch, poplar and spruce. Marsh marigolds and wild sarsaparilla, plants that have disappeared from the area outside the park, grow here. Lakes and sloughs teem with waterfowl—some nesting, others just stopping over during spring and autumn migrations. More than 200 species have been spotted.

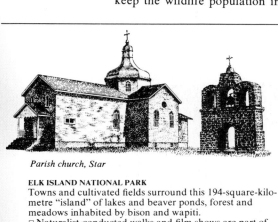

Parish church, Star

ELK ISLAND NATIONAL PARK
Towns and cultivated fields surround this 194-square-kilometre "island" of lakes and beaver ponds, forest and meadows inhabited by bison and wapiti.
□ Naturalist-conducted walks and film shows are part of the park's interpretive program. There are also self-guiding nature trails.
□ At Sandy Beach, on the east side of Astotin Lake, are cabins and campgrounds, a nine-hole golf course, boating, picnicking and supervised swimming. Twenty-one islands are scattered over this four-kilometre-long, six-metre-deep lake, the largest body of water in the park.
□ A thatched Ukrainian farmhouse contains a folk museum, open in summer.
□ Skiers and snowshoers enjoy the park's winter wildlife. There are several well-marked ski trails.

Ukrainian farmhouse,
Elk Island National Park

Astotin Lake, Elk Island National Park

STAR
The oldest Ukrainian Catholic parish in Canada is here, where the first Ukrainian immigrants settled in 1892-94. (At that time, the community was called Edna.) The present church, the third since the parish was founded in 1897, was built in 1926-27. In it, saved from a fire that destroyed the second church in 1922, are enameled paintings of Christ, the Virgin and the four Evangelists.

BEAVER HILLS
Rising some 30 to 60 metres above the surrounding prairie are Alberta's Beaver Hills, a series of ridges, bogs and shallow lakes, all formed by retreating glaciers. (Elk Island National Park is set in the hills.)
□ The bedrock of the hills was formed some 100 million years ago, when a melting ice sheet deposited sand, gravel and mud in an ancient seabed. The present rolling landscape, known as "dead-ice moraine," was created when boulders from the Canadian Shield were laid on this bedrock by a glacier retreating slowly toward the northeast between one million and 10,000 years ago. Bogs, lakes and ponds formed in depressions in this glacial debris.

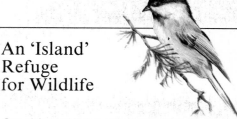

An 'Island' Refuge for Wildlife

One of the world's largest herds of wood bison, a rare species once close to extinction, roams the southern part of Elk Island National Park. Naturalists believe the wood bison no longer needs protection, and the great shaggy beasts are being released in areas they once inhabited.

The park's 194 square kilometres provide sanctuary to several other species once threatened in this region. Wapiti, plains bison and some 2,500 beaver thrive here—since the high fence that surrounds the park keeps out wolves and other large predators. Careful management is needed to control mammal populations in this enclosed environment. Rapidly multiplying deer deplete food supplies; dams built by burgeoning beaver colonies can cause extensive flooding.

Great horned owls and black-capped chickadees (above) are among the more than 200 species of birds that fly over the park's undulating terrain. Common loons, pintail ducks and white-winged scoters nest in sloughs and marshes.

ELK ISLAND NAT PK

UKRAINIAN CULTURAL
HERITAGE VILLAGE

ELK ISLAND

Church Domes and a Giant Egg Gleaming in the Sunshine

Central Alberta

People of Ukrainian origin, the largest ethnic group in this region, arrived here between 1898 and 1910. Deeply religious, hardy and self-reliant, these settlers cleared two to four hectares of land a year. The men bought animals and implements by working in mines or lumber camps, or by laying railway track.

The settlers' first habitations, known as *boordays*, were humble affairs consisting of dugouts roofed with boughs and sod. As their farms prospered, the settlers built

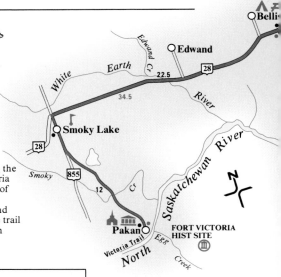

VICTORIA TRAIL
Bushes of prickly rose, Alberta's floral emblem, flank this historic route along the North Saskatchewan River. The Victoria Trail dates from the 1870s. It was part of the route followed by Red River carts hauling supplies between Winnipeg and Edmonton. Today 30 kilometres of the trail west of Pakan offer a panorama of lush valley and steep, wooded riverbanks.

Prickly rose

Thatched Roofs, Blue and Yellow Trim

Most early Ukrainian settlers in Alberta made their first homes in simple dugout huts called *boordays*: metre-deep pits lined with logs and roofed with aspen boughs and sod. Two dark cramped rooms often sheltered several families while they built sturdy log cabins, some of which are preserved at the Shandro Historical Living Village and Pioneer Museum, and in other areas of central Alberta.

Such two-room cabins were usually made of poplar or aspen logs plastered with mud. Whitewash protected the walls from rain. The cabins reflected traditional Ukrainian design— thatched roofs, bright blue and yellow trim on doors and windows, and ornately carved eaves. As soon as their homes were completed the settlers built a church—a simple log structure topped with a distinctive pear-shaped dome.

Thatched log house, Shandro Historical Living Village and Pioneer Museum

PAKAN
Among homemade pioneer objects in th Fort Victoria Museum are a buckwheat sheller, a spinning wheel, a violin and a tooth extractor.
□ A two-story cabin (1864) on the North Saskatchewan River, Alberta's oldest building on its original site, was the hom of the clerk at Fort Victoria, the HBC p established here in 1864.

Miraculous icon, Mundare

A Boorday, the First House, *a painting by William Kurelek*

Ukrainian Orthodox Church, Shandro Historical Living Village and Pioneer Museum

log cabins in a style echoing the architecture of their homeland. Carefully preserved examples of both types of dwellings can be seen today at the Shandro Historical Living Village and Pioneer Museum.

The religious values of the Ukrainians were expressed in their churches, whose domes still gleam in the sunlit prairie air. What were symbols of faith to these pioneers remain as memorials to their fortitude.

Ukrainian traditions have survived, too. Descendants of the settlers keep alive the folk songs and dances, the handicraft skills of embroidery and Easter-egg decoration, and the fine culinary arts. A showcase for this rich cultural heritage is the Ukrainian Pysanka Festival, held in early July at Vegreville. A striking attraction of this community is its giant Pysanka (Easter egg), built to honor the early pioneers. Its design symbolizes prosperity, good harvests and security—all of which the first settlers found here.

Sunset on the North Saskatchewan River, near Wasel

SHANDRO
The Historical Living Village and Pioneer Museum recreates life in an early Ukrainian immigrant community. Among 18 buildings are the 1902 thatched log home of the first settler, Nikon Shandro, a 1926 granary, and one of the province's oldest Orthodox churches—built near Chipman by Russian missionaries in 1904. Other buildings include a blacksmith shop, a wind-driven gristmill, and a replica of a *boorday*—the pioneers' first shelter.

BOIAN
Attracted by the fertile land, Roumanians arrived here in 1899, and named their settlement after a village in their native province, Bukovina. Perched on a hill is St. Mary's Roumanian Orthodox Church (1903), believed to be the oldest Roumanian church still in use in North America. The log structure is sheathed in wood. Nearby are an old stone schoolhouse (now a community hall) and a cemetery—the only remains of the early community. Many families have left the area in recent years for industrial centers in Ontario and Quebec.

St. Mary's Roumanian Orthodox Church, Boian

HAIRY HILL
This village is named for a hill where buffalo shed their hair in spring. The Thompson Canoe Co. annually builds some 50 canoes similar to those made in eastern Canada in the 1880s. The 5-to-5.5-metre-long canoes are made of sitka spruce, oak and maple, and covered with canvas.

TWO HILLS
Natural gas gathering systems and processing plants surround this community west of which runs the main Alberta Gas Trunk Line.
□ A baseball tournament, an indoor rodeo and an agricultural fair are held in August.

VEGREVILLE
An eight-by-six-metre, 2,270-kilogram, aluminum Pysanka (Ukrainian Easter egg) in Heritage Park honors the area's pioneers and the Mounties who protected them. The bronze, gold and silver-patterned egg rotates on a steel and concrete base. Designs of stars, equilateral triangles, six-vane windmills and wolves' teeth symbolize prosperity, good harvests and security.
□ Three days of music, dancing, ethnic food, cultural displays and talent contests highlight the Ukrainian Pysanka Festival in early July. A parade, nightly grandstand shows and a fly-in breakfast for guests arriving at Vegreville Airport are features of a three-day agricultural exhibition in late July.
□ Our Lady of the Highway Shrine, east of town, has a two-metre-high statue of Mary, sculpted in Italy of Carrara marble.

MUNDARE
An unusual collection of East European art, church relics, and Ukrainian artifacts is in a museum at the Basilian Fathers Monastery. Included are a 12th-century gospel handwritten in Old Slavic, four 14th-century icons, copies of the first printed Latin Bible (1520) and the first printed French Bible (1558). Also displayed are a 17th-century altar cloth embroidered in silver and an Italian violin (1723).
□ Stained-glass windows in the monastery's St. Peter and St. Paul Church depict the life of Christ and the history of Mundare and the Ukrainian people. In a chapel-like nook in the vestibule is an enlarged reproduction of an icon (of the Mother of God) at Pochayev in the western Ukraine. (The original icon was investigated by a church commission in 1770 and accredited with 539 miracles.) The church, an octagonal brick building, with a wooden dome, is crowned by eight semi-arches and an aluminum cross.

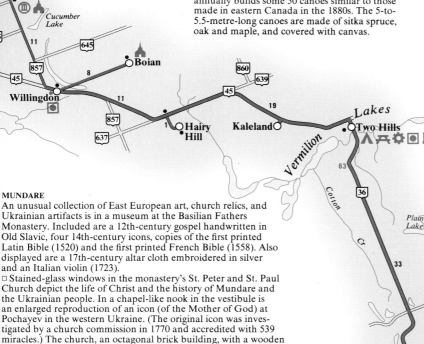

Giant Easter egg, Vegreville

Northern Pike and Grayling from Clear, Island-Dotted Lakes

East-Central Alberta

North of Long Lake Provincial Park, flat, open farmland gives way to rolling, forested countryside. Because this area is thinly populated, many species of birds flourish—white pelicans, blue herons, western grebes, loons, bald eagles, ospreys, hawks, sandhill cranes and owls. Blueberries, cranberries, raspberries and saskatoons carpet the roadsides. (Early settlers dried the berries on blankets in the sun, before storing them for winter's needs.)

In the forested hills are scores of glis-

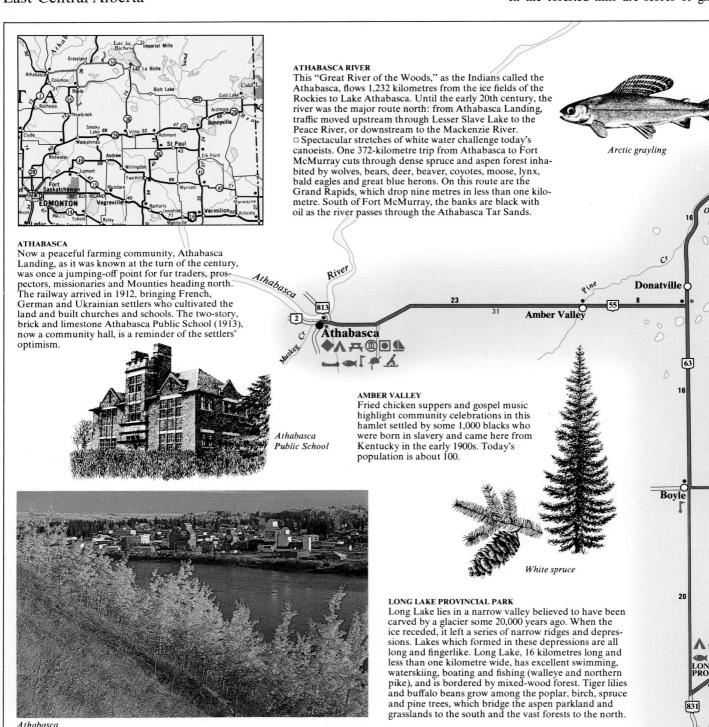

ATHABASCA RIVER
This "Great River of the Woods," as the Indians called the Athabasca, flows 1,232 kilometres from the ice fields of the Rockies to Lake Athabasca. Until the early 20th century, the river was the major route north: from Athabasca Landing, traffic moved upstream through Lesser Slave Lake to the Peace River, or downstream to the Mackenzie River.
□ Spectacular stretches of white water challenge today's canoeists. One 372-kilometre trip from Athabasca to Fort McMurray cuts through dense spruce and aspen forest inhabited by wolves, bears, deer, beaver, coyotes, moose, lynx, bald eagles and great blue herons. On this route are the Grand Rapids, which drop nine metres in less than one kilometre. South of Fort McMurray, the banks are black with oil as the river passes through the Athabasca Tar Sands.

Arctic grayling

ATHABASCA
Now a peaceful farming community, Athabasca Landing, as it was known at the turn of the century, was once a jumping-off point for fur traders, prospectors, missionaries and Mounties heading north. The railway arrived in 1912, bringing French, German and Ukrainian settlers who cultivated the land and built churches and schools. The two-story, brick and limestone Athabasca Public School (1913), now a community hall, is a reminder of the settlers' optimism.

Athabasca Public School

AMBER VALLEY
Fried chicken suppers and gospel music highlight community celebrations in this hamlet settled by some 1,000 blacks who were born in slavery and came here from Kentucky in the early 1900s. Today's population is about 100.

White spruce

LONG LAKE PROVINCIAL PARK
Long Lake lies in a narrow valley believed to have been carved by a glacier some 20,000 years ago. When the ice receded, it left a series of narrow ridges and depressions. Lakes which formed in these depressions are all long and fingerlike. Long Lake, 16 kilometres long and less than one kilometre wide, has excellent swimming, waterskiing, boating and fishing (walleye and northern pike), and is bordered by mixed-wood forest. Tiger lilies and buffalo beans grow among the poplar, birch, spruce and pine trees, which bridge the aspen parkland and grasslands to the south and the vast forests to the north.

Athabasca

0 1 2 3 4 5 Miles
0 2 4 6 8 Kilometres

tening lakes. (There are some 50 of these within a 100-kilometre radius of Lac La Biche.) Most are typical north-country lakes—clear, studded with small wooded islands, and surrounded by splendid, sandy beaches.

Boating, canoeing, sailing, swimming and fishing are excellent. Northern pike, walleye and perch are the principal catch. Pike are present in enormous quantities and sizes—many in the 9-to-13-kilogram range are taken every year. Some of the best arctic grayling fishing in Canada is found in the area around Lac La Biche.

A brief wave of tourism swept this area in 1916, when visitors from Edmonton flocked to the imposing, railway-owned Lac La Biche Inn. During that summer a boating accident claimed the lives of several sportsmen who, ignoring the warnings of Indian fishermen on the shore, had ventured onto Lac La Biche during a squall. The tragedy killed the tourist trade and, except for quarters occupied by the station-master, the inn was abandoned for decades.

Tourists have recently rediscovered the area's scenic beauty and fine fishing, hunting, boating and camping. But the inn is no longer available to them. Converted to hospital use in 1937, it remains part of St. Catherine's Hospital.

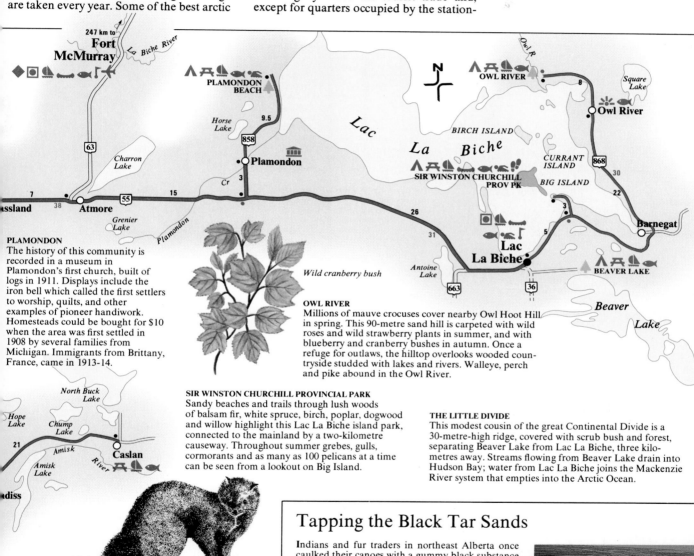

Wild cranberry bush

Mink

PLAMONDON
The history of this community is recorded in a museum in Plamondon's first church, built of logs in 1911. Displays include the iron bell which called the first settlers to worship, quilts, and other examples of pioneer handiwork. Homesteads could be bought for $10 when the area was first settled in 1908 by several families from Michigan. Immigrants from Brittany, France, came in 1913-14.

OWL RIVER
Millions of mauve crocuses cover nearby Owl Hoot Hill in spring. This 90-metre sand hill is carpeted with wild roses and wild strawberry plants in summer, and with blueberry and cranberry bushes in autumn. Once a refuge for outlaws, the hilltop overlooks wooded countryside studded with lakes and rivers. Walleye, perch and pike abound in the Owl River.

SIR WINSTON CHURCHILL PROVINCIAL PARK
Sandy beaches and trails through lush woods of balsam fir, white spruce, birch, poplar, dogwood and willow highlight this Lac La Biche island park, connected to the mainland by a two-kilometre causeway. Throughout summer grebes, gulls, cormorants and as many as 100 pelicans at a time can be seen from a lookout on Big Island.

THE LITTLE DIVIDE
This modest cousin of the great Continental Divide is a 30-metre-high ridge, covered with scrub bush and forest, separating Beaver Lake from Lac La Biche, three kilometres away. Streams flowing from Beaver Lake drain into Hudson Bay; water from Lac La Biche joins the Mackenzie River system that empties into the Arctic Ocean.

LAC LA BICHE
Powwows that Cree Indians held here until the arrival of white settlers are revived in August in conjunction with the Blue Feather Fish Derby. Twice a year, Indians and Métis from a vast area used to gather on the shores of Lac La Biche for dances and games, and to ask the Manitou's blessing. Today's four-day celebration features a parade, native contests, dancing and baseball.
□ Enormous quantities of beaver, fox, lynx, bear, and coyote were trapped and sold here until the late 1800s. Trapping controls were enforced, fur farming developed and mink farming was a major industry here by the 1940s. Only a few mink farms survive but the area is still known for its fine pelts.

Tapping the Black Tar Sands

Indians and fur traders in northeast Alberta once caulked their canoes with a gummy black substance that oozed from the banks of the Athabasca River. Since then engineers have discovered how to extract oil from the sandy ground in the area, and the world's biggest known oil reserve—the Athabasca Tar Sands—is now being commercially exploited.

Conveyor belts move mountains of asphaltlike tar sand, dug from open-pit mines, to an extraction plant. There raw bitumen is withdrawn by a simple process: an oily slush of steaming sand is dropped in hot water, the sand sinks and the oil is skimmed off the top. Intense heat turns the bitumen into synthetic crude oil, ready for further refining.

The Athabasca deposit is thought to hold over twice the recoverable reserves of Saudi Arabia. Since production began in 1967, Fort McMurray has become a boom town.

Open-pit mine near Fort McMurray

Grainfields and Sailboats
Where Cree and Blackfoot Once Traded

East-Central Alberta

MOOSE LAKE PROVINCIAL PARK

A hiking trail from Deadman's Point leads to a mature forest of white spruce underlain with Indian pipe, wintergreen and feather mosses. This is the only portion of the original forest to survive fires in 1927 and 1942. Today jack pine covers much of the rest of this park on the north shore of Moose Lake. (The fires produced the 60°C temperatures necessary to melt open the resin-sealed jack pine cones, releasing seeds which sprout overnight in fire-swept land.)

The park has black bears, red squirrels, striped skunks, white-tailed deer, beaver, coyotes and porcupines. White pelicans nest here, and great crested flycatchers and Blackburnian, Cape May and bay-breasted warblers have been sighted.

Jack pine

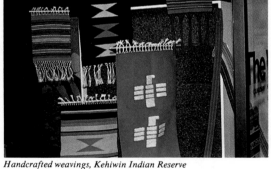

Handcrafted weavings, Kehiwin Indian Reserve

KEHIWIN INDIAN RESERVE

Descendants of Chiefs Big Bear and Poundmaker are among some 500 Indians on this reserve named for another Plains Cree warrior, Kehiwin. Visitors may tour the plants of Kehiwin Steel Industries Ltd., and Kehiwin Cree-ations Ltd. A shop sells blankets, rugs, wall hangings, shawls, vests and shoulder bags woven in the Cree-ations plant and depicting the ancient symbols and geometric patterns favored by the Plains Indians.

□ Kehiwin Lake, southwest of the reserve, and Muriel Lake to the northeast are stocked with perch, walleye and northern pike. Both have picnicking, camping and boat-launching sites, and Muriel Lake has a sandy beach.

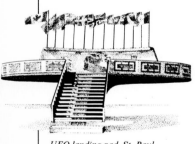

UFO landing pad, St. Paul

ST. PAUL

Before the white man's arrival, this was the territory of the Cree Indians, especially Wood Cree who roamed north of the North Saskatchewan River away from the fierce Blackfoot Indians to the south. The nearby Thérien lakes—then a wilderness haven for waterfowl—were known as Manawan, meaning egg gathering place.

□ The world's first and only flying saucer landing pad was built here in 1967 as a Centennial project. The raised, 12-metre-wide, circular platform displays provincial and territorial flags. The landing pad contains letters to be opened June 3, 2067.

ELK POINT

Rum-barrel hoops, belt buckles, locks, hinges and cast-iron tools in the Fort George Museum date from the 1790s, when the North West and Hudson's Bay companies had rival fur trade posts in the area—Fort George and Buckingham House, both built in 1792. Other exhibits are musket balls, old pistols, flintlock parts and trinkets, rings and factory-made metal arrowheads traded with the Indians for furs.

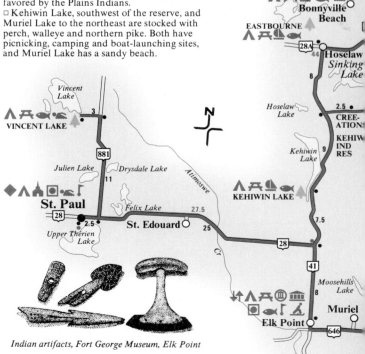

Indian artifacts, Fort George Museum, Elk Point

Clear and moderately warm, the lakes of east-central Alberta are favored by fishermen for their trout, pike, yellow perch, walleye and whitefish. Sandy beaches and good camping facilities further enhance the lakeland region east, west and north of Elk Point.

Some two centuries ago, this was the major fur-trading center on the North Saskatchewan River. Mounds, charred timbers and archaeological digs near Elk Point mark where the Hudson's Bay Company's Buckingham House and the North West Company's Fort George were built in 1792. Canoes and York boats lined the riverbank and teepees dotted the meadows when Cree traded furs and Blackfoot bartered dried buffalo meat here. When the area was depleted of fur-bearing animals, both posts were abandoned. The wilderness remained undisturbed until the early 1900s, when Europeans returned—to fish, trap, log and eventually homestead.

Today roads dip and curve through fields of grain and wooded parkland. North of Moose Lake the countryside is dotted with sloughs, breeding ground for wildfowl that make this a hunter's paradise. Beaches, such as those at Moose Lake and Cold Lake, are characterized by fine sand extending far into the clear water. Cold Lake—at 352 square kilometres one of Alberta's largest lakes—is easily accessible. Sailing, water-skiing, and guided fishing tours are among the activities available here.

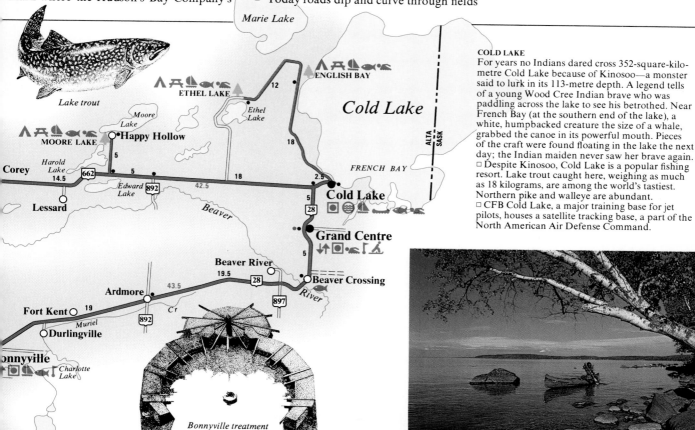

COLD LAKE

For years no Indians dared cross 352-square-kilometre Cold Lake because of Kinosoo—a monster said to lurk in its 113-metre depth. A legend tells of a young Wood Cree Indian brave who was paddling across the lake to see his betrothed. Near French Bay (at the southern end of the lake), a white, humpbacked creature the size of a whale, grabbed the canoe in its powerful mouth. Pieces of the craft were found floating in the lake the next day; the Indian maiden never saw her brave again. □ Despite Kinosoo, Cold Lake is a popular fishing resort. Lake trout caught here, weighing as much as 18 kilograms, are among the world's tastiest. Northern pike and walleye are abundant. □ CFB Cold Lake, a major training base for jet pilots, houses a satellite tracking base, a part of the North American Air Defense Command.

Cold Lake

BONNYVILLE

The circular design of a treatment center for alcoholics opened here in 1976 is symbolic of community co-operation. The cedar building on Moose Lake, designed by Indian architect Douglas Cardinal, contains quarters for single persons and married couples.
□ This area has an airstrip, a nine-hole golf course and good boating, fishing and water-skiing. A snowmobile contest highlights a mid-March winter carnival. Beer gardens, dances, chuckwagon races and a parade are features of a three-day agricultural fair and rodeo in early August.

Bonnyville treatment centre, designed by Douglas Cardinal

LINDBERGH

Up to 345 tonnes of salt are produced daily at the Canadian Salt Co. plant. Discovered in the 1940s, a salt bed 300 metres thick and several kilometres long contains enough salt to supply Canada's needs for the next 200 years. Forty-one grades of salt are refined and packed at the plant. Tours are available.

Majestic Pelicans of Moose Lake

Man's encroachment is endangering the white pelican: a quarter of Canada's nesting colonies have disappeared in the last 25 years. One site in this area where the white pelican can be observed is Moose Lake Provincial Park.

White pelicans feed by opening their long bills and swinging their heads from side to side as they swim, collecting insects, fish and other aquatic animals in bulging bright yellow throat pouches. They swallow the food after squeezing the water out at the sides of their bills. Though clumsy on the ground, white pelicans fly with a majestic, gliding motion, their necks folded back against their shoulders.

The adult birds are pure white except for black wingtips, and have a wingspan up to three metres wide. They winter as far south as Central America, and return each spring to breed by prairie lakes.

Echoes of '85 and Indian Unrest

Northwestern Saskatchewan

FLOTTEN LAKE
The lake has large colonies of ring-billed and California gulls, common terns and western grebes. On the eastern shore are kames—mounds of sand and gravel deposited by glacial meltwater.

MEADOW LAKE PROVINCIAL PARK
The Waterhen River connects some two dozen lakes in this park—where canoes are provided at no cost and experts give canoeing instructions. A canoe route along the Waterhen and Beaver rivers is 112 kilometres of rapids, islands and twisting channels. Roads or trails lead to 15 major lakes. A 172-kilometre self-guiding automobile tour in and south of the park begins at Mustus Lake.

Western grebe,

STEELE NARROWS HISTORIC PARK
The last battle in the Northwest Rebellion was fought here June 3, 1885, between the Cree led by Big Bear and militia led by NWMP Maj. Sam Steele. Big Bear subsequently surrendered, was imprisoned and died Jan. 17, 1888. Plaques in this park describe the battle and the lives of Steele and Big Bear.

Historic plaque overlooking Steele Narrows

FORT PITT HISTORIC PARK
North West Mounted Police led by Insp. Francis Dickens (son of author Charles Dickens) manned Fort Pitt in 1883 in response to Indian unrest. The Cree led by Big Bear besieged the fort in May 1885 and the Mounties were forced to withdraw to Battleford. Plaques in the historic park outline Fort Pitt's history and tell the story of Big Bear.
□ After burning Fort Pitt, Big Bear led several hundred followers east to Frenchman Butte. After an engagement on May 28, the militia withdrew and the Indians fled north with hostages from Fort Pitt. The hill at Frenchman Butte on which the battle occurred is a national historic site. Signposts indicate rifle pits and the positions of artillery, Indians and militia.

LLOYDMINSTER
This city astride the Alberta-Saskatchewan border was founded in 1903 by English immigrants recruited by an Anglican clergyman, the Rev. Isaac M. Barr. Half of the 2,000 colonists defected between London and Saskatoon, where Barr was dismissed for incompetence; under the leadership of the Rev. George Exton Lloyd they settled at Lloydminster.
□ A log church the colonists built in 1904 is now a historic site in Weaver Park. The nearby Barr Colony Museum contains some colonists' furniture and personal effects.
□ Fuchs Wildlife Display in Lloydminster exhibits some 1,000 animals collected and mounted by outdoorsman Nicholas Fuchs (1885-1975). Cougars, wapiti, lynx, mule and red deer, timber wolves, sandhill cranes and great blue herons are displayed in dioramas. An adjoining gallery contains more than 70 paintings by Count Berthold von Imhoff.

St. John's Mission Church, Lloydminster

CUT KNIFE
Tepee poles on a lonely hill mark the grave of Poundmaker who in 1876 signed Treaty Six for his band of Cree Nine years later, during the Northwes Rebellion, the Cree led by Poundmak repulsed some 300 policemen and soldiers. But after the battle, the Cree chief kept his warriors from slaughter the white men. A nearby cairn commemorates the battle site. When the rebellion ended, Poundmaker surrendered, and was sentenced to a year in penitentiary. He died in 188

Memories of Big Bear and Poundmaker, desperate men who made war because they saw their people starving, haunt this part of northwestern Saskatchewan where much of the Northwest Rebellion was fought in 1885. But this is also a pleasant land of farms and lakes, with one community (Lloydminster) that straddles the Alberta-Saskatchewan border and another (St. Walburg) that boasts an unusual art gallery. Still, the echoes of '85 seem to be everywhere.

By 1880 most Prairie Indians were on reserves, some farming, most subsisting on welfare. Rations were cut in 1883 and many Indians died. In March 1885, after the Métis attacked a North West Mounted Police post, Poundmaker's Cree warriors marched on Battleford and burned the settlement. A month later, not far away at Cut Knife Hill, they defeated a force of 300 soldiers and policemen. Big Bear's Cree massacred nine whites at Frog Lake, Alta., and pillaged Fort Pitt (near Lloydminster). A militia force engaged Big Bear's warriors at Frenchman Butte and pursued them to Loon Lake, only to have them escape across Steele Narrows and into the forest of what now is Meadow Lake Provincial Park.

The dream of a Métis-Indian nation ended May 12 when Louis Riel was defeated at Batoche. Soon after that, near present-day Goodsoil, Big Bear released his white prisoners. He and Poundmaker were jailed and lived only briefly after their release.

Von Imhoff murals, Roman Catholic church, Paradise Hill

ST. WALBURG
The Imhoff Art Gallery contains some 200 works by Count Berthold von Imhoff (1866-1939), a German-born painter who lived here from 1913 until his death. On display are *Glory of the Emperor Frederick*, which won him the Berlin Art Academy Medal at age 16, and *The Crucifixion*. Von Imhoff decorated some 90 churches in the United States and Canada, including the Roman Catholic church here. A church at nearby Paradise Hill has 18 panels by von Imhoff.

Fort Battleford — Settlers' Refuge in the Rebellion

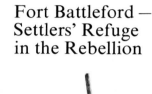

Fort Battleford, established in 1876 as NWMP district headquarters and now restored, was a refuge for 400 settlers who fled their homes as the Cree looted nearby settlements in 1885. The Cree chief Poundmaker surrendered here after the Métis were defeated at Batoche. Eight Indians convicted of murder in the Frog Lake Massacre were hanged at Fort Battleford in Canada's last public execution. In the commanding officer's residence (1877) are original parlor and dining chairs. In the officers' quarters (1886) is the speaker's chair from the Territorial Legislative Assembly (1883-1905) in Regina. In an interpretive center are Poundmaker's war club and Winchester rifle and a 10-barrel Gatling gun used in the rebellion.

Gatling gun, Battleford National Historic Park

COCHIN
The village is named for the Rev. Louis Cochin, a missionary who had a moderating influence on Poundmaker's band in the Northwest Rebellion.
□ A plaque marks a trail which connected the Cochin mission with a Hudson's Bay Company post on Green Lake, 110 kilometres north. The trail was used by troops pursuing Big Bear in 1885.

NORTH BATTLEFORD
Buildings in a prairie village created as a branch of the Western Development Museum include farmhouses, a Battleford Rifle Company building (1879), the Jackfish Lake NWMP post (c. 1890), four churches, a drugstore, a blacksmith shop, a fire hall, a law office, a bank, a leather goods repair shop and a barbershop. A Manitoba and Saskatchewan Coal Company locomotive (c. 1906) and coal car are hitched to an 1883 passenger car and caboose at the onetime Prince Albert train station, built in 1913.

BATTLEFORD
The Battleford Historical Museum displays 18th-century Indian basketwork and a collection of 250 guns.
□ A post office, a courthouse and a land title office—all built in 1911—and the 1886 Gardiner Church and the 1912 town hall have been preserved.
□ Government House, the Northwest Territories council chamber in 1878-83, is an Oblate seminary.

THE BATTLEFORDS PROV PK
Aquadeo Beach
Cochin
Jackfish Lake
Murray Lake
Meota
Saskatchewan River
Turtleford River
Prince
4
36
Delmas
54.5
378
North Battleford
Paynton
5
26
24
Highgate
22
TABLE MOUNTAIN
30.5
FORT BATTLEFORD NAT HIST PK
Battleford
Lambert Lake
Battle R.
CUT KNIFE HILL HIST SITE
Cut Knife

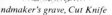

...ndmaker's grave, Cut Knife

Western Development Museum, North Battleford

Once a Temperance Town, Now a Flourishing City

Central Saskatchewan

The only reminder of Saskatoon's sober origins is Temperance Street. In 1882 John Lake was sent to the Northwest Territories (of which Saskatchewan was then part) by an Ontario temperance society to establish a colony. He chose a site overlooking the South Saskatchewan River and named it Saskatoon—the Cree word for a purplish berry that thrives there.

A year later 35 teetotalers arrived from Ontario. The society had sold them homesteads for $320. The buyers were not told

SASKATOON

In July, many Saskatoonians deck themselves in turn-of-the-century dress during Saskachimo Exposition, a week-long fair and pioneer pageant. There are demonstrations of steam and gas tractors, livestock and agricultural shows, and Louis Riel Day.
□ The Western Development Museum has an indoor pioneer village with 26 refurnished buildings. A collection of agricultural machinery and antique automobiles includes the 1926 Derby car, manufactured in Saskatoon.
□ The Mendel Art Gallery and Civic Conservatory has botanical gardens and a permanent collection that includes works by Lawren Harris and A. Y. Jackson.
□ The Ukrainian Museum of Arts and Crafts contains traditional costumes, tapestries and wood-inlaid objects.
□ The Museum of Ukrainian Culture displays ceramics, tapestries and pioneer implements.
□ On the University of Saskatchewan campus are an observatory open to the public, and the restored stone Victoria School (1887).

1 Museum of Ukrainian Culture
2 Western Development Museum
3 Tourist Information (summer only)
4 CAA
5 Tourist Information
6 Tourist Information (summer only)
7 Mendel Art Gallery and Civic Conservatory
8 University of Saskatchewan
9 Ukrainian Museum of Arts and Crafts
10 Tourist Information (summer only)

Looking across the South Saskatchewan River, Saskatoon

Wood inlaid plate and box, Ukrainian Arts and Crafts Museum, Saskatoon

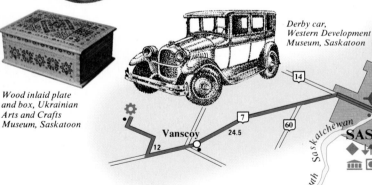
Derby car, Western Development Museum, Saskatoon

VANSCOY

By prearrangement, visitors to the Cominco Potash Mine, 12 kilometres from Vanscoy, are taken a kilometre underground to galleries that honeycomb the world's largest deposit of potash. The evaporation of ancient seas laid down potash in a broad band across central Saskatchewan in layers up to 180 metres thick. Discovered by oil drillers in 1943, it is processed into fertilizer at 11 Saskatchewan mines.

Machines chew tunnels that extend several kilometres from the main shaft. The ore is crushed underground into small chunks and hoisted to the surface. The potash is crushed again, immersed in a brine solution, and separated from other salts and clay particles. It is dried, then graded and stored in immense dome-shaped warehouses until shipped to market.

Potash mine, Vanscoy

the territories were "dry" anyway and homesteads could be purchased from the government for $10. By 1906 the settlement had become a city—but the temperance ideal had withered as Saskatoon flourished.

Today it is the province's second largest city (pop. 140,000), a manufacturing and distribution center, and home of the University of Saskatchewan.

A picturesque view of the city can be seen from the high east riverbank, near a cairn marking John Lake's campsite. Reflected in the river, bordered here with parks, are church steeples, six bridges, and the massive, turreted Bessborough Hotel. Saskatoon's natural setting is enhanced by broad, tree-lined streets and numerous parks.

Canada's highest man-made mountain, Mount Blackstrap (91 metres high), is 40 kilometres south. Built for the 1971 Canadian Winter Games, hosted by Saskatoon, it has facilities for downhill skiing.

Fort Carlton

FORT CARLTON HISTORIC PARK
The most important fur trade fort between the Red River and the Rockies has been reconstructed here. Fort Carlton, built in 1810, was headquarters of the Hudson's Bay Company's Northern Council and a halfway house between Winnipeg and Edmonton.

Reconstructed within the palisades are officers' quarters, a store, a guardroom and a dispensary.
□ A cairn six kilometres east marks the site where, in August 1876, the Cree signed Treaty Six by which they surrendered vast tracts of land.

BATOCHE NATIONAL HISTORIC SITE
Métis making their final stand in the Northwest Rebellion were overwhelmed here by Canadian militia in the Battle of Batoche. Métis rifle pits and militia foxholes can still be seen. Seven interpretive panels explain the conflict.
□ The nearby Church of Saint-Antoine-de-Padoue (1884) and its rectory are the only remains of the Métis "capital." A museum in the bullet-scarred rectory contains some of Louis Riel's personal effects, and Gabriel Dumont's .44 revolver and his bridle of horsehair and leather. Dumont is buried in the church cemetery.

DUCK LAKE
In 1895 a Cree Indian named Almighty Voice shot a stray cow for his wedding feast. He was imprisoned in the North West Mounted Police jail here. He escaped, and one week later shot an NWMP sergeant. After a 19-month manhunt he was killed in a battle with Mounties northeast of Batoche. At the Duck Lake Historical Museum is the restored jail. The museum also has Gabriel Dumont's cane and gold watch, and Louis Riel's shotgun.

ROSTHERN
A plaque six kilometres east identifies the farm where Seager Wheeler grew wheat that won five world championships between 1910 and 1918. For years his 10-B Marquis wheat was the Prairies' most common variety.

Church of Saint-Antoine-de-Padoue, Batoche

FISH CREEK
A road leads six kilometres south along the South Saskatchewan River to a peaceful meadow where militia battled Métis on April 24, 1885, during the Northwest Rebellion. The national historic site is marked by a cairn. A headstone marks the graves of some of the militiamen killed in action.

An 850-man force led by Maj. Gen. Frederick Middleton advanced in the nearby Fish Creek ravine and was ambushed by Gabriel Dumont and 150 Métis on higher ground (depressions used by the sharpshooters can still be seen). Even artillery failed to dislodge the snipers who suffered four casualties (10 soldiers were killed). Before reinforcements arrived the Métis slipped away, ending the Battle of Fish Creek.

Louis Riel

Gabriel Dumont

A Leader of Rebels and the 'Prince of the Plains'

The dream of a Métis state on the prairies ended on May 12, 1885, at the Battle of Batoche. The Métis—offspring of Indian mothers and white fathers—hunted dwindling buffalo herds and farmed in the South Saskatchewan River valley. Batoche became their unofficial capital. In 1884, their leader Louis Riel sent a petition to Ottawa requesting land rights. When it was ignored, Riel formed a provisional government with Gabriel Dumont as his commander in chief.

Some 850 militiamen from Ontario and Quebec were led west by Maj. Gen. Frederick Middleton to put down the insurrection. Although Dumont engineered several brilliant victories, Middleton captured Batoche in a four-day siege.

Riel was tried for treason, and was hanged in Regina. Dumont escaped and joined William "Buffalo Bill" Cody's Wild West Show as the sharpshooting "Prince of the Plains." Granted amnesty, he returned to Batoche where he died in 1906.

Fishing Lakes and a Wilderness River in an Unchanging Northland

North-Central Saskatchewan

A cairn near Montreal Lake marks the geographic center of Saskatchewan. To the west, in Prince Albert National Park, boreal forest gives way to aspen parkland and it, in turn, yields to the prairie that is the familiar face of the province.

North of Montreal Lake is the unknown half of Saskatchewan—a majestic wilderness little changed since it was penetrated by fur traders during the 1700s. The only signs of man's presence are the highway itself and the lakeshore campsites.

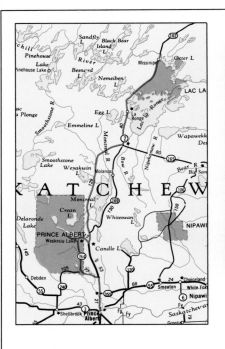

Waskesiu Lake, Prince Albert National Park

Labrador tea

BOUNDARY BOG NATURE TRAIL
This self-guiding trail in Prince Albert National Park skirts muskeg, a sphagnum bog typified by cranberry and Labrador tea (its leaves can be steeped to make a Vitamin-C-rich brew). Insect-eating plants such as round-leaved sundew, bladderwort and pitcher plant thrive in the bog.

WASKESIU LAKE
Prince Albert National Park's only townsite has a golf course, riding stables and an interpretive center with displays of the park's flora, fauna and geological formations. In summer a paddle-wheeler offers daily cruises on Waskesiu Lake.

KINGSMERE LAKE
Bagwa Canoe route passes through Kingsmere Lake. Beaver, moose, wapiti and deer are spotted along marshy channels. Birds seen here are ospreys, belted kingfishers, blue herons, and white pelicans.

Beside an Empty Cabin, Grey Owl's Lonely Grave

A hiking trail deep in Prince Albert National Park leads to the cabin and grave of Grey Owl, the woodsman, author and conservationist who was thought to be an Indian but—after his death in 1938—was proven to have been an Englishman named George Stansfeld Belaney. He came to Canada in 1903, at 15, and learned the language and the lore of the Ojibway in northern Ontario. Lean and dark-skinned, dressed in buckskins and moccasins, he spent much of his life campaigning against the unnecessary killing of animals. Lecture tours took Grey Owl to the United States and Great Britain (where he addressed George VI at Buckingham Palace). He established a beaver colony in Prince Albert National Park, where he spent the last seven years of his life. Several of his books, including *The Adventures of Sajo and Her Beaver People* and *Tales of an Empty Cabin,* have become classics.

Dogsled races, Prince Albert

PRINCE ALBERT
Dogsled races in which contestants drive eight-dog teams 37 kilometres a day for three days are the highlight of a February winter festival. A "king trapper" is chosen for proficiency in log sawing, bannock baking and trap setting.
□ The Presbyterian log church built by the Rev. James Nisbet when he founded Prince Albert in 1866 is in Bryant Park. A table and benches carved by Nisbet are in the Prince Albert Historical Museum.

Lac La Ronge Provincial Park, the province's largest, has outfitters and guides who take adventurous visitors to the park's renowned canoe routes and fishing lakes.

The Churchill River, a maze of lakes connected by raging white water and treacherous rapids, cuts across the park's northern border. This is the only great wilderness river in Canada that can be easily reached by the average traveler.

Lining the river are great banks of pink granite, black basalt and gray metamorphic rock formed two billion years ago. Among the birds found here are gulls, terns, mallards and flocks of white pelicans.

One of the great beauty spots in the Canadian Shield is at Otter Rapids, the only place where the main stem of the Churchill is bridged. Here the river, which drains thousands of square kilometres of northern Saskatchewan, pours through a rocky gorge into the placid waters of Otter Lake.

Fly-in fishing, Otter Lake

LAC LA RONGE PROVINCIAL PARK

This rugged park—almost a third of it water, most of it wilderness—is noted for outstanding walleye, northern pike and rainbow trout fishing. From La Ronge, outfitters fly fishermen to remote areas of the park. A cruise ship plies the lake and an Indian cooperative sells native handicrafts.
□ The Rapid River, emptying Lac La Ronge, ends at Nistowiak Falls which drops 12 metres into the Churchill River. Eight canoe routes—ranging from 35 to 203 kilometres—begin and end in the park. Two are suitable for novices, but white water and long portages restrict the others to skilled canoeists. There are nature and cross-country skiing trails and wilderness camps.

Handcrafted moccasins, La Ronge

OTTER RAPIDS

From a bridge here visitors can see the awesome power and beauty of the Churchill River as it tumbles into Otter Lake.
□ Saskatchewan's first Anglican church (1856) is 29 kilometres southeast at Stanley Mission.

Bald eagle

White pelican

PRINCE ALBERT NATIONAL PARK

Three distinct vegetation zones are found in this park. Badgers inhabit a prairie region typified by meadow rue and prickly rose. Wapiti roam aspen parkland—an area abundant with highbush cranberry and wild sarsaparilla—and woodland caribou range boreal forests. Among 200 bird species found in the park are white pelicans (a rookery of 4,500 is found at Lavallée Lake) and rare bald eagles. There is a small herd of bison.
□ A self-guiding driving tour along the southern shore of Waskesiu Lake passes a beaver pond (a boardwalk leads to the lodge) and ridges left by glaciers. Lobsticks—trees from which Indians and trappers lopped the lower branches when blazing trails—mark some of the park's 240 kilometres of hiking paths.

A Prairie Crop Harvested Every 80 Years

More than half of this "prairie province" is forest. Across central Saskatchewan, between farmland to the south and the Canadian Shield to the north, is a broad belt of provincially owned commercial forest.

Softwoods represent 60 percent of the harvest: jack pine and black spruce are processed into railway ties, fence posts, plywood, and pulp for making newsprint. White spruce is made into lumber. Trembling aspen—the province's commonest tree—is a hardwood used mainly for pulp.

More than three million seedlings are planted annually in cutover areas that cannot regenerate naturally. They reach harvestable size in 80 years.

In summer visitors to the mill near Prince Albert can see softwoods processed into pulp.

Logging operations in Saskatchewan's commercial forest

Lush Lowlands, Blue Ridges...
and Trophy–Sized Trout

Northern Saskatchewan and Manitoba

Until recently the pathless forests of northern Saskatchewan and Manitoba looked much as they did in 1690 to Henry Kelsey, the first European to visit this area.

Now scenic highways such as the Kelsey Trail and the Hanson Lake Road beckon visitors to wilderness fishing, hiking and camping.

The Kelsey Trail skirts the Pasquia Hills, whose rugged ridges can only be explored on foot. Rivers such as the Rice, Pasquia and Waskwei teem with brook trout.

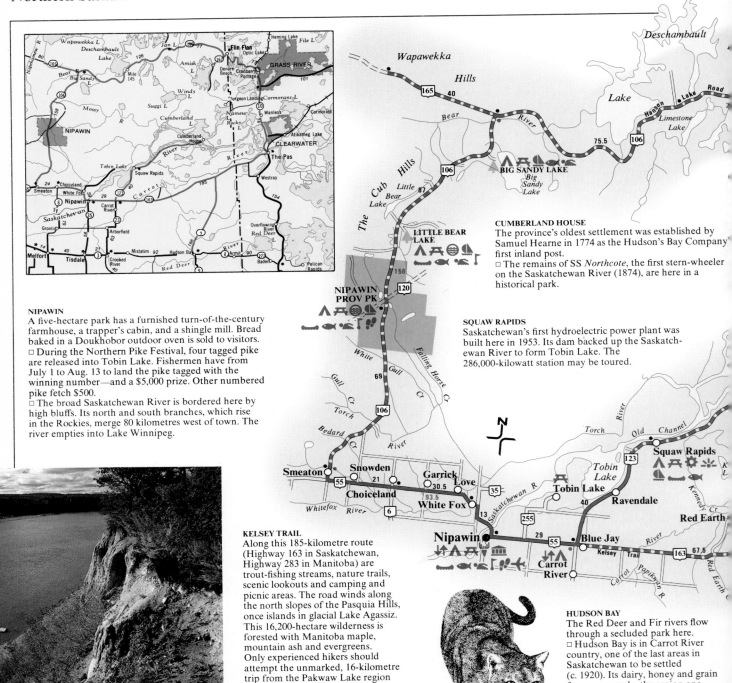

NIPAWIN

A five-hectare park has a furnished turn-of-the-century farmhouse, a trapper's cabin, and a shingle mill. Bread baked in a Doukhobor outdoor oven is sold to visitors.
□ During the Northern Pike Festival, four tagged pike are released into Tobin Lake. Fishermen have from July 1 to Aug. 13 to land the pike tagged with the winning number—and a $5,000 prize. Other numbered pike fetch $500.
□ The broad Saskatchewan River is bordered here by high bluffs. Its north and south branches, which rise in the Rockies, merge 80 kilometres west of town. The river empties into Lake Winnipeg.

High bluffs near Nipawin

KELSEY TRAIL

Along this 185-kilometre route (Highway 163 in Saskatchewan, Highway 283 in Manitoba) are trout-fishing streams, nature trails, scenic lookouts and camping and picnic areas. The road winds along the north slopes of the Pasquia Hills, once islands in glacial Lake Agassiz. This 16,200-hectare wilderness is forested with Manitoba maple, mountain ash and evergreens. Only experienced hikers should attempt the unmarked, 16-kilometre trip from the Pakwaw Lake region to the Wildcat Hill Wilderness Area. Cougars, once thought to be extinct here, have been sighted recently in this game preserve.

CUMBERLAND HOUSE

The province's oldest settlement was established by Samuel Hearne in 1774 as the Hudson's Bay Company' first inland post.
□ The remains of SS *Northcote*, the first stern-wheeler on the Saskatchewan River (1874), are here in a historical park.

SQUAW RAPIDS

Saskatchewan's first hydroelectric power plant was built here in 1953. Its dam backed up the Saskatchewan River to form Tobin Lake. The 286,000-kilowatt station may be toured.

HUDSON BAY

The Red Deer and Fir rivers flow through a secluded park here.
□ Hudson Bay is in Carrot River country, one of the last areas in Saskatchewan to be settled (c. 1920). Its dairy, honey and grain farms now make the region one of the most prosperous in the province.

Cougar

0 4 8 12 16 20 Miles
0 8 16 24 32 Kilometres

Perhaps the most sweeping panorama in northern Saskatchewan is at the junction of the Kelsey Trail and Highway 9. A lookout at the eastern edge of the Pasquia Hills affords a view of the Cumberland Delta, a lush lowland choked with marsh grass and alive with ducks and geese.

The Hanson Lake Road pushes through dense coniferous forests and skirts muskeg and renowned fishing lakes such as Deschambault, Jan and Little Bear. Northwest of Nipawin Provincial Park and Big Sandy

Lake the highway passes the lofty blue ridges of the Wapawekka Hills.

This region's lively, congenial communities love celebrations. Many festivals have fishing themes—not surprising in an area where lakes yield trophy-sized catches. The Flin Flon Trout Festival in June features a fishing derby in which the winning trout may weigh 18 kilograms. Northern pike weighing up to eight kilograms are caught in Clearwater Lake Provincial Park.

Flin Flon Trout Festival

FLIN FLON
A six-metre fiberglass statue by cartoonist Al Capp immortalizes this mining town's namesake. In J. E. Preston-Muddock's novel *The Sunless City* (1905), Josiah Flintabbatey Flonatin descends a bottomless lake and reaches a golden city at the center of the earth. Prospector Tom Creighton found a battered copy of the novel on a Churchill River portage in 1908. When he discovered minerals here six years later, he decided this was where "old Flin Flon" had found his golden city.
□ The Hudson Bay Mining and Smelting Co., which offers tours, refines gold, silver, copper, cadmium and zinc.
□ Much of Flin Flon is built on solid rock. Sewer and water pipes are in aboveground wooden conduits which double as sidewalks.
□ Willowvale Wildlife Park has pheasants, peacocks and guinea fowl.

GRASS RIVER PROVINCIAL PARK
A 130-kilometre stretch of the Grass River Canoe Route links 24 of the park's 154 lakes. Rapids and falls are scattered along the way. Kettle holes eroded in rock by swirling pebbles can be seen in the riverbank. This route, traveled by explorer Samuel Hearne in 1774, cuts through *le pays du rat*, a region where muskrats were once abundant.

Josiah Flintabbatey Flonatin statue by Al Capp

CLEARWATER LAKE PROVINCIAL PARK
Spring-fed Clearwater Lake is noted for its remarkably clear blue water. Dissolved limestone particles in the lake reflect light; cold water and a lack of nutrients discourage the growth of plants and plankton. A hiking trail leads to crevices in a 15-metre-high limestone cliff along the lake's southern shore.
□ A small herd of caribou winters in the northern part of adjacent Cormorant Provincial Forest, where moose, wolves and black bears are common.

HANSON LAKE ROAD
Hundreds of lakes and streams once accessible only by aircraft or canoe can now be reached by the [...]0-kilometre Hanson Lake Road. [F]rom Smeaton, Sask., the road [an]gles north, then east to Flin [Fl]on, Man.
A sidetrip on Highway 165 leads [...]30-metre-high pillars of silica [an]d sand along the Nipekamew [R]iver.

THE PAS
A 240-kilometre dog derby highlights a four-day trappers' festival in February. Other events include muskrat skinning and moose calling.
□ Opasquia Indian Days in August feature native dances and hatchet- and spear-throwing contests.
□ Christ Church (1896) in Devon Park has decorations from an earlier structure. They were carved in 1848 by a rescue party en route to the Arctic to search for Sir John Franklin's missing expedition.
□ The Little Northern Museum displays Inuit miniature ivory carvings.

Flowers and Birds on Birch Bark

Birch-bark biting—an ancient and little-known Indian craft—is still practiced by a few Cree women in northern Manitoba and Saskatchewan. The women fold thin bark into a wedge shape, then bite and rub it with their teeth to produce delicate flower, insect, bird and snowflake designs. Such marks were once used as patterns for beadwork.

The Denare Beach Museum displays and sells birch bark decorated by biting.

Map labels

Wildness Lake
GRANITE LAKE
TYRRELL LAKE
Lake
Leaf Rapids
71
106
167   16
SASK MAN
Creighton
Flin Flon
Denare Beach
Bakers Narrows
82
Amisk Lake
Athapapuskow Lake
10
GRASS RIVER PROV PK
Cranberry Portage
Simonhouse Lake
391
Egg Lake
29
156
Pothier Lake
CORMORANT PROV FOREST
Atik
Rocky Lake
Cormorant Lake
Wanless
Clearwater Lake
Root Lake
CLEARWATER LAKE PROV PK
45
Prospector
Big Eddy Settlement
10
Saskeram Lake
The Pas
79   283
Namew Lake
Cumberland Lake
Cumberland House
CUMBERLAND HIST PK
CUMBERLAND HOUSE
123
Pennican Portage
Bloodsucker River
Goose Lake
Birch River
Bainbridge Lake
38.5   163
193
9
166
Waskwei River
Niska Cr
Pasquia River
87
Chemong Cr
Leaf River
Leaf Lake
Ruby Beach

Hudson Bay

High, Green Hills in a Hot, Dry Plain

Southwestern Saskatchewan

The fascinating, often bizarre Cypress Hills are one of nature's freaks. Surrounded by a sea of shortgrass prairie—sparse, hot and dry—they form a lofty oasis of forests, lakes and verdant pastures.

The hills rise like a narrow wedge above the plains. The thin edge, 1,067 metres above sea level, is near Eastend. The hills extend westward for 100 kilometres and are 1,463 metres above sea level in southeastern Alberta. Two-thirds of their length is in Saskatchewan.

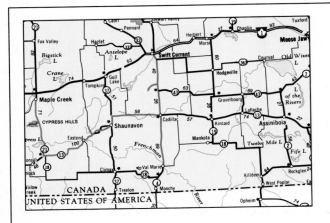

MAPLE CREEK

The "Old Cow Town" is in the heart of the province's ranching country. Northwest of Maple Creek on Highway 1 is a plaque commemorating the "76" Ranch. Organized in 1888, it was one of the largest spreads in the West in the days of the open range. It was broken up in 1921. The office building from ranch headquarters is at the Antique Tractor Museum and Frontier Village south of Maple Creek.
□ Maple Creek's Old Timers' Museum has antique guns, Indian artifacts and an 1890 hand-pumped fire engine.

Hand-pumped fire engine (1890), Maple Creek

CYPRESS HILLS PROVINCIAL PARK

The Gap—a 16-kilometre-wide valley—separates the two sections of Saskatchewan's Cypress Hills Provincial Park. The park's 57-square-kilometre eastern section includes Loch Leven, an artificial lake stocked with brook, brown and rainbow trout. The 148-square-kilometre western section is a provincial forest and wilderness area.
□ At Bald Butte, near Loch Leven, is a view of The Gap. This valley is dotted with knobs (rock and earth pushed into mounds by glaciers) and kettles (depressions formed by melting glacial ice). Near Adams Lake, in the western section, the route passes cliffs of naturally cemented gravel.

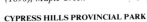

Fort Walsh

FORT WALSH NATIONAL HISTORIC PARK

Two years after the 1873 Cypress Hills Massacre, the North West Mounted Police established Fort Walsh to end the whiskey trade, which fed bad liquor to the Indians and cheated them of their furs.

Named for NWMP Insp. James Walsh, the fort was essential in keeping the peace among Sitting Bull's Sioux. Some 4,000 Sioux escaped into the Cypress Hills in 1876-77 after defeating the U.S. cavalry in the Battle of the Little Big Horn in Montana.

Abandoned in 1883, then burned, Fort Walsh was rebuilt in 1944. For some years the RCMP bred horses there.
□ Reconstructed buildings in Fort Walsh National Historic Park include workshops, a barracks, stable, commanding officer's residence, powder magazine and guardroom. An interpretive center describes a buffalo hunt, the fur and whiskey trades, a policeman's life at Fort Walsh, and the history of the Plains Indians.

FARWELL'S TRADING POST

Abe Farwell's trading post (near Fort Walsh) has been recreated. A warehouse is stocked with furs, tobacco, whiskey kegs and patent medicines, and is staffed by guides in 1870s dress.
□ Assiniboine Indians were killed near here in May 1873 by American wolf hunters. What became known as the Cypress Hills Massacre prompted formation of the North West Mounted Police.

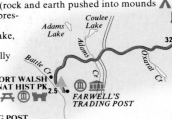

Farwell's Trading Post

| 0 | 3 | 6 | 9 | 12 | 15 Miles |
| 0 | 6 | 12 | 18 | 24 Kilometres |

A broad plateau that caps the hills supports luxuriant grasslands of rough fescue, timber oat grass, bluegrass and bearded wheat grass. In July the plateau is brightened by yellow shrubby cinquefoils, violet silvery lupines and smooth blue beardtongues. Lodgepole pine grows at the highest elevations. French explorers mistook it for jack pine (*cyprès*) and called the hills *Montagne du Cyprès*. This was translated badly into Cypress Hills—although no cypress trees grow here.

Forty million years ago the plateau was a streambed of quartz pebbles and boulders that have since been cemented into a hard, erosion-resistant cap. Narrow north-south valleys cut the plateau into a series of hills. Glaciers have ground the north face of the plateau into steep slopes. Low, rolling hills on the southern face of the plateau merge with the plains.

A lookout near Loch Leven affords a view of surrounding arid flatlands, and of the Great Sand Hills to the north of Maple Creek. These rippled dunes are home to pronghorn antelope, kangaroo rats and western spadefoot toads.

Soaring Storehouses

Clinging to railway lines that crisscross the West, some 4,500 grain elevators give prairie towns their distinctive (and only) skylines. First used in Canada in 1881 at Gretna, Man., elevators replaced low storage sheds. Vertical warehouses take advantage of grain's flow qualities. Gravity, not shoveling, loads railway cars.

Operated by individuals, dealers and co-operatives, elevators have changed little since the early 20th century.

Farmers bring grain to the elevators in trucks. The grain is weighed, graded and dumped into the pit (1). A conveyor (2) carries the grain to one of 20 storage bins (3). For shipment, grain is released into the pit, conveyed to the top, then loaded by chute (4) into a boxcar.

SWIFT CURRENT
Saskatchewan's biggest rodeo is held in July during Swift Current's three-day Frontier Days celebration.
□ A federal research station, established in 1921, develops grasses for livestock pastures and crop strains suitable to the area's semiarid climate. The station is open to the public. Group tours can be arranged.
□ The Swift Current Museum is principally a natural history museum with habitat displays of local wildlife. It also exhibits pioneer and Indian artifacts.
□ Canada's only helium plant, 12 kilometres north of town, can be toured.
□ The Wright Historical Museum, 6.5 kilometres north of Swift Current, boasts North America's largest collection of Nazi artifacts.

PINE CREE REGIONAL PARK
This campground and picnic area is hidden in a deep ravine. A plaque commemorates John Macoun (1831-1920), a botanist with Sandford Fleming's 1872 expedition, which surveyed possible railways routes across the prairies. One of Canada's leading botanists for 50 years, Macoun made excursions to almost every part of the country to gather botanical and other scientific data.

EASTEND
This town nestles in the Frenchman River valley, here 1.5 kilometres wide.
□ The High School Museum displays a lower jawbone of a double-horned titanothere, the only remains recovered of this prehistoric creature. Similar to a rhinoceros, the titanothere grazed on grasslands 40 million years ago.

Frenchman River valley near Eastend

Black-tailed prairie dog

VAL MARIE
A colony of black-tailed prairie dogs east of Val Marie is protected by the Saskatchewan Natural History Society. Enormous "dog towns" were among the wonders of nature. But man decimated prairie dogs, seeing them as a threat to ranching. Today there are only an estimated 6,000, restricted to a few areas in southern Saskatchewan.

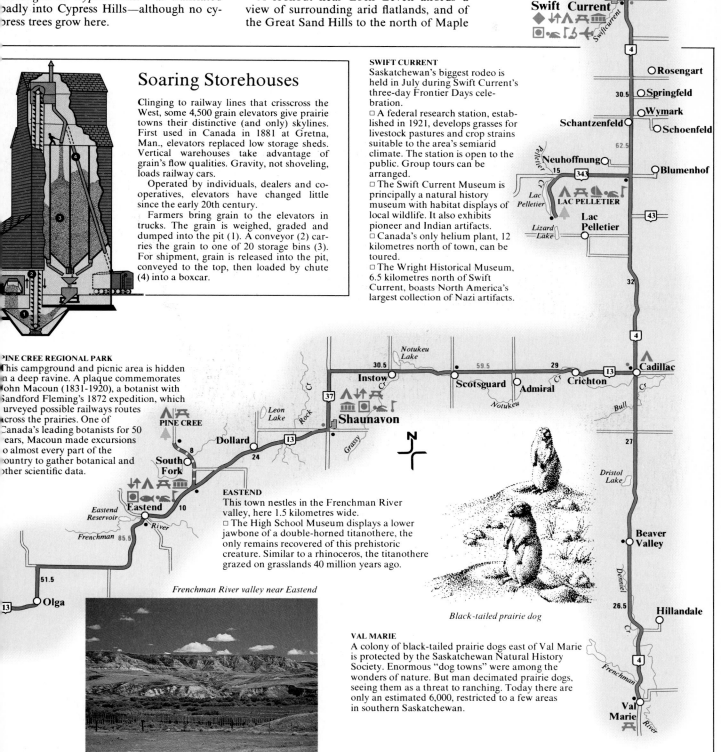

Memories of Desperadoes in the Big Muddy Badlands

South-Central Saskatchewan

Turn-of-the-century outlaws found the Big Muddy Badlands a convenient refuge from the law. The Big Muddy's hoodoos, buttes and secluded coulees were ideal places for losing a posse or hiding stolen livestock.

When drought in 1883 bankrupted many large cattle outfits, some unemployed cowpunchers formed outlaw gangs. Dutch Henry, a rustler, smuggler and horse thief, was chased out of Dodge City, Kans., in the late 1880s. He drifted to Montana and

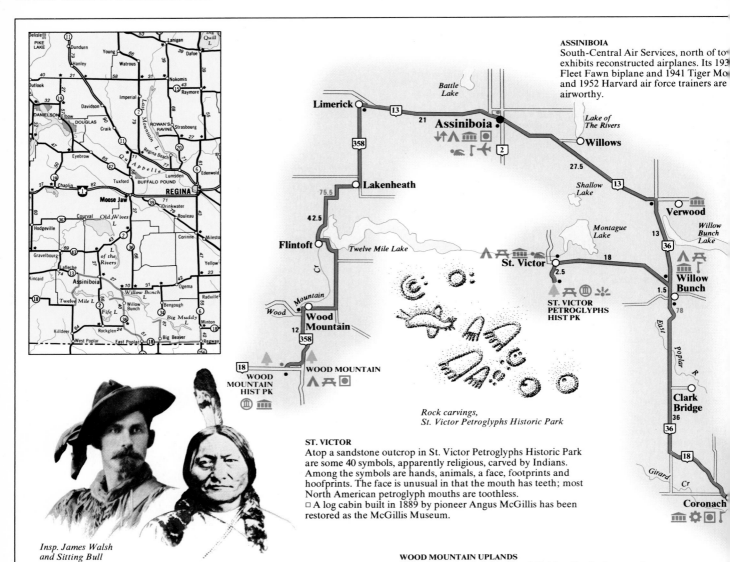

Insp. James Walsh
and Sitting Bull

Rock carvings,
St. Victor Petroglyphs Historic Park

ASSINIBOIA
South-Central Air Services, north of town exhibits reconstructed airplanes. Its 193 Fleet Fawn biplane and 1941 Tiger Moth and 1952 Harvard air force trainers are airworthy.

ST. VICTOR
Atop a sandstone outcrop in St. Victor Petroglyphs Historic Park are some 40 symbols, apparently religious, carved by Indians. Among the symbols are hands, animals, a face, footprints and hoofprints. The face is unusual in that the mouth has teeth; most North American petroglyph mouths are toothless.
□ A log cabin built in 1889 by pioneer Angus McGillis has been restored as the McGillis Museum.

WOOD MOUNTAIN HISTORIC PARK
A barracks and mess hall of a North West Mounted Police post from which Mounties controlled Sitting Bull and his Sioux have been recreated here. After the Battle of the Little Big Horn in 1876, some 4,000 Sioux Indians fled to southwestern Saskatchewan from Montana. Peace was maintained by a handful of Mounties led by Insp. James Walsh, commander of Fort Walsh in the Cypress Hills and of the Wood Mountain outpost. Walsh described the Indian chief Sitting Bull as "the shrewdest and most intelligent living Indian . . . brave to a fault." In 1881 the Sioux surrendered to American authorities.

In the recreated buildings are displays depicting Sioux camp life at Wood Mountain, and NWMP and Indian relics including Sitting Bull's saddle.

WOOD MOUNTAIN UPLANDS
This plateau is a height of land dividing the drainage systems of the Saskatchewan River, flowing northeast to Hudson Bay, and the Missouri River, flowing south to the Gulf of Mexico. Headwaters of the rivers have eroded deep ravines in the uplands' flanks. Wooded with trembling aspen and pussy willow, these gullies are frequented by sage grouse foraging for seeds and berries. In spring pronghorn antelope and mule deer graze on upland grasses such as blue grama, spear, wheatgrass and wild oat.
□ In the Killdeer Badlands, 32 kilometres southwest, are dobbies—eroded, isolated clay hills that support no vegetation. Some are 90 metres high.
□ In July at Wood Mountain Regional Park is the two-day Wood Mountain Stampede. First held in 1912, it is Saskatchewan's oldest regularly operated rodeo.

0 2 4 6 8 10 Miles

0 4 8 12 16 Kilometres

between rustling raids, rested in the Big Muddy, just a gallop across the border. He and partner Tom Owens carved two caves—one large enough for horses, the other for men. Nearby was a year-round source of water and, from Peaked Butte, an uninterrupted view of the approaches to their hideout. Henry and Owens were joined here by several other notorious outlaws, including Bloody Knife and Pigeon Toed Kid.

In 1903 Henry and his men joined the Nelson-Jones gang, part of the West's largest and most feared outlaw band—the Wild Bunch. The gangs terrorized ranchers on both sides of the border. In one raid, 200 horses were stolen and herded into Canada. They were sold, stolen again, and resold in Montana. After the gang rustled 140 cattle from the Diamond Ranch Company, a $1,200 reward was offered for the ringleaders.

In 1906 Dutch Henry was shot dead in a gunfight in Roseau, Minn. Bloody Knife was killed in a drunken brawl, Pigeon Toed Kid was shot by a posse and Jones was shot by a U.S. sheriff. Nelson (alias Sam Kelly) was acquitted of murder, in the United States. He died in North Battleford, Sask., in 1954—in bed with his boots on.

Big Muddy Badlands

WILLOW BUNCH
A life-size papier-mâché model of Edouard Beaupré, an eight-foot three-inch giant born here in 1881, is in Willow Bunch Museum. His clothes, ring and bed are also displayed. Beaupré, 6.4 kilograms at birth, joined P.T. Barnum's circus at age 17. He died six years later.
□ In a regional park southwest of Willow Bunch is a cairn honoring Jean-Louis Légaré, a rancher and trader who supplied food to Sitting Bull's Sioux during their exile in Canada (1876-81).

CASTLE BUTTE
Rising like a fortress from the rolling prairie, this 60-metre-high mound of compressed clay marks the northern extent of the Big Muddy Badlands. Thousands of years ago glacial meltwater eroded soft shale surrounding the butte, leaving an erosion-resistant, flat-topped hill with almost vertical sides.

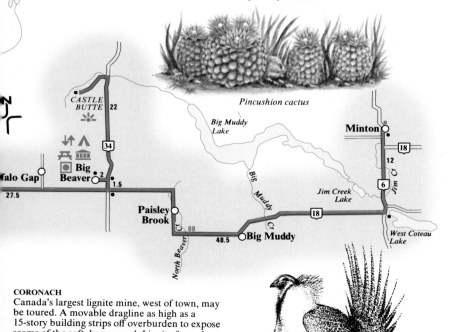

Pincushion cactus

Sage grouse

CORONACH
Canada's largest lignite mine, west of town, may be toured. A movable dragline as high as a 15-story building strips off overburden to expose seams of the soft, brown coal. Lignite from the mine fuels the nearby Poplar River Power Station, which may also be toured. The station's reservoir on the East Poplar River is stocked with fish.

BIG MUDDY BADLANDS
This three-kilometre-wide valley of eroded earth and sandstone winds southeast from near Willow Bunch to Big Muddy Lake. A guided automobile tour, starting at Big Beaver, is offered two weekends in July. The route passes hoodoos (isolated pillars of rock), buttes (flat-topped hills with vertical sides), and coulees (stream-eroded ravines). Also seen are the Sam Kelly outlaw caves, the site of a 1902 North West Mounted Police post, and prehistoric Indian buffalo and turtle effigies (outlines made of stones).

About a million years ago, the area was a slight depression in the plains. Then glaciers gouged the valley. Meltwater streams such as Big Muddy Creek (today a rivulet) excavated the weird rock formations.

Spring comes to the badlands in a rush of color. On dry south-facing slopes, the yellow and purple flowers of prickly pear and pincushion cacti bloom amid white patches of moss phlox. Mixed-grass prairie on western and northern slopes blaze with the western red lily, golden bean and early yellow locoweed.

Soaring above the valley are such bird species as the ferruginous hawk and golden eagle. Mallard, American coot and blue-winged teal nest on Big Muddy Lake in spring.

The Big Beaver Nature Center and Museum displays rocks, petrified wood, and mounted wildlife from the badlands.

A Man-Made Prairie Lake and Oases for Recreation

Central Saskatchewan

Furnished interior of the sod house, Elbow

Sod house, Elbow

ELBOW

Many of the West's early settlers built the walls and roofs of their first dwellings from the most abundant building material available, the deep-rooted sod of the seemingly endless prairie. A replica of a sod house, adjoining the Elbow Museum, was built in 1965. It shows how comfortable the interior (*above*) could be. Furnishings include a hand-cranked record player, a wrought-iron stove, and a butter churn.
□ The Elbow Museum is in a 1908 schoolhouse and contains the original blackboard, desk and organ, and several early bone grinders and coffee grinders.

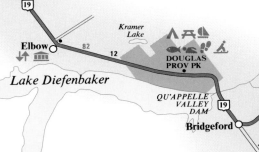

DOUGLAS PROVINCIAL PARK

Visitors to this park on the eastern shore of Lake Diefenbaker can enjoy camping and picnicking facilities and supervised swimming. Fishing is excellent, for the lake is well stocked with sturgeon, trout, northern pike, perch and walleye. Almost a tenth of the park consists of sand dunes. Some are stabilized by scrub brush, but many are constantly shifting. Other areas of the park are patchily forested with trembling aspen and black poplar.
□ On the road north from the park to Elbow is a small fragment of a 362-tonne rock, venerated by Cree Indians, that could not be saved when Lake Diefenbaker was formed by the construction of the Gardiner Dam. The original boulder was thought to have been moved some 322 kilometres by ice age glaciers. The Cree, believing the rock to be the petrified remains of a buffalo dropped by an eagle, named it Mistusinne and made it a shrine. Archaeologists tried in vain to have the rock moved to higher ground to save it from being flooded. The salvaged piece overlooks the lake that hides the rest of Mistusinne.

Earthen Giant on the South Saskatchewan

Gardiner Dam

The earth-fill Gardiner Dam, five kilometres long and 64 metres high, is the largest of its kind in Canada. Begun in 1959 and completed eight years later, it has changed the semiarid face of the South Saskatchewan River valley. Lake Diefenbaker, the 225-kilometre-long reservoir behind the dam, is used for recreation and irrigation.

Visitors to the Gardiner Dam can tour the Coteau Creek hydroelectric station,

designed to produce 800 million kilowatt-hours of energy a year. The self-guiding tour includes a view of the huge generating units, an exhibit on the development of electricity, and displays that explain the workings of the station.

A secondary dam, the Qu'Appelle, was constructed in the 1960s at the southeastern end of Lake Diefenbaker to make possible the release of water into the Qu'Appelle Valley.

0   2   4   6   8   10 Miles

0   4   8   12   16 Kilometres

Centuries before the arrival of whites, Indians used the South Saskatchewan River as a prairie highway. They called it Kisiskatchewan—swift-flowing—and so it must have seemed to them as they launched their frail birchbarks upon its wide waters.

Fur traders used the river and its many tributaries to ship pelts eastward in canoes, later in York boats and stern-wheelers.

The idea of damming the South Saskatchewan originated in 1858 when an expedition surveyed the river and proposed that some of its flow might be diverted to form a commercial water route via the Qu'Appelle and Assiniboine rivers. But when the railway arrived in 1885, the need for a water route was no longer important.

During the dry years of the 1930s, the Prairie Farm Rehabilitation Administration was formed to conserve Saskatchewan's land and water resources. The PFRA was the forerunner of the South Saskatchewan River Project, which developed the river for power, irrigation and recreation.

Control of the South Saskatchewan was achieved with the completion of the Gardiner Dam in 1967. Today a hydroelectric station at the dam provides power. Lake Diefenbaker, the man-made reservoir formed by the dam, supplies water for irrigation. Along the lakeshore are Douglas Provincial Park, Coldwell Recreation Area, and Danielson Provincial Park—three recreational oases in a semiarid region.

PROJECT NISK'U

The Saskatchewan government and Ducks Unlimited, an organization of sportsmen dedicated to the preservation of waterfowl in North America, work together to maintain a breeding flock of 900 Canada geese in Project Nisk'u. Founded in 1969, Nisk'u (Cree for big goose) is located at the east end of Eyebrow Lake. By 1985 some 15,000 goslings will have been raised in the 91-square-kilometre reserve. Project Nisk'u has created an ideal habitat for wildfowl, planting grain for feed and building islands for nesting. Many ducks are caught in baited cages, tagged and set free, helping scientists to monitor the migration of birds on the Central flyway.

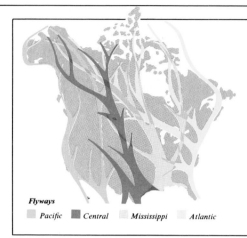

Flyways

Pacific   Central   Mississippi   Atlantic

Flyways Over the Continent

The thousands of birds that stop to rest and to feed at Saskatchewan's Project Nisk'u travel the Central flyway—one of four major North American routes used by migratory birds. In spring some two million ducks and geese follow the Central flyway to northern nesting grounds. In autumn the birds return to southeastern Texas along the same route.

North America's three other main flyways are the Pacific, Mississippi and Atlantic. Birds on the Pacific route winter mainly in California. The floodplains of the Mississippi River and the marshes of Louisiana are the principal wintering grounds on the Mississippi flyway. Birds that migrate along the Atlantic coast winter in Florida and the Caribbean. The four flyways intersect over the Peace-Athabasca Delta in northeastern Alberta.

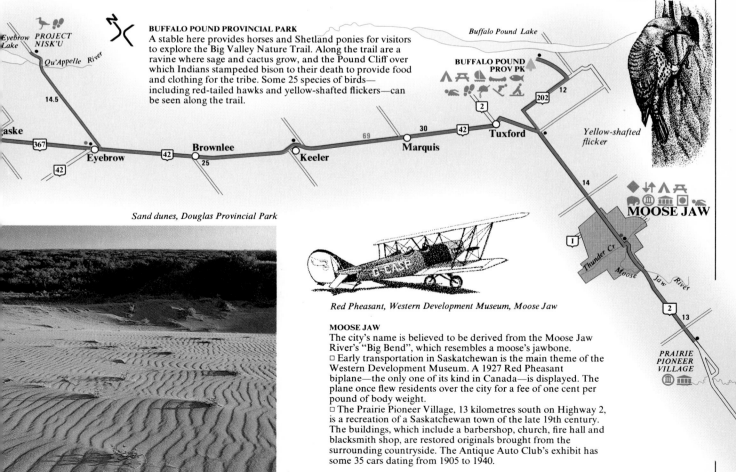

BUFFALO POUND PROVINCIAL PARK

A stable here provides horses and Shetland ponies for visitors to explore the Big Valley Nature Trail. Along the trail are a ravine where sage and cactus grow, and the Pound Cliff over which Indians stampeded bison to their death to provide food and clothing for the tribe. Some 25 species of birds—including red-tailed hawks and yellow-shafted flickers—can be seen along the trail.

Eyebrow Lake   PROJECT NISK'U   *Qu'Appelle River*

Buffalo Pound Lake

BUFFALO POUND PROV PK

14.5

aske   367   Eyebrow   42   Brownlee   25   Keeler   69   Marquis   30   42   Tuxford   2   202   12

42

Sand dunes, Douglas Provincial Park

Yellow-shafted flicker

14

MOOSE JAW

1

Thunder Cr.   *Moose Jaw River*

2   13

PRAIRIE PIONEER VILLAGE

Red Pheasant, Western Development Museum, Moose Jaw

MOOSE JAW

The city's name is believed to be derived from the Moose Jaw River's "Big Bend", which resembles a moose's jawbone.

□ Early transportation in Saskatchewan is the main theme of the Western Development Museum. A 1927 Red Pheasant biplane—the only one of its kind in Canada—is displayed. The plane once flew residents over the city for a fee of one cent per pound of body weight.

□ The Prairie Pioneer Village, 13 kilometres south on Highway 2, is a recreation of a Saskatchewan town of the late 19th century. The buildings, which include a barbershop, church, fire hall and blacksmith shop, are restored originals brought from the surrounding countryside. The Antique Auto Club's exhibit has some 35 cars dating from 1905 to 1940.

A Little Wood and Water– and a Prairie City Blooms

Central Saskatchewan

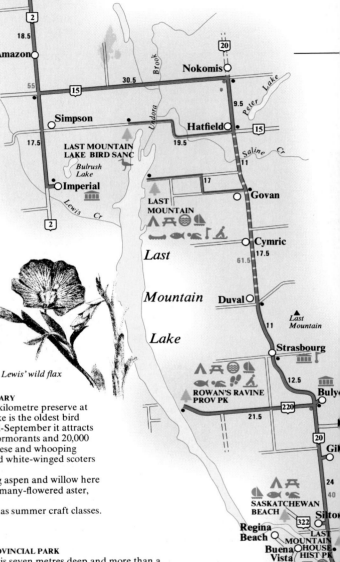

For generations Indian hunters heaped buffalo bones near a creek they called Wascana (Pile of Bones). In 1882 the site was chosen the capital of what was then the Northwest Territories and renamed Regina in honor of Queen Victoria.

The "Queen City of the Plains" did not have a regal setting. Sir John A. Macdonald

Sunset near Last Mountain Lake Bird Sanctuary

MANITOU BEACH
No one has ever drowned in Little Manitou Lake: it is impossible to sink in its buoyant waters, which have greater salinity than the ocean. The 19-kilometre-long lake is fed by mineral-rich groundwater. There is no outlet, and constant evaporation increases the salt content year by year. Indians never fought near this "Lake of the Good Spirit," which they believed had healing properties.
□ An indoor pool in Manitou Beach is filled with heated lake water, which contains sulphates of sodium, calcium, potassium and magnesium and other minerals.
□ A local park has downhill and cross-country skiing.
□ About 400 amateur and professional artists compete in an annual art show in July at nearby Watrous.

Lewis' wild flax

LAST MOUNTAIN LAKE BIRD SANCTUARY
Established in 1887, this 10-square-kilometre preserve at the north end of Last Mountain Lake is the oldest bird sanctuary in North America. In mid-September it attracts as many as 10,000 double-crested cormorants and 20,000 sandhill cranes. Migrating Ross's geese and whooping cranes stop here. White pelicans and white-winged scoters nest on islands in the lake.
□ Grasslands bordered by trembling aspen and willow here are brightened in June and July by many-flowered aster, goldenrod and harebell.
□ A regional park in the sanctuary has summer craft classes.

ROWAN'S RAVINE PROVINCIAL PARK
A ravine in this park is seven metres deep and more than a kilometre long. During spring and fall migrations, waterfowl that nest in a sanctuary at the north end of Last Mountain Lake sometimes feed at the park. Sandhill cranes, white pelicans, ducks, geese and the rare whooping crane can be seen. The narrow, 97-kilometre-long lake has excellent fishing for northern pike, yellow perch and walleye.

Master's house, Last Mountain House Historical Park

LAST MOUNTAIN HOUSE HISTORICAL PARK
This Hudson's Bay Company post was established in 1869 to trade in buffalo meat and hides. Recreated buildings include a master's house, men's quarters and an underground icehouse.
□ A plaque one kilometre south tells of steamships which transported grain and supplies on Last Mountain Lake until about 1910.

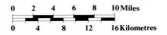

noted in 1886: "If you had a little more wood, and a little more water, and a hill here and there, I think the prospect would be improved."

Farsighted city fathers took Macdonald's advice: when Regina was named the capital of newly formed Saskatchewan in 1905, they decided to make the desolate prairie bloom. A park was established alongside a lake formed by damming Wascana Creek.

Today the park, a verdant playground in the heart of the city, is called Wascana Center. Cycling paths and scenic drives encircle a lake busy with sailboats and canoes. Visitors feed waterfowl in a bird sanctuary. Between the Legislative Building, enhanced with formal gardens and fountains, the University of Regina and a natural history museum, are trees, lawns and picnic areas.

Regina, Saskatchewan's largest city (pop. 150,000), was once dependent on agriculture. Its economy has been broadened by potash mining and other industries.

The city's history is interwoven with that of the Royal Canadian Mounted Police. Once headquarters for the force (1882-1920), Regina still has Depot Division, a recruit-training center.

Fountain from Trafalgar Square and Legislative Building, Regina

WASCANA CENTER
The focal point of this 930-hectare park is Wascana Lake. Visitors can swim, sail, canoe and take a ferry to Willow Island.
□ Wascana Waterfowl Park has walkways through a marsh, boat-launching facilities, and a bird sanctuary.
□ The Legislative Building (1912) has three galleries with portraits of Saskatchewan's lieutenant governors, premiers, Indian chiefs and prominent historical figures. The building is set off by gardens and fountains, including one from London's Trafalgar Square.
□ The boyhood home of John G. Diefenbaker was moved here from Borden, Sask., in 1967. The restored three-room frame dwelling (1906) contains Diefenbaker memorabilia.
□ There are summer tours of the magnificent Saskatchewan Center of the Arts, which includes two theaters and a convention hall.
□ The University of Regina's Norman Mackenzie Art Gallery has Italian Renaissance works and early Egyptian sculpture.
□ Double-decker buses tour Wascana Center in summer.

RCMP DEPOT DIVISION
Some 800 recruits a year are taught law enforcement and are instilled with the traditions of the Royal Canadian Mounted Police here.
□ The RCMP Museum chronicles the history of the force with early weapons, uniforms and documents.
□ The Little Chapel on the Square, Regina's oldest building (1883), has a baptismal font in memory of a Mountie killed during the Northwest Rebellion of 1885.
□ In Sleigh Square, monuments commemorate the force's 100th anniversary (1973), Mounties who died in the line of duty, and the RCMP arctic patrol boat *St. Roch*.

CONDIE NATURE REFUGE
Hundreds of ducks and Canada geese nest near Condie Reservoir. Indian stone effigies—animal and human shapes outlined on the ground with rocks—from the nearby prairie have been reassembled here. A self-guiding trail passes a recreated Indian camp, a prairie dog colony, a nature center and erratics—boulders deposited by glaciers.

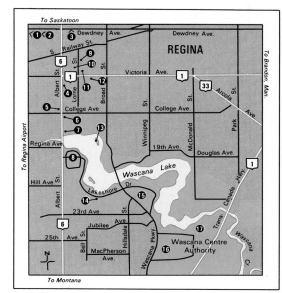

1 RCMP Depot Division
2 Saskatchewan House
3 CAA
4 Tourist Information
5 Telorama
6 Saskatchewan Museum of Natural History
7 Speaker's Corner
8 Legislative Building
9 Tourist Information
10 Dunlop Art Gallery
11 Victoria Park
12 Saskatchewan Power Building
13 Wascana Waterfowl Park
14 Diefenbaker Homestead
15 Saskatchewan Centre of the Arts
16 University of Regina
17 Wascana Centre Authority

REGINA
In July Buffalo Days, in conjunction with Regina's exhibition, features horse racing, a midway, a rodeo and grandstand entertainment. An agricultural exhibition in November has an indoor rodeo and livestock shows and sales.
□ The Dunlop Art Gallery in the Regina Public Library displays works by local artists. In a permanent collection are landscapes and war sketches by English-born Inglis Sheldon-Williams, who lived in the Regina area at various times between 1887 and 1922.
□ Louis Riel's trial for treason is reenacted three nights a week from June to August in Saskatchewan House, once the residence of lieutenant governors.
□ The Saskatchewan Museum of Natural History has dinosaur fossils, prehistoric Indian artifacts and dioramas with mounted animals.
□ The Saskatchewan Power Building has a 13th-floor art gallery and observation area.
□ Telorama in the Saskatchewan Telecommunications Building describes the development of telephone communication—from Alexander Graham Bell's early equipment to satellite systems and videophones.
□ A monument in Victoria Park marks where the inauguration ceremony for the Province of Saskatchewan was held Sept. 4, 1905. There is also a life-size bronze statue of Sir John A. Macdonald.
□ In Wascana Center, Speaker's Corner (dedicated to freedom of speech and assembly) has gas lamps from London and birch trees from Runnymede, England, where King John signed the Magna Carta in 1215.

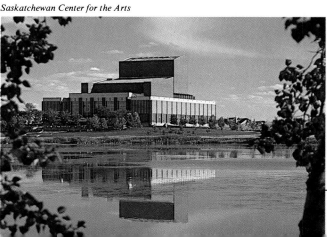
Saskatchewan Center for the Arts

RCMP crest

A Tale of Two Settlements Where Coal Is King

Southeastern Saskatchewan

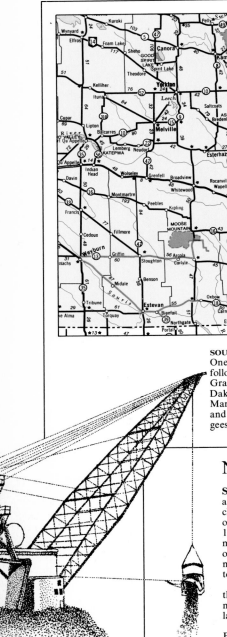

Weyburn's Wheel of Progress

WEYBURN

Mosaic panels between the spokes of a huge, brass-rimmed mahogany wheel at city hall depict the history of Weyburn from Indian days.

□ In the Soo Line Historical Museum are Indian artifacts dating from 5,000 years ago. On display are arrowheads, tomahawks, and coupsticks from which scalps were hung.

□ Weyburn is the home of W. O. Mitchell, author of *Who Has Seen the Wind?*, and politician T. C. Douglas, who was Saskatchewan's premier from 1944 to 1961.

ESTEVAN

Founded in 1892, Estevan is one of Saskatchewan's major coal- and oil-producing cities.

□ The Estevan Brick Wildlife Refuge is a 28-hectare sanctuary where bison, black deer and white-tailed deer roam.

□ In nearby Bienfait is the common grave of three men accidentally killed by police rifle fire during a coal miners' strike in 1931. The shootings occurred when several hundred persons marched on police lines in defiance of a town council ban on public meetings.

SOURIS RIVER

One of Saskatchewan's most popular canoe routes follows 266 kilometres of the Souris River. From the Yellow Grass marshes north of Weyburn, the river dips into North Dakota, then flows into the Assiniboine River in western Manitoba. This extraordinarily scenic route has few rapids and plenty of campsites. Deer, muskrats, beaver, ducks and geese abound along the Souris.

New Life for Scarred Land

Southeastern Saskatchewan's first coal mine was a small pick-and-shovel operation begun by a Roche Percée homesteader in 1895. From this developed a network of underground mines. Then in 1930 a safer and more efficient process—strip mining—was introduced. Instead of tunneling and obtaining only 60 percent of the available coal, miners stripped away the earth above a coal seam to reach more than 85 percent of the mineral.

But strip mining gouged the land, destroying the vegetative cover. Soil and rock were left in massive, unsightly piles. To heal these scars a reclamation program was initiated in the early 1970s.

Reclamation is accomplished in three stages. First the spill piles are bulldozed flat. Then the soil is cleaned of rocks, plowed and fertilized. Finally grass seeds are sown and trees are planted. Many reclaimed areas in Saskatchewan are now pastures or wildlife reserves.

BOUNDARY DAM RESERVOIR

Named because its reservoir extends to the United States border, the Boundary Dam has a generating capacity of 582,000 kilowatts—more than any other dam in the province. Its power station houses the largest lignite-burning plant in Canada and has a ready supply of fuel from southeastern Saskatchewan's vast coal reserves. The lignite is used for firing the boilers to create steam and drive the dam's generators. Tours of the dam are available, and swimming and boating are allowed on Boundary Dam Lake.

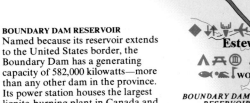

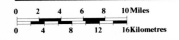

Two sites in this region—Cannington Manor and Hirsch—tell contrasting stories of pioneer days. At Cannington Manor, English aristocrats tried to bring their way of life to the prairie. Persecuted Jews from Europe came to Hirsch in 1892 in search of religious freedom. The two settlements failed—each for different reasons.

Harsh winters and rainless summers doomed the Jewish settlement. By 1894 all but seven of 47 original families had abandoned Hirsch.

The Cannington Manor colony—a "little England on the prairie"—was founded in 1882 by Edward Michell Pierce, a retired British army captain. Here he and his peers lived as English gentry, recreating the grand style of Victorian England. But the settlement failed within a generation. In the late 1890s many of the residents headed for Klondike goldfields, others for battlefields of South Africa to fight in the Boer War. The final blow occurred in 1900 when the CPR bypassed Cannington Manor.

The railway gave rise to new towns and new industries. Coal from underground mines provided fuel for the railway and for domestic heating. In the 1920s, outside competition threatened the local coal industry. But in 1930 the introduction of strip mining—more efficient than underground mining—revitalized the economy of southeastern Saskatchewan.

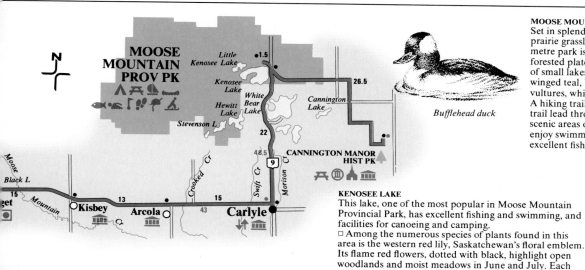

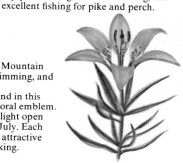

Bufflehead duck

MOOSE MOUNTAIN PROVINCIAL PARK
Set in splendid isolation above the prairie grasslands, this 400-square-kilometre park is located atop an aspen-forested plateau. The park's hundreds of small lakes and marshes attract blue-winged teal, buffleheads, turkey vultures, white-tailed deer and beaver. A hiking trail and a self-guiding nature trail lead through some of the most scenic areas of the park. Visitors can enjoy swimming, horseback riding, and excellent fishing for pike and perch.

KENOSEE LAKE
This lake, one of the most popular in Moose Mountain Provincial Park, has excellent fishing and swimming, and facilities for canoeing and camping.
□ Among the numerous species of plants found in this area is the western red lily, Saskatchewan's floral emblem. Its flame red flowers, dotted with black, highlight open woodlands and moist meadows in June and July. Each plant bears up to five blossoms, which are so attractive that this lily has suffered badly from overpicking.

Western red lily

Roche Percée

ROCHE PERCÉE
Sandstone outcroppings here have been eroded by the elements and mutilated by the knives and axes of autographers. The 7.5-metre-high Roche Percée was venerated by generations of Indians who covered it with petroglyphs. In July 1874 Mounties on their march west camped here for four days and carved their initials in the rock. A cairn records that they held religious services here.

CANNINGTON MANOR HISTORIC PARK
In the late 19th century, English country life was lived to the full here with horse racing, cricket and tennis matches, billiards and a hunt club. All that remains of Cannington Manor, the colony established here in 1882 by English aristocrats, are Maltby and Hewlett houses, a carpenter's shop and a bachelor's shack.
□ All Saints, a log Anglican church (1884), has been restored. Its collection of antique silverware includes a chalice once used as a racing trophy.
□ In the museum are watercolor sketches dating from 1870, a muzzle-loading walking stick for shooting pigeons and a scale model of Cannington Manor in its heyday.

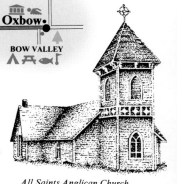

All Saints Anglican Church, Cannington Manor Historic Park

HIRSCH
This tiny community was one of the first Jewish settlements in western Canada. It was founded by Eastern European Jews who came to Canada in the 1890s in search of religious freedom. Their colony was sponsored by the German philanthropist, Baron de Hirsch. A plaque three kilometres west of the town marks the site of the settlers' cemetery.

Maltby House, Cannington Manor Historic Park

In a Tranquil Valley, Echoes of an Indian Legend

Qu'Appelle Valley

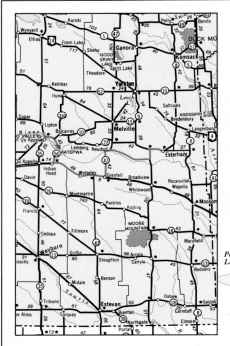

FORT QU'APPELLE
Visitors to the Hansen-Ross Pottery see craftsmen shape Cypress Hills clay (the studio uses about 10 tonnes each year) into distinctive stoneware. Items displayed are for sale.
□ A cabin used by Maj. Gen. Frederick Middleton during the Northwest Rebellion of 1885 now is part of the Fort Qu'Appelle Museum. The cabin contains Middleton's oak desk. The cellars of an NWMP post can be seen on the town's golf course. A plaque nearby records that Fort Qu'Appelle was built in 1875 to protect settlers.
□ In the town park a limestone shaft marks where Indians surrendered vast tracts of southern Saskatchewan by signing Treaty Four (1874).

Hansen-Ross Pottery, Fort Qu'Appelle

LEBRET
Stations of the Cross lead to a hillside chapel overlooking the town, Sacred Heart Church, and Mission Lake. An illuminated cross stands where a wooden cross was placed in 1865 to mark a Roman Catholic mission site.
□ A statue on the grounds of an Indian industrial school commemorates the Rev. Joseph Hugonard, the first principal of one of Canada's oldest Indian residential schools.

Sacred Heart Church, Lebret

ECHO VALLEY PROVINCIAL PARK
The park is between Pasqua and Echo lakes. Two nature trails enter ravines wooded with maple, poplar, elm and birch.
□ Katepwa Provincial Park offers organized programs in sports and crafts. The park is open only during the day.

Plentiful Prairie Crops

Experimental farms such as the one at Indian Head have developed crop varieties that yield bumper harvests.

Hard red spring wheat, Saskatchewan's commonest grain, is ideal for bread flour. This variety, high in protein and rich in color, is the major source of income for Saskatchewan farmers.

Durum, the province's second most common wheat, is excellent for making pasta. It is usually grown in central and southern Saskatchewan.

Flax is processed into linseed oil for use in paints. Second only to cotton as a source of commercial fibers, its by-products are used as livestock feed.

Fall rye is used in flour, whiskey distillation and as livestock feed. It is planted also as a cover crop to prevent soil erosion.

Hard red spring wheat

Durum wheat

Flax

Fall rye

INDIAN HEAD
Visitors to a federal tree nursery here may picnic amid well-tended lawns, flower gardens and ornamental shrubs. The station, established in 1902, has distributed millions of trees to farmers for shelterbelts. By prearrangement, groups can tour the greenhouses, arboretum and packing shed.
□ A round stone stable three kilometres north of Indian Head is on the site of the Bell Farm, established in 1882. The farm was named after Maj. W. R. Bell who managed 100 tenants for the Qu'Appelle Valley Farming Company.
□ In 1887, part of the company's land was sold to the Indian Head Experimental Farm, the first of its kind in what was then the Northwest Territories. Landscaped with trees, shrubs and lawns, and open to visitors, the farm studies crop rotation, weed control and the use of fertilizers.
□ A cairn commemorates the Territorial Grain Growers' Association, founded in Indian Head in 1902. It was the first cooperative established by farmers to improve the shipping and marketing of grain.

The Qu'Appelle River extends across two-thirds of southern Saskatchewan. It meanders eastward from Lake Diefenbaker to join the Assiniboine in Manitoba. The broad and tranquil valley of the Qu'Appelle is best known as a verdant farmland and a well-endowed recreation area.

At Fort Qu'Appelle, the river widens into a chain of sparkling lakes bordered by provincial parks. In this part of the valley, visitors can enjoy swimming and boating. Cottages line The Fishing Lakes—Pasqua, Echo, Mission and Katepwa.

The Qu'Appelle Valley is famous for its poignant legend. The story, told on a marker near Lebret (and in a poem by Pauline Johnson), is of an Indian on his way to see his bride-to-be. The brave was crossing one of the valley lakes when he heard someone call his name. "Qu'appelle?" (Who calls?) he shouted—but only his echo answered. When he reached the camp where his sweetheart lived, he was told that she had fallen ill and died moments earlier. He realized that she had called his name an instant beyond dying. "When the moonrise tips the distant hill," Pauline Johnson wrote in *The Legend of Qu'Appelle Valley*, one seems to hear the echo of the heartbroken brave:

I listen heartsick, while the hunters tell
Why white men named the valley The
Qu'Appelle.

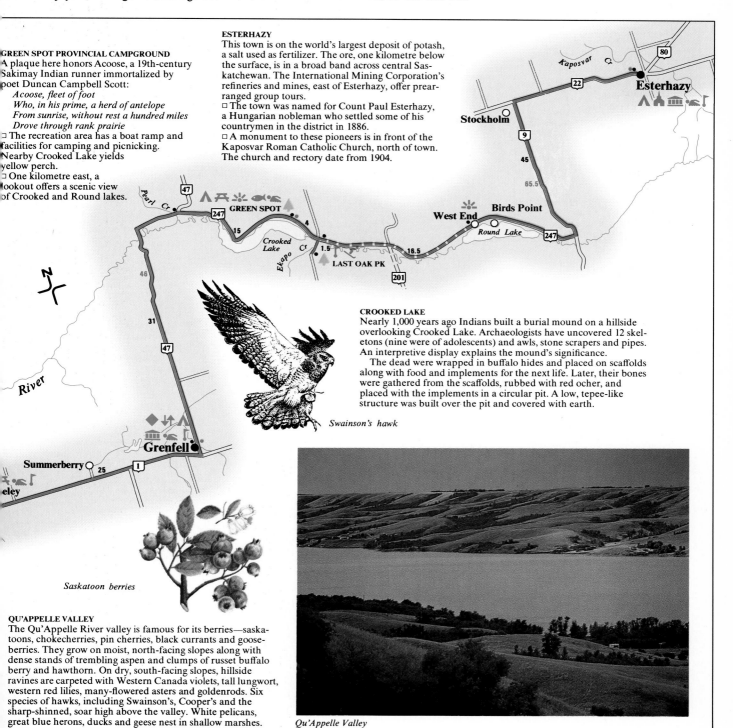

GREEN SPOT PROVINCIAL CAMPGROUND
A plaque here honors Acoose, a 19th-century Sakimay Indian runner immortalized by poet Duncan Campbell Scott:
Acoose, fleet of foot
Who, in his prime, a herd of antelope
From sunrise, without rest a hundred miles
Drove through rank prairie
□ The recreation area has a boat ramp and facilities for camping and picnicking. Nearby Crooked Lake yields yellow perch.
□ One kilometre east, a lookout offers a scenic view of Crooked and Round lakes.

ESTERHAZY
This town is on the world's largest deposit of potash, a salt used as fertilizer. The ore, one kilometre below the surface, is in a broad band across central Saskatchewan. The International Mining Corporation's refineries and mines, east of Esterhazy, offer prearranged group tours.
□ The town was named for Count Paul Esterhazy, a Hungarian nobleman who settled some of his countrymen in the district in 1886.
□ A monument to these pioneers is in front of the Kaposvar Roman Catholic Church, north of town. The church and rectory date from 1904.

Swainson's hawk

CROOKED LAKE
Nearly 1,000 years ago Indians built a burial mound on a hillside overlooking Crooked Lake. Archaeologists have uncovered 12 skeletons (nine were of adolescents) and awls, stone scrapers and pipes. An interpretive display explains the mound's significance.

The dead were wrapped in buffalo hides and placed on scaffolds along with food and implements for the next life. Later, their bones were gathered from the scaffolds, rubbed with red ocher, and placed with the implements in a circular pit. A low, tepee-like structure was built over the pit and covered with earth.

Saskatoon berries

QU'APPELLE VALLEY
The Qu'Appelle River valley is famous for its berries—saskatoons, chokecherries, pin cherries, black currants and gooseberries. They grow on moist, north-facing slopes along with dense stands of trembling aspen and clumps of russet buffalo berry and hawthorn. On dry, south-facing slopes, hillside ravines are carpeted with Western Canada violets, tall lungwort, western red lilies, many-flowered asters and goldenrods. Six species of hawks, including Swainson's, Cooper's and the sharp-shinned, soar high above the valley. White pelicans, great blue herons, ducks and geese nest in shallow marshes.

Qu'Appelle Valley

A Rich Farmland That Lured 'Spirit-Wrestlers' from Russia

East-Central Saskatchewan

Settlement in this area of Saskatchewan started in the late 19th century. Each community has woven its own thread into the ethnic tapestry of the province: Russians at Veregin; Germans at Gorlitz; Scots at Kylemore. Evidence of these early settlers is still apparent. In Kamsack and Yorkton, the silver domes of Ukrainian churches gleam like beacons above rooftops. Lively troupes in ethnic costumes perform traditional songs and dances at a fair

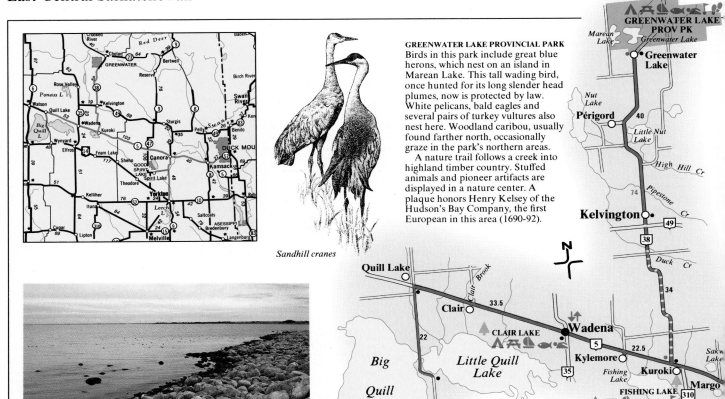

GREENWATER LAKE PROVINCIAL PARK
Birds in this park include great blue herons, which nest on an island in Marean Lake. This tall wading bird, once hunted for its long slender head plumes, now is protected by law. White pelicans, bald eagles and several pairs of turkey vultures also nest here. Woodland caribou, usually found farther north, occasionally graze in the park's northern areas.

A nature trail follows a creek into highland timber country. Stuffed animals and pioneer artifacts are displayed in a nature center. A plaque honors Henry Kelsey of the Hudson's Bay Company, the first European in this area (1690-92).

Sandhill cranes

Big Quill Lake

QUILL LAKES
These shallow lakes are fed by streams laden with mineral salt. There are no outlets, and constant evaporation increases the salt content year by year. Although once fished commercially, Big Quill has not yielded a catch since 1934. Little Quill, half as salty as Big Quill, was fished until the mid-1940s.

In summer much of their water evaporates, leaving dazzling white salt flats whose infertile soil supports only the hardiest rushes and sedges, and a few aspen groves.

Sandhill cranes and thousands of ducks and geese on the continental flyway stop here. Indians once gathered goose feathers from around the lakes and traded them for goods at Hudson's Bay Company posts. The quills were then made into pens—hence the lakes' name.

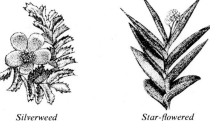
Silverweed

Star-flowered Solomon's seal

Red-osier dogwood

Plants of the Dunes—Roots That Bind the Sand

Few plants survive on the narrow beach along the southern shore of Good Spirit Lake, where sand is tumbled by waves. Fast-growing willows, poplars and grasses take root in sand dunes backing the beach. Yellow-flowered silverweed flourishes in this moist but nutrient-poor soil.

Farther from the beach, red-osier dogwood grows sparsely, poison ivy abun-dantly. Star-flowered Solomon's seal thrives in steep-sided hollows where moisture and nutrients are concentrated. A blanket of moss protects the sand from wind erosion; its roots bind the soil.

Dense brush on the sheltered back slopes of the dunes gives way to stands of trembling aspen and balsam poplar, and moist sedge meadows.

0	4	8	12	16	20 Miles
0	8	16	24		32 Kilometres

in Yorkton each July. This city's Western Development Museum has rooms furnished in different pioneer styles—an English parlor, a German dining room, a Swedish bedroom.

North of Yorkton, near the site of what was once York City, a plaque tells that in 1882 a colonization company bought large tracts of land for $1 an acre and sold it to about 200 settlers from Ontario. York City was their trading post. In 1890, when the railway was built five kilometres south, the settlement was moved and renamed Yorkton. Millstones near the plaque are from the colony's gristmill.

Doukhobors—members of a Russian religious sect whose name means "spirit-wrestlers"—perhaps fought harder than any other group to retain their heritage. And to little avail. In 1899 some 7,400 Doukhobors, financed in part by Russian writer Leo Tolstoy, emigrated from their homeland. Canada had promised them religious freedom and exemption from military service. Yet Doukhobors resented any interference in their way of life. In 1903 some protested in Yorkton against government regulations that would break up their communal farms into individual homesteads. Some members of the sect eventually complied with the demands. Others sought greater freedom in British Columbia.

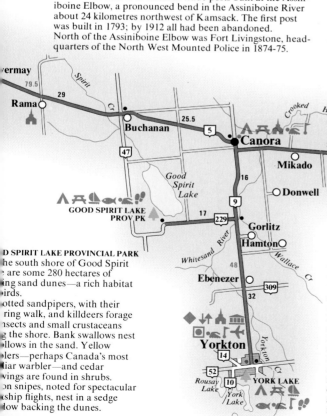

Women Pulled Plows in Solemn, Painful Toil

Most Doukhobors who emigrated from Russia to Canada in 1899 arrived penniless. Men from this pacifist religious sect worked at railway construction to earn money. For lack of draft animals, women harnessed themselves to plows. A Russian playwright, Leopold Soulerzhitsky, observed this toil: "There was something solemn and deeply gripping in these womanly figures as they pulled the heavy plow. Thick sticks, tied to the towline, cut sharply into their stomachs, while their sunburnt hands strove to cushion the pain." Some 60 communities flourished briefly around Yorkton. Doukhobors eventually established individual farms and the settlements disappeared.

A Doukhobor prayerhouse in Veregin (*left*) is still used for services. A second-floor museum has a model of a Doukhobor village.

DUCK MOUNTAIN PROVINCIAL PARK
This rolling, lake-dotted upland marks the southern limit of mixed forest in Saskatchewan. Trembling aspen and balsam poplar grow in the park's sandy soil, white birch beside its lakes and streams, and black spruce and tamarack near marshy areas.
□ Rare turkey vultures, which soar gracefully on long, broad wings, are often seen above Madge Lake. White pelicans, bald eagles and great horned owls also inhabit the park.
□ In a nature center are artifacts from Fort Pelly, a Hudson's Bay Company post built in 1824 on the Assiniboine River. A mushroom display includes a seven-kilogram giant puffball.
□ The park's ski area has four downhill runs. About 80 kilometres of scenic roads skirt Madge Lake and lead to fine beaches.

KAMSACK
In town are the onion-shaped domes of Ukrainian Orthodox and Catholic churches, and a Russian-style meeting hall—evidence of settlers who came here at the turn of the century. An abandoned meeting hall, five kilometres south of Kamsack, is all that remains of Voskrissenie, a turn-of-the-century Doukhobor communal settlement.
□ A marker tells of several fur-trade posts built at the Assiniboine Elbow, a pronounced bend in the Assiniboine River about 24 kilometres northwest of Kamsack. The first post was built in 1793; by 1912 all had been abandoned. North of the Assiniboine Elbow was Fort Livingstone, headquarters of the North West Mounted Police in 1874-75.

Turkey vulture

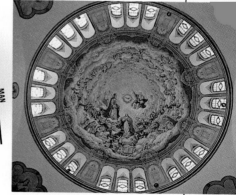

Fresco on the dome of St. Mary's Ukrainian Catholic Church, Yorkton

GOOD SPIRIT LAKE PROVINCIAL PARK
[...]he south shore of Good Spirit [...] are some 280 hectares of [...]ng sand dunes—a rich habitat [...]irds.
[...]otted sandpipers, with their [...]ring walk, and killdeers forage [...]sects and small crustaceans [...]g the shore. Bank swallows nest [...]llows in the sand. Yellow [...]lers—perhaps Canada's most [...]iar warbler—and cedar [...]ings are found in shrubs. [...]n snipes, noted for spectacular [...]ship flights, nest in a sedge [...]low backing the dunes.

YORKTON
A fresco on the dome of St. Mary's Ukrainian Catholic Church depicts the crowning of the Virgin Mary in heaven. The painting, with a diameter of 19 metres, was done by Stephen Meush in 1939-41. The church (1914) has an icon painted in 1964 by Igor Suhacev, who also designed the sanctuary woodwork.
□ The Yorkton branch of the Western Development Museum has a collection of agricultural implements and vintage cars. Rooms furnished in pioneer style include a Ukrainian kitchen with inlaid cedar chests.
□ Harvesting machines are operated at a museum-sponsored Threshermen's Reunion in August. An industrial and agricultural exhibition, held annually since the 1890s, and a rodeo are also in August. An October film festival attracts worldwide entries.

St. Mary's Ukrainian Catholic Church, Yorkton

Two 'Mountain' Peaks Overlooking the Prairie

West-Central Manitoba

Great blue herons

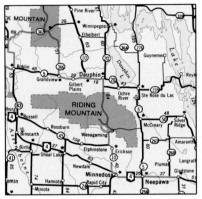

DUCK MOUNTAIN PROVINCIAL PARK

Baldy Mountain (831 metres), Manitoba's highest elevation, is one-seventh as high as the Yukon's Mount Logan, Canada's highest peak. A lookout at Baldy's summit offers a panorama of the Manitoba Escarpment to the north and Dauphin Lake to the southeast.
□ Within Duck Mountain Provincial Park, much of it untouched wilderness, are more than 70 small lakes. Six colonies of great blue herons nest in more than 150 sites.
□ Two plaques and a sundial near Wellman Lake honor Polish astronomer Nicolaus Copernicus (1473-1543).

LAKE OF THE PRAIRIES

This artificial lake flooded 72 kilometres of the broad Assiniboine River valley. Asessippi Provincial Park, at the southern end of the lake, contains several eskers—ridges of gravel and sand deposited by subglacial streams.
□ A plaque near the park commemorates the Shell River Mill, built at the townsite of Asessippi. When the railway was built farther south some 50 Ontario homesteaders, who had settled the area in 1883, left and Asessippi became a ghost town.

Prairie buttercups

Riding Mountain National Park

GRANDVIEW

The Watson Crossley Community Museum has pioneer artifacts and an undated, anonymous book of remedies entitled *Egyptian Secrets*.
□ The Crossley Museum, eight kilometres northwest of town, has an 8,600-year-old musk-ox skull. The museum is housed in an 1898 log schoolhouse.

RIDING MOUNTAIN NATIONAL PARK

Riding Mountain, the focal point of Manitoba's only national park, is part of the Manitoba Escarpment. The park's sharply defined northern and eastern boundaries are some 450 metres above surrounding farmland.
□ Near Lake Audy some 30 bison graze in an enclosure. An interpretive center tells of the bison's role in Plains Indian culture.
□ A hiking trail leads to Beaver Lodge Lake and to a cabin used by Grey Owl who helped reestablish beaver in the park when the once-plentiful animal was threatened by excessive trapping.

ERICKSON

A federal aquaculture field station here seeks to improve a new prairie crop—rainbow trout. The Prairies are dotted with hundreds of thousands of small, water-filled glacial depressions formed some 10,000 years ago. Until recently these potholes were only used, if at all, for watering livestock. The shallow lakes had no permanent fish because of oxygen shortages in the water during winter. In the late 1960s researchers discovered that some potholes could support rainbow trout. In spring farmers and ranchers stock large potholes with fingerlings, which feed all summer on freshwater shrimp, insect larvae and microscopic plankton. In late autumn the fish, then meal-size, are harvested with gill nets, dressed, and sold to local consumers and restaurants. Some 1,500 prairie farmers and ranchers raise rainbow trout, another foodstuff from the breadbasket of the world.

Pothole fishing, Erickson

A great valley separates the low blue ridge of Riding Mountain from the bold outline of Duck Mountain to the north. These "mountains" are part of the Manitoba Escarpment—a series of uplands that angle northwest through Manitoba and into Saskatchewan.

Riding Mountain National Park's varied terrain supports an unusual range of plant life—almost 500 species thrive in meadows, aspen groves and evergreen forests.

The park is believed to be the dividing line of the satyrid butterfly's range. In even-numbered years these insects are seen only east of the park, but in odd-numbered years they are found only west of here—a phenomenon not understood.

More than 160 kilometres of hiking trails lead to remote areas of the park where naturalists conduct wolf-howl sessions on summer nights. Visitors' howls are met with authentic, spine-tingling responses.

Large herds of wapiti and mule deer roam Duck Mountain Provincial Park. The park is also a major nesting ground for great blue herons, turkey vultures and white pelicans.

Manitoba's highest point, Baldy Mountain (831 metres), is in the park's southeast corner. A platform on Baldy's summit affords a view of the great valley to the south, checkered with fields of wheat and sunflowers.

Ukrainian costumes, Dauphin

Traditional Ukrainian Easter basket

DAUPHIN

The town is a swirl of color and excitement during the four-day National Ukrainian Festival in August. Cossack riders parade through the streets and descendants of pioneers wear traditional Ukrainian costumes. Historic and cultural displays include traditional Easter baskets which contain *paska* and *babka* (special Easter breads), ham, cheese and *pysanky*—colorfully painted Easter eggs with intricate plant, animal and geometric designs.

□ A bastion and wooden palisade typical of a fur-trading post surround the Fort Dauphin Museum. Artifacts include a lamp, pieces of musket barrels, and an ax head from the site of the original Fort Dauphin—a North West Company post on the western shore of Dauphin Lake.

Bison, Lake Audy

MINNEDOSA

Nestled in a broad, pastoral valley, Minnedosa has several times been chosen Manitoba's most beautiful town. A dam on the Minnedosa River forms a lake which attracts boaters, swimmers and water-skiers.

□ Tanner's Crossing, a shallow ford where the Saskatchewan Trail crossed the Minnedosa River, is named for John Tanner, the one-armed Métis founder of the town.

The World's Largest Lake Left the Prairies' Richest Soil

The world's largest freshwater lake, larger than the present-day Great Lakes, once covered much of southern Manitoba. Lake Agassiz is no more but its legacy includes lakes Winnipeg, Manitoba, Winnipegosis, Dauphin and Lake of the Woods.

During the past 13,500 years Lake Agassiz formed four times as glaciers advanced and retreated. The first two lakes drained to the Mississippi River; the third flowed to Lake Nipigon; the fourth drained into Hudson Bay. Lake Agassiz dried up 8,000 years ago leaving a thick deposit of silt and clay that now is fertile prairie farmland.

Greatest extent of Lake Agassiz

NEEPAWA

In July during the Holiday Festival of the Arts, professional instructors conduct two-week courses in pottery, painting, photography, drama, drawing, dancing, weaving, writing, sculpting and music. Concerts, art galleries and an auction present the works of students and instructors to the public.

□ Rotary Park, on Park Lake, has camping facilities and a sanctuary for Canada geese. Two other nearby parks also allow camping. Man-made Lake Irwin is stocked with rainbow trout and offers swimming, boating and waterskiing.

GLADSTONE

A plaque commemorates the Pioneer Trail (also called the Saskatchewan Trail) which crossed the Whitemud River near here. (There are also plaques on the former trail in Neepawa and Minnedosa.) A network of trails crisscrossing the Prairies was used until the early 20th century by Indians, fur traders, surveyors and settlers.

□ Williams Park, on the shady banks of the placid Whitemud River, offers facilities for camping, picnicking, tennis and swimming.

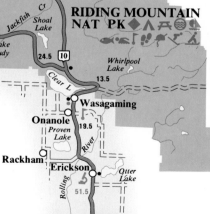

Secluded Valleys and Sparkling Lakes in a Prairie Setting

South-Central Manitoba

Visitors to southwestern Manitoba may expect to see prairie stretching to an unbroken horizon. But this region has another face—secluded river valleys, gently undulating farmland, and wooded hills.

Steep, oak-covered slopes of the Pembina River valley in places plunge deep below surrounding prairie. Eroded in bedrock by glacial meltwater, the broad, 160-kilo-

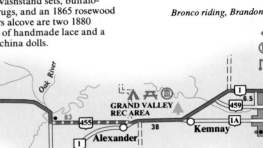
Bronco riding, Brandon

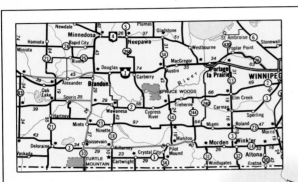

VIRDEN
Discoveries in the 1950s made this the main oil-producing area in Manitoba. Some of the wells are in town.
□ A Victorian residence built in 1888 houses the Pioneer Home Museum. Made of local brick, like many homes in town, the museum is furnished with Limoges china, brass beds, 10-piece ironstone washstand sets, buffalo- and musk-ox-hide rugs, and an 1865 rosewood piano. In an upstairs alcove are two 1880 bridal gowns, items of handmade lace and a nursery containing china dolls.

ASSINIBOINE RIVER VALLEY
Just east of Brandon is a cairn at the former townsite of Grand Valley, a docking place for the "prairie navy"— a fleet of seven stern-wheelers that from 1876 to 1885 sailed the Assiniboine River between Winnipeg and Fort Ellice near the Saskatchewan border. Riverboat traffic declined after the railway reached the area in the early 1880s.

GRAND VALLEY RECREATION AREA
Archaeologists have uncovered the remains of a 1,200-year-old Indian village here whose Algonkian-speaking inhabitants were the first Indians known to have migrated from northern forests to the prairies. An interpretive center displays stone hammers, bone needles and a reconstructed clay vessel.

SOURIS
One of Canada's longest suspension footbridges (177 metres) is a replica of the original built in 1904 by William Sowden, founder of Souris. Sowden's mansion is now the Hillcrest Museum. In a privately owned agate pit, once a glacial riverbed, rock hounds can find fossils, jasper and petrified wood.

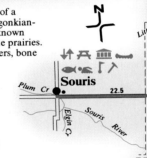

Agate pit, Souris

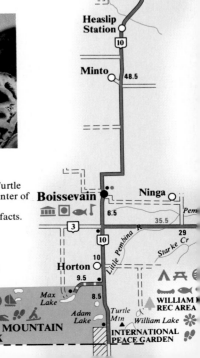

BOISSEVAIN
Each August some 100 turtles race in the Canadian Turtle Derby. The contestants "dash" 15 metres from the center of a circle.
□ The Beckoning Hills Museum contains pioneer artifacts.

INTERNATIONAL PEACE GARDEN
This garden, with its sunken pools and profusions of flowers, was opened in 1932. Dedicated to peace between Canada and the U.S.A., it straddles the border and is midway between the Atlantic and Pacific oceans.

Assiniboine River valley

TURTLE MOUNTAIN PROVINCIAL PARK
The park's rolling, wooded hills and fertile valleys are pitted with 29 kettles—small, rounded lakes formed thousands of years ago by melting glacial ice.
□ The park's International Peace Garden is the site of a summer school of fine arts. Some 2,500 participants study instrumental and choral music, creative writing, art, dance, drama and filmmaking.
□ In August at the peace garden, a Royal Canadian Legion sports camp offers instruction in track-and-field events, sailing, football, basketball and wilderness camping.

| 0 | 3 | 6 | 9 | 12 | 15 Miles |
| 0 | 6 | 12 | 18 | 24 Kilometres |

metre-long valley glitters with a chain of lakes—Pelican, Lorne, Louise and Rock—connected by the Pembina River. These lakes attract large colonies of pelicans in summer. A checkerboard of fields borders the meandering river.

The valley winds through the Pembina Hills, part of the Manitoba Escarpment—a series of uplands extending from North Dakota through Manitoba and into Saskatchewan. Fields of oats, wheat and barley in the Pembina Hills are strewn with stones,

remnants of an ancient glacial beach. Bedrock breaks to the surface here to form whaleback ridges, such as the one at Pilot Mound. The hills flatten into a plateau west of the Pembina River valley. To the southeast the plateau is capped by Turtle Mountain whose crest, nearly 700 metres above sea level, is a maze of lakes, marshes and low mounds left by the last ice sheet.

North of Turtle Mountain is the Assiniboine River valley, broadest of the river valleys that cut through the Manitoba Es-

carpment. More than 100 kilometres wide east of Brandon, the Assiniboine River valley has low hills interspersed with broad, flat plains where wheat and rye are grown. The fields are dotted with potholes—circular water-filled depressions—surrounded by reeds, cattails, willows and trembling aspens.

BRANDON

The oldest prairie city west of Winnipeg is also Manitoba's second largest city. It was founded in 1882 where the CPR crossed the Assiniboine River.
□ The Provincial Exhibition of Manitoba in June has livestock and horticultural exhibits, a midway and a rodeo. The Royal Manitoba Winter Fair (Queen Elizabeth II designated it "royal" in 1970) in April features livestock exhibits, trade displays and horse shows.
□ Brandon University's B.J. Hales Museum of Natural History displays mounted birds and animals, and Indian artifacts and items of pioneer agricultural settlement.
□ Brandon Allied Arts Centre, housed in a turn-of-the-century residence, has an art gallery, and offers courses in painting, pottery, photography, yoga and ballet.
□ Curran Park has facilities for camping, swimming, cross-country skiing, tennis and golf.

NINETTE

This town is on Pelican Lake, part of a chain of lakes formed by broad sections of the Pembina River. Pelican Lake Recreation Area has a beach and camping facilities. There are walleye and northern pike in the lake.

KILLARNEY

Nestled at the foot of a hill wooded with maple and oak is Killarney Lake, once described as "a gem set in jade." Four parks enhance southwestern Manitoba's largest town. In Erin Park is a replica of the Blarney Stone and a shamrock-shaped fountain with a statue of a leprechaun astride a turtle. The old town bell on a cairn honors district pioneers. Erin Park has a beach and public dock.
□ The J.A. Victor David Museum contains pioneer artifacts, stuffed wildlife specimens and an art gallery.

PILOT MOUND

The mound after which this town is named is a 35-metre-high whaleback ridge of bedrock. A plaque records that excavations in 1908 uncovered an Indian burial mound on top of the ridge. In the 1850s Sioux Indians and Métis buffalo hunters battled on the ridge, and Indians once held ceremonial dances there.
□ West of town in Marringhurst Pioneer Park is a refurnished 1892 schoolhouse. A cairn marks where a log schoolhouse (1882) once stood.

Manitoba's Prehistoric Potters

The Indians who made the 1,200-year old Blackduck pottery unearthed in Grand Valley Recreation Area belonged to a trade network stretching across North America. (In southwestern Manitoba have been found shells from the Gulf of Mexico and the Pacific, and copper from north of Lake Superior.) The influence of far-flung tribes that were part of this network can be seen in the pottery created by prehistoric Manitoba Indians. The commonest kinds of Blackduck containers were large, thin-walled, conical or globular pots used

for cooking or food storage. Bowls, platters, lamps and ceremonial vessels have also been discovered.

The pottery was made from riverbank clay. Sand, crushed rocks or shells were added to reduce cracking during drying and firing. Many Blackduck pots were shaped by lining cloth molds with the clay. (Fabric impressions on the pots tell archaeologists much about prehistoric weaving techniques.) Cord-wrapped sticks were used to decorate the soft clay pots with patterns. The pottery was dried, and then fired in a pit of coals.

Blackduck vessel

Prehistoric Indian arrowheads excavated at Grand Valley Recreation Area

ARCHIBALD HISTORICAL MUSEUM

The 1878 log cabin in which suffragette Nellie McClung boarded while teaching at a nearby rural school in 1890-91 is at this museum northwest of Manitou. Refurbished according to the description of it in her book *Clearing in the West*, the cabin has autographed copies of McClung's books.

McClung was a fiery orator. Her motto: "Never retract, never explain, never apologize—get the thing done and let them howl." She led parades, buttonholed premiers and formed the Political Equality League. In 1916, largely through her efforts, Manitoba became the first province to give women the vote. She was the first woman on the CBC Board of Governors (1936-42) and the only woman in the 1938 Canadian delegation to the League of Nations. Despite her active public life, she raised five children and published 17 books.

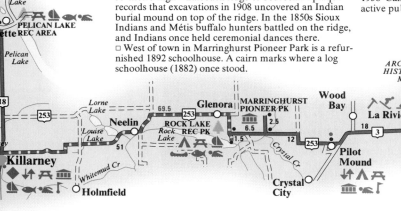

Nellie McClung

MANITOU

A plaque here commemorates Nellie McClung—writer, politician and reformer. She was born in Ontario in 1873 and at age six moved with her parents to Manitoba. In 1911 she moved to Winnipeg where she campaigned for prohibition and women's rights. Her lectures, writing and conferences helped to enfranchise women. She died in British Columbia in 1953.

A Desert of Sandy Hills in the Heart of the Plains

South-Central Manitoba

Only 30 kilometres south of the Trans-Canada Highway is the "desert" known as the Carberry Sandhills, a wild and rugged mix of evergreen stands, deciduous forest bottomlands, grassy plains and low rolling terrain—and, at the heart of it all, the sand dunes of the 40-square-kilometre Bald Head Hills. It is like no other area in Manitoba, and few areas anywhere in Canada. Homesteaders once tried to farm the sandhills, but with little luck, and the land reverted to the Crown in 1895 and

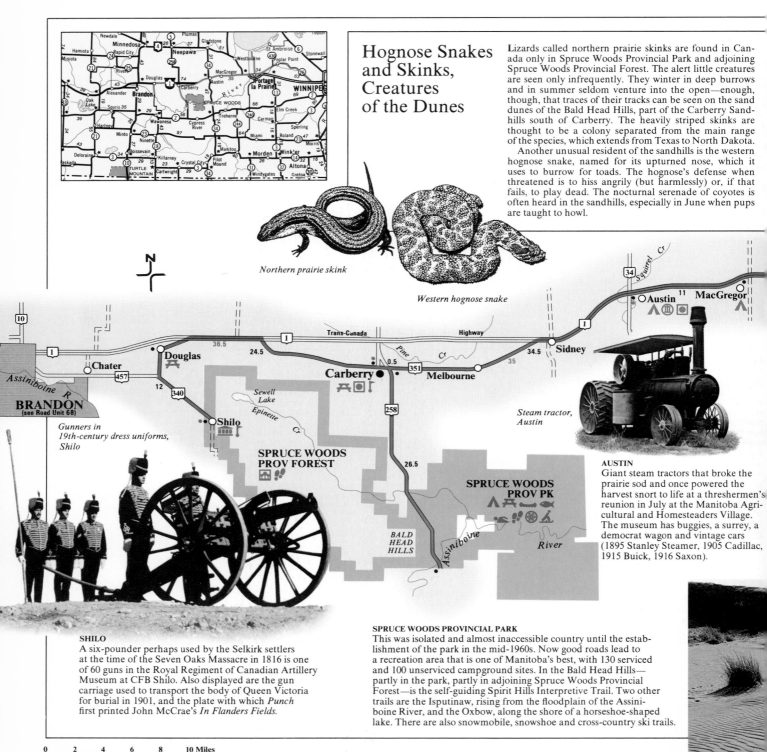

Hognose Snakes and Skinks, Creatures of the Dunes

Lizards called northern prairie skinks are found in Canada only in Spruce Woods Provincial Park and adjoining Spruce Woods Provincial Forest. The alert little creatures are seen only infrequently. They winter in deep burrows and in summer seldom venture into the open—enough, though, that traces of their tracks can be seen on the sand dunes of the Bald Head Hills, part of the Carberry Sandhills south of Carberry. The heavily striped skinks are thought to be a colony separated from the main range of the species, which extends from Texas to North Dakota.

Another unusual resident of the sandhills is the western hognose snake, named for its upturned nose, which it uses to burrow for toads. The hognose's defense when threatened is to hiss angrily (but harmlessly) or, if that fails, to play dead. The nocturnal serenade of coyotes is often heard in the sandhills, especially in June when pups are taught to howl.

Northern prairie skink

Western hognose snake

Gunners in 19th-century dress uniforms, Shilo

Steam tractor, Austin

AUSTIN
Giant steam tractors that broke the prairie sod and once powered the harvest snort to life at a threshermen's reunion in July at the Manitoba Agricultural and Homesteaders Village. The museum has buggies, a surrey, a democrat wagon and vintage cars (1895 Stanley Steamer, 1905 Cadillac, 1915 Buick, 1916 Saxon).

SHILO
A six-pounder perhaps used by the Selkirk settlers at the time of the Seven Oaks Massacre in 1816 is one of 60 guns in the Royal Regiment of Canadian Artillery Museum at CFB Shilo. Also displayed are the gun carriage used to transport the body of Queen Victoria for burial in 1901, and the plate with which *Punch* first printed John McCrae's *In Flanders Fields*.

SPRUCE WOODS PROVINCIAL PARK
This was isolated and almost inaccessible country until the establishment of the park in the mid-1960s. Now good roads lead to a recreation area that is one of Manitoba's best, with 130 serviced and 100 unserviced campground sites. In the Bald Head Hills—partly in the park, partly in adjoining Spruce Woods Provincial Forest—is the self-guiding Spirit Hills Interpretive Trail. Two other trails are the Isputinaw, rising from the floodplain of the Assiniboine River, and the Oxbow, along the shore of a horseshoe-shaped lake. There are also snowmobile, snowshoe and cross-country ski trails.

0	2	4	6	8	10 Miles
0	4	8	12		16 Kilometres

became a provincial forest reserve. Its eastern section is the Spruce Woods Provincial Park.

But all is not "desert" in Manitoba's central plain, from Carberry east to Winnipeg. There is also much rich agricultural land and at the south end of Lake Manitoba is the Delta Marsh, one of North America's great waterfowl breeding areas.

The sandhills were formed some 12,000 years ago when a great river, one kilometre wide, flowed into glacial Lake Agassiz on the southern edge of a retreating ice cap, depositing huge amounts of sand, gravel and silt. The Assiniboine River, a mere trickle compared to the giant it once was, skirts the southern edge of the hills. In 1738, beside the Assiniboine at what now is Portage la Prairie, the French explorer Pierre de La Vérendrye erected the fort that was his base while exploring the prairies.

Settlement started slowly in the 1870s and peaked a decade later as the Canadian Pacific pushed west beyond Portage to Brandon. Because the sandhills were unsuitable for farming, they remain today much as La Vérendrye found them—and as Ernest Thompson Seton knew them. Seton, who was a Manitoba government naturalist, roamed the hills in the 1880s and 90s, and they are the locale of the story he told in his book *The Trail of a Sandhill Stag*, published in 1899.

Lake Manitoba

DELTA MARSH
A long ridge of sand separates Lake Manitoba from the Delta Marsh, a vast bed of tall, yellow reedlike grasses broken by a maze of shallow bays, sloughs and channels. It is a sanctuary and nesting ground for mallards, pelicans, Canada geese, trumpeter swans and other waterfowl—and the site of the Delta Waterfowl Research Station, owned and operated by the North American Wildlife Foundation. Tours of the station are by appointment.

POPLAR POINT
St. Anne's, an Anglican church here built of logs in 1859, is still in use. Today's worshipers occupy the pews of the first parishioners, Red River settlers who had moved west from what now is Winnipeg. St. Anne's has the original organ, pulpit and chancel and a bell, cast in 1871, that once tolled the hour at York Factory, Man., on Hudson Bay. The log walls are lathed with willow and plastered with lime.

...KE MANITOBA
...scovered in 1738 by Pierre La Vérendrye, Lake ...nitoba is 40 kilometres wide ...ts southern end and narrows ...it stretches north. Originally ...led Lac des Prairies, its ...sent name is derived from ...anitou bau"—or Strait of ...God—after the narrows ...t separate it from Lake ...nnipegosis to the north. Waters ...he 190-kilometre-long lake ...in into Lake Winnipeg ...the Dauphin River.

PORTAGE LA PRAIRIE
Cairns near here mark where a great explorer built a key fort in 1738 and where, 134 years later, a farmer from Scotland turned the sod of the first homestead in western Canada. Fort la Reine was Pierre de La Vérendrye's headquarters as he and his sons made their epic journey across the prairies and eventually discovered the Rocky Mountains. It was only a few kilometres from the fort site that John Sutherland Sanderson homesteaded in 1872.
□ The Fort la Reine Museum and Pioneer Village, four kilometres east of Portage, has a replica of La Vérendrye's fort and a house built in 1890 on a farm that was hailed as Manitoba "farm of the century" during the province's 1970 centennial celebrations. Other attractions include a replica of a York boat, a Red River cart that traveled from Joliette, Que., to Portage la Prairie in 1870, and the mahogany-paneled railway car that CPR General Manager William Cornelius Van Horne used in the early 1880s.

Carberry Sandhills

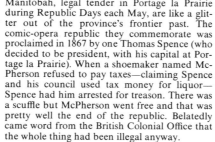

Fort la Reine Museum and Pioneer Village

A Comic-Opera Republic

Newly minted silver coins of the Republic of Manitobah, legal tender in Portage la Prairie during Republic Days each May, are like a glitter out of the province's frontier past. The comic-opera republic they commemorate was proclaimed in 1867 by one Thomas Spence (who decided to be president, with his capital at Portage la Prairie). When a shoemaker named McPherson refused to pay taxes—claiming Spence and his council used tax money for liquor—Spence had him arrested for treason. There was a scuffle but McPherson went free and that was pretty well the end of the republic. Belatedly came word from the British Colonial Office that the whole thing had been illegal anyway.

ST. FRANÇOIS XAVIER
A statue of a white horse *(below)* commemorates an Indian legend that such a creature once roamed the plain here. A Sioux and a Cree both sought the hand of an Assiniboine maiden but, with the gift of a rare white horse, the Cree outbid his rival and took the woman as his bride. The Sioux chased and killed both but the horse escaped. The legend grew that, with the woman's spirit in its body, the great beast would inhabit the White Horse Plain forever.
□ The plain in the 1800s was a gathering place for Métis buffalo hunters who supplied pemmican to the fur brigades.

WINNIPEG
(see Road Unit 71)

Where Festivals and Fairs Seem to Be a Way of Life

South-Central Manitoba

Although a new church now serves the community of Gardenton, special services are still held in nearby St. Michael's, the first Ukrainian Orthodox Church to be built in Canada. Twice a year the bells of the old church summon worshipers—a reminder that once this tiny community had no priest and there were services only at Christmas and Easter. Gardenton, like many southern Manitoba settlements, is proud of its ethnic heritage and preserves its past in ritual and celebration.

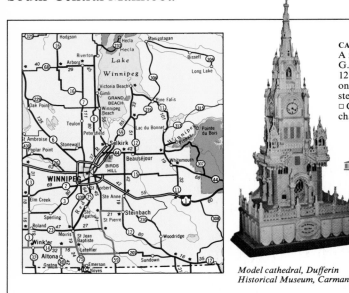

CARMAN

A miniature cathedral, built of balsa wood by handicapped craftsman G. M. Strachan, is in the Dufferin Historical Museum. Strachan took 12 years to carve and assemble the cathedral's 4,514 separate pieces. Also on display is a collection of 24 watercolors by Arthur Brooke, a homesteader of the 1890s. The paintings depict pioneer life on the Prairies.
□ Carman's three-day Harness Racing Festival, in July, includes a rocking chair marathon and an old-time fiddlers' contest.

Model cathedral, Dufferin Historical Museum, Carman

Arthur Brooke watercolor, Dufferin Historical Museum, Carman

Eggs, Skulls and Skins of Mighty Dinosaurs

Dinosaurs thrived here in prehistoric times when this area was covered by a shallow inland sea. They became extinct some 63 million years ago—but their remains, preserved in the shale and sandstone bedrock of southern Manitoba, are frequently unearthed. The first discovery of dinosaur fossils on the prairies was by the Palliser expedition in 1857-60. Since then dinosaur skulls, backbones, eggs and even skins have been found, and more than a hundred skeletons have been removed to museums. The Morden District Museum, which displays bones of birds and reptiles taken from local fossil beds, has among its exhibits the almost complete skeletons of a mosasaur (the largest of these was some 12 metres long) and a plesiosaur, a turtlelike creature with a long neck.

WINKLER

In the heart of the agriculturally rich Pembina Triangle this Mennonite community produces such crops as onions, carrots and cereal grains. During Old Time Value Days, in August, the main street becomes a pedestrian mall attracting as many as 50,000 visitors to booths stocked with local wares.
□ Pioneer artifacts and antique tractors and threshers are displayed at the Pembina Threshermen's Museum. Many of these machines are operated at the Pembina Threshermen's Reunion in September.

MORDEN

A federal research station established here in 1915 by the Department of Agriculture, seeks ways to improve the size, quality and disease resistance of local crops. Visitors will see laboratories, an arboretum and more than 3,000 species of plants on the landscaped grounds.
□ In May Morden celebrates the departure of winter with Spring Blossoms Week. There is plenty of free corn and cider at the Corn and Apple Festival in August.
□ Colert Beach, on man-made Lake Minnewasta, is a popular recreation spot.

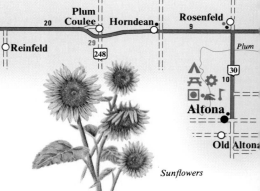

Sunflowers

ALTONA

Sunflower seeds, a major crop here, are processed into vegetable oil at the C.S.P. Foods plant (which may be toured). The Manitoba Sunflower Festival in July features soap and sausage making, parades and agricultural exhibits. Traditional Mennonite dishes are served at the festival.

| 0 | 2 | 4 | 6 | 8 | 10 Miles |

| 0 | 4 | 8 | 12 | 16 Kilometres |

Festivals and rural fairs seem to be a way of life in this region. Winkler's threshermen's reunion, Morris's stampede and Altona's sunflower festival reflect cultural and commercial diversity. The reconstructed Mennonite village at Steinbach reveals the religious way of life of early settlers.

French Canadians, the first settlers in this region, arrived in the 1870s and established such communities as St. Malo and St. Pierre. Immigrants from central and eastern Europe followed soon after, attracted by the promise of religious freedom and the availability of inexpensive farmland.

The land west of the Red River—southern Manitoba's Pembina Triangle—is among the most fertile in North America. Sheltered by the Pembina Hills, it has more frost-free days than anywhere else in the province. Crops that are usually found farther south—potatoes, corn, sugar beets, sunflowers and apples—thrive here.

Farm vacations in this area (and elsewhere in southern Manitoba) are popular with summer visitors. The Manitoba Farm Vacations Association, with some 60 host farms throughout the province, offers holidayers of all ages a taste of country life. Some visitors "live in" with a host family, helping with traditional farm chores and enjoying home-cooked meals. Others camp on farm property. Many farm vacations offer fishing, swimming and riding.

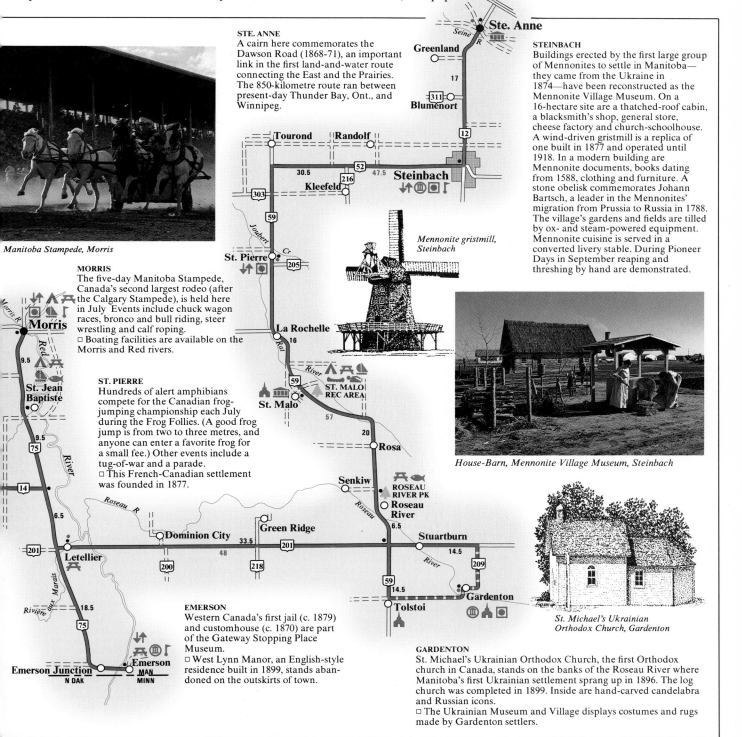

Manitoba Stampede, Morris

STE. ANNE
A cairn here commemorates the Dawson Road (1868-71), an important link in the first land-and-water route connecting the East and the Prairies. The 850-kilometre route ran between present-day Thunder Bay, Ont., and Winnipeg.

MORRIS
The five-day Manitoba Stampede, Canada's second largest rodeo (after the Calgary Stampede), is held here in July Events include chuck wagon races, bronco and bull riding, steer wrestling and calf roping.
□ Boating facilities are available on the Morris and Red rivers.

ST. PIERRE
Hundreds of alert amphibians compete for the Canadian frog-jumping championship each July during the Frog Follies. (A good frog jump is from two to three metres, and anyone can enter a favorite frog for a small fee.) Other events include a tug-of-war and a parade.
□ This French-Canadian settlement was founded in 1877.

EMERSON
Western Canada's first jail (c. 1879) and customhouse (c. 1870) are part of the Gateway Stopping Place Museum.
□ West Lynn Manor, an English-style residence built in 1899, stands abandoned on the outskirts of town.

Mennonite gristmill, Steinbach

STEINBACH
Buildings erected by the first large group of Mennonites to settle in Manitoba—they came from the Ukraine in 1874—have been reconstructed as the Mennonite Village Museum. On a 16-hectare site are a thatched-roof cabin, a blacksmith's shop, general store, cheese factory and church-schoolhouse. A wind-driven gristmill is a replica of one built in 1877 and operated until 1918. In a modern building are Mennonite documents, books dating from 1588, clothing and furniture. A stone obelisk commemorates Johann Bartsch, a leader in the Mennonites' migration from Prussia to Russia in 1788. The village's gardens and fields are tilled by ox- and steam-powered equipment. Mennonite cuisine is served in a converted livery stable. During Pioneer Days in September reaping and threshing by hand are demonstrated.

House-Barn, Mennonite Village Museum, Steinbach

St. Michael's Ukrainian Orthodox Church, Gardenton

GARDENTON
St. Michael's Ukrainian Orthodox Church, the first Orthodox church in Canada, stands on the banks of the Roseau River where Manitoba's first Ukrainian settlement sprang up in 1896. The log church was completed in 1899. Inside are hand-carved candelabra and Russian icons.
□ The Ukrainian Museum and Village displays costumes and rugs made by Gardenton settlers.

Where the West Begins... a Bustling, Cosmopolitan City

Out of turbulent beginnings Winnipeg has become the gateway to the West, capital of Manitoba, and Canada's fourth largest city. Its population of some 600,000 is more than half of Manitoba's total.

The oldest city in western Canada began as the Red River Settlement, an agricultural colony founded in 1812 by Lord Selkirk for displaced Scottish crofters. Despite floods, droughts and grasshopper plagues, the settlement at the forks of the Red and Assiniboine rivers prospered.

The Canadian Pacific Railway linked Winnipeg to the East in 1885, and transformed the city into the West's transportation, manufacturing and financial center.

With the railway came immigrants to settle the Prairies. Many stayed in Winnipeg. Their contribution is remembered during Folklorama, a summer celebration of the city's ethnic heritage.

Winnipeg is justly proud of its lively cultural institutions. The Manitoba Theatre Centre is one of the oldest and most outstanding theater companies in Canada. The city's symphony orchestra provides music for the Manitoba Opera and the Royal Winnipeg Ballet, the city's most famous export.

Assiniboine Park (3)
A zoo here has such rare species as the snow leopard, brush-tailed wallaby and lion-tailed macaque. The Tropical House, a humid jungle of vines and ferns, is home to monkeys and brilliantly colored birds. A children's zoo has farmyard animals. A conservatory houses some 8,000 exotic tropical trees and shrubs.

Centennial Center (15)
It contains the Manitoba Museum of Man and Nature, a concert hall and a planetarium. In the museum, a replica of *Nonsuch*, the first trading vessel into Hudson Bay (1668), stands beside a recreation of London's Deptford Dock. There are guided tours of the concert hall, which is the home of Winnipeg's ballet, opera and symphony. The planetarium produces special effects—from flying saucers to the death of a star.

Grant Gristmill (2)
A working replica of the first mill west of the Great Lakes, built by Métis leader Cuthbert Grant in 1829, grinds flour for sale to visitors.

Kildonan Park (19)
This 40-hectare park on the banks of the Red River was designed by Frederick Olm-stead, an American landscape architect who also designed Montreal's Mount Royal Park and New York's Central Park. Rainbow Stage is a 2,342-seat outdoor theater where musicals and plays are presented. A two-day Highland dancing competition is held here in June.

Living Prairie Museum (1)
An 11-hectare remnant of the uncultivated tallgrass prairie that once covered much of southern Manitoba has been preserved here. Some 150 plant species include gaillardia, prairie crocus, goldenrod and big bluestem grass. An interpretive center has stuffed animals and audiovisual presentations. Naturalists conduct summer hikes.

Macdonald House (10)
The gracious Victorian residence (1895) of Sir Hugh Macdonald, Manitoba's ninth premier (1900) and the son of Sir John A. Macdonald, has been restored. Guides in period costume show visitors the elder Macdonald's desk and clock.

Manitoba Legislative Building (11)
Fountains and flower gardens form a colorful setting for this neoclassic building of Tyndall limestone. Atop its dome is the famous *Golden Boy* by Charles Gardet, a French sculptor. There are guided tours. On the grounds is the Victorian residence of Manitoba's lieutenant governor.

Pan-Am Swimming Pool (6)
Built for the 1967 Pan-American Games, this pool is open to the public. The Aquatic Hall of Fame and Museum of Canada has one of the world's largest sports stamp collections. The Cutty Sark Club has models of 19th-century sailing ships.

Prairie Dog Central (4)
Passengers ride in 19th-century coaches pulled by an 1882 steam engine on a two-hour, 40-kilometre round trip from Winnipeg to Grosse Ile. The PDC operates on summer Sundays and holidays.

Ross House (13)
The Ross House was western Canada's first post office (1855). The refurnished log house has postmaster William Ross's desk and chairs. In front of the Ross House, a cairn marks the site of the HBC's Fort Douglas (1813).

Royal Canadian Mint (21)
This glass-and-metal half-pyramid houses

Broad Portage Avenue (above) is Winnipeg's busiest thoroughfare. More than half the province's total population lives within the city limits. Bronze bison (below) guard the lobby of the Manitoba Legislative Building.

a branch of the Royal Canadian Mint. Guided tours feature a coin museum, a display of ancient minting tools, and an audiovisual presentation describing the production of coins.

Gleaming walls of the Royal Canadian Mint (above) house a coin museum and display of ancient minting tools. Destroyed by fire in 1968, the Roman Catholic St. Boniface Basilica (right) was rebuilt behind the façade of the old (1908) building.

Lively Displays of Diverse Cultures

Much of Winnipeg's vitality stems from its ethnic diversity. Visitors can experience some of the excitement of the city's 30 different cultures during Folklorama, a one-week festival in August. Each group has a pavilion displaying ethnic costumes, food and drink. French-Canadian music and dancing enliven St. Boniface during the Festival du Voyageur in February. Features include dogsled and snowshoe races, snow and ice sculptures—and pea soup at all outdoor activities. The Winnipeg Folk Festival has music workshops and outdoor concerts, featuring old-time fiddling and guitar picking. It is held at Birds Hill Provincial Park in July.

St. Boniface (18)
An 1846 convent is now a museum displaying the coffin which bore Louis Riel's body from Regina to Winnipeg and bars from the Métis leader's Regina cell. Several rooms have period furnishings.

A monument in an adjacent park honors Pierre de La Vérendrye and his sons, who were the first Europeans in this area (1738).

A modern chapel has been built behind the façade of the former St. Boniface Basilica (1908), which was destroyed by fire in 1968. Nearby is the grave of Louis Riel.

Seven Oaks House (17)
The oldest residence in Manitoba, built by merchant John Inkster in 1851-53, has buffalo-hair-bound plaster and many original furnishings. Adjacent is Inkster's store, stocked with period merchandise. A nearby limestone column is approximately where Métis killed 21 settlers in the Seven Oaks Massacre (June 19, 1816).

Ukrainian Cultural and Educational Center (14)
In a room representing a Ukrainian village home are hand-carved furniture and hand-painted ceramics. Another room has woven wall coverings and an ornate fireplace with handmade ceramic tiles. The center's museum exhibits 17th-century church vestments and silverware dating from 1492. A 20,000-volume library includes a 1658 Gospel and 1733 church songbook.

Upper Fort Garry (16)
One gate of this Hudson's Bay Company's fort (1835) still stands. A tablet commemorates this fort and French Fort Rouge (1738), the North West Company's Fort Gibraltar (1804) and an 1821 HBC fort.

Winnipeg Art Gallery (9)
This wedge-shaped structure has nine galleries and a 300-seat auditorium. Its collection of Inuit art is perhaps the world's largest. Guided tours are available.

Winnipeg Centennial Library (8)
More than 300,000 volumes are in this Tyndall limestone building, which is enhanced by pools, sculptures and a solarium.

Winnipeg Commodity Exchange (7)
Visitors may tour the exchange, which deals in futures of grain, oilseeds, gold and beef. A gallery overlooks the trading floor.

Winnipeg

1 Living Prairie Museum
2 Grant Gristmill
3 Assiniboine Park
4 Prairie Dog Central
5 CAA
6 Pan-Am Swimming Pool
7 Winnipeg Commodity Exchange
8 Winnipeg Centennial Library
9 Winnipeg Art Gallery
10 Macdonald House
11 Manitoba Legislative Building
12 Tourist Information
13 Ross House
14 Ukrainian Cultural and Educational Center
15 Centennial Center
16 Upper Fort Garry
17 Seven Oaks House and Monument
18 St. Boniface
19 Kildonan Park
20 Birds Hill Provincial Park
21 Royal Canadian Mint

On the Shores of a Vast Lake, a 'Home of the Gods'

Southwestern Shore, Lake Winnipeg

Lake Winnipeg, an immense expanse of water larger than Lake Ontario, extends 400 kilometres from the prairie north to the Canadian Shield. The lake has a varied shoreline—marshes at the southern end of the lake and near Hecla Island, granite promontories interspersed with sandy bays along the eastern shore, and high clay cliffs on the northwestern shore.

Discovered in 1734 by Pierre de La Vérendrye, Lake Winnipeg was part of a continental waterway used by fur traders.

Stefansson Memorial Park, Arnes

ARNES

Vilhjalmur Stefansson, born here in 1879, demonstrated that Arctic explorers could live off the land as Inuit did. In a memorial park is a statue of Stefansson and a representation of an Inukshuk (an Inuit landmark built of rocks in the form of a man). A quote from his autobiography—"I know what I have experienced, and I know what it has meant to me"—is inscribed on the Inukshuk.

Traditional Icelandic dress, Gimli

GIMLI

The largest Icelandic community outside Iceland, Gimli hosts a three-day festival each August. The *Fjallkona* (Maid of the Mountains) presides over a program of toasts and tributes to Iceland and Canada. Descendants of pioneers wear traditional dress during the festival, which includes drama, poetry, music and athletic competitions.
□ The Gimli Historical Museum displays jiggers for setting nets under ice and a 12-metre whitefish boat, typical of the Lake Winnipeg commercial fishing fleet. Other displays include pioneer household artifacts and the reconstructed log cabin of Alafur Johannsson, the first child born in Gimli.

SELKIRK

A concrete-and-wood replica of a Red River cart in Selkirk Park stands seven metres high (three times actual size). Usually made entirely of wood, the two-wheeled oxcart was the main form of land transportation until railways reached the West.
□ Manitoba's oldest surviving steamship, the MS *Keenora* (1897), and the CGS *Bradbury* (1915), the only icebreaker to sail Lake Winnipeg, are in dry dock at the Manitoba Marine Museum.

York Boats and Steamboats, Successors to Birchbark Canoes

The York boat was heavier and slower than the sleek birchbark canoe of the voyageurs, but by the 1820s the more cumbersome craft had become the main form of transportation in the West. Unlike birchbarks, York boats were durable—and did not require skilled paddlers. They were propelled by six to nine oarsmen and, on large lakes, by a square canvas sail. Too heavy to carry over portages, York boats were dragged or winched overland on rollers to avoid rocks, rapids and falls. There is an authentic York boat at Lower Fort Garry National Historic Park.

York boats were replaced by steamboats on major western rivers in the 1870s. Steamboats brought freight and passengers down the Red River from the railhead in Minnesota, and then into Lake Winnipeg.

Rocks and rapids in rivers and sudden squalls on the lake made navigation treacherous. The SS *City of Winnipeg,* which offered passengers the luxury of a piano and chandeliers, sank in an 1881 gale.

Steamboat traffic declined on Manitoba rivers after the railway reached Winnipeg in 1881 but continued on Lake Winnipeg into the late 1880s. Today, two modern sternwheelers and two cruise ships ply the Red River. The luxury liner *Lord Selkirk II* cruises Lake Winnipeg. It leaves from Selkirk and docks at Gimli, Gull Harbour, and destinations on northern Lake Winnipeg.

York boats

A modern stern-wheeler on the Red River

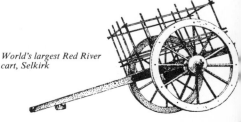

World's largest Red River cart, Selkirk

From rivers flowing into and out of the lake, fur traders paddled their canoes west to the Rockies and east to the Great Lakes.

Birchbark canoes were succeeded by York boats and later by steamboats which transported supplies and trade goods, via the lake and the Saskatchewan River, to Edmonton until the late 1800s. Schooners provisioned settlements bordering the lake and tugboats hauled lumber from mills on the Winnipeg River.

In the 1870s Icelanders settled at

Gimli—"home of the gods" in their language. Today, Lake Winnipeg's fishing fleet, based at Gimli, nets whitefish, sauger, walleye and the famous Manitoba delicacy—goldeye. The lake yields half of the province's commercial catch.

The first resort on the lake, at Winnipeg Beach, opened in 1903. Now cottages and recreation areas stretch as far north as Hecla Island.

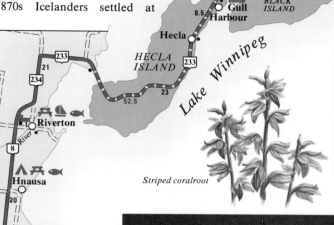

Striped coralroot

HECLA PROVINCIAL PARK

This provincial park consists of islands strewn like stepping stones across Lake Winnipeg. Hecla Island, the park's largest, has stands of red pine, unusual in northern Manitoba. Trembling aspen, jack pine, birch, tamarack and black spruce are found on the western part of the island. Striped coralroot, a vivid lavender orchid, grows in pastures on the eastern shore, where Icelandic farmers once cut hay. At the southern end of Hecla, marshes support Canada, blue and snow geese, whistling swans, bald eagles, and some 15 species of ducks.
□ Hecla Island is linked to the mainland by a causeway. A ferry runs between Gull Harbour on Hecla Island and nearby Black Island. The park's other islands are accessible by boat.

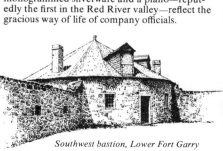
Restored Lutheran church, Hecla

HECLA

A Lutheran church built in 1922 is part of a reconstruction of this Icelandic fishing community in Hecla Provincial Park.

In 1875-76, 1,500 Icelanders immigrated to Manitoba after a volcanic eruption destroyed their farms. They settled on the western shore of Lake Winnipeg and on Hecla Island, where abundant fish, forests and pastures seemed to assure prosperity.

Life in Canada was as harsh as in Iceland. Settlers died of scurvy and smallpox during the first years. After repeated crop failures many families left. In 1878, those settlers who stayed founded the self-governing republic of New Iceland. It had a constitution and a provisional government, which levied taxes and organized schools. The colony's special status ended in 1881 when the northern border of what was then Manitoba was extended to include the republic.

LOWER FORT GARRY

The hustle and bustle of the fur trade is recaptured at Lower Fort Garry National Historic Park, a reconstruction of the Hudson's Bay Company's district headquarters from 1831 to 1837.

Costumed personnel bake hardtack, scones and bannock, spin and card wool, and make soap and candles. The sales shop is stocked with the kinds of goods offered to farmers, trappers and housewives a century ago—sugar, tea, traps, rum, guns and Hudson's Bay blankets, and such luxuries as perfumes and spices. In the shop's third-floor loft are a fur-baling press and hundreds of muskrat, beaver, wolf and fox pelts. The Big House was built of local limestone in 1832 for HBC Governor George Simpson. Its fine china, monogrammed silverware and a piano—reputedly the first in the Red River valley—reflect the gracious way of life of company officials.

Southwest bastion, Lower Fort Garry

Fur Loft, Lower Fort Garry

A Fisherman's Paradise on the Edge of the Shield

Red River Valley/Winnipeg River

Dark and brooding, an endless repetition of rocks, trees and water, the Canadian Shield dips beneath the prairie in southeastern Manitoba. But between prairie and Shield is a vast area of sandy soil that supports jack pine, elm, birch and trembling aspen. A discontinuous chain of provincial forest reserves—Sandilands, Agassiz and Belair—stretches north from the Manitoba-Minnesota border to Lake Winnipeg. Lumber and pulpwood are harvested here for mills on the Winnipeg River,

LOCKPORT
The only lock on the Prairies was opened here in 1910. It bypasses St. Andrews rapids on the Red River near St. Andrews and gives access to Winnipeg and Lake Winnipeg. Above the lock is the Red River Floodway. After winters of heavy snowfall, sudden spring thaws often caused the Red River to flood, turning the flat basin around Winnipeg into a vast lake. In 1950, when the river rose 10 metres above normal, Winnipeg suffered a major flood. Today the Red River Floodway diverts floodwaters around the city. Opened in 1968, the channel is 47 kilometres long and is almost as wide as the Red River is at Winnipeg.
□ Also upstream from the lock is the former home of Arctic explorer Capt. William Kennedy (1814-90). The fieldstone and Tyndall limestone house (1866) is now a museum. Kennedy is buried in the graveyard at St. Andrew's Anglican Church.

Tyndall stone quarries, Garson

GARSON
Tyndall limestone, quarried here since 1895 from of the world's oldest sedimentary rock formations. been used in many important Canadian buildings including the Parliament Buildings in Ottawa and Manitoba Legislative Building in Winnipeg. The grayish limestone contains the fossils of marine animals that lived in warm seas that covered much North America 400 million years ago.

ST. ANDREWS
St. Andrew's Anglican Church (1849) is the oldest stone church in western Canada continuously used for worship. It has original pews and buffalo-hide kneeling pads. Above the altar is a stained-glass window dedicated to the Rev. William Cockran, missionary and founder of the St. Andrews parish. He is buried in the adjoining graveyard.

St. Andrew's Anglican Church, St. Andrews

Prairie crocuses

BIRDS HILL PROVINCIAL PARK
Birds Hill is an esker—a long, narrow ridge of sand and gravel deposited by a glacial stream. Settlers once escaped to this ridge when the Red River flooded. Today a provincial park provides escape from city life in nearby Winnipeg.
□ The prairie crocus, Manitoba's floral emblem, grows on much of the park's uncultivated prairie. In late summer grasslands here are dotted with many-flowered asters, goldenrods and blazing stars.
□ The park is the western limit of the eastern white cedar, which grows here in low-lying peat bogs. Oaks, stunted and gnarled by poor soil and by the short, dry summers, grow in well-drained areas.

COOKS CREEK
Two buildings here are one man's expression of religious faith—the Grotto of Our Lady of Lourdes and the Grotto-Church of the Immaculate Conception. The Rev. Phillip Ruh, Oblate pastor of the Cooks Creek parish for 32 years, supervised their design and construction in the early 1950s. The grotto, the site of an annual August pilgrimage, commemorates the reported 1858 apparition of the Virgin Mary at Lourdes, France.
□ The adjacent grotto-church has a cluster of ornate Byzantine cupolas.

Grotto-Church of the Immaculate Conception, Cooks Creek

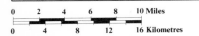

0	2	4	6	8	10 Miles
0	4	8	12		16 Kilometres

which tumbles along the rugged edge of the Canadian Shield from Lake of the Woods to Lake Winnipeg.

The Winnipeg River was a voyageur's nightmare of boiling rapids, dizzying whirlpools and spectacular falls. Seven portages could be seen from one spot alone.

In places, the river has been tamed by hydroelectric dams whose reservoirs drowned many rapids and falls. Although the river is a power source, it is also a fisherman's paradise. It teems with walleye, northern pike, sturgeon and mooneye. Anglers' boats anchor safely in placid coves or by granite outcrops.

Southwest of the river lies a broad forest belt. Beyond is fertile farmland. And to the northeast is the Shield—immutable and untamed.

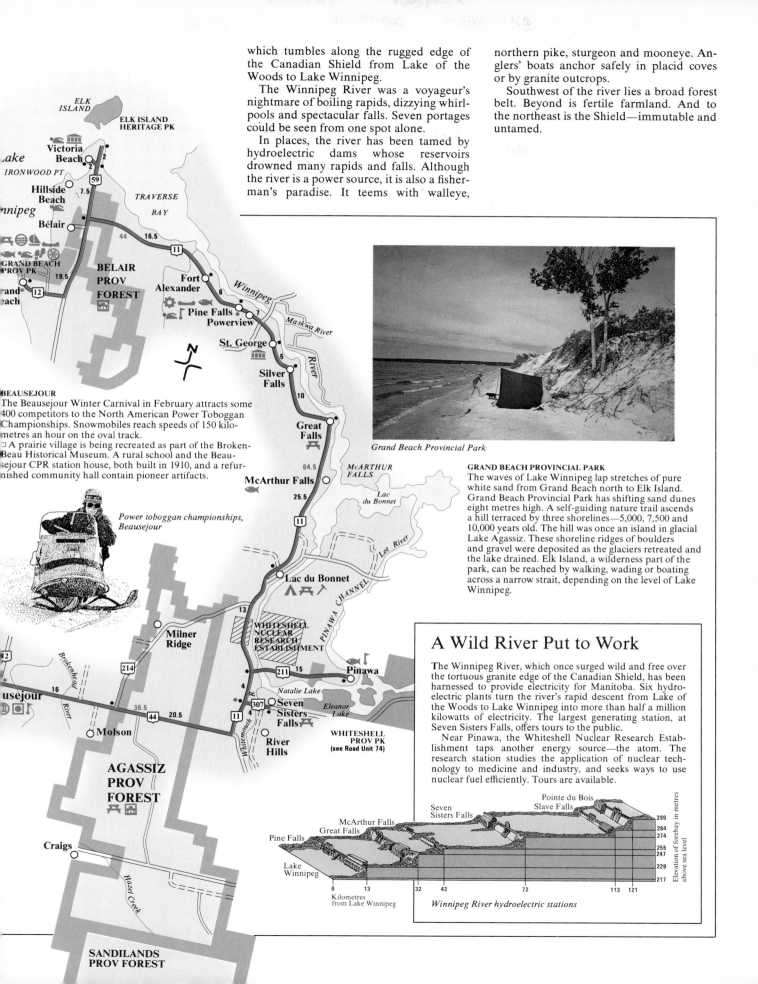

Grand Beach Provincial Park

BEAUSEJOUR

The Beausejour Winter Carnival in February attracts some 400 competitors to the North American Power Toboggan Championships. Snowmobiles reach speeds of 150 kilometres an hour on the oval track.

□ A prairie village is being recreated as part of the Broken-Beau Historical Museum. A rural school and the Beausejour CPR station house, both built in 1910, and a refurnished community hall contain pioneer artifacts.

Power toboggan championships, Beausejour

GRAND BEACH PROVINCIAL PARK

The waves of Lake Winnipeg lap stretches of pure white sand from Grand Beach north to Elk Island. Grand Beach Provincial Park has shifting sand dunes eight metres high. A self-guiding nature trail ascends a hill terraced by three shorelines—5,000, 7,500 and 10,000 years old. The hill was once an island in glacial Lake Agassiz. These shoreline ridges of boulders and gravel were deposited as the glaciers retreated and the lake drained. Elk Island, a wilderness part of the park, can be reached by walking, wading or boating across a narrow strait, depending on the level of Lake Winnipeg.

A Wild River Put to Work

The Winnipeg River, which once surged wild and free over the tortuous granite edge of the Canadian Shield, has been harnessed to provide electricity for Manitoba. Six hydroelectric plants turn the river's rapid descent from Lake of the Woods to Lake Winnipeg into more than half a million kilowatts of electricity. The largest generating station, at Seven Sisters Falls, offers tours to the public.

Near Pinawa, the Whiteshell Nuclear Research Establishment taps another energy source—the atom. The research station studies the application of nuclear technology to medicine and industry, and seeks ways to use nuclear fuel efficiently. Tours are available.

Winnipeg River hydroelectric stations

A Harvest of Wild Rice in Glacier-Carved Lakes

Whiteshell Provincial Park

Some of the world's oldest rocks, an estimated 2½ billion years old, are along the Winnipeg River in Whiteshell Provincial Park. They are the remains of mountains formed millions of years before the Rockies. Repeated glaciation wore down the mountains' soft rock, exposing the ancient outcrops and shaping the low, rolling hills of the Canadian Shield.

Ten thousand years ago glaciers scraped the rock clean of vegetation. First lichen grew on the rock, and then plant seeds from

NUTIMIK LAKE
The Nutimik Lake Natural History Museum displays stuffed animals native to the park. Other exhibits include minerals of the Canadian Shield, and Indian artifacts—rock and bone spearheads and arrowheads, stone axes and shell tools. The Pine Point Hiking Trail passes a series of rapids and falls on the Whiteshell River.

Boulder effigies, Betula Lake

BETULA LAKE
A trail near this lake leads to boulder outlines of birds, turtles, fish and snakes made nearly 1,000 years ago by Algonkian-speaking Indians. The boulder effigies are on a broad, barren granite shelf—an ancient Indian ceremonial medicine ground—alongside the Whiteshell River. The largest outline, 7.5 metres long, is of a turtle.

SANDILANDS PROVINCIAL FOREST
Within this forest reserve the Trans-Canada Highway crosses seven sandridges, former shorelines of glacial Lake Agassiz. Tamarack and cedar swamps between the ridges abound with deer, moose, beaver, lynx, wolves and bears. There are hiking, cross-country skiing and snowshoeing trails, and picnic sites along the highway. Hunting is permitted in the reserve and there is fishing in the Whitemouth River for walleye and northern pike.

Sandilands Provincial Forest was established in 1923 to protect ecologically fragile areas. The forest reserve would erode quickly were it cleared for farmland or logged indiscriminately. Controlled logging of mature trees combined with reforestation helps to preserve the area.

RENNIE
As many as 1,000 geese can be seen here in September and October at the Alf Hole Wild Goose Sanctuary, on the Mississippi flyway migration route. An interpretive center has migratory route maps, stuffed geese and an audiovisual presentation. In 1939 outdoorsman Alfred Hole nurtured four abandoned goslings. Their descendants are part of the sanctuary's resident flock.

Canada geese

Black spruce (left) and trembling aspen

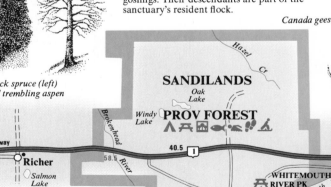

PINELAND FOREST NURSERY
Spruce and pine grown here keep Manitoba forested. Visitors to the nursery, near Hadashville, may tour the seed extraction shed, greenhouses and fields where seedlings are nurtured for three years. Planted in burned or cutover areas, the trees reach harvestable size in 60 years. The nursery has a picnic area on the banks of the Whitemouth River.

HADASHVILLE
In 1955 one of Manitoba's worst fires claimed three lives and ravaged the western edge of Sandilands Provincial Forest. The area has since been reforested.

Visitors to the Manitoba Forestry Association conservation training area, near Hadashville, learn about fire prevention, reforestation and forest ecology. The training area has several nature trails, and a museum that exhibits specimens of local wildlife.

| 0 | 2 | 4 | 6 | 8 | 10 Miles |
| 0 | 4 | 8 | 12 | | 16 Kilometres |

unglaciated areas were scattered on the bleak landscape by winds. Ferns such as rusty woodsia cling precariously to crevices. Along streams boiling over jumbled rock grow eastern white cedar, black ash and mountain maple. Tamarack and black spruce border bogs that cover vast areas of the Shield.

Forests of trembling aspen, jack pine and balsam fir are dotted with some 200 lakes. All but West Hawk Lake—formed by a meteor—are glacial depressions. The lakes attract waterfowl that migrate along the Mississippi flyway. Wild rice is abundant in many of the lakes. At harvest time, Indians bend the tall stalks over canoes and flail the rice with sticks.

Prehistoric Indians used boulders to form outlines of animals and humans on the bare granite near Betula Lake, a ceremonial medicine ground.

The pristine lakes were sought by vacationers at the turn of the century when the area could only be reached by rail. Now several highways, including the Trans-Canada Highway, skirt Manitoba's first provincial park, created in 1962. Still much of the park's wilderness interior is only accessible by air or by water.

An Indian Dish, a Gourmet's Delight

It is known by many names but there is no mistaking its nutlike taste. Wild rice—also known as wild oats, crazy oats and weed of the wheatfields—grows in shallow lakes, marshes and slow streams in Manitoba's Whiteshell Park. In late August or early September Indians in canoes harvest up to 200 kilograms of wild rice a day. Long a staple of the Indian diet, wild rice has become a delicacy popular with gourmets.

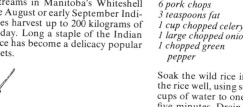

Hunter's Casserole

INGREDIENTS:

1 cup wild rice	1 box mushrooms
6 pork chops	1 can mushroom
3 teaspoons fat	soup
1 cup chopped celery	1 cup milk
1 large chopped onion	½ teaspoon salt
1 chopped green	½ teaspoon oregano
pepper	Pepper to taste

Soak the wild rice in water overnight. Rinse the rice well, using several waters. Using four cups of water to one of rice, boil the rice for five minutes. Drain, rinse, then boil the rice again for 15 to 20 minutes. Drain and rinse again. Put in a casserole. Brown the meat, vegetables and mushrooms until tender. Add seasonings, mushrooms and mushroom soup thinned with milk. Heat well and pour over the rice. Bake for 30 minutes at 350°F.

LILY POND
Named for its myriad fragrant water lilies, Lily Pond (near West Hawk Lake) was carved thousands of years ago by glaciers. One of Canada's sweetest-smelling flowers, the fragrant water lily blooms from June to September. Its white and yellow blossoms open early in the morning and close shortly after noon.

WEST HAWK LAKE
Formed by a meteor some 150 million years ago, this 110-metre-deep lake is Manitoba's deepest. It is stocked with rainbow trout.

Lily Pond, Whiteshell Provincial Park

FALCON BEACH
This town, the focal point of Whiteshell Provincial Park, has riding stables, tennis courts, camping and a golf course. Nearby is a ski resort. Falcon Lake offers boating, waterskiing, swimming and fishing.

EAST BRAINTREE
Eastern white cedar and white and red pine—rare this far north—grow in Northwest Angle Provincial Forest, 40 kilometres south of this town. Granite outcrops rise above the forest's black spruce bogs, where moose often feed. Visitors may camp in the forest reserve.

WHITESHELL PROVINCIAL PARK
Much of Manitoba's first and largest provincial park is wilderness. The Trans-Canada Highway and several provincial highways pass through it, but many of the park's 200 lakes are only accessible by boat, or by plane from Winnipeg, Lac du Bonnet or Pine Falls.

The circular Whiteshell Canoe Route, part of explorer Pierre de La Vérendrye's route to the Red River in 1733, winds deep into the rugged Canadian Shield.

Six hiking and interpretive trails lead park visitors past black spruce swamps, sparkling rivers, beaver ponds and granite outcrops and ridges.

Map labels

WHITESHELL PROV FOREST

River

Eaglenest Lake

Pointe du Bois

Winnipeg River

George Lake

WHITESHELL PROV PK

Turtle Lake

Crowduck Lake

Betula Lake

Whiteshell Lake

Molloy Lake

BOW FALLS

White Lake

Little Whiteshell Lake

Jessica Lake

Lone Island Lake

307

21.5

Brereton Lake

Sailing Lake

St. Claire Lake

44

Bear Lake

South Cross Lake

39.5

THE LILY POND

Caddy Lake

312

8

Star Lake

West Hawk Lake

West Hawk Lake

Barren Lake

Falcon Beach

11.5

301

Falcon Lake

FALCON LAKE SKI RESORT

Falcon River

23.5

1

Boggy River

A Boundary of Lakes and a Thundering Waterfall

Northwestern Ontario

The Rainy River region is a fisherman's paradise which every year yields record-breaking walleye, northern pike and muskellunge. Island-dotted Lake of the Woods is a major waterway in the Rainy River system, taking three-quarters of its flow, then spilling into the Winnipeg River and Lake Winnipeg. Because of the warming influence of the Lake of the Woods, elms, poplars and basswoods grow in an area that might otherwise be dominated by coniferous forest.

Regatta on Lake of the Woods, near Kenora

LAKE OF THE WOODS

This lake, dotted with 14,632 islands, sprawls across parts of Ontario, Manitoba and Minnesota. The first white men in the region sought wealth, not the beauty that now makes this a prime vacation area. Explorers and fur traders pushed west from Lake Superior to harvest what seemed an inexhaustible supply of furs.

Cree, Ojibway and Sioux Indians lived here first. Indian paintings and rock carvings, which have withstood centuries of weathering, have been found at some 20 sites.

Lake of the Woods' permanent population of about 21,000 doubles when summer cottagers arrive, but this is still Indian country. About 2,000 native people live on 10 reserves. Many work as hunters and guides.

Northern pike

KENORA

This mining and pulp and paper town on Lake of the Woods is a popular resort and outfitting center for sportsmen.
□ Nearby Coney Island has picnic facilities, a beach and a boardwalk. The cruiser *Argyle II* stops here.
□ In early August sailboats from Canada, the United States and Britain take part in the Lake of the Woods regatta—a seven-day race from Kenora, around the lake and back.
□ In the chapel of Fort St. Charles is a concrete replica of the fort built in 1732 by Pierre de La Vérendrye.
□ The Lake of the Woods Museum in Memorial Park displays pioneer relics and an extensive collection of local rocks and minerals.

EMO

A regional agricultural fair in this small farming and resort town in mid-August features harness racing, an Ojibway Indian powwow and livestock exhibits.
□ Pioneer artifacts are displayed in the Rainy River District Women's Institute Museum here. The museum is open weekdays and Sundays from mid-May to late September.

RUSHING RIVER PROVINCIAL PARK

The Rushing River tumbles in a series of rapids and falls through this 160-hectare park on the rocky shores of Dogtooth Lake. About 7,500 years ago this area lay beneath glacial Lake Agassiz. Evidence of glaciation can be seen in much of the park's Precambrian bedrock.
□ Rushing River Provincial Park has canoe routes, hiking trails, three sandy beaches, an interpretive center and nearly 200 campsites.

FORT FRANCES

Mainly a pulp and paper town—there are summer tours of the Ontario-Minnesota Paper Company's plant here—Fort Frances is also the access point for a prime vacation, fishing and hunting area. The town is linked by bridge to International Falls, Minn., across the Rainy River.
□ A lookout and museum in the 12-hectare Pithers Point Park, east of town, overlooks the Rainy River.
□ The annual Fun in the Sun Festival in July features log-rolling contests, canoe races, baseball tournaments, skin diving and marathon swimming.

0	8	16	24	32	40 Miles
0	16	32	48	64 Kilometres	

Lake of the Woods, the Rainy River and a string of lakes and rivers along the Canada-U.S. border served as a main route to the furs of the Northwest from about 1780 to 1840. Today the 525-kilometre Boundary Waters Fur Trade Canoe Route, between Kenora and Thunder Bay, evokes the spirit of the voyageur heritage.

Part of the Boundary Waters canoe route follows the southern border of Quetico Provincial Park. Quetico, a rare and special place near the southern limit of the Canadian Shield, is a wilderness with rugged Precambrian ridges, a jumble of lakes, and stands of red and white pine an estimated 200 years old. The only road in the park leads to the Dawson Trail Campgrounds, near where the park's northeastern border meets the Trans-Canada Highway.

East of Quetico, in Kakabeka Falls Provincial Park, the Kaministikwia River roars through a steep-walled gorge after plummeting 33 metres over 100-metre-wide Kakabeka Falls. Below the thundering falls is the Cave of the Winds. Eerie noises believed by the Indians to be spirits are heard when the wind rushes through it. In the shale banks above the falls are fossils 2½ billion years old—among the oldest in the world.

SIOUX NARROWS
Among dozens of Indian rock paintings in this region are representations of a canoe and a fort—perhaps a canoe used by Pierre de La Vérendrye and a fort he may have built on Massacre Island.
□ Moose, deer, bears, wolves and numerous small mammals such as mink roam Sioux Narrows Provincial Park, on Long Point Island in Regina Bay.
□ On summer evenings costumed members of the Whitefish Bay Pow Wow Club perform Indian dances and ceremonies at the Sioux Narrows Teepee Village.

Mink

NESTOR FALLS
A dense forest dominated by aspen, cedar and balsam gives a wilderness flavor to Caliper Lake Provincial Park near here. There is also one of the few remaining stands of red and white pine, trees that were brought by lumbermen from Quebec.

KAKABEKA FALLS
Kakabeka Falls, the "Niagara of the North," is the centerpiece of 387-hectare Kakabeka Falls Provincial Park, 22 kilometres west of Thunder Bay. The park has camping and picnic facilities and a beach. Lookouts provide impressive views of the 33-metre-high falls on the Kaministikwia River.
□ Below the falls, rapids are hemmed in by towering black rock walls, and the wind moans eerily through the narrow entrance of this "Cave of the Winds."

ATIKOKAN
North of Atikokan are iron mines in what was the bed of Steep Rock Lake. It was drained during the Second World War to provide access to the rich iron deposits. From a lookout visitors can view the open-pit mine, pelletizing plant and ore-loading operations of the Caland Ore Company. Steep Rock Iron Mines Ltd. offers group tours by prearrangement.

Round-lobed hepatica

Kakabeka Falls

Osprey

Quetico Provincial Park

QUETICO PROVINCIAL PARK
Only the park's Dawson Trail Campground, on French Lake 48 kilometres east of Atikokan, is accessible by car. The rest of this 4,532-square-kilometre park can be reached only on foot or by canoe.
□ The Quetico wilderness has changed little since the voyageurs paddled through the region in the late 18th and early 19th centuries. The park is still a jumble of pristine lakes and rivers. Here and there rocky outcrops of pink granite contrast with the deep green of pine. On cliffs at 28 sites in the park are primitive Indian paintings of animals and warriors. Most are about 1.5 metres above the waterline, as if done by painters standing in canoes.
Bald eagles and ospreys nest in the park.

A Sleeping Giant on the World's Largest Lake

North Shore, Lake Superior

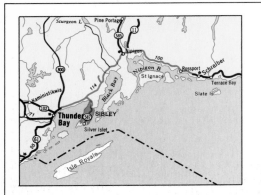

Grain elevators, Thunder Bay

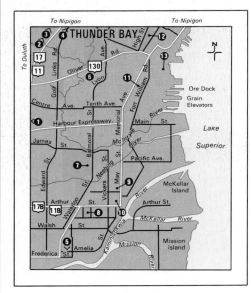

THUNDER BAY

This western terminus of the St. Lawrence–Great Lakes waterway is one of Canada's largest ports. Its main cargoes are iron ore and prairie grain. A drydock here is big enough to accommodate any ship on the Great Lakes. Some of the port's 25 grain elevators may be toured.

□ Formed in 1970 by the amalgamation of Port Arthur and Fort William, Thunder Bay is approximately halfway between Canada's western and eastern limits. The city is also the center of Canada's largest pulp-and-paper-producing area.

□ A granite memorial commemorates the first fort here, built in 1678. Some 125 years later it was named Fort William and became the main post of the North West Company. Fort William Historical Park can be visited in the summer.

□ Boulevard Lake Park, 86 scenic hectares on the Current River, has playgrounds, picnic facilities and a beach. The Black Bay Bridge (1911) over the Current River was the first reinforced concrete bridge in Canada.

□ A recreation of a logging camp (c.1910) is the main attraction of Centennial Park.

1 Fort William Historical Park
2 Boulevard Lake Park
3 Centennial Park
4 Tourist Information (April-October)
5 Chippewa Park
6 Lakehead University
7 Centennial Botanical Conservatory
8 Vickers Park
9 Tourist Information
10 Thunder Bay Historical Museum
11 CAA
12 Hillcrest Park
13 Tourist Information (April-October)

LOON

Visitors to the open-pit mine of the Thunder Bay Amethyst Mining Company at Eagle Lake can dig their own samples of this semiprecious stone. Amethyst, a variety of crystallized quartz is used in jewelry. Large pieces of granite flecked with amethyst are used as decorative building stone.

SILVER ISLET

This dot of rock, some 24 metres in diameter and never more than 2.5 metres above the water, became Canada's first major source of silver when a vertical vein was discovered in 1868. More than $3,000,000 worth of ore was mined before 1884, when the shaft reached a depth of 450 metres and it became impossible to keep the water out of it.

Fort of the 'Great Rendezvous'

In the early 19th century Fort William was the inland headquarters of North West Company fur traders. Every summer more than 2,000 voyageurs and traders met there for the "Great Rendezvous," the company's annual meeting.

Voyageurs, their canoes loaded with furs, had paddled up to 4,830 kilometres from as far west as Fort Chipewyan on Lake Athabasca. Others brought canoes full of trade goods from Montreal. While company partners from the Northwest and from Montreal settled accounts and planned strategy against trading rivals, voyageurs brawled, feasted and drank.

Fort William has been reconstructed as it was in 1816, with 42 buildings inside a palisade. There are storehouses, artisans' shops, a jail, and the Council House where company partners conducted business. Craftsmen build traditional birchbark canoes, and fiddlers play tunes the voyageurs sang.

Piping visitors into Fort William Historical Park

| 0 | 2 | 4 | 6 | 8 | 10 | Miles |
| 0 | 4 | 8 | 12 | 16 | Kilometres |

Ontario's highest cliffs, The Sleeping Giant, Ouimet Canyon (a great gorge that cuts through the wilderness), splendid scenery and abundant wildlife—all are preserved in five provincial parks in this section of Lake Superior's north shore.

The Canadian Shield, the ruggedly beautiful upland that is almost half of Canada, dips into Lake Superior here. Rivers meander through a maze of lakes, dense forests and huge outcrops of the world's oldest rock on their way to the largest freshwater lake in the world. Near Lake Superior many of these rivers surge over sheer precipices or tumble down steplike plateaus, creating cascades such as Rainbow Falls and Middle Falls. The islands that thrust out of Lake Superior still have the look of the primeval.

Ontario's highest cliffs (reaching 1,287 metres) share Sibley Provincial Park with The Sleeping Giant—a long, low hill that resembles a reclining figure. The 243-square-kilometre park includes most of the Sibley Peninsula, except for Silver Islet, a century-old settlement where a major silver discovery was made in 1868.

Northeast of Sibley, arctic plants grow on the floor of Ouimet Canyon. This five-kilometre-long gorge may have been carved millions of years ago by a glacier, or it may be a gigantic fault in the earth's crust.

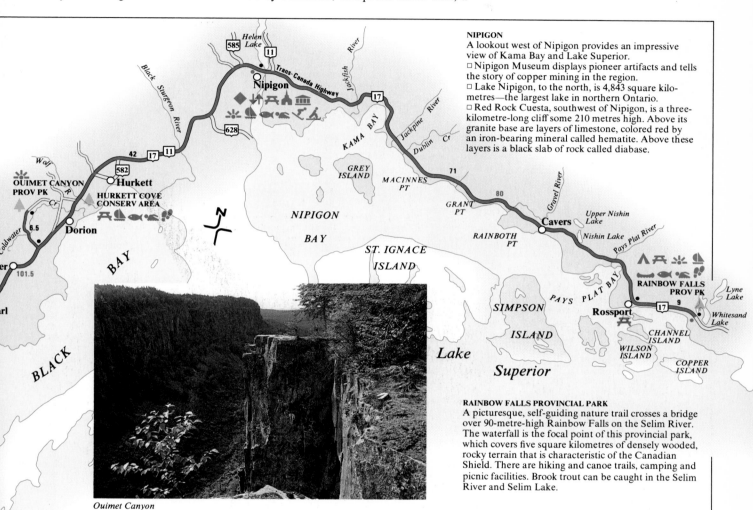

Ouimet Canyon

NIPIGON

A lookout west of Nipigon provides an impressive view of Kama Bay and Lake Superior.
□ Nipigon Museum displays pioneer artifacts and tells the story of copper mining in the region.
□ Lake Nipigon, to the north, is 4,843 square kilometres—the largest lake in northern Ontario.
□ Red Rock Cuesta, southwest of Nipigon, is a three-kilometre-long cliff some 210 metres high. Above its granite base are layers of limestone, colored red by an iron-bearing mineral called hematite. Above these layers is a black slab of rock called diabase.

RAINBOW FALLS PROVINCIAL PARK

A picturesque, self-guiding nature trail crosses a bridge over 90-metre-high Rainbow Falls on the Selim River. The waterfall is the focal point of this provincial park, which covers five square kilometres of densely wooded, rocky terrain that is characteristic of the Canadian Shield. There are hiking and canoe trails, camping and picnic facilities. Brook trout can be caught in the Selim River and Selim Lake.

[SIB]LEY PROVINCIAL PARK

[This] 243-square-kilometre park occupies most of the Sibley [pen]insula. At the tip of the peninsula is The Sleeping [Gia]nt, a hill that, when viewed from Thunder Bay, [rese]mbles a reclining man. The park's Giant Fire Tower [trai]l leads to a fire tower overlooking Thunder Bay. Nearby [Sea] Lion Rock resembles the snout of a seal.
[Th]e three-kilometre Piney Wood [s] Nature Trail, one of 13 trails [in Si]bley, ends at Joe Lake, a [wat]ering ground for moose.
[Pe]regrine falcons, mourning [dove]s, mockingbirds and spotted [sand]pipers are among 200 bird [speci]es found in Sibley. Ravines [in th]e park support green adder's [mou]th and yellow lady's-slipper.

Flying squirrel

OUIMET CANYON PROVINCIAL PARK

The park preserves Ouimet Canyon, a spectacular tree-lined gorge 67 kilometres east of Thunder Bay. Sheer cliffs plunge 90 to 120 metres to rock piles at the floor of the canyon. Several plant species usually found only in the Arctic grow on the canyon floor, which is kept cold by winter ice that persists into summer. Arctic wintergreen and several species of northern liverwort grow among thick carpets of moss. Pussy willows, normally upright, grow horizontally. Stunted cedar and birch trees are also found along the canyon floor. Gnarled jack pine and spruce protrude from the canyon's rim. Looming out of the base of the gorge near the west wall is a high rock pinnacle named Indian Head for its resemblance to a human profile.
□ Ouimet Canyon is 150 metres wide and nearly five kilometres long. There are no camping facilities in the eight-square-kilometre park. A kilometre-long trail leads from a parking lot to the rim of the canyon. Signs warn visitors to explore with caution: there are no fences along the rim and trails that skirt it are often slippery.

Common raven

Where Spectacular Surf Batters Earth's Oldest Rocks

Eastern Shore, Lake Superior

Between Sault Ste. Marie and Wawa the Trans-Canada Highway cuts through rock formations that are among the oldest of the earth's crust. Formed between one and two billion years ago, they are part of the Canadian Shield—rugged, erosion-rounded hills that occupy two-thirds of the surface area of Ontario. Beneath the Shield lies most of the province's mineral resources; on it grows most of Ontario's timber and pulpwood.

Until the Trans-Canada Highway

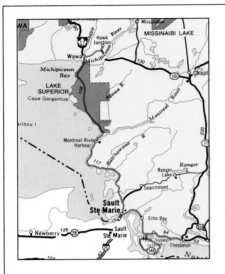

WAWA
The Surluga Loop Road, about a kilometre east of the town of Wawa, winds for 10 kilometres through scenic goldfields. Nine abandoned mines are accessible from the narrow dirt and gravel road. Wawa's short-lived gold rush (1897-1903) produced nuggets and ore worth several million dollars. Today Wawa is an iron-mining and tourist center.
□ A nine-metre steel sculpture of a goose—*wawa* is Ojibway for wild goose—stands at a highway junction south of here. Its predecessor, a smaller concrete statue of a goose, is eight kilometres south at Fort Friendship, a reconstruction of a fur-trading post that once stood beside the Michipicoten River.
□ At Michipicoten, white wooden crosses in an Ojibway burial ground overlook the Magpie River near High Falls. There are picnic facilities beside the 23-metre-high cascade.

HAWK JUNCTION
A spur line of the Algoma Central Railway connects Wawa and Michipicoten with the railway's main north-south line. Motorists can leave their cars at the Hawk Junction station and take the train into the heart of the Algoma wilderness.
□ Canoeists can paddle 72 kilometres of lakes and rivers (with portages) between Hawk Junction and Michipicoten.

LAKE SUPERIOR PROVINCIAL PARK
Sandspits and dunes are common along the beaches in this 1,554-square-kilometre park. Hills rising above Lake Superior offer magnificent views of offshore islands, rocky shorelines and dense forests. Shoreline terraces, some more than 60 metres high, are the remains of ancient beaches raised by shifts in the earth's crust.
□ Several canoe routes wind through this rugged wilderness. The 57-kilometre Sand River Canoe Route drops more than 180 metres along a course that includes Calwin and Lady Evelyn falls.
□ Naturalists conduct walks on the park's many nature trails. At Agawa Bay steps lead down a cliff to Indian rock paintings thought to be more than 200 years old.
□ Many of the park's lakes and rivers are well-stocked with speckled and rainbow trout. Moose, timber wolves and black bears roam the forests. There are two species of nonpoisonous snakes, and several species of frogs, toads and salamanders in the park.
□ Northern birds such as arctic three-toed woodpeckers and boreal chickadees share the deciduous and boreal forests here with such southern birds as boblinks and scarlet tanagers. More than 160 bird species have been spotted in the park.

Muskrat

Indian rock painting, Agawa Bay, Lake Superior Provincial Park

PANCAKE BAY PROVINCIAL PARK
A three-kilometre-long sand beach bordering Pancake Bay on Lake Superior is a feature of this park. Rainbow trout, coho salmon and yellow perch can be caught here. The park has camping and picnic facilities, and hiking trails.

| 0 | 4 | 8 | 12 | 16 | 20 Miles |
| 0 | 8 | 16 | 24 | | 32 Kilometres |

reached Wawa in 1960, much of this region was accessible only by train, floatplane and canoe. Huge tracts of this northland are still as unspoiled as they were when the first explorers arrived 250 years ago.

Brooding mountains, foaming rivers, spring-fed lakes and rock-studded bays give Lake Superior's north shore a character that is unique among the Great Lakes. Spectacular surf usually batters much of Superior's shore. Here and there broad avenues of white sand curl around sheltered coves and bays. In the fall a belt of dense hardwoods, stretching for almost 145 kilometres north and east of Sault Ste. Marie, is a dazzling array of colors.

From May to mid-October the Algoma Central Railway's tour train from Sault Ste. Marie travels to the Agawa Canyon in the heart of this wilderness. The nine-hour return trip includes a two-hour stopover at Agawa Canyon Park where visitors can picnic, fish, climb to a lookout, hike to Bridal Veil Falls, and explore the canyon.

'Snow train' to Agawa Canyon

AGAWA BAY
More than two centuries ago an Ojibway chief led a war party across Lake Superior and recorded his victory in rock paintings on a cliff face in Agawa Bay. In 1851 Henry Schoolcraft, an Indian agent at Sault Ste. Marie, Mich., found the paintings and carefully described them, but neglected to say where they were.

Starting in 1958 a Canadian museum art researcher, Selwyn Dewdney, spent 14 months tracking down clues that finally led him to Agawa Bay and the paintings. Today the pictographs are preserved, and can be seen by the public, in Lake Superior Provincial Park.

AGAWA CANYON
This scenic canyon can be reached by the Algoma Central Railway's excursion train from Sault Ste. Marie (May to mid-October). Passengers have a two-hour stopover to explore the canyon, to fish, picnic and enjoy the beauty of Bridal Veil Falls. A 'snow train' excursion is available on weekends from December to April.

International bridge, Sault Ste. Marie

SAULT STE. MARIE
This is Canada's second largest steel-producing city (after Hamilton) and has one of the busiest canals in the St. Lawrence Seaway system. A lock here and locks on the American side of the St. Mary's River, which links Lakes Huron and Superior, handle more than 100,000,000 tonnes of cargo annually, mostly grain and iron ore. The city is the gateway to the vast Algoma wilderness.
□ A replica of a lock built in 1799 by the North West Company for its freighter canoes is on the Abitibi Paper Company grounds.
□ Ermatinger House, a two-story, Georgian-style stone dwelling built in 1814, has been a residence, hotel, post office, and courthouse. It now is a museum and a national historic site.
□ Visitors to Ontario Air Service, headquarters of the world's largest fleet of planes (45) for fighting forest fires, can see some of the aircraft and fire-bombing apparatus.
□ Military relics and a local history collection are displayed in the Sault Historical Society Museum.
□ A three-kilometre international bridge links the city with Sault Ste. Marie, Mich.

Ermatinger House, Sault Ste. Marie

THESSALON
The lumber town of Thessalon is the access point for a large recreation area to the north.
□ A plaque in Lakeside Park commemorates the capture of the armed American schooners *Tigress* and *Scorpion* in 1814.

ST. JOSEPH ISLAND
The ruins of the most westerly military post in Upper Canada are preserved in Fort St. Joseph National Historic Park. The fort, built in 1796, was an important trading station and British military post in the War of 1812. An interpretive center displays artifacts unearthed by archaeologists and tells the history of the fort. The park is open from mid-May to late October.
□ At the St. Joseph Island Museum, local pioneer artifacts are displayed in a restored church, barn, schoolhouse and log cabin.
□ St. Joseph Island, 30 kilometres long and 24 kilometres wide, lies in the channel between Lakes Huron and Superior. Farmland, dense hardwood forests, and many sheltered bays and inlets characterize the island. Ojibway Indians called it *Anipich*, meaning place of the hardwoods. In early April islanders hold a maple syrup festival.

On a Record-Sized Island, the Home of Gitchi-Manitou

Manitoulin Island

Manitoulin Island is the world's largest island in a lake. It has nearly 1,600 kilometres of picturesque shoreline—most of it facing the open water of Lake Huron and Georgian Bay, the rest along the North Channel that separates the island from the mainland.

A series of bridges and causeways connects the island and the mainland. From spring to fall a 220-car ferry sails regularly between southern Manitoulin and the Bruce Peninsula.

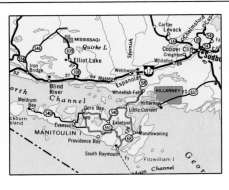

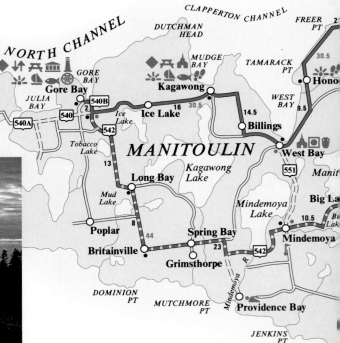

Western Manitoulin Historical Museum, Gore Bay

GORE BAY

The East Bluff Lookout and picnic site near here gives a view of the surrounding hills, the clear waters of Gore Bay and the North Channel of Lake Huron.
□ The Western Manitoulin Historical Museum is in a former courthouse and jail. Some cells, bars and jail furniture remain. There are relics from an ancient Sheguiandah Indian settlement, old coins and pioneer articles, and a collection of objects from a wreck believed to be that of La Salle's *Griffon*, the first ship to sail the upper Great Lakes. (The vessel is thought to have sunk in a storm in Mississagi Strait at the west end of Manitoulin Island in 1679.)
□ Gore Bay, a quiet little town of wide, tree-lined streets, well-groomed lawns and handsome houses, is the government center for the island.

BIRCH ISLAND

Dreamer's Rock, on nearby Little Cloche Island, affords a fine view of the North Channel, Bay of Islands and La Cloche Mountains. A plaque tells that Indian youths were once required to fast here for many days before entering manhood. Through dreams, the youths would receive guidance from a "guardian spirit."
□ A stone monument on this island northeast of Manitoulin Island commemorates a visit by President Franklin D. Roosevelt in 1943.

KAGAWONG

Lake Kagawong, almost at the center of Manitoulin Island, is drained by the Kagawong River which drops over Bridal Veil Falls. A picnic park here has nature trails and, at the brink of the falls, a lookout.
□ St. John's Anglican Church, a small clapboard structure beside the village dock, has a pulpit fashioned from the bow of an old ship. Floats from fishing nets decorate the pews.

Lighthouse, South Baymouth

SOUTH BAYMOUTH

From spring to fall the 110-car ferry M.S. *Chi-Cheeman* (Indian for Big Canoe) sails between here and Tobermory, at the tip of the Bruce Peninsula.
□ The Little Red Schoolhouse Museum, an original school building, contains early school books and desks, pioneer articles and local handicrafts.
□ There are camping and picnic facilities in John Budd Memorial Park. A Fisheries Research Station north of the village welcomes visitors.

Some 800 kilometres of roads skirt the island's shoreline and weave among clear lakes, sparkling streams and waterfalls. Smallmouth bass, northern pike, muskellunge, walleye, and speckled lake trout can be caught in many of the island's 108 lakes. There are many fine sand beaches and the waters off Manitoulin are a favorite with sailors. The town of Little Current is a summer center for divers who come to explore the numerous wrecks in the waters of Lake Huron and the North Channel.

The influence of the Ottawa and Ojibway Indians is still strong on Manitoulin Island, once thought to be the sanctuary of both the good spirit Gitchi-Manitou and his evil adversary Matchi-Manitou. At many places on the island, archaeologists have found 12,000-year-old evidence of Indian habitation. Near some of these sites, local Indians make handmade articles for sale. Local Indian handicrafts are also featured at the Native Arts and Crafts Festival at West Bay in late July. In early August a weekend-long tribal ceremony is held at Wikwemikong, on the 466-square-kilometre Manitoulin Island Indian Reserve, one of the largest Indian settlements in Ontario.

ESPANOLA
A ghost town during the Depression of the 1930s, Espanola revived when a kraft paper mill was established in 1945.
□ The town's nine-hole golf course on the Spanish River is the only one between Sudbury and Sault Ste. Marie. Espanola has public tennis courts and an Olympic-sized swimming pool.

MANITOWANING
Indians believed that this area was the home of the Great Spirit. Gitchi-Manitou. Manitowaning means "den of the Great Spirit."
□ St. Paul's Anglican Church, a white wooden building completed by Indians in 1849, is the oldest church on Manitoulin Island.
□ The Assiginack Museum includes a 19th-century stone jail, a log barn, smithy and one-room schoolhouse. Exhibits detailing the life of Indians and settlers in the region include a beaded wampum belt worn by Chief Assiginack, an Ottawa Indian who sided with the British during the War of 1812.
□ A playground and a beach are near the community dock, where the S.S. *Norisle*—the first car ferry to sail between Manitoulin and Tobermory—is moored.

LITTLE CURRENT
The Little Current-Howland Centennial Museum, 10 kilometres south at Sheguiandah, includes three two-story log houses, a two-story log granary and a blacksmith's shop. The museum displays Indian and pioneer artifacts. There are picnic facilities on the museum's wooded, parklike grounds.
□ Little Current's annual Haweater Festival, held the first weekend in August, features a horse show and riding competitions, handicraft displays, dancing and a midway. The town's September cattle auction is one of North America's largest.
□ A plaque at the R.H. Ripley House tells of an attempt to establish a Hudson's Bay Company post here in 1856. It was abandoned due to opposition from Indians and missionaries. Ripley House was built on the site of the post, whose stone base forms part of the foundation.
□ Near Little Current are the remains of a Jesuit mission operated in 1648-50 by the Rev. Joseph Poncet, the first known European resident of the island.

Thunderbird, *a painting by Francis Kagige*

Woodcock

WIKWEMIKONG
During the first weekend in August, 18 tribes from six North American Indian nations perform Indian songs and dances, and exhibit handicrafts at a tribal ceremony here. Throughout the summer, Indian arts and crafts can be purchased at a crafts center. Wikwemikong is in the Manitoulin Island Indian Reserve.
□ On the walls of a Wikwemikong elementary school are 30 paintings of Canadian wildlife by Indian artist Francis Kagige. The school is open to the public in summer.

McKerrow
17
Spanish River
Espanola
Anderson Lake
Apsey Lake
68
Loon Lake
Lang Lake
West River
West River
Willisville
29
Charlton Lake
Whitefish Falls
49.5
OF ISLANDS
Birch Island
McGREGOR BAY
GREAT LA CLOCHE ISLAND
McGregor Bay
20.5
Little Current
STRAWBERRY ISLAND
Sheguiandah
TEN MILE PT
BAY
24.5
34
SANDY PT
68
Turtle Lake
MANITOWANING
SMITH BAY
CAPE SMITH
Wikwemikong
Buzwah
15
Manitowaning
Two O'Clock
HORSEBURGH PT
Sucker Lake
9
ndfield
44
Hilly Grove
8.5
SOUTH BAY
GEORGIAN BAY
ISLAND
ce
y to ermory e Peninsula
South Baymouth
Huron

Where a Pot of Gold Is
a Basin of Nickel and Copper

Northeastern Shore, Georgian Bay

The Big Nickel, Sudbury

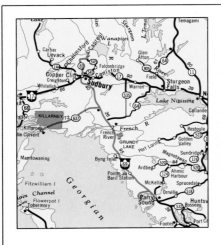

Steam locomotive,
Capreol

CAPREOL
Visitors to this town in the Sudbury Basin can
see the computer heart of the Canadian
National Railways freight system in operation.
□ A railway handcar, a caboose and a steam
locomotive are displayed in Precott Park. Also
in the park is a 12-tonne fragment of an
enormous meteorite that plummeted to earth
near here in 1911 or 1912.
□ Near Capreol there is good fishing for walleye
and northern pike in Burwash, Ferris and Takko
lakes, and in the Groundhog and Vermilion
rivers.

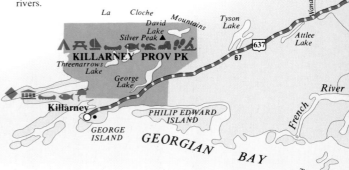

KILLARNEY PROVINCIAL PARK
This primitive park preserves some 345 square kilometres
of prime wilderness on the north shore of Georgian Bay.
Located on the southern part of the Precambrian Shield,
Killarney includes rock formations that are more than two
billion years old. In a small valley are giant, 200-year-old
sugar maple and yellow birch trees—some of the few in
Ontario that escaped the logger's ax.
□ Fishing is poor in the park's acidic lakes but their waters
are so clear that it is possible to see as deep as 30 metres.
□ The 32-kilometre Silver Peak Trail winds through the La
Cloche Mountains to the summit of Silver Peak, 536 metres
above sea level and the highest point in the park. The George
Lake campground has tent and trailer sites, a beach and a
nature interpretation program.

FRENCH RIVER
Most rivers create their own beds by erosion, but the
island-dotted French River follows a complex of natural
fissures and faults as it winds 120 kilometres between
Lake Nipissing and Georgian Bay. The river is a maze
of channels, secluded bays and countless rapids and
falls. Kettles—waterworn holes in rock—can be seen
near Chaudière Dam. There are Indian rock paintings
on granite outcrops near Keso Point. The French River
is a challenge to canoeists. Fishing is excellent for
walleye, muskellunge, bass and northern pike.

POINTE AU BARIL
In the late 1800s, a lantern set on a barrel guided fishing
boats into this sheltered harbor—thus the name Pointe
au Baril (Barrel Point). A wooden lighthouse, still in use,
replaced the makeshift marker in 1889.
□ Six kilometres northwest of Pointe au Baril is 80-hectare
Sturgeon Bay Provincial Park—one of the few places in
Ontario where the massasauga rattlesnake is found. An
endangered species, the massasauga is the only venomous
snake in eastern Canada.

KILLBEAR POINT PROVINCIAL PARK
There are some 4 kilometres of sand beach and 6.5 kilometres of hiking trails in this 11.7-square-kilometre park.
Three rocky headlands provide impressive views of some
of the Thirty Thousand Islands. Some of the islands are
bare, craggy rocks; others are heavily wooded and up to
eight kilometres long. As many as 300 deer winter here.

Killarney Provincial Park

0 2 4 6 8 10   Miles

0 4 8 12 16   Kilometres

From the industrial city of Sudbury to the pristine wilderness of Killarney Provincial Park, from the rushing French River to the placid beauty of the Thirty Thousand Islands, this area, known as "Rainbow Country," is full of contrasts.

Nickel and copper from the Sudbury Basin yield more than a third of Ontario's $1.6 billion annual income from minerals. The price Sudbury has had to pay for its mineral wealth is pollution—and its undeserved reputation as a barren, lunarlike no man's land. However, it is blessed with many parks, forested areas, and lakes.

Glaciation and millions of years of erosion have created the rocky, sparsely treed La Cloche Mountains. These low, rounded hills (once as imposing as the Rockies) cut through Killarney Provincial Park. White quartzite, characteristic of the hills, contrasts starkly with the pink and gray granite common elsewhere on Georgian Bay's northern shoreline.

The wide, fast-flowing French River, particularly favored by fishermen for its large and abundant walleye and northern pike, is part of the historic fur-trade route that linked Montreal and Lake Superior. Every summer hundreds of canoeists paddle this swift river.

The Thirty Thousand Islands hug the east coast of Georgian Bay. A three-hour boat tour from Parry Sound provides a close-up view of the world's largest group of freshwater islands.

Slag pouring, Sudbury

SUDBURY
Bell Park, on the shore of Ramsey Lake—one of four lakes in Sudbury—has a 2,600-seat amphitheater. There are summer concerts and art and handicraft displays. A plaque in the park describes the Sudbury Basin, a 56-by-27-kilometre depression believed formed by the impact of a giant meteorite. Huge deposits of nickel and 15 other elements are mined on the rim of the basin by International Nickel and Falconbridge Nickel Mines. Both companies offer tours of their mining and smelting operations. Inco's smelter at Copper Cliff, six kilometres west of Sudbury, has the world's tallest smokestack (380 metres).
□ From Highway 144, west of Sudbury, visitors can view fiery rivers of slag from the city's smelters sliding down immense slag heaps and lighting up the night sky.
□ Visitors to the Canadian Centennial Numismatic Park can tour a model of an underground mine. The Big Nickel, a nine-metre representation of a five-cent piece, stands in the park.

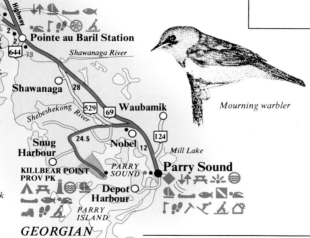

GEORGIAN BAY

Mourning warbler

Grass pink

How Mines Are Worked

In underground mines a main shaft leads to a maze of tunnels on different levels. Miners go down in an elevator cage (1) to one of the levels, then along tunnels, or crosscuts (2), leading to the sections where the ore body is worked. Air is driven into the mine through ventilation shafts (3) by giant fans (4) on the surface.

Drilling and blasting go on in stopes, large openings off the tunnels (5). Ore is mined in various ways. In cut-and-fill mining, one of the commonest methods, miners bore holes into ore-bearing rock with compressed air drills. The holes are loaded with explosives which bring a section of the stope crumbling to the ground. The ore is removed, and the cavity filled with rock, sand or gravel.

Ore is carried along the tunnels by trains running on narrow-gauge tracks or by trackless, rubber-tired trucks (6). It is dropped down a chute (7) to a loading pocket (8). From there, the ore is fed into a crusher (9), where large chunks are broken into smaller pieces for easier hauling. The crushed ore drops to a production shaft (10) and is then hoisted by a skip (11) to the surface, where it is ground, screened, smelted and refined into pure metal.

At Sudbury's Canadian Centennial Numismatic Park a working model of an underground mine has more than 150 metres of tunnels showing stopes with exposed ore bodies, displays of mining procedures, and a room where air is compressed to run the machinery.

PARRY SOUND
From mid-June to mid-September the *Island Queen*, a 30-metre cruise boat, tours Georgian Bay's Thirty Thousand Islands.
□ Ten sets of stairs zigzag up a 24-metre fire tower on a hill in the town. From the top, 76 metres above Georgian Bay, there is a splendid view of the bay and the rolling forest and lake country inland.
□ A plaque in the Parry Sound marketplace records that all 24 persons aboard the side-wheeler *Waubuno* perished when it sank near here in an 1879 snowstorm.
□ Canada's largest public display of live reptiles can be seen at The Reptile House, 16 kilometres south of the town. Exhibited are alligators, lizards, and snakes—including such poisonous species as the massasauga rattlesnake.
□ In the waters of the Parry Sound district, fishermen catch rainbow and brook trout, splake, bass and walleye.

Strongholds of the Past
in a Year-Round Playground

Southeastern Shore, Georgian Bay

On the southeastern shore of Georgian Bay are resorts, marinas and ski hills. But this year-round recreation playground has rich associations with the past. Two sites in this area—Sainte-Marie among the Hurons, and the Royal Navy and Military Establishments—recall events of early Canadian history.

Sainte-Marie among the Hurons, the first European settlement in Ontario, has been reconstructed beside the Wye River east of Midland. From a palisaded stronghold

MEAFORD
The town, heart of a prosperous fruit-farming belt, is surrounded by beaches and ski hills. Every spring trophy-size rainbow trout, coho salmon and hybrid splake are caught in the Big Head River which runs through town. In late April the nearby Beaver River is jammed by a flotilla of bathtubs and homemade boats competing in the annual Beaver River Rat Race.
□ Beautiful Joe, the dog hero of Margaret Marshall Saunders' classic, is buried in a park on the Big Head River. In 1953 the book became the first Canadian work to sell more than a million copies.

THORNBURY
The lovely Beaver Valley is ski hills, orchards and sparkling rivers that harbor rainbow trout. South of town, Eugenia Falls, on the Beaver River, cascades 24 metres over the Niagara Escarpment. The falls, named in 1854 by a former French officer for his Empress Eugénie, was the scene of an 1853 gold rush that yielded worthless pyrites but led to the area's development.

Rainbow trout

CRAIGLEITH PROVINCIAL PARK
Fossilized creatures from a sea that covered the area 375 million years ago are embedded in the limestone terraces of Craigleith Provincial Park on Nottawasaga Bay. An interpretive center, overlooking Nottawasaga Bay, tells how these extinct invertebrates were turned to stone some 200 million years ago.
□ A plaque tells how oil was once extracted from shale here.

Trilobite fossils, Craigleith Provincial Park

OWEN SOUND
Indians called it *Wad-i-need-i-ton,* Beautiful Valley, long before Capt. William Owen sailed into this harbor and named it Owen Sound. Pioneer memorabilia, demonstrations of pioneer crafts and a half-scale model of an Ojibway Indian encampment are features of the County of Grey and Owen Sound Museum.
□ The Tom Thomson Memorial Gallery and Museum of Fine Art commemorates the famous landscape artist who grew up in nearby Leith.

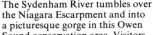

INGLIS FALLS CONSERVATION AREA
The Sydenham River tumbles over the Niagara Escarpment and into a picturesque gorge in this Owen Sound conservation area. Visitors enjoy picnicking, swimming, fishing, boating and hiking, and in winter, snowshoeing and cross-country skiing.

Maidenhair fern

BLUE MOUNTAINS
The scenic caves in the Blue Mountains near Collingwood date from a time when a warm, shallow sea covered Ontario. Although some of the crevices are more than 25 metres deep, handrails allow safe access. A ladder descends to one deep cave where there is year-round ice and snow. Appropriately named for its narrow opening is Fat Man's Misery. The Indian Council Chamber is a reminder that the Hurons lived and worshiped among these rocks. Hart's-tongue, walking and maidenhair ferns are found in Fern Cavern. The pinnacle Ekarenniondi—"where the rock stands out"—was a landmark for the Petun tribes of the Huron nation.

Inglis Falls near Owen Sound

Ekarenniondi, Blue Mountains

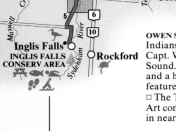

0 1 2 3 4 5 Miles
0 2 4 6 8 Kilometres

on this site, a group of French Jesuits directed their Huronia mission from 1639 to 1649. Here lived Saint Jean de Brébeuf and five other martyred saints.

Indian wars brought the Jesuits' efforts to an early end. Sainte-Marie, though never attacked, became isolated amid deserted Huron villages and increasingly hostile Iroquois. Fearing attack, the Jesuits abandoned their mission, and returned to Quebec. For 300 years, Sainte-Marie among the Hurons—the first bold step into the Ca-

nadian interior—remained a memory. Its recent reconstruction is a tribute to the faith and heroism of its founders.

Five kilometres north of Midland, at Penetanguishene, are the Royal Navy and Military Establishments. Built by the British after the War of 1812, the Establishments—part dockyard, part army camp—

were maintained until the 1850s. A lively settlement of French and English fur traders grew up around these bases. The town of Penetanguishene retains its bilingual character to this day. The bases that were its beginning have been renovated and reconstructed—symbols of the days of British power on the Great Lakes.

Sainte-Marie among the Hurons, with the Martyrs' Shrine in the background

A Lone Outpost and Huron Longhouses

Sainte-Marie among the Hurons was painstakingly reconstructed in the 1960s. Visitors enter through a lobby lined with C. W. Jefferys' illustrations of events in Huronia history, then view a film on life in 17th-century New France. Inside the palisade are residences, a hospital, forge, cookhouse, stables and stockades. A chapel contains the grave of Saint Jean de Brébeuf. The site also preserves the Church of St. Joseph, the oldest Christian shrine in Canada. Overlooking the restoration stands the Martyrs' Shrine, commemorating the Jesuit Fathers.

One of the Huron villages that first drew the missionaries here has been reconstructed in Little Lake Park. Roots, dried corn and herbs hang from bunklined longhouses. Outside are food storage pits and a sweat bath.

Huron longhouse, Midland

PENETANGUISHENE
Many residents of Penetanguishene are descendants of French and English fur traders and pioneers who settled near the Royal Navy and Military Establishments between 1814 and 1856. The one surviving military building, an officers' quarters, has been restored as a museum. St. James-on-the-Lines, a garrison church built in 1836-38, is still used. It has wooden pews carved by soldiers and an aisle wide enough for four men to walk abreast.

Blue Mountain Pottery, Collingwood

COLLINGWOOD
A Great Lakes shipping center for almost a century, Collingwood is now a prosperous year-round resort town. Blue Mountain pottery, developed here in the 1940s, is made with red clay from local creeks. Visitors can watch potters at work.

MIDLAND
A 17th-century Huron Indian Village has been reconstructed beside the Huronia Museum in Midland's Little Lake Park. Indian artifacts and models of Great Lakes ships are displayed in the museum.
□ The Wye Marsh Wildlife Centre has an underwater viewing window, trails, and guided tours.

WASAGA BEACH
The Museum of the Upper Lakes is on an island formed in the Nottawasaga River by silt and sand that collected around the hull of the *Nancy*, a schooner sunk in the War of 1812. The nearby Electronic Theater has a sound-and-light presentation depicting the story of the *Nancy*.
□ Wasaga Beach, 14 kilometres of hard-packed sand on the shore of Georgian Bay, is claimed to be the longest and safest freshwater beach in the world.

WASAGA BEACH PROVINCIAL PARK
Horseshoe-shaped dunes formed 5,000 years ago are preserved in Wasaga Beach Provincial Park. The dunes support plants that are rare in Canada, among them green-leaved rattlesnake plantain and ram's-head and fairy-slipper orchids. The park has supervised swimming, picnic grounds, snowmobile and cross-country ski trails.

Ship's figurehead, Museum of the Upper Lakes, Wasaga Beach

Penetanguishene · Midland · Cawaja Beach · Perkinsfield · Balm Beach · Ossossane Beach · Wahnekewaning Beach · Bluewater Beach · Deanlea Beach · Wendake Beach · Woodland Beach · Allenwood Beach · New Wasaga Beach · Allenwood · Wasaga Beach · Oakview Beach · Springhurst Beach · Brocks Beach · Batteaux · Collingwood · Mair Mills · Pigeon Pt · East Black Bass Bay · Penetang Harbour · Midland Park Lake · Wye Lake · Wye Marsh Wildlife Centre

Bold Headlands, Sheltered Bays, Clear Waters—and Tireless Winds

Bruce Peninsula

Within a few hours' drive of Toronto is an alluring yet accessible wilderness peninsula. Known locally as "the Bruce" this triangle of land jutting into Lake Huron is part of the Niagara Escarpment—a rocky spine arcing northwest from Lake Ontario to Manitoulin Island.

The bold landscape characteristic of the Bruce begins at Wiarton, where Colpoys Bay almost pinches the peninsula into an island. The east coast, on Georgian Bay, is sheer limestone cliffs, pounded and

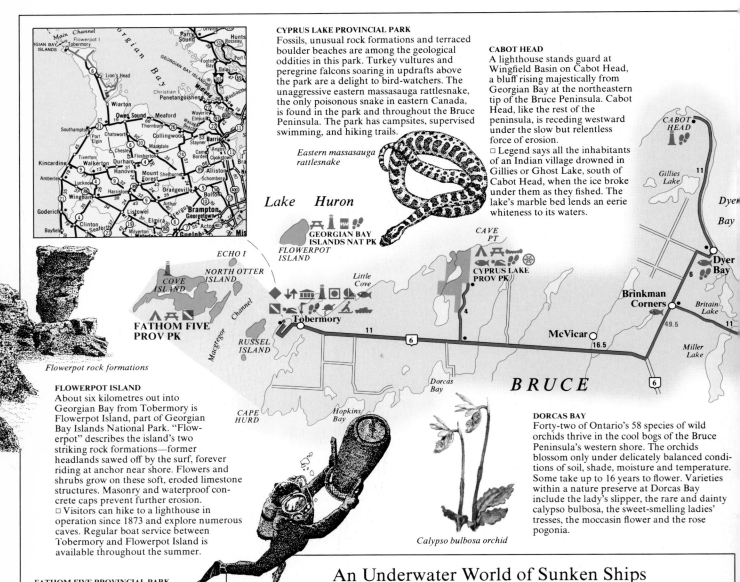

CYPRUS LAKE PROVINCIAL PARK
Fossils, unusual rock formations and terraced boulder beaches are among the geological oddities in this park. Turkey vultures and peregrine falcons soaring in updrafts above the park are a delight to bird-watchers. The unaggressive eastern massasauga rattlesnake, the only poisonous snake in eastern Canada, is found in the park and throughout the Bruce Peninsula. The park has campsites, supervised swimming, and hiking trails.

Eastern massasauga rattlesnake

CABOT HEAD
A lighthouse stands guard at Wingfield Basin on Cabot Head, a bluff rising majestically from Georgian Bay at the northeastern tip of the Bruce Peninsula. Cabot Head, like the rest of the peninsula, is receding westward under the slow but relentless force of erosion.
□ Legend says all the inhabitants of an Indian village drowned in Gillies or Ghost Lake, south of Cabot Head, when the ice broke under them as they fished. The lake's marble bed lends an eerie whiteness to its waters.

Flowerpot rock formations

FLOWERPOT ISLAND
About six kilometres out into Georgian Bay from Tobermory is Flowerpot Island, part of Georgian Bay Islands National Park. "Flowerpot" describes the island's two striking rock formations—former headlands sawed off by the surf, forever riding at anchor near shore. Flowers and shrubs grow on these soft, eroded limestone structures. Masonry and waterproof concrete caps prevent further erosion.
□ Visitors can hike to a lighthouse in operation since 1873 and explore numerous caves. Regular boat service between Tobermory and Flowerpot Island is available throughout the summer.

Calypso bulbosa orchid

DORCAS BAY
Forty-two of Ontario's 58 species of wild orchids thrive in the cool bogs of the Bruce Peninsula's western shore. The orchids blossom only under delicately balanced conditions of soil, shade, moisture and temperature. Some take up to 16 years to flower. Varieties within a nature preserve at Dorcas Bay include the lady's slipper, the rare and dainty calypso bulbosa, the sweet-smelling ladies' tresses, the moccasin flower and the rose pogonia.

FATHOM FIVE PROVINCIAL PARK
Hundreds of scuba divers converge each summer on Canada's first underwater park, where signs guide divers to shipwrecks that include old sailing vessels and early tugs. Fifteen of some 25 wrecks in the 130-square-kilometre park have been explored and identified. An interpretive center pinpoints charted wrecks, some of which are visible from boats. The park will eventually include a land base with campgrounds and picnic areas.

An Underwater World of Sunken Ships

Scores of broken hulls—victims of fierce nor'easters and treacherous shoals—lie beneath the clear waters of Georgian Bay. More than 70 wrecks, ranging from tugs and wooden-hulled schooners to propeller-driven steamers, have been charted near the Bruce Peninsula.

Easiest to locate are the *Sweepstakes,* a schooner lost in 1896, and the *City of Grand Rapids,* which burned in 1907. They are among four hulls lying at depths of three to nine metres in Tobermory's harbor.

The hull of the *China,* a schooner smashed in 1883 on what is now called China Reef, can be seen from

the surface between Wreck Point and China Cove. In 1900 the *Marion L. Breck* went down southwest of Bears Rump. The lighthouse keeper on Flowerpot Island rescued her crew. Capt. John O'Grady of the schooner *Philo Scoville* was not so lucky. He was crushed between his vessel and the rocks during a winter gale in 1889.

In 1901, while towing the schooners *King* and *Brunette,* the steamer *Wetmore* ran aground off Russel Island. All three ships sank. When the water is low, the *Wetmore's* boiler can be seen just above the surface.

chipped by wind and water, and scoured by ancient glaciers. Caves, shoals and rugged rock formations punctuate the ragged shoreline.

Everywhere along the bluff is a view across a bay to distant headlands or offshore islands. Towns and villages surround sheltered bays. Inland are small lakes and, particularly in the north, dense woodlands.

The west side of the peninsula slides into Lake Huron in a series of marshy cedar swamps and shallow inlets. Sand dunes and glacier-scarred ridges parallel the gently sloping shoreline.

One of North America's finest displays of rare wildflowers, ferns and orchids lends a wild beauty to the peninsula. Bears, deer, grouse and coyotes frequent game trails, and eagles are occasionally sighted. Blazed foot trails, including a 145-kilometre section of the famous Bruce Trail, invite visitors off the beaten path to explore ravines, caves, beaches and forest.

The clean, clear waters surrounding the peninsula belie its treacherous reefs and sudden storms. Scores of shipwrecks have been discovered in Georgian Bay and eastern Lake Huron.

A ferry connects Tobermory, at the northern tip of the peninsula, and South Baymouth on Manitoulin Island. In Tobermory, known locally as "the Tub," is a museum displaying pioneer relics and Indian artifacts. The bustling harbor serves as a jumping-off point for visits to Flowerpot Island and Fathom Five Provincial Park.

A Long Trail That Leads Up Into the Clouds

The 700-kilometre Bruce Trail follows the Niagara Escarpment between Queenston in southern Ontario and Tobermory at the tip of the Bruce Peninsula. Weaving through dense cedar and birch forest on the peninsula, the trail passes caves and sheer shale bluffs, and dips down to scenic shoreline villages. Low-lying clouds often envelop hikers at Cabot Head, where the trail traverses some of the highest land in Ontario.

On the Bruce Peninsula, the trail can be entered at Tobermory, Dyer Bay, Cabot Head, Hope Bay, Lion's Head, Cape Croker and Wiarton. A two-kilometre stretch near Halfway Rock Point makes a fine day hike.

A 50-kilometre section between Dunk's Bay and Cabot Head is a tough three-day trek for seasoned backpackers. Hikers are advised to carry canteens: the clean, pure drinking water of Georgian Bay, in full view along much of the Bruce Trail, is often out of reach.

CAPE CROKER
Ojibway Indians have turned the beautiful Cape Croker Indian Reserve into a park. Visitors camp on wooded bluffs overlooking Sydney Bay, or at the water's edge. Nature trails and 24 kilometres of the Bruce Trail run through the park. There are hidden coves, a sandy beach, a playground, picnic areas and good boating and fishing along the rugged coastline. A store near the park entrance offers Indian handicrafts. A lighthouse, reconstructed in 1905, includes part of the original structure erected in the early 1800s to guide ships past the cape's rocky shores.

Limestone cliffs, Bruce Peninsula

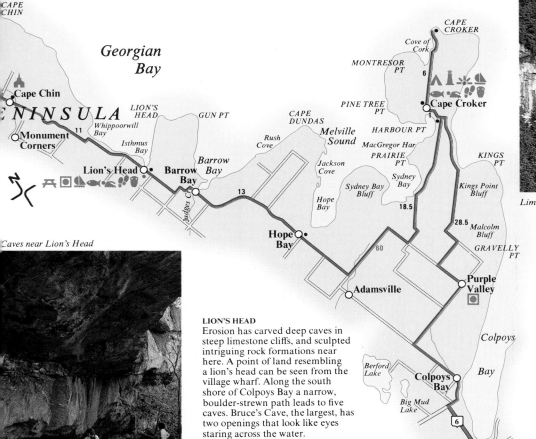

Caves near Lion's Head

LION'S HEAD
Erosion has carved deep caves in steep limestone cliffs, and sculpted intriguing rock formations near here. A point of land resembling a lion's head can be seen from the village wharf. Along the south shore of Colpoys Bay a narrow, boulder-strewn path leads to five caves. Bruce's Cave, the largest, has two openings that look like eyes staring across the water.

WIARTON
A provincial fish hatchery in Wiarton raises three million fish (coho, salmon and species of trout) annually. Visitors see the roe in incubator trays and young fish in holding trays. The hatchery's stocking program has made nearby Colpoys Bay an excellent place to catch rainbow trout. Northern pike inhabit Mountain, Miller and Isaac lakes. Splake (a hybrid trout developed by Canadian biologists) are abundant in the waters off Lion's Head. Lake Huron provides good bass, perch and pike fishing. Bass are found in inland lakes such as Chesley, Gould, Miller, Cyprus, Berford, Cameron and Gillies.

Georgian Bay

CAPE CHIN

Cape Chin

PENINSULA

Monument Corners

LION'S HEAD
Whippoorwill Bay
Isthmus Bay
GUN PT

Lion's Head

Barrow Bay

Judges Cr.

CAPE DUNDAS

Rush Cove

Melville Sound

Jackson Cove

Hope Bay

Sydney Bay Bluff

Sydney Bay

Hope Bay

CAPE CROKER

Cove of Cork

MONTRESOR PT

PINE TREE PT

Cape Croker

HARBOUR PT

MacGregor Har.

PRAIRIE PT

KINGS PT

Kings Point Bluff

Malcolm Bluff

GRAVELLY PT

Purple Valley

Adamsville

Colpoys Bay

Berford Lake

Big Mud Lake

Colpoys Bay

Wiarton

Where Lucky Prospectors Found a 'Golden Stairway' and Fabled Mines

Northeastern Ontario

Thousands of prospectors flocked to thi rugged, mineral-rich region in the earl 1900s. Many failed to find the fortunes the were seeking, while others let wealth sli through their hands. In 1903 two contrac tors, scouting for timber in the forest nea Cobalt (about 130 kilometres south of Kirk land Lake), uncovered glittering sulphide ore. Samples sent to Montreal for analysi revealed high-grade silver. Cobalt wa transformed into a boom town.

A few lucky prospectors stumbled on rich

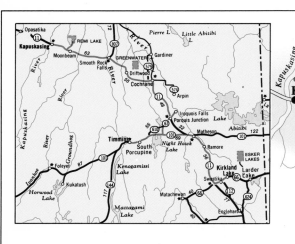

KAPUSKASING
A steam locomotive and two railway coaches house Kapuskasing Public Museum. In one coach is a mo railroad; in the other are furniture and other object dating back to Kapuskasing's settlement about 191(□ Visitors can see how logs are transformed into pap at the Spruce Falls Power and Paper Company.

REMI LAKE PROVINCIAL PARK
This park lies in the Great Clay Belt, an area of deep, fertile soil stretching between Cochrane and Hearst. At the end of the last ice age, glacial meltwater formed a large lake in this area. Eventually, the lake drained, leaving a thick layer of silt and clay sediments. Today moose, bears, wolves and lynx roam the black spruce forests of the Great Clay Belt.

Lynx

All Aboard— for a Journey 'Down North'

Travelers in search of Canada's more remote reaches can go "down north" from Cochrane to Moosonee, near James Bay, on the Polar Bear Express. The express, on the Ontario Northland Railway, winds through more than 300 kilometres of scrub brush and muskeg. Completed in 1932, the railway follows an old Indian canoe route. One-day summer excursions take up to 600 passengers for a five-hour visit to Moosonee.

The railway arranges with Indian guides to take adventuresome passengers the last few kilometres by canoe to Moose Factory—Ontario's oldest fur-trading post—on an island in the Moose River opposite Moosonee. Established in 1673 as a Hudson's Bay Company post, Moose Factory was the first English settlement in what is now Ontario. On the island, the home of Cree Indians, is St. Thomas' Anglican Church (1864), furnished with moosehide altar cloths and Cree hymn books. Moose Factory Museum Park has a restored gunpowder magazine, a log fort and a 1740 blacksmith shop.

TIMMINS
Within Timmins' city limits are some 20 traplines, 200 lakes, three gold mines, Canada's largest copper and silver mine, a nickel mine and three major lumber companies. This city has a population of about 45,000, but its 3,250-square-kilometre territory is roughly equivalent to the combined areas of Winnipeg, Toronto, Montreal and New York.
□ More than 20,000 claims were staked during a copper and zinc strike here in 1964. Lead and silver were also discovered. (The Kidd Creek Mine soon became the world's biggest producer of zinc and silver in concentrates.) The Timmins Chamber of Commerce organizes surface tours of operating mines.
□ The H. H. Costain mineral collection in the McIntyre Community Building displays some of the world's finest specimens of minerals.
□ Competitors from around the world come to Timmins in May for the World Wristwrestling Championships and in September for the World Tug-of-War Championships.

Kidd Creek Mine near Timmins

lodes of silver and gold. In 1903 Harry Preston found a "golden stairway" of yellow-spattered quartz when his boot heel slipped on a mossy knoll. The find became the fabled Dome Mine. A Kirkland Lake claim filed in 1912 by Harry Oakes (later Sir Harry) became the famous Lake Shore Mine, one of the biggest gold producers in Ontario.

Others were less fortunate. One Scots prospector, in need of money for drink, sold his claim in one-eighth shares for as little as $25 apiece. He was Alexander McIntyre—and the McIntyre Porcupine Mine went on to produce gold worth $230 million.

Until the turn of the century lakes and rivers were the main transportation routes here. The Ontario Northland Railway was built in the early 1900s, following rich mineral finds in the Timmins, Porcupine, Cobalt and Kirkland Lake areas. Today, the railway links North Bay and Moosonee near James Bay. (A modern highway parallels the rails as far as Fraserdale, about 115 kilometres north of the town of Cochrane.)

Although rivers here have been dammed, forests hewed and mountains mined, this region still has countless tranquil lakes and vast areas of virgin forest. Between Cochrane and Moosonee civilization has barely touched the fringes of the wilderness.

COCHRANE
The Polar Bear Express, an Ontario Northland Transportation Commission train, winds from Cochrane through 300 kilometres of scrub brush and muskeg to Moosonee on James Bay.
□ Northwest of Cochrane is Greenwater Provincial Park, whose 26 vivid green lakes contain some of Ontario's purest water and finest trout fishing.

Polar bear statue, Cochrane

IROQUOIS FALLS
For a fee, visitors to this pulp and paper town can travel 95 kilometres by bus through woodlands logged by the Abitibi Paper Company. During the seven-hour tour, guides explain modern logging, processing and conservation methods. Visitors watch as trees are cut, trimmed, stacked and hauled to the company's mill. At the mill, visitors see logs turned into pulp, and the pulp into newsprint. The tour includes a hearty logger's lunch at a lumber camp deep in the woods.

MATHESON
When "The Great Fire of 1916" swept through here, it destroyed more than 2,000 square kilometres of forest and the settlements of Porquis Junction, Iroquois Falls and Matheson. A plaque south of Matheson describes the disaster, which claimed 223 lives.
□ Pioneer artifacts, farm implements and pieces of early mining equipment are displayed in the Black River-Matheson Municipal Museum. One exhibit shows the interior of an early one-room schoolhouse.

The Mining 'King' of Kirkland Lake

One of the leading figures in Ontario mining history became the victim in a sensational unsolved murder case. American-born Harry Oakes (later Sir Harry) was a drifter and prospector who eventually became a millionaire. He traveled the mining camps of Australia, South Africa, Colorado and the Yukon, and arrived in the virgin bush area around Kirkland Lake in 1911 to prospect for gold. His second claim, in 1912, became the famous Lake Shore Mine, one of 12 mines along Kirkland Lake's Golden Mile.

Oakes married an Australian girl, built a 37-room mansion in Niagara Falls, and left Canada for the Bahamas in the mid-1930s to avoid taxes. In 1943 he was found brutally murdered in his Nassau home. His son-in-law was charged with the killing, but was acquitted, and the case was never closed.

Kenogami Lake near Kirkland Lake

KETTLE LAKES PROVINCIAL PARK
The two-kilometre Kettle Trail passes several of the more than 20 kettle lakes that give this park its name. These spring-fed, usually circular bodies of water are depressions created at the end of the last ice age by huge blocks of glacial ice.

Because kettle lakes have no natural fish populations, the park's largest lakes are stocked annually with brook and rainbow trout.

Common goldeneye

KIRKLAND LAKE
For centuries the region that now includes Esker Lakes Provincial Park was part of the Ojibways' hunting grounds. In 1912, Harry Oakes staked a claim that became the famous Lake Shore Mine, one of 12 producers along Kirkland Lake's Golden Mile. Soon after, roads and a railway were built, timber was cut and the mining community of Kirkland Lake grew rapidly. Today, only the Macassa gold mine produces. It, and the Adams iron mine, may be toured. In Kirkland Lake's Museum of Northern History are pioneer artifacts and pieces of early mining equipment.

(Map labels: Abitibi River, 574, Canada Highway 47.5, 72, Tunis, Nellie Lake, 578, 67, Iroquois Falls, orquis Junction, 10.5, 577, 11, Frederick House Lake, arbers Bay, 24.5, River, Val Gagné, 67, KETTLE LAKES PROV PK, 32, 16, 101, 101, 16, Shillington, Matheson, Black, 572, 803, Night Hawk Lake, Driftwood, Ranmore, 11, River, Trans-Canada Highway, Bourkes, 72.5, 570, 40.5, Sesekinika, Sesekinika Lake, Kirkland Lake, 8.5, Swastika, 568, Chaput Hughes, 66, 112, Kenogami Lake, 7.5, Kenogami Lake, 11)

Grey Owl's 'Lonely Land'— an Accessible Wilderness

Northeastern Ontario

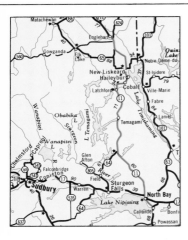

High Falls, Kap-Kig-Iwan Provincial Park, near Englehart

NEW LISKEARD

A lookout south of town provides a superb view of lush, rolling farmland, and in the distance, the forested hills of the Canadian Shield. A clay belt forms a 56-kilometre strip of farmland between New Liskeard and Englehart.
□ In early September the three-day New Liskeard Fall Fair includes livestock, flower and crafts exhibits.

HAILEYBURY

Some 200 students study geology and mining technology at the Haileybury campus of the Northern College of Applied Arts and Technology. Other campuses of the college are at Timmins and Kirkland Lake.
□ Haileybury Centennial Park, on the shore of Lake Timiskaming, has camping facilities and a beach. The lake offers fine fishing for walleye, northern pike and sturgeon.

Jackleg-drill mining competition, Cobalt Festival

Abandoned mine, Cobalt

COBALT

Silver was discovered here in September 1903. According to local legend, Fred LaRose threw a hammer at what he thought were a fox's eyes—and hit the world's richest vein of silver. From a claim that LaRose sold for a mere $30,000 came ore that yielded tens of kilograms of silver to the tonne. (As little as 4.5 kilograms a tonne is a rich yield.) By 1908, with 50 operating mines, the population of Cobalt—the "Town That Silver Built"—was 30,000. But the Depression of the 1930s closed all of the mines. Four were reopened in the 1950s.
□ One remnant of the boom is a 567-kilogram piece of silver. It is part of the Northern Ontario Mining Museum's $250,000 display of raw silver.
□ The 10-day Cobalt Miners' Festival in early August includes displays of miners' skills, fiddlers' contests, parades, dances, a midway and special days for ethnic groups.
□ A cairn marks the site of William Henry Drummond's house. A doctor who wrote English poetry in French-Canadian dialect, Drummond became famous for *The Habitant* in 1898.

LATCHFORD

The Latchford House of Memories Museum has geological and logging displays.
□ At a dam where the Montreal River widens into Bay Lake is the world's largest hydraulic compressed-air plant. A pipeline transmits the air to mines at Cobalt. Excess compressed air is released through a blow-off pipe near the dam, creating a 30-metre geyser.

House of Memories Museum, Latchford

TEMAGAMI

The Temagami Water Carnival in late □ includes canoeing and swimming races a bathtub race and a fishing contest.
□ The town offers summer tours of the lumber mill of W. Milne & Sons Co. L□ and the Sherman open-pit iron mine.
□ A plaque in Finlayson Point Provinc□ Park honors Grey Owl, who lived here 1906-10. On Bear Island, one of 1,200 islands in Lake Temagami, are two buildings of a HBC post founded in 18□ The lake's 600 kilometres of shoreline crown land, all accessible to the public

Ontario's "Near North" is an accessible wilderness within 500 kilometres of Toronto and other major cities. Lumbering, mining and tourism have encouraged the growth of such cities as North Bay. But much of this northern region is still as naturalist and writer Grey Owl described it in the early 1900s: "a great, lonely land of forest, lake and river where moose, deer, bears and wolves roam free."

Sportsmen come here in spring and summer to fish; in fall to hunt ducks, partridge, moose and deer; in winter to fish through the ice, to ski, and to drive snowmobiles on woodland trails.

Lake Nipissing—775 square kilometres of sheltered bays, sweeping beaches, open water and island-dotted shallows—is famous for its walleye. The deep, cold waters of Lake Temagami produce trophy-sized lake trout. Northern pike, muskellunge, sturgeon, whitefish, brook and rainbow trout are among 40 varieties of fishes in the lakes and rivers of the Near North.

Other attractions include a fall fair in New Liskeard, a summer miners' festival in Cobalt, and a winter fur carnival in North Bay. Visitors to Cobalt can tour a mine, and see the world's largest display of raw silver. Museums in Marten River tell of the area's oldest industries—trapping and logging. In North Bay, vacationers can attend a fur auction, cruise Lake Nipissing on the *Chief Commanda II*, or simply bask in the summer sun on any of the city's six public beaches.

ENGLEHART

There is excellent fishing for brook trout, walleye and northern pike in the many lakes and rivers near this lumber and railway town. Mills Lake Fish Hatchery raises some three million brook and lake trout fingerlings annually. Visitors can see how the fish are hatched and raised in 20 raceways and 8 large holding ponds.
□ Kap-Kig-Iwan Provincial Park, set in the deep and beautiful gorge of the Englehart River, has three waterfalls, the highest 21 metres. (*Kap-Kig-iwan* is an Ojibway Indian word meaning high banks.) The river is good for fishing, but is too swift for swimming. There are three self-guiding nature trails in the 317-hectare park.

MARTEN RIVER

The Northern Ontario Trapper's Museum here has a trapper's cabin, a miniature trapline, a beaver house, and a collection of pelts and trapping gear. An audiovisual display tells the story of trapping in northern Ontario.
□ Restored logging equipment in the logging museum at Marten River Provincial Park includes a Crazy Wheel or Barenger Brake—an arrangement of pulleys and rope used to slow the descent of logs down a hill.
□ A nature trail in the 428-hectare park passes 300-year-old white pines.
□ Bass, walleye and northern pike can be caught in the Marten River.

The Famous Quints of Callander

Dionne quintuplets with their physician, Dr. A. R. Dafoe (1938)

The Dionne quintuplets were born in a Callander farmhouse on May 28, 1934. Their birth was unique, their survival a miracle. There had been only two other cases in all medical history of identical quintuplets—and no quintuplet had ever lived more than a few weeks. The Dionne babies, at least two months premature, were each small enough to be held in the palm of a hand.

Yvonne, Annette, Marie, Emilie and Cécile soon became the biggest domestic news item in North America. Two Chicago promoters persuaded their father to sign a contract to exhibit them there at the Chicago Century of Progress Exposition. There was a public outcry and the Ontario government removed the quints from their parents' control and placed them under a board of guardians. They were moved to a specially built hospital, and in 1936 a horseshoe-shaped playground with a public observation gallery was opened. In ten years almost three million persons came to see the quints.

By 1943, the quints' father won a long fight to have the children returned, and the family was reunited in a new home provided by the Ontario government.

NORTH BAY

The world's biggest wild-fur auction, held here five times a year (December, January, March, April, June), attracts buyers from a dozen countries. More than $3 million worth of furs are sold, including beaver, marten and muskrat. The sale, conducted by the Ontario Fur-Trappers Association, is open to the public.
□ In February the four-day North Bay Winter Fur Carnival includes snowmobile and dogsled races, figure-skating competitions and an ice-fishing contest.
□ From May to September the twin-hulled, 300-passenger cruiser, *Chief Commanda II*, follows the route of the voyageurs across Lake Nipissing to French River.
□ North Bay has six public beaches on Lake Nipissing and Trout Lake. The government dock is popular with walleye fishermen. Ouananiche (landlocked salmon) can be caught in Trout Lake.
□ The Dionne homestead, ten kilometres south of North Bay, was moved from its original site in Callander. Inside is the basket in which the Dionne quintuplets were placed immediately after their birth.

Trout Lake, North Bay

LAKE NIPISSING

Abundant furs and an easy passage to the West brought explorers Etienne Brûlé and Samuel de Champlain here in the early 1600s. Today a plaque marks the historic La Vase Portages between the Mattawa River and Lake Nipissing.
□ The lake, 80 kilometres long and up to 56 kilometres wide, is famous for its walleye fishing. In winter, "villages" of ice-fishing huts dot Lake Nipissing.

Pine marten

Marten River
Kaotisinimigo Lake
Marten Lake
99
11
MARTEN RIVER PROV PK
23.5
Tilden Lake
Trans-Canada
37
Cooks Mills
123
63
Lake Talon
Trout Lake
Mattawa R
Tomiko Lake
Little Sturgeon River
Tomiko River
Highway
17
17
94
13
Nipissing Junction
NORTH BAY
Callander
CALLANDER BAY
Lake Nipissing
11

Hell's Gate and a Monster's Cave Along a Waterway to the West

Upper Ottawa River Valley

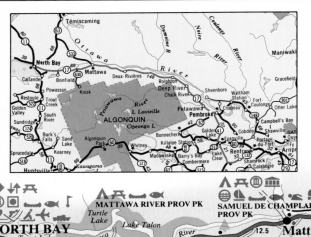

Ottawa River near Mattawa

MATTAWA

Canoeists can paddle on the swift Mattawa River in nearby Mattawa River Provincial Park. On a 30-metre cliff at La Porte de l'Enfer is a rock formation in the shape of an Indian head. Hiking trails lead to wilderness areas in the park.

□ A cairn at Explorers' Point in Mattawa commemorates the voyageurs' canoe route from Montreal to the Great Lakes.

Echoes of Explorers on the Wild Mattawa

The wild Mattawa River—a historic link in the canoe route between the St. Lawrence River and the West—flows through Mattawa River Provincial Park.

For more than 200 years explorers, missionaries and fur traders traveled the Ottawa and Mattawa rivers to Lake Nipissing, then the French River to Georgian Bay. Etienne Brûlé was the first white man to pass this way (in 1611). Later came Champlain, the Jesuit missionaries to Huronia, Radisson and Groseilliers, the La Vérendryes and Alexander Mackenzie. Samuel de Champlain Provincial Park on the Mattawa has a reconstruction of a *canot du maître*, a voyageur freight canoe of birch bark and spruce roots. Audiovisual displays at the park museum tell of canoe construction and the voyageurs.

Canot du maître *replica,*
Samuel de Champlain Provincial Park Museum

Barred owl

DRIFTWOOD PROVINCIAL PARK

An Ottawa River dam built in the late 1940s flooded a forest here, causing great quantities of driftwood to collect on the shores of Holden Lake. Park visitors can hunt for decorative driftwood, and climb to a lookout for a fine view of the Ottawa, its valley and the Laurentian hills across the river in Quebec. Barred owls, kingfishers, Canada jays, broad-winged hawks and black ducks have been spotted here. Several lakes and streams are stocked with brook and rainbow trout.

ROLPHTON

The first nuclear power plant in Canada (1957) can be seen from a lookout here.

□ The 360,000-kilowatt Des Joachims Generating Station is the largest hydroelectric plant on the Ottawa River. It is not open to the public.

□ The Peter A. Nichol Driftwood Museum and Craft Center has some 500 pieces of weirdly shaped driftwood from nearby Holden Lake.

EGANVILLE

Guided tours of the Bonnechere Caves follow twisting passageways deep into a Bonnechere River gorge. The limestone caves, 10 kilometres east of Eganville, were formed by water erosion. Fossils of animals that lived in a tropical sea here 500 million years ago are embedded in the walls.

□ Forests in the rugged Bonnechere River valley are home to white-tailed deer, black bear and gray partridge.

0 2 4 6 8 10 Miles
0 4 8 12 16 Kilometres

The Ottawa and Mattawa rivers were part of Canada's great waterway to the West—a highway used by explorers, missionaries and fur traders for nearly two centuries. Today, travelers can trace the same route along Highway 17.

The Ottawa River, which forms more than half the 1,120-kilometre Ontario-Quebec border, separates rich farmland to the south and an endless expanse of Laurentian hills, lakes and forests to the north.

Near the Chalk River atomic energy plant is long, sandy Pointe au Baptême, where North West Company brigades bound for Fort William stopped to "baptize" new voyageurs. After their initiation, novices treated old-timers to brandy.

The Mattawa River courses through some of the region's most rugged country. In places it slashes between towering granite walls. In cliff faces are weathered rock formations resembling castles.

A plaque in Mattawa River Provincial Park (half the river's 72-kilometre length is in the park) identifies a swift section as Porte de l'Enfer (Hell's Gate). Also in the park, near Portage de la Cave, is a steep-walled corridor darkened by overhanging cedar, spruce and pine. This brooding passage stirred the imaginations of voyageurs, who swore that a man-eating monster dwelt in the black depths of a cave on the north shore of the Mattawa River.

DEEP RIVER
This community was established in 1945 as the main residential center for employees of the Chalk River Nuclear Laboratories.
□ More than 300 mounted animals are in a museum at Ryan's Campsite six kilometres west of Deep River. A horse-drawn stagecoach takes visitors through the 28-hectare campground.

PETAWAWA FOREST EXPERIMENTAL STATION
Canada's oldest forestry research station is used to study tree diseases and the effects of logging and fires. Established in 1918, the 98-square-kilometre Petawawa Forest Experimental Station includes a nursery, a herbarium and greenhouses.
□ A self-guiding one-kilometre walk and eight-kilometre automobile tour teach the rudiments of forest management, geology and soil sciences. An interpretive center has audiovisual presentations. Bunchberry, a type of dogwood with leaves that resemble white petals, brightens forests of red and white pine, balsam fir and yellow birch. Red trillium and jack-in-the-pulpit thrive in moist areas.

CHALK RIVER
This small town is the headquarters of Canada's nuclear energy program.

The Chalk River Nuclear Laboratories, part of the Crown corporation Atomic Energy of Canada Limited, has five reactors. The ZEEP (Zero Energy Experimental Pile), which began operating Sept. 5, 1945, was the first nuclear reactor in Canada and the first in the world outside the United States.

Public tours (June 1 to Sept. 15) begin at an information center. Visitors first learn the basics of nuclear energy with films and displays, then go by bus to one of the research reactors: NRX (National Research Experimental), which began operating in 1947, or NRU (National Research Universal), 1957. NRX and NRU produce radioactive isotopes for medical research.

Other facilities, some of which can be visited on tours arranged at least 24 hours in advance, include a tandem accelerator or atom smasher and "caves" for remote-control handling of radioactive materials.

Chalk River Nuclear Laboratories

PEMBROKE
At the Champlain Trail Museum, Pembroke's first schoolhouse (1838) contains mementos of the great Ottawa Valley lumber industry, including a model of a timber raft, a wooden pulley used to haul logs through rapids, and timber stampers which identified logs for owners. Other buildings at the museum include a furnished log cabin (1872), a smokehouse and an outdoor bake oven. On the grounds are a stump puller, a stone lifter and other pioneer implements.
□ Pansy Patch Memorial Park, on an island in the Muskrat River, has groves of black walnut, Carpathian walnut, larch, butternut and oak—trees not native to the area.
□ Stonehill Farm is a zoo and children's playground.

Bunchberry

RENFREW
The McDougall Mill Museum, housed in a stone gristmill (1855), contains pioneer artifacts and dairy equipment from 19th-century Ottawa Valley farms. The museum is in O'Brien Park on the banks of the Bonnechere River, which is spanned by a suspension footbridge. Summer concerts are held in a band shell.
□ Champlain Storyland is a 16-hectare park with 200 fairy-tale characters in 36 settings. A wildlife museum has dioramas with about 150 stuffed animals. A trail leads to a summit lookout with a panoramic view of the Ottawa Valley.

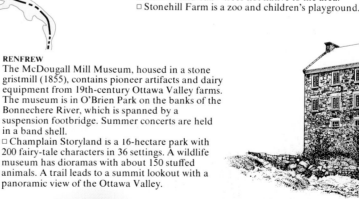
McDougall Mill Museum, Renfrew

DACRE
Ontario's only "magnetic" hill is about one kilometre south of the junction of Highways 132 and 41. Visitors can observe an optical illusion—automobiles appear to roll up a downhill section of road.

White-tailed deer

Beaches, Forest and History: Links Between the Lakes

Southwestern Ontario

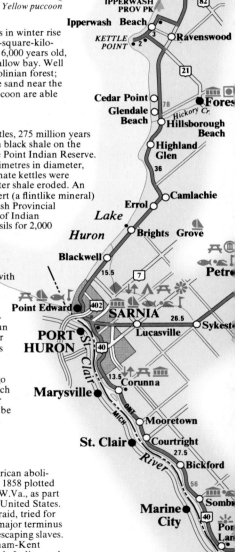

Lake Huron

Grand Be

81

8.5

PINERY PROV PK

Port Franks

2

21

15 82

IPPERWASH PROV PK

Ipperwash Beach

KETTLE POINT • 2

3

Ravenswood

21

78

Hickory Cr.

Cedar Point
Glendale Beach

Fores

Hillsborough Beach

Highland Glen

36

Camlachie

Errol

Lake Huron

Brights Grove

Blackwell

Petr

15.5

7

Point Edward

402

SARNIA 26.5

Sykest

PORT HURON

40

Lucasville

13.5

Corunna

Marysville

Mooretown

St. Clair

Courtright

27.5

Bickford

56

Marine City

Sombr

40

Por Lan

Walpole Isla

Algonac

MICH

GRAND BEND

A wide sandy beach, where the Ausable River angles into Lake Huron, draws some 14,000 summer residents to Grand Bend (winter population, 1,000). The community was originally named Brewster after the owner of a local mill. But the mill dam caused frequent floods, and angry settlers burned the mill and renamed the town in 1860.

Yellow puccoon

PINERY PROVINCIAL PARK

Sand dune ridges so high they are used as ski hills in winter rise three kilometres inland from the beach of this 22-square-kilometre park. The ridges, up to 27 metres high and 6,000 years old, were formed as sandbars when the area was a shallow bay. Well in from the lake is the northern fringe of the Carolinian forest; its trees include eight species of native oak. In the sand near the shore only small, hardy plants such as yellow puccoon are able to survive.

Kettlelike rocks, Kettle Point Indian Reserve

KETTLE POINT

Spheres called kettles, 275 million years old, protrude from black shale on the shore of the Kettle Point Indian Reserve. Averaging 60 centimetres in diameter, the calcium carbonate kettles were exposed as the softer shale eroded. An outcropping of chert (a flintlike mineral) in nearby Ipperwash Provincial Park was a source of Indian weapons and utensils for 2,000 years.

SARNIA

Vertical tanks like great fingers of steel, laced with tubing and ladders and railings, twinkling like fairy castles at night, identify Sarnia and the Chemical Valley south of it as the hub of Canada's oil refining and petrochemical industries. Here are the refineries of Imperial Oil, Sun Oil, Shell and Petrosar, the plant where Polysar Corporation produces 10 percent of the world's synthetic rubber, and the operations of other industry giants such as Du Pont and CIL.
□ Ships sailing the St. Clair River past Sarnia go under the Bluewater International Bridge (which links the city with Port Huron, Mich.) and over the St. Clair Tunnel (a 1,837-metre cast-iron tube built by the Grand Trunk Railway in 1889-91).

Oil refinery, Sarnia

CHATHAM

The First Baptist Church is where American abolitionist John Brown and his followers in 1858 plotted a raid on an arsenal at Harper's Ferry, W.Va., as part of their campaign to end slavery in the United States. (Brown was captured as a result of the raid, tried for treason, and hanged.) Chatham was a major terminus of the Underground Railroad used by escaping slaves. Possessions of Brown's are in the Chatham-Kent Museum. Other museum exhibits include Indian and pioneer relics, an Egyptian mummy and Chatham's first steam fire engine—an 1870 Hyslop-Ronald.
□ Canoe races on the Thames highlight River Days in midsummer.

0	2	4	6	8	10 Miles
0	4	8	12		16 Kilometres

Between the sandy beaches of Lake Huron and Lake Erie is a lush farming region, the northernmost extension of the once great Carolinian forest, some fascinating glimpses of Canadian history, and, at Sarnia, the Chemical Valley that is one of Canada's great industrial areas. All this plus three of Ontario's finest provincial parks—Pinery and Ipperwash on Lake Huron, Rondeau on Lake Erie.

For more than a century vacationers have flocked to this part of southwestern Ontario. Others have come to drill for oil and to make synthetic rubber. But despite human encroachment much of the region remains pastoral and unspoiled. A few kilometres from Grand Bend's nightclubs and midway are forests where deer still roam.

Many groups have found this a welcoming land. United Empire Loyalists established communities here after the American War of Independence. Indians found haven here, settling Moraviantown, about eight kilometres east of Thamesville, in 1792; in the Chatham-Kent Museum at Chatham are a powder horn and war club of Tecumseh, the Shawnee chief who died near Moraviantown in a battle with American invaders in the War of 1812. And it was a refuge for escaped slaves prior to the American Civil War in the 1860s. Chatham was one terminus of the Underground Railroad. Dresden was another. At Dresden is the restored home of the Rev. Josiah Henson, an escaped slave on whom Uncle Tom of Uncle Tom's Cabin was based.

Uncle Tom's Cabin Museum, Dresden

DRESDEN

The two-story house of the Rev. Josiah Henson, after whom Harriet Beecher Stowe modeled the hero of *Uncle Tom's Cabin,* is among seven buildings at the Uncle Tom's Cabin Museum. Henson, born a slave in Maryland in 1789, was ordained in the Methodist Episcopal Church in 1828 and escaped to Upper Canada with his wife and four children two years later. In 1841 he and a group of abolitionists bought property in this area and established the British American Institute, a refuge and vocational school for fugitive slaves. Henson's house, built soon after, still contains some of his furnishings. Other surviving buildings include a house where escaped slaves ate and slept, and a church with a pulpit from which Henson preached. A museum displays a ball and chain, whips, handcuffs, and a club used on slaves. Henson died in 1883 and is buried near his house.

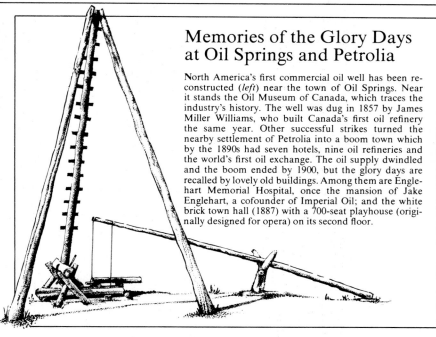

Memories of the Glory Days at Oil Springs and Petrolia

North America's first commercial oil well has been reconstructed (*left*) near the town of Oil Springs. Near it stands the Oil Museum of Canada, which traces the industry's history. The well was dug in 1857 by James Miller Williams, who built Canada's first oil refinery the same year. Other successful strikes turned the nearby settlement of Petrolia into a boom town which by the 1890s had seven hotels, nine oil refineries and the world's first oil exchange. The oil supply dwindled and the boom ended by 1900, but the glory days are recalled by lovely old buildings. Among them are Englehart Memorial Hospital, once the mansion of Jake Englehart, a cofounder of Imperial Oil; and the white brick town hall (1887) with a 700-seat playhouse (originally designed for opera) on its second floor.

THAMESVILLE

Markers and a gravel road 6.5 kilometres east identify the site of Fairfield, established in 1792 by Moravian missionaries and Delaware Indians who had fled the United States. Sacked during the War of 1812, the village was reestablished across the Thames River in 1815 as New Fairfield. The Mission Church, which still stands there, was built in 1848. The Fairfield Museum, at the 1792 site, tells the settlement's story.

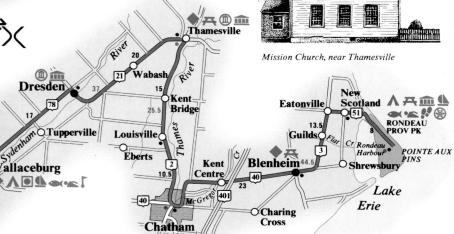

Mission Church, near Thamesville

RONDEAU PROVINCIAL PARK

Exotic plants and wildlife—from the lofty, flowering tulip tree to Ontario's only lizard, the blue-tailed skink—are to be seen in this lush park. Other trees which normally grow much farther south include shagbark hickory, black walnut, sassafras and sycamore. Other reptiles found here include the hog-nosed snake and the spiny soft-shelled turtle. The area includes dense forest, a big marsh, a warm, shallow bay of Lake Erie, and eight kilometres of sandy beach. The forest is tangled with Virginia creeper and wild grape vines, and carpeted with maidenhair fern. This is the main breeding ground in Canada for Acadian flycatchers and prothonotary warblers, and a resting place for migratory birds.

Prothonotary warbler

Giant Industries in a Garden Peninsula

Southwestern Ontario

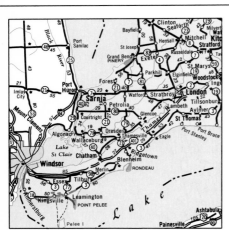

Rosewood melodeon and chair, Hiram Walker Historical Museum, Windsor

Fireboat display on the Detroit River, International Freedom Festival, Wind

WINDSOR

Windsor is Canada's busiest point of entry. Some 30 million persons a year cross from Detroit—by a tunn under the Detroit River, or over the Ambassador Bri (the world's longest international suspension bridge) Thousands of Windsorites commute to Detroit; a smaller number of Detroiters, to Windsor.

□ The cities' joint International Freedom Festival—a week of parades, concerts, picnics, sporting events an fireworks—coincides with Canada's Dominion Day (July 1) and the U.S. Independence Day (July 4).

□ Visitors may tour the Hiram Walker Distillery and the automotive plants of Ford of Canada, Chrysler a General Motors.

□ The Hiram Walker Historical Museum, a two-story Georgian house built in 1811 by Col. François Bâby, is the oldest brick house west of Niagara. The house was used as headquarters by invading Americans in 1812, and the Battle of Windsor was fought on its grounds in 1838. The museum's furniture collection includes a pioneer loom (1830) and a rosewood melodeon made in New York in the 1840s.

□ The Art Gallery of Windsor is in a restored waterfr brewery warehouse. Its permanent collection include Inuit prints and carvings, a bronze by Marc-Aurèle d Foy Suzor-Côté, and works by Emily Carr, Corneliu Krieghoff, Arthur Lismer and David Milne.

Automobile assembly line, Windsor

AMHERSTBURG

Few military sites in Canada have been as strategically important as Fort Malden, now a national historic park here. Built by the British in 1796, the fort was a base in the War of 1812. When the Americans won the Battle of Lake Erie in 1813 the British pulled out of Fort Malden. Recovered from the Americans in 1815 under provisions of the Treaty of Ghent, the fort withstood four attacks by supporters of William Lyon Mackenzie during the Rebellion of 1837.

1 Ambassador Bridge
2 University of Windsor
3 Tourist Information
4 Art Gallery of Windsor
5 Hiram Walker Historical Museum
6 Cleary Auditorium
7 Dieppe Gardens
8 Tourist Information
9 CAA
10 Tourist Information
11 Hiram Walker Distille
12 Chrysler
13 Ford of Canada
14 General Motors

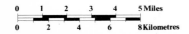

0 1 2 3 4 5 Miles
0 2 4 6 8 Kilometres

Essex County is one of Canada's most industrialized areas. Its major city, Windsor, has an annual manufacturing output of $2 billion—exceeding that of many Canadian provinces. Yet Essex is essentially rural—a great garden peninsula of orchards and farmland, a place for nature study, bird-watching and lolling on sandy shores.

Bounded by Lake St. Clair to the north and Lake Erie to the south, the county has the warmest year-round climate in eastern Canada. Roadside stands here offer fruit and vegetables weeks before produce in other areas is ready for market. Ninety percent of Canada's greenhouse cucumbers, tomatoes and flowers are grown here.

In 1749 farmers from Quebec established Ontario's first permanent agricultural settlement in what is now Windsor. (Some streets follow old farm boundaries.)

Today Windsor, the largest Canadian city on the Canada–United States border, is Ontario's third biggest industrial center (after Toronto and Hamilton). It has large chemical, drug and textile industries, and produces about 25 percent of Canada's motor vehicles and parts. Two companies mine vast deposits of salt under the city.

Windsor's riverfront parks, Centennial and Dieppe, provide a fine view of the Detroit skyline. Thousands of Detroiters cross the border to enjoy Windsor's horse racing and nightclubs. In July, when the two cities host the International Freedom Festival, thousands line both sides of the Detroit River for a grand display of fireworks.

JACK MINER BIRD SANCTUARY

Daily in the migratory season tens of thousands of wild geese and ducks find rest, food and protection in the Jack Miner Bird Sanctuary near Kingsville. Established by the great naturalist in 1904, the sanctuary is open every day, except Sunday, from Oct. 1 to April 15.

The best time to see the migrating geese and ducks is late afternoons the last 10 days of October and the first two weeks of November, and the last 10 days of March and the first 10 of April.

Guides demonstrate banding and feeding and answer questions on wildlife and conservation.

Pink-flowered swamp rose mallow

A Park of Rare Plants, Birds and Butterflies

Point Pelee National Park has many plants usually associated with more southerly areas. Lake Erie moderates the seasonal changes and gives the park one of the longest frost-free growing periods in Canada.

Plant growth is rapid until late June and there is a spectacular succession of abundant flowers. The pink-flowered swamp rose mallow, Canada's only wild hibiscus, grows among marsh ferns and water lilies. During the hot, dry spells in early summer, the prickly pear cactus produces brilliant yellow flowers. The park has such rare shrubs as hop tree, spicebush and fragrant sumac.

The park's biggest attraction is its birds. Two major flyways intersect here and the spring and fall migrations are impressive. At the height of the warbler migration in May, more than 100 species can be seen and the dawn chorus is unforgettable. Hawks, eagles, blue jays, blackbirds, ducks, geese, herons and terns all stop here. Of 300 species of birds that have been seen in the park, 90 stay to nest, including the great blue heron, saw-whet owl, great horned owl and least bittern.

In autumn thousands of monarch butterflies pause in the park on their way to southern wintering grounds.

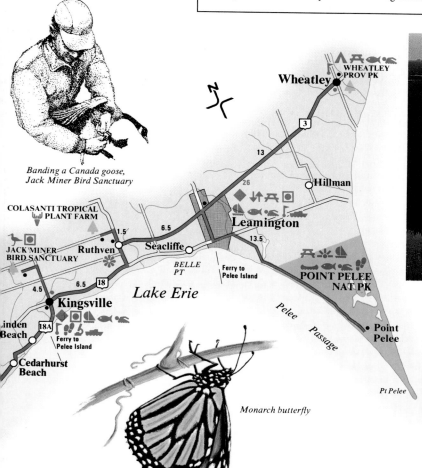

Banding a Canada goose, Jack Miner Bird Sanctuary

COLASANTI TROPICAL PLANT FARM

JACK MINER BIRD SANCTUARY

Ruthven

1.5

6.5

Seacliffe

Lake Erie

4.5

6.5

18

Kingsville

Linden Beach

18A

Ferry to Pelee Island

Cedarhurst Beach

BELLE PT

Ferry to Pelee Island

13.5

Pelee Passage

Leamington

Hillman

13

26

3

Wheatley

WHEATLEY PROV PK

POINT PELEE NAT PK

Point Pelee

Pt Pelee

Monarch butterfly

Boardwalk, Point Pelee National Park

POINT PELEE NATIONAL PARK

Point Pelee is the southernmost part of the Canadian mainland, at the same latitude as northern California. The national park at the tip of this 18-kilometre-long sandy peninsula constantly struggles to maintain its triangular form against the buffeting of Lake Erie. The eastern shore is eroded by as much as half a metre a year in places but waves deposit sand and gravel on the wooded western shore. The park has one of Canada's few remaining stands of Carolinian forest. Hackberry, black walnut, chestnut oak, cottonwood, shagbark hickory and white sassafras grow here.

An interpretive center identifies many of the park's animals, birds, flowers and insects. There is a nature trail through the forest. A boardwalk leads to an observation tower in the park's marsh.

A 'New London' and a Famous Festival

Southwestern Ontario

London was christened by Lieutenant Governor John Graves Simcoe on a 1792 visit to the Thames Valley. He named the site "New London" in the expectation that it would become the capital of Upper Canada. His high hopes were dashed a year later when the capital went to York (Toronto). But London grew into a prosperous industrial and commercial center where streets bear such names as Pall Mall and Piccadilly, reminders of its British namesake.

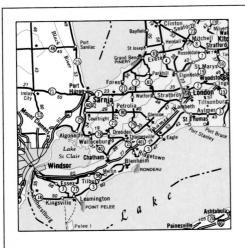

LUCAN
In a shaded corner of St. Patrick's Cemetery is a granite stone whose grim repetition of one date is like the sound of a bell tolling for five dead Donnellys. They were slain Feb. 4, 1880, in the bloody climax to one of Canada's most notorious feuds. It started in Ireland in the 1840s and festered for 40 years until the night vigilantes massacred James and Johannah, John, Thomas and Bridget Donnelly. The six men charged with the murders were acquitted. The stone was erected in the 1960s.

LONDON
Canada's eleventh largest city is in the center of a rich farming area. Fresh local produce attracts thousands of Londoners to Covent Garden, a farmers' market. In September London hosts the Western Fair—Ontario's oldest fall fair, dating from 1868. London's cultural attractions include an art gallery, a symphony orchestra and a professional theater company. Academic quality and scenic beauty are combined on the campus of the University of Western Ontario.
□ Examples of London's early architecture include Eldon House (1834), the fortresslike Middlesex County Courthouse (1831), St. Paul's Cathedral (1846) and the Ridout Street Restoration, a block of restored Victorian homes.
□ London's past is relived in Fanshawe Pioneer Village, a reconstructed crossroad village of the prerailroad era of the 19th century.
□ Springbank Park on the Thames has a bird sanctuary, flower gardens, a zoo and Storybook Gardens, a fairyland of animals and nursery tale characters and scenes.
□ A spring-fed pond and floating mat of sphagnum moss in Sifton Botanical Bog shelter a wide variety of reptiles, birds, and rare orchids.

View of London from the Thames River

ST. THOMAS
Victorian elegance prevails—from the stone towers of City Hall to the Gothic-style shingled beehouse (c. 1826) on the grounds of the Elgin County Pioneer Museum. In the museum building (1848) personal effects of Col. Thomas Talbot recall the city's days as "capital" of the vast Talbot Settlement.
□ Formal gardens, a wildlife sanctuary and a miniature railway can be seen in Pinnafore Park.

Gothic-style beehouse, Elgin County Pioneer Museum

HAWK CLIFF
In late September more than 20,000 migrating broad-winged hawks a day may fly over this Lake Erie vantage point. Between August and December nighthawks, peregrine falcons, bald eagles, loons and Canada geese are seen. In early October blue jays may pass at the rate of 500 a minute.

Broad-winged hawk

ST. MARYS
Overlooking the town is St. Marys District Museum, in a house (1850) built of the local limestone that characterizes many of the town's buildings. Museum has displays of pioneer objects from the region.
□ A disused quarry in Centennial Park provides a 457-by-91-metre swimming pool, Ontario's largest.

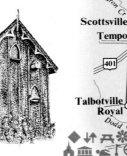

Middlesex County Courthouse, London

Labatt's Pioneer Brewery, London

Lake Erie

Simcoe's dream of settlement was realized by his former secretary, Col. Thomas Talbot, who acquired a vast tract of land north of Lake Erie in 1803. A cantankerous, hard-drinking military man, Talbot was an efficient administrator. A Talbot settler had to clear the roadway in front of his property before receiving the title to his land. Talbot's stipulation helped to create the best roads in Upper Canada.

Because of his despotic ways, Talbot was called the "Baron of Lake Erie." He lost control of his lands in the 1830s, but his imprint on this area is indelible. Many of the towns, including Talbot's "capital" of St. Thomas, owe their origins to his pioneering efforts. The fortresslike courthouse at London was modeled on Malahide Castle, Talbot's ancestral home in Ireland.

About the time Talbot opened up his tract, the land north of London was being settled by other hardworking settlers. Their values and learning came from the Bible and Shakespeare. Adherence to these traditional sources of wisdom may have influenced their decision to name one of their new towns, Stratford, and its river, the Avon.

More than a century later the pioneer dream of transplanting the best of the Old World into the New was fulfilled. In 1953 playgoers came to Stratford for the first Shakespearean festival. This enterprise thrived and has become a world-famous annual theatrical event.

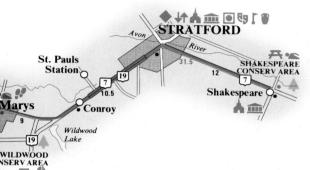

SHAKESPEARE

Sebastian Fryfogel, a Swiss immigrant, was the first settler in this area. He followed road-builders here in 1828 and built a log inn to receive the colonists who were pushing into the wilderness. In 1844-45 Fryfogel replaced the log building with a graceful brick-and-beam structure and adorned the interior with murals. The Fryfogel Inn, 2.5 kilometres east of Shakespeare, has been restored as a museum.

Fryfogel Inn, Shakespeare

STRATFORD

Renowned for its annual Shakespearean Festival, Stratford draws visitors and performers from all over the world. The city's parks and gardens provide a charming setting for this major cultural event. Other attractions in the city include a modern art gallery and one of the finest antique shows in Canada.
□ At the Minnie Thomson Memorial Museum a narrow-gauge steam locomotive and coach run on a kilometre-long railway track.
□ Brocksden School Museum, east of Stratford, recreates an early-19th-century rural school.

Applause on the Avon for Shakespeare, Films, Opera and Pop

In the early 1950s journalist Tom Patterson had an idea—to create a Shakespearean summer festival in his native city of Stratford, Ont. British producer Sir Tyrone Guthrie spent two weeks in 1952 sizing up Stratford and the state of Canadian theater. Patterson and Guthrie put their ideas together, hired a circus tent, and the result was the Stratford Shakespearean Festival.

On July 13, 1953, *Richard III,* with Sir Alec Guinness in the starring role, played to a packed audience. This set the pace for an exciting six weeks of theater, and established a standard that has attracted international acclaim and audiences ever since.

By 1957 the tent was replaced by the present Festival Theater, which seats 2,258. The apron stage jutting into the auditorium gives playgoers a close, unrestricted view of the performers.

Festival facilities were expanded to include two smaller theaters, the Avon Theater and the Third Stage. The scope of the Stratford repertoire was broadened to include plays by Chekhov, Molière and Brecht, and works by Canadian playwrights, such as Stratford-born James Reaney.

Sixteen classical concerts during that first season under the tent have grown into a full program of operas, musicals, and classical, jazz and pop concerts. Art exhibits and film festivals have rounded out the bill of fare. The festival season, which runs from June to October, attracts more than 500,000 theatergoers—20 times the population of the town.

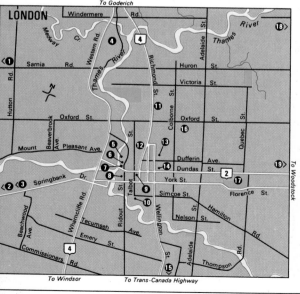

Apron stage, Festival Theatre, Stratford

Where the Faithful Drive Old-Fashioned Buggies

South-Central Ontario

Horse-drawn buggies and their somberly attired passengers remind visitors that the area surrounding the twin cities of Kitchener and Waterloo was settled by Mennonites. Some members of this faith still reject automobiles, electricity, telephones and tractors; will not accept family allowances, medicare and old-age pensions; will not vote, hold public office, or go to war.

Mennonites speak Pennsylvania Dutch, a mixture of German and English. The dia-

Mennonite horse-drawn buggy, Waterloo Region

ELMIRA
In spring this market town's main street becomes a mall where pancakes, fresh maple syrup, sausages, sauerkraut, pies, cakes and apple fritters are sold during a maple syrup festival. Some 30,000 residents and visitors see weaving, quilting, spinning and rug-hooking demonstrations. Visitors can tour a working maple sugar grove in horse- or tractor-drawn sleighs.
□ The Elmira Farmers' Market, held every Saturday, has about 60 booths, most operated by Mennonites. Baked goods, cheeses, and handicrafts are sold.

WOODSIDE NATIONAL HISTORIC PARK
A driveway curves through treed grounds to Woodside, the 10-room boyhood home of Prime Minister Mackenzie King. The impressive Victorian house was built in 1853 and leased by Mackenzie King's father in 1886-93.

The comfortably furnished house has the look of a home, not a museum. Among the highlights are a marble-topped table, a fine old kitchen cookstove, brass spittoons, a brass bed and a grand piano.

Displays include a document Mackenzie King treasured: a government proclamation putting a price of £1,000 on the head of his grandfather, William Lyon Mackenzie, leader of the 1837 rebellion in Upper Canada.

1. Doon Pioneer Village
2. Doon School of Fine Arts
3. Kitchener Farmers' Market
4. Pioneer Memorial Tower
5. Rockway Gardens
6. University of Waterloo
7. Waterloo Park
8. Wilfrid Laurier University

Oktoberfest parade, Kitchener

KITCHENER
With its twin city, Waterloo, Kitchener forms one of Canada's leading industrial communities. It was founded in 1799 by Mennonites from Pennsylvania. With the arrival of settlers from Germany in 1833 the village was called Berlin. That name was dropped at the height of the First World War.
□ The famous Kitchener Farmers' Market enlivens the city on Saturday mornings. Offered for sale are sausages, cheeses, and such Mennonite dishes as shoofly (molasses) pie.
□ The biggest annual celebration is Oktoberfest, nine days of German food and drink, oompah bands and dancing.
□ Doon Pioneer Village, a recreated 1860s settlement, has a Conestoga wagon that brought settlers from Pennsylvania in 1807, and Canada's first production car—the Leroy—built locally about 1899.
□ The stone Pioneer Memorial Tower, overlooking the Grand River, commemorates Mennonite settlers.
□ A plaque at the Doon School of Fine Arts marks the birthplace of Canadian landscape painter Homer Watson.

Pioneer Memorial Tower, Kitchener

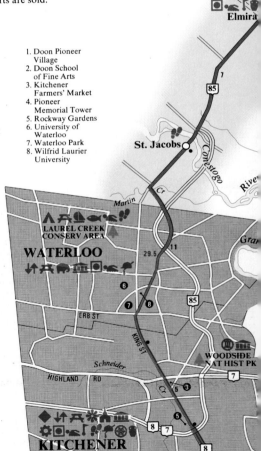

lect evolved among their ancestors, who fled from Switzerland to Germany in the mid-1500s and, 100 years later, to Pennsylvania. In 1784, after the American Revolution, the first group came north to the Waterloo area.

The Amish, another Mennonite sect, came here from Europe after 1822. These and the Old Order Mennonites are the most conservative of more than a dozen sects in the region.

Amish men's garb lacks buttons, collars and pockets, a style originally designed to contrast with military uniforms. The Amish bury their dead in rows according to age and marital status, and grave markers bear only the initials of the deceased.

Women of the Old Order wear no jewelry, not even wedding rings. Most Old Order homes have no indoor plumbing, curtains, pictures or wallpaper.

In sickness or hard times, Mennonites take care of each other. If a barn burns, neighbors replace it within a month. Barn raisings, usually completed in one day, are triumphs of teamwork.

But members of the Old Order have made some concessions to the 20th century: their buggies now display triangular safety reflectors, as required by law. A few drive black, chromeless cars, and transact business by phones—installed in their barns.

ELORA
As the Grand River winds through Elora Gorge Conservation Area, it tumbles over The Cascade, then splits where Islet Rock perches in the middle of another waterfall. It passes Hole-in-the-Rock, a cave leading to the bottom of the gorge, and Hidden Valley, a crevice screened by trees.
□ A museum, antique and gift shops occupy restored turn-of-the-century buildings on Elora's Mill Street. Drimmies Mill, on the Grand River, has been converted into a country inn.

Drimmies Mill, Elora

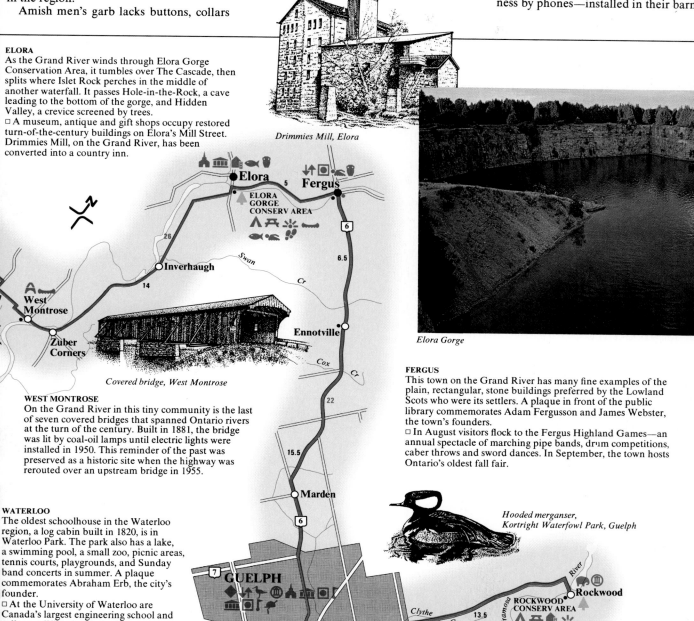

Elora Gorge

WEST MONTROSE
On the Grand River in this tiny community is the last of seven covered bridges that spanned Ontario rivers at the turn of the century. Built in 1881, the bridge was lit by coal-oil lamps until electric lights were installed in 1950. This reminder of the past was preserved as a historic site when the highway was rerouted over an upstream bridge in 1955.

Covered bridge, West Montrose

WATERLOO
The oldest schoolhouse in the Waterloo region, a log cabin built in 1820, is in Waterloo Park. The park also has a lake, a swimming pool, a small zoo, picnic areas, tennis courts, playgrounds, and Sunday band concerts in summer. A plaque commemorates Abraham Erb, the city's founder.
□ At the University of Waterloo are Canada's largest engineering school and colleges affiliated with Anglican, Mennonite, Roman Catholic and United churches. The university's art collection includes William Kurelek's *Haying in Ontario,* and paintings, sculptures, ceramics and tapestries from 20 countries.
□ A plaque at Wilfrid Laurier University commemorates its beginnings (in 1910) as the Evangelical Lutheran Seminary of Canada.

FERGUS
This town on the Grand River has many fine examples of the plain, rectangular, stone buildings preferred by the Lowland Scots who were its settlers. A plaque in front of the public library commemorates Adam Fergusson and James Webster, the town's founders.
□ In August visitors flock to the Fergus Highland Games—an annual spectacle of marching pipe bands, drum competitions, caber throws and sword dances. In September, the town hosts Ontario's oldest fall fair.

Hooded merganser, Kortright Waterfowl Park, Guelph

GUELPH
Fine limestone buildings characterize Guelph, founded in 1827 by John Galt. Off one end of Wyndham Street is the gray limestone city hall, a fine example of classic architecture.
□ The John McCrae House, birthplace of the author of "In Flanders Fields" (1915), contains his personal belongings.
□ Some 2,000 birds inhabit Kortright Waterfowl Park, which has nature trails and picnic areas.

Elora · Fergus · 5 · 26 · Inverhaugh · Swan Cr · 14 · West Montrose · Zuber Corners · Ennotville · 6 · 6.5 · Cox Cr · 22 · 15.5 · Marden · 6 · GUELPH · 7 · Clythe Cr · Speed River · 24 · 7 · 13.5 · Eramosa River · ROCKWOOD CONSERV AREA · Rockwood · ELORA GORGE CONSERV AREA

Through Tobacco Country to a City Named for an Indian Chief

South-Central Ontario

More than 40 percent of Canada's tobacco is grown on the plains of Norfolk County near Simcoe. The flat, well-drained land and the sandy soil are ideal for the cultivation of the crop. Tobacco harvesttime begins about mid-August. Before being shipped to market, the tobacco leaves are dried in the long, red or green curing sheds that are conspicuous on the Norfolk plains.

Visitors to this area are struck by the fine homes and the big barns. But these signs

Can-Amera Games, Cambridge

CAMBRIDGE
This city, created in 1973 from the city of Galt and the towns of Hespeler and Preston, takes its name from Cambridge Mills, an early 19th-century settlement on the Speed River.
□ Some 2,000 amateur athletes compete in the annual Can-Amera Games held alternately in Cambridge and Saginaw, Mich.
□ Mill tours, fashion shows and a parade are features of a textile festival in June. Visitors can arrange to tour Artex Woollens and Dominion Woollens and Worsteds at any time during the year.
□ In August the city's Portuguese community holds a festival, with traditional food and dances.
□ There are campgrounds in the city's Churchill Park. Riverside Park has tennis courts, picnic areas and a zoo.
□ Shade's Mills Conservation Area east of Cambridge offers swimming, fishing, sailing, hiking, snowshoeing and cross-country skiing.

Banded Birds, Tagged Butterflies and Seven Million Seedlings

Bald eagles, piping plovers and Canada geese nest at Long Point, a narrow crescent of shifting dunes and marshes that juts into Lake Erie. More than 270 species of songbirds, shorebirds and waterfowl have been sighted here.

Amateur and professional naturalists are welcomed to weekend workshops at the Long Point Bird Observatory, a year-round research center in the Backus Conservation Area, three kilometres north of Port Rowan. The observatory staff bands birds, tags butterflies and studies seasonal migration patterns. Also in the conservation area is the water-powered Backhouse Mill (1798), the oldest continuously operating gristmill in Ontario.

The St. Williams Forestry Station, Ontario's first tree nursery, raises more than seven million seedlings each year. The station, near St. Williams, can be toured.

PARIS
The Paris Plains Church (1845) is a fine example of cobblestone construction, rare in Canada. Another early structure is Penmarvian (formerly The Stone House), built in 1845-48 in Greek Revival style by Hiram "King" Capron, the town's founder. Capron arrived from Vermont in 1822. Due to his efforts the local gypsum deposits were developed and plaster of Paris made, giving the town its name.

Tobacco plant

Paris Plains Church

SIMCOE
The Eva Brook Donly Museum exhibits pioneer lamps, farm implements and paintings by Norfolk County artists.
□ A cairn in Lynnwood Park commemorates Gen. John Graves Simcoe, first lieutenant governor of Upper Canada, for whom the town is named.

Whistling swans, Long Point

Lake Erie

0   2   4   6   8   10 Miles
0   4   8   12   16 Kilometres

of well-being were not always present, nor was the land as open as it is now. When the first settlers arrived, there were vast stands of white and red pine. The trees were cut down to create farmland. The settlers grew grain, vegetables and fruit in the light soil. Lacking the binding of deep-rooted trees, the hard-won farmland eroded. Fertile fields were transformed into drifting sand, and many farms were abandoned. Fortunes were reversed in the 1920s, when local farmers began growing the tobacco crop that has turned their land into some of the most valuable in Ontario.

To the north of Norfolk County is Brantford. The city owes its name to Joseph Brant, a Mohawk chief, and its renown to the inventor, Alexander Graham Bell. Brant led the Indians of the Six Nations here in 1784 when their allegiance to the British during the American War of Independence cost them their land in upper New York State. Less than a hundred years later, Bell conceived the idea for the telephone here.

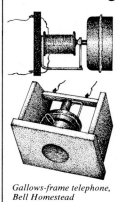

Chapel of the Mohawks, Brantford

When 'Long Distance' Called Mr. Bell

Gallows-frame telephone, Bell Homestead

In the summer of 1874, while visiting his parents' home in Tutela Heights near Brantford, Alexander Graham Bell had an idea that became the basis of the telephone. Returning to Boston where he worked as a speech therapist, Bell took two years to build his first, experimental apparatus. On Aug. 3, 1876, Bell tested his invention at the Dominion Telegraph Company office in Mount Pleasant. He heard his uncle, who was in Brantford, recite Shakespeare's "To be or not to be." This was the first intelligible telephone transmission from one building to another. One week later the first long-distance call was made—from Brantford to Paris, 13 kilometres away. The Bell Telephone Company came into being and by November 1877 it had four subscribers. The fifth request for the new device came from Prime Minister Alexander Mackenzie, who wanted a telephone link between his Ottawa office and the governor-general's residence. The company supplied it—and predated the prime minister's application to make him officially the first subscriber.

F.W.R. DICKSON WILDERNESS AREA
Sassafras trees reach the northern limit of their range in this wilderness area of marsh and meadows, tamarack swamp and hardwood forest. A nature trail passes through the wilderness on an elevated boardwalk through the swamp and close to fox dens in the forest. Feeding stations attract cardinals, woodpeckers and juncos.

Joseph Brant Monument, Victoria Park, Brantford

OHSWEKEN
Iroquois Indians reenact their history in an August pageant in an open-air theater on the Six Nations Reserve. The Haldimand Grant of 1784, assigning the Six Nations their reserve, is displayed in the council house (1864).
□ A plaque commemorates Joseph Brant's son, John, the first Indian elected to the Upper Canada legislative assembly (in 1832).
□ Exhibits at Chiefswood, the restored birthplace of Indian poetess Pauline Johnson, include her writing desk and several of her original manuscripts. Built in 1835 by her father, Chief G. H. M. Johnson, the mansion is furnished in the 1870s style.

NANTICOKE
An Ontario Hydro generating station (the world's largest coal-burning power plant), the blast furnaces of a giant steel processor, and a huge provincial housing development are changing this Lake Erie city of 19,000. By the turn of the century it may be one of Canada's major industrial centers.

Bell Homestead, Brantford

BRANTFORD
A monument in Victoria Park honors Joseph Brant, the Mohawk chief, who gave this city its name. An inscribed sundial in Lorne Park marks the site where Brant and his Indian followers took up land given them by the British Crown in 1784.
□ A monument on West Street commemorates Alexander Graham Bell's invention of the telephone at the family homestead in Tutela Heights. The Bell Homestead, overlooking the Grand River, contains replicas of early telephones and many of the family's original furnishings. Canada's first telephone business office and switchboard (1877)—the Rev. Thomas Henderson's house—are on the grounds.
□ St. Paul's, Her Majesty's Chapel of the Mohawks, was the first Protestant church (1785) built in what is now Ontario. In the churchyard is Brant's tomb.
□ The Brant Historical Society Museum has a collection of Indian artifacts, antique weapons and period furniture.
□ The Art Gallery of Brantford in an 11-room mansion in Glenhyrst Gardens has paintings by Canadian artists Homer Watson and David Milne.
□ Highland Games, featuring pipe bands, Scottish dancing and caber tossing, are held at Brantford in July.

The Steel Capital of Canada in a Land of Blossoms and Wine

Niagara Peninsula

Hamilton is the steel-making capital of Canada. But it is free from the urban blight that afflicts many industrial centers. Old mansions and cobblestone walkways in the heart of the city have been lovingly restored. Handsome modern buildings, such as Hamilton Place, an imposing cultural center, reflect vitality and confidence.

There are some 45 parks in the Hamilton area. At the Royal Botanical Gardens, abandoned gravel pits have been transformed into formal rock gardens and floral

DUNDURN CASTLE
Hamilton's restored and refurnished Dundurn Castle reflects the elegant life-style of Sir Allan Napier MacNab, a lawyer, promoter, financier and politician, who built it in 1832-34.

Among 35 rooms open to the public are a black-walnut-paneled library from which MacNab practiced law, a dining room with a mahogany table seating 20, and a chandelier with 720 crystal prisms. Dundurn Castle Museum (in the mansion) depicts the early history of Hamilton.

Dundurn Castle, Hamilton

HAMILTON
This industrial city is the nation's leading steel producer. Its harbor, spanned at the entrance by the Burlington Skyway, bustles with overseas shipping. Two steel mills, and several of the city's 500 other plants may be toured.
□ Live theater and concerts are presented in Hamilton Place, a multimillion-dollar cultural center. Works by Canadians are prominent in the collection of the Art Gallery of Hamilton. Included are paintings by William Kurelek, Cornelius Krieghoff and Marc-Aurèle de Foy Suzor-Côté.
□ Whitehern, a handsome limestone house built in the 1840s, has been preserved in the heart of the city and is open to the public. In Hess Village, a few blocks west, restored stately homes house specialty shops, galleries and restaurants.
□ McMaster University is noted for its nuclear reactor, and for having the papers of British philosopher Bertrand Russell.

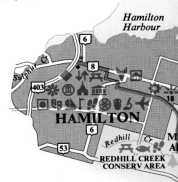

Steel mill, Hamilton

CANADIAN FOOTBALL HALL OF FAME
In the shrine room of the hall of fame are busts of football's builders and great players, a computer that answers questions about Canadian Football League records, and a theater featuring Grey Cup films. Four stages of the game's evolution—1900, 1920, 1950 and the present—are depicted in a stained-glass mural. The hall, located in City Hall Plaza, Hamilton, is open year round.

Stained-glass mural, Canadian Football Hall of Fame

ROYAL BOTANICAL GARDENS
The Royal Botanical Gardens in and near Hamilton have an arboretum and herbarium, a tea house, a children's garden, lectures and guided tours. The vast property includes the famous Rock Garden at the northwest tip of Hamilton; the Spring Garden (in Burlington), with June displays of irises, lilies and peonies, and the nature preserve of Cootes Paradise. Walkways and nature trails crisscross the gardens, which are open every day of the year.

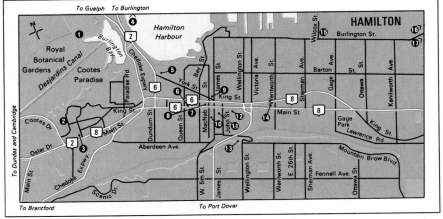

1 Royal Botanical Gardens
2 McMaster University
3 Art Gallery of Hamilton
4 Tourist Information (summer only)
5 Dundurn Castle
6 Hess Village
7 Canadian Football Hall of Fame
8 Hamilton Place
9 Hamilton Market
10 Whitehern
11 Courthouse
12 Tourist Information
13 Sam Lawrence Park
14 CAA
15 Steel Company of
16 Burlington Bay Skyway
17 Burlington Ship Ca

0 1 2 3 4 5Miles

0 2 4 6 8Kilometres

displays. Trails from the gardens lead to nearby Sam Lawrence Park, on the top of Hamilton Mountain. Here visitors can view the city's steel mills, the harbor (one of the largest and busiest on the Great Lakes), the Burlington Skyway and Lake Ontario.

East of Hamilton is the Niagara Peninsula, Canada's fruit belt and major wine-producing region. Most Canadian wine is pressed from grapes grown in its rich soil and mild climate. The scenery here is especially striking in May, when the cherry,

peach and apple trees burst into blossom.

The area was settled by Loyalists, Mennonites, Quakers, Huguenots and at least 20 other groups that followed in their wake. The diverse cultural heritages are honored during a week-long Folk Arts Festival each spring in St. Catharines. The event begins a time of festivals, open-air markets and county fairs. The Niagara Grape and Wine Festival in September celebrates the bountiful harvest with a colorful parade in the streets of St. Catharines.

Lighthouse at Port Dalhousie near St. Catharines

STONEY CREEK
A battle June 6, 1813, in which 700 British regulars routed 2,000 American troops is commemorated in Battlefield Memorial Park. Battlefield House, which served as American headquarters, is a museum with displays relating to the battle and furnishings dating to 1790.

VINELAND
Sick and injured birds of prey receive X rays, surgery, antibiotics, heat-lamp therapy and flight retraining at the unique Owl Rehabilitation Center, operating since 1969 near Vineland. Visitors are allowed by appointment only.
□ Nearby, working demonstrations of historic and modern maple-sugar-making methods are sponsored each spring by the Niagara Peninsula Conservation Authority.

Battlefield Monument, Stoney Creek

Snowy owl

ST. CATHARINES
Many of this city's 117,000 residents are involved in wine production or the fresh and canned fruit business.
□ St. Catharines Historical Museum displays handmade farm tools, butter churns, early Canadian china, and a locally made pitchfork used in the capture of Rudolf Hess in Scotland (1941).
□ A plaque in Centennial Gardens Park describes the building of the first Welland Canal (1824-29) from Port Dalhousie (now part of St. Catharines) to Port Colborne.
□ Mountain Mills Museum is a fine old gristmill (1872) at De Cew Falls. Farther east is a plaque marking the foundations of De Cew House, to which Laura Secord made her famous journey during the War of 1812.
□ The Royal Henley Regatta is held here each July.

Lake Ontario

Marlatt Tavern door, Stone Shop Museum, Grimsby

JORDAN
The Jordan Historical Museum of the Twenty consists of the Vintage (c. 1840) and Jacob Fry (1815) houses, a stone schoolhouse (1859) and churchyard whose headstones mark the graves of Mennonite settlers. A rare, giant cider press on the grounds is a pioneer version of European fruit presses. Lowered by a three-metre screw carved from solid black walnut, the huge press beam exerted a force of 18 tonnes.

GRIMSBY
A farm shop built around 1800 and used by Canadian, British and American blacksmiths during the War of 1812 now houses the Stone Shop Museum. Incorporated into the building is the elaborate door of the Marlatt Tavern (1855-73). Exhibits include a crazy quilt that won first prize at the Chicago World's Fair in 1893, and a Windsor side chair that belonged to Col. Robert Nelles, one of the first settlers in the Grimsby area.

Fruit press, Jordan Historical Museum of the Twenty

Parades and Grape Stomping Contests

For ten days in September, during the Niagara Grape and Wine Festival, St. Catharines lets go in a carnival overflowing with parades, marching bands and floats. The yearly celebration includes a grape-stomping contest between local mayors, and the crowning of a Royal Family to reign over the festival.

Ninety per cent of the wine produced in Canada comes from the Niagara Peninsula. Until the mid-1940s the grapes grown in this area were suitable only for the production of sherry and port. But with the introduction of new grape varieties in the 1970s, Ontario's wines have acquired a subtler flavor and are gaining international recognition. (Barnes Wines Ltd., Canada's oldest winery (1873), and Jordan Wines, both in St. Catharines, and Andrés Wines, in Winona, offer tours by appointment.)

A Mighty Cascade That Has Been 'Conquered,' Tamed and Saved

Niagara Peninsula

A "vast and prodigious Cadence of Water": that was Niagara Falls as described by Jean-Louis Hennepin in 1678. The Belgian-born missionary-explorer was the first eyewitness to write about the two mighty cataracts on the Niagara River— Canada's Horseshoe Falls (670 metres wide,

Where Monuments and Museums Recall a Famous Conflict

Many War of 1812 sites can be seen in the Niagara Peninsula, one of the most fought-over areas of the conflict.

The military figure (*right*) is one of four at the corners of Maj. Gen. Sir Isaac Brock's monument at Queenston. Brock fell at the Battle of Queenston Heights in 1812. In Queenston, the home of Laura Secord, who made a 32-kilometre walk to warn of an American attack, is now a museum.

The McFarland House (1800), a museum at Niagara-on-the-Lake, was used as a hospital by both sides in the war. The town's Fort George (1796-99), which fell to the Americans in 1813, has been restored.

Also restored is Old Fort Erie, the Fort Erie stronghold captured in 1814 by the Americans.

WELLAND CANAL

The 43-kilometre Welland Canal, linking Lake Ontario (Port Weller) with Lake Erie (Port Colborne), crosses the Niagara Peninsula, 21 kilometres west of Niagara Falls. It has eight locks, a total lift of 100 metres, and can handle vessels up to 22 metres long. Transit time is eight to ten hours.

At Thorold, ships are raised 57 metres—43 metres by three twin flight locks, and 14 by a single lock a half-kilometre away. The twin locks are like a double stairway with traffic moving both ways. As westbound ships are stepped up the canal, eastbound vessels are lowered on the other side.

The Welland By-Pass, completed in 1973, cut transit time by about an hour by avoiding five lift bridges and a railway swing bridge in the city. Under the bypass run the Townline Road tunnel (three railway tracks and a two-lane highway) and the East Main Street tunnel (a four-lane highway).

The first Welland Canal (1824-29) was replaced by those built in 1845-86, in 1887-1931, and the present channel, 1913-32.

PORT COLBORNE

The biggest lock on the Welland Canal is here at the Lake Erie end—421-metre Lock 8, one of the longest in the world.
□ Port Colborne also has the world's biggest nickel refinery, a fine harbor, sandy beaches, and a flour mill with tours by appointment.
□ The Historical and Marine Museum has Indian artifacts, a log schoolhouse (1812), relics of early shipbuilding, and glassware produced locally in 1892-94.

Ring-billed gull

NAVY ISLAND

Headquarters of William Lyon Mackenzie's provisional governm[ent] in 1837-38, Navy Island is now pa[rt] of the Niagara Parks system. Floc[ks] of Bonaparte's, ring-billed and he[rring] gulls, and some 20 species of duck[s] are on this uninhabited spot in th[e] Niagara River. Naturalist-conduc[ted] hikes of the island can be arrange[d]

Welland Canal

Lake Ontario

Martindale Pond

ST. CATHARIN[ES]
(see Road Unit 90)

QEW

406

Thorold

Thorold South

58

Turners Corners

20

18

Allanburg

Black Horse Corner

WELLAND

31.5

13.5

Welland Junction

Port Colborne

58

140

3

10.5

Gasline

SUGAR LOAF PT

Gravelly Bay

PINE CREST PT

Sherkston

6.5

Ridgewa[y]

Crystal Beach

Lake Erie

PT ABINO

54 metres high), and the American Falls (305 metres wide, 56 metres high).

The cascade Hennepin saw has been greatly tamed. Power developments on both sides of the border divert waters that would otherwise flow over the falls.

Millions visit the falls every year. The tourist trade at Niagara developed in the early 1800s. With the tourists came daredevils, who defied the falls in barrels, boats and rubber balls. The most celebrated stunter was a French acrobat, the Great Blondin, who walked a tightrope across the Niagara Gorge in 1859. Stunting brought brief fame to some, but others died in their attempts to "conquer" the falls. Stunting was outlawed in 1912.

This legislation was one more attempt to prevent the scenic wonder from becoming a hucksters' paradise. Alarmed that entrepreneurs were grabbing land near the falls, Ontario created Queen Victoria Falls Park (Canada's first provincial park) in 1887, for public enjoyment of the area's natural beauty. Today the Niagara Parks Commission owns all land adjacent to the river and the Niagara Parkway. Along this route, Canada's past can be relived at historic sites in Fort Erie, Chippawa, Queenston and Niagara-on-the-Lake.

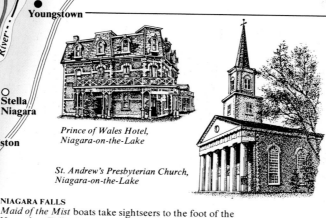

Prince of Wales Hotel,
Niagara-on-the-Lake

St. Andrew's Presbyterian Church,
Niagara-on-the-Lake

NIAGARA-ON-THE-LAKE
Put to the torch by American troops in 1813, rebuilt after the War of 1812, Niagara-on-the-Lake is one of the best preserved early 19th-century towns in North America.
□ St. Andrew's Presbyterian Church is a fine example of ecclesiastical Greek Revival architecture. The Niagara Apothecary, a pharmacy museum, has a hanging golden mortar, the traditional symbol of an apothecary. In the Prince of Wales Hotel's royal suite is a bed used by the Prince of Wales (later King Edward VIII) in the 1920s.
□ The Shaw Festival in summer features plays by George Bernard Shaw, Noel Coward and others.
□ The Royal George Theater is the home of Canada's first professional mime theater.

NIAGARA FALLS
Maid of the Mist boats take sightseers to the foot of the Horseshoe Falls. An aerocar travels 548 metres across the whirlpool below the falls on cables 37 metres above the waters.
□ The Skylon Tower at the Niagara International Center is topped by a revolving restaurant. The observation deck in the seven-story crown of the Panasonic Center has specially tinted glass and built-in light meters as aids to photography.
□ The 37-room Oak Hall, former home of Sir Harry Oakes, the Canadian mining magnate, is open to the public.

NIAGARA GLEN
Downstream from the Whirlpool Rapids Bridge is Niagara Glen, a gorge filled with strangely shaped rocks and potholes. Rare plants, ferns, flowers and trees, including red mulberry and large tulip trees, grow along winding trails.
□ Flora unique to Canada and a rose garden with a floral fountain are among attractions in the adjacent Niagara Parks Commission School of Horticulture.

Leaves and bud of the tulip tree

Aerocar over the gorge at Niagara Falls

A Cataract in Retreat

Some 12,500 years ago, as the last ice age was ending, old lakes were reborn. One was Lake Erie, which first drained southwest into the Mississippi River system.

As the great thaw continued, the lake found a new, lower outlet—north through the channel of the Niagara River into Lake Iroquois, the forerunner of Lake Ontario. When the water plunged some 60 metres over the edge of the Niagara Escarpment, Niagara Falls was born. At that moment, the mighty cataract began retreating some 1.2 metres a year. Already it is some 11 kilometres south of its birthplace at Queenston.

The rapid recession is due to the sedimentary rock structure of the escarpment—soft shale and limestone overlaid by harder limestone and dolomite. Shale at the base erodes quickly, leaving the upper, more resistant ledges jutting out. These, unable to support their own weight, break off and topple into the pool below.

Freshly Painted Gingerbread Trim and Cedar Rail Fences

Central Ontario

This is rural, small-town Ontario caught up in a fling with nostalgia. The pioneer village, the historical plaque, the museum and the restoration have all taken hold and flourished here. The gingerbread trim on brick, story-and-a-half farmhouses is freshly painted. Cedar rail fences, split and erected a hundred years ago by settlers, snake along roads and across fields. In the river towns, restored mansions stand grandly in view on the main streets. Old bank

FORKS OF THE CREDIT
The two main branches of the Credit River tumble through rocky gorges to their confluence at the base of the Niagara Escarpment here.
□ Nearby Rattlesnake Point is a heavily treed bluff, one of the many on the escarpment. Its sheer cliffs, riddled with cracks and fissures, are popular with climbers.

BELFOUNTAIN
A church built here in 1837 by Scottish immigrants, most from the Hebridean islands of Islay and Mull, is preserved by the Credit Valley Conservation Authority. A stone in the church cemetery marks the grave of two men named Duncan McNabb, uncle and nephew, ages 85 and 78, when killed by a falling tree while clearing land.

Old streetcar, Ontario Electric Railway Historical Association, Rockwood

ROCKWOOD
The Ontario Electric Railway Historical Association has reconstructed two kilometres of the Halton County Radial Railway, on which visitors ride in antique streetcars. The association also operates an electric railway museum. Working exhibits include a reversible "stub line" car (1915) with wicker seats, a replica of an 1893 open car with a side running board, a coal-heated wooden streetcar and an early streamlined streetcar that saw service in Toronto from 1938 to 1963.
□ Dozens of large potholes, formed by hard granite stones swirling over soft limestone in glacial meltwater, are seen in the Rockwood Conservation Area. One hole, 4.5 metres wide at the top, is 12 metres deep. Limestone projections as high as 18 metres and three subterranean caves are other features of the park. On the Eramosa River are millponds that once powered a gristmill and a woolen mill.
□ The Rockwood Academy, a pioneer boarding school for boys, was established here in 1850. A surviving three-story stone school building (1853) is now a private residence.

KELSO CONSERVATION AREA
The Halton County Museum was once the homestead of Adam Alexander, who settled here in 1836. The main building is a barn in which the original timber- and woodwork (c. 1867) have been restored. In another building are examples of pioneer weaving, quilting, embroidery, rug making and wood carving. The Centennial Carriage House displays horse-drawn vehicles dating from the early 1800s.

BURLINGTON
A silver gorget—George III's "gift of a friend" to Joseph Brant—is displayed in the Brant Museum. The building is a replica of a cedar house built by the Mohawk chief around 1800. Brant was granted much of the surrounding land as a reward for his loyalty during the American Revolution. He lived here until his death in 1807.
   The museum exhibits spear and arrow points, wampum, French and British trade axes, a copy of Brant's will, one of his muskets, and dishes from the original house.
□ Tall bearded irises are displayed in the Spring Garden of the Royal Botanical Gardens.

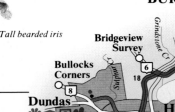

Joseph Brant Museum, Burlington

DUNDAS
Dundas calls itself "The Cactus Capital of Canada." Cacti and succulents in huge numbers are displayed in greenhouses, and a Cactus Festival is held here each June.
□ On the Niagara Escarpment is Webster's Falls Park, where Spencer Creek tumbles 25 metres into a thickly wooded gorge.

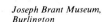

Tall bearded iris

0 1 2 3 4 5 Miles
0 2 4 6 8 Kilometres

barns house the herds of holsteins for which the region is famous, and steam-era machinery is preserved in odd corners of farms.

The Credit Valley is a gently rolling landscape of stony pastures, limestone faults and deep woods crossed by rushing streams. Old dams, still evident on the rivers, once backed up water to run mill wheels geared to saws and grindstones, and later propelled turbines for electric power. It was here in 1883 that the Smith farm became the first electrified house in Ontario, and the old agricultural way of life began to change.

Sunday drivers and antique collectors have helped to preserve the character of the Credit Valley. One-time general stores, haylofts, blacksmiths shops and inns are now antique shops, artists' studios, galleries and restaurants. The Black Creek Pioneer Village recreates rural life of a century ago. The stone and rough-hewn timber galleries of the McMichael Canadian Collection in Kleinburg display the works of the Group of Seven, many of whom lived in this area. These attractions, set in a rich, rolling farmland, give visitors an opportunity to experience the best of the past and the present in rural southern Ontario.

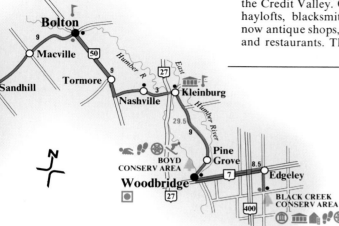

Gristmill, Black Creek Pioneer Village

BLACK CREEK CONSERVATION AREA
This is the site of Black Creek Pioneer Village, which depicts 19th-century life prior to 1867. The nucleus of the village is the Daniel Strong farm of five log farm buildings, all still standing where they were originally built.

Some 25 other buildings here, including a general store, gristmill, weaver's and shoemaker's shops, were brought from elsewhere and reconstructed on their present sites.

Burwick House, built in 1844, has early Ontario furnishings, antique rugs and tapestries. The Daziel Barn Museum, a huge cantilever barn (1809), contains the largest collection of 19th-century toys in Canada.

On educational tours of the village, students dip candles, churn butter, card wool, hook rugs, and bake bread in a wood-burning oven.

A. J. Casson's Kleinburg *(1929)*

A Home for the Group of Seven

One of Canada's largest collections of paintings by the Group of Seven—and the graves of five of the Group's founders—are at Kleinburg in the McMichael Canadian Collection. Formed in 1920, the Group included Frank Carmichael, Lawren Harris, A. Y. Jackson, Frank Johnston, Arthur Lismer, J. E. H. MacDonald and F. H. Varley. Tom Thomson, who drowned in Algonquin Park in 1917, was one of the major influences on the Group. Works by these artists, and by later members of the Group such as A. J. Casson, are displayed at Kleinburg.

The collection was begun as a hobby by Robert and Signe McMichael in a six-room, stone-and-timber house they called Tapawingo (an Indian word meaning "place of joy"). In 1965 the McMichaels turned the collection over to the Province of Ontario. The gallery also houses Indian and Eskimo art, and Tom Thomson's Toronto studio is on the grounds.

Old Post Office Museum, Oakville

OAKVILLE
More than two dozen 19th-century buildings in "Old Oakville" date from an era when shipbuilding flourished here. The Old Post Office Museum (1835) and the adjacent Thomas House (1829) are restored and open to visitors. Other old buildings, most marked with Oakville Historical Society plaques, include a customhouse (1855), St. Andrew's Church (1840), the stone Romain and MacDougald granary (1854), and St. Jude's Church (1883).

BRONTE CREEK PROVINCIAL PARK
Spruce Lane Farm is a working turn-of-the-century homestead with displays depicting pioneer farm life. A separate children's farm has animals to see and touch, and a barn playground full of hay, ropes and barrels.
□ Both the rare eastern bluebird and the red-headed woodpecker are found in the park.
□ The Half-Moon Valley Trail leads past the remains of a 19th-century brick kiln and a millrace and dam.

Eastern bluebird

Soaring Symbols of Progress, Vestiges of a Placid Past

An explosion of development that began in the early 1960s gave this dynamic capital of Ontario a new face and ranked it among the world's fastest-growing cities.

John Graves Simcoe, first lieutenant governor of Upper Canada, established the town of York (later Toronto) in 1793. It was made the capital and presumed safe from attack. But Americans captured the town during the War of 1812 and razed several buildings. York was rebuilt and in 1834 was incorporated as the City of Toronto. As surrounding farmlands were settled, it prospered.

By mid-century, Toronto was a city of 30,000 people, most of them Tories, and 24 churches, most of them Protestant. Until the Second World War, Toronto remained a bastion of Anglo-Saxon rectitude. "The wild and rabid Toryism of Toronto is appalling," wrote Charles Dickens, an 1851 visitor. But postwar immigration transformed "Toronto the Good" into cosmopolitan "People City."

The city's wealth stems from its role as Canada's business and manufacturing center. The Toronto Stock Exchange, one of the world's busiest, is in the heart of the Bay Street financial district with its many banks, office towers and corporate headquarters.

But vestiges of a more placid past remain.

Toronto's architectural heritage is vigorous and unique, and much of it can still be seen: imposing mansions along the Kingsway, Victorian townhouses in Yorkville, and Gothic buildings at the University of Toronto.

Despite building booms, Toronto remains partly wilderness. The city is crisscrossed by a system of largely unspoiled ravines, some with rivers running through them. Signs in the city's parks encourage visitors to "Please Walk *On* the Grass."

Allan Gardens (26)
A statue of poet Robert Burns by Scottish sculptor T. W. Stevenson stands amid floral displays, fountains, and greenhouses filled with tropical and subtropical plants.

Art Gallery of Ontario (11)
Major paintings in Canada's second-largest gallery (after the National Gallery in Ottawa) include Rubens's *The Elevation of the Cross* and Gainsborough's *The Harvest Waggon.* In the Canadian wing are paintings by Krieghoff, Kane, Borduas, Carr, Thomson and the Group of Seven. A sculpture exhibit has works by Picasso and Henry Moore. Part of the gallery is housed in The Grange (1817-20).

Casa Loma (37)
North America's largest castle was built by industrialist Sir Henry Pellatt in 1911-14.

The 98-room building has hidden panels and passageways, and a 240-metre tunnel leading to stables finished in marble.

Chinatown (14)
Surrounding the corner of Elizabeth and Dundas streets are Chinese restaurants, and Oriental shops that sell ivory, jade and silks.

City Hall (17)
The new city hall (1965) epitomizes the spirit of modern Toronto. Its curved twin towers of 27 and 20 stories partially encircle a three-story "flying saucer" that contains the city council chambers.

Craven Foundation
Automobile Collection (36)
A 1906 Sears Highwheeler, a 1917 Stanley Steamer and a sleek 1933 Rolls Royce are among 78 vintage automobiles on display.

Eaton Center (21)
This development comprises shops, offices, a glass-roofed colonnade and Canada's largest department store.

In nearby Trinity Square, surrounded by the modern complex, is the Church of the Holy Trinity (1847).

Prize Steers and Stuffed Pandas at the 'Ex'

All the fun of the fair at the "Ex"

For three weeks in late summer, the "Ex" is a crowded, gaudy, noisy, exciting show that attracts some three million visitors every year.

The largest annual exhibition in the world and a yearly event since 1879, the Canadian National Exhibition (1) has two kilometres of midway, grandstand shows, sports events and flower displays. There are science, education and fashion exhibits, and an agricultural fair that includes livestock judging, horse jumping and dog shows. On the midway, carnival hawkers lure once-a-year gamblers with stuffed pandas and giant balloons.

The Hockey Hall of Fame, open year round, displays sweaters of NHL players, sticks and pucks involved in milestone goals, and pictures of all-time greats. The major NHL trophies, including the Stanley Cup, are on display. In the same building is the Canadian Sports Hall of Fame, where famous athletes are honored.

Fort York (4)
Scarlet-coated guardsmen parade to the music of fife and drum, fire muskets and a six-pounder cannon and perform sunset retreat at restored Fort York (1793).

Gibson House (35)
Restored to its mid-century elegance, this red brick Georgian house was built in 1849.

High Park (34)
Nature trails wind past rock gardens, floral displays, a small zoo and Grenadier Pond. Much of the park was bequeathed to the city by John Howard, one of Toronto's first surveyors and engineers. His house, Colborne Lodge (1836), is now a museum with displays of maps, documents and antiques.

Kensington Market (5)
Not far from downtown high rises is this colorful, European-style street market and cluster of ethnic restaurants.

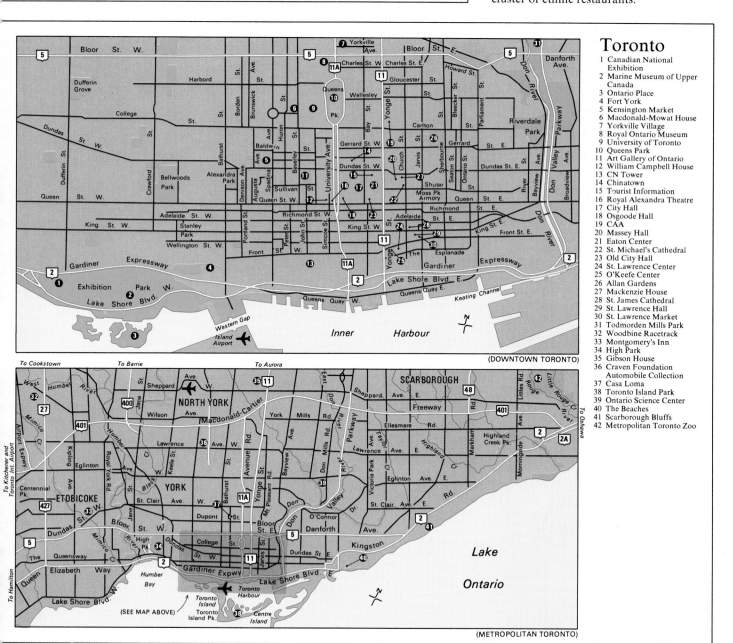

Toronto

1 Canadian National Exhibition
2 Marine Museum of Upper Canada
3 Ontario Place
4 Fort York
5 Kensington Market
6 Macdonald-Mowat House
7 Yorkville Village
8 Royal Ontario Museum
9 University of Toronto
10 Queens Park
11 Art Gallery of Ontario
12 William Campbell House
13 CN Tower
14 Chinatown
15 Tourist Information
16 Royal Alexandra Theatre
17 City Hall
18 Osgoode Hall
19 CAA
20 Massey Hall
21 Eaton Center
22 St. Michael's Cathedral
23 Old City Hall
24 St. Lawrence Center
25 O'Keefe Center
26 Allan Gardens
27 Mackenzie House
28 St. James Cathedral
29 St. Lawrence Hall
30 St. Lawrence Market
31 Todmorden Mills Park
32 Woodbine Racetrack
33 Montgomery's Inn
34 High Park
35 Gibson House
36 Craven Foundation Automobile Collection
37 Casa Loma
38 Toronto Island Park
39 Ontario Science Center
40 The Beaches
41 Scarborough Bluffs
42 Metropolitan Toronto Zoo

(DOWNTOWN TORONTO)

(METROPOLITAN TORONTO)

Macdonald-Mowat House (6)

This brick house (1872) was the residence of Sir John A. Macdonald and later of Sir Oliver Mowat, premier of Ontario (1872-96).

Mackenzie House (27)

This two-story stone building (1859) was the home of William Lyon Mackenzie, Toronto's first mayor (1835) and leader of the Rebellion of 1837.

Marine Museum of Upper Canada (2)

The museum is in the onetime officers' quarters of Stanley Barracks (1841). Preserved in drydock is the tugboat *Ned Hanlan* (1932).

Massey Hall (20)

Built in 1894, Massey Hall is the home of the Toronto Symphony Orchestra. A new Massey Hall is to be opened in the 1980s.

Metropolitan Toronto Zoo (42)

More than 5,000 animals live in huge paddocks simulating their natural environments. Birds fly in walk-through enclosures and nocturnal animals are housed in a darkened tunnel. Slow-moving trains take visitors through the zoo.

Montgomery's Inn (33)

This restored stone inn (1832) is an example of Loyalist Georgian architecture.

O'Keefe Center (25)

Canada's largest theater seats 3,200 for plays, concerts, opera and ballet. The center is home to the National Ballet of Canada and the Canadian Opera Company.

Old City Hall (23)

A 90-metre clock tower crowns the city hall (1891-99), built of brownstone and granite.

Vendors at Kensington Market (right) peddle everything from Rumanian pastries to live rabbits, geese and doves. Ontario Place (below) packs a 38-hectare recreation world on man-made islands and elevated pavilions; its globe-shaped Cinesphere splashes movies across a six-story screen.

Ontario Place (3)

Ontario Place is a May-to-September exposition on three man-made islands in Lake Ontario. Cinesphere's movie screen, six stories high and 24 metres wide, is the world's largest. Music is performed in the Forum. The Children's Village has a punching-bag forest, a foam swamp and a climbing hill. The destroyer HMCS *Haida* is permanently berthed at Ontario Place.

Ontario Science Center (39)

Visitors are invited to participate and learn. Exhibits include a simulated spaceship landing, a computer that plays tic-tac-toe, and a giant seesaw.

Osgoode Hall (18)

The Supreme Court of Ontario occupies the hall, built by the Law Society of Upper Canada in 1829-32.

Queen's Park (10)

The Romanesque-style Ontario Legislative Building was erected in 1886-92. There are statues of Queen Victoria, Sir John A. Macdonald and John Graves Simcoe.

Royal Alexandra Theater (16)

The "Royal Alex" has been a leading Toronto theater since 1907.

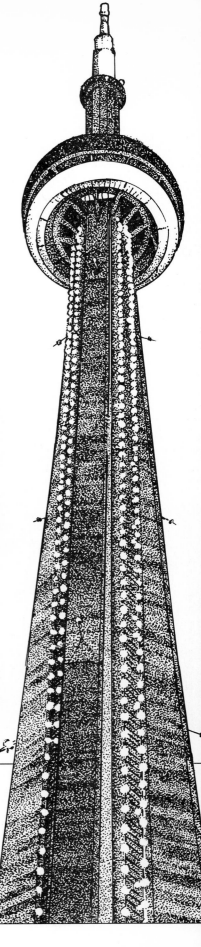

Toronto's 'Cloud Nine'

It has the world's highest elevator ride (477 metres), the longest staircase (2,570 steps) and weighs more than 23,214 bull elephants. On earth, man can stand no higher in an enclosed structure. It is the 553.33-metre CN Tower (add a 5-centimetre stretch in summer heat)—the tallest freestanding structure in the world.

Completed in 1975, the $52 million tower (13) serves as a broadcast and receiving station as well as Toronto's most conspicuous landmark. Into the triangular column went thousands of tonnes of reinforced con-

crete. The result, according to engineers, is the most wind-, ice-, fire-, earthquake-, plane-, suicide- and lightning-proof tower in the world.

Four elevators whisk visitors to the seven-story Sky Pod, 342 metres above the ground. Here are indoor and outdoor observation decks, a revolving restaurant and four floors of broadcast and mechanical equipment. A fifth elevator rises to the 477-metre-high Space Deck, where visitors can look up at the 100-metre transmission mast (lowered by a helicopter during construction) and down on everything else.

Royal Ontario Museum (8)
Canada's largest museum, the ROM has one of the finest collections of Chinese art and archaeology in the western world. Other displays include dinosaur skeletons, furniture from the court of Louis XIV, a roomful of suits-of-armor, tribal masks from New Guinea, a six-story totem pole, and roughly five million other artifacts from all parts of the world.

The McLaughlin Planetarium's Theater of the Stars depicts man's knowledge of the universe.

The Sigmund Samuel Canadiana Building contains silver and glass, ceramics, sculptures, antique furniture and art.

St. James Cathedral (28)
This Anglican cathedral was built in 1853. Its 97-metre steeple is Canada's tallest.

St. Lawrence Center (24)
The center presents a season of drama and, in the Town Hall auditorium, forums on topics of local concern.

St. Lawrence Hall (29)
This Renaissance-style building (1850) is now used for meetings and as a rehearsal hall by the National Ballet of Canada.

The pace of the city slows to a stroll in fashionable Yorkville (right). Wind and water have sculpted the precipitous Scarborough Bluffs (far right). The twin-towered City Hall (below right) rises behind Nathan Phillips Square, alive with people, music and art shows year round. Among the art treasures of the Royal Ontario Museum's Chinese collection is this glazed earthenware statue (bottom). Yonge Street (below) attracts strollers and sightseers both day and night.

St. Lawrence Market (30)
This is the latest version of a public market-place that has occupied the corner of Front and Jarvis streets for more than 170 years.

St. Michael's Cathedral (22)
A 78-metre spire surmounts the bell tower of this Gothic cathedral (1848). Designed by William Thomas, the building has huge stained-glass windows, one an ornate chancel window by French artist Etienne Thevenot. The cathedral has a replica of Michelangelo's *Pieta*.

Scarborough Bluffs (41)
The bluffs rise 90 metres from Lake Ontario in layers of clay and sand that provide a geologic record of the last ice age.

The Beaches (40)
A boardwalk skirts Kew Beach in this east Toronto neighborhood, once a separate re-

sort community. A local landmark is the parklike R. S. Harris Filtration Plant.

Todmorden Mills Park (31)
Water still bubbles into the basement of the Parshall Terry House, built over an artesian spring in 1794. Nearby is the two-story William Helliwell House (1838).

Toronto Island Park (38)
Ferries link the city with 13 islands known collectively as Toronto Island. The park has a wildlife preserve, an amusement park, beaches and lagoons.

University of Toronto (9)
Founded as King's College in 1827, the university has 100 buildings on three campuses.

William Campbell House (12)
The Georgian mansion (1822) of Sir William Campbell, chief justice of Upper Canada (1825-29), has been restored.

Woodbine Racetrack (32)
Woodbine is the site of the continent's oldest regularly run horse race. The first Queen's Plate was held in 1860.

Yorkville Village (7)
Several blocks of Victorian houses have been converted to art galleries, boutiques and restaurants.

Lake Simcoe's 'Smiling Beauty', Muskoka's Autumnal Splendor

Central Ontario

At the point where Lake Simcoe and Lake Couchiching meet is Orillia, immortalized by Stephen Leacock in *Sunshine Sketches of a Little Town*. This humorous classic was one of the many books Leacock wrote in the study of his summer home, now a museum, in Orillia. Explaining his attachment to this area, where he had spent his boyhood, Leacock wrote, "To my way of thinking, nothing will stand comparison with the smiling beauty of the waters, shores and bays of

A Hero Revered by the Chinese

A minister's son born in Gravenhurst in 1890, Norman Bethune interrupted his medical studies in 1914 to join the Canadian army overseas. At the start of the Spanish Civil War in 1936 he established a mobile blood service for the Republican forces. In 1938 Bethune joined the Chinese Communists, then fighting both the Japanese and the Chinese Nationalists. He set up hospitals, organized medical teams and trained army doctors. During a battle-front operation he cut a finger and later died of blood poisoning at Wupaishan, where he was buried. He became a national hero in Communist China. His body was moved to China's Martyrs' Tomb, schools and hospitals were named after him, and his image appeared on Chinese posters and stamps (*right*).

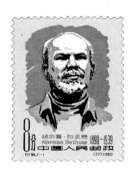

ORILLIA

This industrial and resort city was the model for Mariposa in Stephen Leacock's *Sunshine Sketches of a Little Town*. Economist, historian and humorist, Stephen Leacock (1869-1944) had a summer home here which has been converted into a museum. Many of his papers, including several original, handwritten manuscripts, are displayed.

□ The 12-metre-high Champlain Monument in Couchiching Beach Park is considered one of the finest bronze works in North America.

□ The Anglican Church of St. James (1857) has a memorial to William Yellowhead, an Ojibway chief who fought for the British during the War of 1812.

□ Orillia's Winter Carnival in February includes an ice-fishing derby, a figure-skating show and harness racing on ice.

Stephen Leacock

BARRIE

A marker in Memorial Square indicates the east end of Nine Mile Portage, an important supply route dating back to the War of 1812.

□ The Barrie Winter Carnival, usually held in February, has an air show, parachute drops and dogsled races.

□ Eight kilometres north of Barrie are the Simcoe Museum and Archives. Exhibits include Indian handicrafts, a display on the War of 1812 and a recreated, 19th-century "street" with a general store, toy shop and an undertaker's parlor. Behind the museum is a log house (1834) furnished in pioneer style. Barns contain tools, blacksmithing and barrel-making displays, and a collection of sleighs and buggies. On the grounds is one of Ontario's few remaining wooden windmills.

GRAVENHURST

A plaque outside the two-story frame manse of Trinity United Church identifies it as the birthplace (1890) of Norman Bethune, internationally known for his medical work in Spain and China.

□ The Scottish-built 1887 paddle-wheeler *Segwun*, anchored in Muskoka Bay, displays vintage outboard motors, models of ships that once plied Lake Muskoka, and pioneer household effects.

□ Sixteen kilometres northwest is Woodwinds Historical Museum, consisting of a log cabin with pioneer furniture, a log church and displays depicting early agriculture, hunting, trapping and steamboating in the region.

□ The *Lady Muskoka* makes 3½-hour cruises of Lake Muskoka, passing Rankin and Christmas islands, Lighthouse Narrows and Millionaires Row, and stopping at Port Carling.

ARROWHEAD PROVINCIAL PARK
Deer and moose frequent this lakeside preserve. Nature trails pass beaver dams, waterfalls and plants such as the cardinal flower, normally found farther south. Park naturalists hold interpretive programs throughout the summer in the park amphitheater.

Melissa

ARROWHEAD PROV PK

Lake Vernon

DYER MEMORIAL

Huntsville

Hillside

Peninsula Lake

Dwight

Birkendale

Utterson

Mary Lake

Port Sydney

Port Cunnington

Fox Point

Lake of Bays

Bracebridge

Lake Simcoe and its sister lake, Couchiching." The lakeland remains as attractive now as it was when Leacock described it, more than 50 years ago.

Beyond Orillia, the rolling farmland of southern Ontario gives way to the pine and granite landscape of Muskoka. Lumber, cheap land and rumors of gold attracted settlers to this region. But the old bone-rattling Muskoka Road taxed even the hardiest travelers. At its northern end was the tiny lumbering community of McCabe's Bay (now Gravenhurst) on Lake Muskoka. From here, steamers carried freight and passengers to remote settlements. The last of these ships, the *Segwun*, has become a floating museum at Gravenhurst.

Today's travelers take Highway 11 to reach Gravenhurst, Bracebridge and Huntsville, gateways to Muskoka's lakes and woods. One of Ontario's popular year-round playgrounds, the region is famed for the beauty of its autumn, when foliage becomes a symphony of gold, red and yellow.

HUNTSVILLE
This year-round resort town is a main gateway to the scenic Lake of Bays (160 kilometres of shoreline).
□ Six kilometres south of Huntsville is Madill Church, built in 1872-73 by Wesleyan Methodists. The church, a square-timbered building, is now used only for annual United Church commemorative services.
□ Clustered around the Muskoka Museum is Muskoka Pioneer Village: five houses, a store and a school restored and furnished with pioneer furniture.
□ A chair lift nine kilometres east gives access to Peninsula Peak and a view of hundreds of square kilometres of Muskoka lakes and forests.
□ Northeast of Huntsville is the Dyer Memorial, erected by a Detroit businessman in memory of his wife. A tower rising 13 metres above a flagstone terrace is surrounded by a garden and park overlooking the East River.

BRACEBRIDGE
Among the annual events in this one-time logging town are an international curling bonspiel in February and the Muskoka Arts and Crafts Festival, held in July.
□ The twin generators of the Bracebridge power station were built in 1898 and still produce most of the town's power.
□ Near Bracebridge is St. Peter's on the Rock, a church constructed of hewn timber.

Madill Church, Huntsville

How Leaves Reveal Hidden Hues

Beneath the top layer of a leaf (the cuticle and the epidermis) are chloroplasts, containing the chlorophyll that uses sunlight to produce food. Under the chloroplasts is a layer of spongy cells, in which carbon dioxide, water and nutrients are mixed. (Carbon dioxide enters the leaf through openings, known as stomata, and water and nutrients, through the viens.) When sunlight strikes the chloroplasts, the chlorophyll sets off a reaction (photosynthesis), in which nutrients and carbon dioxide combine to produce sugar that is fed to the tree. In the cooler autumn weather, chlorophyll production slows, and hidden yellow and orange pigments are exposed. Sugar trapped in the leaves works with the sunlight to produce new red and purple pigments. These, in turn, combine with each other, and with tannin (waste products that turn leaves brown) to give the fall hues.

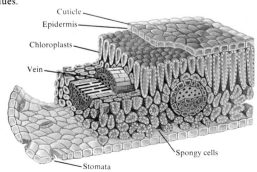

Cuticle
Epidermis
Chloroplasts
Vein
Spongy cells
Stomata

Changing autumn leaves in Muskoka

An Alluring Park—
Inspiration for a Great Painter

Central Ontario

Almost any visitor to Algonquin Provincial Park can see why painter Tom Thomson was inspired by this magnificent wilderness. One need only watch the dance of sunlight on a lake, or the play of shadows among pines, to appreciate what Thomson captured in one of his famous paintings, *The West Wind*.

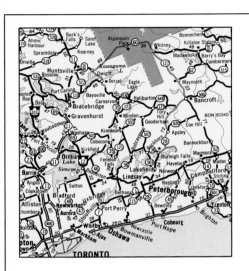

Timber wolves

Tom Thomson's The West Wind

ALGONQUIN PROVINCIAL PARK

This vast park covers some 7,140 square kilometres. Highway 60 runs for almost 60 kilometres through the southern part of the park, but most of this immense wilderness is accessible only by canoe or on foot. The variety of canoe routes on Algonquin's 2,500 lakes is almost endless. Hikes are conducted by park naturalists. Fishing is excellent, for the lakes teem with smallmouth bass, splake, walleye, pickerel, brook trout and lake trout.

□ In a logging exhibit near the highway are a reconstructed loggers' cabin with no windows or chimneys (known as a "camboose"), a "saddleback" locomotive, an alligator boat (capable of traveling on land), and showcases of objects describing 19th-century logging activities in the region.

□ A 12-metre totem pole at Canoe Lake commemorates artist and woodsman Tom Thomson, who drowned here in 1917.

Algonquin Provincial Park

ALGONQUIN PROV PK

Locomotive, Pioneer Logging Exhibit,
Algonquin Provincial Park

**LESLIE M. FROST
NATURAL RESOURCES CENTRE**
Set in a 22,275-hectare estate of forests, lakes, rivers and hills, the Leslie M. Frost Natural Resources Centre offers visitors a fascinating opportunity to study and explore nature. Established in 1974 by the Ontario Ministry of Natural Resources, the center is a major education facility for students, adult groups and professionals in the natural sciences. Casual visitors are welcome at the center. The best visiting time is on a weekday when the full staff is on duty. The estate has well-marked hiking trails, and guides to explain what the visitor will see in the natural surroundings of the estate. Recreational activities at the center include canoeing, cross-country skiing, snowshoeing.

0 2 4 6 8 10 Miles
0 4 8 12 16 Kilometres

A century ago this region was accessible only by canoe. But today visitors arrive by road and air. They can enjoy much of the park from convenient campsites, or they can paddle and camp along its hundreds of canoe routes. Algonquin is the oldest provincial park in Ontario (1893) and one of the biggest in Canada.

Indians roamed the Algonquin region for some 4,000 years without appreciably altering the land; in about 60 years loggers changed it permanently. Early loggers came from Ottawa in the 1840s, attracted by the red, white and jack pines that thrive here. But in felling the pines, the loggers scarred the land and left debris that fed forest fires.

Today some 750,000 trees are cut down annually, but twice that number of saplings are planted each year. Logging roads are built away from shorelines, and in summer loggers are prohibited from working near canoe routes and from hauling after dark.

One of the most distinctive calls of the wild is the high-pitched wail of the timber wolf. In Algonquin Provincial Park, the wolves, hunted to extinction elsewhere in Canada, roam free and unmolested. They respond to humans who imitate their howl. Wolf-howling is used by naturalists to trace their movements. In August visitors can participate in public wolf howls, led by park officials.

The Mystery of Canoe Lake

Canadian artist Tom Thomson spent his last years living alone in Algonquin Park, working as a guide, and sketching and painting. His finest paintings—landscapes which influenced the Group of Seven—were done during this time. Two brilliant canvases from the last year of his life, *The West Wind* (left) and *The Jack Pine*, are among the most frequently reproduced.

Thomson was just 39 when he died mysteriously in Canoe Lake in the summer of 1917. His canoe was found in the lake a day or two after he disappeared—it was said he had gone fishing. Six days later his body surfaced. He had a brutal gash on one temple and a fishing line wrapped around his ankle. The coroner's verdict was accidental drowning. One theory was that Thomson had used the line to support a sprained ankle, then had slipped and hit his head before falling overboard. Others were that he killed himself while under pressure to marry a pregnant girl friend—or that he was murdered.

BANCROFT
Amethysts from Africa, opals from Australia, and a variety of gems found locally are displayed at the Rockhound Gemboree each August. The five-day event, the biggest of its kind in Canada, attracts hundreds of collectors—and thousands of tourists—to this village in the Madawaska Valley. Started in 1963, the Gemboree features field trips (almost 100 different kinds of minerals are found in the immediate vicinity), visits to abandoned mines and demonstrations of gemstone cutting. Other highlights include square dancing, corn roasts and a midway.
□ Pioneer artifacts are displayed in the Bancroft Historical Museum, a log house built in 1857.
□ The countryside surrounding Bancroft is a haven for bird-watchers and nature photographers and offers excellent hunting and fishing.

Bancroft Historical Museum

SILENT LAKE PROVINCIAL PARK
This 12-square-kilometre park has 152 tent and trailer sites, each with a picnic table and a fireplace. The surrounding forest is dominated by sugar maple, hemlock, white pine and white spruce. Wildlife in the forest includes beaver, muskrat, otter, red fox, black bear and deer.
□ Fishing in Silent Lake is excellent: its waters teem with smallmouth and largemouth bass and lake trout. Canoes and rowboats are permitted on the lake; power craft are forbidden.
□ Visitors can explore Silent Lake Provincial Park on foot or, in winter, on cross-country skis. There is a snowmobile trail just west of the park.

Rockhounders near Bancroft

LAKE ST. PETER PROVINCIAL PARK
Visitors to this 810-hectare park can enjoy hiking, canoeing, fishing for rainbow trout, and—in winter—cross-country skiing. Facilities include a beach, a marina and a picnic area.
□ Just west of the park office is a four-kilometre nature trail which leads to a panoramic view at the summit of a mountain in the park.

Rock carvings, Petroglyphs Provincial Park

PETROGLYPHS PROVINCIAL PARK
The petroglyphs in this park are rock carvings believed done by Algonkian Indians between 500 and 1,000 years ago. More than 900 figures etched into a 30-by-50-metre sloping limestone wall are identifiable as animals, humans, mythical forms and fertility symbols. Every summer the park hires anthropology students to conduct an interpretive program on the petroglyphs.
□ A five-kilometre self-guiding nature trail leads to High Falls, on Eels Creek. The 27-metre-high waterfall cascades over a series of cataracts.

Where Canals and Locks Link 'Bright Waters and Happy Lands'

Central Ontario

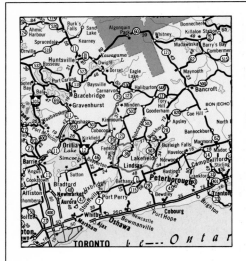

Golden-winged warbler

MINDEN

Founded in 1859, this village was the first settlement in the District of Haliburton, and became the county seat in 1874. The oldest remaining building is the square-timber Clergy House (1870), once used by itinerant Anglican missionaries.
□ Each autumn, when the leaves change to brilliant reds, oranges and yellows, the village celebrates a Fall Festival of Color.

BALSAM LAKE PROVINCIAL PARK

Balsam Lake is the highest point on the Trent-Severn Waterway. Along the park road are huge tree stumps—remnants of a heavy forest of white pine that was harvested many years ago. The entire area has been replanted by the Ministry of Natural Resources. A self-guiding nature trail begins on the road behind the Cedar Grove Camp Area and passes through a swamp, a hardwood forest and open grassland to the top of a lookout hill.

Purdy's Mill, Lindsay

LINDSAY

The first settler in the area, William Purdy, dammed the Scugog River in 1827. In return for a land grant, he built two mills, which still stand. In 1834, a government surveyor named Lindsay was accidentally shot and killed. He was buried in the settlement, and his name was given to the town in 1850.
□ A plaque on the grounds of the Victoria County Historical Society Museum honors Ernest Thompson Seton, naturalist and author, who emigrated from England to a farm near Lindsay in 1866.

"The Highlander," Haliburton

HALIBURTON

This village and the surrounding Haliburton Highlands were named for Judge Thomas Chandler Haliburton, Nova Scotia author and creator of the "Sam Slick" stories. He was chairman of the Canadian Land and Emigration Company which settled the region in the 1860s.
□ Haliburton has an unusual tourist information center: a Grand Trunk Railway steam locomotive and a wooden caboose (1911) which commemorate the opening of the line here in 1878.
□ The Haliburton Highlands Pioneer Museum displays tools once used in lumbering, farming and trapping.

BOBCAYGEON

Built on three islands and the mainland, the village is the midway point on the Trent-Severn Waterway. A monument records the first wooden lock and canal on the waterway were constructed here in 1833-3.

FENELON FALLS

Maryboro Lodge, built in 1837, houses the Fenelon Falls Museum. Displays focus on pioneer life of the mid-19th century.
□ Sturgeon Lake abounds in muskellunge, largemouth bass and walleye.

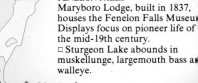

Sycamore

Map labels: 519, Head Lake, Drag River, Haliburton, Soyers Lake, 121, 519, 24, Duck Lake, Kashagawigamog Lake, 40.5, 35, Ingoldsby, Minden, Lutterworth, 35, 121, 16.5, Deep Bay, Kilcoo Camp, Gull Lake, Miners Bay, Miners Cr, Black Lake, Moore Falls, Moore Lake, 11, Gull River, 503, Norland, Shadow Lake, 38.5, 8, Four Mile Lake, Silver Lake, Corben Cr, 7, 1, Coboconk, Corsons, 35, BALSAM LAKE PROV PK, 48, 9, Baddow, Balsam, Kawartha, GRAND ISLAND, Rosedale, 9.5, Cameron Lake, Fenelon Falls, Isaacs Glen, 35A, Bobcaygeon, ISLA, 16, Kenstone Beach, 36, Ancona Point, Birch Point, Lakes, 6.5, 121, Lake, Martin Cr, Sturgeon Lake, 25, 5.5, Cameron, Cambray, 35, McLaren Cr, Scugog, 13, Lindsay, Pigeon Lake, EMILY PROV PK, 7, 36, River, Reaboro, Hillhead, 18.5, 7, Omemee, 35, Stony Cr, 54.5

Scale: 0 2 4 6 8 10 Miles | 0 4 8 12 16 Kilometres

In the Haliburton Highlands, hundreds of lakes are scattered in a rocky, forested expanse of pine, spruce, maple, oak and balsam. Nestling among the ancient hills are Minden and Haliburton. Proximity to lake and forest has made these villages magnets for boaters, campers and harassed city dwellers.

From the Haliburton Highlands, rivers flow south to a chain of 14 lakes known as the Kawarthas—"bright waters and happy lands" in the Huron language. The lakes drain from one to another, over rapids and falls, to Lake Ontario. The entire chain forms a boundary between Haliburton County and the rolling farmlands near Lindsay and Peterborough.

The Kawartha Lakes are linked by the canals and locks of the 380-kilometre Trent-Severn Waterway between Lake Ontario and Lake Huron. The waterway traces a centuries-old canoe route of Indians and explorers. Begun in 1835, the waterway linked early settlements. Bypassing the rapids eased the passage of barges laden with timber from local mills, and the steamers that brought visitors to the area.

Shipping on the Kawartha Lakes declined as the lumber industry died out. Commercial use of the waterway ceased by the 1930s. The remaining waterway trade was transferred to a new system of roads. These made the lakes more accessible to sportsmen, particularly boating enthusiasts. Today, where barges and steamers once plied, pleasure craft sail each summer.

Two Chroniclers of Wilderness Life

Catharine Parr Traill (*left*) and Susanna Moodie (*right*) were two of Canada's "gentle pioneers" who joined the wave of immigration between 1815 and 1855. The two sisters came from England to Upper Canada with their husbands in 1832. Catharine adapted cheerfully to life in Douro Township, near Peterborough, and in *The Backwoods of Canada* (1836) and *The Female Emigrant's Guide* (1854) gave practical advice to would-be settlers.

Susanna was less enthusiastic about frontier life. In *Roughing It in the Bush* (1852) she wrote of feeling like "a condemned criminal." She survived a forest fire and being chased by a bear, and in 1853 produced a more optimistic book, *Life in the Clearings.*

LAKEFIELD

In the cemetery of the village church (1853) is the grave of Major Samuel Strickland, a former British army officer and the founder of Lakefield. After establishing a farm in the wilderness here, he chronicled his adventures in *Twenty-seven Years in Canada West.* His sisters, Susanna Moodie and Catharine Parr Traill, also recorded their pioneer lives in books.

Pleasure craft sailing through the Peterborough Lift Lock

Peterborough Lift Lock

PETERBOROUGH

Officially listed as Lock No. 21 of the Trent-Severn Waterway, the Peterborough Lift Lock is the largest hydraulic lock in the world. When it was opened in July 1904, the concrete-and-steel giant was described by the Peterborough *Examiner* as "the eighth wonder of the world."
□ Among the oldest buildings in Peterborough are the handsome Hutchison House, built in 1837 for the town's first physician, and the Grover-Nicholls House (1847), an excellent example of Greek Revival architecture, rare in Ontario. In striking contrast is the impressive modern architecture of Trent University, established in 1963 on a wooded setting on both sides of the Otonabee River.
□ The Peterborough Centennial Museum has a military exhibit that includes armor, medals and uniforms from the Battle of Waterloo to the Korean War, a collection of photographs that covers a century of local history, and a display of sleighs, carriages and dolls dating from 1800.
□ A marker locates a 2,000-year-old Indian burial site uncovered during excavation for a parking lot.

Hutchison House, Peterborough

Grover-Nicholls House, Peterborough

Trent University, Peterborough

Buckhorn
Lake

Katchewanooka
Lake

28

Lakefield

507

Chemung Lake

Otonabee River

15.5

CHEMUNG LAKE CONSERV AREA

28

7B

17.5

7

Canal

Trent

Meade Cr

ETERBOROUGH

Sawmills by the Stream, Stately Houses by the Roadside

Central Ontario

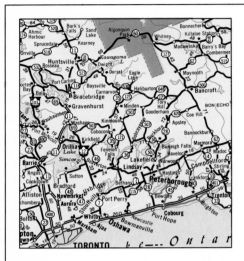

WARSAW CAVES CONSERVATION AREA
Uncounted potholes, passages and underground streams—and a "vanishing" waterfall—have been carved in limestone by the Indian River. On cave walls are fossil remains of prehistoric fish, plants, snails and a giant dragonfly. Above ground are hundreds of potholes, called kettles, formed by boulders caught in river whirlpools. In summer, a four-metre waterfall dries up and the river's reduced flow follows an underground course.

RICE LAKE
This 40-kilometre-long lake takes its name from the wild rice that grows in profusion along its shores. To area Indians, the gourmet delicacy is a principal source of income. Rice Lake is on the route followed by Champlain in 1615 when he journeyed with Huron allies to attack the Iroquois near present-day Syracuse, N.Y.

Victoria Hall courtroom

COBOURG
Palatial summer homes built in the 1800s adorn the town, a Lake Ontario port and popular resort. The birthplace of silent screen star Marie Dressler, restored in the style of the 1830s, is now a tavern and restaurant.
□ A plaque in the Cobourg Conservation Area honors James Cockburn. The Cobourg lawyer was a representative of Upper Canada at the 1864 Quebec Conference, a Father of Confederation, and the first Speaker of the House of Commons.
□ Victoria College (1836) is now a part of the University of Toronto. The college building is part of the Ontario Hospital of Cobourg.
□ Victoria Hall (1860) is one of the province's finest municipal buildings. It was officially opened by the Prince of Wales (later Edward VII). A courtroom is a replica of the Old Bailey in London.

BEWDLEY
In a 19th-century cemetery is an imposing monument to the author of the hymn "What a Friend We Have in Jesus." Irish-born Joseph Medlicott Scriven was drowned in 1886— "found in the attitude of prayer . . . in the flume of a dam near Rice Lake." Three verses of the hymn are inscribed on the memorial.

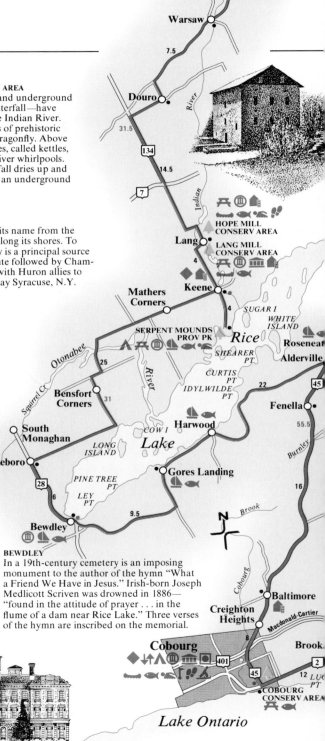

Victoria Hall, Cobourg

Of all pioneer buildings, few are as romantic, or conspicuously practical, as the mill. Near Keene are two fine old mills on the banks of the Indian River. The Lang gristmill, part of Century Village, was built in 1846 to grind flour for local and export markets. Upriver is the Hope sawmill, which milled logs from farmers' woodlots into dressed lumber for barns and houses.

At Keene, rolling farmlands slope down to the inlets and marshes of Rice Lake.

During the 19th century, steamboats from small settlements on the lake, such as Gore's Landing, carried settlers to destinations in the Kawartha Lakes and Haliburton Highlands. Today marinas in the lakeside towns attract boating enthusiasts and fishermen.

South of Rice Lake is Cobourg, whose town hall, opened in 1860, is an impressive reminder of the town's importance during the 19th century, when it was a major port of Lake Ontario. Between Cobourg and Trenton, travelers can take Highway 2. This is part of the Heritage Highway, the historic route that was once the only road link between Upper and Lower Canada. The building of the Macdonald-Cartier Freeway, a few kilometres to the north, has helped to preserve the character of the area. The traveler passes through a tranquil landscape, where red brick and white frame houses built by early settlers in a solid Georgian style stand proudly by the roadside.

Lang gristmill (opposite) and Century Village blacksmith shop (above)

LANG MILL CONSERVATION AREA

The Lang Mill (1846), a stone gristmill beside the Indian River, was the most modern operation of its day. It was here that the first Red Fife wheat, an early hybrid developed in Peterborough, was ground on four large millstones. The grinding bin, scourer, cyclone duster, grain hopper and a fragment of an original millstone are on display.

□ Across the Indian River are the pioneer buildings of Century Village. Restorations include a blacksmith shop, sawmill, shingle mill, a clapboard church, log houses and a general store.

Bones, Beads and Spears from Elaborate Burial Mounds

Under Canada's best preserved and most elaborate burial mounds lie remains of the Point Peninsula Indians who occupied the region 2,000 years ago. They built nine mounds, the largest of which (seven metres high and two metres wide) snakes for 60 metres on a bluff overlooking Rice Lake. Eight smaller, egg-shaped mounds surround it. All contain mass graves associated with elaborate burial rituals. As late as A.D. 1000 small groups of Indians visited the site to bury their dead in pits nearby. Archaeologists have unearthed shell beads, animal bones, copper spears and loon beaks. Some unearthed skeletons are intact; others, fragmented or partially cremated.

An interpretive center displays some of the artifacts found. An excavation in one of the mounds is preserved behind glass.

Excavated skeletons,
Serpent Mounds Provincial Park

GRAFTON

The neoclassic Barnum House was built in 1817 by Col. Eliakim Barnum, a Loyalist who emigrated from Vermont. Restored in the style of a 19th-century gentleman's residence, the building is now a museum. The mansion's showpiece is the elegant, hand-carved mantel.

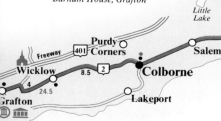

Barnum House, Grafton

TRENTON

This attractive city is at the southern end of the 280-kilometre Trent-Severn Waterway, linking Lake Ontario and Georgian Bay. Originally a trade route, the system of rivers, lakes and canals is now used almost exclusively for recreation. Trenton is the western gateway to Quinte's Isle and the Bay of Quinte.

□ CFB Trenton, one of Canada's largest armed forces air bases, is east of Trenton. Each September an impressive air show draws thousands of spectators.

Common tern,
Presqu'ile Provincial Park

WICKLOW

The oldest Baptist church in Ontario, Wicklow Church (1824), is a simple frame building that served a congregation organized in 1798.

Proctor House, Brighton

BRIGHTON

Presqu'ile Provincial Park, a curved spit of land jutting into Lake Ontario, provides a natural harbor for Brighton and a vast expanse of marshes, forests, meadows and beaches. Presqu'ile Point lighthouse is no longer in service but the lightkeeper's house has been converted into a museum explaining the history and ecology of the region. As many as 10,000 terns and ring-billed gulls breed in summer on a small offshore island. More than 225 species of birds have been sighted; 110 nest in the park.

Trent River
Trenton
BAY OF QUINTE
33
2
14.5
Smithfield
Cankerville
27
Lovett
PROCTOR PARK CONSERV AREA
30
Brighton
Little Lake
12.5
Gosport
PRESQU'ILE BAY
Presqu'ile Point
WELLERS BAY
POPHAM BAY
9
Purdy Corners
401
Salem
Freeway
Wicklow
8.5
2
Colborne
Lake
PRESQU'ILE PROV PK
4
24.5
Lakeport
Grafton
Ontario
CHUB PT

A Lake on the Mountain and a Loyalist Legacy

Southeastern Ontario

Just once in its smooth sweep, the north shore of Lake Ontario dips down into the blue waters. This peninsula appears on the map as Prince Edward County, better known as Quinte's Isle.

With 800 kilometres of shoreline, Quinte's Isle is popular with vacationers. Pleasure craft of all kinds ply its bays and reaches. On the western shore, youngsters romp in the Sandbanks Provincial Park, with its hills of gleaming white sand, or challenge the breakers rolling in on the fine

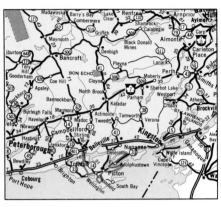

BELLEVILLE

Early Loyalist settlers established two mills on the Moira River here. Belleville, the town that grew up around the mills, became so prosperous that its citizens petitioned Queen Victoria to make their community the capital of Canada.
□ The Hastings County Museum is in Glanmore House, a fine example of Victorian architecture. Lighting devices that range from boat, buggy and bicycle lamps to ancient Roman candles are on display.
□ A monument on the lawn of the Belleville Armory honors Sir Mackenzie Bowell, prime minister of Canada in 1894-96. A printer's apprentice at the Belleville *Intelligencer* as a youth, Bowell later became owner of the newspaper.

Hastings County Museum, Belleville

SANDBANKS PROVINCIAL PARK

A sandy spit of land, this park was once completely covered by water. It was formed when deposits carried by wind and waves created a sand bar across the mouth of a large bay in Lake Ontario. Natural and planted vegetation have taken hold and made permanent this strip of parkland. There is lake swimming along eight kilometres of white beach backed by high sand dunes.
□ A similar reserve in a more developed state is nearby Outlet Beach Provincial Park. Following the self-guiding Cedar Sands Trail, visitors learn how the dunes were formed.

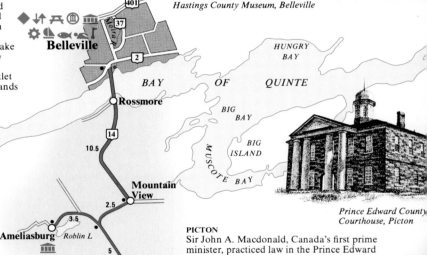

Prince Edward County Courthouse, Picton

PICTON

Sir John A. Macdonald, Canada's first prime minister, practiced law in the Prince Edward County Courthouse, built in 1832-34.
□ Old St. Mary Magdalene's Church (1825-27) is now a museum tracing the history of Prince Edward County.

Sandbanks Provincial Park

Black locust

eaches. On the eastern shore, travelers explore the winding roads that overlook Lake Ontario, and marvel at the Lake on the Mountain, high above the Bay of Quinte. From Glenora, just below the Lake on the Mountain, a free ferry connects Quinte's Isle to Adolphustown. Here, on the shores of Adolphus Reach, is a memorial to the first settlers in this area—the United Empire Loyalists. The first group of pro-British refugees arrived here in 1784.

With determination and patience, these

settlers successfully established themselves here. Reminders of the Loyalist past can be seen today in local museums, Georgian-style houses and old churches kept reverently in repair. Loyalist support for British rule is still reflected in the motto of Ontario: *Ut incepit fidelis sic permanet* (Loyal she began, loyal she remains).

White House, Amherstview

ADOLPHUSTOWN

A plaque that records the landing of one small group of Loyalists on the shores of Adolphus Reach in 1784 bears these words from Exodus—"Put off thy shoes from off thy feet for the place whereon thou standest is holy ground." In a nearby cemetery many Loyalists lie in graves now unmarked. A stone wall, with many of the original headstones embedded in it, and an obelisk were erected in memory of the settlers.

□ The United Empire Loyalist Museum, in an 1877 house, displays maps of the early settlements, "muster rolls" of Loyalists who served in various royal regiments, and pioneer documents, portraits, tools, utensils and furnishings.

□ On the shores of Hay Bay north of Adolphustown is Upper Canada's earliest Methodist chapel, built in 1792. Near the church a cairn marks the site of the boyhood home of Sir John A. Macdonald.

Car ferry to Adolphustown

AMHERSTVIEW

A magnificent example of colonial architecture, the White House was built in 1793 by William Fairfield, Sr., and is still in the Fairfield family five generations later. Few houses of the same period are as well preserved.

□ In nearby Bath is the restored home (1796) of Fairfield's son, William, Jr.

Bonaparte's gull

AMHERST ISLAND

Migratory waterfowl crowd the island's beaches and bays each spring and fall. The gravel beaches of the east end are nesting sites for shorebirds. Bonaparte's gulls are sighted in April and October on the island's southwest tip, accessible only by foot.

□ A plaque at his Amherst Island home honors 19th-century painter Daniel Fowler. A number of the artist's bold watercolors hang in the National Gallery in Ottawa.

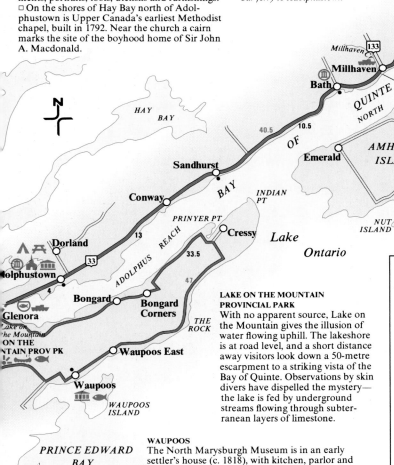

LAKE ON THE MOUNTAIN PROVINCIAL PARK

With no apparent source, Lake on the Mountain gives the illusion of water flowing uphill. The lakeshore is at road level, and a short distance away visitors look down a 50-metre escarpment to a striking vista of the Bay of Quinte. Observations by skin divers have dispelled the mystery— the lake is fed by underground streams flowing through subterranean layers of limestone.

WAUPOOS

The North Marysburgh Museum is in an early settler's house (c. 1818), with kitchen, parlor and bedrooms furnished in rural, 19th-century style. In the restored loft is a display that includes a pedal-operated melodeon (c. 1850), a horse-drawn hay rake (c. 1824), a Quaker doll (1842) and needlecraft, lacework, quilts and handwoven blankets and rugs.

Horse-High, Bull-Strong and Skunk-Tight

Pioneer farmers needed fences that were "horse-high, bull-strong and skunk-tight." They made them from boulders and fieldstones, from tree stumps laid on their sides, and from cedar logs split into rails. One of the most popular was the snake rail fence. With its sharp angles and interlocking joints it was strong and, requiring no posts, easy to build. It zigzagged across the rolling landscape, avoiding obstacles and turning awkward corners. But weeds flourished in its corners and it wasted space. When a snake fence was replaced with a straight rail fence, neighbors disagreed over who owned the newly available land.

Once Canada's Capital, a City Steeped in History

Eastern Ontario

Royal Military College, Kingston

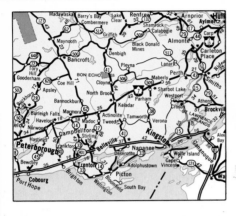

1 Canadian Penitentiary
  Service Museum
2 CAA
3 Bellevue House
  National Historic Park
4 International Hockey
  Hall
  of Fame
5 Queen's University
6 Murney Tower Museum
7 St. Mary's Cathedral
8 St. George's Cathedral
9 City Hall
10 Tourist Information
11 Fort Frontenac
12 Canadian Forces
   Communications and
   Electronics Museum
13 Old Fort Henry
14 Tourist Information
   (summer only)
15 Royal Military
   College
   Museum
16 Stone Frigate

Bellevue House, Kingston

General meeting hall, Kingston City Hall

Sir John A. Macdonald

KINGSTON

In the 1840s when Kingston was the capital of Canada, the city began construction of its city hall in the expectation that it would become the legislative seat. But soon after the build was started, the capital was moved to Montreal; the assembly never used the Kingston building.

□ Bellevue House, an 1840 Tuscan villa, was once the home of Sir John A. Macdonald, Canada's first prime minister.

□ Elizabeth Cottage, at Brock and Clergy streets, is represen tative of the Gothic-style architecture popular in the mid-18

□ Fort Henry, built in 1832-36 and restored 100 years later, presents displays of 19th-century infantry drill. Furnished in the style of the early 1800s, it has extensive collections of cavalry, artillery and naval equipment.

□ The International Hockey Hall of Fame displays skates wi 50-centimetre blades, and a replica of one of the first hockey sticks, used in a game on Kingston harbor ice in the 1880s.

□ Murney Tower, constructed in 1846-51, is a museum of military and pioneer life.

□ The Penitentiary Museum traces the grim story of penal li with displays of instruments of restraint and torture, and prisoner-made weapons.

□ Queen's University, one of Canada's leading universities, founded in 1841.

□ The Royal Military College (1876) is Canada's oldest milit academy.

□ The Canadian Forces Communications and Electronic Museum has exhibits that range from early telephones to modern satellites.

Elizabeth Cottage, Kingston

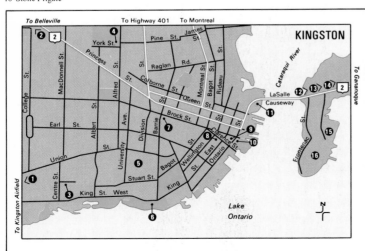

Kingston has been an Indian village, a French fortress, a British citadel—even, briefly, the capital of Canada (1841-44). The past speaks through the gray limestone walls of the old city, through monuments and museums and through the battlements of Fort Henry, where 19th-century military routine is daily reenacted.

Governor Frontenac of New France built a wooden stockade here in 1673. The explorer La Salle, named fort commander, replaced the stockade with stone bastions and called it Fort Frontenac. It was a French trading and military post until 1758, when it fell to the British.

After the American Revolution, in 1784, the site was reoccupied by 1,500 United Empire Loyalists. They called it Kingston in honor of George III. During the War of 1812, Kingston became the major naval base in Upper Canada. It later became an important political center and the home of Sir John A. Macdonald. Today, it is an industrial city of about 60,000.

The Rideau Canal, built in 1826-32, for a time added to Kingston's strategic and commercial importance. For 30 kilometres north of Kingston the canal follows the Cataraqui River through a series of lakes. This stretch of the canal has heavily wooded shores and small rocky islands. Roads lead to picnic sites along many of the canal's hand-operated locks.

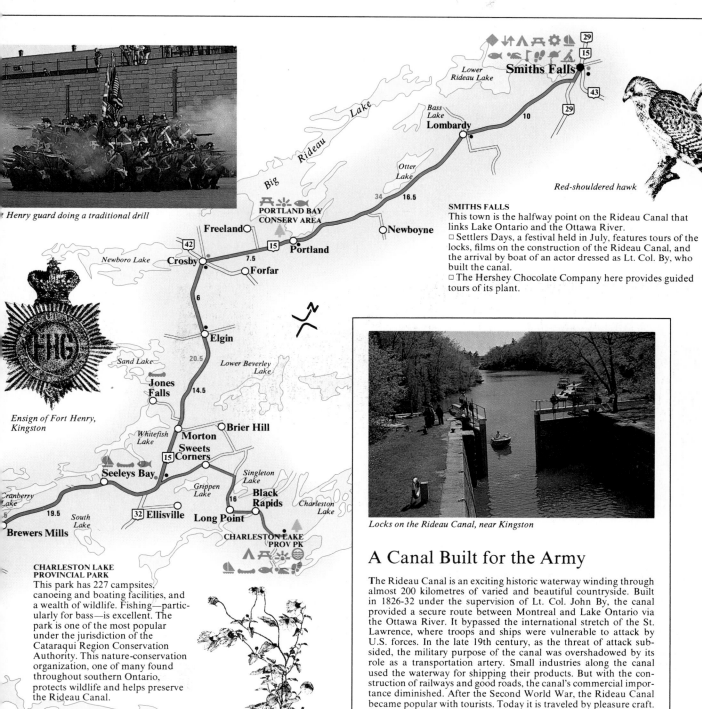

Henry guard doing a traditional drill

Red-shouldered hawk

Ensign of Fort Henry, Kingston

SMITHS FALLS
This town is the halfway point on the Rideau Canal that links Lake Ontario and the Ottawa River.
□ Settlers Days, a festival held in July, features tours of the locks, films on the construction of the Rideau Canal, and the arrival by boat of an actor dressed as Lt. Col. By, who built the canal.
□ The Hershey Chocolate Company here provides guided tours of its plant.

Locks on the Rideau Canal, near Kingston

A Canal Built for the Army

The Rideau Canal is an exciting historic waterway winding through almost 200 kilometres of varied and beautiful countryside. Built in 1826-32 under the supervision of Lt. Col. John By, the canal provided a secure route between Montreal and Lake Ontario via the Ottawa River. It bypassed the international stretch of the St. Lawrence, where troops and ships were vulnerable to attack by U.S. forces. In the late 19th century, as the threat of attack subsided, the military purpose of the canal was overshadowed by its role as a transportation artery. Small industries along the canal used the waterway for shipping their products. But with the construction of railways and good roads, the canal's commercial importance diminished. After the Second World War, the Rideau Canal became popular with tourists. Today it is traveled by pleasure craft.

CHARLESTON LAKE PROVINCIAL PARK
This park has 227 campsites, canoeing and boating facilities, and a wealth of wildlife. Fishing—particularly for bass—is excellent. The park is one of the most popular under the jurisdiction of the Cataraqui Region Conservation Authority. This nature-conservation organization, one of many found throughout southern Ontario, protects wildlife and helps preserve the Rideau Canal.

Black-eyed Susan

Stonemasons' Gems Built Beside Scenic Waterways

Eastern Ontario

Canada has its own Mississippi River—a tranquil, little-known waterway that is a tributary of the Ottawa River. In the last century it was crowded with flat-bottomed barges and log booms. Today, only a few restored mills recall the river's busy past.

Just after the War of 1812, the British government brought settlers here from Scotland and Ireland. Many, ex-soldiers, were rewarded with tracts of land for service to the Crown. Small shipping ports

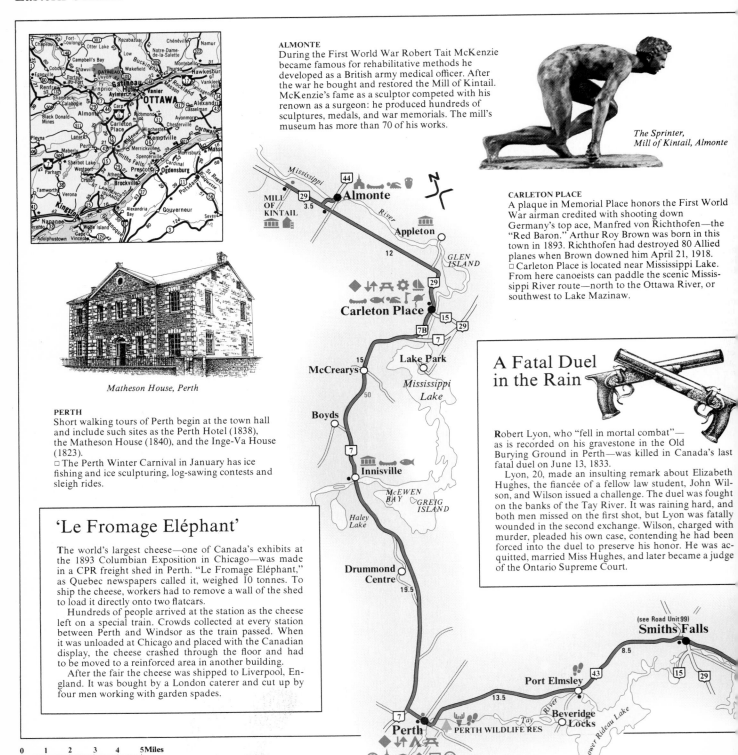

ALMONTE
During the First World War Robert Tait McKenzie became famous for rehabilitative methods he developed as a British army medical officer. After the war he bought and restored the Mill of Kintail. McKenzie's fame as a sculptor competed with his renown as a surgeon: he produced hundreds of sculptures, medals, and war memorials. The mill's museum has more than 70 of his works.

The Sprinter, Mill of Kintail, Almonte

CARLETON PLACE
A plaque in Memorial Place honors the First World War airman credited with shooting down Germany's top ace, Manfred von Richthofen—the "Red Baron." Arthur Roy Brown was born in this town in 1893. Richthofen had destroyed 80 Allied planes when Brown downed him April 21, 1918.
□ Carleton Place is located near Mississippi Lake. From here canoeists can paddle the scenic Mississippi River route—north to the Ottawa River, or southwest to Lake Mazinaw.

Matheson House, Perth

PERTH
Short walking tours of Perth begin at the town hall and include such sites as the Perth Hotel (1838), the Matheson House (1840), and the Inge-Va House (1823).
□ The Perth Winter Carnival in January has ice fishing and ice sculpturing, log-sawing contests and sleigh rides.

A Fatal Duel in the Rain

Robert Lyon, who "fell in mortal combat"— as is recorded on his gravestone in the Old Burying Ground in Perth—was killed in Canada's last fatal duel on June 13, 1833.

Lyon, 20, made an insulting remark about Elizabeth Hughes, the fiancée of a fellow law student, John Wilson, and Wilson issued a challenge. The duel was fought on the banks of the Tay River. It was raining hard, and both men missed on the first shot, but Lyon was fatally wounded in the second exchange. Wilson, charged with murder, pleaded his own case, contending he had been forced into the duel to preserve his honor. He was acquitted, married Miss Hughes, and later became a judge of the Ontario Supreme Court.

'Le Fromage Eléphant'

The world's largest cheese—one of Canada's exhibits at the 1893 Columbian Exposition in Chicago—was made in a CPR freight shed in Perth. "Le Fromage Eléphant," as Quebec newspapers called it, weighed 10 tonnes. To ship the cheese, workers had to remove a wall of the shed to load it directly onto two flatcars.

Hundreds of people arrived at the station as the cheese left on a special train. Crowds collected at every station between Perth and Windsor as the train passed. When it was unloaded at Chicago and placed with the Canadian display, the cheese crashed through the floor and had to be moved to a reinforced area in another building.

After the fair the cheese was shipped to Liverpool, England. It was bought by a London caterer and cut up by four men working with garden spades.

(see Road Unit 99)

0 1 2 3 4 5 Miles
0 2 4 6 8 Kilometres

and mill towns sprang up and, for a time, became thriving commercial centers.

This prosperity is reflected in the fine stone buildings for which the area is noted, many built by the skilled stonemasons who worked on the Rideau Canal. Standing where the Rideau River splits around Long Island at Manotick, Watson's Mill is a splendid five-story gristmill made of river limestone. Equally impressive is the Mill of Kintail, built in 1830 of multicolored fieldstones. Other mills and homes, many of them museums, are treasure houses of local history and Canadiana.

One of the best ways to explore the area is by water. Meandering through historic Lanark County, the Mississippi is at its most active at Almonte, where it drops down Upper and Lower Falls—popular cooling-off spots in summer. The Tay River courses over a pink granite bed, its banks riddled with marine fossils. The Rideau Waterway offers almost 200 kilometres of pleasure boating between Ottawa and Kingston.

This region has attractions for the sportsman and the nature lover. At Rideau River Provincial Park there is fishing for walleye, maskinonge, northern pike and perch. Baxter Conservation Area has interpretive nature trails and programs. A three-kilometre trail at the Perth Wildlife Reserve has been laid out for visitors interested in wildlife management techniques.

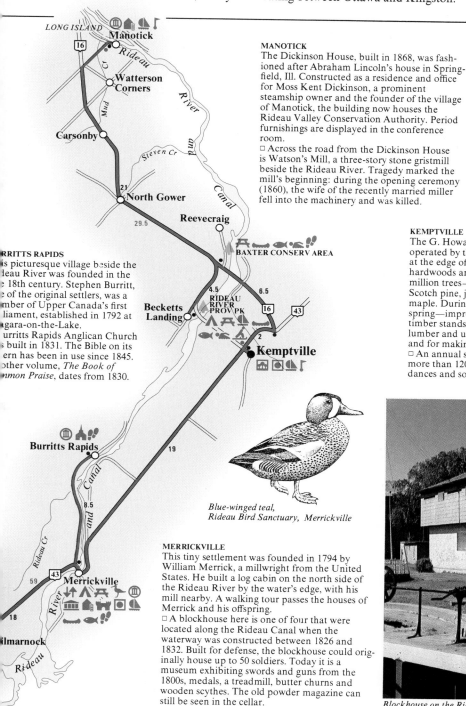

MANOTICK
The Dickinson House, built in 1868, was fashioned after Abraham Lincoln's house in Springfield, Ill. Constructed as a residence and office for Moss Kent Dickinson, a prominent steamship owner and the founder of the village of Manotick, the building now houses the Rideau Valley Conservation Authority. Period furnishings are displayed in the conference room.
□ Across the road from the Dickinson House is Watson's Mill, a three-story stone gristmill beside the Rideau River. Tragedy marked the mill's beginning: during the opening ceremony (1860), the wife of the recently married miller fell into the machinery and was killed.

Watson's Mill, Manotick

KEMPTVILLE
The G. Howard Ferguson Forest Station, a vast tree nursery operated by the Ontario Ministry of Natural Resources, is located at the edge of town. Here nursery stock and mixed and pure hardwoods are grown. Annual production is approximately 10 million trees—the principal species being red pine, white pine, Scotch pine, jack pine, Carolina poplar, white cedar and silver maple. During the nursery's off-season—late fall to early spring—improvement work is done on the hardwood and mixed timber stands. Cuttings taken at this time are processed into lumber and used for the upkeep of buildings and equipment and for making shipping crates.
□ An annual summer festival has been held at Kemptville for more than 120 years. Activities include barbecues, parades, dances and soapbox derbies.

BURRITTS RAPIDS
[Thi]s picturesque village beside the [Rid]eau River was founded in the [lat]e 18th century. Stephen Burritt, [on]e of the original settlers, was a [me]mber of Upper Canada's first [par]liament, established in 1792 at [Nia]gara-on-the-Lake.
[B]urritts Rapids Anglican Church [wa]s built in 1831. The Bible on its [lect]ern has been in use since 1845. [An]other volume, *The Book of [Com]mon Praise*, dates from 1830.

Blue-winged teal,
Rideau Bird Sanctuary, Merrickville

MERRICKVILLE
This tiny settlement was founded in 1794 by William Merrick, a millwright from the United States. He built a log cabin on the north side of the Rideau River by the water's edge, with his mill nearby. A walking tour passes the houses of Merrick and his offspring.
□ A blockhouse here is one of four that were located along the Rideau Canal when the waterway was constructed between 1826 and 1832. Built for defense, the blockhouse could originally house up to 50 soldiers. Today it is a museum exhibiting swords and guns from the 1800s, medals, a treadmill, butter churns and wooden scythes. The old powder magazine can still be seen in the cellar.

Blockhouse on the Rideau Canal near Merrickville

Our 'Westminster of the Wilderness,' a City of History, Parks and Pageantry

Queen Victoria chose Ottawa in 1857, ending the aspirations of Montreal, Quebec, Toronto and Kingston to become the capital of Canada. There was fierce opposition—Ottawa, said author Goldwin Smith, was "a subarctic lumber village converted . . . into a political cockpit." But ground was broken for the Parliament Buildings in 1859 and Ottawa's status was confirmed by the British North America Act of 1867.

The area's first settler had been Nicholas Sparks, who built a farm in the early 1800s near present-day Sparks Street. The homestead he cleared from the Upper Canadian bush remained isolated until 1826, when Col. John By and the Royal Engineers began construction of the Rideau Canal. British Canada had come perilously close to losing the War of 1812, and the canal would enable English ships to avoid American cannon along the St. Lawrence.

When the job was completed in 1832, a small lumbering village called Bytown began to grow. Its name was changed in 1855—Ottawa seemed a better bet in the competition to become the national capital—and two years later the city became the "Westminster of the Wilderness."

Today the sober dignity of Victorian buildings is complemented by striking modern architecture and flower-lined parks, drives and squares. Development of the Ottawa region is carefully supervised by the National Capital Commission, which has redesigned the city center. Among the commission's decisions were to convert the Rideau Canal into an illuminated, seven-kilometre-long skating rink in winter (the world's largest) and to turn Sparks Street into a pedestrian mall. A staid, businesslike seat of government, Ottawa is also a city of history, pageantry, parks, festivals and the arts.

Frozen Rideau Canal (right) attracts about half a million skaters every winter. The seven-kilometre-long rink has six activity centers, each with parking, food and skate sharpening. Strollers and sightseers line the waterway's banks in summer (below).

Billings Estate (7)
Braddish Billings' first home, a small log cabin (1813), became a summer kitchen for a larger home built here in 1828.

Bytown Museum (17)
Housed in Colonel By's three-story stone commissariat store (1827), the museum features relics and documents relating to the building of the Rideau Canal and the history of Ottawa.

By Ward Market (26)
Since the 1830s, farmers have brought their produce to this outdoor market, held on Tuesday, Thursday and Saturday mornings.

Canadian Film Institute (18)
Classic and contemporary films are screened for visitors at the National Film Theater. On display are historic still photographs, books and movie posters. There is also a film library and publication division.

Canadian War Museum (23)
A solid brass cannon cast in 1732 and a Gatling gun, used to suppress the Northwest Rebellion in 1885, are part of a collection tracing Canada's military history.

Carleton University (5)
Fifteen thousand students attend this university (founded in 1942) on the banks of the Rideau River. Elegant modern buildings include the 22-story Arts Tower. In the Henry Marshall Tory Science Building is a 3-by-50-metre mosaic mural by Gerald Trottier.

Central Experimental Farm (3)
A 480-hectare farm in the heart of the city is the headquarters of the Department of Agriculture. Horse-drawn wagon tours pass flower beds, ornamental gardens and the oldest arboretum in Canada.

Changing of the Guard (16)
Rank and file of guardsmen in scarlet tunics and bearskin hats wheel through their precise pageantry on Parliament Hill daily during the summer.

City Hall (30)
Royal swans—a Centennial gift from Queen Elizabeth—and an unusual freestanding stairway finished in white marble and aluminum grace this eight-story building (1958) overlooking the Rideau Falls.

Earnscliffe (29)
This three-story house (1855), Sir John A. Macdonald's home in 1883-91, is the residence of the British high commissioner.

Garden of the Provinces (9)
Provincial flags fly above enameled bronze plaques of the provincial flowers.

Government House (32)
Rideau Hall, the governor-general's residence, is a three-story limestone house built in 1835. The grounds are open to the public when His Excellency is not in residence.

Governor-General's Foot Guards Museum (21)
Regimental colors, trophies, medals, uniforms and weapons date from 1872.

Kitchissippi Lookout (1)
A plaque commemorates the Canadian voyageurs who guided Col. Garnet Wolseley's forces through the rapids of the Nile

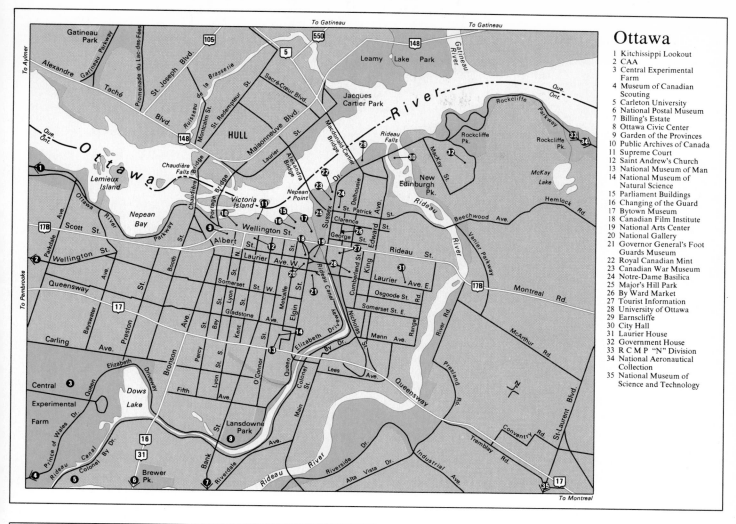

Ottawa

1. Kitchissippi Lookout
2. CAA
3. Central Experimental Farm
4. Museum of Canadian Scouting
5. Carleton University
6. National Postal Museum
7. Billing's Estate
8. Ottawa Civic Center
9. Garden of the Provinces
10. Public Archives of Canada
11. Supreme Court
12. Saint Andrew's Church
13. National Museum of Man
14. National Museum of Natural Science
15. Parliament Buildings
16. Changing of the Guard
17. Bytown Museum
18. Canadian Film Institute
19. National Arts Center
20. National Gallery
21. Governor General's Foot Guards Museum
22. Royal Canadian Mint
23. Canadian War Museum
24. Notre-Dame Basilica
25. Major's Hill Park
26. By Ward Market
27. Tourist Information
28. University of Ottawa
29. Earnscliffe
30. City Hall
31. Laurier House
32. Government House
33. R C M P "N" Division
34. National Aeronautical Collection
35. National Museum of Science and Technology

A Child's Capital

Young visitors explore a War Museum exhibit

There are more museums, galleries, parks and play-grounds per square block in Ottawa than anywhere else in Canada—and most of them are free. Throughout the city, children can browse, picnic, bicycle, skate and, of course, have their pictures taken with a Mountie.

Guided tours show the workings of government on Parliament Hill. In the Museum of Science and Technology are steam whistles, bulb horns and a tilted Crazy Kitchen. Dinosaur skulls bare prehistoric teeth in the Museum of Natural History. The Museum of Man traces the history of the first Canadians—the Indians and Inuit.

Three hangars are filled with vintage airplanes at the Aeronautical Collection, and at the War Museum children can climb on tank turrets and crawl through a battlefield trench. The National Gallery displays everything from art masterpieces to three life-sized stuffed camels.

The former residence of two prime ministers, Laurier House (1878) is now a museum.

National Aeronautical Collection (34)
Among more than 90 historic aircraft on display are a replica of *Silver Dart,* which made the first heavier-than-air flight in the British Empire (1909), and a First World War Sopwith Snipe. The collection is housed at Rockcliffe Airport.

National Arts Center (19)
In this modern complex on the west bank of the Rideau Canal are the 2,300-seat Opera House, the 800-seat Theater, the hexagonal Studio, and the Salon for receptions and recitals. Performances range from symphony concerts to modern jazz, from Shakespearean plays to underground films.

in the 1884 expedition to rescue Gordon of Khartoum.
Laurier House (31)
This stone mansion (1878) is filled with photographs, documents and furniture belonging to the prime ministers who lived here, Sir Wilfrid Laurier and Mackenzie King. A prie-dieu (c. 1550) from Mary Queen of Scots' castle and an oak chair said to have been used at the coronation of James I of England are displayed.

Major's Hill Park (25)
A cannon cast in 1807 is fired at noon on weekdays and 10 a.m. on Sundays in a tradition that dates from 1869. Two stones from the Sappers' Bridge that crossed the Rideau Canal mark the site of Colonel By's house.
Museum of Canadian Scouting (4)
Exhibits tracing the history of the Boy Scout movement in Canada include an illustrated log kept by Lord Baden-Powell on his visit to Canada in 1910.

Blossoming tulips (right) *turn Ottawa into a riot of color. With some three million blossoms, the city has North America's largest tulip display. One of the most stirring sights in Canada is the 45-minute Changing of the Guard on Parliament Hill* (below). *Men of the Governor-General's Foot Guards and the Canadian Grenadier Guards, with two bands, take part. Coats of arms of the provinces are carved in the limestone arches of Confederation Hall* (bottom).

National Gallery (20)
Canada's most extensive art collection displays works from many countries. Canadians Arthur Lismer and Paul-Emile Borduas are represented by *The Guide's Home, Algonquin* and *Sous le vent de l'île,* both oils. The foreign collection includes works by Canaletto, Rubens, Rembrandt, El Greco, Turner, Corot, Dégas, Cézanne and Mondrian. The gallery was founded in 1880.

National Museum of Man (13)
Artifacts, films and dioramas illustrate Indian and Inuit lore, the development of Canada as a nation, and Canadian culture. *The Immense Journey* is a multi-media pre-

A fanciful lion, its fierce stare frozen in stone, is one of many carved figures on Parliament Hill.

sentation of the "poetic and mystic vision of man through the ages." A reconstructed archaeological dig tells the story of prehistoric man in Canada. The museum and the National Museum of Natural Sciences are housed in the castlelike Victoria Memorial Building (1911).

National Museum of Natural Sciences (14)
Preserved specimens of mammals and birds from across Canada are in recreations of their natural habitats. Displays of fossils, minerals, plants and animals illustrate the geologic and natural history of the earth.

National Museum of Science and Technology (35)
Working exhibits ranging from vintage automobiles to a Van de Graaff generator encourage visitors to touch, push, pull, twist, climb and observe. A new observatory has a 37-centimetre refracting telescope.

is paved with stones from the battlefields of France and Belgium.

The Peace Tower entrance to the Center Block leads to Confederation Hall, whose pillars are symbolic of Confederation and the provinces. Hand-painted Irish linen covers the ceiling of the House of Commons. The speaker's chair is a replica of the one in Westminster. In the Commons foyer is a 36-metre-long limestone frieze depicting the history of Canada. Murals of First World War battlefields and a ceiling gilded with gold leaf decorate the ornate Senate Chamber.

When Parliament is in session, visitors may watch the proceedings from the House of Commons gallery.

Public Archives of Canada (10)
On displays are some 100,000 books, paintings, engravings, photographs, manuscripts, recordings, maps and prints relating to Canada's past.

First World War soldiers silhouetted against an Ottawa sky (left) are part of the National War Memorial in Confederation Square. George VI unveiled the memorial in May 1939. Newly minted coins gleam at the Royal Canadian Mint (above). An airmail pioneer of the 1920s (below right) is one of 90 vintage airplanes at the National Aeronautical Collection, housed in three hangars at Rockcliffe Airport. The National Arts Center's grounds are enlivened by an open-air concert (below left).

National Postal Museum (6)
A recreated turn-of-the-century post office and a railway mail car complement an extensive collection of Canadian and world stamps.

Notre Dame Basilica (24)
Above the Gothic-style choir stalls are Philippe Hébert statues of prophets, evangelists and patriarchs of the church. The basilica, begun in 1841, has 54-metre twin towers. There is a memorial to Msgr. Joseph-Eugène Guigues, founder of the University of Ottawa.

Ottawa Civic Center (8)
Among the facilities are a 35,000-seat stadium and a 9,300-seat arena used for sporting events and concerts.

Parliament Buildings (15)
Three huge Victorian Gothic buildings, built between 1859 and 1865, dominate Ottawa's skyline: the Center Block (House of Commons and Senate), the East Block (governor-general's, privy council's and prime minister's offices and cabinet chamber) and the West Block (offices and committee rooms). Much was rebuilt or replaced after a devastating fire swept the buildings in 1916.

Crowning the Center Block is the 87-metre-high Peace Tower with its 53-bell carillon, the largest bell weighing 10,160 kilograms. Atop the tower, a white light burns when Parliament is in session. Below the carillon is the Memorial Chamber, where four Books of Remembrance list the names of Canadians who gave their lives in wars. Carved in sandstone walls that rise to 14 metres are poems by John McCrae, Rudyard Kipling, Victor Hugo, John Bunyan and Laurence Binyon. The chamber

RCMP "N" Division (33)
Visitors can watch rehearsals of the RCMP Band and the Musical Ride, and the training of RCMP horses.

Royal Canadian Mint (22)
The mint produces millions of coins and blanks for other countries. (Canadian bank notes are printed by private firms.) Visitors watch metal being rolled to coin thickness, blanks being annealed and impressions being struck. A small museum has Canadian and foreign coins.

Saint Andrew's Church (12)
The pews in this stone church (1872) are arranged in a semicircle around the pulpit. The lectern was presented to the church by Queen Juliana of the Netherlands, who joined the congregation while living here during the Second World War.

Supreme Court (11)
Tours of this massive stone building include the two Federal Courts, the Supreme Court and the judges' chambers.

University of Ottawa (28)
The oldest bilingual university in Canada (founded as Bytown College in 1848) is also the largest, with an enrollment of 18,000.

A Capital's Playground Nestling in Rolling Wooded Hills

Gatineau Park

A playground set in wilderness, Gatineau Park lies within sight of Ottawa's Parliament Buildings. Neither national nor provincial, the park was established in 1938 and is administered by the National Capital Commission.

The park's rolling hills are the stumps of ancient mountains rounded by glaciers. The ice disappeared about 12,000 years ago, leaving the land bleak and devoid of life. Then began the great invasion of plants and animals that continues even today.

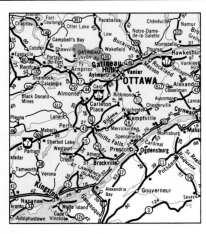

LA PÊCHE
A steam engine, operated in summer along the Gatineau River from Ottawa, is turned 180 degrees on a hand-pushed turntable here. During the stopover, excursionists explore an 88-metre covered bridge spanning the Gatineau, or picnic on the riverbank.
□ The McLaren gristmill, a three-story stone building on the Lapêche River, dates from the 1830s.
□ Lester B. Pearson, Canada's 19th prime minister, is buried in McLaren Cemetery.

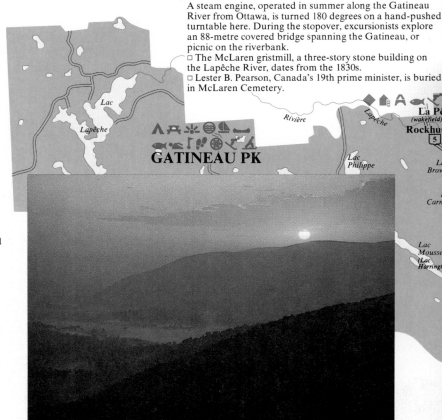

Gatineau Hills

GATINEAU PARK
This 35,640-hectare preserve is a sanctuary for the native wild plants and animals of the Canadian Shield and a year-round recreation area for thousands of visitors.
□ Spring here is heralded by the honk of Canada geese, the croak of wood frogs and the wild sweet music of spring peepers. Blue herons wing over marshes where muskrats swim. Above the hubbub from nesting redwings and swamp sparrows come the clear notes of olive-sided flycatchers. In the mud of a beaver dam, the hiker may chance upon fresh bear tracks, or glimpse a deer, a fox or an otter on the banks of a stream.

Wild herbs abound in the park, which has some 100 species of wild flowers. The showy lady's-slipper and the insect-trapping sundew and pitcher plants grow in boggy woods.
□ The official summer residence of Canadian prime ministers is at Harrington (Mousseau) Lake. It is not open to the public.

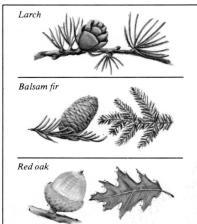

Larch

Balsam fir

Red oak

From Hilltop to Lowland— a Forest Renewed

Centuries of logging, land clearing, fires and floods have left their mark on the three types of forest in Gatineau Park. Half the trees grow in shallow soil along ridgetops and upper slopes. Fires have swept away many older stands, and most trees are less than 60 years old. Here are the hardwoods—gnarled red oak, ironwood and white ash, and the aspens and white birch which take over cleared land. There are mixed-wood stands of hemlock and red maple, and a few softwood groves of white, red and jack pines.

Shade-tolerant hardwoods such as sugar maple and beech thrive on moist middle and lower slopes. Balsam fir and white spruce grow in softwood thickets on abandoned farmland.

Along streams and wet lowlands, mixed woods—black ash and cedar—and softwood stands of black spruce, larch and tamarack are most common.

AYLMER
Vintage golf balls, one-piece wooden clubs and the brassies and mashies, spoons and niblicks, forerunners of today's numbered woods and irons, are in the Canadian Golf Museum at the Kingsway Park Golf and Country Club. Other exhibits include a leather-faced wooden spoon used by Willie Park, winner of the first British Open in 1860.
□ Among some 170 historic buildings in the Aylmer-Lucerne area are Symmes Inn (1832), the British Hotel (1841) and the Town Hall (1851), formerly a courthouse.
□ A public marina can accommodate several hundred boats.

Indians settled in the valley of the Ottawa River 4,000 years ago, but it was not until the fur-trade era that man's presence was felt in the Gatineau region in a major way. Settlers and loggers arrived early in the 19th century. Because the terrain was suitable only for sheep grazing, most settlers had left by the turn of the century. But the loggers stayed until lumbering ended in the 1920s. With their departure, man invaded the Gatineau Hills, this time for the sheer enjoyment of the wooded terrain.

Today the Gatineau Parkway, a 35-kilometre scenic drive from Hull to the Champlain Lookout, offers a panoramic view of the hills. More than 97 kilometres of hiking trails crisscross the slopes. In winter, skiers (cross-country and downhill) and snowshoers follow these trails. Forty-four lakes beckon to canoeists and fishermen. The park has family and group camping and is studded with picturesque picnic sites. There is an atmosphere of timelessness that only a wilderness can impart.

Gatineau River

GATINEAU RIVER
This tributary of the Ottawa River, into which it empties near Hull, is named after Nicolas Gatineau, a fur trader and notary from Trois-Rivières, Que., who explored the river in 1650, and is believed to have drowned here in 1683. Hydroelectricity is generated at four sites along this 386-kilometre-long waterway.

LAC-MEACH
In 1911 Lac-Meach became the research headquarters for Thomas "Carbide" Willson, who had discovered the process for manufacturing calcium carbide and acetylene gas. Ruins of the experimental station where Willson worked remain.
□ A frame house built here in 1823 by one of the area's first settlers, Asa Meech, has been restored.

The Great Days of the Gatineau Logger

Lumbering was Canada's biggest industry during most of the mid-19th century—and some of the finest stands of white pine needed for the British square-timber trade were in the Gatineau forests.

Trees were felled in winter, when logs could be skidded along the frozen ground. The men who felled and squared the logs also shepherded them on the long river drives, and so were hired "from freeze-up to Quebec."

Loggers worked in pairs, taking alternate swings at a tree. Logs were hauled to a river's edge by oxen and stacked there for the spring drive. When the ice broke, the tumbling logs had to be herded down rivers and streams to the Ottawa River, where they were bound into rafts to be guided to Quebec. It was dangerous, exhausting work. Lumbermen in town after being paid off in July were like "a roistering plague." Many a man's pay—up to $300—was lost in a few nights of drinking, wenching and brawling.

KINGSMERE
The Cloisters (*below*) is the most striking of the ruins that Mackenzie King, prime minister in 1921-30 and 1935-48, collected at his Kingsmere estate, now part of Gatineau Park. Part of The Cloisters is a bay window taken from the demolished Ottawa home of Simon-Napoléon Parent, premier of Quebec in 1900-05. Other buildings consist of re-assembled stone walls from demolished 19th-century Ottawa office buildings and the bombed Houses of Parliament in London.
□ King's summer residence, Moorside, is now a museum.

HULL
This city was founded in 1800, more than two decades before Ottawa (Bytown) began to develop across the Ottawa River. The first settler was Philemon Wright, an American, who cleared a farm near Chaudière Falls. He is commemorated by a stone column bearing a bronze medallion of his likeness. The Georgian farmhouse he built in 1839, and which was later owned by his son-in-law Thomas Brigham, is now a restaurant, La Ferme Columbia.
□ One of North America's biggest lumber, pulp and paper centers, Hull is the home of the E.B. Eddy Company, which began as a pine match factory in 1851.
□ There are tours of Place du Portage, the Government Printing Bureau, where Hansard, the record of parliamentary business, is produced.
□ The Trail of the Voyageurs, a portage at Chaudière Falls, used by early explorers, is one of Canada's oldest preserved hiking routes.

Place du Portage, Hull

Patterson
○ Cascades
○ Chemin-des-Pins
○ Burnet 20
Larrimac 22
River
Kirks Ferry
Gleneagle
Lac-Meach
Tenaga
6
307
2 Chelsea
Old Chelsea
3
Kingsmere
Lac Pink
105
Gatineau Parkway
Ruisseau Chelsea
14
Touraine
307
GATINEAU
ILE KETTLE
Pointe-Gatineau
Ottawa River
148
5
24.5
HULL
148
Lucerne
Queensway
CMER
148
10.5
Lac Deschênes
Deschênes
PTE ROCHEUSE
Queensway
OTTAWA
(see Road Unit 101)

Legendary Pieces of Paradise Dropped from a God's Blanket

The Thousand Islands

Some are lushy forested. Others support only a few ragged pines perched precariously over the water. These are the lovely Thousand Islands (perhaps 995, maybe 1,010) that lie in a 56-kilometre stretch between Gananoque and Brockville. They range in size from a protruding boulder to large islands with attractive summer homes and marinas.

By day the islands appear as splashes of green on a river whose blues change color with every different shade of light; when

By Boat to Boldt Castle

George Boldt, an immigrant from Germany in the late 1800s, began work in North America as a dishwasher. His rise from poverty to riches was quick. He helped establish the Waldorf-Astoria Hotel in New York City, acquired control of several major businesses—and became a millionaire.

Boldt's dream was to build a castle for his wife. In the 1890s he purchased one of the Thousand Islands, had it reshaped as a heart, and ordered the construction of his castle. But before the structure was completed, Boldt's wife died. Grief-stricken, he ordered the work halted. Boldt never returned to his ornate dream castle on Heart Island. Boats to the island leave from Gananoque, Ivy Lea, Kingston and Rockport.

Boldt Castle, Heart Island

Thousand Islands International Bridge

THOUSAND ISLANDS PARKWAY
Trees along the 38-kilometre parkway sometimes screen the St. Lawrence but lookouts every few kilometres give fine views of the river. Above the road, near Brown's Bay, is a kilometre-long slab of rare light gray sandstone atop the reddish granite common in this area.

The largest stand of pitch pine in mainland Canada grows along this route; the trees are especially thick among the red and white oaks between Rockport and Ivy Lea. Great blue herons and American bitterns feed in roadside marshes.

Pitch pine

MALLORYTOWN LANDING
Located on the north shore of the St. Lawrence River, this is the only part of St. Lawrence Islands National Park accessible by car. Swimming, fishing and fine beaches are major attractions.

GANANOQUE
This picturesque waterfront resort is the chief Canadian approach to the Thousand Islands.
□ Three rooms of the Gananoque Historical Museum—bedroom, parlor and kitchen— are furnished in Victorian style. Exhibits include a wooden flute (c. 1750) and an 1885 gramophone.
□ A plaque describes the exploits of "Pirate" Bill Johnson, a Canadian-born renegade who settled in New York State and, during 1838, led armed raids on the Canadian shore and on British shipping from a base in Thousand Islands.

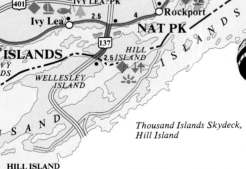

Thousand Islands Skydeck, Hill Island

HILL ISLAND
Hill Island is between spans of the Thousand Islands International Bridge. A plaque commemorates the opening of the bridge by Prime Minister Mackenzie King and President Franklin D. Roosevelt in 1938.
□ The view from the Thousand Islands Skydeck, 120 metres above the St. Lawrence River, is 65 kilometres on a clear day. Three observation levels are reached by an elevator.

0 1 2 3 4 5 Miles
0 2 4 6 8 Kilometres

night descends, cottage lights and campfires wink from among the trees and cast flickering reflections across the water.

Indians called the Thousand Islands the Garden of the Great Spirit and believed the region was once a great expanse of open water. According to legend, the Great Spirit created a garden paradise along the shore in an effort to bring peace to warring tribes. Still they fought. So he bundled paradise into a blanket and flew toward his home in the heavens. But the blanket tore and paradise crashed into the water, breaking into hundreds of pieces.

There is also a geological explanation. Some 900 million years ago mountains as majestic as the Rockies rose where the St. Lawrence River now flows. Rivers and glaciers reduced the peaks to low hills that now are islands and shoals.

In the late 19th century the islands were a millionaires' playground where tycoons built lavish waterfront mansions and spent summers in idyllic luxury. Today the islands are among Canada's most popular tourist areas. Scenic boat tours, nature trails, country fairs, water sports and some of the world's best freshwater fishing make the Thousand Islands a near perfect family vacationland.

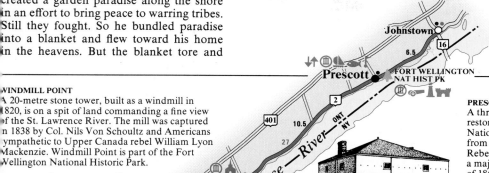

WINDMILL POINT
A 20-metre stone tower, built as a windmill in 1820, is on a spit of land commanding a fine view of the St. Lawrence River. The mill was captured in 1838 by Col. Nils Von Schoultz and Americans sympathetic to Upper Canada rebel William Lyon Mackenzie. Windmill Point is part of the Fort Wellington National Historic Park.

BUELL'S CREEK CONSERV AREA

Brockville

Maitland

Morristown

Butternut Bay

Blockhouse, Fort Wellington National Historic Park

PRESCOTT
A three-story blockhouse built in 1838 has been restored as the main attraction of Fort Wellington National Historic Park. The fort itself, which dates from 1812, saw service during the Upper Canada Rebellion of 1837 and the Patriot War of 1838, was a major defensive position during the Fenian raids of 1866 and was last garrisoned in 1885.

The blockhouse has stone walls 1.3 metres thick. The ground floor, consisting of a guardroom, storeroom, armory and powder magazine, serves as a museum. Exhibits include rifles, pistols, swords, cannon and historical documents and pictures.
□ Loyalist buildings in Prescott include the Jones and Peck houses, both in neoclassic style.
□ At Johnstown, 6.5 kilometres east, is the Ogdensburg-Prescott International Bridge.

MAITLAND
At the Blue Church, a wooden building erected in 1845 on the site of two previous chapels, are the graves of many of Ontario's earliest settlers, including Barbara Heck, the founder of Methodism in North America. Born in Ireland, she emigrated to New York in 1760; there she founded a Methodist society and the continent's first Wesleyan church. She came here after the American Revolution, formed Upper Canada's first Methodist society and lived here until her death.
□ The Old Distillery Tower, built as a gristmill by George Longley in 1828, was also used as a distillery and a shot tower.

Blue Church, Maitland

Red-breasted merganser

Mayapple

Shaggymane

BROCKVILLE
Founded in 1784, Brockville was one of the first Loyalist settlements in Upper Canada. It was named after Maj. Gen. Sir Isaac Brock, the War of 1812 hero.
□ Along the city's clean, tree-lined streets are many fine old homes. Brockville Courthouse, constructed in 1842, is one of Ontario's oldest public buildings. Other well-preserved structures include The Carriage House Hotel (1820), Victoria School (1855) and the Orange Lodge (1825).
□ The Brockville Railway Tunnel, Canada's oldest, was built in 1854-60 to enable trains of the Brockville and Ottawa Railway to reach the riverfront. The tunnel was last used in 1954.
□ Nearby Blockhouse Island was used as a quarantine station during a cholera outbreak in the 1830s.

A Boater's Paradise in a Park of Islands

A small mainland area, 18 heavily wooded islands and 80 rocky islets between Kingston and Brockville form St. Lawrence Islands National Park. Its scenic beauty and sheltered waters have earned it a reputation as a boater's paradise.

The park supports a rich diversity of flora and fauna, much of it usually found farther south. Among 800 plant species are black oak, mayapple and shaggymane, Canada's only deerberry and the world's most northerly growth of rue anemone. Some 65 species of birds sighted here include cardinals, Carolina wrens, wild turkeys, bald eagles and red-breasted mergansers; 28 species of reptiles and amphibians include eastern ribbon snakes and blue-spotted salamanders. There are some 35 species of fish in this region.

The islands, with such poetic names as Camelot, Mermaid and Endymion, were rounded by glaciers and rivers some 500 million years ago. Almost all of the islands have docks, campsites, wells and kitchen shelters.

Hiking, canoeing and supervised swimming are among the park's main attractions.

Across an 1840 Bridge
to a Village of Yesteryear

Southeastern Ontario

Sightseeing barge, Upper Canada Village

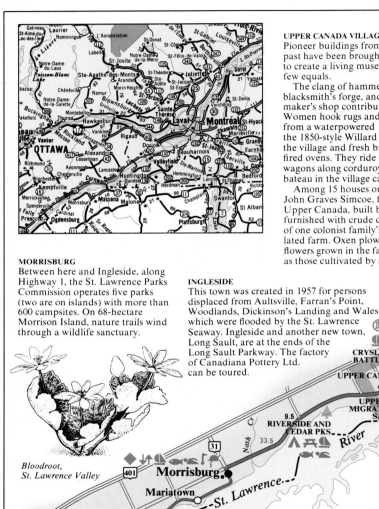

UPPER CANADA VILLAGE
Pioneer buildings from Ontario's past have been brought together here to create a living museum that has few equals.

The clang of hammer on anvil rings from the blacksmith's forge, and a sawmill and cabinet-maker's shop contribute to the village's upkeep. Women hook rugs and make blankets with wool from a waterpowered 1840 mill. Visitors can eat in the 1850-style Willard Hotel, buy cheese made in the village and fresh bread baked daily in wood-fired ovens. They ride on oxcarts or horse-drawn wagons along corduroy, plank and dirt roads. A bateau in the village canal is pulled by a horse.

Among 15 houses on the site is the residence of John Graves Simcoe, first lieutenant governor of Upper Canada, built before 1783. A log school is furnished with crude desks and benches. The story of one colonist family's success is told on a simulated farm. Oxen plow the fields; vegetables and flowers grown in the farm gardens are the same kind as those cultivated by settlers.

Cheese factory, Upper Canada Village

MORRISBURG
Between here and Ingleside, along Highway 1, the St. Lawrence Parks Commission operates five parks (two are on islands) with more than 600 campsites. On 68-hectare Morrison Island, nature trails wind through a wildlife sanctuary.

Bloodroot, St. Lawrence Valley

INGLESIDE
This town was created in 1957 for persons displaced from Aultsville, Farran's Point, Woodlands, Dickinson's Landing and Wales which were flooded by the St. Lawrence Seaway. Ingleside and another new town, Long Sault, are at the ends of the Long Sault Parkway. The factory of Canadiana Pottery Ltd. can be toured.

IROQUOIS
When the St. Lawrence Seaway was constructed, Iroquois was the largest of several villages relocated: about 1,100 residents and 157 buildings were moved to a site about one kilometre north of the original.
□ The 1½-story Carman House (c. 1810)—built of stone on high ground—was the only Iroquois building not moved. Now a craft shop and museum, it contains many original furnishings, a stone sink and a Dutch oven and hearth.
□ Straddling the Canada-U.S. border is a huge international dam which maintains the St. Lawrence River at the best level for navigation.

Carman House, Iroquois

CRYSLER'S FARM BATTLEFIELD PARK
The centerpiece of this park is a 15-metre mound of battlefield soil topped by an obelisk commemorating those killed in the 1813 Battle of Crysler's Farm. An interpretive center describes the battle in which some 800 British, Canadians and Indians routed 4,000 invading American soldiers.
□ The nearby Pioneer Memorial has gravestones of pioneers built into its walls.
□ A memorial to Loyalist settlers has a bronze figure of a soldier in a tattered uniform.

Iroquois lock, St. Lawrence Seaway

Houses, churches, taverns and shops of the era from 1784 to 1867 have been restored and reconstructed at Upper Canada Village, east of Morrisburg. Some of the buildings were moved here when their original sites were submerged during construction of the St. Lawrence Seaway in the late 1950s. The authentic flavor of village life involved painstaking research by architects, historians and horticulturists.

Visitors enter the village's main street—the King's Highway—over an 1840 bridge.

Clustered along one side of the highway are houses whose interiors mirror pioneer existence in the smallest detail. Fabrics, paints and wallpapers match those in use before Confederation. Every hand-forged nail and door latch, every hand-dipped candle is authentic or was reproduced with 19th-century tools and methods.

Lunaria, hollyhocks, love-in-a-mist and McIntosh apple trees—the first McIntosh Reds were produced north of here at Dundela—bloom at Crysler Hall. This imposing

mansion was built by a son of John Crysler, whose farm was the site of a decisive victory in the War of 1812. The site was submerged, but the battle is commemorated in Crysler's Farm Battlefield Park next to the village.

A few kilometres east, the Long Sault Parkway links a series of islands, each of which was a hilltop before the flooding.

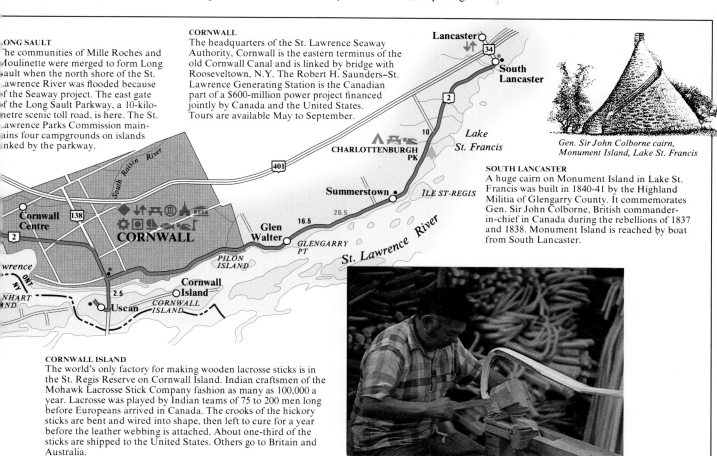

LONG SAULT
The communities of Mille Roches and Moulinette were merged to form Long Sault when the north shore of the St. Lawrence River was flooded because of the Seaway project. The east gate of the Long Sault Parkway, a 10-kilometre scenic toll road, is here. The St. Lawrence Parks Commission maintains four campgrounds on islands linked by the parkway.

CORNWALL
The headquarters of the St. Lawrence Seaway Authority, Cornwall is the eastern terminus of the old Cornwall Canal and is linked by bridge with Rooseveltown, N.Y. The Robert H. Saunders–St. Lawrence Generating Station is the Canadian part of a $600-million power project financed jointly by Canada and the United States. Tours are available May to September.

Gen. Sir John Colborne cairn, Monument Island, Lake St. Francis

SOUTH LANCASTER
A huge cairn on Monument Island in Lake St. Francis was built in 1840-41 by the Highland Militia of Glengarry County. It commemorates Gen. Sir John Colborne, British commander-in-chief in Canada during the rebellions of 1837 and 1838. Monument Island is reached by boat from South Lancaster.

CORNWALL ISLAND
The world's only factory for making wooden lacrosse sticks is in the St. Regis Reserve on Cornwall Island. Indian craftsmen of the Mohawk Lacrosse Stick Company fashion as many as 100,000 a year. Lacrosse was played by Indian teams of 75 to 200 men long before Europeans arrived in Canada. The crooks of the hickory sticks are bent and wired into shape, then left to cure for a year before the leather webbing is attached. About one-third of the sticks are shipped to the United States. Others go to Britain and Australia.

Lacrosse factory, Cornwall Island

The St. Lawrence Seaway— Gateway to North America's Heartland

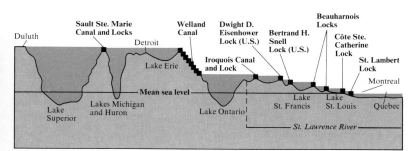

When the Great Lakes–St. Lawrence Seaway was completed in 1959, large, oceangoing ships could travel to the heartland of North America—from the Atlantic Ocean all the way to Lake Superior. Until then, passage had been limited to canal boats, using channels dug before 1903 to bypass shoals and rapids on the St. Lawrence between Montreal and Prescott. In 1954 Canada and the United States agreed upon a joint project to improve the St. Lawrence–Great Lakes System, in all some 3,800 kilometres of canals, lakes and river.

Seven new locks were built, and existing channels dredged to deepen the waterway. Ontario and New York State carried out their own joint project, building three huge dams to harness the power of the International Rapids section near Cornwall.

Today, the seaway raises vessels 183 metres from the Atlantic into Lake Superior through 20 locks. Computers regulate traffic. The ships now accommodated carry loads three times greater than the largest of the old canal boats. Grain and iron ore account for more than half the cargo.

A Wee Bit of Scotland on the Raisin River

Southeastern Ontario

Glengarry County was the first Scottish settlement in Ontario. Western Highlanders arrived in 1784 from New York's Mohawk Valley, where they had settled before the American Revolution. Two years later 500 parishioners of the Rev. Alexander Macdonell of Glengarry, Scotland, joined them. Others followed in the next 50 years, including 400 Highlanders in 1802, one quarter of them named MacMillan.

The preponderance of Scottish names was a postmaster's nightmare. At one time

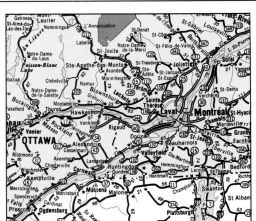

L'ORIGNAL
The first seigneury in what is now Ontario was granted here in 1674 but significant development did not start for 100 years.
□ Ontario's oldest remaining courthouse, for many years the judicial and administrative center of the old Ottawa district, is in this town. The central portion, built in neoclassic style, was completed in 1825.

County courthouse, L'Orignal

DUNVEGAN
In three square-timber buildings here are artifacts of Scottish and Loyalist pioneers who settled Glengarry County nearly 200 years ago. The restored Glengarry Pioneer Inn (c. 1830) has its original bar, wainscoting and broad pine floors. In a coach shed are early 19th-century sleighs, wagons and a log pump drill. Hand tools are displayed in a log barn (c. 1850).

Massed pipe bands, Maxville

Pioneer Life in Best-Selling Yarns

Ralph Connor liked good yarns about people who worked hard and fought well. Others liked them too—and bought five million copies of books he wrote. But writing was only a hobby: Connor was the pseudonym of Charles William Gordon (1860-1937), a prominent Presbyterian clergyman.

Gordon's first ministry, in the Rockies near Banff, Alta., provided the background for *Black Rock* (1898). *The Sky Pilot* (1899), a tale of prairie settlers, and *The Man from Glengarry* (1901) and *Glengarry School Days* (1902)—both set in the backwoods of the author's boyhood—enhanced his popularity. Gordon wrote 25 books in all, but obligations to his church came first. He was pastor of a Winnipeg church from 1895 to 1915, and from 1919 until his death, in the First World War.

MAXVILLE
The Glengarry Highland Games, bigger than any comparable gathering in North America, have been held here since 1948. The games, in early August, include the North American Pipe Championships, and drumming and drum majors' contests.
□ This is the part of southeastern Ontario in which Ralph Connor (the Rev. Charles William Gordon) set his novels *The Man from Glengarry* and *Glengarry School Days*. The Rev. Dr. Gordon was born in St. Elmo, north of Maxville, in 1860. He died in 1937 and was buried on the grounds of his home church.

ST. ANDREWS
The oldest remaining stone structure in Ontario erected as a place of worship is old St. Andrew's Church (1801), now a parish hall. It was the first church built by Roman Catholic Scottish Highlanders in Upper Canada. In a graveyard opposite new St. Andrew's Church (1860) is the grave of Simon Fraser, the explorer for whom the Fraser River is named.

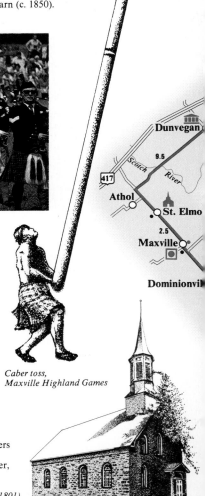

Caber toss, Maxville Highland Games

St. Andrew's Church (1801), St. Andrews West

Dunvegan

Scotch River

9.5

417

Athol

St. Elmo

2.5

Maxville

Dominionvi

0 1 2 3 4 5 Miles
0 2 4 6 8 Kilometres

as many as 500 Macdonalds received mail from the Alexandria post office. The town of Maxville may have been so named because most of its residents had names beginning with "Mac."

These Scottish settlers carved today's prosperous dairy farms out of a forest wilderness on the Raisin River. Some sought further adventure and, as partners and employees of the fur-trading North West Company, helped open up Canada's North and West. They were replaced here by farmers from Quebec and half of today's population is French-speaking.

Glengarry's pioneers achieved prominence in education, politics, industry and business. A proud military history, dating from the Glengarry Light Infantry's role in the War of 1812, has been handed down to the present-day Dundas, Stormont and Glengarry Highlanders. The traditions of Scottish music, dance and athletics live on in the Glengarry Highland Games, held annually at Maxville.

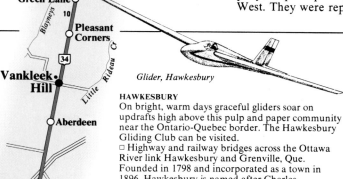

Glider, Hawkesbury

HAWKESBURY
On bright, warm days graceful gliders soar on updrafts high above this pulp and paper community near the Ontario-Quebec border. The Hawkesbury Gliding Club can be visited.
□ Highway and railway bridges across the Ottawa River link Hawkesbury and Grenville, Que. Founded in 1798 and incorporated as a town in 1896, Hawkesbury is named after Charles Jenkinson, Baron Hawkesbury and Earl of Liverpool. Most of the town's residents are of French origin.
□ Hawkesbury Mills is on the site of Hawkesbury's first gristmill and sawmill. Both were built by Thomas Mears, who also built the *Union*, the first steamship to navigate the Ottawa.

ST. RAPHAELS
A three-day classical concert in the ruins of St. Raphael's Church marks the summer solstice in late June. The stone church, destroyed by fire in 1970, dated from 1821.
□ A cairn commemorates the Most Rev. Alexander Macdonell, first Roman Catholic bishop of Upper Canada and founder of the Glengarry Light Infantry.
□ A plaque marks the birthplace of John Sandfield Macdonald, joint prime minister of Canada in 1862-64 and first premier of Ontario in 1867-71.

MARTINTOWN
The Raisin River, its level raised more than two metres by spring meltwaters, becomes a white-water canoe route each April. Some 100 persons compete in races from here to St. Andrews.
□ A favorite of artists is a three-story, fieldstone gristmill, built at the turn of the century. It is occupied by descendants of the original miller.

Alaistair Mhor, Priest and Patriot

A leading spokesman for Glengarry's settlers was the Most Rev. Alexander Macdonell, known as Alaistair Mhor (Big Alexander)—to distinguish him from a predecessor at St. Raphaels. Father Macdonell was 42 when he led the disbanded Glengarry Fencibles—a Roman Catholic Highland regiment he had organized—from Scotland in 1804. The Glengarry Light Infantry he formed in the War of 1812 fought in 14 battles.

After the war Macdonell opened his home to students for the priesthood. He became Upper Canada's first Roman Catholic bishop in 1820, and a member of the legislative council in 1831. He died in 1840 in Scotland.

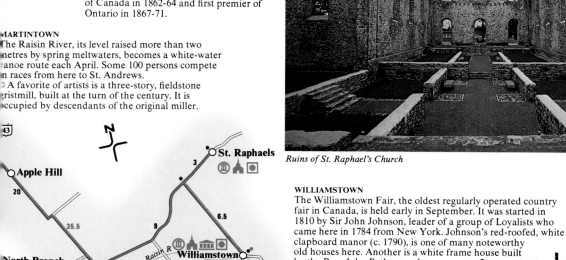

Ruins of St. Raphael's Church

WILLIAMSTOWN
The Williamstown Fair, the oldest regularly operated country fair in Canada, is held early in September. It was started in 1810 by Sir John Johnson, leader of a group of Loyalists who came here in 1784 from New York. Johnson's red-roofed, white clapboard manor (c. 1790), is one of many noteworthy old houses here. Another is a white frame house built by the Rev. John Bethune, who founded Ontario's first Presbyterian congregation in 1787. Fraserfield (c. 1812), a 23-room stone structure, was one of the finest country houses of its day.
□ The Nor'Westers and Loyalist Museum is in a red brick Georgian building (1862).

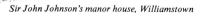

Sir John Johnson's manor house, Williamstown

Where Voyageurs Once Sang Their 'Parting Hymn'

Lac Saint-Louis

In the late 1700s and early 1800s Lachine was the embarkation point of the North West Company fur brigades heading west. The starting point was above the treacherous Lachine Rapids, near present-day Promenade du Père-Marquette. In spring voyageurs loaded food, supplies and trade goods into birchbark canoes. (In autumn they would return, their canoes laden with beaver pelts.) As the voyageurs paddled off, they sang rousing songs that gave rhythm to their strokes. Their first stop was

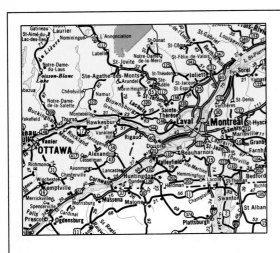

18th-century windmill, Pointe-Claire

SAINTE-ANNE-DE-BELLEVUE
A two-story stone house that dates from 1798 was the home of Simon Fraser, a fur trader and partner in the North West Company (and a relative of the explorer of the same name). It is now a restaurant, the Petit Café. Fraser is buried in a nearby cemetery.
□ The Church of Sainte-Anne-de-Bellevue is believed built on the foundations of a chapel where voyageurs starting for the Northwest stopped to pray. On the grounds is a nine-by-four-metre wooden model of the building. It was demolished in 1880, the year the present church was built.
□ Macdonald College, the agricultural school of McGill University, Montreal, is here. The Morgan Arboretum on the property has some 150 species of Canadian trees, 350 kinds of flowering plants and wildflowers and 100 species of birds. There are 17 kilometres of nature trails.
□ At Senneville, some two kilometres north on the shore of Lac des Deux Montagnes, is a cairn commemorating a battle between the French and the Iroquois in 1689.

Vaudreuil Historical Museum

VAUDREUIL
A stone school built in 1847 houses the Vaudreuil Historical Museum. It has documents, sculptures and paintings dating back to the 1600s, and pine furniture used by early settlers.
□ A tabernacle, candlesticks and a statue in Saint-Michel Church (1787) were carved in 1792 by sculptor Philippe Liébert.
□ A plaque in the registry office honors Pierre de Rigaud, marquis de Vaudreuil-Cavagnal, last governor of New France, who surrendered this region to the British in 1760.
□ The area offers sailing, duck hunting, ice fishing and horseback riding.

COTEAU-DU-LAC
The ruins of a tiny canal, the forerunner of the St. Lawrence Seaway, are the focal point of Fort Coteau-du-Lac, a national historic site. Earthworks and the remains of various buildings are also preserved. In an eight-sided blockhouse, a reconstruction of one built in 1812, is an exhibition of artifacts unearthed during restoration. A model of the fort is displayed in an information center.
  The canal was cut through rock in 1779-80 and was North America's first with locks—its three locks were later reduced to two. Extensive defenses were built around the canal during the War of 1812, including a cloverleaf-shaped bastion and several blockhouses. These and a barracks, bakery, guardhouse, magazine, hospital, cookhouse and officers' quarters eventually fell into ruins. Only a few remains were visible when restoration was started in 1965.

Octagonal blockhouses, Coteau-du-Lac

POINTE-DES-CASCADES
This village is divided by the Soulanges Canal, built in the 1890s to bypass rapids in the St. Lawrence River between Lac Saint-François and Lac Saint-Louis. The canal became obsolete with the construction in 1959 of the Beauharnois Canal and the St. Lawrence Seaway. From the village may be seen rapids, locks and powerhouses along the seaway.

at Sainte-Anne-de-Bellevue. It was here, in 1804, that Thomas Moore, the Irish poet, may have heard the "parting hymn" of the voyageurs, which inspired his *Canadian Boat Song*:

Faintly as tolls the evening chime,
Our voices keep tune and our oars keep time.
Soon as the woods on shore look dim,
We'll sing at St. Ann's our parting hymn.
Row, brothers, row, the stream runs fast,
The Rapids are near, and the daylight's past.

The fur trade was waning when the Lachine Canal was opened in 1825. The canal, built to bypass the hazardous rapids, became a gateway to the Great Lakes. For 130 years it carried more shipping traffic than any other Canadian canal.

During the 19th century running the Lachine Rapids was a major attraction for thrill-seekers. (A traveler of 1854 described it as "terror in its most exhilarating form.") Canada Steamship Lines introduced daily cruises on the *Rapids' King*, the *Rapids'* *Prince* and the *Rapids' Queen*. The last passenger vessel to make the run was the *Rapids' Prince* in 1940. Less than two decades later the rapids were tamed by the construction of the St. Lawrence Seaway.

Only pleasure craft bound for Dorval, Pointe-Claire and Baie-d'Urfé on Lac Saint-Louis use the Lachine Canal today. In summer, billowing sails are mirrored in the lake that once resounded to the songs of the voyageurs; in winter, swift iceboats skim its frozen surface.

POINTE-CLAIRE
Stewart Hall is a half-scale model of a castle on Mull Island, Scotland. Now a community center, it was one of the mansions built here at the turn of the century by wealthy Montrealers.
□ On the point for which this city is named is a windmill dating from the early 1700s. It was used for grinding grain and as a refuge during Indian raids.

Lachine Canal—A Gateway to the Great Lakes

In the early 1600s fur brigades traveling from the Northwest to Montreal either challenged the treacherous Lachine Rapids on the St. Lawrence River or trekked 13 kilometres around them. Many coureurs de bois who risked the swift downstream run lost their canoes, their cargoes, their lives.

A channel to bypass the rapids was proposed in 1680. It was to be just wide enough and deep enough to float fur-trade canoes, but too little money and manpower, and a lack of government interest thwarted construction of the canal.

The War of 1812 emphasized the need for British steamers and warships to sail between Montreal and the Great Lakes in defense of Upper Canada. Construction of the Lachine Canal finally began in 1821. Four years later the 13-kilometre waterway opened the St. Lawrence to shipping between Montreal and the Great Lakes. Its seven locks were 30 metres long and 6 metres wide, and 1½ metres in depth. The town of Lachine, once the departure point for fur traders heading to the Northwest, grew into a thriving center.

In 1959 the St. Lawrence Seaway replaced the Lachine Canal. Today only small pleasure craft sail the canal, and picnic tables and a cycling path line its banks.

Lachine Canal in the 19th century

ILE-PERROT
At Pointe-du-Moulin on this island are a stone windmill and a house that date from about 1700. At the northeast corner of the island is the Lotbinière windmill (1778) which once stood at Vaudreuil. It was dismantled and rebuilt here in the late 1950s.
□ The Church of Sainte-Jeanne-Françoise-de-Chantal, in Notre-Dame-de-l'Ile-Perrot on the south shore, dates from 1753. Near it is a chapel built from the stones of Ile-Perrot's original chapel (1740).

LACHINE
Explorer and fur trader René-Robert Cavelier de La Salle believed that he could find a way across North America to China. The land he was given near Montreal when he arrived in New France in 1667, age 23, was called La Chine (China) by his detractors. He sold it to finance an expedition to the Ohio River. A 37-metre stone monument to La Salle stands outside city hall.
□ Plaques near the La Salle monument describe the 1689 Lachine massacre. On Aug. 4, a few hours before dawn, Lachine was awakened to the frightful screams of 1,500 Iroquois warriors from the Finger Lakes region of present-day New York State. They killed at random, burned the settlement, then retired to the south shore of the St. Lawrence with 90 prisoners. Montreal watched the smoke of their victory bonfires that night, knowing that captives were being burned alive. Forty-eight of the prisoners escaped; the rest were never seen again.
□ The Lachine Museum, in a house built by Charles Le Moyne and Jacques Le Ber, dates from about 1670 and is one of Canada's oldest buildings. In it is a six-metre-long model of the *Dorchester* (1836), the first locomotive in Canada, and equipment used by the voyageurs.

Iceboats on Lac Saint-Louis

Lac St-Louis

MONTRÉAL (see Road Unit 108)

LACHINE

CANAL DE LACHINE

St. Lawrence River

RAPIDES DE LACHINE

POINTE-CLAIRE

Dorval

Old Conflicts and Fur Trading on the 'Grand River of the North'

Lower Ottawa River Valley

Interior of the old Carillon Barracks

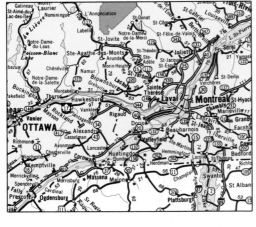

GRENVILLE
English settlers first established a trading post here in 1809. A stone cairn marks the site of the old Carillon, or Grenville, Canal, built in 1819-33 by the Royal Engineers. Almost all work on this project was done by hand. The canal permitted uninterrupted water travel between Montreal and Ottawa, and was replaced in 1963 by the present canal at Carillon.

CARILLON
A monument to Adam Dollard des Ormeaux and his 16 companions who were massacred by the Iroquois in 1660 stands near the Ottawa River at the reputed site of the battl □ The original doors, stairs and woodwork of the Old Carillc Barracks, built in 1829 for soldiers guarding the first Carillor Canal, have been preserved. The four-story stone structure, now a museum, displays Indian artifacts, articles from the French seigneurial days, and furniture and dishes of the firs English settlers.
□ The Carillon Canal, built in the early 1960s as part of the Carillon power project, has a single lift of 20 metres, making it the highest conventional lock in Canada. There are tours of the power plant.

PAPINEAUVILLE
A farming and industrial village, Papineauville is named for the *Patriote* leader and chief architect of the Rebellion of 1837, Louis-Joseph Papineau.

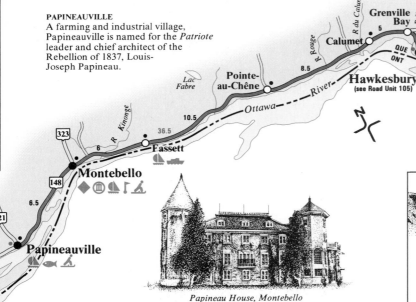

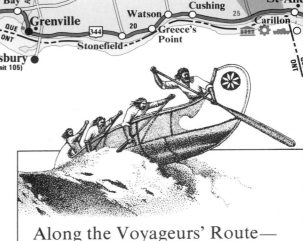

Papineau House, Montebello

MONTEBELLO
This resort and farming town takes its name from the imposing stone manor built in 1850 by Louis-Joseph Papineau, leader of the 1837 rebellion in Lower Canada. The manor, now a museum, and the chapel in which Papineau is buried are on the grounds of the Chateau Montebello Hotel here.
□ Trained as a lawyer, Papineau was a member of the Lower Canada Legislative Assembly from 1808-37 and served as Speaker for much of that period. Although Papineau admired British political institutions, he was an opponent to British rule in Canada. He became the leader and spokesman for the *Patriotes* and other radical reformers. When the *Patriote* party rebelled against the British in 1837, Papineau fled into exile in the United States, but returned to Canada and re-entered political life in 1844. He retired to Montebello ten years later.

Along the Voyageurs' Route— the First 'Trans-Canada'

The Ottawa River was a key artery of the fur trade, and the first "Trans-Canada Highway" carrying Indians, missionaries, merchants, trappers and farmers to and from the interior. From the Hudson's Bay Company warehouse in Lachine, brigades of great *canots du maître* would start out in early May to rendezvous at remote northern outposts. The voyageurs made their first night's camp by Lac des Deux Montagnes. The next day the canoes, each loaded with three tonnes of trade goods and supplies, would negotiate the 20 kilometres of rapids known as the Long Sault. Passing the riverside settlements of Carillon and Grenville, the voyageurs caught their first glimpse of the Laurentian Hills that marked the edge of the vast wilderness ahead. Today the Ottawa is paralleled by modern highways, and visitors can share the scenes viewed by the voyageurs as they paddled and portaged along the river.

0 1 2 3 4 5 Miles
0 2 4 6 8 Kilometres

To the early French explorers and fur traders, the Ottawa River was the "Grand River of the North." The first European to ascend the river was Etienne Brûlé, in 1610. Champlain followed in 1613 and again in 1615 on what later became Canada's main fur-trade route—up the Ottawa to the Mattawa River and across to Lake Nipissing. Echoes of the colorful and sometimes violent history of the river still linger at certain places on its north shore.

Lac des Deux Montagnes, where the Ottawa widens at its outlet, was once a stopping place for fur traders heading into the West. The French and Indians clashed fiercely along the river. Monuments at Carillon commemorate one of the bloodier battles—the heroic stand of Adam Dollard des Ormeaux in 1660. Hostilities impeded the settlement of the Ottawa River until the 18th century. One of the few French seigneuries in this area, La Petite Nation, was acquired in the early 1800s. Here, in 1850, Louis-Joseph Papineau, leader of the 1837 rebellion in Lower Canada, built his manor at Montebello, now a museum.

In the early 19th century the fur trade gave way to the lumber industry. Canals and, later, railways were built to bypass the hazardous rapids between Carillon and Grenville. Loyalists, Scots and Americans came to the banks of the Ottawa and established communities that have become farming, industrial and resort towns. In this century, the Ottawa has been turned to modern use by vast power developments.

SAINT-PLACIDE
A plaque in this resort center on the Lac des Deux Montagnes marks the birthplace of Sir Adolphe-Basile Routhier (1839-1920), author of the French lyrics to *O Canada*. A lawyer, poet, novelist and playwright, Routhier served as chief justice of Quebec and president of the Royal Society of Canada.

SAINT-ANDRÉ-EST
This was the first settlement of the seigneury of Argenteuil and birthplace of Sir John J. C. Abbott, the first Canadian-born prime minister (1891-93).
□ A plaque records that Canada's first paper mill was built here in 1803-05 by a group of New England immigrants.

SAINT-EUSTACHE
This old French-Canadian village was a *Patriote* stronghold, and the site of the decisive battle of the Rebellion of 1837. The walls and landmark twin towers of the village church (1813) still bear the marks of cannon shot. The church was rebuilt in 1841. The town preserves several examples of old French-Canadian homes.
□ Built in 1762 to serve the Rivière-du-Chêne seigneury, the Légaré gristmill has been restored.
□ The Chénier House, home of the rebel leader, has been renovated and is now a private residence.
□ The Festival of Old Saint-Eustache in August recalls the colorful history of the area.

OKA
La Trappe, established here in 1881, is one of the largest Cistercian (Trappist) monasteries in the world. In 1893 the monks founded a school of agriculture affiliated with the University of Montreal and established an experimental farm. On this farm, no longer in operation, originated the widely known Oka cheese.
□ Seven stone chapels on a mountain here were built in 1740-42 as a Way of the Cross, the oldest calvary in Canada. There is a procession to the remaining three chapels on Holy Cross Day, Sept. 14.
□ The Manoir d'Argenteuil, built around 1720, became a convent in 1864 but is now again a private residence.

Scars of a Brave Rebellion

Pockmarked by cannon shot, the walls of the Saint-Eustache church bear witness to the bloodiest battle of the Rebellion of 1837. General Sir John Colborne, commander of British forces in Lower Canada, marched to Saint-Eustache to crush the French-Canadian rebel movement. Some 250 *Patriotes*, led by Jean-Olivier Chénier, barricaded themselves into the church. The British troops slowly advanced behind heavy cannon and musket fire, broke into the church and set it aflame. Some 100 rebels were killed, among them Chénier, whose monument stands at Sacré-Coeur School. In 1841 the reconstructed church was blessed by the Bishop of Montreal.

Cannon marks, Saint-Eustache Church

The Chapel, La Trappe monastery, Oka

Stone chapels near Oka

PARC PAUL-SAUVÉ
This large provincial park on Montreal's doorstep was once part of the Deux Montagnes seigneury, ceded to the Gentlemen of Saint-Sulpice in 1733 by Louis XIV. Hickory, linden, ash, walnut and oak trees comprise the lovely hardwood forest in the park. A few scattered elms survive. The beach is nearly two miles long and slopes gently into the lake. In spring, anglers fish for pike, perch and bullhead on Lac des Deux Montagnes and in the Rivière aux Serpents. In summer, thousands are attracted to the swimming, camping, canoeing and sailing here. Winter draws snowshoers, snowmobilers, cross-country skiers and ice fishermen to the park.

Canada's Great 'World City': Varied, Vibrant and Ever-Changing

Bonsecours Market (27)
This cut-stone building housed the Parliament of Canada in 1849-52 and was the city hall until 1878, when it was converted to a market. It now houses municipal offices.

Château de Ramezay (1705), now a museum, once served as the seat of government for New France.

Château de Ramezay (26)
This fieldstone château (1705) was the government seat of French Canada until 1724. It became headquarters of the American Continental Army during its occupation of Montreal in 1775-76. It is now a museum of Quebec history.

Cité du Havre (3)
In this part of Montreal's waterfront are the International Broadcast Center, the Museum of Contemporary Art, Habitat, Olympic House and Expo Theater. At the broadcast center visitors watch the taping of CBC television programs. The museum exhibits the work of Quebec artists such as Paul-Emile Borduas (1905-60), founder of painting's automatiste school. Habitat, designed by Moshe Safdie for Expo 67, is a cluster of 158 modular apartments. A museum at Olympic House, the office of the Canadian Olympic Association, has photos, medals and trophies of Canadian athletes. The Expo Theater presents plays in English and French.

Complexe Desjardins (22)
Three office towers and a hotel surround a glassed-in mall with shops, fountains, sculptures and bright, open promenades.

Dominion Gallery (12)
Two life-size statues, Henry Moore's *Upright Motive No. 5* and Auguste Rodin's *Jean d'Aire*, stand outside the city's largest private gallery. Inside are more than 400 sculptures and paintings by about 200 Canadian artists.

Dow Planetarium (15)
The aluminum dome of the planetarium serves as a screen on which photographs of planets and about 9,000 stars are projected, along with special effects such as meteor showers, comets and northern lights.

Lafontaine Park (6)
The Garden of Wonders children's zoo has more than 550 small animals set in storybook scenes. The 32-hectare park has two lagoons (boating in summer, skating in winter) and an open-air theater for puppet shows, concerts and plays.

This dynamic city on a 50-kilometre-long island in the St. Lawrence River is known above all for its diversity—its mélange of French and English, of old-world sophistication and North American get-up-and-go.

Montreal's population of 2,800,000 (roughly equal to that of Toronto) has about 45 percent of Quebec's inhabitants. But one Montrealer in three is non-French, and the combination of Gallic and Anglo-Saxon culture, plus the traditions of numerous ethnic groups, contribute to the city's cosmopolitan atmosphere.

In 1535 when Jacques Cartier reached what is now Montreal he found the Indian village of Hochelaga. He named the 232-metre mountain behind the settlement for the cardinal of the Medicis, once bishop of Monreale in Sicily. Monreale in French became Mont Réal. In 1611 Champlain established a trading post on the island. In 1642 Sieur de Maisonneuve founded a mission which he named Ville-Marie. The tiny fortified settlement survived a half-century of Iroquois attacks and grew into the capital of the fur trade in the 1700s, and a transportation, manufacturing and financial center in the 19th and 20th centuries.

Montreal's international reputation has soared with its skyscrapers. Expo 67 and the 1976 Olympic Games brought increased convention and athletic facilities, hotels and the ultramodern Métro, with subway stations that seem like art galleries.

Montreal's port, at the head of the St. Lawrence Seaway, is eastern Canada's largest. The harbor handles about 3,500 commercial ships a year. The head offices of Air Canada, and Canadian National and Canadian Pacific railways are here. Mirabel International Airport, the world's largest in area, is 55 kilometres west.

Montreal's distinguished educational institutions include the Université de Montréal, renowned for its faculties of medicine and law, and a campus of the Université du Québec. McGill University is noted for its schools of engineering and medicine. Concordia University is Quebec's largest (enrollment 25,000).

Orchestras, singers, and ballet and theater troupes perform at the three magnificent halls of Place des Arts. Cafés, bars and discothèques keep the city's exciting nightlife alive until the early hours of the morning.

Bank of Montreal Museum (23)
Canada's first bank (1817) has collections of early coins, bills, banking documents and maps of Montreal. The museum is in a new building beside the bank's main office, an elegant domed edifice (1848) with a classic portico of Corinthian columns.

McGill University (16)

Founded in 1821 and one of Canada's largest universities, McGill occupies 30 hectares in downtown Montreal. Its McCord Museum has artifacts from the city's fur-trading days, dolls, china, furniture and native art. A costume gallery includes Canadian clothes from 1770. The extensive Notman collection has photographs taken between 1856 and 1934.

Man and His World

Man and His World (5)

Successor to Expo 67, this exhibition has national pavilions and others on themes such as the environment, humor and antique cars—all amid breezy avenues, flower gardens and spacious lawns.

Mary Queen of the World Cathedral (14)

Modeled after St. Peter's in Rome with about one-quarter of its area, this cathedral (1875) has an altar of marble and ivory.

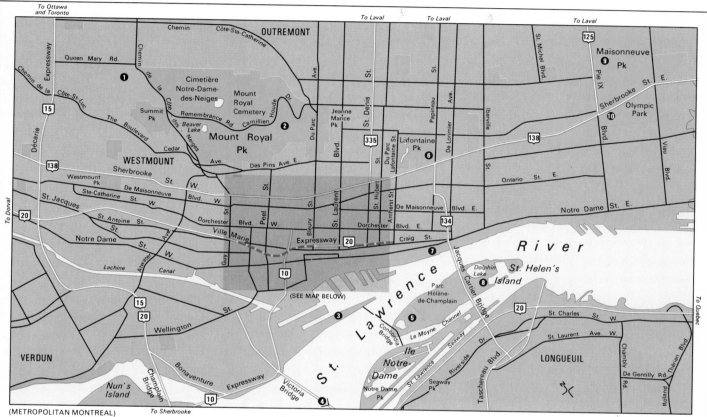

(METROPOLITAN MONTREAL)

Montreal

- - - - - Underground Highway

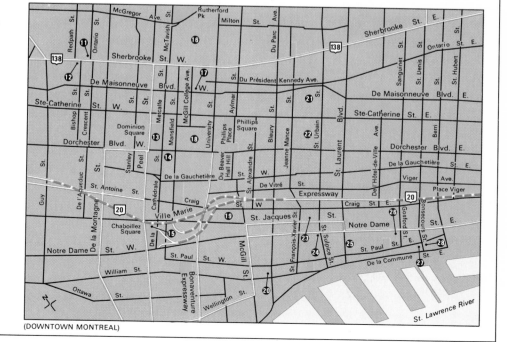

(DOWNTOWN MONTREAL)

Molson Brewery (7)

Tours may be taken through the oldest brewery in continuous operation in Canada (1786). The reception room has an antique gun collection.

Montreal Botanical Gardens (9)

The third largest botanical garden in the world (after those in Berlin and London) is noted for its cactus and begonia collections. Individual gardens range from miniature deserts to lush tropical forests. There are rock, shrub and aquatic gardens, and an arboretum with some 15,000 species from many parts of the world.

Montreal Museum of Fine Arts (11)

Among the most valuable pieces in Canada's oldest art museum are Henry Moore's sculpture *Reclining Figure: Internal and External Forms* and Pablo Picasso's oil *La Lampe et les Cerises*. The museum has

Old and new, side by side, lend charm to historic Place Jacques-Cartier (above). Ultramodern Habitat 67 (left) rises on Cité du Havre, berthing place for oceangoing freighters. Montreal town houses of a bygone era (below) extend gingerbread roofs and balconies railed with wrought iron. Masterworks of the wood-carver's art glorify Notre-Dame Church (below left), built in 1829 to replace Montreal's first parish church. Sculptured hedges and colorful floral displays line the tree-shaded walks of the Botanical Gardens (bottom).

paintings by Dutch and English masters, 16th-century sculpture, European tapestries, Oriental art objects and an unusual collection of ancient Roman and Syrian glassworks. There are displays of native art and handicrafts, and early Canadian wood carving and furniture. The museum was built in 1912 in Greek neoclassic style and renovated in 1973-76.

Mount Royal Park (2)

Wooded slopes, unsurpassed views of Montreal, and man-made Beaver Lake help to make this 200-hectare park a favorite retreat mere minutes from big-city bustle. In winter Beaver Lake becomes a skating rink and there are ski trails, toboggan hills and horse-drawn sleighs. A 30-metre-high illuminated cross commemorates the erection of a wooden cross by de Maisonneuve in 1643. The Mount Royal Art Center holds exhibitions in an old stone farmhouse.

Notre-Dame Church (24)

This church (1829), which resembles Paris' Notre-Dame Cathedral, has 67-metre twin towers. It accommodates 7,000 worshipers and has exquisite interior decoration by French-Canadian artists such as Ozias Le-

duc and Victor Bourgeau. Stained-glass windows depict early Montreal history. A museum behind the church has 17th-century silverware. The adjacent Sulpician Seminary (1685), Montreal's oldest building, has a roof clock which dates from 1700.

Notre-Dame-de-Bon-Secours Chapel (28)

A copper statue of the Virgin Mary with a crown of stars faces Montreal harbor from behind this church (1773), known as the sailors' chapel.

Old Montreal (25)

Historic fieldstone dwellings and warehouses hug narrow cobblestone streets in this 40-hectare quarter that was the opulent center of the fur trade. The Quebec government declared Old Montreal a historic district in 1963. Scores of buildings have been renovated and occupied. Some have become restaurants, museums and art studios. Old Montreal's focal point is Place Jacques-Cartier, once a busy marketplace, now a wide boulevard bordered by restaurants and hotels. A monument erected in 1809 honors Rear Adm. Horatio Nelson. The nearby City Hall (1926), an ornate five-story example of French Renaissance architecture, resembles the city hall in Paris.

Olympic Park (10)

The 55,000-seat Olympic Stadium was the main site of the 1976 Olympic Games. The immense cement structure, designed by French architect Roger Taillibert, is now used for football, baseball and special events. In winter the infield becomes a skating rink. A swimming pool and diving towers are part of the stadium. The adjacent Velodrome is used for cycling, judo and other athletics. The Olympic Park may be toured. Nearby is the former Olympic vil-

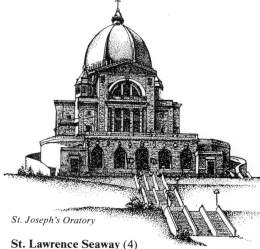

Olympic Stadium

lage, four 20-story, half-pyramid towers. They will eventually become a housing complex.

Place des Arts (21)

Elegant, 3,000-seat Salle Wilfrid-Pelletier is the home of the Montreal Symphony Orchestra and is used for opera, ballet and concerts. The other theaters in this complex are the 1,300-seat Maisonneuve and the 800-seat Port Royal.

Place d'Youville (20)

The Youville Stables—three restored 18th-century fieldstone warehouses—now house offices, boutiques and a restaurant. They face an inner court with tables and park benches amid trees, lawns and flowers.

Place Victoria (19)

A 47-story tower here contains financial offices and the Montreal Stock Exchange. The world's tallest glass sculpture, four stories high, is suspended from the ceiling of the lobby. Hand-blown in Murano, Italy, the colorful sculpture contains 3,000 pieces of cubed and oblong glass.

Place Ville-Marie (18)

Four large office buildings surround a business and entertainment area. The main structure is the 45-story Royal Bank of Canada complex, the world's largest cruciform building, with some 1,000 offices.

St. Helen's Island (8)

The Montreal Aquarium has sharks, sea turtles, and performing dolphins. The St. Helen's Island Museum, in the arsenal of a fort built in 1820-24, displays 17th-century military equipment and a model of 18th-century Montreal. Students drill in uniforms of the Fraser Highlanders and the Compagnie Franche de la Marine, a unit founded by Cardinal Richelieu in 1683. La Poudrière, once the fort's powder magazine, is now a theater.

St. Joseph's Oratory (1)

In 1904, on the west slope of Mount Royal, Brother André of the Congregation of Holy Cross built a wooden chapel to honor Saint Joseph. He began to treat the afflicted, preaching that complete faith in the saint would relieve suffering. His reputation for miraculous healing was such that when he died in 1937, age 91, an estimated one million persons filed past his coffin. The oratory's basilica, a Montreal landmark and Canada's largest church, was begun in 1924 and completed in 1967. The octagonal dome is second in size only to that of St. Peter's in Rome. Brother André's tomb is in the oratory's Crypt Church. In his restored mountainside chapel is a replica of the austere room he occupied for 38 years.

St. Joseph's Oratory

St. Lawrence Seaway (4)

An observation deck atop the Seaway Authority building overlooks the Saint-Lambert lock. The seaway handles 6,000 ships each year.

Underground Retreats, Spacious Promenades

Beneath Montreal's soaring skyscrapers and bustling streets is an underground city—a network of passageways connecting office towers, more than 300 shops, theaters, countless restaurants and bars, hotels and the Métro, an ultra-modern subway. Even a downtown extension of the Trans-Canada Highway is underground.

This subterranean network covers more than 16 hectares in the heart of the city alone. In winter many Montrealers seem to hibernate in this underground, retreating from an average 240-centimetre snowfall and freezing temperatures. One can travel underground along spacious promenades from Place Ville-Marie to Central Station, below the Queen Elizabeth Hotel, and to Place Bonaventure, several blocks away. Similar shopping malls are also located in Place du Canada, Complexe Desjardins (*left*) and the Alexis Nihon Plaza.

Linking it all with speed—and in near silence—is the Métro (*far left, bottom*). Its rubber-tired trains travel on 30 kilometres of track between 37 stations, each decorated differently. The station at Place des Arts is perhaps most striking, with a stained-glass mural (*far left, top*) designed by Montreal artist, Frédéric Back.

Year-Round *Joie de Vivre* in a Vital Vacationland

The Laurentians

Quebec's Laurentian region is one of the most highly developed resort and ski areas in North America. In and around some 20 major winter sports communities are more than 100 ski lifts and tows. Interlinking cross-country trails abound. Accommodation ranges from modestly priced *pensions* to luxurious hotels.

At the Laurentian Snow Festival, which begins in December and ends in March, residents and visitors in Sainte-Agathe-des-Monts don red tuques and multicolored

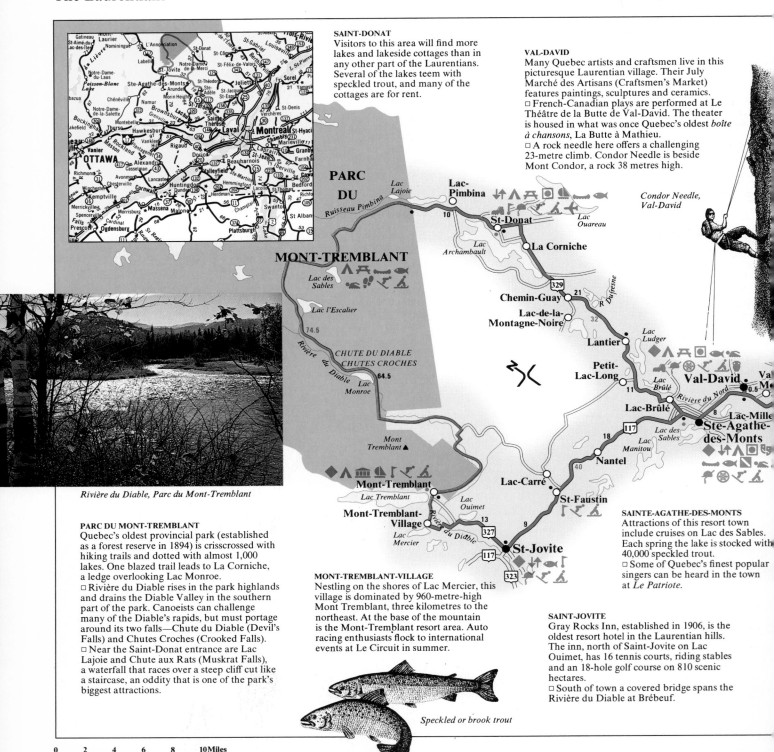

Rivière du Diable, Parc du Mont-Tremblant

SAINT-DONAT
Visitors to this area will find more lakes and lakeside cottages than in any other part of the Laurentians. Several of the lakes teem with speckled trout, and many of the cottages are for rent.

VAL-DAVID
Many Quebec artists and craftsmen live in this picturesque Laurentian village. Their July Marché des Artisans (Craftsmen's Market) features paintings, sculptures and ceramics.
□ French-Canadian plays are performed at Le Théâtre de la Butte de Val-David. The theater is housed in what was once Quebec's oldest *boîte à chansons*, La Butte à Mathieu.
□ A rock needle here offers a challenging 23-metre climb. Condor Needle is beside Mont Condor, a rock 38 metres high.

Condor Needle, Val-David

PARC DU MONT-TREMBLANT
Quebec's oldest provincial park (established as a forest reserve in 1894) is crisscrossed with hiking trails and dotted with almost 1,000 lakes. One blazed trail leads to La Corniche, a ledge overlooking Lac Monroe.
□ Rivière du Diable rises in the park highlands and drains the Diable Valley in the southern part of the park. Canoeists can challenge many of the Diable's rapids, but must portage around its two falls—Chute du Diable (Devil's Falls) and Chutes Croches (Crooked Falls).
□ Near the Saint-Donat entrance are Lac Lajoie and Chute aux Rats (Muskrat Falls), a waterfall that races over a steep cliff cut like a staircase, an oddity that is one of the park's biggest attractions.

MONT-TREMBLANT-VILLAGE
Nestling on the shores of Lac Mercier, this village is dominated by 960-metre-high Mont Tremblant, three kilometres to the northeast. At the base of the mountain is the Mont-Tremblant resort area. Auto racing enthusiasts flock to international events at Le Circuit in summer.

Speckled or brook trout

SAINTE-AGATHE-DES-MONTS
Attractions of this resort town include cruises on Lac des Sables. Each spring the lake is stocked with 40,000 speckled trout.
□ Some of Quebec's finest popular singers can be heard in the town at *Le Patriote*.

SAINT-JOVITE
Gray Rocks Inn, established in 1906, is the oldest resort hotel in the Laurentian hills. The inn, north of Saint-Jovite on Lac Ouimet, has 16 tennis courts, riding stables and an 18-hole golf course on 810 scenic hectares.
□ South of town a covered bridge spans the Rivière du Diable at Brébeuf.

0 2 4 6 8 10 Miles

0 4 8 12 16 Kilometres

Skiing in the Laurentians

sashes and recapture the spirit of habitant days. Horses pull old farm sleighs down streets lined with ice sculptures. The festival includes an international dogsled race, speed- and figure-skating competitions, hockey games and toboggan races.

In summer, fresh mountain air, clear lakes and forested hills delight vacationers. Many resorts offer water sports, horseback riding, tennis and golf. During cool, restful evenings visitors can enjoy plays presented in theaters in Sainte-Adèle and Val-David.

Popular French-Canadian musicians perform in the relaxed and intimate atmosphere of the area's *boîtes à chansons*.

Parc du Mont-Tremblant provides more rugged summer recreation. The park's northern wilderness forest, unmarked by roads or trails, is a paradise for fishermen and canoeists.

PRÉVOST
This quiet resort town, also known as Shawbridge, boasts 75 kilometres of cross-country ski trails. Between 1932 and 1935, the famous cross-country skier, Herman "Jack Rabbit" Johannsen organised the Maple Leaf Trail from Prévost to Mont-Tremblant, a distance of 96 kilometres, through some of the most beautiful wilderness in the Laurentians. Part of the trail is still open to the public.
□ Canada's first ski tow was built here in 1932. It was improvised from an automobile engine, lines and tackles, and heavy concrete blocks, but it worked. The price of being towed up the hill was five cents.

SAINT-SAUVEUR-DES-MONTS
This oldest of the Laurentian ski resorts (it started attracting skiers in 1930) has nearly 30 lifts within three kilometres of town. North America's second rope tow was erected here in 1934; the first was at nearby Prévost. Skiers almost double the town's 2,000 population every winter weekend.

Labelle of the Laurentians — A Priestly 'King of the North'

In 1870 there were barely a dozen communities north of Saint-Jérôme and settlers were steadily leaving Quebec to work in the United States. But by 1891 the Most Rev. Antoine Labelle had changed all that. This fiercely determined leader traveled into the Laurentian wilderness, exploring sites for new settlements and creating some 20 new parishes. He brought European settlers to Quebec and persuaded the government to route the Montreal-Quebec railway through Saint-Jérôme. Curé Labelle once told his struggling parishioners: "You who with infinite toil have carved yourselves farms from the wilderness, stay on! Persevere! In another 50 years strangers will flock here, and they will scatter gold by the handful." Today Saint-Jérôme is the gateway to one of Quebec's finest year-round resort areas.

SAINT-JÉRÔME
The impressive triple-spired Cathédrale de Saint-Jérôme, the largest church in the Laurentians, was built in 1897-99 and opened in 1900. A massive portable altar, a silver chalice presented by Pope Leo XIII and other mementos of the Most Rev. Antoine Labelle are housed here. During the 1870s and '80s Curé Labelle founded 20 parishes in the Laurentians. A bronze statue by Canadian sculptor Alfred Laliberté honors Curé Labelle.

SAINTE-ROSE
This tranquil rural village was founded in 1845. Sainte-Rose Church (1856) was designed by Victor Bourgeau, a prominent French-Canadian architect. Inside is a handsomely carved altar dating from the late 18th century. Near the church are several well-preserved, old houses. One contains an antique shop, another a handicraft shop.

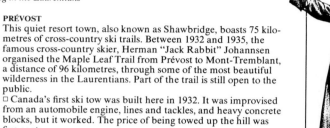

Village de Séraphin, Sainte-Adèle

MIRABEL
This municipality was created in 1970 (from Sainte-Scholastique, Belle-Rivière, Sainte-Monique and 11 other towns and villages) to accommodate Montreal's second international airport. Mirabel has a 361-room hotel, parking for 3,000 cars and two runways built for the largest jet airplanes.

Mirabel is the world's largest airport in size. It can handle 10 million passengers a year—60 million by the year 2025. The maximum distance between the terminal's entrances and boarding gates is only 100 metres (about 130 paces). Special vehicles shuttle passengers between aircraft and terminal.

Terminal building, Mirabel International Airport

SAINTE-ADÈLE
Sainte-Adèle, a writers' and artists' colony, is built around Lac Rond and on the slopes of Mont Sainte-Adèle. Local craftsmen make wood sculptures, furniture and jewelry.
□ The Village de Séraphin is a reconstructed mid-19th-century hamlet inspired by Claude-Henri Grignon's book *Un homme et son péché.* A miniature train takes visitors past the village's old, Laurentian-style post office, general store, blacksmith shop, school, church and doctor's office.

A Quiet Corner of Quebec Where Laurier Spent His Boyhood

The Laurentians

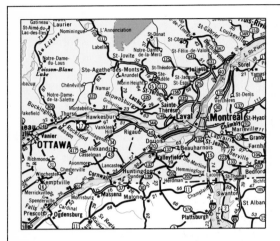

Northeast of Montreal, across the Rivière des Prairies, is a region of quiet farming towns and picturesque Laurentian lakes and woods. Highway 138 follows the north shore of the St. Lawrence River through L'Assomption County, one of the smallest in Quebec, and Berthier County.

The road passes through Repentigny,

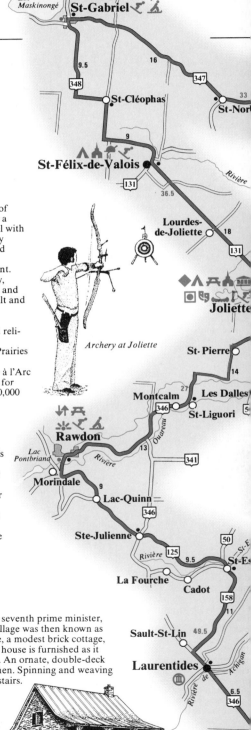

SAINT-GABRIEL-DE-BRANDON
This early settlement, set in magnificent Laurentian scenery, was known as the Mission of Lac Maskinongé until 1837 when its name was changed to Saint-Gabriel-du-Lac-Maskinongé. In 1840 it was renamed Saint-Gabriel-de-Brandon, after an English village.
□ Lac Maskinongé is popular with swimmers, water-skiers and fishermen.

JOLIETTE
In the provincial house of the Brothers of Saint-Viateur, built in 1939 to resemble a 13th-century Norman abbey, is a chapel with stained-glass windows and sculptures by Marius Plamondon. There are also wood sculptures by artist Sylvia Daoust. The ceramic altar was crafted by Louis Parent.
□ Designed by the Rev. Pierre Conefroy, Saint-Paul Church was built in 1803-04 and decorated by Jean-Chrysostôme Perrault and Amable Charron.
□ The Joliette Museum of Art exhibits European and Canadian paintings, and religious art dating from the Middle Ages.
□ In a converted barn the Théâtre des Prairies presents a summer season of plays.
□ The scenic grounds of the Club de Tir à l'Arc de Joliette, site of archery competitions for the 1976 Olympics, contain some $1,250,000 worth of archery equipment.

Archery at Joliette

Joliette Museum of Art

A Mighty Fighter

The deep waters of the lakes and rivers in this region teem with muskellunge, Canada's second largest freshwater fish (after sturgeon). The powerful fish is a fighter, and landing one is a thrilling experience. The average fish caught is between 2 and 16 kilograms but some 45-kilogram giants, 183 centimetres long, have been recorded.

Muskellunge are caught mainly by trolling, but it takes patience: the angler may fish for days without a strike. But when the fish are hungry, they will bite at anything, and several can be caught in a day.

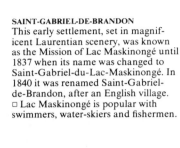

RAWDON
A one-room schoolhouse, a settler's cabin, a smithy and an ice cream parlor are among the 19th-century buildings in Canadiana Village. A covered bridge (1888) spans a river that flows through the village.
□ At nearby Darwin Falls is a rock formation in the shape of an Indian's head. Legend says it is the head of a sorcerer who, shunned by a maiden, pushed her into the falls and was turned to stone.

LAURENTIDES
Sir Wilfrid Laurier, Canada's seventh prime minister, was born here in 1841. The village was then known as Saint-Lin. His boyhood home, a modest brick cottage, is a national historic site. The house is furnished as it was when Laurier lived there. An ornate, double-deck wood stove stands in the kitchen. Spinning and weaving rooms and a bedroom are upstairs.

Wilfrid Laurier House, Laurentides

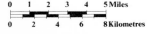

where the modernity of Notre-Dame-des-Champs Church contrasts with the simplicity of the town's 18th-century parish church, and Lanoraie, whose Hétu and Hervieux houses are fine examples of 19th-century Quebec architecture. At Berthierville, there is the Cuthbert Chapel, the first Presbyterian church in Lower Canada. The town is linked by bridge and road to Ile Dupas and other small, tranquil islands.

This route passes through tobacco-growing country. Hothouses, curing sheds and shrubbery windbreaks, essential to the crop's cultivation, dot the landscape. (Near Berthierville, tobacco thrives on a strip of reclaimed land, once marshy channels of the St. Lawrence.) The tobacco belt extends to the farmlands near Joliette. Sandy soil, some 125 frost-free days annually, and adequate rainfall during the growing season have made this one of Canada's major tobacco-growing areas.

North of Joliette is the wooded and mountainous landscape of the Laurentians.

Both Saint-Gabriel-de-Brandon and Rawdon offer year-round recreational activities. Rawdon boasts five waterfalls; the most spectacular is the 30-metre-high, 15-metre-wide Darwin Falls. In Laurentides (formerly Saint-Lin) is the boyhood home of Sir Wilfrid Laurier. The brick cottage is now open to the public.

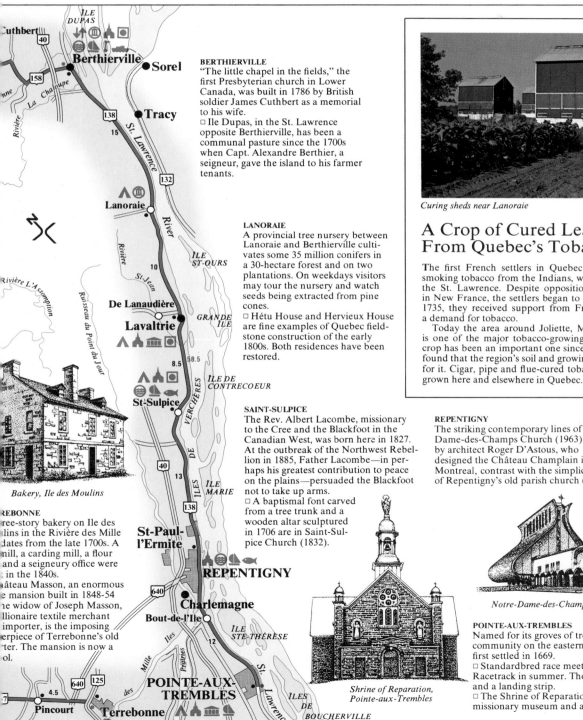

Bakery, Ile des Moulins

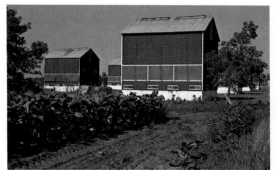

Curing sheds near Lanoraie

A Crop of Cured Leaves From Quebec's Tobacco Belt

The first French settlers in Quebec acquired the habit of smoking tobacco from the Indians, who grew the crop along the St. Lawrence. Despite opposition from the authorities in New France, the settlers began to cultivate tobacco. After 1735, they received support from France, where there was a demand for tobacco.

Today the area around Joliette, Montcalm and Lanoraie is one of the major tobacco-growing areas in Canada. The crop has been an important one since the 1930s, when it was found that the region's soil and growing conditions were ideal for it. Cigar, pipe and flue-cured tobacco are the main types grown here and elsewhere in Quebec.

BERTHIERVILLE
"The little chapel in the fields," the first Presbyterian church in Lower Canada, was built in 1786 by British soldier James Cuthbert as a memorial to his wife.
□ Ile Dupas, in the St. Lawrence opposite Berthierville, has been a communal pasture since the 1700s when Capt. Alexandre Berthier, a seigneur, gave the island to his farmer tenants.

LANORAIE
A provincial tree nursery between Lanoraie and Berthierville cultivates some 35 million conifers in a 30-hectare forest and on two plantations. On weekdays visitors may tour the nursery and watch seeds being extracted from pine cones.
□ Hétu House and Hervieux House are fine examples of Quebec fieldstone construction of the early 1800s. Both residences have been restored.

SAINT-SULPICE
The Rev. Albert Lacombe, missionary to the Cree and the Blackfoot in the Canadian West, was born here in 1827. At the outbreak of the Northwest Rebellion in 1885, Father Lacombe—in perhaps his greatest contribution to peace on the plains—persuaded the Blackfoot not to take up arms.
□ A baptismal font carved from a tree trunk and a wooden altar sculptured in 1706 are in Saint-Sulpice Church (1832).

REPENTIGNY
The striking contemporary lines of Notre-Dame-des-Champs Church (1963) by architect Roger D'Astous, who designed the Château Champlain in Montreal, contrast with the simplicity of Repentigny's old parish church (1725).

Notre-Dame-des-Champs Church, Repentigny

Shrine of Reparation, Pointe-aux-Trembles

POINTE-AUX-TREMBLES
Named for its groves of trembling aspen trees, this community on the eastern tip of Montreal Island was first settled in 1669.
□ Standardbred race meets are held at Richelieu Racetrack in summer. The town also has a marina and a landing strip.
□ The Shrine of Reparation features a grotto, a missionary museum and a chapel.

TERREBONNE
[...]ree-story bakery on Ile des [Mou]lins in the Rivière des Mille [...] dates from the late 1700s. A [...]mill, a carding mill, a flour [...] and a seigneury office were [...] in the 1840s.
[...]âteau Masson, an enormous [...]e mansion built in 1848-54 [...]e widow of Joseph Masson, [...]llionaire textile merchant [...] importer, is the imposing [...]erpiece of Terrebonne's old [...]ter. The mansion is now a [...]ol.

Farms and Orchards in a Region Graced with Serenity

Southwestern Quebec

After the bustle of nearby Montreal, the peaceful orchards and fertile valleys of southwestern Quebec offer a pleasant change of pace.

Across the St. Lawrence River from Montreal, the Indian village of Caughnawaga reflects the region's history. French Jesuits established a mission here in the late 17th century for Indian converts to Christianity. In the days of New France the mission Indians carried on a lively contraband trade in furs with the Dutch settlers

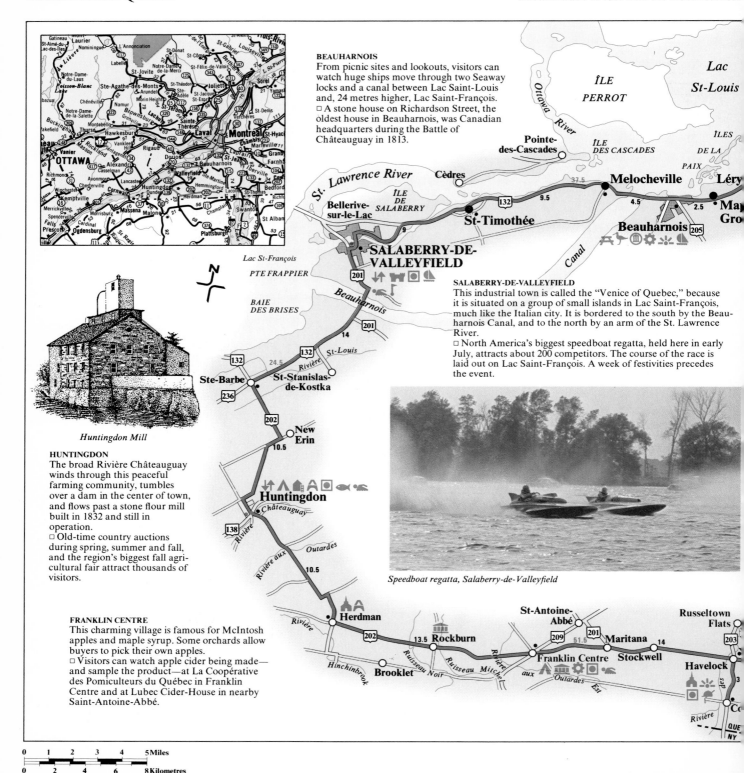

Huntingdon Mill

BEAUHARNOIS
From picnic sites and lookouts, visitors can watch huge ships move through two Seaway locks and a canal between Lac Saint-Louis and, 24 metres higher, Lac Saint-François.
□ A stone house on Richardson Street, the oldest house in Beauharnois, was Canadian headquarters during the Battle of Châteauguay in 1813.

SALABERRY-DE-VALLEYFIELD
This industrial town is called the "Venice of Quebec," because it is situated on a group of small islands in Lac Saint-François, much like the Italian city. It is bordered to the south by the Beauharnois Canal, and to the north by an arm of the St. Lawrence River.
□ North America's biggest speedboat regatta, held here in early July, attracts about 200 competitors. The course of the race is laid out on Lac Saint-François. A week of festivities precedes the event.

Speedboat regatta, Salaberry-de-Valleyfield

HUNTINGDON
The broad Rivière Châteauguay winds through this peaceful farming community, tumbles over a dam in the center of town, and flows past a stone flour mill built in 1832 and still in operation.
□ Old-time country auctions during spring, summer and fall, and the region's biggest fall agricultural fair attract thousands of visitors.

FRANKLIN CENTRE
This charming village is famous for McIntosh apples and maple syrup. Some orchards allow buyers to pick their own apples.
□ Visitors can watch apple cider being made— and sample the product—at La Coopérative des Pomiculteurs du Québec in Franklin Centre and at Lubec Cider-House in nearby Saint-Antoine-Abbé.

0 1 2 3 4 5 Miles
0 2 4 6 8 Kilometres

A Mohawk maiden, Kateri Tekakwitha, expected to become the first
North American Indian saint, is
revered in this village where she died
in 1680. Her relics lie in a white
marble tomb in the Mission Church
of St. Francis Xavier (1717).
□ In the sacristy chapel of the mission
church is an elegant tabernacle
believed built in France about 1700.
In the adjacent fieldstone presbytery
(1717-18) are an old Iroquois
grammar book (1813-53), and
dictionaries.

Statue of Kateri Tekakwitha,
Tekakwitha School, Caughnawaga

in what is now New York State. Today the
men of Caughnawaga, representing seven
Indian tribes, are famous for their work
as high-steel riggers on skyscrapers.

The clays and silts of Rivière Châteauguay support the most intensive dairy farming in Canada. Forerunners of the black
Canadian breed were imported by Champlain before 1610 and flourished in
southwestern Quebec. Today herds of
black-and-white holsteins are a familiar
sight in roadside fields.

Along the winding roads are other samples of an agricultural way of life almost
three centuries old. The Grey Nuns of Châteauguay were the first to cultivate apple
trees here in the late 1700s; dozens of orchards now prosper. In spring, wisps of
smoke curl from sugar shacks deep within
area maple groves. Silhouettes of huge old
elm trees—dead but still standing—punctuate fields that have been tilled, seeded and
harvested since the 17th century.

[Map showing Caughnawaga, Île St-Bernard, Châteauguay, St-Constant, Delson, Candiac, La Prairie, Brossard, Île des Soeurs, Île au Héron, St. Lawrence River, routes 138, 6, 132, 15, 202, 219, distances 23.5, 9.5, 8, 13.5]

LA PRAIRIE
La Prairie was one terminus (the other was Saint-Jean)
of Canada's first railway. A plaque records that this
25-kilometre line was built in 1836.
□ The Church of the Nativity, in Italian baroque style,
dates from 1839. The pulpit was carved by Victor
Bourgeau.
□ A cairn commemorates a 1691 battle in which French
settlers repelled an invading force of New Englanders
and averted an attack on Montreal. The ruins of a fort
erected four years earlier, to protect against Iroquois
raids, can be seen in the middle of town.

Saint-Joachim Church, Châteauguay

CHÂTEAUGUAY
Southwest of here on Oct. 26, 1813, Lt. Col. Charles-
Michel de Salaberry's 460 Canadian Voltigeurs defeated
invading Americans and saved Montreal from attack.
□ Saint-Joachim Church in nearby Châteauguay-Center
is more than 200 years old. The Lang House, built by the
Hudson's Bay Company, can be visited. A windmill on
Île Saint-Bernard dates from 1687.

Sleepers, Cabooses, and a Schoolhouse on Wheels

A locomotive that was built in 1887 and—73
years later—was the last steam engine to haul
a CPR train is exhibited in the Canadian Railway Museum at Saint-Constant.

A sleek, powerful 1937 locomotive of the type
that set a world record of 126 miles an hour (202
kilometres an hour) for steam locomotives is also
here.

The museum has many Montreal streetcars,
including the city's first electric tram (1892) and
the Golden Chariot open cars used on scenic
tours. There are cabooses, sleepers, tank and
freight cars and a carriage once used in northern
Ontario as a mobile schoolhouse. On the museum site are a turntable, a water tank, a round-
house and a rural station of the 1880s.

The *John Molson* (right), similar to the locomotive used on Canada's first railway in 1836,
operates on scheduled days.

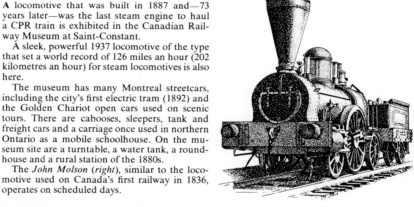

HEMMINGFORD
Parc Safari Africain at Hemmingford has one of
the largest collections of wildlife in Canada. The
162-hectare park has about nine kilometres of road
winding through open country, where lions, tigers,
baboons, elephants, giraffes and zebras roam. (No
convertibles are allowed in the park, and visitors
are warned to remain in their cars.) An
area where children can pet tame animals
is called the Friendly Forest.
□ The park has rare square-lipped
rhinoceros, popularly known as "white
rhinos" which are the largest of the
species with a weight of three tonnes.

White rhino,
Parc Safari Africain, Hemmingford

Parc Safari Africain, Hemmingford

Echoes of Wars Past
on the Banks of a Welcoming River

Richelieu River Valley

The 130-kilometre-long Richelieu River has its source in Lake Champlain on the Quebec-Vermont border. It flows almost due north and merges with the St. Lawrence at Sorel. Pleasure boats and commercial vessels that transport goods between Montreal and New York State ply the river in summer.

In 1609 Champlain ascended the Richelieu to make the first fateful French attack on the Iroquois. The river was known as the "River of the Iroquois" until it was re-

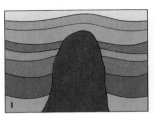

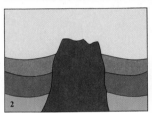

Eight Peaks of the Plain

The Monteregian Hills rise abruptly from the flat lowlands of southwestern Quebec. There are eight peaks in all: Johnson, Brome, Shefford, Yamaska, Rougemont, Saint-Bruno, Saint-Hilaire and Montreal's Mount Royal. The name derives from the Latin *Mons Regius*—royal mountains.

Geologists believe the hills were formed when molten rock rose from below the earth's crust some 120 million years ago. The molten rock thrust into layers of soft, porous sedimentary rock near the earth's surface (Figure 1), then cooled and solidified into igneous rock. Millions of years of erosion wore down the sedimentary rock, exposing the hard igneous rock (Figure 2). Ancient sea beaches and marine shells indicate that the hills were once partially submerged by the Champlain Sea—a body of water that covered the St. Lawrence lowlands when glaciers were receding. Fossils can be found in the sand on the foothills of Mont Saint-Hilaire.

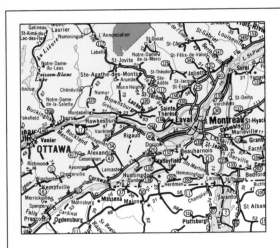

Fort Chambly

CHAMBLY
The great, square fort here was built by the French and abandoned to the British in 1760. It was held by American invaders in 1775-76, and served as a prison for American soldiers during the War of 1812 and for rebels during the 1837 uprising. Today Fort Chambly is a national historic park. Three walls and a dungeon have been restored.
□ Near the fort are the oldest locks of the Chambly Canal (c. 1843). River traffic still uses the canal to bypass rapids here.
□ In Chambly is a statue and the grave of Charles-Michel de Salaberry, who commanded the Canadian forces that defeated the Americans at Lacolle and Châteauguay in 1813.

SAINT-JEAN
A cairn marks the site of Fort Saint-Jean besieged in 1775 by American forces for 45 days. The Americans occupied the fort before burning it down the following year.
□ Weapons, uniforms and documents from the fort are in the museum of the Collège Militaire Royal.
□ A tablet at the CN station commemorates the building of Canada's first railway between here and La Prairie in 1836.

ÎLE-AUX-NOIX
Fort Lennox stands on Ile-aux-Noix in the Richelieu River. The island, a national historic park, is reached by ferry.
□ The French fortified the island in 1759. The British took possession the next year and held Ile-aux-Noix until it was captured in 1775 by an American army. The Americans abandoned the island in 1776 after their failure to capture Quebec.
□ The British built a fort here in 1783. Following the War of 1812, the British reinforced this stronghold as part of a defense against a possible future American invasion. They renamed it Fort Lennox. A barracks, commissary, guardhouse, officers' quarters, and canteen have been restored.

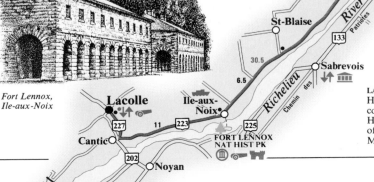

*Fort Lennox,
Ile-aux-Noix*

Carignan   St-Mathi
Chambly   *Bassin de Chambly*
Riche

St-Luc   Ile-Ste-Thérèse
Talon   *ÎLE STE-THÉRÈSE*
Grand-Bernier
ST-JEAN
Iberville
St-Blaise
Sabrevois
St-Noix
Lacolle   Ile-aux-Noix
Cantic
FORT LENNOX NAT HIST PK
Noyan

LACOLLE
Here, 260 Canadian Voltigeurs, commanded by a Major Hanock, forced the retreat of 4000 American soldiers on May 13, 1814.

0 1 2 3 4 5 Miles
0 2 4 6 8 Kilometres

named, in 1642, in honor of French Cardinal Richelieu.

During the early days of settlement, the Richelieu served as the route by which French and English colonists repeatedly attacked each other. In 1760 an English army advanced up the river to Montreal and, in 1775, invading Americans followed the same course. During the War of 1812 American forces were again repelled at present-day Lacolle.

Rising some 400 metres above the Riche-

lieu is Mont Saint-Hilaire, one of the eight Monteregian Hills that lie between Montreal and the Appalachian uplands of the northern United States. Visitors can drive as far as Lac Hertel at the side of the mountain. A footpath leads from there to a summit lookout that gives a panoramic view of the Richelieu River valley extending as far south as Lake Champlain.

Patriote monument, Saint-Denis

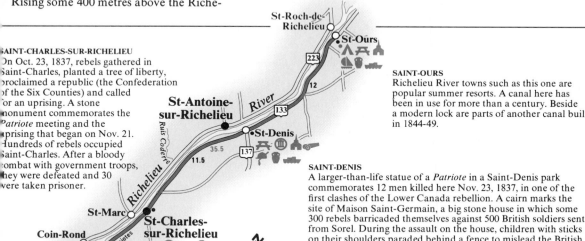

SAINT-CHARLES-SUR-RICHELIEU
On Oct. 23, 1837, rebels gathered in Saint-Charles, planted a tree of liberty, proclaimed a republic (the Confederation of the Six Counties) and called for an uprising. A stone monument commemorates the *Patriote* meeting and the uprising that began on Nov. 21. Hundreds of rebels occupied Saint-Charles. After a bloody combat with government troops, they were defeated and 30 were taken prisoner.

SAINT-OURS
Richelieu River towns such as this one are popular summer resorts. A canal here has been in use for more than a century. Beside a modern lock are parts of another canal built in 1844-49.

SAINT-DENIS
A larger-than-life statue of a *Patriote* in a Saint-Denis park commemorates 12 men killed here Nov. 23, 1837, in one of the first clashes of the Lower Canada rebellion. A cairn marks the site of Maison Saint-Germain, a big stone house in which some 300 rebels barricaded themselves against 500 British soldiers sent from Sorel. During the assault on the house, children with sticks on their shoulders paraded behind a fence to mislead the British as to the number of armed rebels in the village. The ploy succeeded and the British soldiers retreated. A year later, the British returned and set fire to the village.

MONT SAINT-HILAIRE
This is one of the eight Monteregian Hills of southwestern Quebec. Near the center of Mont Saint-Hilaire is Lac Hertel, surrounded by a network of nature trails, all part of the Gault Estate, owned by McGill University. Part of the estate—the Mont-Saint-Hilaire Nature Conservation Centre—is used for biological research. Another sector of the estate is open to the public, and guided hikes can be arranged.
□ In a small quarry near Mont Saint-Hilaire, geologists have discovered 20 minerals yet to be reported anywhere else on earth. In another Mont Saint-Hilaire quarry are clearly defined strata of shells and fossils, some estimated to be 50 million years old.
□ The 1837 church in the town of Mont-Saint-Hilaire has a Gothic interior and a fieldstone exterior. On the interior walls are 11 frescoes, murals, Stations of the Cross, and bas-reliefs by Osias Leduc. The presbytery dates from 1798. Several water mills from about 1800 have been converted into houses at the foot of the mountain. Two imposing stone manor houses along the Rivière des Hurons date from about 1850.

Cerulian warbler

Seigneurial land pattern: an aerial view, near Saint-Denis

A Land of Loyal Seigneurs and Industrious Habitants

Some Quebec farmers still pay rent under contracts laid down in the 17th century. The fertile land along the St. Lawrence and Richelieu rivers was distributed to seigneurs, "persons of rank," by Louis XIV. Seigneurs who pledged loyalty to the King were granted waterfront lots which they parceled out to tenant farmers, who had to clear the land. (Seigneurs divided their land into thin strips so that each tenant had river frontage.) The seigneur was obliged to live in a manor house on his land and to run a flour mill for his tenants, who paid about $35 a year for a 40-hectare farm. Industrious habitants grew wheat, oats, peas and beans, and raised cattle, sheep, pigs and chickens—and prospered; impoverished seigneurs often went hungry to keep up an appearance of gentility.

Lac Hertel, Mont Saint-Hilaire

Apples, Cheeses and Mushrooms From the 'Garden of Quebec'

Eastern Townships

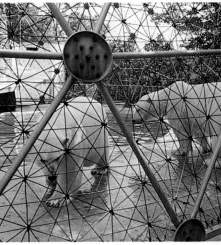

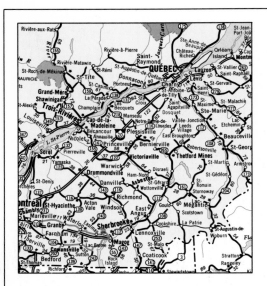

GRANBY
This industrial city has about a dozen European fountains acquired after the Second World War. A 3,200-year-old Greek fountain is on Leclerc Boulevard and a first-century Roman fountain is the centerpiece of Pelletier Park.
□ In Granby Zoo, one of Canada's largest zoos, are more than 1,300 animals representing some 300 species.
□ The Granby Car Museum has a 1931 Buick limousine used for 10 years by Louis St. Laurent before he became prime minister. Other vehicles include a 1903 Holsman, 1906 Reo, 1914 McLaughlin and 1929 Rolls-Royce.

Granby Zoo

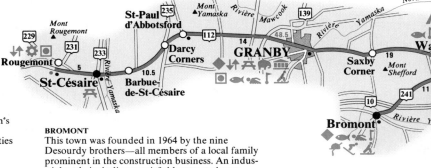

ROUGEMONT
An interpretive center on Rougemont's main street describes apple-growing and cider-making, this town's main industries.
□ Visitors to La Cidrerie du Québec taste local varieties of cider.

Rural Charm and Superb Skiing

The Eastern Townships (or *Les Cantons de l'Est*) extend east from the Richelieu River to the Chaudière River, and south from the St. Lawrence lowlands to Quebec's border with the United States. The area is famed for its rural charm. Its scenic lakes, rivers and mountains make it a year-round resort area, and its ski hills, such as Mont Orford, rival those of the Laurentians.

BROMONT
This town was founded in 1964 by the nine Desourdy brothers—all members of a local family prominent in the construction business. An industrial park, including an airfield, attracted new business to the area and the venture prospered. With 10 mountain peaks and two lakes near at hand, the town has become a popular resort.

American woodcock

COWANSVILLE
Red brick houses in the part of Cowansville that was once the village of Sweetsburg are among Quebec's finest examples of Victorian gingerbread architecture. Cowansville (originally Nelsonville) and Sweetsburg (at first called Churchville) were United Empire Loyalist villages.

STANBRIDGE EAST
Cornell Mills, a three-story brick structure built in 1930, is part of Missisquoi County Museum at Stanbridge East. The second floor of the mill has been converted into the interior of a 19th-century home. There are displays of village life a century ago, including replicas of a blacksmith's shop and a cobbler's shop.
□ Near the museum is Hodge's Store, a two-story brick house (1843). It has been renovated as an "Old Time Country Store." Most of the merchandise on display was found intact during the renovation of the building in the early 1970s.

| 0 | 2 | 4 | 6 | 8 | 10 Miles |
| 0 | 4 | 8 | 12 | | 16 Kilometres |

Quebec's Eastern Townships were first settled by United Empire Loyalists who fled here in the 1790s after the American War of Independence. (The region was given its name to distinguish it from the townships to the west of Montreal in what is now Ontario.) During the early 19th century the Loyalists were followed by successive waves of immigrants: Americans, Irish, Scots and English. After 1840, French Canadians came to the townships, where they predominate today.

Known as the "Garden of Quebec," the townships have many of the province's best dairy and livestock farms. The abundance of local produce is the foundation of food industries at Granby and Rougemont. The Benedictine Abbey at Saint-Benoît-du-Lac makes two distinctive cheeses, *Ermite* and *St. Benoît*. Canada's largest producer of mushrooms is at Waterloo. Ducks are raised commercially at Lac Brome.

In summer and early autumn roadside stands offer farm produce, maple-sugar products, homemade preserves—and apples. The largest apple orchards in Quebec are found in this region. The first orchards were planted near Rougemont in the 1860s by the Sulpician Fathers. Early apple varieties, such as the Fameuse or Snow apple, have been replaced by the Melba, Lobo, McIntosh and Cortland. From the plentiful apple crop, hard cider is made. Some local cideries can be toured and their delicious product sampled.

WATERLOO
This industrial community on the shores of Lac Waterloo is the home of Slack Bros., Canada's largest mushroom producer. This family-owned business was begun in 1880 by Thomas Slack, who raised flowers and vegetables. Mushrooms were first grown here in 1924. Today the firm raises more than three million kilograms of mushrooms each year.
□ Waterloo, first settled in 1786, was incorporated as a village in 1867. The town's oldest building, a stone store built in 1829, now houses a restaurant and a bus terminal.

Young musicians at Parc du Mont-Orford

PARC DU MONT-ORFORD
Orford Arts Centre, home of the Jeunesses Musicales du Canada, covers a 90-hectare area in this provincial park. The center, established in 1951, is open year round. During the summer, more than 300 students attend music and theater classes here. The annual Orford Festival offers a varied program of public concerts and recitals. Art exhibitions are also held throughout the summer.

The center has a 500-seat concert hall and a central building, where visitors can dine and enjoy a spectacular view of Mont Orford. The Man and Music Pavilion, built for Expo 67 in Montreal, was moved here in 1972. It has assembly and exhibition halls, and large classrooms.
□ Mont Orford, one of the highest peaks (738 metres) in the Eastern Townships, is a ski center. A chair lift carries skiers and sightseers to the summit.

Brown trout

Benedictine Abbey, Saint-Benoît-du-Lac

SAINT-BENOÎT-DU-LAC
The Benedictine Abbey overlooking Lake Memphrémagog here is a striking combination of octagonal and square towers, triangular gables and long, thin, pointed windows. Inside are intricately tiled floors and graceful arches in mosaics of brick. The abbey's design was influenced by French-born Dom Paul Bellot, who immigrated to Canada in 1937, and became one of Quebec's foremost ecclesiastical architects. His most famous work is the dome of St. Joseph's Oratory in Montreal. His grave is in the abbey grounds.
□ Visitors can pick apples in the abbey's orchard and buy cheese made by the monks. Their distinctive *Ermite* is a blue cheese. *St. Benoît* has a nutty, somewhat sweet flavor, and looks like Swiss cheese.

BROME
A three-day festival in early September features handicraft displays and square dancing.
□ In the annex of the museum is a Second World War German Fokker aircraft, its camouflaged fabric skin intact. Pioneer artifacts and archives are in the Brome County Historical Museum, a white brick building that was the Knowlton Academy (1854), the village's first school. Other museum buildings include a schoolhouse (1854) and a 19th-century fire station and tower.

Benedictine Abbey, Saint-Benoît-du-Lac

Where Backwoods Roads Lead to Country Fairs and Covered Bridges

Eastern Townships

This lively and picturesque corner of the Eastern Townships offers year-round recreation. In summer visitors enjoy fishing and boating on the sparkling waters of Lac Memphrémagog and its smaller neighbor, Lac Massawippi. Hikers are drawn to the high wooded hills surrounding the lakes. In winter skiers flock to Parc du Mont-Orford, one of Quebec's major winter sports centers, near the town of Magog.

Entertainment as well as recreation thrives here. Festival Lennoxville, held

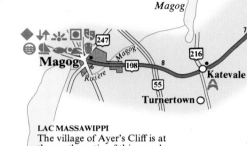

The Piggery, North Hatley

NORTH HATLEY

This all-seasons resort town north of Lake Massawippi is home to numerous painters, sculptors, potters and writers. The Piggery offers a summer program of drama and musicals. Evening concerts are combined with exhibitions of local art and handicrafts.
□ Two of North Hatley's oldest houses, Hovey Manor and the Hatley Inn, have been converted into hotels. Both were built about 1900.
□ Hatley, south of here, has clapboard houses and two wooden churches, all dating from 1850.

MAGOG

Established in 1799 by United Empire Loyalists, Magog is a popular year-round sports center. Northwest of the town is a major ski center at Parc du Mont-Orford.
□ To the south of the town is Lac Memphrémagog—an Indian word meaning great stretch of water. (The name of the town is an abbreviation of this word.) One fifth of this 52-kilometre-long lake lies in Vermont. Boat tours of the lake are available from Magog. The cruises offer views of local scenic landmarks such as Mont Orford, Owl's Head and Three Sisters Islands.
□ At Magog Lac Memphrémagog empties into the Magog River which, in turn, flows into the Saint-François River at Sherbrooke. During the 19th century, commercial shipping traffic traveling from the United States crossed the lake to reach the Saint-François.

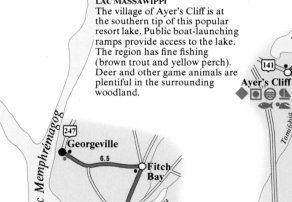

LAC MASSAWIPPI

The village of Ayer's Cliff is at the southern tip of this popular resort lake. Public boat-launching ramps provide access to the lake. The region has fine fishing (brown trout and yellow perch). Deer and other game animals are plentiful in the surrounding woodland.

Haskell Opera House, Rock Island

ROCK ISLAND

The Haskell Opera House in the twin towns of Rock Island, Que., and Derby Line, Vt., straddles the international border. Theatergoers sit in the United States to watch performances on a stage in Canada. Downstairs in the Haskell Library the adult section is in the U.S., and the children's section is in Canada. The Opera House, built in 1901-04, is a replica of the old Boston Opera House.
□ The Barn Museum displays a pioneer system that carried spring water through connected hollow logs. It also has tools for hollowing logs. There are a stagecoach and sleigh (c.1850), and a colonist kitchen with dishes, churns, stoves and looms.
□ The Stanstead Historical Museum, five kilometres west in Beebe Plain, has a collection of Canadian military insignia from 1914 on.

Bishop's University, Lennoxville

each summer at the 650-seat Centennial Theater of Bishop's University, presents a season of Canadian plays. Theatrical and musical attractions are offered at the Piggery, North Hatley, and the Théâtre du Vieux Clocher, Magog.

In this area are towns and villages that tempt the traveler to linger and enjoy the rural charm and peace of a bygone age. Mementos of the past are displayed in museums at Rock Island, Beebe Plain and Coaticook. Lively country fairs and festivals are still held every autumn in towns like Ayer's Cliff and Magog.

Outside the towns the visitor can explore quiet backroads winding through woodlots, meadows and furrowed fields. Covered bridges still span the rivers near Fitch Bay, Coaticook and Lennoxville. At the turn of the century there were more than a thousand covered bridges in Quebec, but today only 80 remain. Those that survive in this unspoiled region are eloquent reminders of horse-and-buggy days.

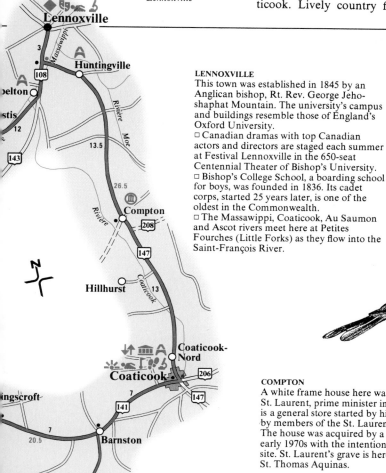

LENNOXVILLE
This town was established in 1845 by an Anglican bishop, Rt. Rev. George Jehoshaphat Mountain. The university's campus and buildings resemble those of England's Oxford University.
□ Canadian dramas with top Canadian actors and directors are staged each summer at Festival Lennoxville in the 650-seat Centennial Theater of Bishop's University.
□ Bishop's College School, a boarding school for boys, was founded in 1836. Its cadet corps, started 25 years later, is one of the oldest in the Commonwealth.
□ The Massawippi, Coaticook, Au Saumon and Ascot rivers meet here at Petites Fourches (Little Forks) as they flow into the Saint-François River.

Birds of the Townships

Red-breasted nuthatches and downy woodpeckers are year-round residents in the wooded Eastern Townships. The downy woodpecker, a black and white bird, is the smallest of its species found in Canada. It nests in a hole drilled high in a tree. A strong skull enables the woodpecker to withstand the pounding of its bill as it bores into trees.

Abandoned woodpecker holes are favorite nesting places of the tree-climbing red-breasted nuthatch. It lines the nesting cavity with shredded bark, grasses and roots. The nuthatch feeds on nuts and, using its long toes and claws to climb, it forages up and down tree trunks for insects.

In early May the first Baltimore orioles appear in the Eastern Townships. The male has fiery orange markings. The female is a duller, dusky orange. Other birds found in this area include yellow-throated vireos, warbling vireos, chestnut-sided warblers, scarlet tanagers and pine siskins.

Baltimore oriole

Red-breasted nuthatch

Downy woodpecker

COMPTON
A white frame house here was the birthplace of Louis St. Laurent, prime minister in 1948-57. Adjoining the house is a general store started by his father in 1879 and operated by members of the St. Laurent family until the late 1960s. The house was acquired by a private foundation in the early 1970s with the intention of preserving it as an historic site. St. Laurent's grave is here, in the parish cemetery of St. Thomas Aquinas.

COATICOOK
A lookout in Carillon Park provides a view of the Coaticook River where it cuts through a deep, tree-lined gorge. A nearby covered bridge (19 metres long) crosses the gorge. Coaticook is from the Indian word *Koakitchou*, meaning "river of the land of pines."
□ Norton House is typical of the mansions built by farmers who prospered here in the early 1900s. It can be visited.
□ Beaulne Museum, in the town's former post office, displays local pioneer artifacts.

WAY'S MILLS
Rozynski Pottery, in this small farming community on the Rivière Niger, offers a series of two-week summer courses in pottery.
□ South of here, at Baldwin Mills, a provincial fish hatchery rears splake—a crossbreed of speckled and lake trout. Visitors see a variety of game fish in the hatchery's aquariums. Splake and rainbow, brown, speckled and lake trout all can be caught in nearby Lac Lyster.

Rozynski Pottery, Way's Mills

Coaticook River gorge

Asbestos, Hockey Sticks and Scenic Hardwood Forests

Eastern Townships

The region between Sherbrooke and Victoriaville exudes rural tranquillity. Here are rolling, forested hills; poultry and dairy farms and lush meadows; weathered wooden barns, old mills and covered bridges. But here, too, are the bustling pulp-and-paper towns of Bromptonville and Windsor, the mining center of Asbestos, and Victoriaville, which has the world's leading manufacturer of hockey sticks.

The largest center in this region is Sherbrooke, unofficial "capital" of the Eastern

Restored gristmill, Denison Mills

RICHMOND
A cairn here commemorates the first road to connect the Eastern Townships and Quebec City. Construction of the Craig Road, a crude trail that was impassable much of the year, was begun in 1809 under the direction of Sir James Craig, governor of Lower Canada. The route was built to encourage British settlement in the Eastern Townships. Today parts of the Craig Road near Quebec City are paved, but much of the original route has been abandoned.

1 Université de Sherbrooke
2 Jacques-Cartier Park
3 Floral Mosaics
4 Mount Bellevue
5 Mena'Sen (Illuminated Cross)
6 St. Peter's Church
7 Court House
8 St. Michael's Cathedral
9 Tourist Information
10 Aylmer Bridge

Festival des Cantons de l'Est, Sherbrooke

Sanctuary of the Sacred Heart, Beauvoir

BEAUVOIR SHRINE
The Sanctuary of the Sacred Heart, a fieldstone shrine overlooking Rivière Saint-François, is at Beauvoir Hills. Erected in 1920, it fulfilled a vow made by a parish priest, the Rev. J. A. Laporte, who held services on this hilltop for some 30 years.

From Easter Sunday to the end of October more than half a million persons visit the shrine, which is maintained by the Assumptionist Fathers.

SHERBROOKE
Founded by Loyalists in the 1790s, Sherbrooke (pop. 81,000) now is Quebec's sixth largest city.
□ Rivière Magog tumbles 45 metres through a series of rapids in the city before emptying into Rivière Saint-François.
□ More than 50,000 plants are grown each year for colorful mosaic floral displays. Some 15,000 are in a garden near the courthouse; 25,000 form an abstract design along King Street West, the main thoroughfare.
□ The one-week Festival des Cantons de l'Est (Festival of the Eastern Townships) in August has livestock displays and harness racing.
□ Université de Sherbrooke, founded in 1954, has eight faculties, a postgraduate school, and extensive medical research facilities.
□ St. Peter's Church, built in 1844, is one of the oldest Anglican churches in the Eastern Townships.

SHERBROOKE

To Drummondville
Prospect St.
Portland Blvd.
King St. W.
Des Nations Lake
Roy St.
Galt
Jogues St.
King St. E.
Conseil St.
Woodward
Galt St. E.
To Montreal
To Lennoxville

Richmond
Melbourne
Upper Melbourne
Windsor
St-Grégoire-de-Greenlay
Bromptonville
BEAUVOIR SHRINE
SHERBROOKE

Townships. It is attractively situated on hills at the point where Rivière Magog plunges into the Saint-François. (There is a magnificent view of the city from Mont Bellevue on the southern outskirts.) The city's founder was Gilbert Hyatt, a Loyalist from Vermont, who built a gristmill by Rivière Magog in 1794. The community that grew up around it was named for Sir John Sherbrooke, governor-general of Canada in 1816-18. Today it is Quebec's sixth largest city (pop. 81,000) and a major manufac-

turing center. Almost all of its inhabitants are bilingual French Canadians.

North of Sherbrooke is Warwick, the gateway to the Bois-Francs, a scenic region of maple and hardwood forests. Here, the agricultural lowland stretching south from the St. Lawrence River gives way to the rugged hills of the Eastern Townships.

Arthabaska, in the heart of Bois-Francs country, claims two famous sons: the painter Marc Suzor-Côté, and Sir Wilfrid Laurier. (The house where Laurier lived

from 1876 to 1897 is a museum.) Asbestos, south of Warwick, takes its name from the fibrous mineral extracted locally from a vast, terraced open-pit mine, one of the largest in the world. Its size dwarfs the men and machines that continually enlarge it.

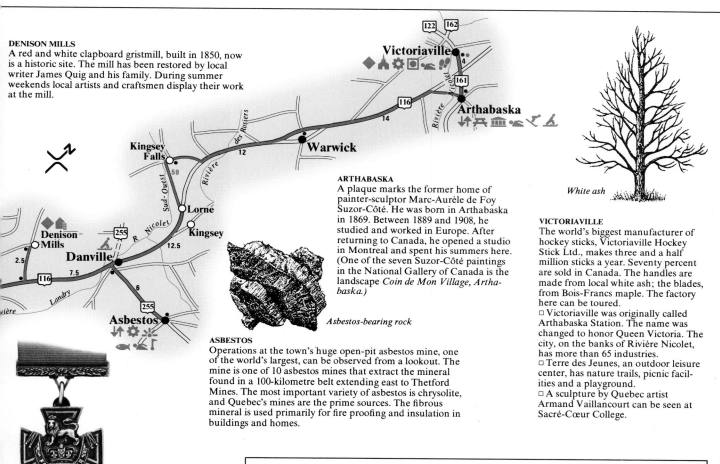

DENISON MILLS
A red and white clapboard gristmill, built in 1850, now is a historic site. The mill has been restored by local writer James Quig and his family. During summer weekends local artists and craftsmen display their work at the mill.

White ash

ARTHABASKA
A plaque marks the former home of painter-sculptor Marc-Aurèle de Foy Suzor-Côté. He was born in Arthabaska in 1869. Between 1889 and 1908, he studied and worked in Europe. After returning to Canada, he opened a studio in Montreal and spent his summers here. (One of the seven Suzor-Côté paintings in the National Gallery of Canada is the landscape *Coin de Mon Village, Arthabaska.*)

Asbestos-bearing rock

VICTORIAVILLE
The world's biggest manufacturer of hockey sticks, Victoriaville Hockey Stick Ltd., makes three and a half million sticks a year. Seventy percent are sold in Canada. The handles are made from local white ash; the blades, from Bois-Francs maple. The factory here can be toured.
□ Victoriaville was originally called Arthabaska Station. The name was changed to honor Queen Victoria. The city, on the banks of Rivière Nicolet, has more than 65 industries.
□ Terre des Jeunes, an outdoor leisure center, has nature trails, picnic facilities and a playground.
□ A sculpture by Quebec artist Armand Vaillancourt can be seen at Sacré-Cœur College.

ASBESTOS
Operations at the town's huge open-pit asbestos mine, one of the world's largest, can be observed from a lookout. The mine is one of 10 asbestos mines that extract the mineral found in a 100-kilometre belt extending east to Thetford Mines. The most important variety of asbestos is chrysolite, and Quebec's mines are the prime sources. The fibrous mineral is used primarily for fire proofing and insulation in buildings and homes.

Victoria Cross

DANVILLE
Ten years after Queen Victoria instituted the Victoria Cross "for conspicuous bravery in the presence of the enemy," a 20-year-old British soldier won the Empire's highest award far from the scene of combat. On June 9, 1866, a train stopped at Danville. Locked in converted boxcars were 800 immigrants. In another boxcar was ammunition for use against Fenian raiders. Private Timothy O'Hea suddenly noticed that the ammunition car was on fire. He shouted an alarm, but nearby railwaymen and soldiers fled. O'Hea ripped burning covers off ammunition cases. Then, for almost an hour he carried buckets of water from a nearby creek. He fought the flames and he won. A plaque in Danville honors O'Hea.

An Elegant Home for a Leader

Wilfrid Laurier, prime minister of Canada in 1896-1911, lived in Arthabaska for some 20 years. The elegant brick house he built here in 1876 is now a museum. The house—perhaps a bit beyond Laurier's means at the time—is furnished as in his day. Historical documents and many personal possessions of Laurier and his wife, Zoë, are displayed.

Laurier practiced law and ran a weekly newspaper in Arthabaska—the chief town of Quebec's Bois-Francs region. The voters of Drummond-Arthabaska, attracted by Laurier's moderate political views, elected him their Member of Parliament in 1874. For the next 13 years, Laurier's eloquence and ability won the respect of the Liberal Party. In 1887 the Liberals made him national leader.

Living room, Laurier House, Arthabaska

Lively Folk Songs and Sugar Shacks Along the Chaudière

Eastern Townships

Pottery making, Saint-Joseph-de-Beauce

Gentle Lullabies, Drinking Songs, and the Famous *Alouette*

Writer and folklore expert Marius Barbeau—born at Sainte-Marie in 1883—collected, recorded and transcribed thousands of French-Canadian folk songs.

Barbeau traveled Quebec, the Maritimes and New England in his search for traditional songs. Many of the songs had been passed down for generations, but had never been put in written form. The singers were fishermen, lumbermen, and women who sang as they worked at spinning and weaving. Some had memorized more than 100 songs. There were songs of the fur traders, voyageurs and coureurs de bois; work songs of the habitant farmers who cleared land along the St. Lawrence; lullabies and drinking songs. Old French songs—brought to Quebec by early settlers—sometimes dated back to the 16th century.

One of the best known Canadian songs in Barbeau's collection is *Alouette*, in which an unfortunate lark is told: "I will pluck your head, your beak, your nose, your eyes . . ."

Barbeau studied at Université Laval then at Oxford and the Sorbonne. He worked as an anthropologist at the National Museum of Canada from 1911 to 1958, and produced a number of books on French-Canadian and Indian folklore and arts and crafts, collections of legends and folk tales, and two novels. Barbeau died in 1969 in Ottawa.

SAINTE-MARIE
The shrine of Sainte-Anne-de-Beauce is between two historic houses. One, built in 1811, was the birthplace of Elzéar-Alexandre Taschereau (1820-1898), the first Canadian cardinal. The other was built in the early 1800s by the cardinal's father, Jean-Thomas Taschereau, a judge.

SAINT-JOSEPH-DE-BEAUCE
Local clay is used to produce pottery by La Céramique de Beauce, a cooperative. The plant and an exhibition hall may be toured.
□ Saint-Joseph-de-Beauce was named for Joseph de la Gorgendière who was granted the seigneury in 1736. Saint-Joseph-de-Beauce Church was built of local fieldstone in 1867.

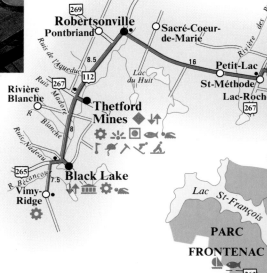

THETFORD MINES
The first asbestos mine in Quebec was opened here in 1878. Today Thetford Mines has five open-pit and two underground mines. The mining area may be viewed from four observation posts. Other asbestos mines have been developed along a 100-kilometre belt that extends west through the Eastern Townships.
□ A monument at city hall honors Joseph Fecteau, who discovered asbestos here in 1876.
□ In late August livestock, produce and handicrafts are exhibited at an agricultural fair. Local musicians provide lively dance music during the four-day event.

Open-pit asbestos mine, Thetford Mines

During the American invasion in the winter of 1775-76, Gen. Benedict Arnold led 1,100 American troops along the Rivière Chaudière from northern Maine to Quebec City. (Plaques in present-day Lac-Mégantic, Saint-Georges and Sainte-Marie mark his route.) Nearly half the invaders died in forests and swamps. Starving survivors ate soap, grease and boiled moccasins. They reached Quebec City, but were repulsed on Dec. 31, 1775, by the troops of Gov. Guy Carleton.

The forests have been cleared and the swamps drained in what now is known as the Beauce Country. The Chaudière, which flows through gently rolling terrain, is bordered by long, narrow farms. (During the French regime seigneurs divided their land into thin strips so that each tenant farmer had river frontage.) Quebec's longest covered bridge (155 metres) spans the river at Notre-Dame-des-Pins. The Chaudière's source is Lac-Mégantic, noted for its ouananiche (landlocked salmon).

Maple trees here yield most of the maple syrup produced in Canada. Wooden shacks (*cabanes à sucre*) in the hills are used for "sugaring off" parties. Families and friends gather to dance, sing and sample maple syrup in celebration of spring.

NOTRE-DAME-DES-PINS
Some 80 artists and craftsmen of Créativités Beauceronnes, a cooperative, produce fine linen and woolen goods, pottery and wood sculptures, handmade toys and dolls. Members grow flax to produce linen, and raise sheep for wool. Spring visitors can watch sheep being shorn and the fleece being carded and spun into wool.

SAINT-GEORGES-OUEST
A five-metre-high bronze statue of Saint George, sculpted in 1912 by Louis Jobin, stands in front of the church here.
□ Three kilometres north is Parc des Sept Chutes, named for seven waterfalls that drop 38 metres in a gorge of the Rivière Pozer.

Tire sur la neige—
Hot Maple Syrup on Snow

Maple trees were the only source of sugar for the early settlers in New France. Before their arrival, the Indians had been familiar with the process of making maple syrup and sugar. Each spring, when the sap began to run freely, the Indians tapped the maple tree by cutting a diagonal incision in the trunk. In the lower end of the incision, they placed a concave piece of bark which piped the sap into a hollowed log.

The pioneers borrowed and improved upon the Indian techniques of tapping the maples and refining its sap. (The earliest record of Canadian maple-sugar production is dated 1706.) After the sap was gathered, it was boiled in a large kettle over an open fire. The maple sugar was formed into cakes for later use.

Today the sap is processed in sugar shacks, where evaporator pans over furnaces convert it rapidly into syrup and sugar. Modern production methods yield some 4.5 million litres of maple syrup annually in Canada. Ninety percent comes from rural regions of Quebec, such as the Beauce Country.

Although maple syrup is now produced commercially in large quantities, many families save small amounts for "sugaring off" parties each spring. The hot syrup is poured on clean snow and the sweet taffy (called *tire*) is eagerly eaten.

Maple syrup is often associated with Canadian cuisine, especially that of Quebec. Two famous recipes are maple sugar pie, a custardlike dish with maple syrup thickened with cornstarch, and *grands-pères au sirop d'érable* (maple syrup dumplings).

Sugaring-off party, Saint-Benoit-Labre

PARC FRONTENAC
Created in 1976, 150-square-kilometre Parc Frontenac is dotted with lakes and rivers, and borders Lac Saint-François. Furnished cottages which can accommodate up to ten adults, are scattered throughout the park. Fishing is good for walleye, perch, and smallmouth bass.

Gray partridge

LAC-MÉGANTIC
A plaque in city hall notes that American Revolutionary troops led by Gen. Benedict Arnold camped here on their way to join Gen. Richard Montgomery's army for an attack on Quebec City. The American invasion was unsuccessful.
□ A dozen plays are presented in August at the Quebec Student Drama Festival. Throughout summer students study theater arts.

Rivière-des-Plantes
16
50
Rivière-Gilbert
Notre-Dame-des-Pins
auceville-Est
eauceville
108
Chaudière
16
204
173
St-Georges
Lacroix
12
St-Georges-Ouest
271
St-Benoît-Labre
Lac-Poulin
31
-Ephrem-Station
12.5
St-Ephrem-de-Tring
Rancourt
5
269
adeloupe
St-Evariste-de-Forsyth
20
Courcelles
108
ambton
263
St-Romain
des-Indiens
10.5
Felton
Stornoway
161
13
25.5
Lac Whitton
Nantes
12.5
Lac de l'Orignal
263
204
Lac Mégantic
Lac-Mégantic

Work in Silver and Wood
by Quebec's Early Artisans

South Shore, St. Lawrence River

The south shore of the St. Lawrence River is redolent with history. This was the land Jacques Cartier saw in 1535. Chagrined that the broad blue river was not a route to the Orient, Cartier sailed away. But other Frenchmen followed—explorers, fur traders and missionaries. These adventurous men pushed westward from New France until, by the early 1700s, they had explored the vast interior of North America.

A monument in a Boucherville park honors one of these explorers—the Rev. Jac-

Short-billed marsh wren

Sorel shipyard

LAC SAINT-PIERRE
A seafood fricassee, *gibelotte de poissons,* is the regional specialty in restaurants on a cluster of islands opposite Sorel, and just north of the town. The islands, favorite haunts of duck hunters and fishermen, are at the entrance to Lac Saint-Pierre, a shallow, 11-by-22-kilometre bulge in the St. Lawrence River.
□ Common gallinules, long-billed and short-billed marsh wrens are found by the shores of Lac Saint-Pierre. Large colonies of seabirds, ducks, bustards and snipes also breed in the reedy, lakeside marshes. This is the only place in the St. Lawrence Valley inhabited by red-spotted turtles, which normally avoid subzero winters. They are believed to be survivors from a warmer, wetter period that followed the last ice age.

Common gallinule

SOREL
On the St. Lawrence River at the mouth of the Richelieu, Sorel is an inland seaport humming with naval construction and related industries.
□ La Maison des Gouverneurs, built by Governor-in-Chief Sir Frederick Haldimand in 1781, was for many years a summer residence of the governors-general of Canada. It now is a conference and exhibition hall.
□ Boat cruises (from Sainte-Anne-de-Sorel) include a tour of the offshore islands and a moonlight trip to the Saint-Ours lock on the Richelieu River.
□ Canada geese, ducks and snipe are plentiful in this area, and there is good perch fishing.
□ A provincial marina can berth 315 boats.

(see Road Unit 110)

BOUCHERVILLE
Sainte-Famille Church, built in 1801, contains an important collection of religious art and has been designated an historic monument. Among many wood sculptures is a tabernacle carved about 1745 by Gilles Bolvin. Side altars (1807-08) are by Louis Amble Quevillon, and baptismal fonts (c. 1880) by Nicolas Manny.
□ Other historic monuments are La Chaumière (1741), the oldest house in Boucherville, and the Lafontaine House (1780), birthplace of Louis-Hippolyte Lafontaine, joint premier (with Robert Baldwin) of the Province of Canada in 1842-48.

VERCHÈRES
Three times life size, this bronze statue of Madeleine de Verchères commemorates the 14-year-old's defense in 1692 of her father's seigneurial fort. Sculpted in 1913 by Philippe Hébert, the statue is at the site of the girl's heroic encounter with the Iroquois.
□ A plaque marks the site of a house in which Ludger Duvernay, founder of the Saint-Jean-Baptiste Society (1834), was born in 1799. Verchères was also the birthplace of Calixa Lavallée (1841-1919), who composed the music of *O Canada.*
□ A round, stone windmill (c. 1700) is two kilometres northeast.

VARENNES
A huge wooden calvary overlooks the St. Lawrence River here. The figure of Christ is on a cross 24 metres high, those of the two thieves on crosses about 23 metres high. The calvary was sculpted in 1776 by Michel Brisset.
□ A shrine honors Mother Marguerite d'Youville, foundress of the Order of the Gray Nuns, who was born here.

Madeleine de Verchères statue, Verchères

0 2 4 6 8 10 Miles

0 4 8 12 16 Kilometres

ques Marquette. The Jesuit was interpreter to Louis Jolliet on his 1673 voyage of discovery down the Mississippi River. In the parish archives at Boucherville is a baptismal certificate of an Indian child, dated May 20, 1668, and signed by Marquette.

Sainte-Famille Church, at Boucherville, contains the work of one of Quebec's greatest wood-carvers, Louis Amble Quevillon (1749-1823). By drawing on the Canadian scene for motifs and designs, Quevillon and his contemporary, François Baillargé

(1739-1819), created a distinctive and original style of church decoration. At Lotbinière, examples of Baillargé's sculpture can be seen in Saint-Louis Church—one of the most richly decorated in Quebec.

Church silver was another craft that was brought to a high state of artistic development in Quebec during the late 1700s and the early 1800s. The fine work of François Ranvoyzé (1739-1819), the foremost silversmith of his time, is found in Saint-Edouard Church at Gentilly.

LES BECQUETS
This summer resort town offers a panoramic view of the St. Lawrence River as far upstream as Trois-Rivières. Vegetable stands here offer produce from the area's market gardens.
□ Le Manoir de Saint-Pierre-les-Becquets (Manoir Baby-Méthot), a private residence, dates from 1792.

GENTILLY
Saint-Edouard Church, built of fieldstone in 1848 and classified as an historic building, contains fine oil paintings, and works by silversmiths François Ranvoyzé and Laurent Amyot.
□ A renovated 18th-century windmill here still grinds flour.
□ Audiovisual presentations are given at a nuclear generating station operated by Hydro-Quebec.

Saint-Louis de Lotbinière Church

LOTBINIÈRE
Saint-Louis Church, which dates from 1818, was designed by Abbé Jérôme Demers and François Baillargé. Sculptures are by André Paquet.
□ A plaque on a roadside chapel commemorates Léon Pamphile Lemay, a poet, novelist and jurist born here in 1837.

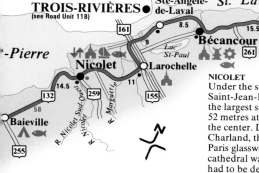

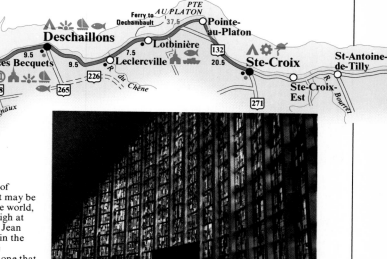

NICOLET
Under the sweeping white front arch of Saint-Jean-Baptiste Cathedral is what may be the largest stained-glass window in the world, 52 metres at the base and 21 metres high at the center. Designed by Nicolet artist Jean Charland, the window was produced in the Paris glassworks of Max Ingrand. The cathedral was built in 1963 to replace one that had to be demolished after a landslide in 1955.
□ A Quebec Police Force training school here is in a onetime seminary built in 1827-30.

PIERREVILLE
Canada's biggest producer of fire engines, Pierre Thibault Ltd., offers tours by appointment.
□ Indians on the nearby Odanak reserve maintain campgrounds, a handicraft center, and a museum containing a model of the 17th-century Abenaki fort at Odanak, a traditional Abenaki skin tent, the Scriptures in Abenaki, and basketwork. A stone chapel (1828) has a sheet-metal interior engraved with fleur-de-lis and sacred vessels by early craftsmen.

Stained-glass window, Saint-Jean-Baptiste Cathedral, Nicolet

Stone chapel, Odanak Indian Reserve

A Heroine of New France

Madeleine de Verchères, who led the defense of her father's seigneury against an Iroquois war party in 1692 when she was 14, wrote the best-known account of her feat 30 years later. She claimed she ran in from the fields ahead of 45 Indians, repaired the fort and, with two soldiers, an old man and two younger brothers, held out for seven days (*right*) until help arrived from Montreal. In 1699 she had written a more plausible account: she struggled free of one Iroquois who grabbed her neckerchief, and with one soldier she fought off attackers for two days. Whichever story is to be believed, Madeleine remains a heroine. In 1722 when her husband, Pierre-Thomas de La Pérade, was attacked by two Indians, she disabled one and saved her husband's life.

Canada's First Iron Foundry and Second Oldest City

Saint-Maurice River Valley

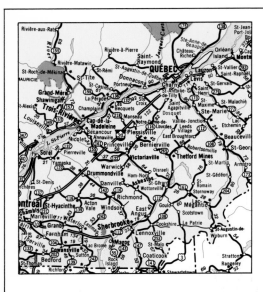

Common loon

LA MAURICIE NATIONAL PARK
This heavily wooded, 544 square-kilometre park in the Saint-Maurice River valley has campsites, beaches, wilderness and wildlife areas, and 154 lakes. Lac Wapizagonke, a favorite of canoeists and sailing enthusiasts, is the park's chief lake. It is boxed into a narrow valley by cliffs formed millions of years ago by a massive movement of the earth's crust. Here and there are tiny coves with waterfalls and sandy beaches.
□ A 23-kilometre scenic road divides the park into two sections. One remains in its wild state; the other, developed for campers, has an interpretive center.
□ Moose, bear, deer, lynx, beaver, wolves, and many small mammals inhabit the park's rolling hills.

Lac Wapizagonke, La Mauricie National Park

SHAWINIGAN
A promenade along the Saint-Maurice River provides a spectacular view of thundering 45-metre Shawinigan Falls. The falls provide inexpensive electrical power for this major industrial city. A Hydro-Québec plant, which may be visited, has a capacity of 313,000 kilowatts.
□ On tours of a Consolidated-Bathurst mill visitors see the processes by which logs are converted into fine paper.
□ The Shawinigan Cultural Center art gallery has paintings by Léo Ayotte and François Déziel and sculptures by Claude Descoteaux. The Church of Notre-Dame-de-la-Présentation in Shawinigan-Sud has paintings by Osias Leduc.

Anchors, Plowshares and Pots From Master Ironworkers

A towering stone chimney (*right*), once part of Canada's first iron foundry, dominates Les Forges du Saint-Maurice National Historic Park. The foundations of the *Grande Maison*—home of the ironmasters—are also in the six-hectare park.

The foundry, established in 1730, marked the start of industrialization in the region. Local iron ore and wood were used to produce stoves, pots, tools, plowshares and anchors.

François Poulin de Francheville, seigneur of Saint-Maurice, built the ironworks after he was granted iron-mining rights by Louis XV. By 1741, with the help of master ironworkers from France, the foundry had become the most important industry in New France. At peak production, its blast furnaces were fired around the clock by stokers working in six-hour shifts. In 1833 the plant produced 1,500 cast-iron stoves in only four months. Competition from modern foundries and a dwindling supply of local raw materials eventually forced the Saint-Maurice works to close. The foundry was abandoned in 1883.

| 0 | 1 | 2 | 3 | 4 | 5 Miles |
| 0 | 2 | 4 | | 6 | 8 Kilometres |

In Quebec, major cities have developed where important tributaries flow into the St. Lawrence River, the backbone of Canada's transportation system for more than three centuries. Canada's second oldest city, Trois-Rivières was established in 1634 at the confluence of the Saint-Maurice and the St. Lawrence. There was a fur market at Trois-Rivières as early as 1610, and the settlement was a major fur-trading center until 1665, by which time Montreal had become the primary marketplace.

Les Forges du Saint-Maurice, the first iron foundry in Canada, was established north of Trois-Rivières in 1730. It became the most important industry in New France, but competition from more modern foundries forced it out of business in 1883.

In 1852 a slide was built at the falls upstream at Shawinigan so that logs from the immense forests of the Saint-Maurice Valley could be floated to the mouth of the river. By 1854 some 80 sawmills were operating at Trois-Rivières. Today about 25 per-

cent of the city's work force is in the pulp and paper industry.

North of the industrial centers of Trois-Rivières, Shawinigan and Grand-Mère is the wild grandeur of the Laurentian hills. This wilderness is preserved in La Mauricie National Park. Here, in a pristine forest that is ablaze with color in the fall, are 25 kinds of deciduous trees and 10 evergreen species. In spring and summer the park is bright with asters, goldenrod, fireweed, violets and numerous other wildflowers.

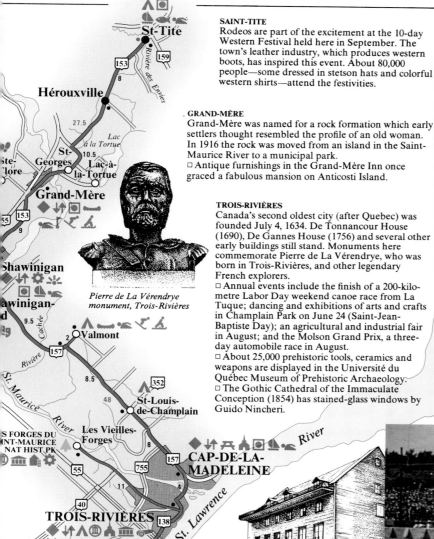

Pierre de La Vérendrye monument, Trois-Rivières

De Tonnancour House, Trois-Rivières

SAINT-TITE
Rodeos are part of the excitement at the 10-day Western Festival held here in September. The town's leather industry, which produces western boots, has inspired this event. About 80,000 people—some dressed in stetson hats and colorful western shirts—attend the festivities.

GRAND-MÈRE
Grand-Mère was named for a rock formation which early settlers thought resembled the profile of an old woman. In 1916 the rock was moved from an island in the Saint-Maurice River to a municipal park.
☐ Antique furnishings in the Grand-Mère Inn once graced a fabulous mansion on Anticosti Island.

TROIS-RIVIÈRES
Canada's second oldest city (after Quebec) was founded July 4, 1634. De Tonnancour House (1690), De Gannes House (1756) and several other early buildings still stand. Monuments here commemorate Pierre de La Vérendrye, who was born in Trois-Rivières, and other legendary French explorers.
☐ Annual events include the finish of a 200-kilo-metre Labor Day weekend canoe race from La Tuque; dancing and exhibitions of arts and crafts in Champlain Park on June 24 (Saint-Jean-Baptiste Day); an agricultural and industrial fair in August; and the Molson Grand Prix, a three-day automobile race in August.
☐ About 25,000 prehistoric tools, ceramics and weapons are displayed in the Université du Québec Museum of Prehistoric Archaeology.
☐ The Gothic Cathedral of the Immaculate Conception (1854) has stained-glass windows by Guido Nincheri.

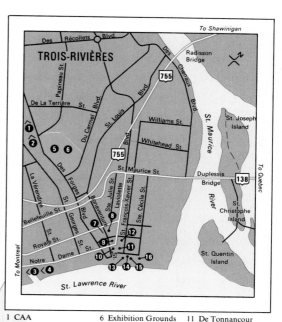

1 CAA
2 Université du Québec à Trois-Rivières
3 Tourist Information (summer only)
4 Vieux Moulin à Farine
5 Molson Grand Prix
6 Exhibition Grounds
7 Champlain Park
8 Cathedral of the Immaculate Conception
9 Tourist Information (summer only)
10 Le Flambeau
11 De Tonnancour House
12 Place d'Armes
13 St. James Anglican Church
14 Sieur des Groseilliers
15 Ursuline Convent
16 Turcotte Terrace

POINTE-DU-LAC
The Church of the Visitation (c.1883) has Stations of the Cross sculpted in stone by Léo Arbour about 1950. Arbour's studio at Pointe-du-Lac may be visited. The first seigneurial manor here, built of stone in 1736, has been used as a presbytery since 1791.
☐ A 1721 stone flour mill with a bright red tin roof is open to the public.

Molson Grand Prix, Trois-Rivières

An Old Royal Road, Graceful Houses and Winter Carnivals

North Shore, St. Lawrence River

French Canada's religious spirit, history and *joie de vivre* pervade this stretch of the St. Lawrence shore. Highway 138 follows Canada's first carriageway, *le Chemin du Roy* (King's road). Opened in 1734, the road linked Montreal and Quebec. One of 30 relay stations where travelers changed horses was at Deschambault. The habitant homes where they rested still line the road. These lovingly restored houses are fine examples of the stout masonry and harmonious lines of early Quebec architecture.

LA PÉRADE
Between December and February the frozen Rivière Sainte-Anne blossoms with the cabins of thousands of anglers fishing for tommycod through holes in the ice. Singing and dancing enliven the proceedings. A Mr. Tommycod, a festival queen and princesses preside over a two-month carnival. Prizes are awarded for the best catch (the average per hut is 45 fish a day), and the best decorated cabin.
□ In La Pérade are the ruins of the seigneurial manor house built in 1676 and the well-preserved Gouin (1669), Tremblay (1669), Dorion (1719) and Baribeau (1717) houses.

Tommycod

Cabins on the frozen Rivière Sainte-Anne, La Pérade

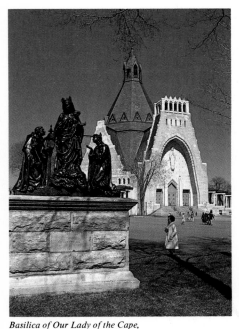
Basilica of Our Lady of the Cape, Cap-de-la-Madeleine

BATISCAN
Near here in 1609 Champlain first met with the Huron Indians, who thereafter were allies of the French.
□ A handsome 17th-century fieldstone house—the rectory and manor house of Jesuit priests who were Batiscan's first seigneurs—is preserved in a small provincial park.
□ Canoe races are held on Rivière Batiscan in midsummer, and there is tommycod fishing in winter.

CAP-DE-LA-MADELEINE
Since 1888, when three witnesses said they saw her eyes become momentarily animated, a Madonna in the Shrine of Our Lady of the Cape has been considered miraculous.
□ Near the little stone chapel (1714) housing the statue is the magnificent, octagonal Basilica of Our Lady of the Cape. The Bridge of the Rosaries, over a stream in the grounds, commemorates a St. Lawrence River ice bridge across which parishioners carried stones in 1879 to build the church.
□ Candlelight processions are held nightly from mid-May to Mid-October.

CHAMPLAIN
A sanctuary lamp carved in maple and painted white with gilt trim serves as a baptismal font in the Church of Notre-Dame-de-la-Visitation. It was used in an earlier church (1710). In the present church, built in 1879, Mass is said on a consecrated stone given to the parish in 1681 by Jean-Baptiste de la Croix de Chevrières de Saint-Vallier, second Roman Catholic bishop of Quebec.

Yet few are marked with plaques or other indications of historical value. But the imposing chimneys, multipaned dormer windows, steep roofs with bell-cast curves and finials on the ridges are easily identified.

Also seen here are ancient, richly decorated churches, many executed by the famous craftsmen of New France. In the church at Deschambault (designed by Thomas Baillargé) is a statue of St. Joseph by Thomas Berlinguet. Antoine Plamondon paintings and François Baillargé sculptures

are in a church at Neuville. Belfries in a little stone chapel at Cap-de-la-Madeleine, built in 1714 by master mason Pierre Lafond, are believed to be the oldest in Canada. The chapel, on the site of a wooden chapel built in 1659, has been a place of pilgrimage since 1883. Now Canada's national shrine to the Virgin Mary, it is visited by thousands of pilgrims each year.

A carnival mood reigns at Champlain, Batiscan and La Pérade at tommycod spawning time. At La Pérade, where the fish wriggle up from the St. Lawrence about mid-December, a cabin village sprouts on the frozen Rivière Sainte-Anne, touching off a round of fishing and merrymaking that continues into mid-February. Visitors can sample the tasty fish at roadside stands, or rent cabins equipped with stove, ice-cutting tools, fishing tackle and bait.

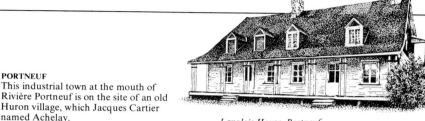

Langlois House, Portneuf

PORTNEUF

This industrial town at the mouth of Rivière Portneuf is on the site of an old Huron village, which Jacques Cartier named Achelay.
□ Langlois House, built of wood in the early 19th century, is a fine example of domestic architecture from this period.
□ Once noted for eel and sturgeon fishing, the area is now popular with tommycod anglers. There are campgrounds and snowmobile trails.

NEUVILLE

A half-domed sanctuary that dates from 1697 is part of Saint-François-de-Sales Church. The church's treasures include a wooden baldachin (altar canopy) dating from 1775, three late-18th-century altars sculpted by François Baillargé and 21 Antoine Plamondon paintings.
□ Neuville's fine old buildings include a convent (1716), a procession chapel (1735), and the Soulard (1760-80), Denis (c. 1780), Darveau (1785), Poitiers (1795) and Anger (1797) houses.

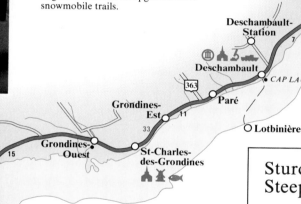

DESCHAMBAULT

Saint-Joseph-de-Deschambault Church (1837) and the rectory (1815), now a cultural center, are historic monuments.
□ Descendants of thoroughbred horses and of purebred cattle brought to New France by Intendant Jean Talon in 1665-71 are raised at a provincial government experimental farm which may be visited.
□ The ruins of a small fort built by Champlain are on an island in the St. Lawrence River.
□ A third of Deschambault's houses are at least one century old.

CAP-SANTÉ

The site of historic Fort Jacques-Cartier, the last place in New France to capitulate to the English, is marked by a stone at the head of a private road three miles east of the village. The fort held out until Sept. 13, 1760, five days after Montreal surrendered.
□ Cap-Santé's church was built in 1755. A house on the Morisset farm, at the village's outskirts, dates from 1696.
□ A costume ball, poetry readings, an auction, and exhibition of antiques highlight a two-day festival in early August.

Sturdy Stone Walls, Steep-Slanted Roofs

Jesuit rectory, Batiscan

Manor house, Neuville

Gorgendière House, Deschambault

Stone houses of 17th-century New France were square and sturdy, with single chimneys and steep-slanted roofs. Walls sloped inward to support the roof better. Dormers were added when growing families needed top stories for bedrooms.

Typical of this style of architecture is the Gorgendière House, built in the 1660s in Deschambault. A modification of this style is the Jesuit rectory at Batiscan—rectangular with triple chimneys and eaves flared to protect the walls from the elements. By the 18th century, the projection of the eaves became larger—and was supported by posts. This created a veranda, as in the manor house on Neuville's main street.

Examples of styles favored by 19th-century builders are the steep roof, multipaned dormer windows and two chimneys of Langlois House at Portneuf.

Where New France Was Born, an Ancient City Thrives

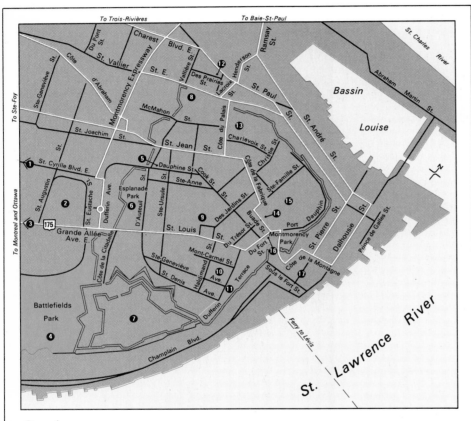

Cradle of New France, Quebec sprawls atop Cape Diamond, discovered in 1535 by Jacques Cartier. Turreted Château Frontenac was built in 1893-95.

Quebec

1 Grand Théâtre de Québec	5 Jesuit Chapel	10 Wolfe-Montcalm Monument	14 Basilica of Notre-Dame
2 National Assembly	6 Tourist Information	11 Dufferin Terrace	15 Quebec Seminary
3 CAA	7 The Fortifications	12 Talon's Vaults	16 Musée du Fort
4 Battlefields Park	8 Artillery Park	13 Hôtel-Dieu Hospital	17 Place Royale
	9 Ursuline Convent		

Where sheer cliffs rise above the narrowing St. Lawrence River, Samuel de Champlain founded Canada's oldest city in 1608. From its first buildings snuggled between the river and scarp, the settlement burgeoned to the heights of Cape Diamond. Its expanding institutions—religious, military and cultural—imbued it with an old-world flavor that lingers still.

Grayed by the brush of time, the tile roofs and old stone of the Lower Town still throb with life. Ancient stone houses huddle next to venerable churches and historic monuments on narrow, cobbled streets. The city's stormy history (it was besieged six times) is reflected in its fortifications and city gates and the low, brooding Citadel on towering Cape Diamond.

On the rolling, windswept Plains of Abraham, now a national historic park, a 10-minute battle in 1759 between French and English sealed the fate of New France—and set the course for Canadian history.

Artillery Park (8)
In this park are the Dauphine Redoubt (begun in 1712), the New Barracks (1749-54) and the Captain's House (1820), formerly the residence of the garrison commanding officer.

Basilica of Notre-Dame (14)
The church of Canada's oldest parish (1659) was begun in 1647. The façade was designed by Thomas Baillargé.

Dufferin Terrace (11)
This boardwalk, dotted with Victorian pagodas, affords a view of the St. Lawrence, some 70 metres below. It extends from Place d'Armes to the Citadel. There con-

nects with another boardwalk called the Governor's Promenade, which follows the clifftop to National Battlefields Park.

Grand Théâtre de Québec (1)
This new (1971) complex is the home of the Quebec Symphony Orchestra, Théâtre du Trident and Club musical de Québec.

Grand Théâtre de Québec

Hôtel-Dieu Hospital (13)
A museum in Canada's first hospital, founded in 1637, has antique furniture, silverware and paintings.

Jesuit Chapel (5)
A reliquary contains some bones of three Canadian martyr saints: Jean de Brébeuf, Charles Garnier and Gabriel Lalemant.

Musée du Fort (16)
The six sieges of Quebec are reenacted with a sound-and-light show and a 40-square-metre model of 18th-century Quebec.

National Battlefields Park (4)
Granite markers in this 95-hectare park trace the course of the Battle of the Plains of Abraham (Sept. 13, 1759), the most decisive clash in Canadian history. Outside the park is a statue of the Marquis de Montcalm, at the place where the French general was mortally wounded. The St. Joan of Arc Monument honors those who fought at the Plains of Abraham and at nearby Sainte Foy the following spring. A flower garden flanking a statue of Joan of Arc is the si-

On a former sheep pasture (above) French and English armies met in the most decisive battle in Canadian history. Soldiers, fur-traders and priests walked the streets of Place Royale (right) in the early days of New France.

of the first public performance of "O Canada" (June 24, 1880).

National Assembly (2)

The elegant Renaissance-style seat of the provincial government, completed in 1886, may be toured. Fifteen bronze statues of Quebec historical figures by French-Canadian sculptor Philippe Hébert are in niches on the façade. In the National Assembly Chamber is a painting depicting the sitting of the first parliament of Lower Canada in 1792. It is the work of Charles Huot.

Place Royale (17)

A showcase for the architecture of New France is being created at Place Royale,

the site of Champlain's 1608 Habitation. About 80 houses dating from the 17th and 18th centuries are being restored or rebuilt. Among those completed are the two-story stone Hôtel Chevalier (1725), now a museum housing early French-Canadian furniture, and Hazeur House (1685), the oldest in Place Royale. The Fornel House contains a historical display. Tours leave from an interpretive center at Le Picard House (1763). An altar in the form of a fortress is in the Notre-Dame-des-Victoires Church (1688). A bronze bust of Louis XIV, in whose honor the square is named, was presented by the French government in 1928.

The Quebec Seminary (above) was founded in 1663 by François de Laval, the first bishop of Quebec.

Quebec Seminary (15)

A museum has paintings by Plamondon and Suzor-Coté; silverware by Ranvoyzé and Amiot; and a display of playing card money (legal tender in New France in 1658-1717 and 1729-59).

Talon's Vaults (12)

Hoping to curb drunkenness in Quebec—by having colonists drink beer instead of brandy—Intendant Jean Talon had Canada's first commercial brewery built in 1688. Its vaults, beneath a present-day brewery, are now a museum containing 17th-century guns and furniture.

The Fortifications (7)

Visitors can stroll along sections of the 5.6-kilometre-long fortifications surrounding North America's only walled city. Although defense works have existed since 1608, most surviving ramparts were constructed by the British in 1823-32. The remaining city gates—Saint-Louis, Kent and Saint-Jean—are reconstructions (c.1880).

Ursuline Convent (9)

Founded in 1642 by Madame de La Peltrie and Mother Marie de l'Incarnation, Canada's oldest nunnery has Montcalm's tomb within its walls. The convent's museum has one of Canada's oldest beds (1686).

Wolfe-Montcalm Monument (10)

In the Governors' Garden is an obelisk bearing the Latin inscription: "Valour gave them a common death, history a common fame, posterity a common monument."

Parades, Giant Snowmen and an Icy Canoe Race

Launched by winter-weary Quebecers, the world-famous Quebec Winter Carnival doubles the city's population for 10 days in February as Quebec erupts with street dances, beauty contests, hockey tournaments, winter sports and parades (above). Streets are ablaze with lights and decorations during the pre-Lent festival, and fanciful ice sculptures (left) are carved in parks and squares. One highlight is a canoe race across the ice-choked St. Lawrence River. The celebrations are presided over by Bonhomme Carnaval, a jovial giant snowman.

A Famous Flagship
Beyond the City Walls

Around Quebec City

In suburbs and towns surrounding Quebec City are a modern aquarium, zoo and university campus—and buildings as historic as those in the walled capital.

Sillery, an elegant residential suburb, has one of Canada's most important historic sites. In front of the Old Jesuit House (c. 1700) are the foundations of an older Jesuit House (1637) and Saint-Michel Church (1644), the first stone church built in New France. Bois de Coulonge park, once the estate of Quebec's lieutenant governors,

Artisan at work,
Village-des-Hurons

UNIVERSITÉ LAVAL

The oldest French-language university in North America (1852) is located on a new campus at Sainte-Foy. About 12,000 full-time and 3,000 part-time students attend Laval, which is noted for its summer school language programs. On campus are a botanical garden and a fountain made of blocks of asbestos. The Koninck Pavilion has collections of Inuit and Greek artifacts. A museum displays coins from ancient Egypt, Greece and Rome. A mural on the Pouliot Pavilion is by Jordi Bonnet. There are prearranged group tours of the campus.

VILLAGE-DES-HURONS

Visitors to this Indian reserve, founded in 1697, can see Huron artisans make snowshoes much as their ancestors did three centuries ago.
□ The whitewashed stone chapel of Notre-Dame-de-Lorette was built in 1730 by François Vincent, a Huron who apprenticed to sculptor François-Noël Levasseur. In the chapel are a silver sanctuary lamp (1730) by François Ranvoyzé and a wooden statue of the Madonna sculpted by Levasseur. The Stations of the Cross are by Médard Bourgault.

AQUARIUM DE QUÉBEC

This aquarium at Sainte-Foy which exhibits more than 170 species of fish, has a splendid setting on a cliff overlooking the St. Lawrence River. Sturgeon, northern pike, cod, eel and salmon and tropical fish such as angelfish and piranha are in 48 freshwater and 20 saltwater tanks. Snakes, crocodiles, turtles and lizards are exhibited in four terraria. Marine mammals, such as harbor and gray seals, are in four outdoor pools.

PONT DE QUÉBEC

This bridge, spanning the St. Lawrence near Quebec City, was one of Canada's most daring—and tragic—engineering feats. Construction began in 1899. A section collapsed in 1907, killing 71 steelworkers. Another 13 died in 1916 when a central section plunged into the river as it was being hoisted into position. When completed, the bridge was the world's longest cantilever span (548 metres). It is still the longest bridge of this kind in North America. Officially inaugurated in 1918 by the Prince of Wales (the future King Edward VIII), the bridge has a railroad track, a highway and a footpath.
□ Nearby is the modern Pont Pierre-Laporte, Canada's longest suspension bridge (668 metres).

Pont de Québec

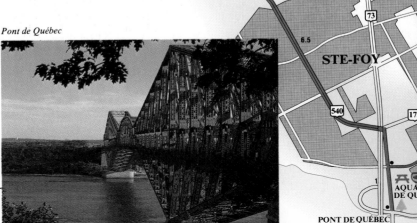

| 0 | 0.5 | 1 | 1.5 | 2 | 2.5 Miles |

| 0 | 1 | 2 | 3 | 4 Kilometres |

PONT DE QUÉBEC

delights the eye with flower gardens, trees, lawns and a splendid view of the St. Lawrence River.

The Sainte-Foy campus of Université Laval has distinctive modern architecture: a striking, flat-roofed church has towers and arched windows that give it the appearance of a Gothic cathedral. The Sainte-Foy aquarium overlooks the Pont de Québec, which spans the St. Lawrence.

Rivière du Berger flows through the lush gardens and wooded grounds of the Orsain-ville zoo, where zebras, wapiti and caribou graze.

Charlesbourg, settled in 1659, has a central square with streets radiating from it like spokes.

Jacques Cartier, the first European here, wintered beside the Rivière Saint-Charles in 1535-36. A national historic park at the site has a replica of his flagship, *La Grande Hermine.*

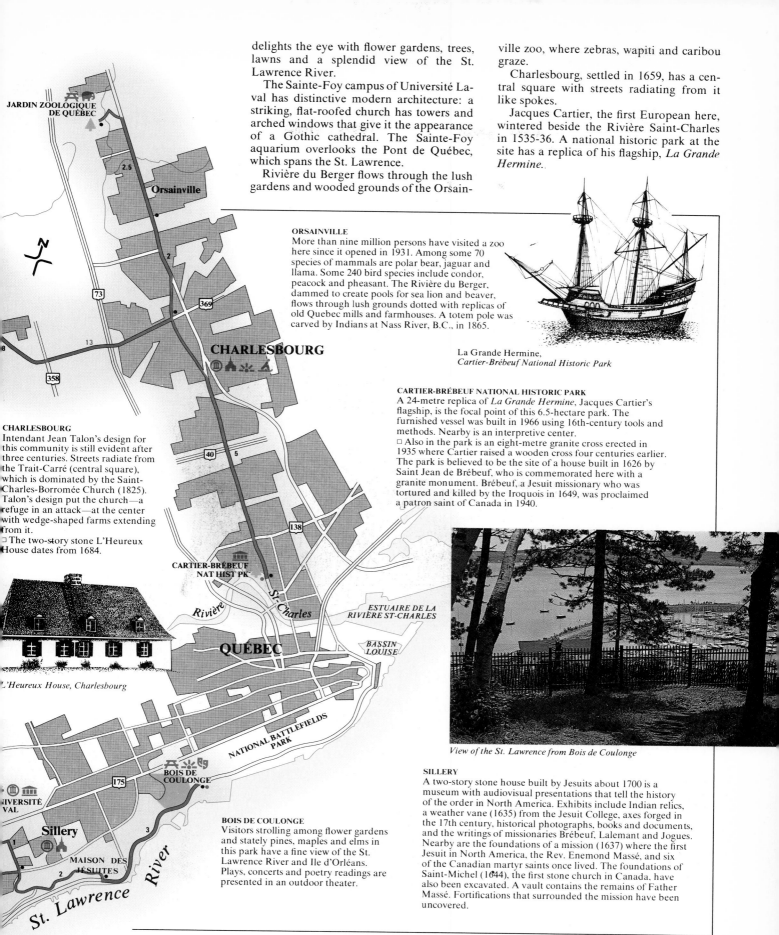

La Grande Hermine,
Cartier-Brébeuf National Historic Park

JARDIN ZOOLOGIQUE DE QUÉBEC

Orsainville

CHARLESBOURG

ORSAINVILLE
More than nine million persons have visited a zoo here since it opened in 1931. Among some 70 species of mammals are polar bear, jaguar and llama. Some 240 bird species include condor, peacock and pheasant. The Rivière du Berger, dammed to create pools for sea lion and beaver, flows through lush grounds dotted with replicas of old Quebec mills and farmhouses. A totem pole was carved by Indians at Nass River, B.C., in 1865.

CARTIER-BRÉBEUF NATIONAL HISTORIC PARK
A 24-metre replica of *La Grande Hermine*, Jacques Cartier's flagship, is the focal point of this 6.5-hectare park. The furnished vessel was built in 1966 using 16th-century tools and methods. Nearby is an interpretive center.
□ Also in the park is an eight-metre granite cross erected in 1935 where Cartier raised a wooden cross four centuries earlier. The park is believed to be the site of a house built in 1626 by Saint Jean de Brébeuf, who is commemorated here with a granite monument. Brébeuf, a Jesuit missionary who was tortured and killed by the Iroquois in 1649, was proclaimed a patron saint of Canada in 1940.

CHARLESBOURG
Intendant Jean Talon's design for this community is still evident after three centuries. Streets radiate from the Trait-Carré (central square), which is dominated by the Saint-Charles-Borromée Church (1825). Talon's design put the church—a refuge in an attack—at the center with wedge-shaped farms extending from it.
□ The two-story stone L'Heureux House dates from 1684.

CARTIER-BRÉBEUF NAT HIST PK

Rivière St-Charles

QUÉBEC

ESTUAIRE DE LA RIVIÈRE ST-CHARLES

BASSIN LOUISE

L'Heureux House, Charlesbourg

NATIONAL BATTLEFIELDS PARK

BOIS DE COULONGE

UNIVERSITÉ VAL

Sillery

MAISON DES JÉSUITES

St. Lawrence River

View of the St. Lawrence from Bois de Coulonge

BOIS DE COULONGE
Visitors strolling among flower gardens and stately pines, maples and elms in this park have a fine view of the St. Lawrence River and Ile d'Orléans. Plays, concerts and poetry readings are presented in an outdoor theater.

SILLERY
A two-story stone house built by Jesuits about 1700 is a museum with audiovisual presentations that tell the history of the order in North America. Exhibits include Indian relics, a weather vane (1635) from the Jesuit College, axes forged in the 17th century, historical photographs, books and documents, and the writings of missionaries Brébeuf, Lalemant and Jogues. Nearby are the foundations of a mission (1637) where the first Jesuit in North America, the Rev. Enemond Massé, and six of the Canadian martyr saints once lived. The foundations of Saint-Michel (1644), the first stone church in Canada, have also been excavated. A vault contains the remains of Father Massé. Fortifications that surrounded the mission have been uncovered.

An Idyllic, Fertile Island Where Time Stood Still

Ile d'Orléans

Ile d'Orléans is so vital a reminder of Quebec rural life in the 1700s that the entire island has been designated a historic region. Its centuries of isolation in the St. Lawrence River ended in 1935 when a bridge linked it with the north shore. But islanders still cling to old ways, proud of churches, houses and farms that have been here for two to three hundred years—symbols of French Canada's beginnings.

Jacques Cartier first called the island Bacchus, for the Roman god of wine, be-

SAINTE-PÉTRONILLE

This town has a splendid view of the heights of Quebec on the north shore of the St. Lawrence. Several hundred Hurons, refugees from Iroquois attacks at Trois-Rivières, lived here in the 1650s. The first French settlers also chose the western end of Ile d'Orléans.

□ The two largest wooden ships built in Canada, *Columbus* (1824) and *Baron Renfrew* (1825), were launched from a dry dock here, which is commemorated with a plaque.

SAINT-PIERRE-D'ORLÉANS

The parish church (1720) is built in early Norman style. Altar and sanctuary carvings by Charles Vézina date from the 1730s. In summer, chamber music recitals are held in the church.

□ A barn has been converted into a theater. Productions are staged in summer, along with poetry readings, concerts, and exhibitions of paintings and photography.

SAINT-LAURENT-D'ORLÉANS

An art center in a century-old barn displays local painting, sculpture, weaving, ceramics and tapestry. Visitors can watch artists at work.

□ The church (1732) in Saint-Laurent has a pulpit carved by Jean Gosselin. A nearby plaque is at the site where Gen. James Wolfe landed during the 1759 siege of Quebec.

□ A four-story stone water mill built about 1635 is now a restaurant.

Evening, Ile d'Orléans, by Horatio Walker

A Painter of Island Scenes

Artist Horatio Walker lived and worked on Ile d'Orléans for more than 50 years. By 1907 he had become the most famous Canadian-born painter, winning international acclaim for his portrayals of the island's farming life.

Walker was born at Listowel, Ont., in 1858, and moved to Toronto at age 15 to work as a staff artist at the Notman and Fraser photographic studios. A few years later he went to New York to study and paint, made several visits to European art galleries, and in 1883 settled on Ile d'Orléans. In 1915 he became president of the Canadian Art Club, and in 1925 president of the Royal Canadian Academy. Walker died at Sainte-Pétronille in 1938.

Artisans at work, Saint-Laurent-d'Orléans

Restaurant L'Atre, Sainte-Famille

cause of its wild grapes, then renamed it in honor of the Duke of Orléans, son of Francis I. Settlement started in 1648 and the first chapel was built five years later. By 1712 there were five prosperous parishes. There are now six, each with a beautiful stone church.

The island's finest church, at Sainte-Famille, was built in 1734. It has magnificent wood carvings and three bell towers. Some of the island's old barns and sturdy field-stone houses with their steep, Norman-style roofs are now restaurants, art galleries and theaters.

Potatoes and other vegetables are grown on long, narrow farms, each extending to the river. Orchards yield apples and plums. The island is noted for its strawberries.

Near Saint-Pierre is a splendid view of Chute Montmorency on the north shore of the St. Lawrence. North of Saint-François, visitors can look across the river to Cap-Tourmente and the Laurentians.

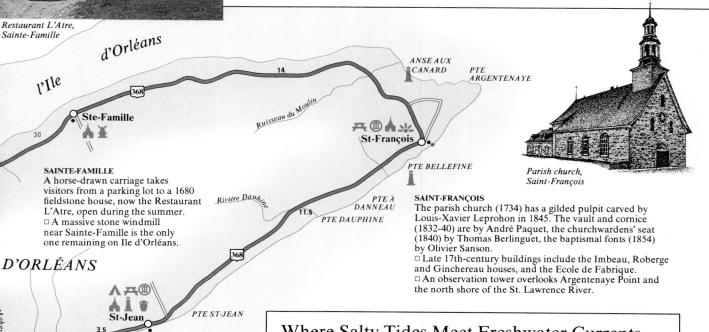

Parish church, Saint-François

SAINTE-FAMILLE
A horse-drawn carriage takes visitors from a parking lot to a 1680 fieldstone house, now the Restaurant L'Atre, open during the summer.
□ A massive stone windmill near Sainte-Famille is the only one remaining on Ile d'Orléans.

SAINT-FRANÇOIS
The parish church (1734) has a gilded pulpit carved by Louis-Xavier Leprohon in 1845. The vault and cornice (1832-40) are by André Paquet, the churchwardens' seat (1840) by Thomas Berlinguet, the baptismal fonts (1854) by Olivier Sanson.
□ Late 17th-century buildings include the Imbeau, Roberge and Ginchereau houses, and the Ecole de Fabrique.
□ An observation tower overlooks Argentenaye Point and the north shore of the St. Lawrence River.

Mauvide-Genest Manor, Saint-Jean

SAINT-JEAN
Mauvide-Genest Manor (1734) bears the scars of English cannonballs fired during the siege of Quebec in 1759. It was built by Jean Mauvide, Ile d'Orléans' first doctor, who lived in the house for almost 50 years until his death in 1782. Now a private home with period furniture, the manor may be visited in summer.
□ An artisans' shop in a stone house (1708) displays blown glass, ceramics, metal work and wooden dolls.
□ The parish church (1734) has paintings by Antoine Plamondon. The Dubuc House dates from about 1750.

Where Salty Tides Meet Freshwater Currents

Ile d'Orléans marks the tidal divide of the St. Lawrence River. Here is the "brackish zone" where saltwater tides meet and mix with freshwater river currents. In the zone is a community of marine life that can live in both fresh and salt water.

All fish need dissolved salts to survive. In fresh water, where the concentration of salt is low, a fish retains salt and keeps out water; in salt water, a fish must reverse this process. The passage through the brackish zone is impossible for most fish. A fish swimming from fresh to salt water could take in too much salt and shrivel. In salt water, the fish could take in too much water and become bloated. In the brackish zone, certain fish overcome these problems by eliminating excess salt when they are in the ocean, and by retaining salt in the river. This ability to adapt is common to the sea-run brook trout, stickleback, lamprey and American eel.

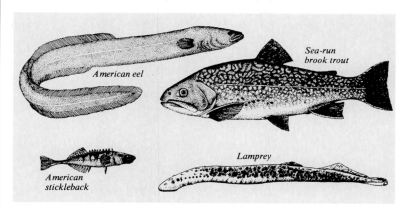

A Faith-Healing Shrine on the Broad Beaupré Coast

North Shore, St. Lawrence River

The Beaupré Coast—a broad plain on the north shore of the St. Lawrence River between Quebec City and Cap-Tourmente—is most famous for a faith-healing shrine in Sainte-Anne-de-Beaupré.

In 1658 a lumbago-ridden man building the town's first chapel was reportedly cured by the intercession of Saint Anne. In 1665 Marie de l'Incarnation, founder of Quebec's Ursuline Convent, wrote "Seven leagues from here is . . . a church of Saint Anne (where) paralytics walk, the blind re-

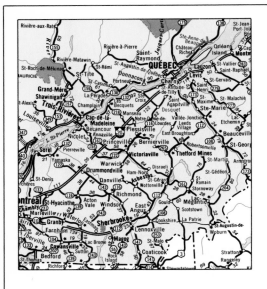

Where Oven-Fresh Bread is Still Baked Outdoors

Bread is still baked in two old outdoor ovens—*les fours Turgeon*—alongside the highway in Château-Richer. Outdoor ovens, once common in Quebec villages, were often shared by several families to bake bread, beans and tourtières. The ovens—traditionally made of hard-packed earth or clay, or of stones or bricks—burned wood. Wooden roofs keep off rain and snow.

Old masonry root cellars, embedded in steep slopes along the north side of the road through Château-Richer and L'Ange-Gardien, can also be seen. Some of the cellars are still used for winter storage of vegetables.

Outdoor oven, Château-Richer

MONTMORENCY
A suspension bridge overlooks Chute Montmorency. The 84-metre cataract, 30 metres higher than Niagara, was named by Champlain in 1603. There are picnic and observation areas at its base and summit.
□ Kent House, also known as Maison Montmorency, was built in 1781 by Sir Frederick Haldimand, Governor-General of Canada from 1778 to 1786.
□ A plaque near the Montmorency church commemorates a 1759 battle in which defenders of Quebec City repulsed British troops led by Gen. James Wolfe.

Kent House, Montmorency

Montmorency Falls

BEAUPORT
This is the first parish (1634) on the Beaupré Coast. Part of the Aimé Marcoux House was built in 1655. The Cléophas House is about 300 years old. A plaque identifies another house as the birthplace of Lt.Col. Charles-Michel de Salaberry, whose victory in the 1813 Battle of Châteauguay, near Montreal, stopped an American attack on that city.

L'ANGE-GARDIEN
Chapels commemorate the La Berge and Brisson families who came here in the 1660s. Part of the La Berge House, a private residence, is thought to date ▸ the 1670s. A monument is at the site the Trudelle House in which the town first Mass was celebrated in 1664.

0   ·5   1   1.5   2   2.5 Miles

0   1   2   3   4 Kilometres

cover their sight, and the sick, whatever be their malady, recover their health."

More than a million persons visit the shrine each year—some merely curious, some pious, and some hoping for a miraculous cure.

Farmers had settled on the Beaupré Coast before the shrine at Sainte-Anne-de-Beaupré was built. Some of the region's whitewashed dwellings date from the 1700s. Along Highway 360 are old outdoor ovens, stone root cellars and wayside chapels.

Thousands of migrating geese gather in spring and fall at Cap-Tourmente, where Samuel de Champlain once grazed cattle. Nearby Mont Sainte-Anne is renowned as a ski resort. Mists from Chute Montmorency, eastern Canada's highest waterfall, form a 30-metre-high cone of ice in winter. Nineteenth-century revelers tobogganed down the cone and dispelled winter chills with whiskey and "other strong waters" served at a bar excavated in its side.

Cross-country skiing, Parc du Mont-Sainte-Anne

SAINTE-ANNE-DE-BEAUPRÉ
A shrine dedicated to Saint Anne has attracted pilgrims for three centuries. Many arrive during the week preceding July 26, feast day of Saint Anne.

□ The shrine has four buildings. Inside the Basilica of Sainte-Anne-de-Beaupré, a massive Gothic and Romanesque structure, is a statue of Saint Anne on a marble pedestal atop an onyx shaft. The church displays what are said to be the saint's finger, wrist bone and forearm. Memorial Chapel contains an altar carved by Charles Vézina in 1702 and a pulpit erected by Thomas Baillargé in 1807. Scala Santa, a three-story building, has a replica of the 28 steps Christ ascended to meet Pontius Pilate. The Historial, a museum and art gallery, displays 20 waxwork tableaux depicting the life of Saint Anne.

Basilica of Sainte-Anne-de-Beaupré

Raccoons

PARC DU MONT-SAINTE-ANNE
This park, one of eastern Canada's prime ski areas, has 28 downhill runs and 130 kilometres of cross-country ski trails. Gondolas carry skiers to the summit of 800-metre Mont Sainte-Anne in 13 minutes. Park trails wind through woods of yellow birch where raccoons and deer may be seen at dusk.

...TEAU-RICHER
...e of the dwellings here—
...Côté, Caughon, Simard and
...vel houses—are nearly as
...nded in 1640.
... summer maple syrup,
...etables, and bread baked
...utdoor ovens are sold at
...dside stands.

SAINT-JOACHIM
A house called La Petite Ferme, once Bishop François de Laval's seigneurial manor, is on the site of a farm operated by Samuel de Champlain in 1626. The building houses a visitor reception center for the wildlife area at Cap-Tourmente.

□ The Saint-Joachim parish church (1779) has wood sculptures by François and Thomas Baillargé.

PARC DU
MONT-STE-ANNE

▲ Mont
Ste-Anne

Snow geese, Cap-Tourmente National Wildlife Area

ÎLE D'ORLÉANS

St. Lawrence River

Ste-Anne-de-Beaupré-Ouest
10.5
360 138
Sault-à-la-Puce
Château-Richer

Beaupré
4.5
Ste-Anne-de-Beaupré
22
aux Chiens

4.5
138
360
CHUTES STE-ANNE
R. Jean Larose
du Nord
Ste-Anne

St-Joachim
4
Cap-Tourmente
3
CAP TOURMENTE
NAT WILDLIFE AREA

La Petite Ferme, Saint-Joachim

CAP-TOURMENTE NATIONAL WILDLIFE AREA
A trail leads to a cliff where visitors can observe some 100,000 snow geese dappling the St. Lawrence River for six weeks in spring and fall. Geese stop at Cap-Tourmente on their migration between breeding grounds on Baffin Island and wintering grounds in Virginia and North Carolina. At low tide they feed on bullrushes that grow in the mudflats. Some 22 other bird species, including Canada geese, are also found in the sanctuary. An interpretive center gives the life history and habits of snow geese and local songbirds. Naturalists conduct walks through the wildlife area. A trail leads to the summit of Cap-Tourmente.

Where the Wild Laurentians Overlook a Quaint Town and Its Broad Bay

North Shore, St. Lawrence River

Charlevoix County—on the north shore of the St. Lawrence between Baie-Saint-Paul and Baie-Sainte-Catherine—is a region of stunning beauty. Its rugged hills and coast, fertile river valleys, and picturesque fishing and farming communities have long inspired artists—and have been an irresistible lure to tourists.

Baie-Saint-Paul's narrow streets and fieldstone houses were captured on canvas by Quebec artist Clarence Gagnon at the turn of the century. Wild, broken Lauren-

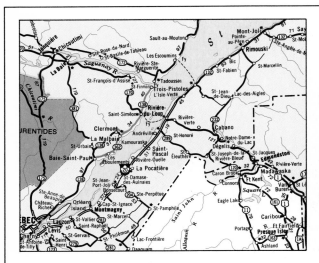

Baie-Saint-Paul

La Maison Croche, Ile aux Coudres

ÎLE AUX COUDRES
Time seems to have stopped on Ile aux Coudres. The metre-thick stone walls of its farmhouses, the lazy look of its windmills, the pace and the peace of this little island keep it a living miniature of 18th-century New France. Eleven kilometres by three, Ile aux Coudres is linked by ferry with Saint-Joseph-de-la Rive on the north shore.
□ Jacques Cartier gave the island its name (for its abundance of hazelnut trees) when he landed Sept. 7, 1535. The first Mass on Canadian soil, celebrated that same day, is commemorated by a granite cross at Saint-Bernard-sur-Mer.
□ Among buildings classified as historic monuments are the Bouchard House (1654), the Desgagné windmill (1777) and procession chapels (1806, 1836), all at Isle-aux-Coudres. The Leclerc House (1780) at La Baleine is a museum, open in summer.
□ La Maison Croche (the crooked house) at La Baleine is a local architectural curiosity. Built in 1963, it is open to the public.
□ Bogs between Saint-Bernard and La Baleine support a variety of plant life and provide a livelihood for islanders who harvest peat moss.

BAIE-SAINT-PAUL
A superb setting, between two promontories at the mouth of the Rivière du Gouffre and opposite Ile aux Coudres, has made the Baie-Saint-Paul landscape a favorite of some of Canada's best-known artists. (Among Quebec places, only Montreal and Quebec City appear oftener than Baie-Saint-Paul in paintings in the National Gallery of Canada.) Every year, hundreds of visitors paint and photograph the fertile fields, the bold hills, old farm buildings and picturesque town houses. Not far inland are the highest of the Laurentians (about 1,240 metres).
□ Two French regime gristmills, the Michel Perron and the de La Rémy mills, are still in use. The César Mill (1722) has an art gallery and a shop specializing in Canadian furniture and sculpture.
□ The area has good cross-country skiing, fishing, (arctic char and speckled trout), and hunting (bear, hare, moose and partridge). There are a beach, a campground, a marina, and a nine-hole golf course.

Arctic char (Quebec red trout)

LES ÉBOULEMENTS
The village is named for landslides caused by a 1663 earthquake reputedly so violent that a mountain on the shore became an island in the St. Lawrence River.
□ From a lighthouse on the promontory of Cap aux Oies, beluga whales are frequently seen in the Lawrence.
□ In Notre-Dame de L'Assomption Church are the remains of a finely carved altar shelf (c.1775).

Windmill, Ile aux Coudres

tian hills that overlook the town and its broad bay are softened by green farmland in the valley of the Rivière du Gouffre.

Guarding the entrance to Baie-Saint-Paul is a haven of tranquillity and tradition—Ile aux Coudres. In 1535 Jacques Cartier celebrated Canada's first Mass on this island. New France seems to live on in its stone windmills, wayside chapels and apple and plum orchards.

La Malbaie, North America's oldest resort, has long attracted visitors. (The first were Scottish soldiers who came to fish in the area during the late 1760s.) The town is dominated by the baronial towers of Château Richelieu. This hotel overlooks the St. Lawrence, its opposite shore merely a narrow blue line on the horizon.

The coast is more rugged at Saint-Siméon, where craggy granite cliffs line the river. Here Highway 138 turns inland, climbs the Laurentians and skirts sparkling lakes amid forests of cedar and white spruce.

Devastating Tremors That Toppled a Mountain

In 1663 a series of devastating earthquakes shook New France. An Ursuline nun in Quebec wrote of "a horrible confusion of overturning furniture, falling stones, parting floors, and splitting walls." Frightened Indians believed that "the streams were full of firewater and the forests were drunk."

The first quake, one of the worst ever in North America, was centered near the mouth of the Saguenay River. Thirty-two more followed during the next seven months, transforming the countryside. Waterfalls vanished, forests were destroyed, crevices opened and swallowed up whole houses. The face of a mountain toppled into the St. Lawrence River near the present-day town of Les Eboulements (French for landslides).

Many colonists believed the tremors were the result of God's displeasure, and priests were kept busy day and night with confessions. Dishonest fur traders cleaned up their business dealings, and the liquor trade was abolished. When the earthquakes finally ended, not one person had been killed or injured—and many penitents no doubt returned to their sinful ways.

BAIE-SAINTE-CATHERINE
The base of the parish church altar is a gilded cedar stump with intertwining roots.
□ From a wharf carved in rock, a year-round, toll-free ferry crosses the Saguenay River to Tadoussac. Passengers have a magnificent view of the Saguenay.

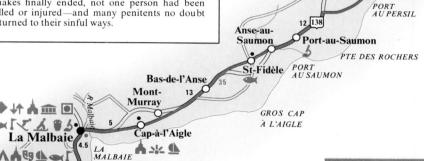

Brown-headed cowbird

SAINT-SIMÉON
At Les Palissades, a provincial nature appreciation center northwest of here, are glacial lakes, waterfalls and 244-metre-high jagged cliffs with magnificent views of the valley of Rivière Noire. Roadside stands offer fresh-caught fish during a smelt festival in late July.

PORT-AU-PERSIL
A brook cascades into this small harbor, dominated at low tide by a rocky islet. The waterfall is a favorite playground of children. Thousands annually visit this charming hamlet. A hotel here has a fine collection of early works by Quebec artist Jean-Paul Lemieux.

LA MALBAIE
Champlain came here in 1608, anchored at high tide, found his ship hard aground by morning, and called the place *malle baye* (bad bay). Many visitors know the village as Murray Bay.
□ A local museum honors Laure Conan, Canada's first woman novelist of renown. The author of *L'Oublié*, whose real name was Félicité Angers, was born here in 1845.

POINTE-AU-PIC
Perched on a 213-metre cliff is the imposing Château Richelieu (c.1910), one of Quebec's oldest resort hotels. Scores of splendid old summer homes are in this village.
□ The grave of William Hume Blake, a lawyer who wrote *Brown Waters*, *In a Fishing Country*, and *A Fisherman's Creed*, is in the yard of the Murray Bay Protestant Church. A plaque in the church honors U.S. President William Howard Taft, who summered here.

Port-au-Persil

Wood-Carvers and Famous Sons of an Island-Dotted Shoreline

South Shore, St. Lawrence River

The road from Lévis to Rimouski climbs and dips along the rugged south shore of the island-dotted St. Lawrence River. On the north shore is the blue outline of the Laurentian hills.

Many islands, including Ile aux Grues, Ile du Bic and Les Pèlerins, are frequented by thousands of seabirds and shorebirds. Grosse Ile was a 19th-century immigrant quarantine station. On Ile aux Basques are furnaces used by 16th-century Basque fishermen to extract whale oil.

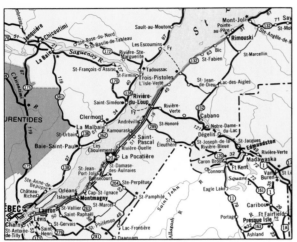

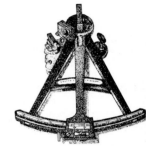

Capt. Joseph-Elzéar Bernier's octant, Musée Maritime de L'Islet-sur-Mer

L'ISLET-SUR-MER
Almost three centuries of seafarers born and raised here have earned this village the name *la patrie des marins,* the sailors' homeland. A marine museum especially honors Capt. Joseph-Elzéar Bernier, a native son whose seven voyages between 1904 and 1925 established Canada's sovereignty over the Arctic islands. An octant (a navigational instrument) from his ship *Arctic* is in the museum. A monument to Bernier in a park next to the museum is an aluminum globe on which his Arctic voyages are indicated.

Wood carvings of St. Paul and St. Peter, Saint-Romuald-d'Etchemin Church

BERTHIER-SUR-MER
A lookout affords a view of the St. Lawrence River, Grosse Ile and Ile de Bellechasse. A monument on Grosse Ile marks where an immigrant quarantine station was established during an 1832 cholera epidemic. Some 5,000 Irish immigrants died there during an outbreak of typhus in 1847-48.
□ The town's beach is one of the finest on the south shore of the St. Lawrence River.

SAINT-ROMUALD-D'ETCHEMIN
A wood sculpture by Lauriat Vallière, *Le Père Jean de Brébeuf évangélisant deux jeunes Indiens,* is in Saint-Romuald-d'Etchemin Church (1854).
□ Busts of St. Peter and St. Paul decorate the ornate wooden pulpit done by Ferdinand Villeneuve and Louis Saint-Hilaire.

LÉVIS
The Church of Notre-Dame-de-la-Victoire (1850) was designed by Thomas Baillargé in Louis XVI style and decorated by André Paquet. A plaque and two cannons near the church mark where English artillery fired across the St. Lawrence River to bombard Quebec in 1759.
□ A plaque marks the home of Alphonse Desjardins, who developed the idea of caisses populaires (cooperative saving and loan associations) here in 1900. A monument with a bust of Desjardins is on the grounds of the Fédération de Québec des Caisses Populaires Desjardins.

MONTMAGNY
The restored two-story wooden Manoir Couillard-Dupuis, built in 1768, has a large stone bread oven. The house is a tourist information center. The second floor has local handicrafts for sale.
□ A granite statue honors Sir Etienne-Paschal Taché, prime minister of the Province of Canada in 1856-57 and 1864-65 and a Father of Confederation. He was born and practiced medicine here. The statue was carved by Jean-Julien Bourgault in the style of the miniature wooden figures done by his Saint-Jean-Port-Joli family for two generations. The 18th-century Taché House may be visited.
□ In the St. Lawrence River here are Ile aux Grues and Ile aux Oies, where as many as 200,000 white geese gather in spring. Mallard, snipe and blue-winged teal are also seen.
□ Montmagny hosts a White Goose Festival in October.

Manoir Couillard-Dupuis, Montmagny

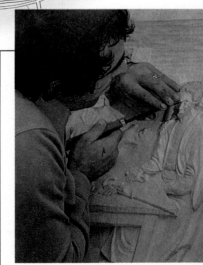

A wood-carver in his studio, Saint-Jean-Port-Joli

Sandy beaches line many of the area's bays and coves. At Rivière-du-Loup visitors can picnic beside a 38-metre waterfall.

This region is famous for its wood-carvers, many of whom live in Saint-Jean-Port-Joli. They follow a tradition that goes back three centuries in Quebec. Local churches, museums and other public buildings are decorated with their meticulous carvings.

Arctic explorer Joseph-Elzéar Bernier is honored by a monument and museum in his hometown of L'Islet-sur-Mer. The Montmagny residence of Sir Etienne-Paschal Taché, a Father of Confederation, may be visited. The house of Louis Fréchette, the first French-Canadian poet honored by the Académie française, still stands in Lévis. A plaque in Rivière-du-Loup marks the birthplace of the Most Rev. Alexandre-Antonin Taché, bishop of the Red River settlement that grew into Winnipeg.

Weir traps for eels, Kamouraska

KAMOURASKA
In the St. Lawrence River here eels are caught in weir traps—rows of stakes that divert the fish into enclosures where they are netted. Most of the catch is shipped to Europe.
□ One of North America's largest colonies of black-crowned night herons occupies rocky ledges and reefs on six islands opposite Kamouraska.
□ One of several fine old residences in Kamouraska is Maison L'Anglais, built in 1725.

ÎLE DU BIC
As many as 8,000 eider ducks nest on islands in the St. Lawrence River here; sea otters and harbor and harp seals sun on reefs and rocky shores.
□ Ile du Massacre, where 200 Micmacs were trapped and slaughtered by Iroquois in 1533, is accessible at low tide. Visitors can see the cave in which the Micmacs hid.

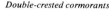

SAINT-JEAN-PORT-JOLI
This town is the wood-carving capital of Quebec. Some 50 studios (many are open to the public) display life-size religious and historical figures, sculptured murals, Quebec landscapes, miniature birds and animals, abstract forms, and some of the finest miniature sailboats in the world. Many sculptures have rustic themes: a trapper on snowshoes, a logger swinging an ax, the ever-popular habitant. Other artists and craftsmen produce copper-enamel art, jewelry and leather goods.

RIMOUSKI
Art treasures of eastern Quebec are exhibited in the bright, open galleries of the Rimouski Regional Museum, housed in a former church. Works by Quebec artists Antoine Plamondon, Charles Huot, Rodolphe Duguay and Frédéric Taylor are displayed along with Stations of the Cross by Médard Bourgault, who helped to revive the province's ancient craft of wood carving.

TROIS-PISTOLES
On Ile aux Basques in the St. Lawrence River are the restored remains of three stone furnaces that early Basque whalers used to convert blubber to oil. A monument on the island and a plaque at Trois-Pistoles commemorate the Basques who hunted baleen whales at the mouth of the Saguenay River in the 1500s.
□ Ile aux Basques and the two Razade islands are a sanctuary where double-crested cormorants may be photographed.
□ The work of Trois-Pistoles artisans—weaving, knitting, painting and pottery—is displayed in La Maison du Notaire.

Double-crested cormorants

A Tradition Revived

Most of the wood carving in Saint-Jean-Port-Joli's church (1779) was done in the late 18th and early 19th centuries. But the magnificent pulpit, installed in 1937, is the work of the Bourgault brothers. The tradition they follow goes back to the 1670s when Bishop Laval encouraged the teaching of arts and crafts. For two centuries artists in wood were in demand for decorating public buildings. Wood carving declined with the mass production of furniture and building materials but farmers and seamen kept it alive as a pastime. One seaman, Médard Bourgault, opened a studio in 1928 with brothers André and Jean-Julien. Among the Bourgaults' works are André's *Evangeline* (it is in his shop in Saint-Jean-Port-Joli), Médard's Stations of the Cross in the L'Islet-sur-Mer Church, and Jean-Julien's *Town Council* in l'Auberge du Faubourg in Saint-Jean-Port-Joli.

RIVIÈRE-DU-LOUP
The Park of the Luminous Cross overlooks the town, the St. Lawrence and five islands called Les Pèlerins. The islands are frequented by thousands of seabirds and shorebirds including black guillemots and great blue herons. Canada's largest colony of double-crested cormorants nests on Grand Pèlerin.
□ A plaque downtown marks the site of the house in which the Most Rev. Alexandre-Antonin Taché was born in 1823. He was sent to the Red River as a missionary in 1845 and became bishop of St. Boniface, Man., in 1853. Deeply sympathetic to the Métis, Taché was influential in restoring order after the Red River Rebellion in 1870.

St. Lawrence River near Rivière-du-Loup

A Sportsman's Paradise in Cartier's 'Saguenay Kingdom'

Lac Saint-Jean

Rich, fertile plains and ancient hills border 523-square-kilometre Lac Saint-Jean. It is a part of the immense territory on which Jacques Cartier conferred the name "Saguenay Kingdom," but it is perhaps the most impressive part, the richest in contrasts.

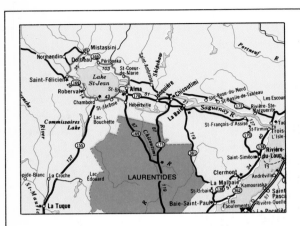

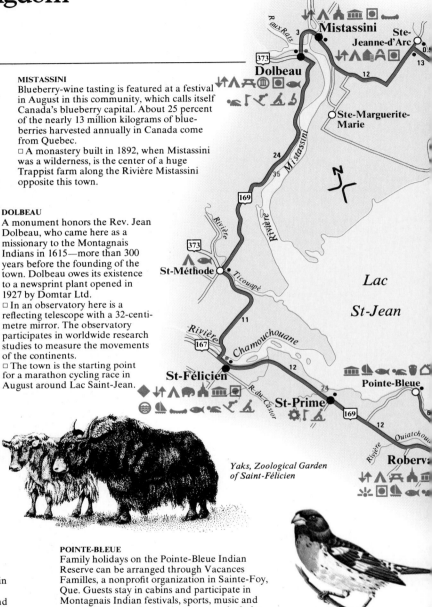

MISTASSINI
Blueberry-wine tasting is featured at a festival in August in this community, which calls itself Canada's blueberry capital. About 25 percent of the nearly 13 million kilograms of blueberries harvested annually in Canada come from Quebec.
□ A monastery built in 1892, when Mistassini was a wilderness, is the center of a huge Trappist farm along the Rivière Mistassini opposite this town.

DOLBEAU
A monument honors the Rev. Jean Dolbeau, who came here as a missionary to the Montagnais Indians in 1615—more than 300 years before the founding of the town. Dolbeau owes its existence to a newsprint plant opened in 1927 by Domtar Ltd.
□ In an observatory here is a reflecting telescope with a 32-centimetre mirror. The observatory participates in worldwide research studies to measure the movements of the continents.
□ The town is the starting point for a marathon cycling race in August around Lac Saint-Jean.

Yaks, Zoological Garden of Saint-Félicien

Zoological Garden, Saint-Félicien

SAINT-FÉLICIEN
The Zoological Garden of Saint-Félicien is on Ile du Jardin in the Rivière aux Saumons, a tributary of Rivière Chamouchouane which races through turbulent rapids and waterfalls at Saint-Félicien. An Indian village, a fur-trading post and logging camp have been reconstructed in the 120-hectare Zoological Garden.
□ The International Regatta on Lac Saint-Jean, on the Chamouchouane in late June or early July, is preceded by a week of sailing, kayak and waterskiing contests, dances and a torchlight boat parade.
□ At Saint-Félicien is the main entrance to Chibougamau Reserve. Within the 11,025-square-kilometre park Chute de la Chaudière tumbles some 60 metres on the Chamouchouane.
□ Saint-Félicien Church, an ornate stone structure that resembles a cathedral, has two steeples.

POINTE-BLEUE
Family holidays on the Pointe-Bleue Indian Reserve can be arranged through Vacances Familles, a nonprofit organization in Sainte-Foy, Que. Guests stay in cabins and participate in Montagnais Indian festivals, sports, music and dance. The reserve's vacation program includes canoeing, sailing, swimming, archery, and arts and crafts. There are hiking trails, playgrounds, a gymnasium and a beach. Indian fishing and hunting guides can be hired.

Rose-breasted grosbeak

ROBERVAL
Swimmers from more than a dozen countries compete in the Lac Saint-Jean marathon in August, a 40-kilometre race from Péribonka to Roberval. The race, first held in 1955, has become a marathon classic, with prize money of close to $20,000. It marks the end of Roberval's *Huitaine de gaieté*, an eight-day festival.
□ Life-size concrete figures of the eight North American martyr saints were sculpted in 1940 for a monument in Parc Saint-Jean-de-Brébeuf.

0	1	2	3	4	5 Miles

0	2	4	6	8 Kilometres

The almost circular lake is an ancient glacial trough that was once an arm of the sea. The Péribonca, largest of the rivers that cascade down from the Laurentians to feed Lac Saint-Jean, is 494 kilometres long. The Métabetchouane is 142; the Chamouchouane, 178; and the Mistassini, 286. All this tumbling water, temporarily stilled by the lake, soon rushes through two channels worn in the bedrock of the Canadian Shield. Then the two become one: the seething, torrential Saguenay.

A tour around the lake crosses all these rivers. At the western end of the lake the road leads to Saint-Félicien, gateway to the vast Chibougamau and Mistassini reserves, then bends northeast toward the logging town of Mistassini.

The north shore, on the edge of the Laurentian hills, is strewn with granite outcrops and glacial debris as high as three-story buildings. The south shore is gently rolling and fertile. Here, good pastures and clear waters support prosperous dairy farms. In unspoiled towns such as Hébertville (where settlement of the region began in 1849), charming 19th-century houses hug the narrow streets.

For the sportsman, Lac Saint-Jean is a region of fine fishing and hunting, of hiking, climbing and horseback riding. The lake provides some of the province's best fishing for landlocked salmon. Here and there are sparkling waterfalls and lakeside recreation areas. And everywhere is the wild beauty of the countryside.

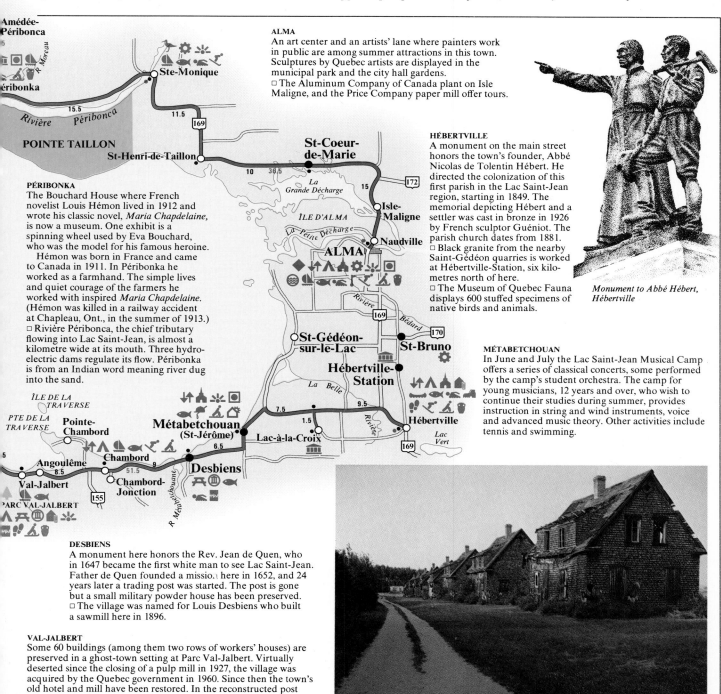

ALMA
An art center and an artists' lane where painters work in public are among summer attractions in this town. Sculptures by Quebec artists are displayed in the municipal park and the city hall gardens.
□ The Aluminum Company of Canada plant on Isle Maligne, and the Price Company paper mill offer tours.

HÉBERTVILLE
A monument on the main street honors the town's founder, Abbé Nicolas de Tolentin Hébert. He directed the colonization of this first parish in the Lac Saint-Jean region, starting in 1849. The memorial depicting Hébert and a settler was cast in bronze in 1926 by French sculptor Guéniot. The parish church dates from 1881.
□ Black granite from the nearby Saint-Gédéon quarries is worked at Hébertville-Station, six kilometres north of here.
□ The Museum of Quebec Fauna displays 600 stuffed specimens of native birds and animals.

Monument to Abbé Hébert, Hébertville

PÉRIBONKA
The Bouchard House where French novelist Louis Hémon lived in 1912 and wrote his classic novel, *Maria Chapdelaine*, is now a museum. One exhibit is a spinning wheel used by Eva Bouchard, who was the model for his famous heroine.
Hémon was born in France and came to Canada in 1911. In Péribonka he worked as a farmhand. The simple lives and quiet courage of the farmers he worked with inspired *Maria Chapdelaine*. (Hémon was killed in a railway accident at Chapleau, Ont., in the summer of 1913.)
□ Rivière Péribonca, the chief tributary flowing into Lac Saint-Jean, is almost a kilometre wide at its mouth. Three hydroelectric dams regulate its flow. Péribonca is from an Indian word meaning river dug into the sand.

MÉTABETCHOUAN
In June and July the Lac Saint-Jean Musical Camp offers a series of classical concerts, some performed by the camp's student orchestra. The camp for young musicians, 12 years and over, who wish to continue their studies during summer, provides instruction in string and wind instruments, voice and advanced music theory. Other activities include tennis and swimming.

DESBIENS
A monument here honors the Rev. Jean de Quen, who in 1647 became the first white man to see Lac Saint-Jean. Father de Quen founded a mission here in 1652, and 24 years later a trading post was started. The post is gone but a small military powder house has been preserved.
□ The village was named for Louis Desbiens who built a sawmill here in 1896.

VAL-JALBERT
Some 60 buildings (among them two rows of workers' houses) are preserved in a ghost-town setting at Parc Val-Jalbert. Virtually deserted since the closing of a pulp mill in 1927, the village was acquired by the Quebec government in 1960. Since then the town's old hotel and mill have been restored. In the reconstructed post office an audio-visual presentation tells the history of the town. A trail leads from the mill to the top of spectacular 64-metre Val-Jalbert Falls on the Rivière Ouiatchouane.

Ghost town, Parc Val-Jalbert

A Mighty 'Fjord'
Where the Sea Surges Inland

Saguenay River

For centuries the Saguenay River was the only gateway to the furs and forests of the region around Lac Saint-Jean. Today Highway 170, leading to the bustling centers of Chicoutimi and Jonquière, parallels the Saguenay River. From the road the spectacular grandeur of its steep south bank can be glimpsed.

The Saguenay once leaped and plunged for 56 kilometres of rapids and falls from Lac Saint-Jean to Chicoutimi, dropping more than 90 metres along the way. Now

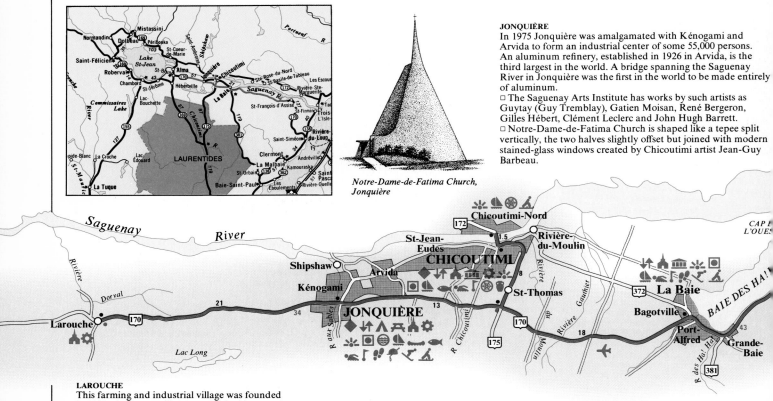

JONQUIÈRE
In 1975 Jonquière was amalgamated with Kénogami and Arvida to form an industrial center of some 55,000 persons. An aluminum refinery, established in 1926 in Arvida, is the third largest in the world. A bridge spanning the Saguenay River in Jonquière was the first in the world to be made entirely of aluminum.
□ The Saguenay Arts Institute has works by such artists as Guytay (Guy Tremblay), Gatien Moisan, René Bergeron, Gilles Hébert, Clément Leclerc and John Hugh Barrett.
□ Notre-Dame-de-Fatima Church is shaped like a tepee split vertically, the two halves slightly offset but joined with modern stained-glass windows created by Chicoutimi artist Jean-Guy Barbeau.

*Notre-Dame-de-Fatima Church,
Jonquière*

LAROUCHE
This farming and industrial village was founded in 1921 after a sawmill was established here. Saint-Gérard-Majella Church, built in 1960, is distinctively modern in architecture but traditional in form. The roof, sweeping up in two curved planes to its highest point above the altar, is supported by white concrete walls. They describe four quarter-arcs to form the conventional cross-shaped ground plan.

CHICOUTIMI
The city stands on the hilly south shore of the Saguenay at the end of deep-water navigation. Chicoutimi-Nord has a magnificent view of the Saguenay River.
□ The development of Chicoutimi began in 1842 when Peter McLeod built a sawmill on the Rivière du Moulin. A gold watch and other personal possessions belonging to McLeod are displayed in the Saguenay Museum.
□ Each year Chicoutimi celebrated the settlement of the region in the mid-1800s. During an eight-day Carnaval-Souvenir, just before Lent, the city is filled with the sights and sounds of wood-chopping contests, snowshoe races, tugs-of-war and a torchlight parade. Many of the city's residents wear period costumes during the festivities.
□ From Chicoutimi there are eight-hour Saguenay cruises to Cap Trinité and Cape Eternité and four-hour trips to Sainte-Rose-du-Nord.

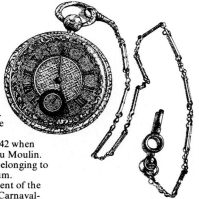

*Peter McLeod's gold watch,
Saguenay Museum,
Chicoutimi*

Carnaval-Souvenir, Chicoutimi

modern hydroelectric dams have tamed the mighty torrent.

Between Chicoutimi—an inland seaport and a chief city of the region—and the St. Lawrence River the Saguenay is a "fjord," an ice age relic by which the sea penetrates deep into the continent. In the fjord, cold seawater from the St. Lawrence pushes under warmer freshwater from Lac Saint-Jean and the Saguenay becomes a two-level river: on top it is warm and slightly saline; the lower level is icy and almost as salty as the sea itself. The river's depth, which averages 240 metres, makes the waters appear deep amber or black. Much of the fjord is flanked by barren, ash-colored rocks. Here and there are patches of vegetation: a clump of birches, a lone spruce, a slender poplar.

Near L'Anse-Saint-Jean a trail leads to the top of the Cap Trinité, some 500 metres above the water. It offers an impressive view of the Saguenay. Beyond the river's austere cliffs, the forested Laurentians—ancient hills that cradle some 1,500 lakes and 700 rivers—seem to undulate to the ends of the earth.

Monument to pioneers, La Baie

LA BAIE
Port-Alfred, Bagotville and Grande-Baie were amalgamated to form La Baie. This commercial and agricultural center is a rail terminal and deep-water port at the head of Baie des Ha! Ha! on the Saguenay River. About 500 freighters annually bring in bauxite for aluminum smelters at Arvida, and take away newsprint from paper mills in La Baie.
□ A stone statue of a settler commemorates the region's pioneers, who came here in 1838.

L'ANSE-SAINT-JEAN
This picturesque agricultural village is on a bay where Rivière Saint-Jean flows into the Saguenay. Before the first colonists arrived here in 1838, L'Anse-Saint-Jean was the site of an Indian mission.
□ In the village, a 37-metre covered bridge spans Rivière Saint-Jean. There are picnic areas and lookouts beside waterfalls on the river.

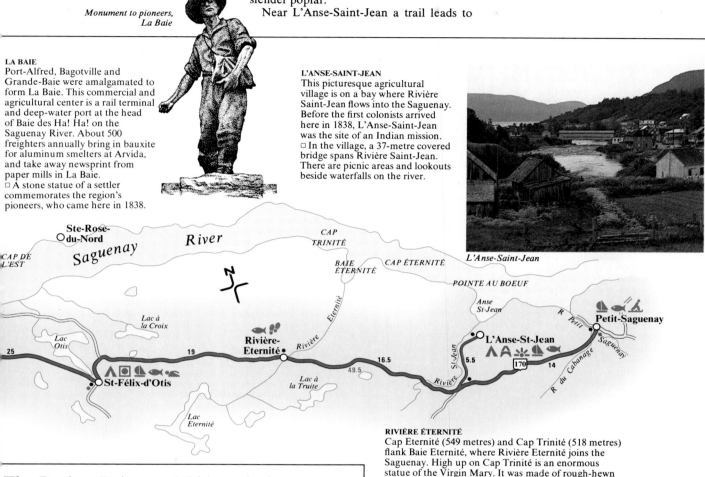

L'Anse-Saint-Jean

RIVIÈRE ÉTERNITÉ
Cap Eternité (549 metres) and Cap Trinité (518 metres) flank Baie Eternité, where Rivière Eternité joins the Saguenay. High up on Cap Trinité is an enormous statue of the Virgin Mary. It was made of rough-hewn wood covered with lead by sculptor Louis Jobin, and erected in 1881.

The Barber-Painter of Chicoutimi

In 1957 Arthur Villeneuve, a Chicoutimi barber for 31 years, decided to become a painter. He started on his house and didn't stop until he had run out of walls—inside and out—and ceilings. His wife forbade him to paint the stove and refrigerator. Some years later she said, "I even bought two gallons of white paint to cover up what he had done to the walls."

His neighbors called him a fool. But Villeneuve was not discouraged. He painted for two years, and then opened his house to the public. Scenes of Chicoutimi spread from room to room; the Saguenay River flowed beside the staircase. Visitors left with growing respect for Villeneuve's talent.

When he ran out of walls, Villeneuve switched to canvas. His paintings, lauded as "authentic primitives," began to sell. In 1972, a one-man show at the Montreal Museum of Fine Arts confirmed the art world's acceptance of the barber-painter.

Le train de la parenté, by Arthur Villeneuve

Le Conte's sparrow

PETIT-SAGUENAY
In 1848 William Price purchased a sawmill and established a warehouse and an administrative center here for his logging operations in the area.
□ This tiny village nestles in the steep-sided valley of Rivière Petit Saguenay. Salmon use a fish ladder to bypass two nearby waterfalls on the Petit-Saguenay.
□ From June to the end of August speckled trout can be caught in a government fishing reserve here.

An Awakening Frontier—
Rich in Minerals and Power

North Shore, St. Lawrence River

Until the 1930s settlement of this stretch of the St. Lawrence, called the "North Shore," was limited to a string of small fishing villages joined by primitive roads and connected with the outside world by coastal vessels. But exploitation of the region's vast natural resources—wood and water in a 200-kilometre-wide coastal strip and iron ore in the northern hinterland—led to spectacular developments.

Pulp mills came first, in the 1930s. Two decades later iron ore was discovered near

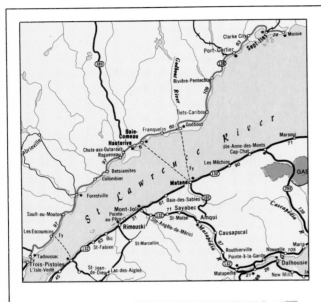

Whale-Watching on the St. Lawrence

Whales by the score can often be seen where the Saguenay joins the St. Lawrence. The shallow waters at the confluence of the two rivers are a rich feeding ground. The Saguenay is the home of the beluga whale, a variety of white arctic porpoise, once known as the St. Lawrence whale. The beluga is attracted by abundant shrimp and capelin, and its young are believed to be born in the Baie Sainte-Marguerite area. Whalers once hunted and killed the beluga for its oil. Now, if hunted at all, belugas are taken alive for shipment to zoos.

Other species of whale reported near the mouth of the Saguenay include finbacks, humpbacks and blues.

Trips can be arranged at Tadoussac. Saguenay cruise ships provide opportunities to catch sight of the beluga.

Cruise ships near the Saguenay River

Sand dunes, Tadoussac

TADOUSSAC
Summer skiers climb 550 wooden steps to the top of a 112-metre sand dune and schuss down.
□ The xenon lamp in a lighthouse, eight kilometres offshore in the St. Lawrence River, is visible for 48 kilometres.
□ A wooden chapel (1747) in Tadoussac is the oldest in North America. In its tower hangs the bell from a Jesuit church (1641) that once stood on the same site.
□ Pierre Chauvin's fortified house (1600)—Canada's first trading post—has been reconstructed at the mouth of the Saguenay River. Chauvin chose this location for a headquarters after being granted a ten-year fur trade monopoly.

CHUTE-AUX-OUTARDES
A 1.6-kilometre pipe made from British Columbia pine carries water from a dam on the Rivière aux Outardes here to a generating station which powers a Baie-Comeau paper mill. Hydro-Québec built two more dams upriver in the late 1960s as part of a plan to harness all of the 483-kilometre Rivière aux Outardes.
□ Pointe-aux-Outardes, across the river on the Manicouagan Peninsula, has a 31-metre-long covered bridge.

Wooden chapel, Tadoussac

FORESTVILLE
The world's highest-capacity pulpwood loading system is here. A current, created by opening a power dam gate, pulls logs to a flume entrance. The 1.6-kilometre flume carries the wood to a loading plant in nine minutes. There the logs are diverted into chutes which slide them onto barges.
□ During the town's Capelin Festival in May, smeltlike capelin can be scooped up by the bucketful along the St. Lawrence River shore.

0 4 8 12 16 20 Miles
0 8 16 24 32 Kilometres

Schefferville (Que.) and Wabush (Labrador). Railway links between the mines and the natural harbors of the North Shore such as Port-Cartier and Sept-Iles brought radical economic change. Sept-Iles, for instance, was a fishing village of 1,500 persons in 1950. It is now a bustling shipping and administration center of 31,000 people.

In the 1960s came hydroelectric developments. Dams and generating plants harnessed rivers such as the Betsiamites, Outardes, Manicouagan and Toulnustouc. A dam at Labrieville on the Betsiamites (some 90 kilometres northwest of Forestville) creates a reservoir 770 square kilometres large. The 214-metre-high Manic 5 Dam on the Manicouagan, 210 kilometres north of Baie-Comeau, is one of the world's largest. High-energy-consuming aluminum refineries and other industries are located near this source of electric power. Despite these developments, much of this region remains a wilderness offering thrilling experiences for canoeists and fishermen.

Robert R. McCormack statue, Baie-Comeau

IE-COMEAU

e industrial development of the once-isolated North Shore d its beginning here in 1936 when Chicago publisher Col. bert R. McCormick built a pulp-and-newsprint mill to feed newspapers in the United States. McCormick is honored a statue at Baie-Comeau. Development boomed in the 50s and 1960s: an aluminum refinery and grain elevators re built here, and the Rivière Manicouagan and the Rivière x Outardes were harnessed to produce electricity.
he Daniel Johnson (Manic 5) Dam, 210 kilometres north Baie-Comeau on the Manicouagan, may be visited in mmer.

POINTE-AUX-ANGLAIS

When Saint-Paul-de-Pointe-aux-Anglais Church was erected in 1962, some 120 parishioners each carried 40 stones five kilometres from a Gulf of St. Lawrence beach to the construction site. Bas-relief Stations of the Cross by Médard Bourgault are of basswood on walnut backgrounds. Above the altar is an oak crucifix, also sculpted by Bourgault.

MOISIE

East of Moisie, the Natashquan and Moisie rivers spill into the Gulf of St. Lawrence. Each river offers challenges to experienced canoeists. The 384-kilometre Natashquan requires few portages: most of its many rapids can be run. Waterfalls, rapids and difficult portages mark the 304-kilometre Moisie—one of the best salmon rivers in eastern North America.

SEPT-ÎLES

The city is on the almost circular Sept-Iles Bay, some 35 kilometres in diameter and deep enough for oceangoing vessels.
□ Vast quantities of iron concentrate, brought by remote-controlled trains from New Quebec and Labrador, are shipped from the year-round natural harbor of Sept-Iles to steel mills in Canada, the United States and Europe. Giant conveyer belts transport the metal directly from the railway cars into waiting ships.
□ A log fort built in 1661, once owned by explorer Louis Jolliet and burned in 1692 by English troops, has been reconstructed near the Vieux Fort River. It has a 27-metre guard tower, two dwellings, a chapel, powder magazine, store and stable.

Northern Iron Ore for the World's Steel Mills

Each year the rusty red earth of Labrador and northern Quebec yields millions of tonnes of iron ore for the giant blast furnaces of Canada, Europe, Japan and the United States.

Although iron ore was discovered along Rivière Moisie in 1866, Canada mined little iron until 1939. Then, for five years, the Helen Mine in the Michipicoten area of Ontario was the chief producer. In 1944 the great open-pit mine at Steep Rock, Ont., came into production. Ten years later development of the rich iron deposits in Labrador and northern Quebec was begun.

Today iron concentrate from Schefferville, Wabush and Labrador City is hauled by railway cars to ports such as Sept-Iles *(right)* and Port-Cartier. Much of the ore is further refined at pelletizing plants in these centers.

Visitors to Sept-Iles can watch ships being loaded with iron concentrate and pellets.

Arctic Flowers on the Mountain, Rare Caribou in the Park

Gaspé Peninsula

The Gaspé Peninsula is a world of delightful variety: tiny fishing villages, pastoral farmland and rugged mountains. The region was isolated until a highway called the Perron Boulevard (now Highway 132) was built around the perimeter of the peninsula in 1929. The Gaspé still retains its traditional charm and natural beauty.

Parc de Métis has formal gardens that were once part of the estate of George Stephen, first president of the Canadian Pacific Railway. In summer Stephen angled in the

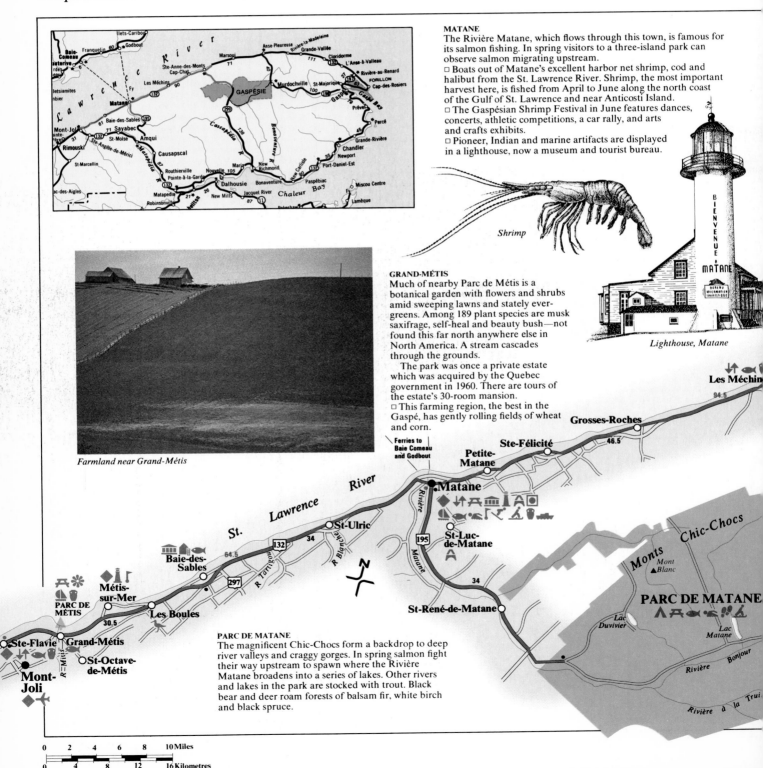

MATANE

The Rivière Matane, which flows through this town, is famous for its salmon fishing. In spring visitors to a three-island park can observe salmon migrating upstream.
□ Boats out of Matane's excellent harbor net shrimp, cod and halibut from the St. Lawrence River. Shrimp, the most important harvest here, is fished from April to June along the north coast of the Gulf of St. Lawrence and near Anticosti Island.
□ The Gaspésian Shrimp Festival in June features dances, concerts, athletic competitions, a car rally, and arts and crafts exhibits.
□ Pioneer, Indian and marine artifacts are displayed in a lighthouse, now a museum and tourist bureau.

Shrimp

Lighthouse, Matane

GRAND-MÉTIS

Much of nearby Parc de Métis is a botanical garden with flowers and shrubs amid sweeping lawns and stately evergreens. Among 189 plant species are musk saxifrage, self-heal and beauty bush—not found this far north anywhere else in North America. A stream cascades through the grounds.

The park was once a private estate which was acquired by the Quebec government in 1960. There are tours of the estate's 30-room mansion.
□ This farming region, the best in the Gaspé, has gently rolling fields of wheat and corn.

Farmland near Grand-Métis

PARC DE MATANE

The magnificent Chic-Chocs form a backdrop to deep river valleys and craggy gorges. In spring salmon fight their way upstream to spawn where the Rivière Matane broadens into a series of lakes. Other rivers and lakes in the park are stocked with trout. Black bear and deer roam forests of balsam fir, white birch and black spruce.

0 2 4 6 8 10 Miles
0 4 8 12 16 Kilometres

region's excellent salmon-fishing rivers. In 1910 his niece, Elsie Reford, inherited the estate and established the gardens. Nearby Métis-sur-Mer, the region's oldest resort, has fine beaches and many beautiful old summer homes.

Inland are wild rolling highlands and the Chic-Chocs, eastern Canada's highest mountains. From the summit of Mont Jacques-Cartier (1,268 metres), the loftiest peak in the range, visitors can see the St. Lawrence River 25 kilometres away.

About 20 Chic-Choc peaks exceed 1,070 metres; some of these are snowcapped as late as July. The summit of Mont Albert, a lake-dotted plateau, has mosses, lichens and stunted shrubs that are usually found in the Arctic.

Parc de Matane in the Chic-Chocs has rivers teeming with salmon, and lakes and streams stocked with trout. One of Quebec's largest herds of moose range the park's black spruce forests.

Much of Parc de la Gaspésie is wilderness—home to one of the world's last herds of woodland caribou.

Highway 132 near Sainte-Anne-des-Monts

SAINTE-ANNE-DES-MONTS
This farming, cod-fishing and lumbering community is on the rocky shore of a bay named by Champlain for Pierre de Monts, the first governor of Acadia (1604).
□ A stately granite church here is dedicated to Saint Anne, patron saint of sailors.

CAP-CHAT
The town overlooks the St. Lawrence from a cape whose profile, when seen from the river, resembles a cat sitting on its haunches.
□ A July arts and crafts festival features folksingers, storytellers and Gaspésian cuisine. Artisans offer instruction in handicrafts.
□ Mont Logan, 24 kilometres south, has downhill and cross-country skiing. The 1,148-metre peak is part of the Chic-Choc range. The Rivière Cap-Chat is noted for its salmon.

Lapland rosebay

SAINT-JOACHIM-DE-TOURELLE
Two craggy granite pillars stand about five kilometres apart on a beach near here.
□ This agricultural and fishing community, founded in 1916, was partially destroyed by a landslide in 1963.
□ East of town Highway 132 winds between the St. Lawrence River and sheer cliffs.

Rock formation, Saint-Joachim-de-Tourelle

PARC DE LA GASPÉSIE
One of the world's last herds of woodland caribou lives on the slopes of 1,268-metre Mont Jacques-Cartier, the highest peak in the Chic-Chocs. This rugged region is also inhabited by moose, deer and black bear. As many as 150 species of alpine flowers—plants that survived here above the reach of ice-age glaciers—grow on the 30-square-kilometre summit of Mont Albert. They include alpine azalea and alpine camion. Lapland rosebay, a shrub with pink and purple flowers, blooms from June to September.
□ More than 240 kilometres of hiking trails include three paths to the top of Mont Albert. Guides take visitors to the summit of Mont Jacques-Cartier. Fishermen angle for ouananiche (landlocked salmon) and trout in the park's rivers.

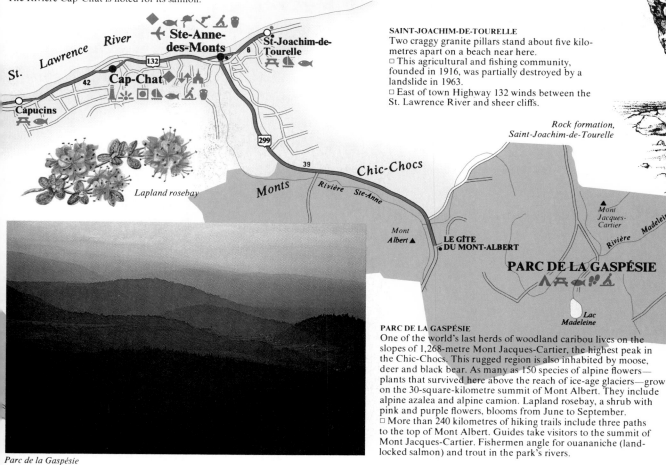
Parc de la Gaspésie

Wild Beauty and Sheltering Bays 'Where the Land Ends'

North Shore, Gaspé Peninsula

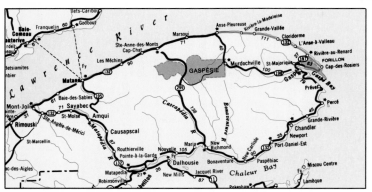

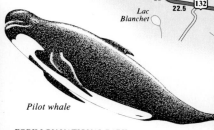

Vigneaux at Cloridorme

CLORIDORME

Large, sonar-equipped trawlers have replaced small wooden fishing boats in recent years, but *vigneaux*—wooden tables with metal trellises used for drying cod—still line the shores of Cloridorme. A portion of the catch, cleaned and salted, is spread out on these racks to dry in the sun.
□ On display in a shed in Saint-Yvon are the remains of a torpedo fired by a German submarine Sept. 4, 1942. The torpedo missed its mark—a schooner—and exploded on a rock.

ANSE-PLEUREUSE

A lovely fishing village at the head of a small bay, Anse-Pleureuse ("sighing bay") is named for the sound of the wind along the shore.
□ Nearby Mont-Louis was burned to the ground by General Wolfe's soldiers on their way to besiege Quebec in 1759.

Rusty blackbird

SAINT-HÉLIER

Thousands of eels wriggle across the 90-metre *portage de l'étang* (pool portage) here each autumn forsaking this freshwater pool for the St. Lawrence River and the long journey to spawning grounds in the mid-Atlantic Sargasso sea. Millions of migrating eels, forming a metre-wide phalanx several kilometres long, have been observed at sea. Young eels are about two centimetres long when they head north in the spring. The North American eel's journey to fresh water takes roughly a year.

Limestone cliffs, Forillon National Park

Pilot whale

FORILLON NATIONAL PARK

One of Canada's newest national parks, Forillon was established in 1971 with the official theme "Harmony between man, land and sea."
□ Black spruce and reindeer moss, usually found 800 kilometres to the north, grow on Penouille, a long peninsula facing the Baie de Gaspé. Some 36 species of lichen thrive on sandy soil. Nearby are sand dunes and salt marshes. Fractured limestone cliffs as high as 200 metres face the Gulf of St. Lawrence. They support herring gulls, black guillemots and double-crested cormorants. The park has more than 160 bird species in all. Pilot whales are the most common of the 12 whale species in the waters off Forillon.

The northeast coast of the Gaspé Peninsula is a rich landscape of limestone cliffs, shingly beaches, streams, coves and thickly forested highlands. Small villages dot the coastline in sheltered bays. Fishing boats cluster around wharves much as they have since the 1700s. Cod is still split, salted and dried on wooden racks along the beach.

The wild beauty of the Gaspé (from an Indian word, *Gaspeg*—"where the land ends") reaches its climax at Forillon National Park. Here, visitors stand at one end of the Appalachian Mountains, a chain that extends deep into the southeastern United States. The park appears as a massive, tilted block emerging from the sea. Wind and surf have sculpted 200-metre-high escarpments on sections of the eastern shore. The coast facing the Baie de Gaspé is indented with beaches and small coves hidden between the rocky headlands. On the cliffs grow species of vigorous alpine flora—species whose presence here is not yet understood by botanists. Sheltered from the harsh weather of the gulf are long stretches of sandy beach. Within a hundred metres of shore is a heavy cover of evergreen forest crisscrossed by nature trails.

Thousands of birds visit the peninsula—some migrating from the Arctic to winter in the park, others flying on. Seals in great numbers return each summer to the waters off Forillon, as do pilot whales. Such yearly migrations, like the rugged scenery, give the region a timeless quality.

Forillon: A Stepping-Stone Between Land and Sea

Life between the deep waters of the Gulf of St. Lawrence and the highlands of Forillon National Park is inextricably linked to the rise and fall of the tide. Along the rugged, rocky shore are three life zones: the splash zone, high on the rocks; the intertidal zone, flooded at high tide and exposed at ebb tide; and the subtidal zone, uncovered by only the lowest tides.

Forillon has countless tide pools, each a marine world in microcosm. On and near the rocks are countless communities of sea plants and animals, each specifically adapted to the rigors and demands of its environment. Together the zones illustrate the progress of life from sea to land.

SPLASH ZONE
Only the highest spring tides reach the splash zone. Life here relies on spray for its seawater needs. The rough periwinkle eats minute blue-green algae, scraping them from the rocks with an abrasive tongue. Its rows of microscopic thorns can wear down even rocky surfaces.

Rough periwinkle

INTERTIDAL ZONE
The intertidal zone is covered with water about half the time and animals and plants retain enough to sustain them when the tide is out. Creatures here must be able to anchor themselves against the push and pull of the waves. Each barnacle secretes a strong adhesive and attaches itself to the spot it will occupy the rest of its life.

Barnacle

SUBTIDAL ZONE
Covered by water most of the time, plants and animals of the subtidal zone are poorly adapted to dry land. The starfish eats mussels, oysters and other bivalve mollusks, curving itself around each victim and pulling the shells apart with its hundreds of "suction-tube" feet.

Starfish

RIVIÈRE-AU-RENARD
Many residents of this fishing community are descendants of Irish sailors shipwrecked off Cap-des-Rosiers in 1856.
□ Paintings of the Stations of the Cross by Hungarian artists Edith and Isabella Piczek adorn Saint-Martin-de-la-Rivière-au-Renard. The church, with marble altars and walls of pink granite, is in the modern style of architect Dom Bellot.

CAP-DES-ROSIERS
Named by Champlain for the wild rose bushes that thrive here, Cap-des-Rosiers is considered to be the point where the St. Lawrence River ends and the Gulf of St. Lawrence begins.
□ The Cap-des-Rosiers lighthouse, completed in 1858, is the highest (33 metres) of a series of lighthouses built to guide ships safely along the treacherous coast of the St. Lawrence River. Before the use of wireless in the early 1900s, incoming ships signaled their passing to the station by means of flags. The notice of arrival was then telegraphed to Quebec. Until recently a nine-pounder cannon was fired every hour in fog and snow.

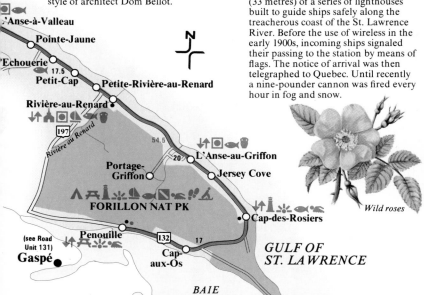

Wild roses

Cap-des-Rosiers

A Great, Shiplike Rock, Sweeping Views of the Gulf

South Shore, Gaspé Peninsula

At the tip of the Gaspé Peninsula, the irregular coastline blends into limestone and shale formations which have been pushed, folded and squeezed by tremendous geological forces. Nowhere is the effect more striking than at Percé Rock, a great shiplike block of limestone rising 86 metres from the sea. Off the mainland near Percé, the French explorer Jacques Cartier anchored his three ships in 1534 to claim the region for France.

Offshore from Percé village is another

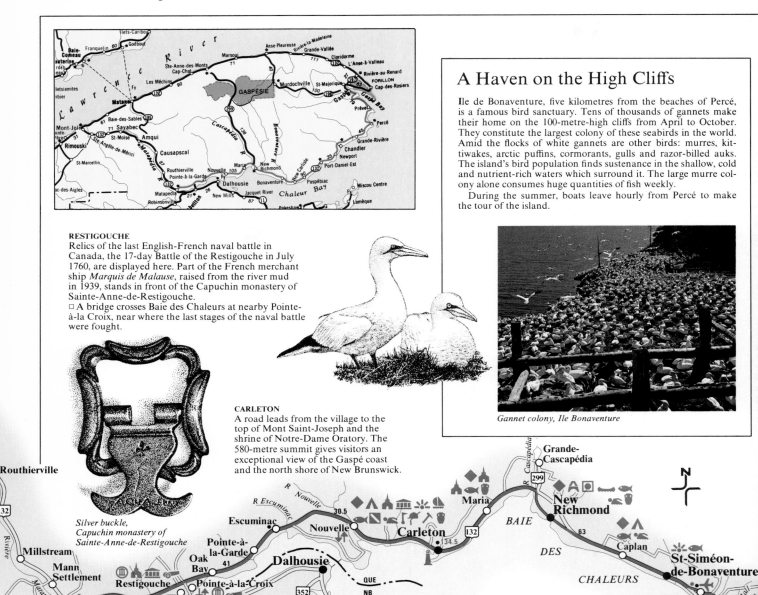

A Haven on the High Cliffs

Ile de Bonaventure, five kilometres from the beaches of Percé, is a famous bird sanctuary. Tens of thousands of gannets make their home on the 100-metre-high cliffs from April to October. They constitute the largest colony of these seabirds in the world. Amid the flocks of white gannets are other birds: murres, kittiwakes, arctic puffins, cormorants, gulls and razor-billed auks. The island's bird population finds sustenance in the shallow, cold and nutrient-rich waters which surround it. The large murre colony alone consumes huge quantities of fish weekly.

During the summer, boats leave hourly from Percé to make the tour of the island.

Gannet colony, Ile Bonaventure

RESTIGOUCHE
Relics of the last English-French naval battle in Canada, the 17-day Battle of the Restigouche in July 1760, are displayed here. Part of the French merchant ship *Marquis de Malause*, raised from the river mud in 1939, stands in front of the Capuchin monastery of Sainte-Anne-de-Restigouche.
□ A bridge crosses Baie des Chaleurs at nearby Pointe-à-la-Croix, near where the last stages of the naval battle were fought.

Silver buckle, Capuchin monastery of Sainte-Anne-de-Restigouche

CARLETON
A road leads from the village to the top of Mont Saint-Joseph and the shrine of Notre-Dame Oratory. The 580-metre summit gives visitors an exceptional view of the Gaspé coast and the north shore of New Brunswick.

MATAPÉDIA
The highway between Matapédia and Routhierville follows the former Kempt Military Road through the beautiful Matapédia Valley. The Rivière Matapédia, flanked by steep mountain slopes, is nicknamed the "River of 222 Rapids." The river offers fine canoeing and fishing for Atlantic salmon.

BONAVENTURE
An historical museum here is in a 200-year-old building that was among the first built by the community's Acadian settlers. Displays include Acadian cradles, spinning wheels, looms and tools, and a collection of fossils.
□ A 36-kilometre boat race across Baie des Chaleurs from Petit Rocher, N.B., to Bonaventure highlights the Festival of Saint-Bonaventure in early summer.

```
0   2   4   6   8   10 Miles
0   4   8   12   16 Kilometres
```

of Canada's most spectacular natural sights: the gannet colony of Ile de Bonaventure. As the tour boat rounds a corner of the island, the great gannet ledges come into view, painted white with thousands of nesting birds. From the island's flat top the birds' fighting, courting, nest building and take-offs can be viewed at close range.

Toward the Baie des Chaleurs, the highway winds past the sheltered bays of the Gaspé's south shore. In season, scores of salmon fishermen line the banks of the Dartmouth, York and Saint John rivers. The scenic Matapédia and Cascapédia rivers, known for their salmon fishing, drain into the Baie des Chaleurs. The Chic-Chocs, the mountains with the highest peaks in eastern Canada, rise behind the fishing villages and resort centers strung along the coast. Hiking trails wind through the forested slopes leading to sweeping views of the Gulf of St. Lawrence and Baie des Chaleurs.

Gaspé fishermen

GASPÉ

A nine-metre granite cross erected here in 1934 commemorates Jacques Cartier's landing on July 24, 1534. He took possession of the Gaspé in the name of the King of France and erected a nine-metre wooden cross on the Pointe de Penouille. The fishing port that grew at the mouth of the York River overlooking the Baie de Gaspé was destroyed by British troops under James Wolfe in 1758. In the late 1700s many United Empire Loyalists settled in the area.
□ A provincial fish hatchery, Canada's oldest (1876), produces a million salmon and trout fry annually for Quebec lakes and rivers.
□ The Gaspé Museum has exhibits tracing the peninsula's history from the time of the Vikings, through the French regime to the present. Folklore and music of the Gaspé are featured in an audiovisual presentation.
□ Christ-Roi Cathedral is an ultra-modern structure built of wood in 1960.

Christ-Roi Cathedral, Gaspé

RÉSERVE PORT-DANIEL

From its headwaters in the Gaspé interior, the Rivière Port-Daniel flows through a deep, forested valley, part of which has been preserved in this park. Most of the lakes in the park have excellent brook trout fishing, and angling for Atlantic salmon is popular on the Rivière Port-Daniel.

Porcupine,

Map labels
Rivière-au-Renard
Morris
L'Anse-au-Griffon
FORILLON NAT PK (see Road Unit 130)
PTE DE PENOUÏLLE
Cap-des-Rosiers
Gaspé
Cap-aux-Os
Haldimand
R York
R St-Jean
Douglastown
BAIE DE GASPÉ
PARC FORT-PRÉVEL
St-Georges-de-Malbaie
Bridgeville
Coin-du-Banc
Percé
PERCÉ ROCK
L'Anse-au-Beaufils
PARC DE L'ÎLE BONAVENTURE
Grande-Rivière
Cap-d'Espoir
Pabos
Lac des Sept Iles
Chandler
GULF OF ST. LAWRENCE
RÉSERVE PORT-DANIEL
Pabos-Mills
Newport
Anse-aux-Gascons
Port-Daniel
Godefroi
Hope Town
ébiac

(see Road Unit 130)

Salmon Pie, Gaspé Style

This version of shepherd's pie is a regional dish of the Gaspé, whose rivers are among the finest Atlantic salmon waters in the world.

INGREDIENTS:

2 cups flaked cooked fresh salmon
(or 2 cups canned salmon)
2½ to 3 cups mashed potatoes
½ cup finely chopped onion
3 tablespoons butter
¼ teaspoon savory
pastry dough for one pie crust
salt and pepper

Combine the potatoes, onion, butter, and seasoning. Place half the potato mixture in the bottom of a greased, nine-inch pie plate or individual casseroles. Add salmon, and top with remaining potato. Cover with prepared pastry.

Bake in a 400°F oven for 25 to 30 minutes, or until golden brown. Makes six servings.

PERCÉ

Percé, once the largest fishing port in the Gaspé, is now a tourist and resort town. Behind the village are scenic hills and mountains. Atop 360-metre Mont Sainte-Anne is a statue of the saint, a landmark for fishermen at sea.
□ Percé Rock was named by Champlain for the soaring natural arch that distinguishes this enormous block of limestone in the Gulf of St. Lawrence.

Percé Rock

A Mountain Wilderness and Sandy, Pine-Clad Shores

Northern New Brunswick

By late spring the Atlantic salmon are running in the Restigouche Valley. Anglers and their guides, in long, green canoes, head upriver toward the sheltered pools and backwaters where the fish will rest on their way to the spawning grounds. The salmon run continues into early July, and the season ends with a gala festival in Campbellton.

Downriver, the Restigouche flows past Dalhousie into Chaleur Bay. Here, in summer, tourists sunbathe on the bay's sandy,

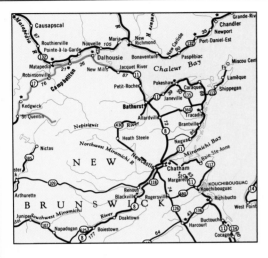

MORRISSY ROCK PROVINCIAL PARK
A high vantage point here provides a sweeping view of the Restigouche River valley, Quebec's Gaspé coast, and Sugarloaf—a volcanic peak that towers (305 metres) above Campbellton. In the Restigouche River fighting Atlantic salmon run large (the record is 25 kilograms). Though most salmon spawn in the fall, some enter fresh water in spring or early summer. In addition to superb sportfishing, the Restigouche provides some of New Brunswick's finest wilderness canoeing. A 149-kilometre route between Cedar Brook and Campbellton has fast water, rapids, tight turns and magnificent upland scenery.

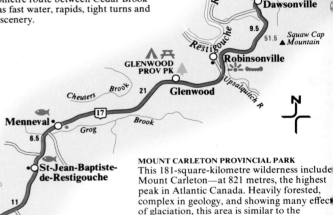

SQUAW CAP MOUNTAIN
Robinsonville, where the Upsalquitch River meanders toward its confluence with the Restigouche, offers a fine view of this 483-metre peak. In the heavily forested uplands of north-central New Brunswick, high peaks are often cloaked in mist while valleys are bright with sunshine.

Squaw Cap Mountain

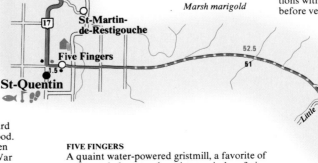

Marsh marigold

MOUNT CARLETON PROVINCIAL PARK
This 181-square-kilometre wilderness include Mount Carleton—at 821 metres, the highest peak in Atlantic Canada. Heavily forested, complex in geology, and showing many effec of glaciation, this area is similar to the Appalachians of New England.
□ About 100 species of birds and 30 species of mammals have been reported in the park. At Nictau Lake are the park headquarters an a primitive camping area with fireplaces and picnic tables. The clear, cold waters of Nictau and Nepisiguit lakes are good for swimming, canoeing and trout fishing. (Canoes and fishi guides are available for hire.) Old logging roa form a network of trails for snowmobiling, cross-country skiing and snowshoeing.
□ Roads to the park are closed at certain time of the year. Visitors should check on road con tions with the provincial tourism department before venturing to the park.

SAINT-QUENTIN
The Saint-Quentin area produces millions of board feet of lumber, and thousands of cords of pulpwood. The town, called Anderson Siding until 1919 when it was renamed to commemorate a First World War battle, is a seasonal headquarters for hunters and fishermen.

FIVE FINGERS
A quaint water-powered gristmill, a favorite of artists and photographers, is a reminder of pioneer days when local farmers brought grain for custom grinding. A 48-kilometre logging road leads east to Mount Carleton Provincial Park.

| 0 | 2 | 4 | 6 | 8 | 10 Miles |
| 0 | 4 | 8 | 12 | 16 Kilometres |

pine-clad shores; swim in its salt water; fish offshore for cod and mackerel; sail before a brisk ocean breeze; or dig for clams on sandbars at the mouth of the Eel River.

In autumn, inland from Campbellton, brilliant foliage transforms the vast forest into a dazzling tapestry splashed with gold and scarlet. Mount Carleton, Atlantic Canada's highest mountain, looms over the land. In this rugged wilderness, outdoor enthusiasts find pleasure in camping, canoeing, hiking, mountain climbing, photography,

bird-watching, rock hounding and fishing. Big-game hunters make their headquarters in villages such as Saint-Quentin, Kedgwick and Robinsonville.

In winter the snow-covered slopes of Sugarloaf, on the outskirts of Campbellton, are speckled with hundreds of brightly clad downhill skiers. At the base of the mountain there are skating ponds and a toboggan run. Cross-country skiers and snowshoers are invigorated by the scent of the pines and the clear, crisp air.

From salmon fishing to big-game hunting, from saltwater swimming to mountain climbing, northern New Brunswick offers an almost unlimited variety of outdoor activities. It is an uncrowded vacationland, and a place for all seasons.

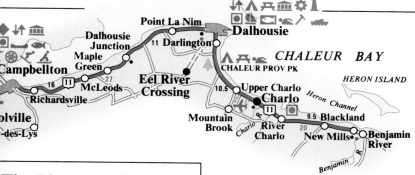

DALHOUSIE

This year-round port at the mouth of the Restigouche River offers deep-sea fishing and swimming in Chaleur Bay. Displays in the Chaleur Area History Museum deal with pioneer days in northeastern New Brunswick and with the growth of fishing, farming, and local industry. Tourists may also visit the New Brunswick International Paper Company plant.
□ At New Mills, 19 kilometres southeast, is a rearing pond where huge Atlantic salmon may be seen.

The Phantom Ship of Chaleur Bay

On stormy nights a mysterious, burning, square-rigged warship is said to haunt Chaleur Bay between Campbellton and Bathurst. Is it a ghostly reincarnation or is it a mirage? Witnesses have reported seeing a large, fully rigged, four-masted ship, with masts and sails ablaze. Some claim to have seen men scurrying about the flaming rigging. Those who have tried to approach the ship say it stays out of clear viewing distance. Eventually, it disappears.

Some say the phenomenon is merely the reflection of heat waves. Others insist it is a phantom—the ghost of a French ship that burned and sank in 1760 during the Battle of the Restigouche.

CAMPBELLTON

Campbellton is New Brunswick's fourth largest seaport and the commercial center of the province's north shore. In early July the city's annual salmon festival attracts thousands of visitors for several days of revelry. Restaurants serve huge salmon suppers, and there are flycasting contests, a trade fair, and cruises on the Restigouche River.
□ Sugarloaf, a mass of volcanic rock 305 metres high, overlooks the city, and is the highlight of Sugarloaf Provincial Park, where skiing, skating and tobogganing are popular.
□ A cairn in Riverside Park commemorates the last naval encounter of the Seven Years' War. In the 1760 Battle of the Restigouche, a French squadron was trapped and defeated by an overwhelming British force.

Skiing at Sugarloaf Provincial Park

Mount Carleton: A Mixed Forest of Hardwoods and Evergreens

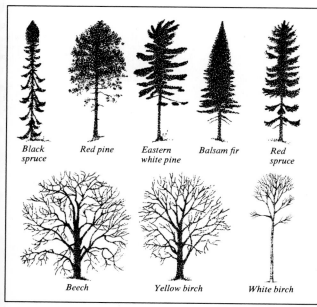

Black spruce *Red pine* *Eastern white pine* *Balsam fir* *Red spruce*

Beech *Yellow birch* *White birch*

More than half of Mount Carleton Provincial Park is, at high, dry elevations, burned-over forest that has regenerated into nearly pure stands of fire-resistant hardwoods. Yellow and white birches grow near lakes and streams. Beeches, with smooth, gray bark and dark green leaves, produce edible, three-cornered nuts. In autumn the vivid foliage of sugar maples brightens the landscape.

Softwoods thrive in the moist, low-lying areas. Stands of black spruce seldom exceed 15 metres. Red pines may reach 38 metres but usually grow to about 20. Moose eat the leaves of the trembling aspen and beavers feed on its pale, greenish white bark. Ground vegetation in the burned-over forest includes Dutchman's-breeches, bloodroot, wild ginger, trilliums and orchids.

The park area untouched by fire is mainly coniferous forest. The balsam fir,

a common Christmas tree, has upright seed-bearing cones. The red spruce has narrow, pendulous, egg-shaped cones that open in autumn and usually remain attached to the tree through winter. The eastern white pine grows to 30 metres and may live 450 years. Its seed cones mature in autumn and drop off in winter; the cones are food for squirrels, chipmunks and birds. Bunchberries, dainty evergreen twinflowers, club mosses and ferns grow on the floor of the park's coniferous forest.

In spring, the brilliant yellow flowers of the marsh marigold or cowslip brighten swamps, marshes and wet meadows. Fragrant water lilies, which float on ponds and slow-moving streams, bloom from June to September. Fish and mammals eat their leaves and protein-rich seeds. Alders, red-osier dogwoods and willows border marshy areas.

Farms, Fishing Villages and Picturesque Seascapes

The Acadian Peninsula

All along the Chaleur Bay coast is evidence of Acadian *joie de vivre*, self-reliance and determination to preserve a unique heritage.

The richness of this people's history is captured at the Acadian Historical Village (Village Historique Acadien), near Caraquet. Sod dikes have reclaimed marshes near the river for wheat, oats and hay. Reconstructed houses and public buildings mirror the tiniest details of early Acadian architecture. Small log farmhouses, their

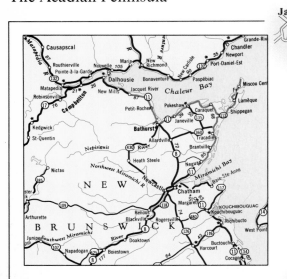

JACQUET RIVER
This town was probably named after James "Jock" Doyle who, despite threats and harassment by local Indians, settled near here in 1790 and for many years was the area's only white inhabitant.
□ Overlooking Chaleur Bay is Jacquet River Provincial Park, with picnicking and camping facilities.

BELLEDUNE
Silver and lead concentrate are produced here at the huge smelter of the Brunswick Mining and Smelting Corp. The minerals are extracted by melting down ore from the company's mine at Middle River.

PETIT-ROCHER
A grueling race across Chaleur Bay highlights the annual Festival des Rameurs (Rowers' Festival), here in early July. New Brunswick rowers line up the Quebec side of the bay and row 35.5 kilometres the finish line in Petit-Rocher harbor.

BATHURST
This fast-growing city, long prominent in the manufacturing of pulp and paper, has been at the heart of a base metals mining boom since 1953.
□ On a hill overlooking the city is the Collège de Bathurst, an affiliate of the Université de Moncton. Another landmark is Sacré-Cœur Cathedral.
□ A cairn honors Nicolas Denys, French "Governor of the coasts and islands of the St. Lawrence," who founded a trading and fishing post at Bathurst (then Nepisiguit) in 1652.
□ Beresford Beach and Youghall Beach provincial parks, north of Bathurst, offer warm saltwater swimming in Chaleur Bay. West of the city, beside Tetagouche Falls, is a scenic rest area. Upstream on the Nepisiguit River is Pabineau Falls; farther upstream is Grand Falls, a series of cataracts where the river drops 43 metres.

An Underground 'City,' and a Man-Made Canyon

A steel cage takes visitors 400 metres down into a subterranean "city" at the below-ground workings of Brunswick Mining and Smelting Corp., 37 kilometres southwest of Bathurst. During a tour of the mine visitors learn about hard-rock mining, watch drilling operations and see the heavy machinery that is used to haul zinc, lead, silver and copper ore to the surface.

About 10 kilometres south is an open-pit mine—a man-made canyon 100 metres deep. From the top of the pit, huge trucks and bulldozers look like toys as they wind their way up a curved roadway.

Gull Island, Pokeshaw

POKESHAW
Offshore is Gull Island, where hundreds of seabirds rest on the branches of trees killed years ago when the island was struck by lightning. The stark, flat-topped island is a favorite of artists and photographers.
□ Nearby Stonehaven was once a major producer of grindstones.

| 0 | 2 | 4 | 6 | 8 | 10 Miles |
| 0 | 4 | 8 | 12 | 16 Kilometres |

vegetable gardens planted in neat rows, nestle in clearings cut in stands of white birch. Costumed staff demonstrate pioneer skills: men square timbers, make shingles, dry and barrel salted cod; women spin wool, hook rugs, churn butter and bake bread. Visitors can eat homemade meals and sip wine in a public house that dates from 1875, and tour the village in a *carriole* drawn by horses or oxen.

Acadian gaiety and enthusiasm enliven annual festivals in Pointe-Verte, Nigadoo, Petit-Rocher, Shippegan, Lamèque and Caraquet—where the famous blessing of the fishing fleet highlights the Acadian Festival in mid-August. Also in Caraquet is a bustling fishermen's market, an Acadian museum and a historic chapel more than two centuries old. Elsewhere along the coast are farms, fishing villages, picturesque seascapes, and occasional reminders of the past—an abandoned farmhouse, old and gray, its windows shuttered; or the beached, battered hulk of a fishing boat.

CARAQUET
A ritual blessing of the fishing fleet of northeastern New Brunswick, symbolic of Christ's blessing of the fishermen of Galilee, opens the annual eight-day Acadian Festival here in mid-August. As many as 60 boats, from draggers to small craft, all decorated with flags and bunting, are blessed by the bishop of Bathurst. On succeeding days there are sports events and parades; the nights are filled with Acadian songs, poetry and dances.
□ Charter boats take tourists deep-sea fishing for giant bluefin. Fresh-caught shellfish and groundfish are sold at the fishermen's market on the town wharf. Visitors to a canning factory can watch the processing of queen crabs.
□ One of many exhibits in the Acadian Museum is a violin brought here from Nova Scotia at the time of the expulsion in 1755.
□ Most of Caraquet's 3,000 persons live close to its 13-kilometre main street, the longest in the Maritimes.

Where Acadia's Homespun Heritage Lives On

Acadian haystacks

La Maison Godin, Acadian Historical Village

A pioneer Acadian community has been recreated on a 10.5-square-kilometre site between Grande-Anse and Caraquet. In addition to 10 dwellings, Acadian Historical Village has a smithy, a warehouse, a general store, a one-room schoolhouse, a chapel, and a public tavern. Along the banks of the Rivière du Nord are diked farmlands.

The men, women and children of the village wear colorful homespuns and live as their Acadian forebears lived. Some tend fields and cattle; others churn butter, make clothing, build furniture, split shingles, and perform a myriad of other chores.

Expelled from the Maritimes by the British in 1755, thousands of Acadian refugees spent years of exile in Massachusetts, Virginia, Louisiana and France. Most of them returned to the Maritimes, and between 1780 and 1880 they built primitive settlements along the coast of northeastern New Brunswick.

Some of the reconstructed buildings in the Acadian Historical Village come from as far away as Fredericton and Edmundston. The oldest building is the Martin farmhouse (1783). A log cabin with an earthen floor, it stood for nearly two centuries at French Village, near Fredericton.

MISCOU ISLAND
This "Land's End" of New Brunswick—only 18 kilometres long and 13 kilometres wide—has changed little since its first settlers arrived from France and the Channel Islands. Spruce trees, dwarfed by wind and salt spray, overlook deserted white sandy beaches. In summer and fall, local fishermen offer deep-sea fishing charters.
□ A free government-operated ferry links Miscou with Ile Lamèque and the mainland.
□ Miscou islanders speak a unique *patois* that some linguists claim is pure Old French.

Queen crab

ÎLE LAMÈQUE
Vast bogs here are among Canada's major sources of peat moss. Most of the local product is shipped to the United States as soil conditioner, stable and poultry litter, insulation and packing material.
□ The village of Lamèque holds a Peat Moss Festival in late July.

SHIPPEGAN
Delicious seafood platters are served here during the July Fisheries Festival which also features street dancing, deep-sea fishing trips, and tours of fish-packing plants and nearby peat bogs.
□ Shippegan Provincial Park, west of town, has camping and picnicking facilities, and a beach.

Fishermen's wharf, Shippegan

Lumberjacks, Legends and a Wild Waterfall

Upper Saint John River Valley

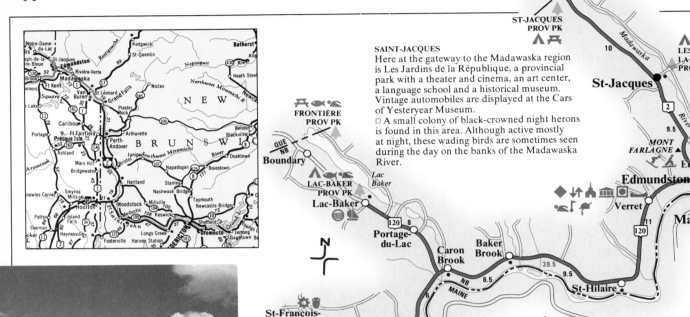

Black-crowned night heron

SAINT-JACQUES
Here at the gateway to the Madawaska region is Les Jardins de la République, a provincial park with a theater and cinema, an art center, a language school and a historical museum. Vintage automobiles are displayed at the Cars of Yesteryear Museum.
□ A small colony of black-crowned night herons is found in this area. Although active mostly at night, these wading birds are sometimes seen during the day on the banks of the Madawaska River.

Tau cross by Claude Roussel

SAINT-FRANÇOIS-DE-MADAWASKA
Visitors may tour a furniture plant and a handicraft center here. Lac Baker, north of the town, is bordered by sandy beaches. The town's two provincial parks, Lac Baker and Frontière (day-use only), have marinas, permit waterskiing and the trout fishing is excellent.
□ At nearby Clair an international bridge leads to Fort Kent, Maine.

EDMUNDSTON
Straddling the junction of the Madawaska and Saint John rivers, this predominantly French-speaking community was named in 1853 after New Brunswick governor, Sir Edmund Head. Today it is a thriving pulp-producing center. (The Fraser plant here may be toured.)
□ At the Church of Our Lady of Sorrows are intricate wood carvings of the 14 Stations of the Cross by Claude Roussel. One of these is a pre-Christian tau cross, which resembles the Greek capital T.
□ The twin-spired, stone and marble Cathedral of the Immaculate Conception is a fine example of rich architectural design.

Saint-François-de-Madawaska

Six Red Stars and an Eagle— Symbols of 'la République'

In 1837 the timber-rich Madawaska region was involved in a boundary dispute between New Brunswick and Maine. Lumbermen on both sides of the Saint John River fought in what became known as the Aroostook or "Pork and Beans War." The conflict was resolved in 1842 under the Webster-Ashburton Treaty, but five years of tug-of-war tactics between the American and Canadian governments had created a concept of an independent Madawaska—a *republic* of Madawaska.

The title is thought to have originated with a response given by a colonist to a French official. Thinking the official too inquisitive, the colonist remarked: "I am a citizen of the Republic of Madawaska." The name stuck.

In 1949, recognizing the publicity value of this historical quirk—a republic in the heart of a constitutional monarchy—two New Brunswickers prepared a coat of arms for Madawaska. Edmundston became the republic's capital (mayors of Edmundston automatically hold the title of president of the republic) and an official flag was designed. The flag features a bald eagle, symbol of Madawaska's independent spirit. Six red stars represent the republic's cultural groups: Indian, Acadian, Canadian, English, American and Irish.

Important visitors to the republic are often presented with honorary citizenships, and may even be addressed in the republic's own dialect—known as "Brayon."

The Saint John River winds through forest and field and primeval gorge on its journey across Madawaska County. It dominates the rich, gently rolling landscape of this region and at Grand Falls plunges 25 metres over the province's highest escarpment. The river forms almost 110 kilometres of the Canada–United States border, and is skirted for most of its length in New Brunswick by the Trans-Canada Highway.

Malecite Indians were here when explorers de Monts and Champlain named the river on June 24, 1604—the feast day of St. John. The region was later inhabited by settlers from Quebec.

In the 1800s Madawaska was a land of riotous lumber camps. But today the rip-roaring life of the lumberjacks is little more than folklore among a people whose love of dancing and music, work and independence is instantly recognizable.

An effortless bilingualism unites residents of Madawaska—conversations often switch back and forth between French and English. Architectural styles reflect differences between the two cultures. English towns tend to have tree-lined roads, ornate houses set well back from the road, and several small wooden churches. The French towns have few roadside trees, and houses are often simple frame structures built close together. A single stone church usually overlooks each French community.

SAINT-BASILE

Founded in 1792, this tiny parish is the oldest in Madawaska County. The Saint-Basile Chapel Museum, a log replica of the area's first chapel (1780), displays pioneer household utensils. A nearby Malecite Indian reserve, established in 1824, may be visited. Saint-Basile hosts the Madawaska County Fair in late August. North of the town is Saint-Basile Provincial Park.

'Main John' Glasier, the First Man to Drive Logs Over Grand Falls

John Glasier was a pioneer lumberman in the Madawaska region. Born in 1809, he was the first to drive logs over Grand Falls, and the first to explore the Squatec Lakes in Quebec. A rugged bear of a fellow, he towered over other men and added to his height by wearing a tall black hat—even in bed, according to legend.

Early in life Glasier employed some 600 men to run New Brunswick's largest lumbering operation. As his reputation grew, he acquired the nickname "Main John"—a title that identified him as the man in charge. The expression was later used throughout North America to designate the manager of any large lumber camp.

Glasier became a member of the New Brunswick legislature in 1861. Seven years later he was named to the Canadian Senate. He died in 1894 and was immortalized in a poem by H. A. Cody:

Don't you see the "Main John" striding in the lead?
Clear-eyed, strong and fearless, kith of Bluenose breed;
First to bring a timber drive through the wild Grand Falls;
First to sight the Squattook Lakes where the lone moose calls.
Haunter of the silent ways,
Spirit of the glen,
Dauntless as in olden days
Glasier leads his men.

SAINT-LÉONARD

Linked to the United States by an international bridge over the Saint John River, this busy rural community is a communications center for the large lumbering and agricultural area that surrounds it. Potatoes are the main crop. Local schools open in early August so that students can leave in September to help with the harvest.
□ Saint-Léonard is the home of the famous Madawaska Weavers, whose colorful hand-loomed skirts, scarves and ties are worn throughout the world. The Weavers' store-workshop on Main Street may be visited.
□ Saint-Léonard Provincial Park, about two kilometres northeast of town, has picnic and camping sites.

Weavers at Saint-Léonard

GRAND FALLS

Here the mighty Saint John River plunges into a gorge of half-billion-year-old rock. The river's power is channeled through a hydroelectric station in a lower basin. Malecite Indians named the falls *Chik-un-il-pe*—"the destroying giant"—probably because of its awesome appearance. Legend attributes the name to the time a band of invading Mohawks perished in the torrent. In lumbering days logs caught in a whirlpool (known as "the coffee mill") below the falls were ground to a point.
□ Grand Falls' 38-metre-wide main street, originally a military parade ground, is believed to be the widest in Canada. In early summer the town hosts a potato festival.

Grand Falls

A Tradition of Hospitality in Bountiful Potato Country

Upper Saint John River Valley

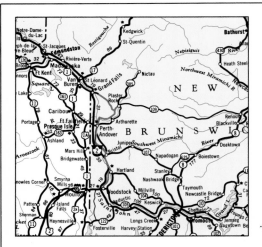

DRUMMOND

Since the 1860s, Drummond and its surroundings have prospered from potato farming. The first bushel of potatoes grown here was planted by Barney McLaughlin, an Irishman. Today most Drummond farmers are of French descent. Schools here open in early August so that students can leave for three weeks in September to help with the harvest. The crop is stored in potato barns—storage sheds partly buried in the ground to protect against frost.

Potato barn, Drummond

Greens for Gourmets

Fiddleheads, unopened fronds of the ostrich fern, are harvested in New Brunswick when they poke through the moist woodland floor and on riverbanks moist from spring runoff. Harvesters gather about 114 tonnes of the fast-growing shoots each spring. The plants are packaged and frozen in Florenceville. When boiled, the greens are a succulent delicacy. For centuries, New Brunswick's Malecite Indians have prized fiddleheads as food and medicine. Now the plant is big business and something of a provincial symbol: Fredericton stages an annual fiddlehead festival; a radio station boasts of serving "fiddlehead country," and the University of New Brunswick publishes a literary magazine called *The Fiddlehead*.

BEECHWOOD

Visitors to Beechwood's hydro-electric plant may watch a fish elevator lifting Atlantic salmon over an 18-metre dam on the Saint John River. The plant's grounds feature a floral clock.

□ North of Beechwood, a hillside setting of beech and maple adds to the picnicking and camping pleasures of Muniac Provincial Park.

FLORENCEVILLE

Canada's largest frozen food plant is operated by family-owned McCain Foods Ltd. The company processes potato specialties, fiddleheads, vegetables and desserts. Tours are available.

□ Visitors are welcome at a federal fish hatchery in this town.

□ Once known as Buttermilk Creek, Florenceville was renamed for nurse Florence Nightingale, heroine of the Crimean War.

UPPER WOODSTOCK

Historic documents, costumes, photographs, paintings, an old law book and a blotting sand bottle are preserved in the Old Carleton County Courthouse (1833), whose courtroom, jury and lawyers' rooms have been restored. This elegant, two-story, clapboard museum was the seat of New Brunswick's first county council. It has also been a stagecoach stop, and the scene of agricultural fairs, political rallies and governors' levees. One exhibit recalls Edwin Tappan Adney, a local author, artist, naturalist, authority on heraldic design and expert on North American Indian crafts. Another exhibit includes 1,000 lead soldiers, replicas of British regiments of the 18th and 19th centuries.

Old Carleton County Courthouse, Upper Woodstock

Toy soldiers, Old Carleton County Courthouse

| 0 | 2 | 4 | 6 | 8 | 10 Miles |

| 0 | 4 | 8 | 12 | 16 Kilometres |

The Saint John River: *Oo-lahs-took* the Indians called it—the goodly river. And goodly it remains to those who till its valley soil. This is potato country—a peaceful, prosperous land where potato-blossom festivals (at Grand Falls and Hartland) pay homage to the bounty of the soil, and where bushels of the vegetables roll off production lines as french fries, hash browns and instant mashed. The fields that produced them stretch to the horizon.

Agriculture is a common bond uniting diverse communities in this region. Between Perth-Andover and Woodstock gospel tents dot the countryside, and Bible texts on billboards and barn gables exhort repentence. Stately homes set among elms and maples are the hallmark of Woodstock, "the hospitality town." Its settlers decreed that "no visitor, known or unknown, should pass through this community without sharing its hospitality."

Woodstock's hospitality is particularly warm during Old Home Week, an annual July celebration that includes horse-pulling contests and harness racing. In Woodstock, visitors can see the house outside which, in 1860, Charles Connell, the eccentric provincial postmaster general, lit a bonfire and burned half a million stamps on which he had printed his own portrait.

In spring, travelers on this route can pluck and savor fiddleheads. In any season they can explore one of New Brunswick's most famous landmarks—the world's longest covered bridge at Hartland.

NEW DENMARK

Many of the 1,000 persons in this town wear Danish dress and enjoy traditional dances each June 19—Founders' Day in Canada's largest Danish community. The festivities commemorate 29 immigrants who settled at the junction of the Saint John and Salmon rivers in 1872.
□ The New Denmark Memorial Museum, on the site of the original clearing, displays early tax records, and settlers' clothing, including an old wedding dress and boots from an immigrant's army service in Denmark.

Folk dancing, New Denmark

PLASTER ROCK

At Plaster Rock, gateway to the highlands of northern New Brunswick, the Tobique River loops green and swift through red gypsum hills for which this lumbering and agricultural town is named. The Tobique, main tributary of the Saint John, provides a 137-kilometre canoe route through wilderness inhabited by black bears, moose, white-tailed deer, marten, ruffed grouse and black ducks. The route includes fast water, rapids, tight turns and the calm waters of the Tobique Reservoir. Upriver from Plaster Rock, guides and outfitters cater to hunters and fishermen.

PERTH-ANDOVER

Originally logging and portage centers, settled in 1851 by British soldiers who received land in lieu of pay, Perth and Andover were amalgamated in 1966.
□ The Aroostook Valley Country Club hosts international golf tournaments. Its 18-hole course is partly in New Brunswick, partly in Maine.

HARTLAND

Where the world's longest covered bridge (391 metres) spans the Saint John River at Hartland, you may cross your fingers, hold your breath and make a wish: according to local lore, dreams come true for those who cross the seven-span giant without exhaling. Built in 1896, it was a toll bridge until 1904. Upstream is the Hugh John Flemming Bridge, erected in 1955 as part of the Trans-Canada Highway.

WOODSTOCK

A two-story wooden dwelling built in the 1820s by Charles Connell is one of several stately old homes here. Connell, postmaster general of New Brunswick in 1858-61, is famous for substituting his own likeness for one of Queen Victoria on an 1860 issue of stamps. In the ensuing protest Connell burned the stamps and resigned.
□ Harness racing, golf, swimming and a weekly farmers' market are among the attractions in Connell Park.

Tobique River, Plaster Rock

Sheltering Spans of Yesteryear

Wishing or kissing bridges are romantic relics of a bygone age. Wishin' may indeed have become kissin' under those wooden rafters of yesteryear, but it was common sense not dreams and romance that inspired the building of Canada's covered bridges.

An uncovered wooden bridge lasted only 15 years before rot weakened its underpinnings and broad deck planks. Horses, frightened by rushing waters glimpsed through the timber floor, shied and bolted. With a roof and siding—cheap and easy to install—a bridge was good for 80 years. And animals, reassured by the stablelike structure, trotted docilely through.

Covered bridges were "high enough and wide enough to take a load of hay." Snow was spread on the carriageway in winter to ease sled traffic. The bridges

World's longest covered bridge, Hartland

served as notice boards for circuses and patent medicines.

Of the thousands of covered bridges built at the turn of the century, fewer than 200 are still standing and most of these are in Quebec and New Brunswick. At Hartland, N.B., the world's longest covered bridge (*above*) is a 391-metre giant whose seven spans leap the Saint John River. The original cedar log abutments and rock-filled piers of 1899 were replaced by concrete in 1920.

A City of Stately Elms
Where Past and Present Merge

Lower Saint John River Valley

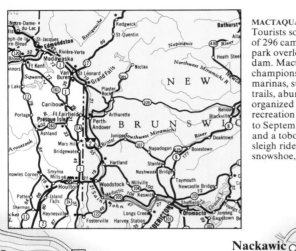

Glass blower, Opus Craft Village

MACTAQUAC PROVINCIAL PARK

Tourists sometimes wait in line all night for one of 296 campsites in New Brunswick's all-seasons park overlooking the head pond of the Mactaquac dam. Mactaquac Provincial Park has an 18-hole championship golf course, sailboat and powerboat marinas, supervised beaches, hiking and nature trails, abundant picnic grounds, playgrounds with organized activities, an amphitheater, a rainy-day recreation building, and a campers' store (May to September). There are winter campsites, too, and a toboggan run, lighted skating ponds, sleigh rides, ice fishing, and snowmobile, snowshoe, and cross-country ski trails.

OPUS CRAFT VILLAGE

Blacksmiths, candlemakers, glassblowers, leather-crafters and potters make all the merchandise in New Brunswick's only contemporary craft village—a cluster of privately owned studios near the entrance to Mactaquac Provincial Park. The village is open daily, throughout the year, and visitors may watch the craftsmen at work.

MEDUCTIC

A cairn records that here were a church built by Malecite Indians in 1717, a Malecite village, and a fort that was the chief Indian stronghold on the Saint John River in the 17th and 18th centuries. John Gyles, the nine-year-old son of a New England judge, was seized by the Malecites in 1689 and held captive here for six years. In 1698, three years after being sold to a French trader, Gyles was reunited with his family in Boston.

Warm Hearths and Creaking Oxcarts

The sights and sounds of New Brunswick's past are everywhere in Kings Landing Historical Settlement at Prince William. Many of the buildings were moved here when the Mactaquac dam, 22.5 kilometres downstream, flooded the Saint John River valley. There are about 60 buildings, including 13 houses, a water-powered sawmill (right), a smithy, a carpenter's shop and a general store.

The settlement and its costumed staff recreate New Brunswick community life of 1790-1870. Fires crackle on open hearths in houses where women do spinning and weaving, churn butter and make soap. Guests down mugs of draft beer in the cozy taproom of the Kings Head Inn, or sample 1850s-style fare in its dining room.

The elegantly furnished Ingraham House typifies the surroundings of a wealthy New Brunswick family of the 1840s. The plush parlor and formal dining room of the Hagerman House mirror the life of the well-to-do of the 1870s. Joslin Farm shows how a farm family of the 1860s lived. Scythes swish through the farm's meadows; oxcarts and horse-drawn buggies creak along its dirt lanes.

Kings Landing Historical Settlement is open from June 1 to Labor Day.

WOOLASTOOK PROVINCIAL WILDLIFE PARK

Nature trails in Woolastook Provincial Wildlife Park pass enclosures where caribou, moose, lynx and panthers roam in natural surroundings. There are some 30 species of wildlife in this provincial park at Longs Creek on the Mactaquac head pond. There are picnic facilities, a boat ramp, a lake that serves as a waterfowl sanctuary, and a gift shop featuring New Brunswick crafts.

□ Woolastook, the name early settlers gave the Saint John River, comes from the Indian Oo-lahs-took, goodly river.

Monuments, cairns and the Kings Landing Historical Settlement are reminders that this region is proud of its rich past. Sophisticated tourist attractions and a major hydroelectric plant are evidence of people attuned to today.

Past and present merge in Fredericton, provincial capital of New Brunswick. Stately elms, gracious homes and historic buildings recall the wealthy 19th-century merchants and lumber barons who built this city.

Fredericton's modern structures include the Centennial Building, a provincial government office complex. A handsome art gallery, a theater, an arena and a gymnasium were endowed by Lord Beaverbrook.

Now the hub of prosperous farming country, Fredericton was a wilderness when Loyalists settled at Sainte-Anne's Point in 1783-84. In 1785 they renamed it for a son of George III and founded the college from which sprang the University of New Brunswick, Canada's oldest provincial university.

The nation's first astronomical observatory (1851) and first engineering school (1854) are here.

A memorial on the UNB campus honors poets Bliss Carman, Sir Charles G. D. Roberts and Francis Joseph Sherman, all New Brunswickers. Odell Park is named for another poet, Jonathan Odell, the first provincial secretary. The stone house he built in 1785 is now the residence of the Anglican dean of Fredericton. It is the oldest dwelling in a city that treasures its past.

FREDERICTON

New Brunswick's majestic Legislative Building, a silver-domed, Victorian edifice built in 1880, is the most celebrated of Fredericton's historic buildings. The city's military and social history is enshrined in the officers' quarters (1839-69), barracks and guardhouse of the Military Compound, across from Officers Square. In the York-Sunbury Historical Society Museum in the officers' quarters are fine collections of coverlets, furniture and uniforms.

□ Christ Church Cathedral, a Gothic structure built in 1845-53, houses a gold altar cloth used at the coronation of William IV of England, a pulpit hanging made from part of Queen Victoria's coronation robe, and the letters patent issued by Queen Victoria in 1845, constituting Fredericton as a city.

□ Opposite Wilmot Park is Old Government House, the imposing Georgian home of colonial governors from 1828, and of lieutenant governors from 1867 to 1893. Now the headquarters of an RCMP division, the building is not open to the public.

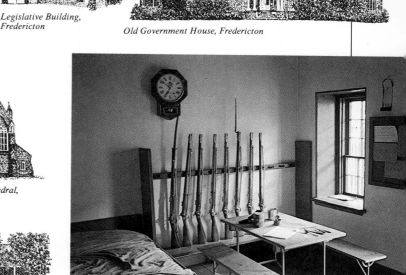

Legislative Building, Fredericton

Old Government House, Fredericton

Christ Church Cathedral, Fredericton

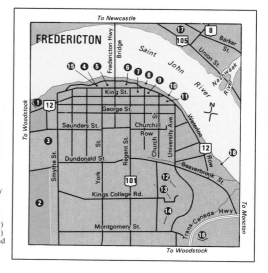

Orderly room, Fredericton Military Compound

Purple martins

Officers' quarters, Fredericton

Beaverbrook's Gift— a Gallery of Great Pictures

Lord Beaverbrook said that the best picture in Fredericton's Beaverbrook Art Gallery was the view of the Saint John River from the great window in the main gallery. But the painting that attracts most visitors is Salvador Dali's large *Santiago el Grande*. The gallery, one of Beaverbrook's gifts to the city, houses a collection of British art. There are paintings by Reynolds, Gainsborough, Constable, Romney, Turner and Hogarth. Several of Sir Winston Churchill's canvases are here. The Canadian collection includes 34 Krieghoffs, and works by Tom Thomson, Arthur Lismer, Paul Kane and Emily Carr. In the Lucile Pillow Room are 130 porcelain pieces representing the best of English artistry between 1743 and 1840. *Right:* a Chelsea Goat and Bee jug (1743).

1 Old Government House
2 Odell Park
3 Exhibition Grounds
4 City Hall
5 Military Compound
6 Officers' Square
7 The Playhouse
8 Beaverbrook Art Gallery
9 Legislative Building
10 The Green
11 Christ Church Cathedral
12 Poets' Corner
13 University of New Brunswick
14 St. Thomas University
15 Tourist Information Center
16 Tourist Information (open in summer only)
17 Fort Nashwaak (cairn)
18 Loyalist Burial Ground

Line-Busting Salmon in a Land of Song

Nashwaak-Miramichi Trail

All morning the angler has been casting over his favorite stretch of water on the Southwest Miramichi.

Suddenly there is a flash of silver and a tug that bows the angler's rod. The reel screams as a salmon takes out line, dashes almost to the opposite shore, then downstream. The fish leaps far out of the water, hangs poised for a breathless second, then falls with a splash. Again the salmon leaps and strikes the water on its side with a sound like breaking glass. With luck, patience will

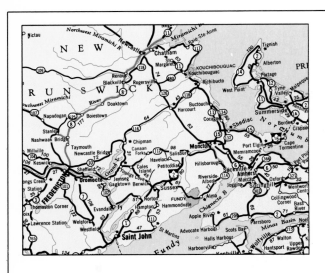

BOIESTOWN

This village, a lumbering and outfitting center, is at the geographical midpoint of New Brunswick. For travelers heading northeast from Fredericton on Route 8, Boiestown provides the first glimpse of the world-renowned salmon river, the Southwest Miramichi. Sport fishermen flock to the area from April to May during the spring run of Atlantic salmon, although the "early-run" fish are not so firm or tasty as the silver salmon taken from May to September.

□ Red Pines Provincial Park has picnic and camping sites on the banks of the Southwest Miramichi River. Thirteen kilometres northeast is the village of McNamee, where the river is spanned by a 200-metre swinging footbridge, the only one in New Brunswick.

□ Fishing and hunting camps operated by outfitters abound in and around Boiestown, Ludlow, McNamee, Doaktown, Blissfield, Upper Blackville and Blackville.

Salmon angling on the Southwest Miramichi

STANLEY

The mid-August Stanley Fair, established in 1851, celebrates the harvest with square dancing and old-time fiddle playing. Local farmers (most are descendants of Scottish and Welsh settlers) display produce and livestock. The fair's motto is "Speed the Plow!"

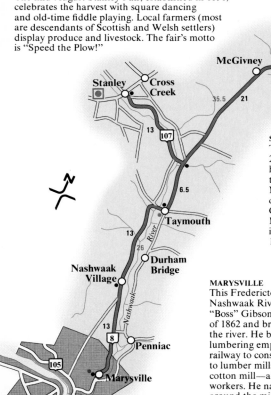

SOUTHWEST MIRAMICHI RIVER

This world-famous salmon river flows 217 kilometres from the heavily forested highlands of central New Brunswick to the rolling lowlands hugging Northumberland Strait and the Gulf of St. Lawrence. Newcastle and Chatham, on opposite banks of the Miramichi, lie near the estuary. The river is up to one kilometre wide and up to 14 metres deep.

MARYSVILLE

This Fredericton suburb near the mouth of the Nashwaak River was founded by Alexander "Boss" Gibson, who arrived here in the summer of 1862 and brought the first log drive down the river. He built sawmills and an extensive lumbering empire, and even constructed a railway to consolidate his holdings. In addition to lumber mills, Gibson built a large red brick cotton mill—along with row housing for his workers. He named the town which grew up around the mill, Marysville, in honor of his wife.

Southwest Miramichi River

(see Road Unit 136)

FREDERICTON

| 0 | 2 | 4 | 6 | 8 | 10 Miles |
| 0 | 4 | 8 | 12 | 16 Kilometres |

soon pay off handsomely for yet another sportsman, lured to the Southwest Miramichi River by tales of line-busting Atlantic salmon.

Northbound highway travelers on the Nashwaak-Miramichi Trail first glimpse the Southwest Miramichi at Boiestown, the geographical center of New Brunswick. The trail follows the Nashwaak River north from Fredericton, then heads along the Southwest Miramichi—through the spectacular scenery of central New Bruns-

wick—to the sea, and the thriving ports of Newcastle and Chatham.

Basque and French fishermen came to Miramichi Bay in the early 1500s, though the first recorded voyage was that of Jacques Cartier in 1534. In 1686, Baptiste Franquelin, a French engineer-cartographer, mapped the river and its numerous tributaries, and recorded their Indian names.

Then came the valley's hardy pioneers—lumbermen and shipbuilders—and with them, their songs. Singing remained a major

part of Miramichi life in horse-and-buggy days, when songs were carefully chosen to last the length of a journey. Today the people of the region celebrate their love of music at the three-day Miramichi Folk Song Festival in Newcastle in June.

McDonald farmhouse, Bartibog Bridge

BLACKVILLE
The 61 kilometres between Blackville and Boiestown are the legendary haunt of the Dungarvon Whooper, the ghost of a lumber camp cook who was robbed and murdered on the bank of the Dungarvon River in the 1860s. After the young man was buried in a shallow grave, people in the area began to hear loud, blood-curdling screams. Unwary travelers are warned to "beware of the smell of frying bacon"—with which the Whooper tries to lure his murderer.

BARTIBOG BRIDGE
Overlooking Miramichi Bay is an eight-room sandstone house built in the 1820s by Alexander McDonald, a Scottish soldier who settled here after serving with MacDonald's Highlanders in the American Revolution. His handsome 2½-story house has been chosen for restoration as the centerpiece of a provincial historic park, which will recreate a complete working farm of the 1800s.

NEWCASTLE
This town of large frame buildings, many of them built by 19th-century lumber barons after the 1825 Miramichi Fire leveled all but 12 of the town's 260 buildings, is the birthplace of the British newspaper baron, Lord Beaverbrook. Born Max Aitken, he grew up in the Old Manse—now a library and museum—adjacent to St. James Church.
□ When his title was bestowed, Aitken chose the name Beaverbrook in honor of a small stream where he used to fish near his home. A bronze bust of Beaverbrook stands on a pedestal in the Town Square. When Beaverbrook died in 1964, his body was cremated and his ashes were placed in the base of the monument.

Lord Beaverbrook monument, Newcastle

Governor's Mansion, Nelson-Miramichi

CHATHAM
Cunard family documents and records are displayed in the Miramichi Natural History Museum. Joseph Cunard, a member of the family which founded the steamship line, came here in 1820 from his native Halifax to establish a branch of the family's banking, shipping, iron, lumber and coal business. At one time almost the whole population of the Miramichi area depended on the Cunards for a living. The splendor of the Cunard empire in Chatham lasted for 28 years—until the advent of steel ships and the steam engine.
□ Middle Island, joined to the mainland by a causeway, is a provincial park and picnic site.
□ Chatham is linked with Douglastown and Newcastle by the Miramichi Centennial bridge. CFB Chatham, one of Canada's largest jet-training facilities, is southeast of the town.

NELSON-MIRAMICHI
Loyalist ladder-back chairs that were brought to New Brunswick after the American Revolution are among antiques displayed in the Governor's Mansion and an adjacent museum, on the former estate of a wealthy lumberman. Other furnishings in the two buildings include a grandfather clock that stood for more than a century in the old Royal Hotel in Saint John; oriental rugs from the summer home of Sir William Cornelius Van Horne on Ministers Island near St. Andrews, N.B.; and a military chest that belonged to Colonel Rainsford, commander of the 104th New Brunswick Regiment on its march from Fredericton to Kingston, Ont., during the War of 1812.

Biplane "air tankers," Upper Blackville

UPPER BLACKVILLE
An airstrip here is maintained by the Forest Protection Branch of New Brunswick's Natural Resources Department. The strip is provincial headquarters for light aircraft, which patrol vast tracts of forest, and one of the bases for monitoring forest fires. A fleet of biplane "air tankers" is used for bombing trees with chemical fire retardants.

Come All Ye Down to the Miramichi . . .

Acadian step dances and the traditional songs of New Brunswick's colorful lumbermen are highlights of the Miramichi Folk Song Festival at Newcastle in late June. Long narrative chants about great feats and lost loves are sung to the foot-tapping music of fiddle, banjo, accordion and mouth organ.

The Jones Boys, a one-verse ditty, was a favorite of Lord Beaverbrook. The bells he

gave to the University of New Brunswick at Fredericton ring out that chorus on the hour. Another popular ballad is *Peter Emberley,* a tale of a young man fatally injured in the Miramichi woods.

Other festival favorites include ballads that begin with "Come all ye jolly lumbermen . . ." and "good night" songs—those once sung at public executions.

My name 'tis Pe - ter   Em - ber - ley.

I landed in New Brunswick in a lumbering counterie,
I hired to work in the lumber woods on the Sou-West Miramichi.
I hired to work in the lumber woods where they cut the tall spruce down,
While loading teams with yarded logs I received a deadly wound.

The World's Lobster Capital and Its Largest Hayfield

Southeastern New Brunswick

ESCUMINAC

A striking concrete sculpture by Acadian artist Claude Roussel stands in memory of 35 fishermen l in a storm on Miramichi Bay in June 1959. Paid for the New Brunswick Fishermen's Memorial Fund, t monument was commissioned by Sir Max Aitken, s of Lord Beaverbrook.

Sculpture by Claude Roussel at Escumina

RICHIBUCTO

St. Louis of Aloysius Roman Catholic Church symbolizes this community's ties with the sea. The contour roof of the circular building represents ocean waves; the bell tower suggests a lighthouse.
□ Portraits of prominent local citizens hang in the Kent County courthouse.
□ The Richibucto River Museum features the history of Kent County.

KOUCHIBOUGUAC NATIONAL PARK

Boardwalks in this park on Kouchibouguac Bay lead to a 25-kilometre sweep of offshore sandbars, tidewater lagoons and grassy salt marshes. Marram grass and false heather anchor shoreline dunes. Peat bogs, underlying the marshes and dunes, encourage the growth of bog laurel, lambkill, white-fringed orchids, and insect-eating sundews and pitcher plants. Inland is mixed forest of black spruce, white pine, jack pine, yellow birch and trembling aspen. More than 200 species of birds and 15 species of mammals have been sighted in the 241-square-kilometre park. There is good swimming in the warm water of Northumberland Strait. Other park activities include camping, canoeing, hiking, fishing and cross-country skiing.

Sundew

Bog laurel

REXTON

A stone cairn here commemorates Andrew Bonar Law, a Rexton native who became prime minister of Britain. The gabled farmhouse where he was born in 1858 still stands. At age 12 Bonar Law went to live in Glasgow, Scotland. Elected to British Parliament in 1900, he was prime minister in 1922-23.

Specialities from Acadian Kitchens

For centuries Acadians have reaped the sea's harvest and tilled the fertile soil of the Maritimes. Fish and vegetables are important ingredients in traditional Acadian cooking. Mackerel, herring or cod is boiled in salted water and served with potatoes; hearty chowder is made with clams, oysters or lobsters, and potatoes and onions. Turnips, cabbages or red beans are often combined with bacon.

Several Moncton area restaurants prepare Acadian specialities like *pot-en-pot*, a chicken stew cooked with homemade noodles, and *poutines râpées*, large balls of grated and mashed potato embedded with diced salt pork and simmered in water. *Poutines râpées* are served with salt and pepper for a main course, or with molasses for a tasty dessert.

MONCTON

New Brunswick's second largest city (pop. 87,000) is the largest rail center east of Montreal. A third of its residents are French-speaking and its Université de Moncton is the only French-language university east of Quebec City.
□ Attractions include Bore View Park, where twice daily a small tidal bore rushes up the Petit-codiac River; Centennial Park, with 71 hectares of woodland and lakes; and Magnetic Hill, where vehicles seem to coast uphill.
□ Places of historical interest include Moncton's oldest building, the Free Meeting House (c. 1821), a one-story, frame structure where early German and Dutch settlers worshiped; the Moncton Civic Museum, which displays the city's past from Micmac Indian days to the present; and an Acadian Museum (at the university) containing old looms, spinning wheels, paintings, a smithy and a 1614 French pipe organ.
□ Harness races are run year round at Brunswick Downs Raceway in neighboring Dieppe.

0 2 4 6 8 10 Miles
0 4 8 12 16 Kilometres

Lobster traps, homespun sweaters, sea gulls, vesper bells and front-porch rocking chairs—these are the sights and sounds of the Northumberland Shore, in southeastern New Brunswick.

In Kouchibouguac National Park, set in gently rolling mixed forests of spruce, birch, aspen and pine, side roads lead seaward to sand dunes, quiet lagoons and sandy beaches. South of the park are Richibucto, famed for scallops; Rexton, birthplace of Andrew Bonar Law (1858-1923)—the only British prime minister born outside the British Isles; and Buctouche, home of the Acadian literary character "La Sagouine." Near Shediac, "lobster capital of the world," fine beaches offer warm saltwater swimming.

A bustling terminus of one New Brunswick–Prince Edward Island ferry is at Cape Tormentine. Inland, across the Isthmus of Chignecto, the ruins of Fort Beauséjour overlook the vast, barn-dotted Tantramar marshes—known as the world's biggest hayfield. For 13 grim days in 1755, the marshes were the scene of bitter fighting as 270 British regulars and 2,000 New England volunteers attacked and captured Beauséjour.

Sackville is a quiet, tree-shaded university town; Dorchester boasts some of the province's finest Classical Revival architecture; and Moncton, the transportation hub of the Maritimes, combines English reserve with Acadian *joie de vivre*.

"La Sagouine" as portrayed by New Brunswick actress, Viola Léger

BUCTOUCHE

Wild and beautiful beaches, warm sands and the temperate water of huge Buctouche harbor make this Acadian fishing village a tourist favorite. There is excellent lobster fishing and the area is known as "the oyster bed of New Brunswick."
□ Buctouche is the birthplace of Acadian novelist Antonine Maillet, author of *La Sagouine* (1971), a volume of 16 monologues in Acadian French. La Sagouine (The Slattern)—a 72-year-old charwoman, former prostitute, and wife of an Acadian fisherman—recites grievances, recollections, anecdotes and homilies in a rich argot that is descended from 16th-century French.

Ruins at Fort Beauséjour National Historic Park

SHEDIAC

The "lobster capital of the world" stages a five-day festival in mid-July with parades, folk songs and dancing, sports events and lobster dinners. One of New Brunswick's principal yachting and resort areas, Shediac has several fine beaches on the Northumberland Strait, whose waters are among the warmest north of Virginia. Parlee Beach Provincial Park offers spacious camping facilities and excellent saltwater swimming.

AULAC

Fort Beauséjour, one of the few military posts in Canada to see heavy fighting, was built by the French in 1751-55 to counter the British at Fort Lawrence, near present-day Amherst, N.S. In June 1755 Beauséjour was taken by the British, renamed Fort Cumberland and its defenses extended. The old name Beauséjour was reinstated in 1926 when the site was designated a national historic park.

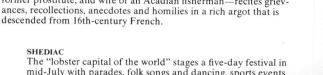
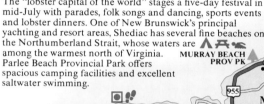

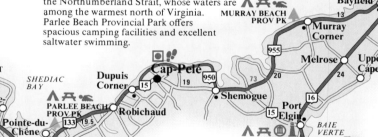

TANTRAMAR MARSHES

Protected from the sea by old Acadian dikes, these 207 square kilometres of fertile land are known as the world's biggest hayfield. Tantramar may be from the French *tintamarre* (loud noise), referring to the sound of the tides or the cacophony of marsh birds.

Tantramar marshes, near Sackville

Keillor House, Dorchester

DORCHESTER

Locally quarried stone was used in the construction of Keillor House, a nine-fireplace mansion built in 1813 by a Yorkshire settler. This magnificent example of Regency architecture now is a museum containing furniture from the late 18th and early 19th centuries.
□ Nearby is Chandler House, a Classical Revival stone mansion built about 1831 for Edward Barron Chandler, a Father of Confederation who was lieutenant governor of New Brunswick from 1878 until his death in 1880.

SACKVILLE

Near the center of town is the parklike campus of Mount Allison University, whose Owens Art Gallery has one of Canada's finest collections of graphics. The gallery has three silk-screened prints by realist painter Alex Colville, who studied at Mount Allison. There are also works by the Group of Seven; pre-1880 English watercolors, etchings and paintings; and 10 prints and a self-portrait in oils by Newfoundland artist Christopher Pratt. Graduates of the university include Grace Ann Lockhart, the first woman in the British Empire to be granted a bachelor's degree (1875).
□ A small harness shop on Main Street is the only one in North America still producing handmade horse collars.

A Friendly Border
Where Old Angers Are Forgotten

Southwestern New Brunswick

The industry and conservatism of Loyalist forebears are imprinted along this route, which is broken by gentle bays and belted by spruce and fir and rolling farmland. Scorned and threatened by the victors of the American Revolution, the Loyalist residents of Castine, Maine, fled from the United States and settled these rugged shores. The Crown rewarded their loyalty with liberal land grants and they prospered.

In St. Andrews, stately homes and quaint inns exude colonial charm, and reflections

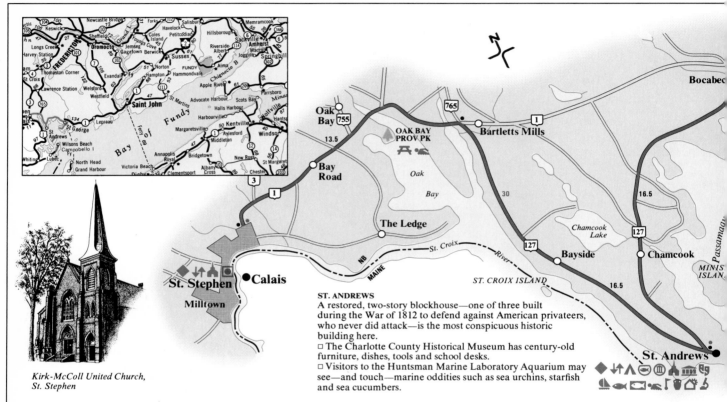

Kirk-McColl United Church, St. Stephen

ST. ANDREWS
A restored, two-story blockhouse—one of three built during the War of 1812 to defend against American privateers, who never did attack—is the most conspicuous historic building here.
□ The Charlotte County Historical Museum has century-old furniture, dishes, tools and school desks.
□ Visitors to the Huntsman Marine Laboratory Aquarium may see—and touch—marine oddities such as sea urchins, starfish and sea cucumbers.

ST. STEPHEN
A bridge across the St. Croix River links St. Stephen with Calais, Maine. The towns celebrate each other's national holidays, share the same water supply, and answer each other's fire alarms.
□ Kirk-McColl United Church is named for Rev. Duncan McColl, a Methodist minister who helped to keep peace between the towns during the War of 1812.
□ St. Stephen was founded in 1786 as a shipbuilding center; masts were once hauled down King's Mast Road, now King Street. Today the town's biggest industry is the candy plant of Ganong Bros., Ltd. Here in 1906 Arthur Ganong concocted snacks for a fishing trip—blocks of chocolate separated by paper—and the chocolate bar was born.

Ganong's chocolate box (1920)

Canada's First 'Prefabs' Came by Sea

When the Loyalist founders of St. Andrews fled Castine, Maine, after the American Revolution, some brought their houses, section by section, on barges. A green-roofed, white clapboard dwelling built in Castine in 1770 and reassembled here in 1783 is at 75 Montague Street. Of the 13 other 18th-century buildings in the town, the best preserved one is at Adolphus and Queen streets. It was built about 1790 for John Dunn, county sheriff. A rarer, saltbox design—two-storied front, one-storied rear—is the frame dwelling on Queen Street, near Edward Street, built in 1785 by ship's carpenter Joseph Crookshank. The Pagan-O'Neill House at Queen and Frederick streets was one of the first in the settlement. Chestnut Hall at King and Montague streets was built about 1810 for Col. Christopher Hatch, commander of the garrison.

But the town's architectural gem is Greenock Presbyterian Church, built in 1824 by a shipbuilder, Capt. Christopher Scott. On its white tower is carved a green oak tree (emblem of Scott's Greenock, Scotland, birthplace).

Joseph Crookshank House (1785)

Pagan-O'Neill House (1784)

John Dunn House (1790)

0 1 2 3 4 5 Miles
0 2 4 6 8 Kilometres

of the town's English-American heritage are in historic buildings on almost every street.

For many years tensions ran high between the Loyalists and their American neighbors. The wooden blockhouse opposite Centennial Park was built early in the War of 1812. (Capt. Christopher Scott, a wealthy shipbuilder, paid for construction of the blockhouse when military funds were withheld.)

The Americans never attacked St. Andrews. By the mid-19th century old angers were spent and American vacationers flocked to this Loyalist bastion. The Shiretown Inn (1881), one of Canada's oldest summer hotels, and the gabled Algonquin Hotel (1888, rebuilt 1915) are reminders of St. Andrews's era as the summer playground of wealthy Bostonians and New Yorkers.

Today on Campobello Island an international park dedicated to the memory of U.S. President Franklin Delano Roosevelt symbolizes friendship between Canada and the United States.

ST. GEORGE
Granite markers in a Loyalist cemetery and granite outcrops are reminders of a once-thriving industry, when this was "the red granite town." Now the main industry is fishing.
□ Near picturesque Magaguadavic Falls, Atlantic salmon bound for upstream spawning grounds use a concrete fish ladder that bypasses the falls.

Magaguadavic Falls, St. George

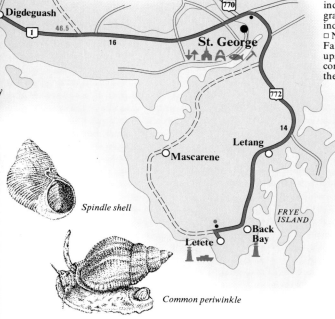

Spindle shell

Common periwinkle

Waved whelk

Lobster pound, Deer Island

PASSAMAQUODDY BAY
Sheltered Passamaquoddy Bay has a rich variety of marine life. Periwinkles, barnacles, limpets, sand dollars and poisonous moon snails can be found on its shores at low tide. In warm weather, rocky areas yield waved whelks. (Warnings are posted any time these normally edible mollusks contain toxins.)

Spindle shells, whose shells once served as whale-oil lamps, are occasionally found here. Clams can be dug from muddy sand. Moon jellyfish float on the water in summer. Sea anemones and starfish cling to rocks at or below the low-tide line. The starfish extends its stomach through its mouth to devour barnacles and shellfish. Toad crabs hide in weeds. Shore crabs will threaten intruders but rarely attack. Whales, porpoises, seals, eels and lobsters are found in the bay.

DEER ISLAND
The world's three biggest lobster pounds are here, at Northern Harbour. The pounds are inlets converted by fences and nets into corrals whose salt water is changed daily by surging Bay of Fundy tides. Lobsters trapped during strictly enforced seasons are put into the pounds alive, to be shipped fresh as markets demand.
□ Old Sow, a whirlpool that rivals the Maelstrom in Norway, is seen to advantage from the high ground of a campsite at Deer Island Point.

CAMPOBELLO ISLAND
President Franklin D. Roosevelt's 34-room "summer cottage"—a red-shingled, green-roofed Dutch colonial mansion—is the centerpiece of Roosevelt-Campobello International Park. FDR spent most of the summers of his youth on the island until 1921, when he was stricken with polio. During his presidency, Roosevelt visited the island three times during the 1930s.
□ In the Campobello Library at Welshpool are mementos of the Owen family, who owned the island from 1767 to 1881.
□ A toll ferry links Campobello and Deer islands.

FDR statuette, Roosevelt-Campobello International Park

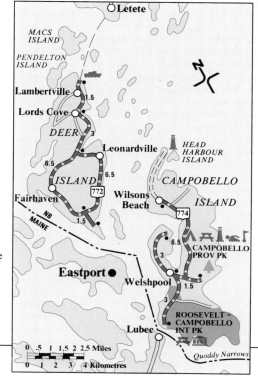

A Storybook Island
Off a Coast of Sheltered Coves

Southwestern New Brunswick

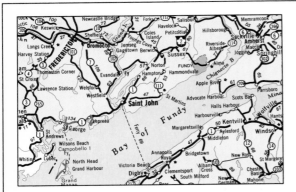

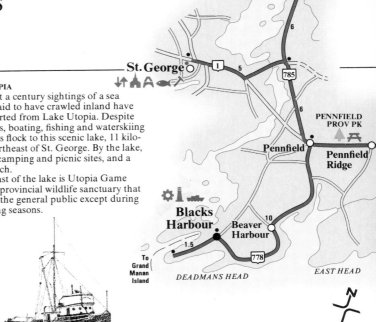

LAKE UTOPIA

For almost a century sightings of a sea monster said to have crawled inland have been reported from Lake Utopia. Despite the rumors, boating, fishing and waterskiing enthusiasts flock to this scenic lake, 11 kilometres northeast of St. George. By the lake, there are camping and picnic sites, and a sandy beach.

Northeast of the lake is Utopia Game Refuge, a provincial wildlife sanctuary that is open to the general public except during the hunting seasons.

BLACKS HARBOUR

The biggest sardine and herring canning operation in the Commonwealth ships more than 50 million tins of sardines each year. Visitors may tour three plants of Connors Bros. Limited, whose 10 canneries—eight on the Bay of Fundy—process 95 percent of Canada's sardines.

The fish are caught near shore in giant weirs—circular fenced traps—or in open water by seiners. A seine—60 metres deep and up to 500 metres long—is set around a school of sardines. Then the bottom of the net is drawn tight to form a purse and the catch is emptied by suction hoses.

Seining for sardines, Bay of Fundy

GRAND MANAN ISLAND

Geological curiosities and the unhurried pace of life are among the attractions of picturesque Grand Manan, the biggest (142 square kilometres) of the Fundy isles. Its 2,500 inhabitants harvest dulse (an edible seaweed), and trap lobsters.

There are no neon signs or public drinking places here. But there are tranquil forests of spruce, balsam, birch and poplar; awesome cliffs; craggy trails, bright with wildflowers; and off the sheltered east shore a forest of underwater tree stumps.

Grand Manan is a fine place for whale-watching, beachcombing or basking on a lonely stretch of seaside sand. A ferry links the island and the mainland.

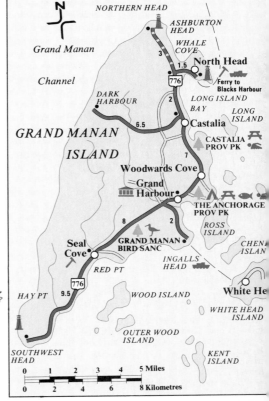

Swallowtail Lighthouse, Pettes Cove, Grand Manan Island

DARK HARBOUR

Soft or leathery, pink or purple, dulse is a seaweed delicacy—and dulse from Dark Harbour (36 tonnes of it a year) is rated the best in the world. This tangy, salty seaweed, rich in iron and iodine, is eaten raw, toasted over a flame, or powdered for use in chowders, casseroles and gravies. It is picked from the rocks at low tide and dried in the sun for five hours. An experienced picker gathers about 56 kilograms of dulse between tides. Most of Dark Harbour's harvest is shipped throughout Canada and the United States.

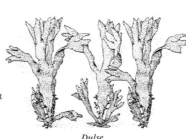

Dulse

St. George and Blacks Harbour snuggle in a rugged coastline worn by mighty Bay of Fundy tides. Fishing villages cling to sheltered coves along Fundy's north shore. Lakes and streams teem with fish, and woodlands shelter black bears, moose and white-tailed deer. The swift current and white water of the Lepreau River challenge experienced canoeists.

At St. George, settled nearly 200 years ago, Atlantic salmon dart up a concrete fish ladder on their way to spawning grounds in the northern reaches of the Magaguadavic River.

Blacks Harbour, center of Canada's sardine industry, is a company town where public utilities, a supermarket, an arena, a hotel and many houses are cannery-owned.

A ferry links Blacks Harbour and Grand Manan Island. A favorite haunt of naturalists, geologists, writers and artists, Grand Manan is a storybook setting of towering cliffs, pirate coves, white lighthouses, and rose-covered cottages.

Tourists can accompany fishermen to herring, pollock, haddock or bluefin tuna grounds; visit a smokehouse where salted herrings hang above smoldering, sawdust-smothered logs; or dig for Captain Kidd's treasure where Money Cove Brook plunges down a 244-metre ravine near Dark Harbour. Offshore there are numerous shipwrecks to interest experienced divers.

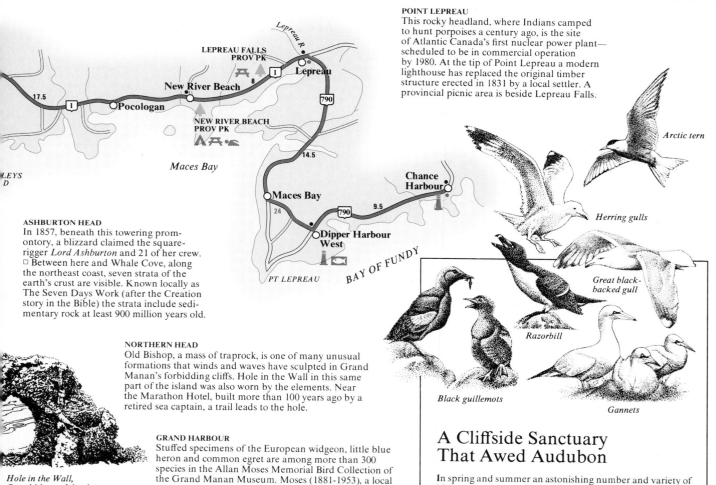

POINT LEPREAU
This rocky headland, where Indians camped to hunt porpoises a century ago, is the site of Atlantic Canada's first nuclear power plant—scheduled to be in commercial operation by 1980. At the tip of Point Lepreau a modern lighthouse has replaced the original timber structure erected in 1831 by a local settler. A provincial picnic area is beside Lepreau Falls.

Arctic tern

Herring gulls

Great black-backed gull

Razorbill

Black guillemots

Gannets

ASHBURTON HEAD
In 1857, beneath this towering promontory, a blizzard claimed the square-rigger *Lord Ashburton* and 21 of her crew. □ Between here and Whale Cove, along the northeast coast, seven strata of the earth's crust are visible. Known locally as The Seven Days Work (after the Creation story in the Bible) the strata include sedimentary rock at least 900 million years old.

NORTHERN HEAD
Old Bishop, a mass of traprock, is one of many unusual formations that winds and waves have sculpted in Grand Manan's forbidding cliffs. Hole in the Wall in this same part of the island was also worn by the elements. Near the Marathon Hotel, built more than 100 years ago by a retired sea captain, a trail leads to the hole.

Hole in the Wall, Grand Manan Island

GRAND HARBOUR
Stuffed specimens of the European widgeon, little blue heron and common egret are among more than 300 species in the Allan Moses Memorial Bird Collection of the Grand Manan Museum. Moses (1881-1953), a local naturalist, participated in two scientific expeditions—one to East Africa, one to the South Atlantic.

A Cliffside Sanctuary That Awed Audubon

In spring and summer an astonishing number and variety of birds stop to feed and nest on Grand Manan Island, a northern terminal of the Atlantic flyway. When naturalist John James Audubon visited here in 1833, he was awed by tens of thousands of nesting gulls and songbirds. Cliffsides give arctic terns, gannets, black guillemots and razorbills ready access to fish and shelter their nests from predators.

More than 245 species of birds have been sighted in the 81-hectare Grand Manan Bird Sanctuary, between Grand Harbour and Seal Cove. During a typical nesting season, ornithologists have counted more than 2,000 black ducks, 1,200 brant, 200 goldeneyes and 100 buffleheads. Other species here include geese, teal, eiders, ring-necked ducks, mergansers, scaup and pintail. The sanctuary, a refuge in the hunting season and a wintering place, consists of wet heath, spruce and fir woods, and two ponds separated from the sea by a grassy sandbar.

RED POINT
Grand Manan Island, a rockhound's paradise, consists of two major geologic structures formed 700 million years apart. The rugged, uninhabited west is of volcanic origin; the flatter, eastern island is of older, sedimentary rock. At Red Point, on the southeast shore, a line can be seen where gray, volcanic rock overlapped red, sedimentary slabs millions of years ago. Between Dark Harbour and North Head, the collector can find such semiprecious minerals as amethyst, agate, jasper, hornstone and apophyllite.

Specular hematite, Grand Manan Island

A New Life for an Old Seaport
Where Loyalist Memories Linger

Loyalist House

Saint John

1 Reversing Falls
2 Carleton Martello Tower
3 New Brunswick Museum
4 Reid's Point
5 Fort Howe
6 Loyalist Landing Place
7 University of New Brunswick
8 Samuel de Champlain
9 Saint John's Stone Church
10 Loyalist House
11 Trinity Church
12 Old City Market
13 King Square
14 County Courthouse
15 Tourist Information
16 Loyalist Burial Ground
17 Barbour's General Store
18 CAA
19 Saint John Dry Dock
20 Rockwood Park
21 Mispec
22 Atlantic National Exhibition
23 Rothesay Collegiate School

A walk along the "Loyalist Trail" through downtown Saint John is a walk into the history of one of North America's oldest cities. The trail, about five kilometres long, leads past 18th- and 19th-century houses, stores, churches, a burial ground, and a bustling indoor market more than a century old.

Champlain anchored in the harbor of Saint John in 1604 and Charles de la Tour established a fortified trading post here in 1631. The first permanent English settlement dates from 1762 but Saint John received its first main influx of settlers when a few thousand Loyalist refugees arrived from the United States in the summer of 1783. Timber and shipbuilding brought fame and fortune to Saint John in the 19th century. But when wooden shipbuilding declined, so did the city, although it remained an important year-round port.

New life came to Saint John in the 1960s and 1970s with major renewal projects in the heart of the city and huge investments in mining, manufacturing and shipping.

Atlantic National Exhibition (22)
There are fish and livestock shows at eastern Canada's largest fair, in late August.
Barbour's General Store (17)
Clerks and "customers" play checkers near a potbellied stove in this building, which dates from 1867.
Carleton Martello Tower (2)
Dating from the War of 1812, this circular stone fort affords sweeping vistas of Saint John and its harbor.

Carleton Martello Tower

Tea chests, cracker barrels and hand scales evoke the past at Barbour's General Store.

County Courthouse (14)
Completed in 1829, the building has a self-supporting, three-story spiral stone stairway. Next door is the old City Gaol (c.1830).
Fort Howe (5)
Overlooking Saint John Harbour is a reconstructed blockhouse originally built in 1777 as part of British defenses against marauding Indians and American raiders.

King Square (13)
A memorial cross bears a plaque commemorating the founding of New Brunswick on Aug. 16, 1784.

Loyalist Burial Ground (16)
The oldest gravestone is that of Coonradt Hendricks, who died July 13, 1784.

Loyalist House (10)
This former home of a prosperous 19th-century Loyalist merchant has double parlors with Grecian swooning sofas, a piano organ and Duncan Phyfe tables from 1818.

Loyalist Landing Place (6)
A boulder memorial marks the landing place of the Loyalists of 1783.

Mispec (21)
A lookout provides a panoramic view of North America's first deep-water oil terminal, which opened in 1970.

Aromas of sweet hay, dulse and fresh fish mingle at the Old City Market (below). Loyalists who helped create Saint John in the 1780s are remembered in the Old Loyalist Burial Ground (right).

New Brunswick Museum (3)
Outstanding displays include an important nautical collection (ship models, whaling dioramas and whalebone carvings), an exhibition of mounted birds and animals, the J. C. Webster collection of pictorial Canada, and supplies and equipment from the clipper ship *Marco Polo*, sunk off Cavendish, P.E.I., in 1883.

Old City Market (12)
The block-long structure, built in 1876, survived a fire the next year that destroyed more than half the city.

Reid's Point (4)
The Three Lamps were erected on an iron standard in 1848 as a navigation guide for ships entering the harbor of Saint John.

A Celtic cross stands in memory of 2,000 Irish immigrants who died of cholera during voyages from Ireland in 1847. Some 600 were buried on nearby Partridge Island.

Reversing Falls (1)
Twice a day the sea boils into the Saint John River through a deep, narrow gorge. Rising in one of the world's highest tides, the sea throws the river back and sweeps upstream in a fury of foam, rapids and whirlpools.

Rockwood Park (20)
This expanse of parkland and lakes near the city center offers boating, camping, nature trails, and a children's farm.

Rothesay Collegiate School (23)
New Brunswick's only independent private school for boys was founded in suburban Rothesay in 1877. Nearby is Netherwood School (1891), the province's only independent private school for girls.

Saint John Dry Dock (19)
One of the largest in the world, the main dock is 350 metres long and 38 metres wide.

Reliving Loyalist Days in Old Saint John

Early in May 1783, seven ships were anchored in the Bay of Fundy off the mouth of the Saint John River. On board were Loyalist refugees—all fleeing persecution at the hands of victorious American rebels in the War of Independence. Today, during Saint John's annual Loyalist Days celebration in late July, children and adults don 18th-century dress and proud tales are told of the Loyalists' arrival some 200 years ago. The five-day celebration opens with a reenactment of the first Loyalist landing. Bedecked in velvet and a white periwig, the Mayor of Saint John receives the disembarking Loyalists and their Indian guides. After a ceremonial raising of the Union Jack, the pageantry continues with street parades, a beauty contest and a gala Colonial Ball. There are sidewalk breakfasts, outdoor barbecues, beer gardens, fireworks and horse-and-buggy tours of old Saint John. Tea is served in memory of settlers who could seldom afford such a luxury.

Reenactment of the first Loyalist landing

Viewed from across Saint John Harbour, a new generation of bridges and buildings rises in the downtown area above the sea-worn façade of the city.

Saint John's Stone Church (9)
The city's first stone structure was completed in 1825 with stone brought from England as ship's ballast.

Samuel de Champlain (8)
A monument recalls the explorer who named the Saint John River on June 24, 1604, after the saint whose feast day it was.

Trinity Church (11)
The royal coat of arms over the great west door was brought here in 1776 by Loyalists who stole it from the Boston council chamber of the former colony of Massachusetts.

University of New Brunswick (7)
The university's Saint John campus was established in 1964.

In Serene Beauty, a Great River Flows Down to the Sea

Lower Saint John River Valley

Tranquil and ever more picturesque as it approaches the sea, the Saint John River flows east past Fredericton and then on to Oromocto. Here it widens before flowing southward on a winding course to the city of Saint John and the Bay of Fundy. Travelers can cross the lower reaches on a bridge at Maugerville, or via several free, government-operated ferries.

Downriver from Oromocto is Gagetown, a charming, elm-shaded town surrounded by woodlands of white cedar, pine, maple,

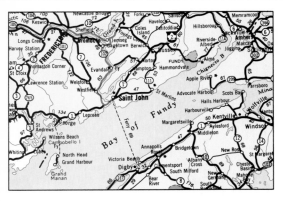

SHEFFIELD

Puritans from Massachusetts built New Brunswick's first Protestant church in nearby Maugerville in 1775. Thirteen years later, after a land dispute, they moved the wooden structure to Sheffield, pushing it eight kilometres along the Saint John River ice. Rebuilt in 1840 with the original lumber, the church is still in use. A cairn commemorating the church's founders was erected in 1926.

Blue flag

OROMOCTO

This town is at the north end of CFB Gagetown, the Commonwealth's third largest military camp. A small military museum is open to the public.
□ Fort Hughes, a British blockhouse (1781), was rebuilt in 1970. It protected local settlers during the American Revolution, and it deterred marauding Machias Indians. In summer a guard squad wears uniforms of the Royal Fencible Americans, the British regiment stationed here during the Revolutionary War.
□ Oromocto Pioneer Days, usually in early July, features street dances, fireworks and a 16-kilometre canoe race from Fredericton to Oromocto.

Fort Hughes blockhouse

MAUGERVILLE

The town of Maugerville (pronounced "Majorville") was named after Joshua Mauger, a Halifax merchant who helped New England settlers acquire land here during the early 1760s.
□ The surrounding area is known as New Brunswick's "garden patch." So rich is the silt brought from the upper Saint John River by spring floods that local farmers sometimes harvest two crops in a single growing season.
□ A modern, single-span bridge over the Saint John River links Maugerville with Burton and Oromocto.

Fine Homemade Tartans From Traditional Hand Looms

Handweaving on a four-harness floor loom

The Loomcrofters of Gagetown, designers and weavers of fine tartans, demonstrate handweaving and sell their products in a onetime trading post that is one of the oldest existing buildings on the Saint John River. The hand-split cedar shingles of the small two-story structure are held together with wooden pegs (no nails were used). It is known as the Blockhouse (firearms and ammunition were stored in the cellar) and as the Loomcrofters Inn (meals were once served by the weavers).

Begun as a government-sponsored youth training program in 1939, Loomcrofters has woven tartans for members of the Royal Family, presidents of the United States, Lord Beaverbrook and American movie stars. As many as 35 weavers, working at looms in their own houses, produce Loomcrofter tartans, clothing, afghans, draperies and upholstery materials. Tartans woven by Loomcrofters are designed by the owner of the enterprise, Miss Patricia Jenkins. Her best-known tartans were created for the Royal Canadian Air Force and the province of New Brunswick.

0	2	4	6	8	10 Miles
0	4		8	12	16 Kilometres

spruce, poplar, and great oaks that sprouted before the first United Empire Loyalists arrived in the 1780s. Lilies of the valley and orchids grow in the woods, but the most abundant flower is the blue flag, a wild iris.

The river is quiet here, so filled with long, low islands that it is often difficult to distinguish the main channel. The islands, swept by floodwater, ice and driftwood in the annual breakup, are used for pasture and hay but seldom for homesteads. Silt dumped by the river each spring makes farmland in the lower Saint John River valley among the most fertile in Canada. Wildlife is abundant. There are deer, muskrat and almost every species of duck and wading bird native to eastern Canada.

South of Evandale is Long Reach. This lake, flanked by impressive hills covered in hardwood and laced with trout streams, is a 32-kilometre stretch of the river. Here, in autumn, the river's placid surface mirrors the brilliant gold-and-scarlet foliage of the Kingston Peninsula on the eastern shore.

Yellow warbler

WHITES COVE
Fruit-and-vegetable stands line the highway here. A one-room schoolhouse has been converted into a shop selling handwoven articles, pottery, blown glass and other New Brunswick crafts.
□ Lakeside Provincial Park has sandy beaches, camping and picnicking sites, and fishing for alewife (a fish resembling the herring) and Atlantic salmon.

LOWER JEMSEG
A cairn marks the site of Fort Jemseg (1659). Built by the British and used for trade with the Indians, it was taken over by the French in 1670. Captured by the Dutch in 1674, the fort was soon retaken by the French, who rebuilt it in 1690, then abandoned it two years later.

GAGETOWN
Tilley House is the birthplace of Sir Samuel Leonard Tilley (1818-96), a druggist who entered politics and became one of the Fathers of Confederation. The house, now a national historic site, has been restored as the Queens County Museum. A parlor and bedroom are restored in early Victorian fashion; older parts of the house are in Loyalist style. The house was built in 1786 by Dr. Frederick Stickles, the town's first physician.
□ The Loomcrofters, designers and weavers of tartans, demonstrate weaving and sell their products in a onetime trading post that is the oldest existing building (c. 1760) on the Saint John River. As many as 35 persons, working in their own homes, produce Loomcrofter tartans, clothing, afghans, draperies, upholstery materials, place mats, napkins and wool cushions.

OAK POINT
On a low-lying strip of land jutting into the Saint John River is Oak Point Provincial Park, with tree-shaded campsites, a beach and an old lighthouse.
□ Offshore lies Caton's Island, named for Isaac and James Caton—Englishmen who were granted the island in 1760. Traders from France began a short-lived settlement here in 1610. They were New Brunswick's first European settlers.

Queens County Museum, Gagetown

SAINT JOHN RIVER
Until the 1940s the Saint John River was New Brunswick's principal transport route. Riverboats with names like *May Queen* and *Majestic* chugged and throbbed up this broad and scenic inland waterway. Nowadays, except for farmers' boats and scows, and some ferries, the river carries little but pleasure craft. Canoeing and sailing are popular activities near Gagetown, where the lower Saint John is dotted with long, low-lying islands. Provincial parks at Queenstown and Oak Point are ideal spots to enjoy the river's serene beauty.

Lower Saint John River

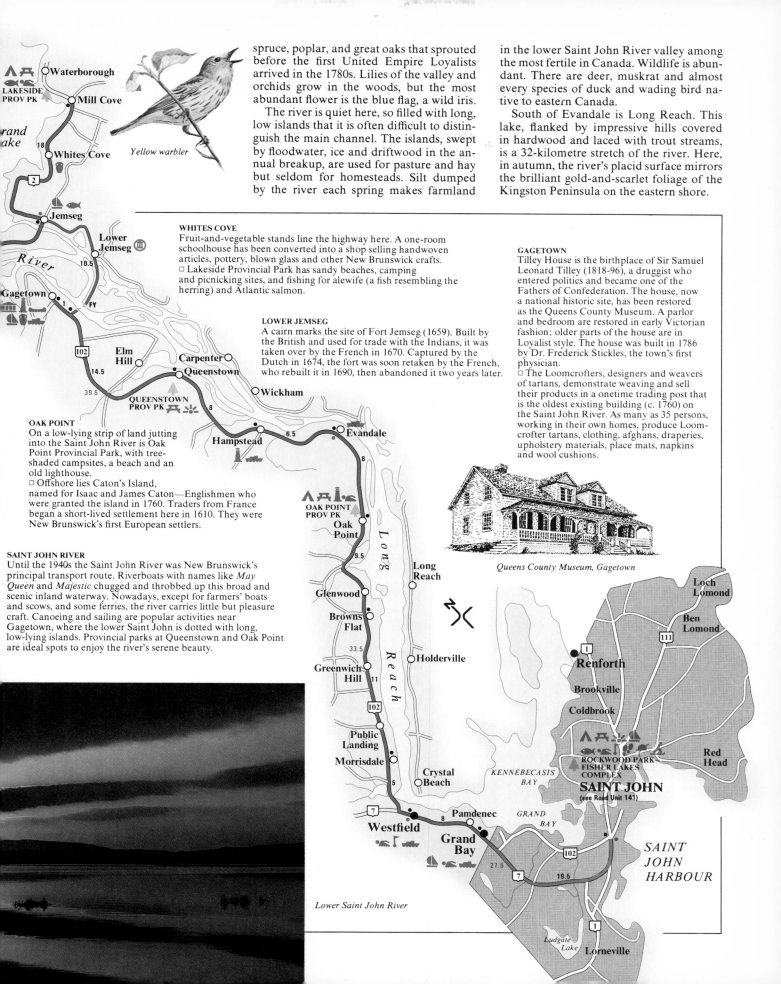

Where Surging Tides Sculpt Towering 'Flowerpots'

Southeastern New Brunswick

Southeastern New Brunswick has dramatic rock formations, rugged cliffs battered by the highest tides in the world, serene dairy farms and woodlands, and sparkling trout streams spanned by quaint covered bridges.

In Fundy National Park coves and inlets cut into steep sandstone cliffs along a spectacular 13-kilometre shoreline. Inland the park is an undulating plateau of forested hills, tumbling brooks, placid lakes and flowered meadows. Armed with cameras

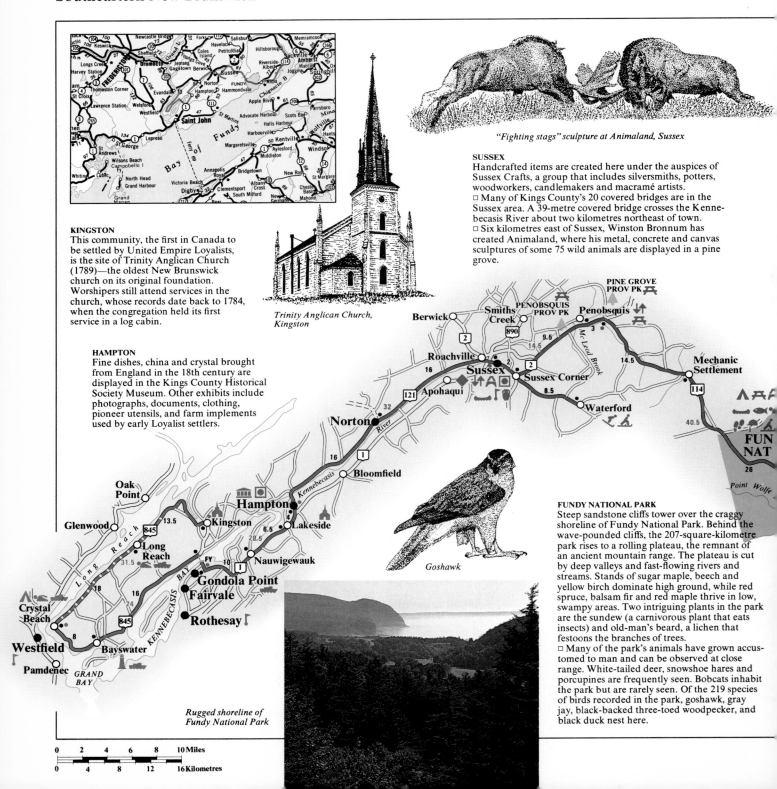

"Fighting stags" sculpture at Animaland, Sussex

KINGSTON
This community, the first in Canada to be settled by United Empire Loyalists, is the site of Trinity Anglican Church (1789)—the oldest New Brunswick church on its original foundation. Worshipers still attend services in the church, whose records date back to 1784, when the congregation held its first service in a log cabin.

Trinity Anglican Church, Kingston

HAMPTON
Fine dishes, china and crystal brought from England in the 18th century are displayed in the Kings County Historical Society Museum. Other exhibits include photographs, documents, clothing, pioneer utensils, and farm implements used by early Loyalist settlers.

SUSSEX
Handcrafted items are created here under the auspices of Sussex Crafts, a group that includes silversmiths, potters, woodworkers, candlemakers and macramé artists.
□ Many of Kings County's 20 covered bridges are in the Sussex area. A 39-metre covered bridge crosses the Kennebecasis River about two kilometres northeast of town.
□ Six kilometres east of Sussex, Winston Bronnum has created Animaland, where his metal, concrete and canvas sculptures of some 75 wild animals are displayed in a pine grove.

Goshawk

FUNDY NATIONAL PARK
Steep sandstone cliffs tower over the craggy shoreline of Fundy National Park. Behind the wave-pounded cliffs, the 207-square-kilometre park rises to a rolling plateau, the remnant of an ancient mountain range. The plateau is cut by deep valleys and fast-flowing rivers and streams. Stands of sugar maple, beech and yellow birch dominate high ground, while red spruce, balsam fir and red maple thrive in low, swampy areas. Two intriguing plants in the park are the sundew (a carnivorous plant that eats insects) and old-man's beard, a lichen that festoons the branches of trees.
□ Many of the park's animals have grown accustomed to man and can be observed at close range. White-tailed deer, snowshoe hares and porcupines are frequently seen. Bobcats inhabit the park but are rarely seen. Of the 219 species of birds recorded in the park, goshawk, gray jay, black-backed three-toed woodpecker, and black duck nest here.

Rugged shoreline of Fundy National Park

0 2 4 6 8 10 Miles
0   4   8   12   16 Kilometres

and binoculars, amateur naturalists can watch for some of the park's 185 bird species, or some of its many mammals. Beachcombers can tread 250-million-year-old rocks and explore caves, beaches and tidal pools. In a spruce grove on a rocky bluff overlooking the Bay of Fundy is an arts and crafts school where students, young and old, learn enameling, weaving, pottery, wood turning, leatherwork, silk-screening, jewelry-making and rug hooking.

East of the park, on the beach at Alma, are rare rock specimens. Countless driftwood souvenirs can be found in a sheltered bay near Cape Enrage. At Riverside-Albert is a museum in an old jail. Nearby are a picnic site and lookout where the view of Crooked Creek is unexcelled. Farther east, at Hopewell Cape, are tide-sculpted rocks.

From Penobsquis, northwest of the park on the Kennebecasis River, a pleasant day trip leads past dairy farms and through small villages such as Sussex, Norton and Hampton, where skilled weavers produce the Kings County tweed. In Sussex exquisite handmade silver jewelry and delicious locally made ice cream can be purchased. At Gondola Point a car ferry crosses the Kennebecasis River to the picturesque Kingston Peninsula.

A circle tour around the peninsula leads through Loyalist settlements dating back to 1783. Here are some of the oldest churches—and some of the finest autumn scenery—in the Maritimes. Here, too, is unforgettable calm and tranquillity.

HILLSBOROUGH
When he immigrated here in 1766, Heinrich Steeves (or "Stief" as the name was spelled then) had seven sons. Now more than 150,000 of their descendants live all over the world. Each July the Steeves Family Reunion is held in Hillsborough—complete with parade floats depicting events in the early life of the family. William H. Steeves (1814-73), a Father of Confederation, and many other members of the family are buried in the Hillsborough cemetery.

Former county courthouse, Hopewell Cape

HOPEWELL CAPE
The Albert County Museum is in a former county jail (1846) and courthouse (1904). The jail has cut-stone walls nearly a metre thick, barred windows and an iron-reinforced wooden door. The museum features models and photographs of ships and plans and tools used in building sailing ships. In other rooms are pioneer candlesticks, whale-oil lamps and chandeliers.
□ A monument in Hopewell Cape Park honors Richard Bedford Bennett, born at his grandfather's home near here, raised at Hopewell Cape and the only New Brunswicker to become prime minister of Canada (1930-35).

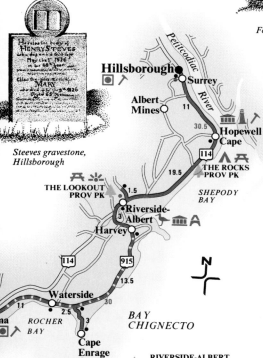

Steeves gravestone, Hillsborough

Bobcat

Low tide at The Rocks Provincial Park

RIVERSIDE-ALBERT
A picnic site and Lookout Provincial Park provide a spectacular view of Crooked Creek, which winds through a steep ravine.
□ South of town, in Shepody National Wildlife Area, circular water-filled trenches serve as feeding and resting stations for migratory birds.
□ In nearby Harvey is an imposing green and yellow wooden schoolhouse (1905) with metal fire-escape chutes that lead from the second floor to the ground.

CAPE ENRAGE
A lighthouse warns ships away from this rocky promontory in Chignecto Bay. A sheltered bay on the west side of the cape is noted for its abundance of driftwood.
□ At Alma, 15 kilometres west, rock hounds can find colorful and rare specimens near the mouth of the Salmon River. The shoreline site is accessible at low tide.

THE ROCKS PROVINCIAL PARK
Top-heavy formations of soft rock resembling grotesque, overgrown flowerpots stand near the mouth of the Petitcodiac River at Hopewell Cape. The reddish pillars capped by balsam fir and dwarf black spruce have been shaped by centuries of frost and wind, and the 35-metre-high tides that surge up the Bay of Fundy. At high tide the towering "flowerpots"—up to 15 metres high—become small islands. At low tide park visitors can descend a set of stairways and walk along the shore to explore caves and crevices in the cliffs. A warning whistle sounds when the tide is coming in. At the top of the cliff are a restaurant and a gift shop. Nearby are picnicking and camping facilities, and a supervised beach.

Where Life Moves to the Rhythms of the Sea and the Seasons

Northwestern Prince Edward Island

Spring is a lively season in northwestern P.E.I.—especially in and around Bloomfield and other farming communities in Prince County, where half of the province's potato crop is grown. While potato farmers work through the short planting season—plowing, seeding and fertilizing the red soil—fishermen at Tignish Shore and Northport sort gear, prepare bait, and load their boats with lobster traps and brightly painted buoys. In early May on the first day of the north shore's spring lob-

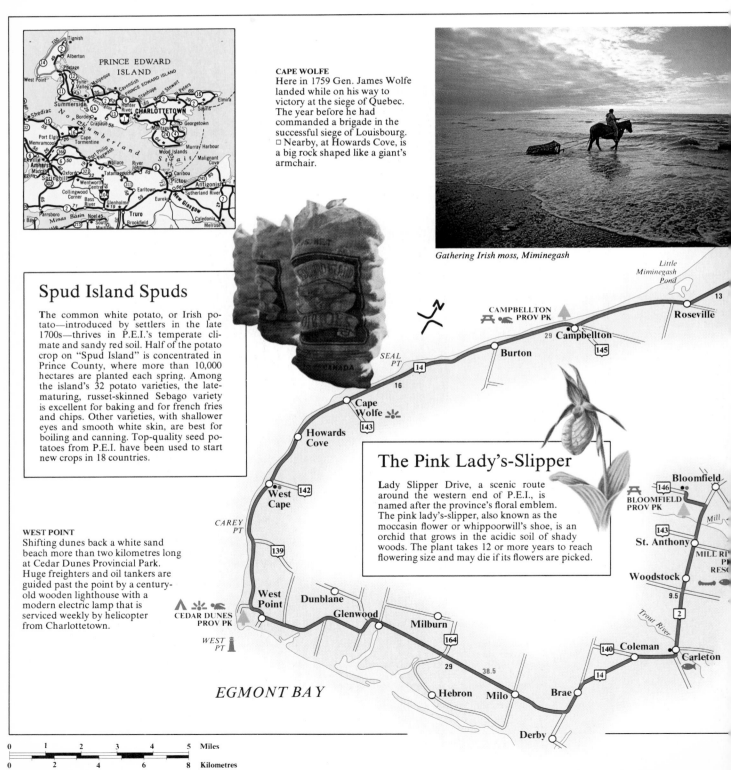

CAPE WOLFE
Here in 1759 Gen. James Wolfe landed while on his way to victory at the siege of Quebec. The year before he had commanded a brigade in the successful siege of Louisbourg. □ Nearby, at Howards Cove, is a big rock shaped like a giant's armchair.

Gathering Irish moss, Miminegash

Spud Island Spuds

The common white potato, or Irish potato—introduced by settlers in the late 1700s—thrives in P.E.I.'s temperate climate and sandy red soil. Half of the potato crop on "Spud Island" is concentrated in Prince County, where more than 10,000 hectares are planted each spring. Among the island's 32 potato varieties, the late-maturing, russet-skinned Sebago variety is excellent for baking and for french fries and chips. Other varieties, with shallower eyes and smooth white skin, are best for boiling and canning. Top-quality seed potatoes from P.E.I. have been used to start new crops in 18 countries.

WEST POINT
Shifting dunes back a white sand beach more than two kilometres long at Cedar Dunes Provincial Park. Huge freighters and oil tankers are guided past the point by a century-old wooden lighthouse with a modern electric lamp that is serviced weekly by helicopter from Charlottetown.

The Pink Lady's-Slipper

Lady Slipper Drive, a scenic route around the western end of P.E.I., is named after the province's floral emblem. The pink lady's-slipper, also known as the moccasin flower or whippoorwill's shoe, is an orchid that grows in the acidic soil of shady woods. The plant takes 12 or more years to reach flowering size and may die if its flowers are picked.

EGMONT BAY

| 0 | 1 | 2 | 3 | 4 | 5 | Miles |
| 0 | 2 | | 4 | | 6 | 8 | Kilometres |

ster season, the trim boats chug out to the fishing grounds at 5 a.m.

Summer arrives. Colts frolic on new pasture grass. And thousands of tourists, drawn here by the sun and the tang of salt air, enjoy fishing, golfing and clam digging and swimming off magnificent beaches. There are museums and handicraft shops to visit. On bustling wharves, fishermen unload lobsters from rounded traps. The midsummer Potato Blossom Festival in O'Leary (near Bloomfield) and the Prince County Exhibition in Alberton have midways, displays of livestock and farm produce, home-cooking competitions and fiddling and square dancing contests.

Autumn comes early. Under darkening skies farmers now race against time to harvest late-maturing potato crops before the first killing frost. (Even after dark the headlights of tractors trace eerie patterns in the potato fields.) At Howards Cove and other ports along the Northumberland Strait coast, lobster traps are neatly stacked on wharves as the fall season ends in mid-October; then fishermen gather a different harvest—Irish moss that has been uprooted by the ocean's fury. Autumn's chill brings a consolation prize of vivid color in fields and woodlots. With summer visitors gone and winter not yet upon the land, this is the favorite season of Islanders.

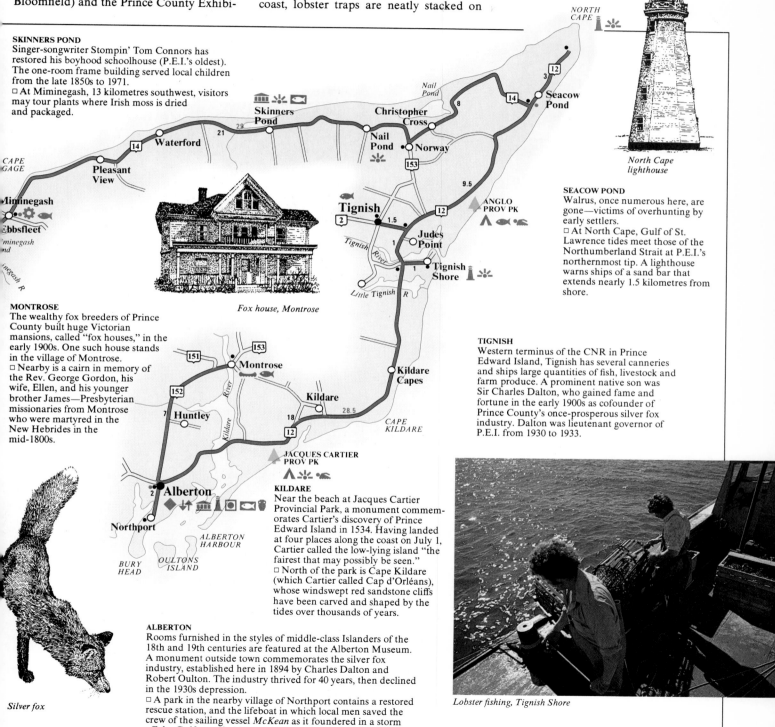

SKINNERS POND
Singer-songwriter Stompin' Tom Connors has restored his boyhood schoolhouse (P.E.I.'s oldest). The one-room frame building served local children from the late 1850s to 1971.
□ At Miminegash, 13 kilometres southwest, visitors may tour plants where Irish moss is dried and packaged.

Fox house, Montrose

MONTROSE
The wealthy fox breeders of Prince County built huge Victorian mansions, called "fox houses," in the early 1900s. One such house stands in the village of Montrose.
□ Nearby is a cairn in memory of the Rev. George Gordon, his wife, Ellen, and his younger brother James—Presbyterian missionaries from Montrose who were martyred in the New Hebrides in the mid-1800s.

Silver fox

KILDARE
Near the beach at Jacques Cartier Provincial Park, a monument commemorates Cartier's discovery of Prince Edward Island in 1534. Having landed at four places along the coast on July 1, Cartier called the low-lying island "the fairest that may possibly be seen."
□ North of the park is Cape Kildare (which Cartier called Cap d'Orléans), whose windswept red sandstone cliffs have been carved and shaped by the tides over thousands of years.

ALBERTON
Rooms furnished in the styles of middle-class Islanders of the 18th and 19th centuries are featured at the Alberton Museum. A monument outside town commemorates the silver fox industry, established here in 1894 by Charles Dalton and Robert Oulton. The industry thrived for 40 years, then declined in the 1930s depression.
□ A park in the nearby village of Northport contains a restored rescue station, and the lifeboat in which local men saved the crew of the sailing vessel *McKean* as it foundered in a storm off the Gulf coast in November 1906.

North Cape lighthouse

SEACOW POND
Walrus, once numerous here, are gone—victims of overhunting by early settlers.
□ At North Cape, Gulf of St. Lawrence tides meet those of the Northumberland Strait at P.E.I.'s northernmost tip. A lighthouse warns ships of a sand bar that extends nearly 1.5 kilometres from shore.

TIGNISH
Western terminus of the CNR in Prince Edward Island, Tignish has several canneries and ships large quantities of fish, livestock and farm produce. A prominent native son was Sir Charles Dalton, who gained fame and fortune in the early 1900s as cofounder of Prince County's once-prosperous silver fox industry. Dalton was lieutenant governor of P.E.I. from 1930 to 1933.

Lobster fishing, Tignish Shore

Memories of the Acadians
Near a Bay Famed for Oysters

Western Prince Edward Island

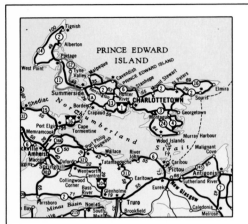

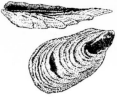

Malpeque oyster

BIDEFORD
As many as 30 million Malpeque oyster larvae are reared each year at an Environment Canada research station here. Visitors see displays of oysters, lobsters and other shellfish in a small museum.
□ At nearby Tyne Valley, a midsummer oyster festival features not only oysters but also clams and quahog—and fiddling and step-dancing contests.

Tonging oysters, Malpeque Bay

Farming Oysters in Malpeque Bay

Prince Edward Island pioneers knew the clean, sharp taste of Malpeque oysters long before it was savored by gourmets around the world. An epidemic in 1917 all but wiped out the tasty mollusks in Malpeque Bay. By the 1930s they had developed a resistance to the disease that was killing them. Today some five million Malpeque oysters are harvested annually. Modern farming techniques involve the collection of larval oysters, and their subsequent cultivation in tidal bays and estuaries. In spring, when mature oysters begin to spawn, fishermen set down artificial collectors in the water to which the tiny larval oysters attach them-selves. Collectors are usually disks of cardboard or plywood coated with concrete and strung on wires between stakes that are planted in the ocean floor. In autumn the young oysters are pried from the collectors and planted out in growing beds, where they feed on minute food particles brought in by the tides. After about 18 months the beds are raked or dredged and the oysters taken to fattening grounds, also in the estuary. The oysters are allowed to grow for about five years, each year adding a new layer to their shell. Then they are gathered and, before marketing, left for a few days in sterile seawater to cleanse them.

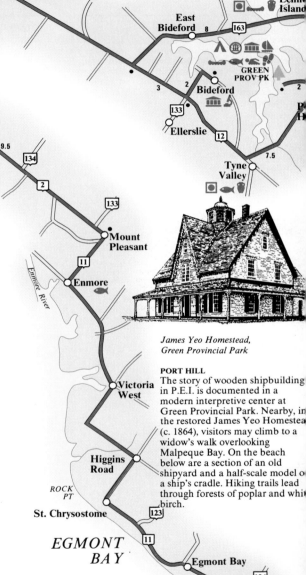

James Yeo Homestead, Green Provincial Park

PORT HILL
The story of wooden shipbuilding in P.E.I. is documented in a modern interpretive center at Green Provincial Park. Nearby, in the restored James Yeo Homestead (c. 1864), visitors may climb to a widow's walk overlooking Malpeque Bay. On the beach below are a section of an old shipyard and a half-scale model of a ship's cradle. Hiking trails lead through forests of poplar and white birch.

ABRAMS VILLAGE
Acadian handicrafts, prize livestock and farm produce are displayed at the annual Egmont Bay and Mount Carmel Exhibition in late August. The village also hosts an annual Acadian Festival in September.
□ Fresh lobster can be bought in late summer and early fall at the Acadian Fishermen's Cooperative, 10 kilometres south in Cape Egmont.

0 1 2 3 4 5 Miles

0 2 4 6 8 Kilometres

West of Summerside, the low-lying central portion of Prince County is thinly populated yet rich in history. Much of this region was molded by the hands of hardy Acadians, experts at reaping harvests from land and sea.

Twin-spired churches tower by the roadside in seaside villages such as Egmont Bay and Mount Carmel, where French is still spoken in the tradition of the Acadian pioneers of two centuries ago. This people's culture, their music and dance, food and handicrafts, can be seen and appreciated at the Acadian Pioneer Village in Mount Carmel; at the Acadian Museum in Miscouche; and at the Acadian Festival, held in Abrams Village each September.

Early Acadians survived famine and plague. After the island came under British control in 1763, Acadians often fled to the woods to escape persecution by British soldiers. During harsh winters, Acadians shared meager rations of eel and walrus with starving settlers from Scotland.

The troubled history of the Acadians is in sharp contrast to that of shipbuilders who prospered here in the 19th century, when almost every cove and inlet around the island was the scene of bustling shipbuilding activity. Island-built ships sailed to all corners of the world, and for some Islanders lumbering and shipbuilding were sources of great wealth. In Green Provincial Park is the restored home of James Yeo, whose family ranked among the island's leading shipbuilders.

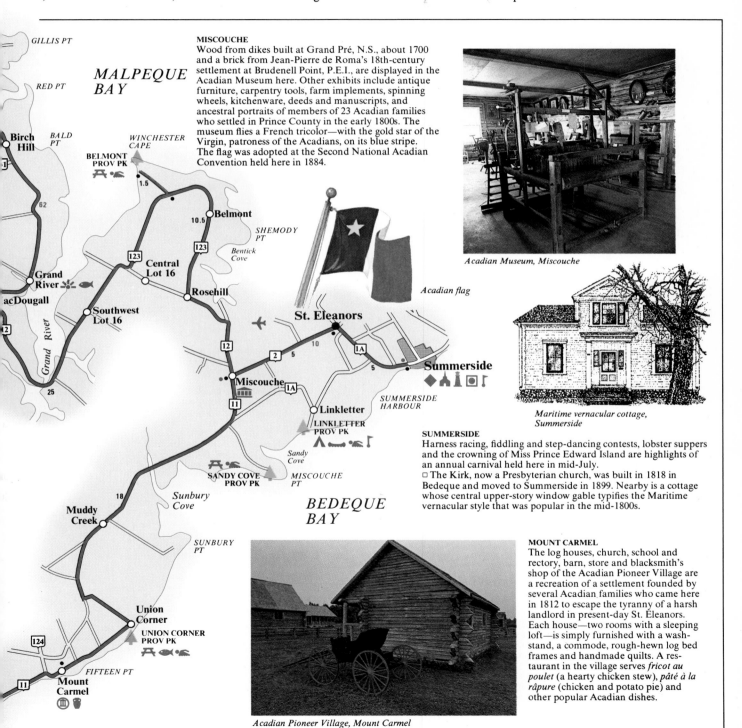

MISCOUCHE
Wood from dikes built at Grand Pré, N.S., about 1700 and a brick from Jean-Pierre de Roma's 18th-century settlement at Brudenell Point, P.E.I., are displayed in the Acadian Museum here. Other exhibits include antique furniture, carpentry tools, farm implements, spinning wheels, kitchenware, deeds and manuscripts, and ancestral portraits of members of 23 Acadian families who settled in Prince County in the early 1800s. The museum flies a French tricolor—with the gold star of the Virgin, patroness of the Acadians, on its blue stripe. The flag was adopted at the Second National Acadian Convention held here in 1884.

Acadian Museum, Miscouche

Acadian flag

Maritime vernacular cottage, Summerside

SUMMERSIDE
Harness racing, fiddling and step-dancing contests, lobster suppers and the crowning of Miss Prince Edward Island are highlights of an annual carnival held here in mid-July.
□ The Kirk, now a Presbyterian church, was built in 1818 in Bedeque and moved to Summerside in 1899. Nearby is a cottage whose central upper-story window gable typifies the Maritime vernacular style that was popular in the mid-1800s.

MOUNT CARMEL
The log houses, church, school and rectory, barn, store and blacksmith's shop of the Acadian Pioneer Village are a recreation of a settlement founded by several Acadian families who came here in 1812 to escape the tyranny of a harsh landlord in present-day St. Éleanors. Each house—two rooms with a sleeping loft—is simply furnished with a washstand, a commode, rough-hewn log bed frames and handmade quilts. A restaurant in the village serves *fricot au poulet* (a hearty chicken stew), *pâté à la râpure* (chicken and potato pie) and other popular Acadian dishes.

Acadian Pioneer Village, Mount Carmel

Warm Beaches, Shifting Dunes, Rugged Cliffs–and a Tireless Wind

North-Central Prince Edward Island

The great dune lands of Prince Edward Island's north shore are like a strip cut from the mighty Sahara and set down between a storybook sea and a neat country garden. The best place to experience both the naturalist's awe at the creation of the dunes and the sunny comfort of some of the finest beaches in North America is in Prince Edward Island National Park. This 40-kilometre stretch of sand, bluffs, salt marshes and freshwater ponds is one of the smallest of the national parks. Yet, each

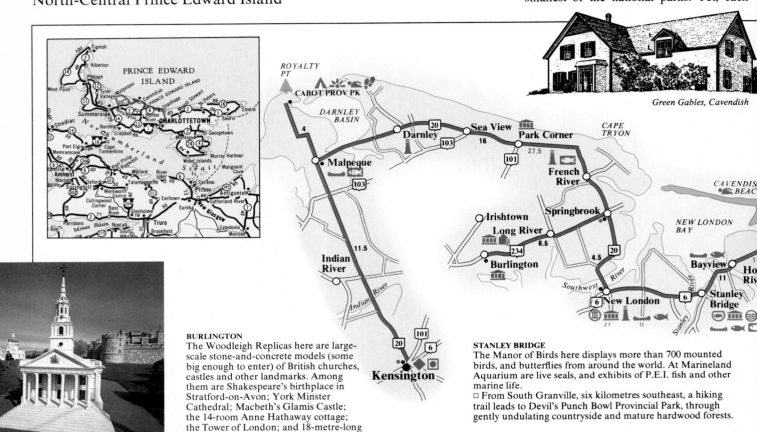

Green Gables, Cavendish

Woodleigh Replicas, Burlington

BURLINGTON

The Woodleigh Replicas here are large-scale stone-and-concrete models (some big enough to enter) of British churches, castles and other landmarks. Among them are Shakespeare's birthplace in Stratford-on-Avon; York Minster Cathedral; Macbeth's Glamis Castle; the 14-room Anne Hathaway cottage; the Tower of London; and 18-metre-long Dunvegan Castle (with antique furnishings, Scottish artwork and a dungeon).
□ At Long River, three kilometres east, Ye Olde Mill Museum displays a Scottish wool-carding machine, a weaving loom (c. 1820), spinning wheels, a variety of wagons and sleighs and antique furniture and kitchenware.

STANLEY BRIDGE

The Manor of Birds here displays more than 700 mounted birds, and butterflies from around the world. At Marineland Aquarium are live seals, and exhibits of P.E.I. fish and other marine life.
□ From South Granville, six kilometres southeast, a hiking trail leads to Devil's Punch Bowl Provincial Park, through gently undulating countryside and mature hardwood forests.

NEW LONDON

A green-trimmed white cottage here was the birthplace of Lucy Maud Montgomery, author of *Anne of Green Gables* (1908), the first in a popular series of warm, lively novels for young girls. In the house, now a provincial historic site, are Miss Montgomery's wedding dress, scrapbooks and a replica of the blue chest she wrote about in *The Story Girl* (1911).
□ At Park Corner, 10 kilometres north, is The Story Girl and Silver Bush House which gets its name and fame from *The Story Girl* and another novel written by Miss Montgomery, who lived here with her aunt and uncle after her parents died. It was in this house, in 1911, that she married the Rev. Ewan MacDonald, a Presbyterian minister. *Pat of Silver Bush* (1933) and *The Story Girl* were based on incidents that occurred here.

Sand-Loving Marram Grass

The botanical name for marram grass, *Ammophila arenaria*, means "sand loving." On north-shore Prince Edward Island the sand desperately needs loving—just to stay put. Marram grass obliges. It is the first growth in nature's system for turning sand into something that can support life. Marram roots reach as much as three metres down in search of water, then spread into a deep, stringy network that helps hold great sand dunes together. The grass survives because it can grow quickly to the surface after being blanketed with sand and because it is impervious to salt spray. But it is not hardy enough to withstand heavy human traffic. Once the grass has gone, the wind often carves small depressions into giant holes called "blowouts." Too many blowouts turn stable dunes into constantly shifting hills unable to support vegetation.

year, more than a million persons come here. Hundreds of thousands make the pilgrimage to Green Gables, the house that helped inspire Lucy Maud Montgomery's classic *Anne of Green Gables*. Other hundreds of thousands find a deeper meaning in the park: a sense of the incredible complexity in the natural forces that make the dune country what it is.

A few metres from the shoreline, white spruce fight to grip the sand. Winds prune them, salt spray stunts them. Strange, twisted, older than they look (some trees 75 years old are less than a metre high), they are the tough handiwork of the violent elements. Yet farther inland, where the high dunes offer shelter from winds and salt spray, the white spruce grow straight and tall, heralding the start of the coastal forest, with its carpet of rich, emerald-green ferns and mosses.

Along the park's seaward edge great waves roll relentlessly to the land. White breakers curl, collapse, and foam up on the beaches, each in turn tracing a delicate new line of sand at high water. The wind teases and sweeps and scours the dunes and the spits, digging some depressions deeper, filling in others, tirelessly reshaping the sandy shore.

Sandstone cliffs, Prince Edward Island National Park

CAVENDISH
Green Gables, the old farmhouse immortalized in *Anne of Green Gables* and other novels by Lucy Maud Montgomery, is a museum in the Cavendish section of Prince Edward Island National Park. Green Gables was the home of Lucy Maud's friends David and Margaret MacNeill. In the novels this house became Anne's home. Places such as Anne's Babbling Brook, the Lake of Shining Waters, the Haunted Woods and the Lovers' Lane are on or near the park's 18-hole golf course. Close by, in Cavendish cemetery, is Miss Montgomery's grave. The world-famous author died in Toronto in 1942.

RUSTICO ISLAND
This island in P.E.I. National Park is summer home to hundreds of great blue herons—some with wingspreads of almost two metres. They nest high in spruce trees and forage for fish in marshes and ponds.

Great blue heron

P.E.I. NATIONAL PARK
Fringed by the Gulf of St. Lawrence, this park has some of North America's finest white sand beaches. Near Cavendish is sand tinted pink by the erosion of bleached red clay. Between North Rustico Harbour and Orby Head are more than nine kilometres of red sandstone cliffs up to 30 metres high. At Brackley Beach, wooden walkways pass sand dunes up to 18 metres high. Red foxes prowl the dunes, and mink, muskrat and raccoons are common. Among 210 species of birds are the northern phalarope, Swainson's thrush, marsh hawk and slate-colored junco.
□ In addition to cottages and camping facilities, the park has an elegant and historic summer hotel: Dalvay-by-the-Sea, built in 1895, was once the summer estate of Alexander Macdonald, a Cincinnati oil tycoon.

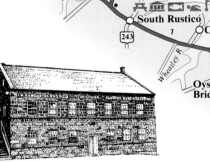
Farmers' Bank, South Rustico

NORTH RUSTICO
Animals native to the Maritimes are exhibited in P.E.I. Wildlife Park here.
□ At South Rustico, a monument to the Rev. Georges-Antoine Belcourt stands between Saint Augustine's Church where he was parish priest from 1859 to 1869 and the Farmers' Bank he founded in 1864. The bank, the smallest ever chartered in Canada, operated on the credit union principle, although credit unions as such were not introduced in Canada until 1900. The two-story brown sandstone bank building (1861-64), now the parish hall, contains a small museum. Exhibits include the bank's own $5 notes.

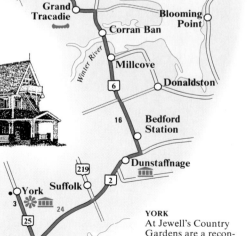
Dalvay-by-the-Sea Hotel, Prince Edward Island National Park

DUNSTAFFNAGE
A 1916 Buick, a 1921 Chevrolet touring car, a 1925 Studebaker, a 1929 Durant, a 1933 Dodge sedan and a 1938 Packard hearse are among the 40 restored automobiles at the Spoke Wheel Car Museum here. A 1931 Ford cabriolet—the last sequence of the Model A line—has a four-cylinder engine, rumble seat, slanted windshield, black fenders and convertible top, beige body and chocolate-brown trim.

YORK
At Jewell's Country Gardens are a reconstructed 19th-century general store, smithy, one-room schoolhouse and chapel. Also among the flowers is an antique glass museum.

CHARLOTTETOWN
(see Road Unit 147)

The Peaceful Island Capital Where Canada Was Born

South-Central Prince Edward Island

Charlottetown, the cradle of Confederation—with its Victorian homes, stately churches and tree-shaded squares—is the peaceful urban counterpart of Prince Edward Island's idyllic farmlands and seaside villages.

The city's most impressive modern building is the Confederation Center for the Arts, which was officially opened by Elizabeth II in 1964. Within the center's great slabbed stone walls, a museum displays contemporary Canadian fine arts, and an art gal-

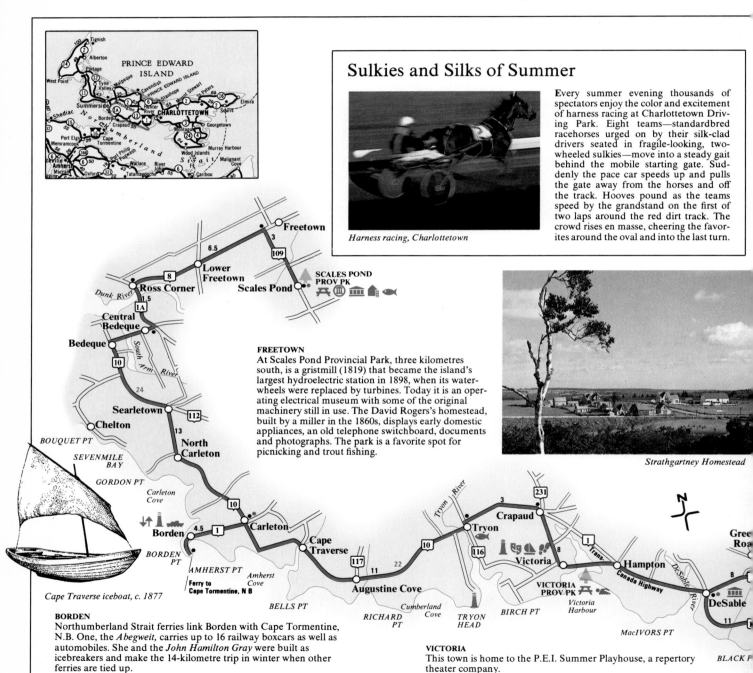

Sulkies and Silks of Summer

Every summer evening thousands of spectators enjoy the color and excitement of harness racing at Charlottetown Driving Park. Eight teams—standardbred racehorses urged on by their silk-clad drivers seated in fragile-looking, two-wheeled sulkies—move into a steady gait behind the mobile starting gate. Suddenly the pace car speeds up and pulls the gate away from the horses and off the track. Hooves pound as the teams speed by the grandstand on the first of two laps around the red dirt track. The crowd rises en masse, cheering the favorites around the oval and into the last turn.

Harness racing, Charlottetown

Strathgartney Homestead

Cape Traverse iceboat, c. 1877

FREETOWN
At Scales Pond Provincial Park, three kilometres south, is a gristmill (1819) that became the island's largest hydroelectric station in 1898, when its waterwheels were replaced by turbines. Today it is an operating electrical museum with some of the original machinery still in use. The David Rogers's homestead, built by a miller in the 1860s, displays early domestic appliances, an old telephone switchboard, documents and photographs. The park is a favorite spot for picnicking and trout fishing.

BORDEN
Northumberland Strait ferries link Borden with Cape Tormentine, N.B. One, the *Abegweit*, carries up to 16 railway boxcars as well as automobiles. She and the *John Hamilton Gray* were built as icebreakers and make the 14-kilometre trip in winter when other ferries are tied up.
□ At Cape Traverse, six kilometres east, a replica of an ice-boat is on display. These 5.5-metre wooden boats, with iron runners on both sides of the keel, were towed across ice and rowed or sailed across water. For most of a century (1827-1917) they were the only winter transportation link between P.E.I. and the mainland.

VICTORIA
This town is home to the P.E.I. Summer Playhouse, a repertory theater company.
□ Vacationers can enjoy sailing excursions off Victoria Harbour aboard a traditionally rigged schooner.
□ The 32-kilometre Bonshaw Hills Trail, between Victoria and St. Catherines, leads hikers through farm fields and cool, dark hemlock forests.

0   1   2   3   4   5 Miles

0   2   4   6   8 Kilometres

lery houses more than 1,500 works, such as oil paintings by Canadian masters Robert Harris and Jean-Paul Lemieux. The center's 1,000-seat theater highlights its year-round program with a gala summer festival of musical theater, whose repertoire includes *Anne of Green Gables,* and colorful performances by Canada's exuberant folk-dance troupe, Les Feux-Follets.

Across the street is a reminder of the past: the old legislative building with the chamber where the Fathers of Confederation first met, in 1864. The chairs they used stand neatly around the table at which they deliberated. A plaque tells that

In the hearts and minds of the delegates who assembled in this room on September 1st 1864 was born the Dominion of Canada. Providence being their Guide, they builded better than they knew.

In August, Old Home Week in Charlottetown features one of Canada's best rural fairs, at the Provincial Exhibition Grounds, and harness racing at Charlottetown Driving Park. West of the city there is fishing, hiking, sailing in Northumberland Strait, and summer theater at Victoria. There are museums to visit at Scales Pond, Bonshaw and Strathgartney. And at Rocky Point, in Fort Amherst National Historic Park, is the site of Port la Joie—the island's first white settlement, founded in 1720 by 300 French colonists. The British took it in 1758 and six years later, across the harbor, founded Charlottetown.

Province House, Charlottetown

CHARLOTTETOWN

Canada's smallest provincial capital and the only city in Prince Edward Island. Charlottetown calls itself the birthplace of Canada, for here in September 1864 the Fathers of Confederation met for the first time.
□ Confederation Center, built in 1964, is a national memorial to the Fathers of Confederation. This center, covering two downtown blocks, contains a memorial hall, theater, art gallery, museum and a provincial library.
□ Opposite the center is Province House, a three-story, Georgian-style stone structure built in 1843-47. In a high-ceilinged room, now known as the Confederation Chamber, delegates of Britain's North American colonies signed the articles that led to the uniting of present-day Nova Scotia, New Brunswick, Ontario and Quebec into one nation in 1867. Province House also houses the P.E.I. Legislative Assembly.
□ Government House, an imposing white colonial building, home of P.E.I.'s lieutenant governor, was erected in 1834. Beaconsfield, headquarters of the P.E.I. Heritage Foundation, is a Victorian mansion built in 1877. Both buildings overlook Charlottetown harbor and Victoria Park, where a plaque marks the site of Fort Edward, a six-gun battery (c. 1800). The fort was one of a series of strongholds guarding the entrance to the harbor in the early 19th century.
□ St. Dunstan's Basilica, one of Canada's largest churches, is known for its twin Gothic spires, an impressive altar and fine Italian carvings. Murals in St. Peter's Anglican Cathedral are by Robert Harris, the famous Canadian portrait painter.
□ The baptismal register of St. Paul's Anglican Church contains the name of Margaret Gordon, sweetheart of Thomas Carlyle and heroine of his masterpiece *Sartor Resartus.*

BONSHAW

The prize exhibit in the Car Life Museum is an 1898 Mason Steamer, a two-cylinder, five-horsepower car that runs on naphtha.
□ Visitors to Strathgartney Homestead, two kilometres north, can tour a 16-room house (c. 1847) that is richly furnished in the Victorian style of pioneer Prince Edward Island. Farm implements and household items are displayed in barns and a coach house on the estate. Adjacent to the homestead is Strathgartney Provincial Park.
□ Nearby is Churchill, whose white-frame Presbyterian church (1862) was originally called the Church of Scotland.

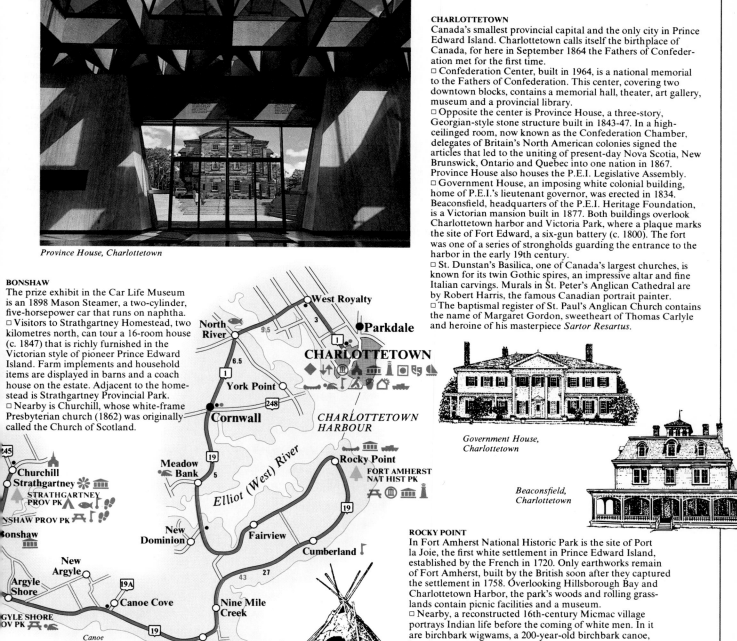

Government House, Charlottetown

Beaconsfield, Charlottetown

ROCKY POINT

In Fort Amherst National Historic Park is the site of Port la Joie, the first white settlement in Prince Edward Island, established by the French in 1720. Only earthworks remain of Fort Amherst, built by the British soon after they captured the settlement in 1758. Overlooking Hillsborough Bay and Charlottetown Harbor, the park's woods and rolling grasslands contain picnic facilities and a museum.
□ Nearby, a reconstructed 16th-century Micmac village portrays Indian life before the coming of white men. In it are birchbark wigwams, a 200-year-old birchbark canoe, hunting and fishing implements and displays of Indian crafts.

Birchbark wigwam at Rocky Point

A Trim and Tranquil Corner in the 'Garden of the Gulf'

Southeastern Prince Edward Island

Life is green and calm and unhurried in this southeastern corner of Canada's "Garden of the Gulf." In the summer sun the land is undulating, trim, as picturesque and ordered as a patchwork quilt. It is close to what much of Canada was like at the turn of the century: placid, homespun and friendly.

Visitors experience this sense of the past at the restored 19th-century country crossroads hamlet at Orwell Corner, and in neat, farming communities such as Belfast (prob-

ORWELL CORNER HISTORIC SITE

Hayrides and musical evenings highlight the summer program at Orwell Corner, where crops and livestock are raised and tended much as they were a century ago. This small rural crossroads, restored to the late 1800s, contains a combined store, post office and farmhouse, with a dressmaker's shop upstairs. There are also barns, a school and a church. The shingled buildings, all on their original sites, date from 1864 to 1896.

Nearby is Sir Andrew Macphail Provincial Park, named after the celebrated author-physician who was born in Orwell in 1864. The park contains a campground, a trout pond and a nature trail.

Orwell Corner Historic Site

MONTAGUE

Among relics of early Prince Edward Island at the Garden of the Gulf Museum are farm implements, a 1698 Bible, clock with wooden works and letters written by Lucy Maud Montgomery, author of *Anne of Green Gables*.
□ A cairn at nearby Brudenell Point commemorates Jean-Pierre de Roma. Depressions in the ground—they were once cellars—are all that remain of his dream of a French settlement in Prince Edward Island 250 years ago. De Roma built wharves, bridges, storehouses and dwellings on the point. But some of his people defected, then crops were destroyed by field mice. In 1745, when the settlement was burned by New England, de Roma and his family hid in the forest and eventually escaped to Quebec.

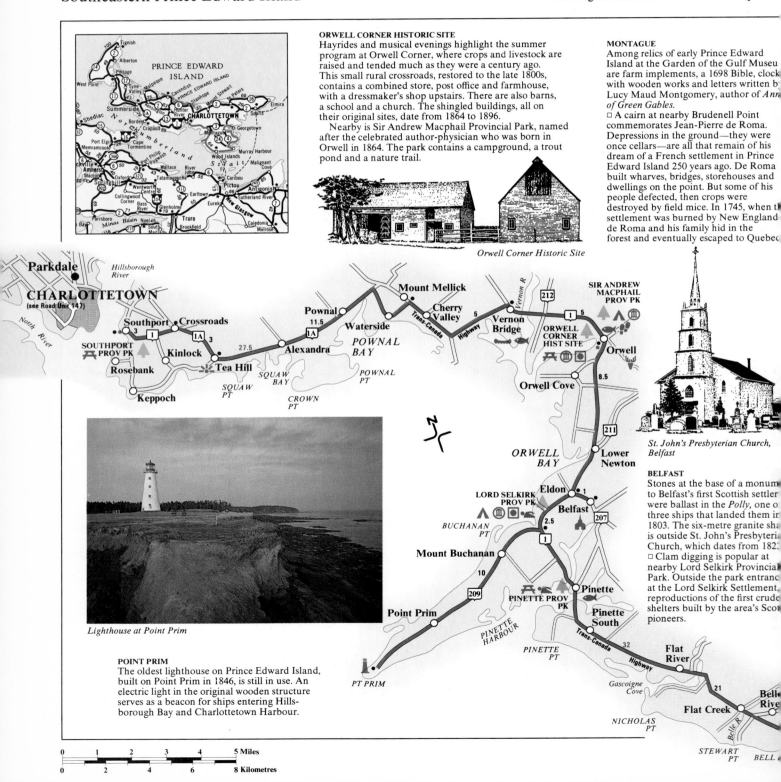

St. John's Presbyterian Church, Belfast

BELFAST

Stones at the base of a monument to Belfast's first Scottish settlers were ballast in the *Polly*, one of three ships that landed them in 1803. The six-metre granite shaft is outside St. John's Presbyterian Church, which dates from 1823.
□ Clam digging is popular at nearby Lord Selkirk Provincial Park. Outside the park entrance at the Lord Selkirk Settlement, reproductions of the first crude shelters built by the area's Scottish pioneers.

Lighthouse at Point Prim

POINT PRIM

The oldest lighthouse on Prince Edward Island, built on Point Prim in 1846, is still in use. An electric light in the original wooden structure serves as a beacon for ships entering Hillsborough Bay and Charlottetown Harbour.

0 1 2 3 4 5 Miles
0 2 4 6 8 Kilometres

ably a corruption of *la belle face* to denote the lovely view). On a knoll in Belfast is a memorial to the Selkirk Settlers—800 impoverished crofters brought out from the Isle of Skye by Lord Selkirk in 1803, in one of numerous infusions of Scottish blood. Nearby is a 150-year-old church the settlers built. Its archives contain Selkirk's deed of land for the church and the nearby cemetery.

Some visitors come to the island "from away" and never want to leave. Many families spend summer or fall vacations as paying guests in farm homes. There are farms everywhere, with ample wooden houses, big barns, sturdy fences, fat cattle. Fields surge with golden grain, and, near little places such as Cherry Valley, with great green leaves of tobacco.

Teeming Life Along the Seashore

A myriad of small marine creatures lives close to the water's edge along Prince Edward Island's long stretches of sandy beach.

The starfish, usually found in tidal pools, feeds upon clams, mussels and oysters. It attaches its five powerful arms to the shell of its prey by means of hundreds of suction-tube feet on the underside of each arm. Forcing the shell open by pulling from opposite sides, it lowers its stomach to envelop the prey.

Low tide is best for digging clams. Watch for small round holes in the sand, from which burrowing clams—up to 30 centimetres below the surface—eject streams of water when one walks near.

Hermit crabs, often seen scurrying along tidal pools, are beach scavengers that inhabit the empty shells of marine snails. The crab's rear appendages grasp the inside of the shell; when danger threatens, its two front claws block the shell opening.

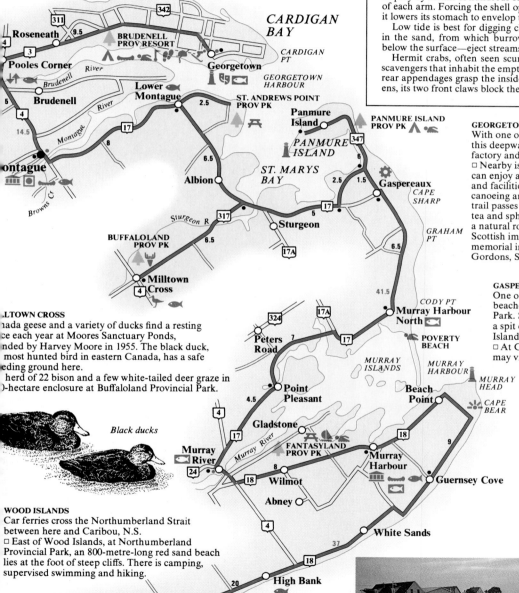

GEORGETOWN

With one of the finest harbors on Canada's east coast, this deepwater port has a modern fish processing factory and a shipbuilding plant.

□ Nearby is Brudenell Provincial Resort, where visitors can enjoy an 18-hole golf course, tennis courts, chalets, and facilities for camping, supervised swimming, canoeing and horseback riding. A self-guiding nature trail passes a spruce bog where sheep laurel, Labrador tea and sphagnum moss grow. Offshore but linked by a natural rock causeway is Brudenell Island, where Scottish immigrants settled in the late 1750s. A stone memorial in their cemetery bears the names of Gordons, Stewarts, MacLarens and other pioneers.

GASPEREAUX

One of Prince Edward Island's finest white sand beaches is at nearby Panmure Island Provincial Park. Sand dunes are up to six metres high on a spit of land between Smith Point and Panmure Island.

□ At Graham Point, south of Gaspereaux, tourists may visit a lobster cannery.

MURRAY HARBOUR

This village is home to a fleet of some 35 fishing boats, much of whose catch of lobster, hard-shell clams and other fish is canned at a local factory.

□ The Log Cabin Museum, two kilometres south, houses antiques up to 200 years old. Featured are old spinning wheels, crockery, lamps, gramophones and a collection of dolls dating to 1850.

□ Near Gladstone, sculptures of storybook characters are displayed in natural settings in Fantasyland Provincial Park.

MILLTOWN CROSS

Canada geese and a variety of ducks find a resting place each year at Moores Sanctuary Ponds, founded by Harvey Moore in 1955. The black duck, most hunted bird in eastern Canada, has a safe feeding ground here.

A herd of 22 bison and a few white-tailed deer graze in a 60-hectare enclosure at Buffaloland Provincial Park.

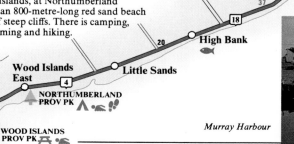

Black ducks

WOOD ISLANDS

Car ferries cross the Northumberland Strait between here and Caribou, N.S.

□ East of Wood Islands, at Northumberland Provincial Park, an 800-metre-long red sand beach lies at the foot of steep cliffs. There is camping, supervised swimming and hiking.

Murray Harbour

An Old Lighthouse, a Modern Ark and a Sea Full of Bluefins

Northeastern Prince Edward Island

At Savage Harbour, Morell, Naufrage, North Lake and other north-shore ports in Prince Edward Island, brightly painted fishing vessels seldom slumber against sunlit wharves. After the lobster season ends in late June, most boats head out to deep-sea fishing grounds in the Gulf of St. Lawrence. Many local skippers welcome tourists aboard for a day spent "jigging" multihooked lines in waters that are alive with mackerel, haddock, cod and herring.

In late summer and early fall, sport fish-

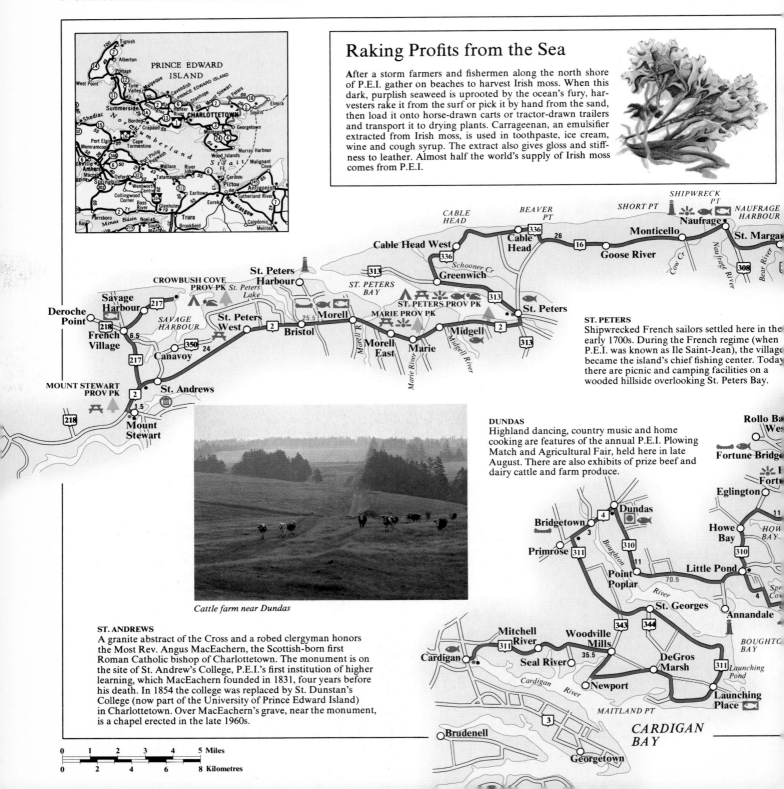

Raking Profits from the Sea

After a storm farmers and fishermen along the north shore of P.E.I. gather on beaches to harvest Irish moss. When this dark, purplish seaweed is uprooted by the ocean's fury, harvesters rake it from the surf or pick it by hand from the sand, then load it onto horse-drawn carts or tractor-drawn trailers and transport it to drying plants. Carrageenan, an emulsifier extracted from Irish moss, is used in toothpaste, ice cream, wine and cough syrup. The extract also gives gloss and stiffness to leather. Almost half the world's supply of Irish moss comes from P.E.I.

ST. PETERS
Shipwrecked French sailors settled here in the early 1700s. During the French regime (when P.E.I. was known as Ile Saint-Jean), the village became the island's chief fishing center. Today there are picnic and camping facilities on a wooded hillside overlooking St. Peters Bay.

DUNDAS
Highland dancing, country music and home cooking are features of the annual P.E.I. Plowing Match and Agricultural Fair, held here in late August. There are also exhibits of prize beef and dairy cattle and farm produce.

Cattle farm near Dundas

ST. ANDREWS
A granite abstract of the Cross and a robed clergyman honors the Most Rev. Angus MacEachern, the Scottish-born first Roman Catholic bishop of Charlottetown. The monument is on the site of St. Andrew's College, P.E.I.'s first institution of higher learning, which MacEachern founded in 1831, four years before his death. In 1854 the college was replaced by St. Dunstan's College (now part of the University of Prince Edward Island) in Charlottetown. Over MacEachern's grave, near the monument, is a chapel erected in the late 1960s.

ermen are lured here by the chance of hooking a giant bluefin tuna. (Some of the world's largest bluefins have been caught in these waters, and more than a thousand have been boated in a single season.) When a tuna is hooked, the ensuing battle can last mere seconds or stretch into a marathon of endurance. A successful day ends with the traditional weigh-in ceremony, and photographs of the victor and his prize.

The annual P.E.I. Plowing Match and Agricultural Fair is held in the cattle-raising

Tuna fishing, North Lake

center of Dundas, in late August. At East Point, visitors may tour a lighthouse built in 1867. At Spry Point, Sunday visitors may tour the Ark—an experimental house of the future that is heated by solar energy. At Basin Head, there are guided walks over magnificent sand dunes; here too is one of the province's finest museums—a tribute to the proud, independent spirit of P.E.I.'s commercial inshore fishermen.

NORTH LAKE
Sport fishermen from around the world come here each year (from August to early October) to pit their strength against fighting bluefin tuna. A 538-kilogram giant—the world's largest to date—was caught off North Lake in 1976. Boats can be chartered for deep-sea fishing.
□ Three kilometres south is Elmira Station. Restored as a railway museum, this green, one-story frame structure (c. 1911) has two waiting rooms, a baggage depot and an agent's office.

EAST POINT
Centuries ago Micmac Indians named this area Kespemenagek—"the end of the island." Today the East Point lighthouse, a wooden colonial structure that may be visited, marks this easternmost tip of Prince Edward Island. Built in 1867, the white tower is one of the province's four manned lighthouses (the other three are on Panmure, Souris and Wood islands). All other lighthouses in P.E.I. are automatic.

East Point lighthouse

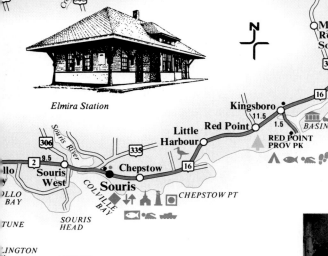

Elmira Station

BASIN HEAD
High on a sandy bluff overlooking the Atlantic Ocean, the Basin Head Fisheries Museum recounts the history of inshore commercial fishing in Prince Edward Island. The museum displays photographs and marine equipment, including ropes, hooks, nets, drying racks and a dory. On the beach below are four reconstructed fish shacks; and on the wharf stands an old lobster cannery.
□ The museum's interpretive program features guided walks over sand dunes where beach grass, lichens and other vegetation fight for life. Cranberries grow in sheltered spots. Foxes roam the dunes hunting meadow voles, shrews and woodland jumping mice. Herring gulls, great black-billed gulls and crows are seen on the barren open center part of the dune system.

SOURIS
This town is noted for its deep-sea fishing and lobster industry and for its fine beach on Northumberland Strait. A car ferry links Souris with Cap-aux-Meules in the Magdalen Islands.
□ The Black Pond Bird Sanctuary, maintained by the Canadian Wildlife Service, is eight kilometres northeast of the town. Great blue herons, black ducks, blue-winged teals and American goldeneyes visit ponds and a lagoon in the sanctuary.

SPRY POINT
Heated by the sun and powered by wind turbines, the Ark at Spry Point is an experimental "bioshelter" built in 1976 by an international team of researchers with funds provided by the Canadian government. A prototype for houses of the future, the structure contains greenhouses for growing vegetables, and aquaculture tanks for raising fish. Visitors may tour the Ark on Sunday afternoons.

Basin Head Fisheries Museum

Windjammer Lore, Scallops and the Picturesque 'French Shore'

Southwestern Nova Scotia

Sunset, Sandy Cove

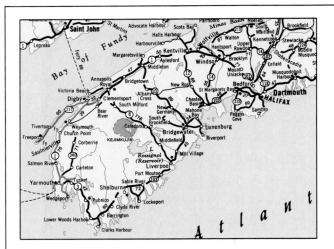

WESTPORT
South of this fishing village on Brier Island, columns of rock march to the water's edge, then extend for hundreds of metres into the sea. In spring and summer, the rocks are enlivened by streaks of green lichens and dazzling blue, white and yellow wildflowers. Many species of sea and land birds congregate on the island during migration.
□ A plaque commemorates Capt. Joshua Slocum, the first man to sail around the world alone—between April 1895 and June 1898. Slocum lived in Westport until he went to sea as a 16-year-old. His famous voyage, when he was 51, was in the oyster sloop *Spray*—less than 12 metres long. About a decade after he returned to his home in Newport, R.I., the captain was lost at sea.

YARMOUTH
A 181-kilogram stone at the Yarmouth County Museum may have been inscribed by Norsemen 1,000 years ago. Ship paintings and models in the museum reflect Yarmouth's prominence as a shipbuilding center during the late 1800s, and a chart locates the 20 shipyards in the area at that time.
□ The Firefighters' Museum of Nova Scotia has two Hunneman engines made in 1840 and an 1880 Silsby steamer. The museum's 34 engines form Canada's largest such collection.
□ The Western Nova Scotia Exhibition, in August, has horse shows, displays of crafts and livestock, and a midway. A 10-day tuna festival is held in August and September.
□ The Yarmouth light, on Cape Forchu near Yarmouth harbor, can be seen from 48 kilometres at sea. Champlain named the "forked" cape in 1604. It has had a lighthouse since 1840.
□ The road between Yarmouth and Hebron is called the Lupine Trail—for the blue-violet and pink lupines which are common throughout Yarmouth County.

Amoskeag steamer (1863), Firefighters' Museum, Yarmouth

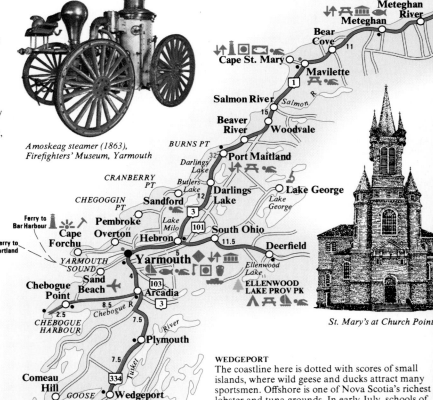

St. Mary's at Church Point

Monument in Town Point Cemetery

CHEBOGUE POINT
In Town Point Cemetery, a life-size marble monument of a woman resting on sheaves of wheat is a Canadian doctor's memorial to his Scottish wife. Frederick Webster, a medical student at the University of Edinburgh, met Margaret McNaught while walking in the Scottish countryside. Some say that when she died in Yarmouth, N.S., in 1864, aged 45, Webster had the monument carved as he remembered her from their first meeting.

WEDGEPORT
The coastline here is dotted with scores of small islands, where wild geese and ducks attract many sportsmen. Offshore is one of Nova Scotia's richest lobster and tuna grounds. In early July, schools of bluefin tuna feed on herring and mackerel among the rocky Tusket Islands. The tuna are found in the powerful flow of the Tusket riptide—a six-knot current about 1.6 kilometres wide.

A century ago, when 3,000 Nova Scotian windjammers made up one of the world's largest mercantile fleets, the town of Yarmouth was the richest port per capita on the Atlantic coast. Now, Yarmouth thrives on the summer tourists arriving on the daily car ferries from Portland and Bar Harbor, Maine. From this southwest tip of the province, a road leads north along the "French Shore," where picturesque Acadian villages line St. Mary's Bay.

This district of Nova Scotia was settled in 1768 by Acadians who had been expelled by the English 13 years before. The first to return was Joseph Dugas, who walked some 483 kilometres from New England to Church Point, leading his wife and daughter on a horse. Other Acadians straggled back by canoe or schooner and established communities such as Mavillette, Meteghan, Saulnierville, Comeauville, Belliveau Cove and St. Bernard. Most of the nearly 9,000 people who live in these places are of Acadian descent. In mid-July an Acadian festival alternates between Church Point and Meteghan River.

Farther north are the seaside resorts of Smiths Cove and Digby, the latter famed for its scallop fleet and a superb 18-hole championship golf course. Possible side trips from Digby include a day-long excursion out to Westport, on Brier Island. This tiny island at the mouth of the Bay of Fundy was the boyhood home of Capt. Joshua Slocum, the first man to sail around the world alone—between April 1895 and June 1898.

SANDY COVE
Deep-sea fishing for cod, pollack, haddock and halibut makes Sandy Cove, a picturesque village 32 kilometres southwest of Digby, a sportsmen's favorite. Fishing boats are available for charter here and farther out on Digby Neck—at Tiverton and Freeport on Long Island, and at Wesport on Brier Island. Ferries run regularly between the mainland and the islands.

DIGBY
One of the world's great scallop fleets is based in Digby, close to the Bay of Fundy scallop grounds. (A scallop festival is held here in August.) The town is also famous for its smoked herring, called "Digby chicks."
□ One of Nova Scotia's most popular summer resorts, Digby offers golfing, boating, deep-sea fishing, saltwater swimming and horseback riding. The Pines is a resort hotel run by the province. A car ferry operates daily between here and Saint John, N.B.

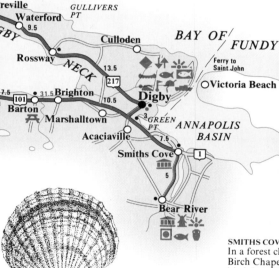

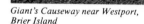

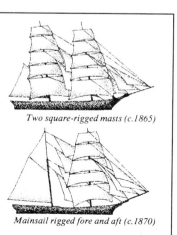

Giant's Causeway near Westport, Brier Island

METEGHAN
La Vieille Maison, an Acadian house built in the 1760s, is a private museum containing 18th-century sea chests, butter churns and spinning wheels.
□ Trees from a parishioner's woodlot became the pillars that support the soaring arches of St. Mary's Church, 18 kilometres north, at Church Point. Built in 1905, St. Mary's seats 750 and is called the largest wooden church in Canada.
□ The village of Grosses Coques is named for big St. Mary's Bay clams that kept the first Acadian settlers alive through a long bitter winter.
□ An Acadian cemetery at nearby Belliveau Cove was the first established in Nova Scotia after the expulsion of the Acadians in 1755.
□ St. Bernard (pop. 324) has a great stone church that seats 1,000 persons.

Digby scallop

SMITHS COVE
In a forest clearing in this quiet resort town stands Birch Chapel, built in 1919 with rough-hewn yellow birch logs. Anglican services are held in summer.
□ Bear River, eight kilometres southeast, is noted for its cherry trees and for a cherry carnival usually held in July. Highlands above the town provide a fine view of the Annapolis Basin.

Unloading Irish moss, Wedgeport

Yarmouth's Golden Age

Shipbuilding in Yarmouth flourished during the Golden Age of Sail in the late 19th century, when thousands of wooden vessels of all shapes and sizes were built in bays and harbors along the Nova Scotia coast. By the late 1870s Canada ranked fourth among shipbuilding and shipowning countries—and Yarmouth led the nation. While the ships and men of the "Bluenose Fleet" won fame around the world, wealth flowed into Yarmouth's two banks and its insurance companies, and to ship chandlers and sailmakers. Ships of the 19th century carried great clouds of sail. Square rigging (hung from transverse yards) caught lots of wind but required big crews working aloft. Fore-and-aft-rigged ships needed fewer men and were more maneuverable near shore. Designs of various ships changed over the years; those pictured (*right*) are typical of the years indicated.

Two square-rigged masts (c.1865)

Mainsail rigged fore and aft (c.1870)

Good Cheer, a Bloodied Fort and a Deep, Woodland Haven

Southwestern Nova Scotia

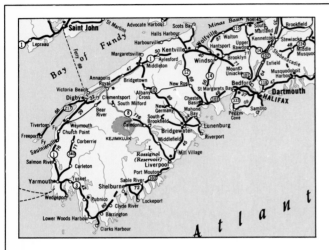

Port Royal Habitation

VICTORIA BEACH

A pony express that helped speed news from Britain to the United States is commemorated by a national historic plaque here. The express operated in 1849, the year after a telegraph line linked New York with Saint John. Cunard ships brought British dispatches to Halifax. From there the messages were sped 232 kilometres west to Victoria Beach (with fresh horses every 20 kilometres), then by steamer across the Bay of Fundy to Saint John for relay to the United States. At the end of 1849, when Halifax and Saint John were linked by telegraph via Amherst, N.S., the express was suspended.

PORT ROYAL

Here stands a reconstruction of the Habitation that de Monts, Champlain and Poutrincourt established in 1605. The buildings of Port Royal National Historic Park are faithful in every detail to the originals, designed by Champlain. They form a compact square around a courtyard and are fortified by a palisade and a cannon platform. The buildings include the governor's residence, a chapel, a kitchen, a blacksmith shop and a fur-trading room.

Here, in 1606, Champlain formed North America's first social club, the Order of Good Cheer. Each member took his turn as Grand Master, responsible for the daily feast of game and wine. Marc Lescarbot, a Paris lawyer, wrote and produced North America's first play here. *Le Théâtre de Neptune* was performed in 1606.

CORNWALLIS

Built during World War II (as HMCS *Cornwallis,* the Commonwealth's biggest naval training base), CFB Cornwallis is now a basic training school. Tours can be arranged. □ In Clementsport, 2.5 kilometres east, is Old St. Edward's Church, consecrated in 1797 to serve United Empire Loyalist settlers. Coins, household effects, prayer books and a silver communion set from that period are displayed in the church.

Scarlet tanager

Blanding's turtle

A Generous Oasis for Plants and Wildlife

Because Kejimkujik National Park is in a region that has longer, hotter summers than the rest of Nova Scotia, unusual plants and animals exist here: in a lush mixed forest that contains huge hemlocks centuries old, there are greenbrier and witch hazel and such birds as the scarlet tanager, great crested flycatcher and wood thrush. The ribbon snake, Blanding's turtle and the southern flying squirrel—species found nowhere else in the Atlantic provinces—inhabit the park. Kejimkujik has five species of snakes and salamanders, three of turtles and eight of frogs and toads—one of the most varied reptile and amphibian populations in eastern Canada. Several lakes support whitefish, a species common farther west.

Eastern hemlock

Kejimkujik National Park

KEJIMKUJIK NATIONAL PARK

This 380-square-kilometre park was opened in 1969 to preserve some of Nova Scotia's finest interior woodlands. Island-dotted lakes are surrounded by low-lying forested hills that were molded by glaciers thousands of years ago. A network of seven canoe routes provides the best means of exploring the park's forested depths. There are more than 100 kilometres of hiking trails, and an interpretive program includes guided walks, canoe outings, nature films and lectures. For snowshoers and cross-country skiers the Kejimkujik wilderness is a haven of tranquility.

0   1   2   3   4   5 Miles
0   2   4   6   8 Kilometres

Overlooking the broad Annapolis Basin is Port Royal National Historic Park, site of the first successful French colony in the New World. In 1605 Pierre de Monts, and a boatload of French colonists, built a stockaded Habitation in what was then called "Acadie." To brighten their lives, explorer Samuel de Champlain created *l'Ordre de Bon-Temps* (the Order of Good Cheer), which featured banquets of moose pie, roast duck and much wine, followed by songs and music. Today visitors can explore a replica of Port Royal Habitation, with its original well, studded oaken doors, and cobblestoned room where Indians traded beaver pelts.

A few kilometres away, on the south side of the basin, is Fort Anne National Historic Park at Annapolis Royal. The existing earthworks, built by the French in 1690-1708, were later strengthened by the British. The fort has a violent history and was the most fought over place in Canada. In the streets of Annapolis Royal are historic buildings that reveal glimpses of the past.

From Annapolis Royal, the traveler can continue northeast through the verdant Annapolis Valley, a 130-kilometre-long orchard whose fertile land was farmed by French-speaking Acadians as long ago as 1630. But nature lovers take the road which leads south from Annapolis Royal to Kejimkujik National Park. In this woodland haven visitors will find deep solitude and a seemingly endless network of tree-shaded hiking trails and calm canoe routes.

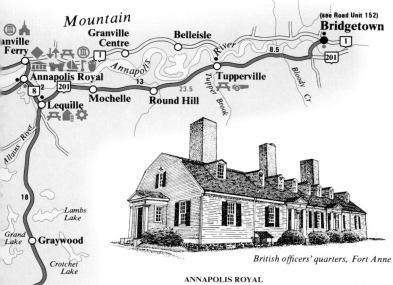

British officers' quarters, Fort Anne

TUPPERVILLE

Two ambushes, in 1711 and 1757, in which French and Indians killed a total of 54 British soldiers from Annapolis Royal, are commemorated by a cairn at nearby Bloody Creek.
□ Col. James Delancey, the "Outlaw of the Bronx" who led pro-British partisans in raids around New York during the American Revolution, settled in this area after being banished from the United States in 1783. His grave is in a private family plot.

GRANVILLE FERRY

The restored Amberman House (c.1730), one of Nova Scotia's oldest, has the "saltbox" exterior and "H and L"-shaped hinges common in early 18th-century New England. These "Holy Lord" hinges were thought to fend off the powers of witchcraft. Hand-hewn beams in the old house are more than nine metres long.

Interior of British officers' quarters, Fort Anne

ANNAPOLIS ROYAL

Near the earth ramparts of Fort Anne National Historic Park is a monument with a bust of Pierre de Monts, founder in 1605 of the original Port Royal Habitation. The French moved their post here in the 1630s, and lost it to the British for good in 1710. In the intervening years, it was the most fought over place in Canada. A powder magazine dating from 1708 (Canada's oldest building outside Quebec) has a door reflecting a violent history that includes some 15 sieges and numerous raids: the top hinge is French, the other English. In 1710 the English renamed the fort and town that had grown up around it, Fort Anne and Annapolis Royal. A reconstructed officers' quarters (1797) displays 18th-century pistols and muskets.
□ Historic buildings on St. George Street include the restored McNamara House—it was a school in the 1790s—and the O'Dell Inn and Tavern, a stagecoach stop in the mid-1800s. It is now a museum. The Banks House (c.1709) is thought to be the town's oldest dwelling.

Indian Petroglyphs: Traces of Prehistory

Here and there on the shores of Kejimkujik Lake is fascinating evidence of early human existence. The slate is so soft that, with a harder rock, a knife or piece of bone, men could carve pictures and symbols on it. Some of these petroglyphs, done by Indians, may predate the arrival of the Europeans. There are pictures of animals, of men fishing and hunting, ancient Micmac symbols, and a four-legged bird encircled by stars (probably an Indian god). Later drawings show European traces in Micmac dress and one figure resembles a French cavalier. Some petroglyphs portray sailing ships with flawless rigging (*left*).

A Fertile Valley Famed for Apples, and a Tidy Farm Still Plowed by Oxen

Annapolis Valley

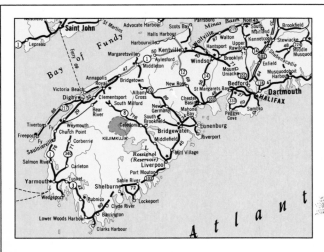

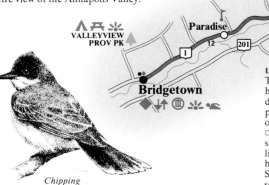

Halls Harbour

St. Mary's Anglican Church, Auburn

HALLS HARBOUR
Overlooking the Minas Channel, where Bay of Fundy tides are among the highest in the world, this picturesque fishing village is named for the captain of the *Mary Jane*, a pirate ship which ravaged the settlement twice in the early 1800s. It came a third time, in 1813, but the settlers, having been warned by an Indian, were waiting in ambush. They defeated the pirates, seized a chest of gold on the *Mary Jane*, and are said to have buried it on shore. The place of burial was forgotten, and the legendary treasure was never found.

AUBURN
Loyalist settlers built St. Mary's Anglican Church in 1790. They made plaster for the walls of the church by powdering the shells of mussels that Acadian refugees ate while in hiding during the winter of 1755-56. (The Acadians had escaped deportation by the English in 1755.) A plaque at St. Mary's commemorates the Rt. Rev. Charles Inglis, first bishop of Nova Scotia (1787), who lived near Auburn for many years.
□ At Morden, 11 kilometres north, a large cross of beach stones honors the estimated 250 Acadians who wintered here in 1755-56. Some of the Acadians died; the survivors escaped by canoe to the north side of Minas Channel in March 1756.
□ Berwick, east of Auburn, is Nova Scotia's largest apple-processing center.

BRIDGETOWN
Fine old houses line the streets of this town, near the head of navigation on the Annapolis River. Acadians settled the area in the 1650s; then came New Englanders and, after 1776, United Empire Loyalists.
□ Valleyview Provincial Park, on the brow of North Mountain, gives a spectacular 80-kilometre view of the Annapolis Valley.

Chipping sparrow

LAWRENCETOWN
The Annapolis County Exhibition, held here in mid-August, has displays of livestock and farm produce, ox and horse pulls, tugs of war and home-cooked meals.
□ Student surveyors are a common sight along highways and railway lines near Lawrencetown: it is the home of the Nova Scotia Land Survey Institute, Canada's only school devoted exclusively to cartography, land surveying and photogrammetry.

GREENWOOD
This town was established for families of airmen stationed at CFB Greenwood, a long-range maritime patrol base. Tours of the base may be arranged through the public relations officer.
□ In the nearby village of Kingston, an annual steer barbecue in early July features sports events, a midway, pony rides and a stage show.

MIDDLETON
Old Holy Trinity Anglican Church, built in 1788 by Loyalist settlers from New England, still has its original straight-backed pews, each with a numbered door. It is no longer in use but may be visited. In Holy Trinity Church (1893) are objects from the old church: a Bible and prayer book dating from 1783, a paten and flagon made in 1792 and a bell cast in 1792.
□ Antiques and other secondhand goods are offered for sale at outdoor flea markets held at Middleton in July and August.
□ Near the seaside village of Margaretsville, 12 kilometres north, visitors enjoy bathing, boating and saltwater fishing in the Bay of Fundy.

0 1 2 3 4 5 Miles
0 2 4 6 8 Kilometres

More than three centuries ago, the fertile land of the Annapolis Valley was farmed by Nova Scotia's first permanent settlers, the French-speaking Acadians. Following their expulsion to the Thirteen Colonies in 1755, the area was settled by New Englanders, and then by United Empire Loyalists fleeing persecution at the hands of American revolutionaries. Many of the Loyalists' descendants remain here today, enjoying an easygoing pace of life, in what has become one of the most well-known apple-producing regions in Canada.

Between Bridgetown and Kentville are peaceful farming communities such as Lawrencetown, Middleton, Aylesford, Berwick—and even a village named Paradise. Along the valley road, sea and woodland bird species give way to farm and orchard species such as the ruby-throated hummingbird, the eastern kingbird and the chipping sparrow. In late May and early June, the valley is filled with the fragrance of blossoming trees.

The main highway runs parallel to the Bay of Fundy shore, which is never more than 15 kilometres due north. Side roads branch off to picturesque seaside hamlets such as Hampton, Port George and Margaretsville, where sunny beaches are washed by Fundy's surging tide.

From Kentville, famed for its springtime Apple Blossom Festival, a road leads south to Nova Scotia's "living museum" of agriculture: New Ross Farm, fully restored and operating as it did a century ago.

Apple Blossom Festival parade, Kentville

KENTVILLE
When orchards are in full bloom in late May or early June the annual Annapolis Valley Apple Blossom Festival is held in Kentville or in one of several other towns in the valley. (The first festival was held in Kentville in 1932.) Each town sponsors a princess in the festival queen competition, and the people of more than a dozen communities participate in five days of parade and pageantry.
□ The Canada Department of Agriculture research station at Kentville specializes in horticulture and poultry research. Nearby CFB Aldershot, once the home of the Black Watch (Royal Highland Regiment) of Canada, is a reserve training base.

NEW ROSS FARM
Plows are pulled by oxen and grain is cut by scythe and sickle at this living museum of agriculture. Ross Farm dates from 1816, when Capt. William Ross of the Nova Scotia Fencibles undertook to settle 172 discharged soldiers in the area.
□ In an 1892 red wooden barn are implements illustrating farm technology from 1600 to 1925. In the collection are cant hooks for removing tree stumps, plows and reapers, and threshing and winnowing machines powered by horse or dog treadmills.
□ Barrels and casks are made and repaired in the cooperage at the farm workshop. There are demonstrations of yoke and shingle making and ox shoeing.
□ Rosebank is a two-story frame house built by Captain Ross in 1817 to replace his first log house. It has five fireplaces. Exhibits include a piano (c.1820) that four soldiers carried from Chester, 24 kilometres south.

Crimson Beauties from the Annapolis Valley

Almost all of Nova Scotia's apple orchards are in the Annapolis Valley, where the soil is rich and the climate mild. Settlers who came here from New England in 1760 planted Canada's first commercial orchards. The trees they grew are gone, but many descendants of those settlers still tend Annapolis Valley orchards.

McIntosh, Red and Gold Delicious (*left to right, above*), and Northern Spy are the commonest varieties of apples here; other types include Crimson Beauty, Melba, Bough Sweet and Honeygold. Apples that bruise easily are sold locally; hardier varieties are exported, mainly to Great Britain and the United States. Most types are used for applesauce, juice, jelly and cider.

Eastern kingbird

Rosebank cottage, New Ross Farm

Memories of a Tragic Acadian Heroine and a Comical Yankee Clock Peddler

Central Nova Scotia

Sandstone cliffs overlooking Minas Basin near Blomidon

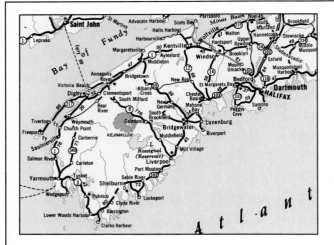

CAPE BLOMIDON

A 14-kilometre hiking trail between Blomidon Provincial Park and Cape Split runs atop 200-metre sandstone cliffs. Lookouts provide sweeping views of the Annapolis Valley, Minas Basin and the Bay of Fundy. Amethyst and agate can be found along the trail. Blomidon may be a corruption of Blow-me-down, as the cape was known to early sailors.

STARRS POINT

In a magnificent garden setting, Prescott House is a Georgian mansion built in 1799-1802 by Charles Ramage Prescott, a pioneer horticulturist. The 21-room structure has a steep hip roof with four dormers and two massive chimneys. The whitewashed brick walls are nearly a metre thick. Furnishings include four-poster beds, a grandfather clock, Coalport china of the early 1800s, an 18th-century maple desk, Regency dining-room chairs and a portrait of Prescott.
□ At nearby Port Williams, tides rise and fall as much as 12 metres. Ships loading apples and potatoes at low tide are high and dry beside the wharf.

Prescott House, Starrs Point

Fertile Farmland Rescued From the Sea

Old Acadian dikes still remain along the Minas Basin shore near Grand Pré, N.S. (*below*). The dikes held back Bay of Fundy tides and eventually transformed marshes into farmland. More than three metres wide, the dikes were made of stones and logs packed with clay. Built into the base were *aboiteaux*—wooden boxes with clappers hinged to seaward—which prevented sea water from entering at high tide, but allowed marshes to drain at low tide.

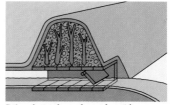

Dikes drained marshes at low tide—

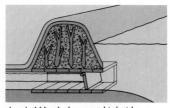

then held back the sea at high tide

WOLFVILLE

Some 2,500 students attend classes in the gracious classical buildings of Acadia University, founded by Nova Scotia Baptists in 1838. In Vaughan Memorial Library are the sermons and journal of evangelist Henry Alline, whose preaching in 1775-83 helped keep Nova Scotia from joining the American Revolution. Theater Arts Festival International is held at Acadia in mid-July.
□ The Wolfville Historical Museum contains furnishings from the late 1700s, when the area was resettled by New Englanders following the expulsion of the Acadians in 1755.
□ A plaque at Wolfville United Baptist Church (1912) honors the Rev. Ebenezer Moulton, who organized Canada's first Baptist congregation here in 1763.

The flag of Acadia, a French tricolor with a yellow star in the blue field, flies proudly at Grand Pré National Historic Park, the principal scene of *le grand dé-rangement*—the expulsion of 1755. That year, as the struggle for North America grew hotter, the Acadians of Nova Scotia refused to swear allegiance to England lest they be forced to fight other Frenchmen. As a result, thousands were shipped south to the English colonies, and abandoned. Ironically, the most moving account of that sad episode, Longfellow's epic *Evangeline*, was written about a girl who lived mainly in the poet's imagination. Yet today, by an ivy-covered chapel, on the very site where the Acadian expulsion was ordered, visitors can toss coins into "Evangeline's well" and gaze at her bronze statue.

Three of Nova Scotia's finest museums are in this area. At Starrs Point is Prescott House, a Georgian mansion built in 1799-1802 by a pioneer horticulturist. At Mount Uniacke is a 19th-century mansion, part of the former estate of one of Nova Scotia's most prominent political families. And at Windsor is the frame house in which Thomas Chandler Haliburton wrote his Sam Slick stories, beginning in 1836 with *The Clockmaker*. It was Sam, the fictional Yankee clock peddler, who first said: "the early bird gets the worm." He coined "jack of all trades and master of none" and countless other "wise saws" on "human nature"—bringing Haliburton international fame as a humorist.

GRAND PRÉ

Old willow trees in Grand Pré National Historic Park are said to have survived from the 1600s and 1700s, when this small community was a major Acadian settlement. A chapel in the park commemorates the church in which the 1755 expulsion notice was read to the Acadians. Outside is a bronze statue of Long-fellow's fictional heroine, *Evangeline*. Nearby is "Evangeline's well," a restoration of one that was found when English settlers occupied the lands left by the Acadians.
□ A monument near the park commemorates the 1747 Battle of Grand Pré, in which some 240 Frenchmen and 20 Indians routed an occupying force of 500 New Englanders.
□ Covenanters' Church, built by Loyalists in 1804, has box pews, sounding boards and a pulpit reaching halfway to the ceiling. Square-headed nails join its hand-sawn boards.
□ A marker identifies the boyhood home of Sir Robert Borden, prime minister during the First World War.

Haliburton's Sam Slick

Evangeline: The Story Behind the Poem

In 1847 American poet Henry Wadsworth Longfellow published *Evangeline: A Tale of Acadie*. With its memorable opening ("This is the forest primeval"), the epic poem about the dispersal of the Acadians became one of his most popular works. Millions now know the story of Evangeline's romance with Gabriel, their separation, and her long, sad search for her lover. The idea to publish the tale came from a Boston minister named Horace L. Conolly. Having heard an account of parted Acadian lovers, Conolly approached novelist Nathaniel Hawthorne to write the story. When Hawthorne declined, Longfellow offered to tell it. The poet began writing *Evangeline* in 1845 at his home in Cambridge, Mass. He relied on published accounts of the Acadian expulsion and never visited Grand Pré.

The Evangeline *statue, Grand Pré National Historic Park*

WINDSOR

"Clifton," the 15-room frame house in which Judge Thomas Chandler Haliburton wrote the Sam Slick stories, is now the Haliburton Memorial Museum. Built in 1834-36, the house contains Haliburton's desk and a Sam Slick shelf clock.
□ Atop a hill overlooking Windsor stands a split-log blockhouse, the oldest in Canada. It was built by the British in 1750 as part of the defenses of Fort Edward.
□ The Hants County Exhibition, first held in 1765 (and run annually since 1815), is North America's oldest agricultural fair. The September exhibition has horse shows, displays of livestock, fruit, vegetables and local crafts, and an ox-pulling event.

SOUTH RAWDON

Nineteenth-century rural Nova Scotia artifacts in the South Rawdon Museum include ice skates (steel blades secured in blocks of wood that were strapped to the skater's boots) and a press for making straw hats. The museum is in a former Sons of Temperance hall, built in 1867.

MOUNT UNIACKE

Original furnishings still grace Uniacke House, an elegant colonial mansion that was once at the center of a huge country estate. Irish-born Richard John Uniacke built the house in 1813-15 while serving as Nova Scotia attorney general. The two-story, eight-bedroom white wooden house later became the summer home of his son, James Boyle Uniacke, a fiery Tory leader who resigned from the Legislative Council in 1837 to join Joseph Howe's reform party. In 1848 Uniacke became Nova Scotia's premier and attorney general—in the British Empire's first responsible government.

Pine grosbeak

HANTSPORT

Ship models and other maritime mementos are displayed at the Hantsport community center in a great three-story house built in 1860 by Ezra Churchill, a shipyard owner who prospered when Hantsport was a major shipbuilding town.
□ A cairn marks the grave of William Hall, the first black and the first Canadian sailor to win the Victoria Cross. The son of a slave brought from Virginia, he served with the Royal Navy in the Crimean War and during the 1857 Indian Mutiny.

Avonport Station

onport
12
101
32.5
Hantsport
Avon River
Mount Denson
11.5
Halfway R
101
DIMOCK PT
Falmouth ● Windsor
St. Croix River
215
14.5
101
14
9
Three-Mile Plains
St. Croix
Ellershouse
30
Willow Hill ▲
1
Ardoise Hill ▲
Meander R
South Rawdon
8.5
Hillsvale
Cockscomb Lake
Pigott Lake
Lakeland
Lily Lake
Mount Uniacke ▲
6.5
Mount Uniacke
Oland
South Uniacke
1
Lewis Lake
101

White Crescents of Sand Where Pirates Once Roamed

Southwestern Nova Scotia

On a street corner in the village of Milton, just north of Liverpool, is a privateer cannon placed muzzle down. It was probably placed there to keep carriages to the road and away from a front garden. But the old gun is a reminder of less peaceful times along Nova Scotia's south shore. Settlers from Cape Cod who founded Liverpool in the 1760s spent much of the next 50 years protecting homes, fisheries and shipping from French and Spanish raiders and Yankee privateers. They fought for sur-

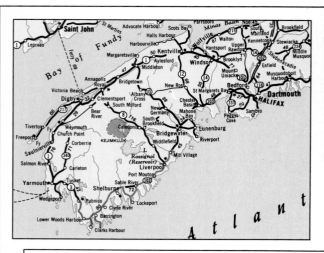

Wool mural at Barrington Woolen Mill

BARRINGTON

Eastern Canada's last water-operated woolen mill, built in the 1880s, is now a museum. Exhibits include machines that were used for twisting and winding yarn. A wool mural depicts the history of sheep-raising in Nova Scotia.
□ Canada's oldest nonconformist house of worship is Barrington's Old Meeting House, built in 1765 by members of a strict fundamentalist sect who came here from Massachusetts. The structure served as town hall as well as church until about 1838. Narrow steps lead to a wall pulpit (c. 1790). Ceiling beams are braced by "ship's knees," common when most carpenters were shipbuilders.

Cape Sable: Graveyard of the Atlantic

Near the rocky southern tip of Nova Scotia, in the village of Centreville on Cape Sable Island, a self-bailing lifeboat (c. 1890) outside the Archelaus Smith Museum is a reminder of the crews who fought through crashing surf to rescue shipwreck victims—and salvage what they could from disaster. As soon as a ship was in trouble offshore, "wrackers" would launch boats—to save lives, but also to recover food and furnishings.

Hundreds of ships have been lost off Cape Sable, where submerged, ship-destroying ledges extend hundreds of metres to sea, and powerful tides sweep around shoals and islands. For centuries the cape has been known to sailors as one of the graveyards of the Atlantic. (It is not to be confused with another Atlantic graveyard that is just as notorious and has a similar name: Sable Island is a treacherous strip of shifting sand more than 300 kilometres east of Halifax.)

Cape Sable's worst wreck occurred in February 1860, when the steamship *Hungarian*, en route from England to Portland, Maine, foundered on a rocky shoal. All 125 passengers and 80 crewmen drowned. But much of *Hungarian*'s cargo was salvaged, and Cape Sable Islanders considered the rich wreck a gift from providence.

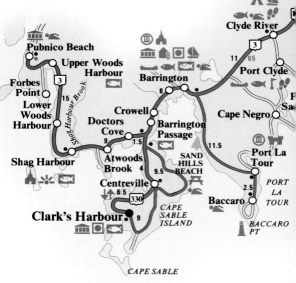

SHAG HARBOUR

A fine view of islands off Nova Scotia's south coast is had from Chapel Hill, where the beacons of five lighthouses can be seen. Boats may be chartered to Seal Island, 25 kilometres offshore. The island's octagonal timber lighthouse was built in 1830—at the insistence of two families who had settled there to aid distressed mariners. It was fired by seal oil, then petroleum vapor, and was electrified in 1959.

White ibis

CAPE SABLE ISLAND

At Barrington Passage, a 1,200-metre causeway leads to Cape Sable Island, Nova Scotia's most southerly point.
□ In the Archelaus Smith Museum at Centreville, artifacts salvaged from shipwrecked vessels include a quilt made of cloth retrieved from the *Hungarian*, a steamship that sank in 1860.
□ Clark's Harbour is the birthplace of the Cape Island boat, famed for its stability and good handling in shallow water and swells. It was developed in the early 1900s by Ephraim Atkinson. Modern versions of the boat, up to 12 metres long and powered by inboard engines, are used mostly for inshore fishing.

PORT LA TOUR

Nearby are traces of two 17th-century forts. A cairn a few kilometres south of here marks the site of Fort Saint-Louis, built about 1627 by French trader Charles La Tour. Northwest of Port La Tour are traces of Fort Temple (1658), the first English stronghold on the coast of southwestern Nova Scotia.

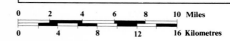

| 0 | 2 | 4 | 6 | 8 | 10 Miles |
| 0 | 4 | 8 | | 12 | 16 Kilometres |

vival, once in their own streets, often on the high seas, outfitting their own privateers with Royal Navy cannon, and taking wars of retaliation to the New England coast and the Caribbean.

The road south from Liverpool leads past White Point and Hunts Point—resorts fringed by flawless white crescents of sand. Farther on lies Shelburne, a drowsy little shipbuilding town of 2,700 that was briefly the most populous place in British North America when some 10,000 Loyalists ar-rived after the American Revolution. At Barrington is the Old Meeting House where these settlers gathered more than 200 years ago; here, too, is one of Canada's first water-driven woolen mills. A causeway at Barrington Passage leads to Cape Sable Island, long notorious among sailors as one of the deadliest hazards on the Atlantic coast. At this southernmost tip of Nova Scotia, exotic birds such as the white ibis are sometimes spotted among flocks of Canada geese, black ducks and blue-winged teal.

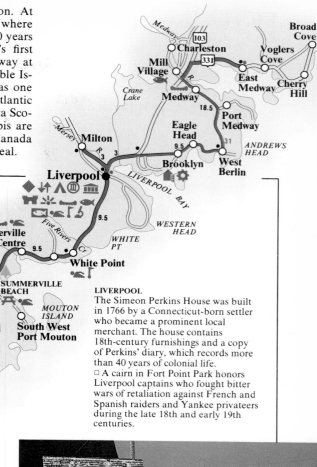

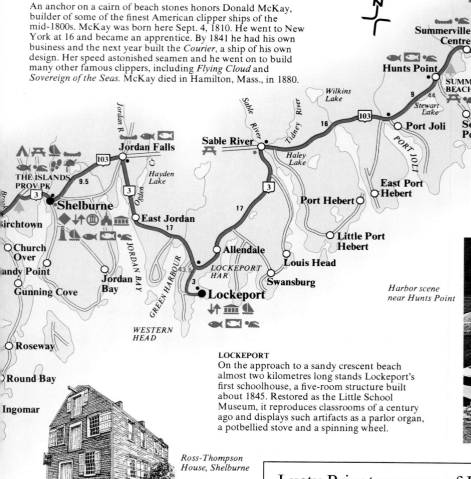

JORDAN FALLS

An anchor on a cairn of beach stones honors Donald McKay, builder of some of the finest American clipper ships of the mid-1800s. McKay was born here Sept. 4, 1810. He went to New York at 16 and became an apprentice. By 1841 he had his own business and the next year built the *Courier*, a ship of his own design. Her speed astonished seamen and he went on to build many other famous clippers, including *Flying Cloud* and *Sovereign of the Seas*. McKay died in Hamilton, Mass., in 1880.

LIVERPOOL

The Simeon Perkins House was built in 1766 by a Connecticut-born settler who became a prominent local merchant. The house contains 18th-century furnishings and a copy of Perkins' diary, which records more than 40 years of colonial life.
□ A cairn in Fort Point Park honors Liverpool captains who fought bitter wars of retaliation against French and Spanish raiders and Yankee privateers during the late 18th and early 19th centuries.

Harbor scene near Hunts Point

LOCKEPORT

On the approach to a sandy crescent beach almost two kilometres long stands Lockeport's first schoolhouse, a five-room structure built about 1845. Restored as the Little School Museum, it reproduces classrooms of a century ago and displays such artifacts as a parlor organ, a potbellied stove and a spinning wheel.

Ross-Thompson House, Shelburne

SHELBURNE

This shipbuilding town of 2,700 enjoyed a brief, elegant heyday when some 10,000 United Empire Loyalists settled here in 1783. (A cairn at the foot of King Street marks their landing place.) The Ross-Thompson House, built in 1784, has been restored and is now a branch of the Nova Scotia Museum. The front part of the two-story frame house is a store with period merchandise.
□ Cape Roseway Light on McNutt Island in the harbor is one of Nova Scotia's oldest lighthouses, dating from 1788. The island, accessible by boat from Shelburne, is a favorite picnic spot. Camping, fishing, canoeing, hiking and horseback riding are popular activities at nearby Islands Provincial Park.

Lusty Privateersmen of Liverpool

Nova Scotia's dreaded privateer ship, the Liverpool Packet

Nova Scotians practiced privateering with gusto and profit between 1756 and 1815. They turned to this legalized piracy mainly because their trade in the West Indies was threatened by enemy ships from France, Spain and the United States—during the American Revolution, the Napoleonic wars and the War of 1812.

Liverpool privateersmen included Capt. Alexander Godfrey of the brig *Rover*, who routed a Spanish squadron and captured its flagship in the Caribbean in 1800; and Capt. Joseph Barss of the schooner *Liverpool Packet*, who captured nearly 100 American ships off the New England coast during the War of 1812.

Smugglers' Haunts, Buried Treasure and the Ghost of a Privateer

Southwestern Nova Scotia

From the rugged shore at Prospect, southwest of Halifax, Nova Scotia's "Lighthouse Route" stretches down a coast where many houses of the old sailing men still have a "widow's walk" looking out to sea. One favorite stop is rockbound Peggy's Cove, the most photographed fishing village in Canada, with about 90 residents and 1,000 sightseers on a typical summer day.

Here the road turns north, winding around the indented shoreline of St. Margaret's Bay, where rumrunners loaded boot-

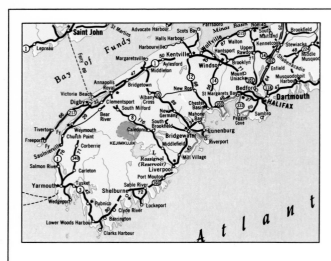

BRIDGEWATER
The focal point of a town park that also contains nature trails, a pond and bird sanctuary, the DesBrisay Museum documents the story of Lunenburg County with artifacts collected by Judge Mather Byles DesBrisay. Displays include a birchbark cradle, ornamented with dyed woven porcupine quills; made in 1841, it is a fine example of Micmac Indian quill work. German Bibles in the museum date from 1669.
□ The International Ox-pulling Championships are held in early August at the South Shore Exhibition.
□ At New Germany, 24 kilometres northwest, is the Anglican Church of St. John in the Wilderness. The frame structure was built in 1844 as an offshoot of St. John's Church in Lunenburg.

A 'Living Museum' of Ships and Seafaring

Veteran fishermen guide visitors through a historic ship moored to a quay at the Lunenburg Fisheries Museum, a branch of the Nova Scotia Museum. *Theresa E. Connor* (launched in 1938), last of the Lunenburg dory schooners, has been converted below decks to house exhibits of the era of the deep-water fleet and

Schooner Theresa E. Connor

Nova Scotia schooner men. Built by the Lunenburg shipyard of Smith and Rhuland (as were *Bluenose* and her Halifax-based replica, *Bluenose II*), she contains exhibits on the story of the offshore fishery, and *Bluenose's* wheel and trophies. Also part of the museum are the Prohibition rumrunner *Reo II* and the dragger *Cape North*, both built at Meteghan, N.S. An aquarium at the museum displays fish native to Nova Scotia.

Belted kingfisher

LAHAVE
One of Canada's earliest settlements stood here, on a point overlooking the LaHave River. A cairn marks the site of a fort built in 1632 by Isaac de Razilly, lieutenant general of Acadia. Later captured by the English, the post was burned by Boston privateers in 1705.
□ At nearby Risser's Beach Provincial Park are dunes up to three metres high.

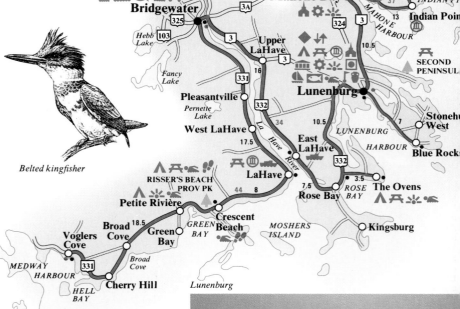

leg liquor for the New England coast in the 1920s and early 1930s. Farther on is Mahone Bay, where pirate treasure has been sought on Oak Island since 1795, and where the U.S. privateer *Young Teazer* was blown up in 1813 but still "reappears" in flames on dark, dreadful nights. Some 350 islands and coves make Mahone Bay fascinating to explore.

The most famous port along this coast is Lunenburg, which 50 years ago owned the largest deep-water fishing fleet plying the Grand Banks off Newfoundland. Best of all was the schooner *Bluenose*, whose likeness is on the Canadian dime; she outraced the fastest Yankee ships in the 1920s and 1930s. Now those billowing windjammers have vanished, replaced by modern trawlers. But Lunenburg remains among the most prosperous fishing towns on the Atlantic seaboard.

Nearby is a picturesque haven called Blue Rocks, where fish-drying houses are built on stilts and reached by dory. On the opposite side of Lunenburg Harbour are The Ovens—a series of caves or "blow-holes" carved into the cliffs by the pounding sea. The caves can be seen from a concrete viewing platform.

Not far inland, on wooded hills overlooking the LaHave River, lies Bridgewater, the biggest town in Lunenburg County. International horse and ox pulls are an exciting highlight at the South Shore Exhibition held here each August.

CHESTER

Now a popular resort, Chester was first settled by New Englanders in 1759. The Sword and Anchor Inn was built in the early 1800s as a private home; its annex, Sheet Anchor House, dates from 1783. A ferry links Chester with Big Tancook Island, famed for sauerkraut made from locally grown cabbages. Across Mahone Bay is Oak Island, frequented by treasure seekers. Farther south, in the town of Mahone Bay, three old churches stand in a row: St. James' Anglican (1883), St. John's Lutheran (c. 1869) and Trinity United (1862).

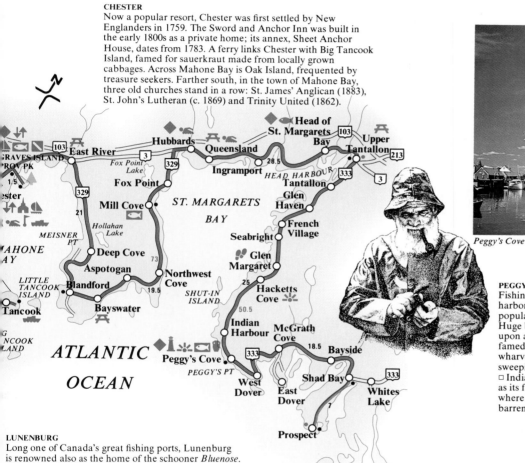

Peggy's Cove

PEGGY'S COVE

Fishing boats rest peacefully in a sheltered little harbor at Peggy's Cove, one of Canada's most popular spots with artists and photographers. Huge boulders are strewn about and piled one upon another around the quaint, rustic cove—famed for its trim houses, its weatherworn wharves and a lighthouse point that provides a sweeping view of the ocean.
□ Indian Harbour, although not as well known as its famous neighbor, is a similar settlement where weather-beaten fishing shacks perch on a barren shoreline.

LUNENBURG

Long one of Canada's great fishing ports, Lunenburg is renowned also as the home of the schooner *Bluenose*. An inscription on a local monument calls the schooner a symbol of "the transformation of an inland people." Planted here as farmers in 1783, German, French and Swiss immigrants cleared the wilderness, fished first off the coast, then gradually went on to the Grand Banks to vie with the best of deep-sea fishermen.
□ Among restored vessels moored at the Lunenburg Fisheries Museum is the *Theresa E. Connor*, the last Canadian schooner to fish the Banks (in 1962).
□ Among the town's churches are some of the oldest in Canada. St. Andrew's Church (1828) has one of Canada's first Presbyterian congregations, founded in 1783. St. John's Anglican Church (1754) was presented with communion vessels by George III. The steeple of Zion Lutheran Church (1776) contains the bell that once rang in the chapel of the French fortress at Louisbourg.
□ The annual Lunenburg Fisheries Exhibition in early September includes contests in fish filleting and scallop shucking, and international dory races. The Fishermen's Memorial Room at the Exhibition grounds is dedicated to men and ships of Lunenburg lost at sea.

Sour Cream and Cabbages

The people of Lunenburg—many of them descended from Germans who settled in Nova Scotia in the 1750s—speak with a musical lilt, keep their houses freshly painted and their gardens neat, and love German cooking.

The fertile soil here nourishes bumper crops of vegetables. Local cabbage, when shredded, salted and fermented, makes tart and tasty sauerkraut. Hodge-podge, a Lunenburg specialty for the past 200 years, is made with fresh, young vegetables. Carrots, onions, green beans, peas and small new potatoes are steamed together, then combined with cream (sweet or sour) and butter and diced salt pork fried to a crisp.

Salt cod, soaked overnight, is boiled with potatoes and garnished with fried onions and crisped salt pork to make hugger-in-buff, a traditional dish of Newfoundland. Lunenburg cooks add a German touch: a cup of sour cream.

An Anchorage in Peace and War ... and the Leader of Atlantic Canada

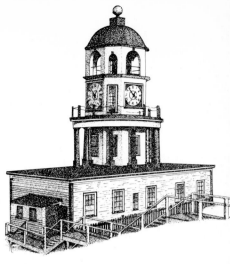

The biggest city in the Atlantic provinces and the capital of Nova Scotia, Halifax is a year-round seaport, and the financial, educational, medical, cultural and business leader of Atlantic Canada. The city is on a peninsula, with tidewater on three sides. The outer harbor, almost 1.5 kilometres wide, has 32 berths on a frontage of more than 5 kilometres. The port's Ocean Terminals are big enough to have berthed the *Queen Mary* and the *Queen Elizabeth* end to end, and its modern container port provides docking space for the largest freighters. A narrow passage leads to the inner harbor, Bedford Basin. (It is big enough and deep enough to accommodate the combined navies of the world.) The entire harbor is ice-free and is busiest in winter when St. Lawrence ports are closed. More than 3,400 ships dock annually in Halifax.

Throughout this modern city are reminders of its storied past. In a Halifax of skyscrapers and expressways are little streets where Wolfe and Captain Cook walked—and Royal Navy press gangs

hunted. Joseph Howe stands in bronze where, in 1835, he won a historic courtroom battle for freedom of the press. In a north-end cemetery are long rows of *Titanic* graves. Two modern bridges leap the great harbor where the munitions ship *Mont Blanc* exploded in 1917 in the biggest non-nuclear blast ever. And in Bedford Basin, the ghosts of vast Second World War convoys ride at restless anchor.

All Saints Cathedral (18)
It was built in 1907-10 to commemorate the 200th anniversary of the first Anglican service in Nova Scotia.
CFB Stadacona (4)
The Maritime Command Museum is in Admiralty House, once the home of the British commander of the Halifax naval base.
Chapel Built in a Day (19)
Two thousand persons built the chapel of Our Lady of Sorrows in Holy Cross Cemetery on Aug. 31, 1843.
Citadel Hill (16)
Overlooking Halifax and its harbor is the

A dignified Halifax landmark since 1803, the Old Town Clock (above) has different peals for the quarter hour, half hour and hour. Once dominated by the cannon of Citadel Hill, the city's skyline now blossoms with highrise buildings.

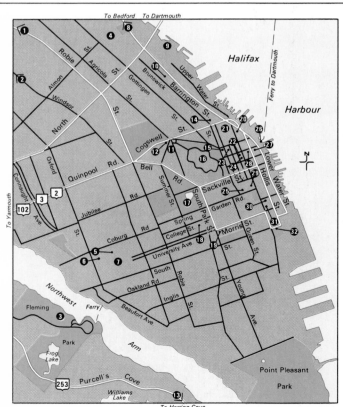

Halifax

1 Prince's Lodge
2 Fairview Cemetery
3 Fleming Park
4 CFB Stadacona
5 University of King's College
6 Public Archives of Nova Scotia
7 Dalhousie University
8 Halifax Shipyards
9 Naval Dockyard
10 Old Dutch Church
11 Nova Scotia Museum
12 Tourist Information
13 York Redoubt
14 St. George's Church
15 CAA
16 Citadel Hill
17 Public Gardens
18 All Saints Cathedral
19 Chapel Built in a Day
20 Historic Properties
21 Scotia Square
22 Grand Parade
23 Halifax Metro Center
24 St. Paul's Church
25 Halifax North Memorial Library
26 Province House
27 Government House
28 St. Mary's Basilica
29 St. Matthew's Church
30 Henry House
31 Edward Cornwallis
32 Point Pleasant Park

Citadel, a massive, star-shaped stone fortress built in 1828-56. It contains military and maritime exhibits, a museum of furniture and farm implements, and the Centennial Art Gallery of Nova Scotia.
Dalhousie University (7)
The university, founded in 1818, is noted for its law and medical schools. The Arts Center contains a gallery with displays that range from pre-Inca pottery to modern abstract paintings.
Edward Cornwallis (31)
In a small park near the Hotel Nova Scotian is a statue of Governor Edward Cornwallis, who founded Halifax in 1749.
Fairview Cemetery (2)
Here are numbered graves of 125 persons who died in the 1912 sinking of the *Titanic*. Memorials mark the common grave of 249 unidentified victims of the Halifax explo-

An oasis of calm and stubborn nostalgia in the heart of bustling, modern Halifax, the Public Gardens (left) were opened in 1867. Visitors may arrange harbor tours aboard Bluenose II *(below), a replica of the famous fishing schooner that won many international races in the 1920s and 1930s. Cobbled streets of the Historic Properties (bottom) once echoed the steps of privateersmen and navy press gangs; today they attract shoppers, office workers and sightseers.*

sion of Dec. 6, 1917. (The French munitions ship *Mont Blanc* caught fire and exploded after a collision with a Norwegian freighter. The blast killed 1,600 persons, injured thousands and leveled the city's north end.)

Fleming Park (3)
The Dingle, as Fleming Park is popularly known, overlooks the North West Arm—a saltwater inlet that is the city's main aquatic playground. A memorial tower (1908-12) commemorates Canada's first legislative assembly (in Halifax, Oct. 2, 1758).

Government House (27)
This stone mansion, residence of Nova Scotia's lieutenant governor, was built in 1800-05. It is closed to the public.

Grand Parade (22)
Originally the garrison parade ground (where the town crier read the news), this is the site of the Halifax War Memorial,

by Scottish sculptor John Massey Rhind.

Halifax Metro Centre (23)
Sports events, shows and exhibitions are held in this modern, 11,000-seat coliseum.

Halifax North Memorial Library (25)
The library is a monument to victims of the 1917 explosion. Outside, a Jordi Bonet sculpture, incorporating a fragment from the *Mont Blanc*, symbolizes the catastrophe and the city's subsequent reconstruction.

Halifax Shipyards (8)
More than 7,000 damaged ships were repaired here during the Second World War. Since then giant oil rigs and a variety of modern vessels have been built in the yards. Tours may be arranged.

Henry House (30)
The home of William Alexander Henry (1816-88), a Father of Confederation and mayor of Halifax, is a national historic site.

Historic Properties (20)
Restored waterfront buildings—including the Privateers' Warehouse, where cargoes captured by 19th-century privateers were stored before auction—now house offices, restaurants, and stores.

Naval Dockyard (9)
Modern warships berth in North America's oldest naval dockyard, begun in 1759 under the supervision of Capt. James Cook. (Entry is restricted to bus tours.)

Nova Scotia Museum (11)
It maintains 15 branches throughout the province. The theme of the main museum here is Man and His Environment in Nova Scotia.

Old Dutch Church (10)
Only 12 metres by 6, it was built in 1756 by German settlers and was the first Lutheran church in Canada.

Point Pleasant Park (32)
Tree-shaded walking trails lead past the ruins of five batteries which date from 1762. The Prince of Wales Martello Tower, begun in 1796, has been fully restored. The National Sailors' Memorial honors Canadian seamen who died in two world wars and have no known graves.

Prince's Lodge (1)
A small rotunda (closed to the public) remains from a villa constructed on Bedford Basin by Prince Edward for Julie de Saint-Laurent, his mistress.

Province House (26)
The courtroom in which journalist Joseph Howe successfully defended himself in 1835 against a charge of criminal libel is now the library of Canada's oldest (1818) legislative building. The nation's first responsible government, in which Howe was provincial secretary, met in this sandstone building Feb. 2, 1848.

Public Archives of Nova Scotia (6)
Exhibits include presses on which Joseph Howe printed the *Novascotian* between 1827 and 1841.

Public Gardens (17)
Opened in 1867, the gardens are an oasis of calm and 19th-century charm in the heart of bustling, modern Halifax.

St. George's Church (14)
Prince Edward oversaw the design of this round, Byzantine-style Anglican church. It was built in 1800-12.

St. Mary's Basilica (28)
One of Canada's oldest stone churches (c.1820), it has the tallest polished granite spire (58 metres) in the world.

St. Matthew's Church (29)
This United Church, built in 1858, is the home of the oldest dissenting (non-Anglican Protestant) congregation in Canada.

St. Paul's Church (24)
Built with timbers shipped from Boston in 1749, it is Halifax's oldest building, and was the cathedral of Loyalist Charles Inglis, the first Anglican bishop of Nova Scotia.

Scotia Square (21)
This downtown development has a 305-room hotel, office and apartment buildings, a trade mart and more than 100 stores and boutiques.

University of King's College (5)
Established in Windsor, N.S., in 1789, King's is the oldest university in the Commonwealth outside the British Isles. It was moved to Halifax in 1923.

York Redoubt (13)
A fortified position since 1793, this seaward extension of the Halifax defense complex is a national historic site.

High Tides and Gemstones in the Land of Glooscap

Central Nova Scotia

This scenic drive follows the north shore of Cobequid Bay and Minas Basin, where tides are among the highest in the world. The drive is part of Nova Scotia's Glooscap Trail—named for the legendary man-god of the Micmac Indians. Glooscap's anger was thunder and flashing lightning; his peace, the tranquillity of Indian summer; and his friends, the Micmac Indians, whose lands these were before the settlers came. He is said to have held court atop Cape Blomidon, across Minas Basin.

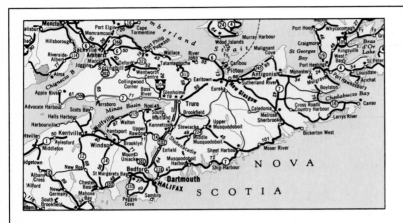

Miners' Monument, Springhill

SPRINGHILL

Coal mining began at Springhill in 1872; a 1,220-metre shaft here was once the deepest in Canada. On Main Street a monument topped by a statue of a coal miner commemorates three tragic mine disasters. An explosion in 1891 killed 125 miners; another in 1956 killed 39; a "bump" in 1958 claimed 76 lives. In the 1958 disaster 12 miners were saved after being entombed for six days; seven more were rescued two days later. Fewer than 150 men now work in two small mines.

Disasters have not been limited to the mines. A fire destroyed the business district the day after Christmas 1957. Another major fire struck in 1975.

A Roundup for Rockhounds

Amethysts from the Parrsboro region

Amethysts, agates, zeolites, jasper and other semiprecious stones are found on the miles of public beaches near Parrsboro. Many of the gemstones and minerals are displayed at the Parrsboro Geological Museum. The cutting, polishing and setting of rough stones are demonstrated here. Collectors and craftsmen gather here during a three-day Rockhound Roundup in mid-August. It features cabochon cutting and polishing, tumbling, faceting and micromounting, and an exhibit and sale of Nova Scotia gemstones, handcrafted jewelry and other items.

Visitors also take field trips to nearby East Bay, where fossils of prehistoric plants, fish, lizards and amphibians are found in cliffs along the shore. The 250-million-year-old footprints of a small dinosaur were discovered here in 1902.

SPENCERS ISLAND

The brigantine *Mary Celeste,* which figures in one of the great mysteries of the sea, was built in this village in 1861. A cairn records that in 1872 she was discovered in the Atlantic—between the Azores and Gibraltar—"with all sails set and everything in order, but not a person was on board or ever found." The ship had been on a voyage from New York to Genoa.
□ At nearby Advocate Harbour is a rock formation known as the Three Sisters—the legendary sisters of Glooscap who were turned to stone by the man-god as a punishment.

PARRSBORO

When the tide ebbs in Minas Basin, an arm of the Bay of Fundy, it drains Parrsboro's harbor. Falling as much as 15 metres, the water recedes more than 1.6 kilometres, leaving vessels hard aground. Fishermen here string nets on poles in the sand, catching fish at high tide, harvesting them at low tide.
□ The Parrsboro Golf Club, with the Cobequid Mountains in the background, provides a fine view of rocky inlets and island-dotted bays along the coast.
□ Moose, deer, and black bears inhabit Chignecto Game Sanctuary, 17 kilometres inland.

West of Truro the Glooscap Trail runs along Cobequid Bay to Great Village, where traces of Acadian dikes may still be seen along the marshy shore. From Bass River, where a century-old factory still turns out chairs made from birch and maple, the highway climbs to village of Economy, which offers a panoramic view of Glooscap's legendary Five Islands—Moose, Diamond, Long, Egg and Pinnacle.

Along the shore near Parrsboro, collectors hunt for semiprecious stones—from amethyst and agate to zeolite. Seabirds nest in marshy areas behind the beaches. Visitors to Parrsboro may tour a small shipyard where yachts are built, watch weir-fishing, dig for clams or gold along a rocky shore that offers one of Nova Scotia's finest ocean views. To the west lies the village of Spencers Island, where the famous mystery ship *Mary Celeste* was launched in 1861. Farther on is Advocate Harbour, where the French explorer Pierre de Monts found copper in June 1604.

From Parrsboro the road leads inland to Springhill, where coal-mining operations began in 1872. Since then, this courageous town has survived three mine disasters and two major fires. (Guides at the Miners' Museum here are retired miners who have a wealth of stories and a staunch pride in their work.) Here, too, in the highlands called the Cobequid Mountains, the lands of Glooscap remain much as they were—breathtaking in their beauty, and steeped in Indian legend and folklore.

A Town Famed for Courage in the Face of Disaster

The story of a coal-mining town's courage in the face of disaster is told at the Springhill Miners' Museum. Among mining equipment of many kinds—some picks and shovels date from 1885—are rubber air pipes, handsaws, and breathing apparatus dating from the early 1900s. There are a diary and letters of trapped men, and other relics of Springhill's three worst mine accidents. At the museum are a washhouse with miners' clothes, hats and boots, and a lamp cabin with a display of miners' lamps from the 1930s to the present. Retired miners conduct a museum tour that includes a 274-metre descent into a mine shaft.

A view of Five Islands, Minas Basin

FIVE ISLANDS PROVINCIAL PARK
Vast stretches of red sand are laid bare here at low tide. A four-kilometre hiking trail winds along the crest of 45-metre cliffs facing Minas Basin. According to Micmac legend, the fire islands offshore are great clumps of earth which the god Glooscap threw in anger at mischievous beaver.

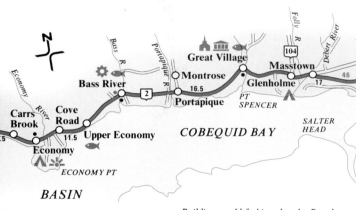

Bobolink

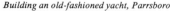

Building an old-fashioned yacht, Parrsboro

GREAT VILLAGE
Shipwrights built St. James United Church in 1884. It contains a small museum devoted to shipbuilding. The Robert F. Layton general store has a display of relics of a different sort: from hatpins and hardware to "kidney flushers, guaranteed to cure the ills of man."
□ Wentworth Valley, 22 kilometres north, is the oldest ski development in the Atlantic provinces, dating from the 1940s.

TRURO
In Victoria Park wooden walkways cling to the edge of a ravine and lead to two picturesque waterfalls on Lepper Brook. The Colchester Historical Society Museum has displays ranging from oceanography to Micmac Indian history. The Nova Scotia Provincial Exhibition is held at Truro each August.
□ The Truro tidal bore, a surge of water sometimes 1.5 metres high, rushes up the Salmon River twice daily.
□ Across the river, at Bible Hill, visitors may tour a demonstration farm at the Nova Scotia Agricultural College.
□ Nearby is Canada's only Islamic cemetery east of Alberta. Weekly services are held in a mosque that accommodates 70.

Giants and Gristmills, Blueberries and Tidal Bores

Central Nova Scotia

At Amherst, just below the New Brunswick border, highway travelers are greeted by Gaelic signs bidding them *Ciad Mile Failte*—"a hundred thousand welcomes." It is a warm and typical Nova Scotia greeting, and a sentimental farewell.

Leaving the Trans-Canada Highway at Amherst, this is a delightful route across north-central Nova Scotia at its best. It links Joggins (and its fossils), on Chignecto Bay, with the charming Balmoral Mills (and its historic gristmill). It cuts across the narrow

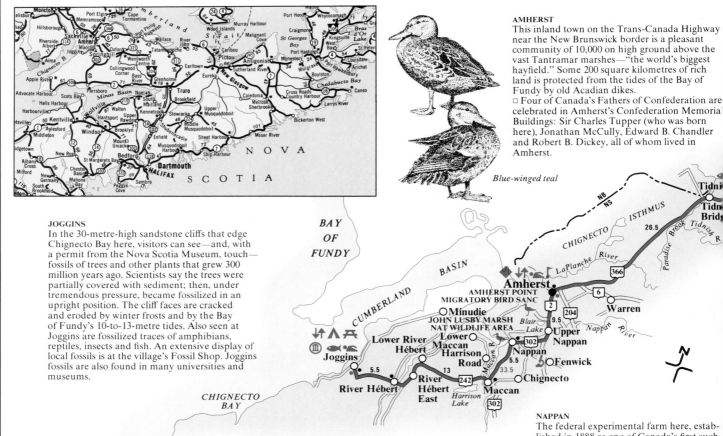

Blue-winged teal

AMHERST
This inland town on the Trans-Canada Highway near the New Brunswick border is a pleasant community of 10,000 on high ground above the vast Tantramar marshes—"the world's biggest hayfield." Some 200 square kilometres of rich land is protected from the tides of the Bay of Fundy by old Acadian dikes.
□ Four of Canada's Fathers of Confederation are celebrated in Amherst's Confederation Memorial Buildings: Sir Charles Tupper (who was born here), Jonathan McCully, Edward B. Chandler and Robert B. Dickey, all of whom lived in Amherst.

JOGGINS
In the 30-metre-high sandstone cliffs that edge Chignecto Bay here, visitors can see—and, with a permit from the Nova Scotia Museum, touch—fossils of trees and other plants that grew 300 million years ago. Scientists say the trees were partially covered with sediment; then, under tremendous pressure, became fossilized in an upright position. The cliff faces are cracked and eroded by winter frosts and by the Bay of Fundy's 10-to-13-metre tides. Also seen at Joggins are fossilized traces of amphibians, reptiles, insects and fish. An extensive display of local fossils is at the village's Fossil Shop. Joggins fossils are also found in many universities and museums.

NAPPAN
The federal experimental farm here, established in 1888 as one of Canada's first such farms, is devoted to livestock research and the growing of feed crops. About 40 of its 240 hectares were once farmland. This had been drained by dikes with gates that swing freely outward. Water pressure keeps them closed at high tide; at low tide, water behind the dikes forces the gates open and flows into the sea. The farm welcomes visitors.

MACCAN
Here visitors can witness the force of the Fundy tides. The tidal bore forms north of Minudie and, moving at about 10 kilometres per hour, becomes two bores as it thrusts into the Hébert and Maccan rivers; in about 15 minutes both rivers rise more than a metre. The bores' heights vary from 40 centimetres at high tide to 20 centimetres at medium; at low tides there is a small but perceptible change of direction of the water. A fine viewpoint from which to watch the bore is the Lower Maccan Tidal Bore Picnic Area, about six metres above the water, on Lower Maccan Road.

Blueberry harvest in Cumberland County

Come September, It's Blueberry Time

For three days in early September, "blueberry" is the most often-heard word in Amherst. This is the heart of Cumberland County, which is also the center of Nova Scotia's blueberry country. At the annual Blueberry Harvest Festival visitors eat blueberry pancakes, watch a blueberry pie-eating contest, see a Blueberry Queen chosen, and enjoy street-dancing, fiddling, golf, track and field, topped off by the blueberry harvest ball. Blueberries, Canada's most valuable native fruit (a multimillion-dollar cash crop), are harvested with hand rakes, air-cleaned (to remove green berries and leaves), then quick-frozen before shipment to processors—most in the United States. The end result: pies, muffins, tarts, wine, syrup and—for the purist—blueberries and cream.

Chignecto Isthmus and skirts the Northumberland Strait shore. Along the route are the town of Tidnish and the old French community of Tatamagouche.

Attractions here are both interesting and unique: the Fundy tides in action, a century-old operating gristmill, the giantess of Nova Scotia, the "world's biggest hayfield" near Amherst, the ruins of an ambitious ship railway. At various places there are cairns and plaques recording the stormy history of the area in Acadian times. There are trout streams, deep-sea fishing, golf, swimming, a colorful Scots gathering at Pugwash, and in September, a blueberry festival to remember. Also near Amherst are the John Lusby Marsh, a 6.5-square-kilometre national wildlife area visited by as many as 6,000 Canada geese in March and April; and the Amherst Point Migratory Bird Sanctuary, with its widgeons, pintails and green- and blue-winged teal.

Ship railway culvert at Tidnish

TIDNISH

Men dreamed great dreams here in the 1890s—of a 27-kilometre railway that would carry 5,000-tonne schooners between Tidnish and the Bay of Fundy. With the long, 1,040-kilometre haul around the southern tip of Nova Scotia thus eliminated, the savings would have been tremendous. But so was the cost of such a railway. Four thousand men were employed building the Cumberland Ship Railway. Some track was laid but, after five years, money ran out and the project died. Some remains of the dream can still be seen: the old roadbed, crumbling masonry, and a culvert in Tidnish.

PUGWASH

Bagpipes skirl and Highland dancers whirl at the annual July 1 Gathering of the Clans in Pugwash, a community whose street signs are in English and Gaelic. □ Pugwash has one of Nova Scotia's best harbors—the big freighters and tankers are a major tourist attraction—and nearby golf, boating and fine sand beaches, all enriched by the tang of salt air. Charter boats are available for deep-sea fishing; several streams in the area have trout and salmon. In the fall, lakes and marshes are popular with waterfowl hunters.

WALLACE

This tiny village is famous for its sandstone and for a native son little known in his own land. Wallace has quarried stone for a century; it was used in Province House in Halifax and the Parliament Buildings in Ottawa. Near the ruins of his boyhood home is a monument to Simon Newcomb (1835-1909) who, after emigrating to the United States, became a world-famous astronomer.

Drysdale Falls, near Balmoral Mills

BALMORAL MILLS

Many old millstones survive in Nova Scotia—as doorsteps and curios—and there are a few derelict mills to be seen. But the Balmoral Gristmill, nearly 100 years old, has been rescued from disuse and is back in operation on Matheson's Brook. The gristmill is one of the historic buildings lovingly tended by the Nova Scotia Museum. Its original 1.5-tonne stones still grind wheat, oats, barley and buckwheat for visitors between mid-May and mid-October. Nearby, on Baileys Brook, is seven-metre-high Drysdale Falls.

TATAMAGOUCHE

The startlingly large clothing of Anna Swan, 2.41-metre (7 feet, 11 inches) "giantess of Nova Scotia," is displayed in the Sunrise Trail Museum. Swan was born in nearby New Annan in 1846—an eight-kilogram baby—and for years was in P. T. Barnum's "Greatest Show on Earth." Later she took a giant husband, 2.35-metre Capt. Martin Van Buren Bates, an American and another of Barnum's oddities. The museum's collection also includes detailed records of an 1867 open vote (no secret ballot) won by Charles Tupper, later Canadian prime minister. Opposite each Cumberland riding voter's name is the name of the candidate who received the vote.

Balmoral Mills

A Pride in Old Ways, in a Land Like Home

Central Nova Scotia

The Scots who settled this part of Nova Scotia in the late 1700s and early 1800s found a land that reminded them of home. Thousands, drawn by the promise of free land, came to Nova Scotia in the wake of political unrest in Scotland. They sank deep roots in the rolling hills and, while visitors here will encounter many an Indian and French place-name, the shores of Northumberland Strait and St. George's Bay are truly a bit of old Scotland.

Loch Broom, New Glasgow, MacPher-

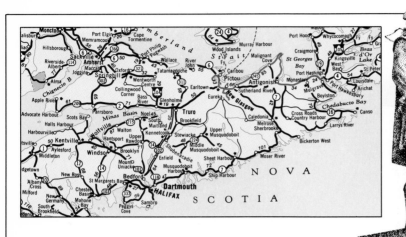

PICTOU

Pictou's monument to colonists who came from Scotland in the bark *Hector* in 1773 is a statue of a bonneted and kilted Scot, rifle in one hand, ax in the other. The people it salutes—farmers bent on a new life in a hostile land—began Pictou's real settlement.

□ Pictou Academy, still functioning, dates from 1816. McCulloch House, home of the Rev. Thomas McCulloch, first president of the academy, contains exhibits tracing Pictou's Scottish heritage.

*Pictou's monument
to early Scottish settlers*

LOCH BROOM

A small Presbyterian church built in 1973 is a replica of one erected in 1787 by Gaelic-speaking Scots settlers. Summer Sunday services are at 3 p.m.; the church can be visited on weekdays. The original log structure was 12 by 7 metres. It too was used only in summer because it could not be heated.

Historic Pictou Homes

Settlement began at Pictou June 10, 1767, with the arrival of six families from Pennsylvania and Maryland. Six years later, in the bark *Hector*, came some 180 Scots—33 families and 25 unmarried men. This was the first of many waves of immigrants from Old Scotland to "New" Scotland—Nova Scotia. The town was named Coleraine, then New Paisley, Alexandria, Donegal, Southampton and Walmsley, until Pictou (the original Indian name) was chosen in 1790. Pictou's oldest building is a cottage built in 1788 by John Patterson, a *Hector* passenger. Other historic sites include such Scottish-style stone buildings as the 1816 Thomas McCulloch House (*above*); Norway House (1813), Lord Strathcona's home in the 1880s and now an Odd Fellows' home; and an 1827 structure that once housed the Bank of British North America, and later an American consulate.

STELLARTON

Coal and steel and early railroading play important roles in the history of Stellarton and the neighboring towns of New Glasgow and Trenton.

□ Coal was discovered at Stellarton in 1798 and was mined continuously until recent years. The Foord Seam (no longer mined) was up to 14 metres thick, thought to be the world's thickest. Canada's first stationary engine went into operation here in 1827; the first iron rails in North America were cast here a year later.

□ In the Stellarton Miners Museum are helmets and equipment dating from the early days of coal mining, and the locomotive *Albion*, which went into service in 1854 for the General Mining Association. Another historic locomotive, the first to run on steel rails, is the *Samson*, on display at the Pictou County Historical Museum in New Glasgow.

MacPHERSONS MILLS

The wide boards and hand-hewn beams of this old gristmill, its cogwheels and belts, are all clues to busy days long ago when the mill ran day and night—when season and water were right. It was first a sawmill (1861); later its three sets of millstones ground oats, wheat and buckwheat. For years it also served as a post office, barbershop, general store and community center. Nearby is the restored MacPherson homestead, a fine representation of a 19th-century Pictou County farm dwelling.

MacPhersons Mills

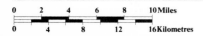

sons Mills, Heatherton, Auld Cove . . . all speak of Scottish origins. But there are Scots in Pictou as well, and Antigonish, Tracadie and Merigomish—all towns with Indian names—and at Pomquet and Havre Boucher and other old Acadian settlements. Gaelic is still heard—although less and less—as are the pipes in all their glory at Antigonish's famous Highland games. It is a land of seascapes and fine beaches; of old churches and simple, certain beliefs; of miners museums and modern manufac-

turing; of lobster suppers and a superb coastal drive past Cape George.

In rural districts, and in towns like Pictou, visitors will discover century-old houses, barns, gristmills, iron foundries, and stores that are being carefully restored to their original state. Many of these buildings are associated with major occupations of a hundred years ago—spinning and weaving, coal mining and iron forging, shipbuilding, and, of course, fishing and farming. Two 19th-century locomotives, the *Samson* (at

New Glasgow) and the *Albion* (at Stellarton Miners Museum), once hauled local ores to foundries and mills that produced everything from cast-iron kettles and ship's knees to stoves and fancy tombstones. This pleasant corner of Nova Scotia is pure delight for history buffs and vacationers—whether Scots-descended or not. It offers swimming and beachcombing, hiking and fishing, sight-seeing and a hundred other pursuits—with pride in its rich past and enjoyment of the present.

The Caber, the Kilt, and the Wail of the Pipes

Highland dances, Antigonish

They are called "Canada's Braemar," after the world-famous Highland Games of the Royal Braemar in Scotland. The Antigonish games, oldest in Canada, have been held each July since 1863, an explosion of caber tossing, hammer throwing (and today high jumping, broad jumping, shot putting) in which young and old still feel the pull of Highland origins. Scots (and "the others") revel in this pageant of Highland history and customs, all to the wondrous wail of Scottish bagpipes.

NORTH SHORE DRIVE
A scenic 40-kilometre drive between Malignant Cove and Antigonish Harbour is part of Nova Scotia's Sunrise Trail along Northumberland Strait. The North Shore Drive leads over the tip of Cape George at the head of St. George's Bay. Along the way are the communities of Georgeville and Livingstone Cove, Ballantynes Cove, Lakevale, Morristown and Crystal Cliffs. Near most of these towns are good swimming beaches; some have fishing. The drive is through pastoral and forested countryside, often within sight and sound of the sea.

Cape George, high point of the North Shore Drive

LISMORE
On a beach near here is a cairn in memory of Angus MacDonald, Hugh MacDonald and John MacPherson—"soldiers of Prince Charlie," who were among the Scots defeated by the English at Culloden in 1746. They settled here around 1790. St. Mary's Church, built by Roman Catholic Scots, dates from 1834.

ANTIGONISH
This is the home of St. Francis Xavier University (1853) and its renowned Antigonish Movement (cooperative self-help through adult education), of Canada's oldest Highland games, and of the Maritimes' oldest continuing weekly newspaper, with the unusual name *The Casket*. (The paper and the name date from 1852, when casket meant jewel chest.) In the university's Angus L. Macdonald Library is the Hall of Clans, its walls decorated with Scottish crests. St. Ninian's Cathedral, of local blue limestone, was built in 1868-75. Near Antigonish are Riverside Speedway and Keppoch Mountain ski resort.

Red-winged blackbird

MONASTERY
St. Augustine's Monastery, the Augustinians' first in Canada (1938), was originally a Trappist institution. That order came here in 1825 and built a monastery that gave the community its name. None of the original buildings remain. Behind the altar in the Augustinians' modern chapel are oil paintings and stained glass depicting the life of Saint Augustine and saints of the order named after him.

Where a Stately House Recalls the Age of Sail

Central Nova Scotia

In the 19th century, the forests of Nova Scotia supplied lumber for shipyards that launched thousands of barks, brigs and schooners—and the province's worldwide reputation for shipbuilding. One of Canada's largest wooden ships, a magnificent windjammer named the *William D. Lawrence*, was built virtually at the doorstep of her owner's house beside the Shubenacadie River at Maitland. The elm-shaded W.D. Lawrence House is now a museum and national historic site. This 2½-story

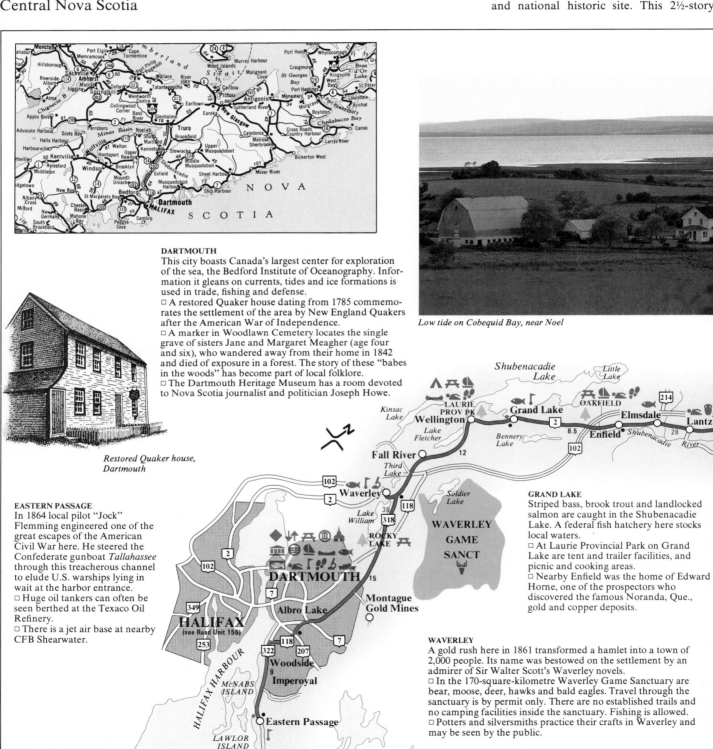

Low tide on Cobequid Bay, near Noel

Restored Quaker house, Dartmouth

DARTMOUTH
This city boasts Canada's largest center for exploration of the sea, the Bedford Institute of Oceanography. Information it gleans on currents, tides and ice formations is used in trade, fishing and defense.
□ A restored Quaker house dating from 1785 commemorates the settlement of the area by New England Quakers after the American War of Independence.
□ A marker in Woodlawn Cemetery locates the single grave of sisters Jane and Margaret Meagher (age four and six), who wandered away from their home in 1842 and died of exposure in a forest. The story of these "babes in the woods" has become part of local folklore.
□ The Dartmouth Heritage Museum has a room devoted to Nova Scotia journalist and politician Joseph Howe.

EASTERN PASSAGE
In 1864 local pilot "Jock" Flemming engineered one of the great escapes of the American Civil War here. He steered the Confederate gunboat *Tallahassee* through this treacherous channel to elude U.S. warships lying in wait at the harbor entrance.
□ Huge oil tankers can often be seen berthed at the Texaco Oil Refinery.
□ There is a jet air base at nearby CFB Shearwater.

GRAND LAKE
Striped bass, brook trout and landlocked salmon are caught in the Shubenacadie Lake. A federal fish hatchery here stocks local waters.
□ At Laurie Provincial Park on Grand Lake are tent and trailer facilities, and picnic and cooking areas.
□ Nearby Enfield was the home of Edward Horne, one of the prospectors who discovered the famous Noranda, Que., gold and copper deposits.

WAVERLEY
A gold rush here in 1861 transformed a hamlet into a town of 2,000 people. Its name was bestowed on the settlement by an admirer of Sir Walter Scott's *Waverley* novels.
□ In the 170-square-kilometre Waverley Game Sanctuary are bear, moose, deer, hawks and bald eagles. Travel through the sanctuary is by permit only. There are no established trails and no camping facilities inside the sanctuary. Fishing is allowed.
□ Potters and silversmiths practice their crafts in Waverley and may be seen by the public.

frame dwelling, typical of many 19th-century Nova Scotia houses owned by sea captains and shipbuilders, recalls the prosperity and elegance of the age of sail.

Some of Dartmouth's earliest houses and buildings were built by New England Quakers who set up a whaling company here in 1785, after the American War of Independence. In what was reputedly Canada's first urban renewal project, they revised the first town plan to include a common, now called Dartmouth Park.

Dartmouth's 26 lakes are aquatic parks surrounded by flowers and trees, and freckled with sailboats, water-skiers and sleek racing canoes. Regattas are held throughout the summer, and war-canoe races on Lake Banook are part of Dartmouth's Naval Day celebrations.

The city is connected with Halifax, its twin community, by two bridges and Canada's oldest saltwater ferry system, established in 1752. The ferry affords today's visitors close-up views of Halifax Harbour.

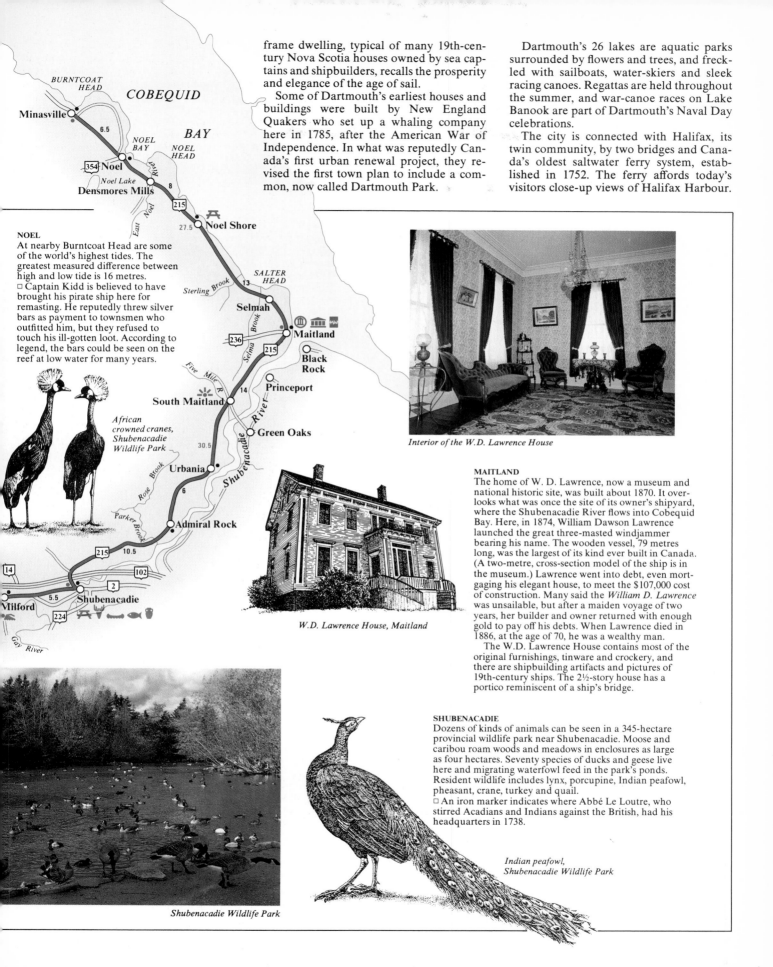

NOEL
At nearby Burntcoat Head are some of the world's highest tides. The greatest measured difference between high and low tide is 16 metres.
□ Captain Kidd is believed to have brought his pirate ship here for remasting. He reputedly threw silver bars as payment to townsmen who outfitted him, but they refused to touch his ill-gotten loot. According to legend, the bars could be seen on the reef at low water for many years.

African crowned cranes, Shubenacadie Wildlife Park

Interior of the W.D. Lawrence House

W.D. Lawrence House, Maitland

MAITLAND
The home of W. D. Lawrence, now a museum and national historic site, was built about 1870. It overlooks what was once the site of its owner's shipyard, where the Shubenacadie River flows into Cobequid Bay. Here, in 1874, William Dawson Lawrence launched the great three-masted windjammer bearing his name. The wooden vessel, 79 metres long, was the largest of its kind ever built in Canada. (A two-metre, cross-section model of the ship is in the museum.) Lawrence went into debt, even mortgaging his elegant house, to meet the $107,000 cost of construction. Many said the *William D. Lawrence* was unsailable, but after a maiden voyage of two years, her builder and owner returned with enough gold to pay off his debts. When Lawrence died in 1886, at the age of 70, he was a wealthy man.

The W.D. Lawrence House contains most of the original furnishings, tinware and crockery, and there are shipbuilding artifacts and pictures of 19th-century ships. The 2½-story house has a portico reminiscent of a ship's bridge.

SHUBENACADIE
Dozens of kinds of animals can be seen in a 345-hectare provincial wildlife park near Shubenacadie. Moose and caribou roam woods and meadows in enclosures as large as four hectares. Seventy species of ducks and geese live here and migrating waterfowl feed in the park's ponds. Resident wildlife includes lynx, porcupine, Indian peafowl, pheasant, crane, turkey and quail.
□ An iron marker indicates where Abbé Le Loutre, who stirred Acadians and Indians against the British, had his headquarters in 1738.

Indian peafowl, Shubenacadie Wildlife Park

Shubenacadie Wildlife Park

On a Shore of Strange Place-Names— a 'Wine Harbour' and a 'Sober Island'

Southeastern Nova Scotia

From Lawrencetown to Auld Cove is a drive that combines history, recreation and magnificent scenery. Much of this route winds along Nova Scotia's eastern shore—a region of sheltered coves, friendly fishing villages, and quiet woodlands embroidered by brooks and streams.

History is alive here—in museums, festivals and old-fashioned craft shops. At Sherbrooke Village an extensive restoration provides a glimpse of community life in the 1880s. Visitors can stroll among some

SHEET HARBOUR

The small, fish-smoking business of Willy Kraunch is a popular attraction in the nearby village of Tangier. Salmon, mackerel and eels are smoked here and sold abroad as delicacies. Visitors may watch as the fish are thawed, salted, dried and smoked.
□ The 453-square-kilometre Liscomb Game Sanctuary, an example of virgin Nova Scotia forest, has abundant wildlife and excellent trout fishing.
□ A cairn at Moose River Gold Mines recalls the dramatic rescue of two of three men trapped in an abandoned gold mine in 1936. The men were rescued after 10 days. The mine is considered too dangerous to be visited.

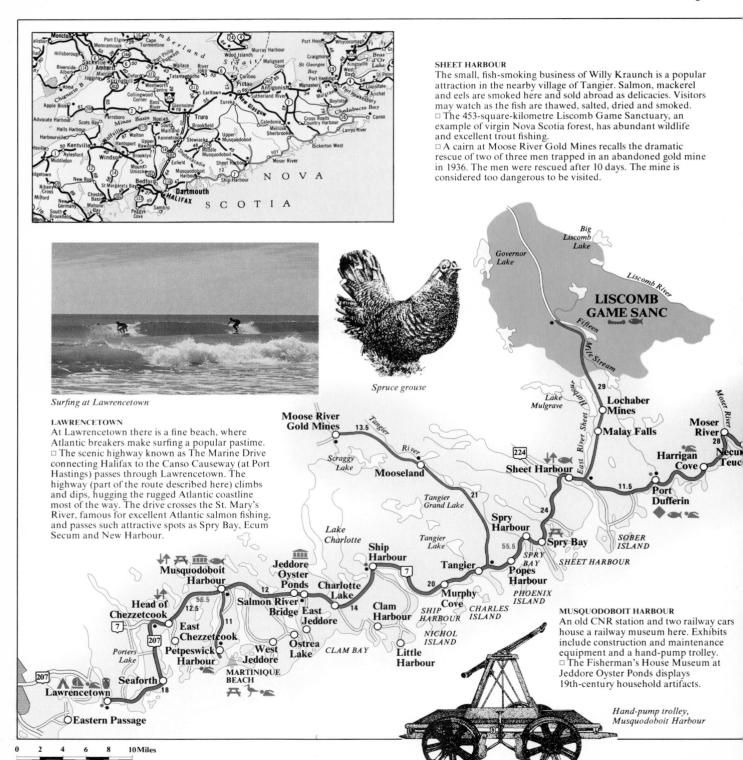

Surfing at Lawrencetown

Spruce grouse

LAWRENCETOWN

At Lawrencetown there is a fine beach, where Atlantic breakers make surfing a popular pastime.
□ The scenic highway known as The Marine Drive connecting Halifax to the Canso Causeway (at Port Hastings) passes through Lawrencetown. The highway (part of the route described here) climbs and dips, hugging the rugged Atlantic coastline most of the way. The drive crosses the St. Mary's River, famous for excellent Atlantic salmon fishing, and passes such attractive spots as Spry Bay, Ecum Secum and New Harbour.

MUSQUODOBOIT HARBOUR

An old CNR station and two railway cars house a railway museum here. Exhibits include construction and maintenance equipment and a hand-pump trolley.
□ The Fisherman's House Museum at Jeddore Oyster Ponds displays 19th-century household artifacts.

Hand-pump trolley, Musquodoboit Harbour

20 pioneer buildings, sample meals from an 1880s menu and learn about 19th-century crafts.

Equally popular with vacationers are sailing, surfing, swimming and scuba diving. Hikers and photographers can take advantage of the low hills above the coastline, following trails through meadows of wildflowers. Hunters and fishermen delight in the region's abundant wildlife.

At almost every turn along the eastern shore, strange place-names greet travelers.

Among the more unusual: Musquodoboit (Indian for rolling out in foam); Necum Teuch (Indian for a beach of fine sand); Sober Island (named by early surveyors unable to obtain intoxicants on the island); and Wine Harbour (named because a cargo of wine was spilled in this area).

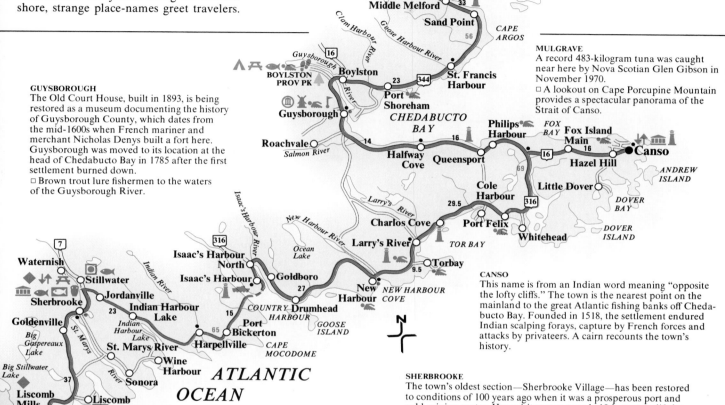

GUYSBOROUGH

The Old Court House, built in 1893, is being restored as a museum documenting the history of Guysborough County, which dates from the mid-1600s when French mariner and merchant Nicholas Denys built a fort here. Guysborough was moved to its location at the head of Chedabucto Bay in 1785 after the first settlement burned down.
□ Brown trout lure fishermen to the waters of the Guysborough River.

MULGRAVE

A record 483-kilogram tuna was caught near here by Nova Scotian Glen Gibson in November 1970.
□ A lookout on Cape Porcupine Mountain provides a spectacular panorama of the Strait of Canso.

CANSO

This name is from an Indian word meaning "opposite the lofty cliffs." The town is the nearest point on the mainland to the great Atlantic fishing banks off Chedabucto Bay. Founded in 1518, the settlement endured Indian scalping forays, capture by French forces and attacks by privateers. A cairn recounts the town's history.

SHERBROOKE

The town's oldest section—Sherbrooke Village—has been restored to conditions of 100 years ago when it was a prosperous port and gold-mining center. Here visitors can sample 19th-century life by carding wool and spinning it into yarn. They can also weave on an antique loom, make quilts and hook rugs. The village has a blacksmith shop, general store, courthouse and jail, woodworking shop, residences, two churches and a school. The Jordan Barn, moved from its original location 20 kilometres from the village, can also be seen. Guides in period costume escort visitors through the complex.

Sawmill, Sherbrooke Village

Blacksmith shop, Sherbrooke Village

The Swordfish— a Tasty Fighter

The highly prized swordfish is common in waters off eastern Nova Scotia. Its flat, rapierlike snout and upper jaw are up to one-third its body length. It feeds by thrashing its sword among a school of fish, then cruising back and forth to eat chunks of flesh. Averaging 320 kilograms, this pugnacious fish has been known to pierce ships' timbers and even whales (probably accidentally) with its sword. Sport fishermen eager to land this tasty fighter can charter boats along the southeastern coast of Nova Scotia.

A Spectacular Highland Trail and a Misty Island's Beauty

Cape Breton Island

Lone Shieling,
near Pleasant Bay

Women doing petit point embroidery,
Acadian Museum, Chéticamp

A Breathtaking Drive by the Sea

The Cabot Trail is a modern two-lane highway along 296 kilometres of magnificent Cape Breton Island. Named for explorer John Cabot, who may have sighted the northern tip of the island in 1497, the trail threads lush glens, passes white gypsum bluffs and skirts headlands pounded by surf. Seldom far from the sea, always breathtakingly lovely, it is one of Canada's most exciting highways. The trail is at its best in September and October when the highlands are bright with autumn color.

From South Gut St. Anns, the Cabot Trail parallels Cape Breton's Atlantic coast, with its rocky coves wet with spindrift. At Sunrise Valley, along the North Aspy River, the trail turns west to the Gulf of St. Lawrence. Now vista after vista unfolds along the rugged shore. The road goes south through small Acadian communities (Chéticamp, Grand Etang, Belle Côte), winds through the pastoral Margaree Valley, and then returns to Baddeck and South Gut St. Anns.

Cabot Trail by Pleasant Bay

CHÉTICAMP
French-Canadian antiques, spool beds, spinning wheels, looms, wooden farm implements and glassware are displayed at the Acadian Museum. There are demonstrations of spinning, carding, weaving and petit point embroidery. Chéticamp is noted for colorful rugs, hand-woven from the wool of local sheep.
□ There are summer guided tours of this historic village, settled in 1778 by 14 Acadian families.
□ St. Peter's Church was built in 1893 of freestone quarried on Chéticamp Island and hauled by horse and sleigh across the harbor ice.

MARGAREE HARBOUR
Boats can be chartered to nearby Margaree Island National Wildlife Area. Colonies of black guillemots, common terns and great cormorants roost on pinnacles and ledges along the island's 20-metre-high cliffs. Forests of spruce and fir are home to a rookery of great blue herons. The noisy greater yellowlegs (also called the tattler) forages in tidal flats. Its long, bright yellow legs make it one of the area's most conspicuous shorebirds.

MARGAREE FORKS
The Forks, Thornbush, Hut and Long pools along the Margaree River are among Canada's best salmon grounds. The Salmon Museum at North-East Margaree contains anglers' and poachers' rods, spears, jig hooks and *flambeaux* (torches used for night fishing). Displays in the museum's aquarium explain the life histories of trout and salmon.
□ The Museum of Cape Breton Heritage has tartans, pioneer spinning tools, and a rare collection of drafts (Scottish weaving patterns).

Alexander Graham Bell wrote, "I have traveled around the globe. I have seen the Canadian Rockies, the Andes and the Highlands of Scotland. But for simple beauty, Cape Breton outrivals them all."

Bell's accolade is supported by the spectacular Cabot Trail, the highway around the northern part of Cape Breton Island.

The route curves around sea-swept headlands, clings to the edge of cliffs that drop 300 metres to the sea, and threads dark river gorges amid ancient hills. More than one-third of the road's length is in Cape Breton Highlands National Park.

Cape Bretoners are fiercely proud of their island, yet share their ancestors' yearning for the Highlands of Scotland, the homeland of many of the earliest settlers.

A lament for the old country is expressed near Pleasant Bay at the Lone Shieling, a replica of a stone hut used by crofters when tending sheep. On a plaque are these words from the "Canadian Boat Song":

From the lone shieling of the misty island
Mountains divide us, and the waste of seas—
Yet still the blood is strong, the heart is High-
land,
And we in dreams behold the Hebrides!

These ties are renewed at St. Anns during an August celebration alive with Highland dancing and the skirl of bagpipes. The town's Gaelic college ensures that the language and lore of the clans live on among descendants of 19th-century pioneers.

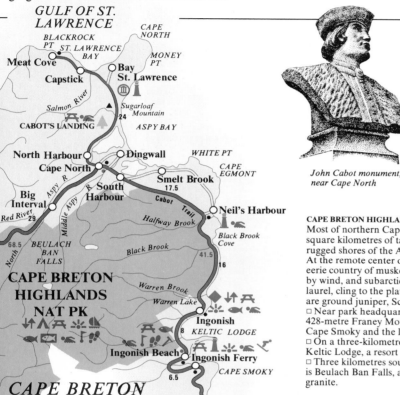

Greater yellowlegs

CAPE NORTH
At nearby Cabot's Landing are a cairn and a bust of John Cabot. A trail leads to the summit of Sugarloaf Mountain, which some think was the explorer's landfall in 1497.
□ The western terminus of the first cable between Nova Scotia and Newfoundland (1856) is commemorated by a plaque at Aspy Bay.
□ From surrounding hills there is a splendid view of fertile farmland, stands of elm, and brightly colored houses in the Sunrise Valley along the North Aspy River.

John Cabot monument, near Cape North

CAPE BRETON HIGHLANDS NATIONAL PARK
Most of northern Cape Breton Island is national park—1,050 square kilometres of tableland rising wild and high above the rugged shores of the Atlantic Ocean and the Gulf of St. Lawrence. At the remote center of the park is the Everlasting Barren—an eerie country of muskeg, ponds and heath barrens. Spruce, gnarled by wind, and subarctic plants such as reindeer moss and sheep laurel, cling to the plateau's thin soil. Atop salt-sprayed headlands are ground juniper, Scotch lovage and black crowberry.
□ Near park headquarters at Ingonish Beach, a hiking trail ascends 428-metre Franey Mountain with its splendid view of the coast, Cape Smoky and the lighthouse on Ingonish Island.
□ On a three-kilometre-long peninsula called Middle Head is Keltic Lodge, a resort owned by the Nova Scotia government.
□ Three kilometres southwest of the Big Intervale warden station is Beulach Ban Falls, a lacy ribbon of water that slips over smooth granite.

CAPE SMOKY
This majestic 365-metre headland, often shrouded in mist, is best seen from across South Bay Ingonish at Middle Head, a peninsula that is part of Cape Breton Highlands National Park. A chair lift takes visitors near the cape's summit. A hiking trail leads to a lookout, which affords stunning panoramas of the Cape Breton coast.

ENGLISHTOWN
Earthworks here date from 1713, when the French fortified the settlement of Sainte-Anne and renamed it Port Dauphin. Sainte-Anne, founded in 1629, was Cape Breton Island's first French colony. A cairn marks its site.
□ In a cemetery here is the grave of the Cape Breton giant, Angus McAskill (2.4 metres tall and more than 180 kilograms). He died at St. Anns in 1863, aged 38.

ST. ANNS
The Gaelic College, founded in 1939 to help preserve Scottish culture, offers summer courses in Highland dancing, arts, crafts, bagpipes and the weaving of tartans.
□ The Giant McAskill-Highland Pioneers Museum on the college grounds tells of early settlers and of the mighty giant, Angus McAskill, who operated a mill here in the 1850s. The museum displays his chair and bed, and some of his clothing.
□ Boat tours cruise near Bird Islands, nesting grounds for bald eagles, common puffins and razor-billed auks. Gray seals often sun on the rocks.

Beulach Ban Falls, Cape Breton Highlands National Park

Canada's Scotland by the Sea Bids '100,000 Welcomes'

Cape Breton Island

Highland piper, Iona

WHYCOCOMAGH

Several lookouts on the southwest slope of 300-metre-high Salt Mountain in Whycocomagh Provincial Park offer spectacular views of Bras d'Or Lake. The park is heavily forested with beech, maple, spruce, pine and horse chestnut, and is crossed by several nature trails.
□ Native craftsmen do basketry, wood carving and silk-screening at the Micmac Indian Reserve here. Examples of their work are sold at four local handicraft shops.
□ The Whycocomagh Summer Festival in July features woodsmen's competitions and Scottish music and dance.

PORT HASTINGS

The 1,370-metre Canso Causeway linking mainland Nova Scotia with Cape Breton Island is the world's deepest. Rising 66 metres from the floor of the Strait of Canso, it is 243 metres wide at its base, 24 metres wide above the surface, and carries a two-lane highway, a railway track and a pedestrian walkway. Ships use a navigation lock at the Port Hastings (northern) end. The causeway, opened in 1955, keeps ice from entering the strait from the north and thus creates an ice-free harbor 16 kilometres long.
□ Giant supertankers, some longer than three football fields, discharge crude oil at a 600-metre-long deep-water terminal dock at Point Tupper. A ship can berth here, unload and sail within 24 hours. One 2,350,000-barrel cargo satisfies the local refinery for almost a month.
□ Looming 260 metres above St. Georges Bay and the Strait of Canso, Creignish Mountain affords spectacular views of the strait, the bay and mainland Nova Scotia.

IONA

This village has a pioneer museum, stages a summer festival of Scottish music and art, and is the home of the Highland Village Pipe Band.
□ The museum, in which settlers' belongings are labeled in English and Gaelic, is the nucleus of the Nova Scotia Highland Village. Among several reconstructed buildings are a 19th-century carding mill, a country store, a forge, and *Tigh Dubh*, a crofter's stone cottage.

Oil refinery at Point Tupper near Port Hastings

ISLE MADAME

Settled by Acadians after the fall of Louisbourg in 1758, Isle Madame is ringed by rocky coves and picturesque fishing villages.
□ When Thomas LeNoir came from the Magdalen Islands in the early 1800s, Arichat was a prosperous ship-building town. The forge that he and his family built at nearby Petit-de-Grat served the builders and trained new craftsmen; eventually the LeNoirs established Nova Scotia's first blacksmith school. When shipbuilding declined, so did the forge, but it was restored in 1967 as a museum with exhibits of ship chandlery and anchor making.
□ Arichat's twin-towered, wooden L'Assomption Church, built in 1837, was a cathedral until 1886, when the diocesan seat was moved to Antigonish. The original bishop's palace is now a hospital.

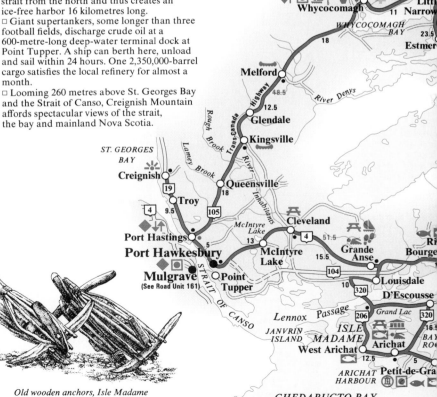

Old wooden anchors, Isle Madame

When the Strait of Canso was bridged by a 1,370-metre causeway in 1955, one Nova Scotian wrote to a newspaper, claiming that the link would unify Canadians from Atlantic to Pacific. "For now," he declared, "we're *all* Cape Bretoners."

After crossing the causeway, the Trans-Canada Highway sweeps around sparkling Bras d'Or Lake, a 640-square-kilometre inland sea that almost splits Cape Breton Island. Encircled by superb highland scenery, the virtually tideless lake resembles a Scot-

tish loch. To the south, a strip of land less than a kilometre wide (now traversed by St. Peters Canal) separates Bras d'Or Lake from the sea. To the north, the Atlantic comes and goes on both sides of Boularderie Island. Low mountains rise behind the channels, bays and harbors, and the salty lake has excellent fishing, sheltered anchorages and scores of fine beaches.

This is Scottish Nova Scotia, fiercely proud of its heritage—of the Gaelic language that is still spoken here; of strath-

speys, sword dances, bagpipes, caber tossing at Highland games, and the ancestral virtues of industry and thrift. Here Scottish-born Alexander Graham Bell spent his summers in a mansion overlooking Baddeck Bay, and a dozen Cape Bretoners witnessed the birth of Canadian aviation.

Nestling by the shore of Bras d'Or Lake, towns named Iona and Ben Eoin speak of Scottish origins. Gaelic signs bid visitors "100,000 welcomes," and kilted pipers skirl "Will Ye No Come Back Again?"

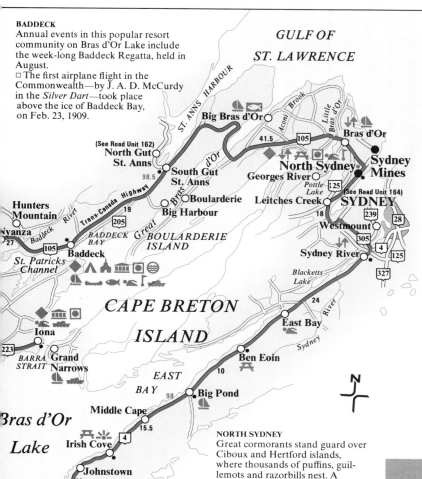

BADDECK
Annual events in this popular resort community on Bras d'Or Lake include the week-long Baddeck Regatta, held in August.
□ The first airplane flight in the Commonwealth—by J. A. D. McCurdy in the *Silver Dart*—took place above the ice of Baddeck Bay, on Feb. 23, 1909.

GULF OF
ST. LAWRENCE

ST. ANNS HARBOUR

Big Bras d'Or
41.5
105
Bras d'Or
(See Road Unit 162)
North Gut
St. Anns
98.5
South Gut
St. Anns
Georges River
North Sydney
Sydney Mines
125
Pottle Lake
(See Road Unit 164)
Leitches Creek
SYDNEY
Boularderie
18
239
Big Harbour
19
205
Westmount
28
Hunters
Mountain
305
4
125
St. Patricks
Channel
105
Baddeck
BADDECK BAY
BOULARDERIE
ISLAND
Sydney River
327
Blacketts
Lake
Nyanza
27
CAPE BRETON
ISLAND
24
East Bay
Iona
223
BARRA
STRAIT
Grand
Narrows
Ben Eoin
10
EAST
BAY
98
Big Pond
Middle Cape
15.5
N
Bras d'Or
Lake
Irish Cove
4
Johnstown
13
Loch
Lomond
Red Islands
ST. PETERS
INLET
Hay Cove
Soldiers
Cove
Barra
Head
17.5
St. Peters
BATTERY
PROV PK

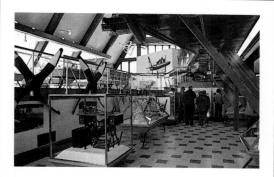

The Genius of *Beinn Breagh*

The centerpiece of 10-hectare Alexander Graham Bell National Historic Park in Baddeck is a museum (*above*) which mirrors the genius of the Scottish-born inventor of the telephone—whose research led to important contributions to medicine, aeronautics, marine engineering and genetics. Displayed are replicas of early telephone equipment and examples of Bell's lesser-known inventions, including a "vacuum jacket" (an early iron lung), surgical probes, manned kites and a hydrofoil boat.

Bell first visited Baddeck in 1885. Seven years later he built a summer home, *Beinn Breagh* (Gaelic for beautiful mountain), on a headland overlooking Baddeck Bay. There he did much of his research. He died at *Beinn Breagh* in 1922 and was buried on the summit of his beautiful mountain amid scenery that had reminded him of Scotland.

NORTH SYDNEY
Great cormorants stand guard over Ciboux and Hertford islands, where thousands of puffins, guillemots and razorbills nest. A 2½-hour boat tour circles the uninhabited islands.
□ Fairy Hole, a limestone cavern lined with stalactites and stalagmites, has a 15-metre-wide mouth but narrows abruptly to a mere crawlway.

ST. PETERS
A cairn marks the site of a fort and trading post established here in 1650 by Nicholas Denys, of which only earth mounds remain. Micmac Indian and pioneer artifacts are displayed in the Nicholas Denys Museum, built in the architectural style of the original fort.
□ One of Nova Scotia's most beautiful beaches—three kilometres of level white sand—is at Point Michaud. Gray seals are often seen on and around the Basque Islands nearby.
□ The St. Peters Canal, completed in 1869, cuts across a kilometre-wide isthmus to connect Bras d'Or Lake with the Atlantic. Before the canal was built, vessels were pulled over the narrow strip of land by oxen and the area was referred to on early charts as "Haulover Isthmus."

Sailing on Bras d'Or Lake, near Baddeck

'Impregnable' Louisbourg...
and Towns Built by Coal

Cape Breton Island

The Fortress of Louisbourg, a great gray ghost on the rocky Cape Breton coast, was built to guard the Gulf of St. Lawrence and France's dwindling empire in the New World. Begun in 1720, it was ringed with three-metre-thick stone walls nine metres high, armed with 148 cannon, and built at such cost that Louis XV said he expected to see the towers of Louisbourg rising over the Paris horizon.

Yet, as a stronghold it was a failure. In 1745 a ragtag army of 4,000 Yankee volun-

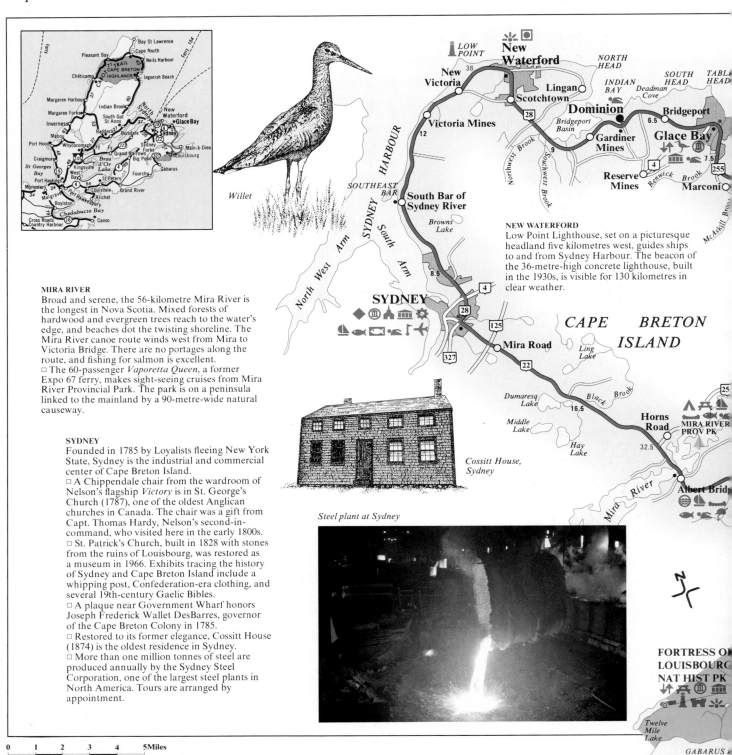

Willet

Cossitt House, Sydney

Steel plant at Sydney

MIRA RIVER
Broad and serene, the 56-kilometre Mira River is the longest in Nova Scotia. Mixed forests of hardwood and evergreen trees reach to the water's edge, and beaches dot the twisting shoreline. The Mira River canoe route winds west from Mira to Victoria Bridge. There are no portages along the route, and fishing for salmon is excellent.
□ The 60-passenger *Vaporetta Queen*, a former Expo 67 ferry, makes sight-seeing cruises from Mira River Provincial Park. The park is on a peninsula linked to the mainland by a 90-metre-wide natural causeway.

SYDNEY
Founded in 1785 by Loyalists fleeing New York State, Sydney is the industrial and commercial center of Cape Breton Island.
□ A Chippendale chair from the wardroom of Nelson's flagship *Victory* is in St. George's Church (1787), one of the oldest Anglican churches in Canada. The chair was a gift from Capt. Thomas Hardy, Nelson's second-in-command, who visited here in the early 1800s.
□ St. Patrick's Church, built in 1828 with stones from the ruins of Louisbourg, was restored as a museum in 1966. Exhibits tracing the history of Sydney and Cape Breton Island include a whipping post, Confederation-era clothing, and several 19th-century Gaelic Bibles.
□ A plaque near Government Wharf honors Joseph Frederick Wallet DesBarres, governor of the Cape Breton Colony in 1785.
□ Restored to its former elegance, Cossitt House (1874) is the oldest residence in Sydney.
□ More than one million tonnes of steel are produced annually by the Sydney Steel Corporation, one of the largest steel plants in North America. Tours are arranged by appointment.

NEW WATERFORD
Low Point Lighthouse, set on a picturesque headland five kilometres west, guides ships to and from Sydney Harbour. The beacon of the 36-metre-high concrete lighthouse, built in the 1930s, is visible for 130 kilometres in clear weather.

FORTRESS OF
LOUISBOURG
NAT HIST PK

teers, backed by three British ships, captured Louisbourg in seven weeks—only to see it returned to the French in 1748. Ten years later, the British took it again, this time blasting the fortress to rubble.

Some of the massive fortifications of Louisbourg have risen again near the eastern tip of Cape Breton Island, in a $20 million recreation of one-fifth of the garrison area and enclosed town. An echo of 18th-century New France, Louisbourg is a cluster of faithfully restored stone bastions and wooden houses and barracks. The tools, materials and methods of 250 years ago are used wherever possible to mirror the tiniest historical detail. Uniformed officers stroll along the cobblestone, fishermen salt and dry their catch, soldiers patrol the bastions, and costumed staff hold auctions, launder clothes, bake bread, mold bullets, and operate taverns and blacksmith shops.

Though short-lived, Louisbourg was a toehold for settlement in eastern Canada. Rich seams of bituminous coal—first mined in 1720 to supply the garrison at Louisbourg—were discovered under much of northeastern Cape Breton. Full-scale mining operations began in the 1850s, and the names of such towns as Sydney, Glace Bay, Dominion, Donkin and New Waterford became synonymous with coal.

Today these highland and harbor towns supplement traditional trades with manufacturing and tourism. But their heritage—a rich blend of French and English traditions—is reverently preserved.

GLACE BAY

A coal mine under the floor of the Atlantic is the realistic main attraction of the Miner's Museum in this historic coal town. Retired miners guide visitors down a sloping tunnel and through three levels of the Ocean Deeps Colliery, where mining machinery is in place and coal samples can be dug as souvenirs. On the top level, 15 metres below the sea, a flower garden grows in the rock. Among the exhibits in the museum building on the surface are wrought-iron sculptures depicting miners at work, a model of a Sydney and Louisbourg Railway coal train, a coal-burning street lamp, mining augers, borers, shovels, and a mine telephone.

PORT MORIEN

A rocky slope near here is the site of a 1720 French coal mine, said to be the first in North America.
□ The Cape Breton Steam Railway has two operating steam locomotives, several vintage railway cars and a recreated 19th-century depot.

A Fortune From the Deep

Alex Storm (above right) with treasure from Le Chameau

For 236 years the cold Atlantic near the Fortress of Louisbourg hid a fortune in gold and silver coins. The treasure—pay for the French army in Quebec—had been strewn over the rocky ocean floor in 1725 when the 48-gun naval transport *Le Chameau*, seeking refuge from a sudden gale, was wrecked on a reef.

In 1961, skin diver Alex Storm found a silver coin with the bust of Louis XV and the date 1724. Convinced that he had stumbled upon *Le Chameau*, Storm mapped a system of grids to search, in water 22 to 30 metres deep, more than 250,000 square metres of sea bottom. Finally, on Sept. 22, 1965, the bulk of the treasure was discovered. Within days some $300,000 in silver and gold coins was recovered—the largest treasure find in Canadian history.

LOUISBOURG

The Fortress of Louisbourg, begun by the French in 1720 to protect New France, was captured by the English in 1758 and destroyed in 1760. Now Canada's biggest historical reconstruction and the focal point of 51-square-kilometre Fortress of Louisbourg National Historic Park, it includes some 50 buildings, the blackened shells of other structures (giving the impression of a city under siege) and extensive stone fortifications.

Plans and drawings of the original fort and accounts of the sieges of 1745 and 1758 are displayed in the Fortress of Louisbourg Museum. Other exhibits explain how Louisbourg is being restored. The three-story King's Bastion Barracks, once the New World's largest building, contains the governor's luxurious 10-room suite, officers' quarters, a chapel, a prison and an artillery school. Typical 18th-century meals are served in the Hôtel de la Marine, a waterfront tavern.
□ A plaque from Canada's first lighthouse (1734), stating that the beacon was built by order of Louis XV, is on a lighthouse built in 1923 on the foundations of the original.

King's Bastion Barracks, Louisbourg

ATLANTIC OCEAN

Costumed staff recreate the past at Louisbourg

Coastal Barrens, a Bay of Islands and a World-Famous Salmon Stream

Southwestern Newfoundland

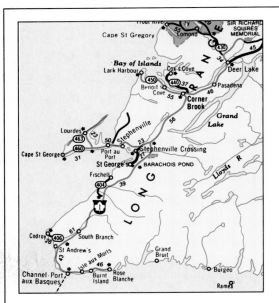

Cape St. George, Port au Port Peninsula

PORT AU PORT PENINSULA
Here live descendants of French fishermen who used the peninsula as their base of operations as early as 1713.
□ Evidence of forces that shaped this region some 500 million years ago is seen in layered, folded and faulted rock in cliffs along the peninsula's south shore. Mostly dolomite and limestone, the formations contain fossils of marine animals. Wind and waves batter Cape St. George, the peninsula's westernmost point.
□ At Piccadilly Head Provincial Park visitors dig for clams from the sand flats at low tide. A walking trail leaves the beach and penetrates a forest of balsam fir. Some limestone cliffs in the park drop more than 12 metres to the sea. Blue- and green-winged teal may be seen here in the fall.

CODROY VALLEY
Migrating Canada geese—as many as 500 at a time—stop on the banks of the Grand Codroy River, near Grand Codroy Provincial Park.
□ In Mummichog Provincial Park, 12 kilometres south, a lagoon supports the tiny mummichog, a fish found in few other places in Newfoundland. The lagoon is a mixture of fresh water from the Little Codroy River and salt water from the Atlantic. Great blue herons and American woodcocks are seen in the park.

Rose Blanche

CHANNEL-PORT AUX BASQUES
A monument commemorates 133 persons who died in 1942 when a German submarine torpedoed the ferry *Caribou*. A scenic, 45-kilometre drive leads east to the picturesque fishing village of Rose Blanche.
□ A sandbar shelters a saltwater inlet from the Atlantic's thundering surf, northwest of Channel-Port aux Basques at John T. Cheeseman Provincial Park. Surrounding the park are the desolate barrens of Cape Ray. Strong winds funnel down from Table Mountain and across a dry gulch at nearby Red Rocks; the winds have frequently upset railway cars.
□ Car ferries connect Channel-Port aux Basques with North Sydney, N.S.

Newfoundland pine marten

BARACHOIS POND PROVINCIAL PARK
A 3.2-kilometre self-guiding nature trail climbs through a forest of birch, spruce and fir to the barren summit of Erin Mountain. Moose, caribou and, occasionally, the rare Newfoundland pine marten, are sometimes spotted. The 305-metre peak provides a panoramic view of the surrounding area.

Southwestern Newfoundland is a region of stark coastal barrens, broad headlands pounded by surf, placid wilderness lakes and densely forested mountains. East of the ferry terminus at Channel-Port aux Basques is Newfoundland's sparsely settled south coast, a vast area served only by boat. Ships from the port travel 400 kilometres east to Terrenceville, stopping at remote fishing villages.

The Trans-Canada Highway goes north from Channel-Port aux Basques, past the desolate barrens of Cape Ray, to Red Rocks and McDougall Gulch. Farther on is the Codroy River valley, a bird-watcher's paradise in spring and fall; and the Crabbes River, where salmon anglers can try their luck in June and early July. A trek to the summit of Erin Mountain in Barachois Pond Provincial Park will reward hikers and photographers with a spectacular view of sea and shore—and perhaps a glimpse of a moose or a caribou. To the west, farms and fishing hamlets line the coast of the Port au Port Peninsula—where residents speak French with a Newfoundland accent.

Still farther north, nestled in the lush valley of the Humber River, is the pulp mill city of Corner Brook. Some of Newfoundland's finest scenery is west of the city, where towering cliffs rise sharply out of the water on both sides of Humber Arm and in the Bay of Islands.

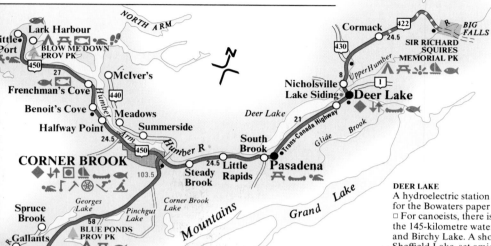

SIR RICHARD SQUIRES MEMORIAL PARK

Spawning salmon use a fish ladder to bypass Big Falls on the Humber River. Fishing near the falls is among the best in Newfoundland. North of the park the Upper Humber flows between narrow canyon walls up to 91 metres high. Farther upstream are wilderness lakes, turbulent rapids and shoreline forests of spruce and white birch. A canoe route from the park leads downstream to Corner Brook.

DEER LAKE

A hydroelectric station at the town of Deer Lake supplies power for the Bowaters paper mill at Corner Brook.
□ For canoeists, there is magnificent scenery south of here along the 145-kilometre waterway formed by Grand Lake, Sandy Lake and Birchy Lake. A short portage extends the waterway into Sheffield Lake, set amid heavily forested mountains.
□ From Deer Lake roads lead northwest to Bonne Bay and Gros Morne National Park, and then north 460 kilometres to the tip of Newfoundland's Great Northern Peninsula.

BAY OF ISLANDS

Blow Me Down Provincial Park provides a stunning view of this bay. Wooden stairs, set in a steep rock overhang, lead to a lookout tower. Woods Island lies at the head of the bay. Guernsey, Tweed and Pearl islands are strung across the horizon at the bay's outer reaches. The densely forested park is reputed to have buried treasure.

CORNER BROOK

Worldwide demand for newsprint has made Corner Brook the second largest city in Newfoundland, with a population approaching 30,000. On one of several hills overlooking the city, a cairn honors Capt. James Cook, who made the first detailed map of Newfoundland's west coast and sailed up the Humber River as far as Deer Lake in 1767. From the cairn is a fine view of the Bowaters paper mill, one of the world's largest, with a capacity of more than 500,000 tonnes a year. Visitors may arrange tours of the mill, which ships newsprint around the world.
□ Among the city's striking buildings is the 10-story Government Building. The Centennial Arts and Culture Center contains a theater, a swimming pool, an art gallery and exhibition areas.
□ Humber Valley salmon streams and big-game hunting are easily accessible from Corner Brook. Parks include Margaret Bowater Park (in the city) and the Bowater Park at South Brook, 24 kilometres northeast. Blue Ponds Provincial Park, 13 kilometres southwest, contains two lakes whose limestone bottoms account for their deep turquoise color.

Atlantic Salmon— Surviving All Obstacles

Revered by sportsmen and esteemed by gourmets, the Atlantic salmon (*below*) is world renowned as a game fish and a commercial species.

The Atlantic salmon is the classic migratory fish. After spawning in the freshwater streams of Newfoundland in October and November, the adults head for the sea. (Unlike Pacific salmon, Atlantic salmon usually survive after spawning and may return to spawn more than once.) The young remain in fresh water for two or three years, then descend to the sea to spend one or more years feeding and growing before coming back to the streams of their birth to spawn.

The ability of the salmon to surmount falls and other obstacles on their return is a fascinating sight. At Big Falls, in Sir Richard Squires Memorial Park, the salmon can be seen thrashing tirelessly as they mount a fish ladder built to ease their passage.

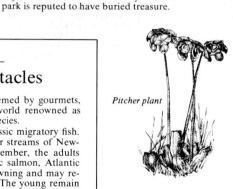

Pitcher plant

Corner Brook

The Misty Heights of Gros Morne...
and (Perhaps) the Norse Vinland

Northwestern Newfoundland

Along the craggy coast of Bonne Bay in Gros Morne National Park, the peaks of some of the most spectacular mountains in eastern North America drop sharply to long narrow fjords. Close to the bay, tiny fishing hamlets dot the sloping landscape. A car ferry takes travelers across the bay to Norris Point, where Highway 430 continues along the west coast of Newfoundland's Great Northern Peninsula. The brooding, flat-topped Long Range Mountains rise dramatically from a low coastal

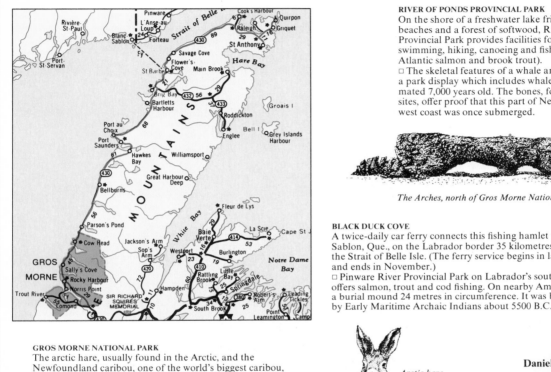

RIVER OF PONDS PROVINCIAL PARK
On the shore of a freshwater lake fringed by sand beaches and a forest of softwood, River of Ponds Provincial Park provides facilities for camping, swimming, hiking, canoeing and fishing (for Atlantic salmon and brook trout).
☐ The skeletal features of a whale are described in a park display which includes whale bones an estimated 7,000 years old. The bones, found at nearby sites, offer proof that this part of Newfoundland's west coast was once submerged.

The Arches, north of Gros Morne National Park

BLACK DUCK COVE
A twice-daily car ferry connects this fishing hamlet with Blanc Sablon, Que., on the Labrador border 35 kilometres across the Strait of Belle Isle. (The ferry service begins in late spring and ends in November.)
☐ Pinware River Provincial Park on Labrador's southeastern coast offers salmon, trout and cod fishing. On nearby Amour Point is a burial mound 24 metres in circumference. It was built by Early Maritime Archaic Indians about 5500 B.C.

GROS MORNE NATIONAL PARK
The arctic hare, usually found in the Arctic, and the Newfoundland caribou, one of the world's biggest caribou, inhabit this 1,943-square-kilometre park. Set in the most spectacular portion of the Long Range Mountains, the park is named for Newfoundland's second highest peak, Gros Morne (806 metres), which dominates the Bonne Bay area.
☐ North of the bay, between the sea and the mountains, lies a low coastal plain crisscrossed by small rivers and covered with bogs and grassland. Along the shore are sand dunes up to 12 metres high. Rock cliffs tower above Western Brook Pond, one of several fjordlike lakes cradled in river gorges that were deepened by glaciers during the last ice age.
☐ South of Bonne Bay is the Serpentine Tableland, a barren upland plain littered with ocher-brown volcanic boulders. A car ferry crosses the bay, linking the village of Woody Point with the park headquarters at Rocky Harbour.
☐ Among more than 175 bird species sighted in Gros Morne are the endangered peregrine falcon and the gyrfalcon, American golden plover, osprey and whimbrel. Fish species include Atlantic salmon, brook trout, cod and mackerel.

Arctic hare

Arctic rhododendron

plain. Along Gros Morne's rugged 65-kilometre coastline are fine beaches and broad expanses of shifting dunes. Inland are dense forests, narrow mountain lakes, a tidal inlet, and streams noted for salmon.

Past Gros Morne's northern boundary, travelers may return to the dawn of recorded Canadian history. In L'Anse aux Meadows, at the northern tip of Newfoundland, is the only known site of Viking settlement west of Greenland. Norsemen came to these rocky shores about A.D. 1000 and established what may have been the first European colony in North America.

Another important archaeological site is at Port au Choix. An interpretive center displays skeletons and relics of "red paint people" who lived here 5,000 years ago.

A memorable side trip begins at Black Duck Cove, where summer travelers can take a car ferry across the Strait of Belle Isle and explore the southern coast of Labrador.

Red Paint People, *a mural at*
Port au Choix National Historic Park

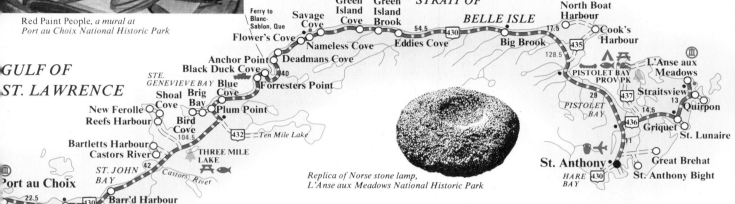
Replica of Norse stone lamp,
L'Anse aux Meadows National Historic Park

PORT AU CHOIX

Skeletons and relics of "red paint people" who roamed between Maine and Labrador some 5,000 years ago are displayed in an interpretive center at Port au Choix National Historic Park. Burial sites uncovered here in the late 1960s tell most of what is known about the red paint people. Graves were lined with red ocher and contained bundles of artifacts for use by the dead in the afterlife. Weapons of slate, bone and ivory show that the red paint people lived by hunting and fishing. Awls, gouges, axes and cutting tools show there was a well-developed wood-carving industry, and fine bone needles demonstrate the existence of sewn garments. Also on display are relics of Dorset Inuit who lived on nearby Pointe Riche about A.D. 100.
□ Picnic grounds at Pointe Riche lighthouse provide fine sunset views of the Gulf of St. Lawrence.

Western Brook gorge, Gros Morne National Park

L'ANSE AUX MEADOWS

A Viking settlement, possibly the Vinland of Norse sagas, was established here about A.D. 1000. Remains of seven buildings, a smithy and two cook pits have been unearthed in L'Anse aux Meadows National Historic Park. The site was discovered by a Norwegian archaeological team in 1961. Research has left a pattern of shallow, sod-covered diggings approximating the layout of the original Norse buildings. Displays in the park's interpretive center include the floorboard of a Norse boat, iron rivets excavated at the site, and a soapstone flywheel used for spinning wool. The flywheel, the earliest European household article unearthed in North America, is identical to those found at Viking sites in Greenland, Iceland, Norway and Sweden.

ST. ANTHONY

In recent years the rallying point for groups protesting the annual Gulf of St. Lawrence seal hunt, St. Anthony is a beacon of hope for the people of northern Newfoundland and Labrador. It is headquarters of the Grenfell Mission, which provides medical aid along a bleak 2,400 kilometres of coast. Sir Wilfrid Grenfell founded the mission in 1893. He died in 1940, aged 75, and is buried here. Grenfell's work goes on here and in a network of clinics and nursing stations linked by ships and aircraft. Ceramic murals by Jordi Bonet adorn the foyer of Curtis Memorial Hospital, named for Dr. Charles S. Curtis, another devoted missionary. Handcrafted items sold at St. Anthony include embroidered parkas and soapstone carvings.

When Seafaring Norsemen Found the New World

About A.D. 800, Norwegians began voyages of exploration in the North Atlantic, and eventually settled in Iceland. In A.D. 982 an Icelander named Erik the Red murdered a man and was banished for three years. He spent his exile exploring the shores of Greenland, where he established two colonies. Men from these settlements sailed farther west. One ship was driven off course in 986 and sighted strange new wooded lands—apparently Newfoundland and Labrador.

Leif Eriksson, son of Erik the Red, heard of the discovery. Attracted by the possibility of timber close to Greenland, he sailed (about A.D. 995) and landed at a fertile spot he called Vinland. He remained there for a year. Archaeologists have proved there was a Norse settlement at L'Anse aux Meadows. But was it Eriksson's Vinland or the settlement of Norsemen who came after him? That question will probably tantalize scholars for years to come.

A 'Road to the Isles' and a World-Famous Airport

Central Newfoundland

About midway along the Newfoundland portion of the Trans-Canada Highway lies Grand Falls, the province's fourth largest urban center. The town was established in 1909 when Lord Northcliffe, the British

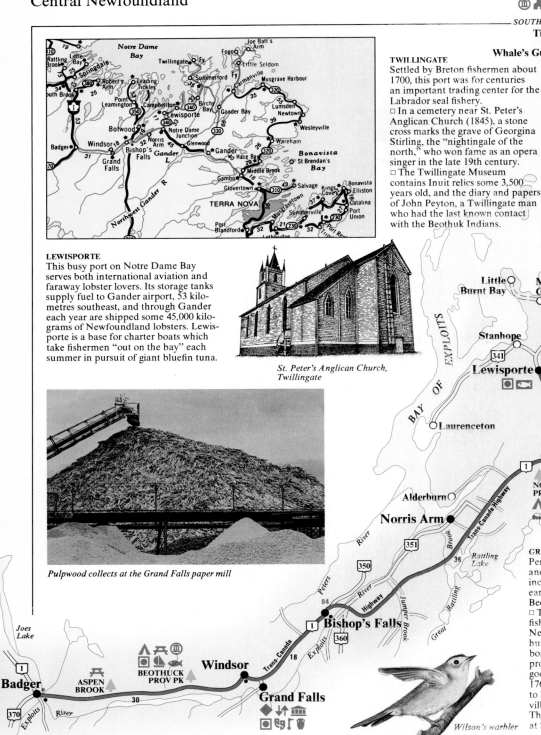

TWILLINGATE
Settled by Breton fishermen about 1700, this port was for centuries an important trading center for the Labrador seal fishery.
□ In a cemetery near St. Peter's Anglican Church (1845), a stone cross marks the grave of Georgina Stirling, the "nightingale of the north," who won fame as an opera singer in the late 19th century.
□ The Twillingate Museum contains Inuit relics some 3,500 years old, and the diary and papers of John Peyton, a Twillingate man who had the last known contact with the Beothuk Indians.

LEWISPORTE
This busy port on Notre Dame Bay serves both international aviation and faraway lobster lovers. Its storage tanks supply fuel to Gander airport, 53 kilometres southeast, and through Gander each year are shipped some 45,000 kilograms of Newfoundland lobsters. Lewisporte is a base for charter boats which take fishermen "out on the bay" each summer in pursuit of giant bluefin tuna.

St. Peter's Anglican Church, Twillingate

Pulpwood collects at the Grand Falls paper mill

BISHOP'S FALLS
The Beothuk Indians used the Exploits River, south of here, to travel to and from the Atlantic. From early spring through fall they camped on the coast, hunting seabirds and seals, gathering eggs and fishing. In late fall they move inland to hunt caribou.

GRAND FALLS
Permanent exhibits in the Mary March Museum and National Exhibition Center, opened in 1977, include a model of a sealing ship, photographs of early logging in Newfoundland and a mural of a Beothuk Indian village.
□ The Beothuks, a tribe of nomadic hunters and fishermen who lived in this area of central Newfoundland, were exterminated by settlers who hunted them like animals. When Beothuks borrowed fishing gear they thought was public property, English and French killed to recover their goods. It was not a crime to murder a Beothuk until 1769—but the killing went on. It became popular to hunt the tribe and profitable to wipe out entire villages and take valuable furs and caribou hides. The last Beothuk, a girl named Shanawdithit, died at St. John's in 1829.

Wilson's warbler

0   2   4   6   8   10 Miles
0   4   8   12   16 Kilometres

newspaper magnate, acquired forests in the area and started a pulp and paper plant. It now produces more than 1,100 metric tons of newsprint a day.

From Grand Falls, highways 1 and 340 lead northeast to the bustling commercial center of Lewisporte, also a popular tuna-fishing base. Farther on, at Boyd's Cove, the "Road to the Isles" begins—a series of bridges and causeways crossing Dildo Run, linking the mainland with Chapel, New World and South Twillingate islands. In June and July, north of the historic town of Twillingate, giant icebergs off Long Point Lighthouse appear menacing when they loom through fog, enchanting when they sparkle in bright sunshine.

Farther south lies Gander Bay, the starting point for hunting and fishing expeditions up the Gander River. East of Gander and its famed international airport is the village of Gambo, set in prime hunting and fishing country, a popular base for campers and canoeists.

Tizzard's Harbour, New World Island

FOGO ISLAND

A twice-daily car ferry crosses Hamilton Sound, linking Fogo Island with the mainland village of Carmanville. A shipbuilding cooperative on the island transforms rough timber into sturdy fishing boats, ranging from skiffs to long-liners.

Arctic char

GANDER

In the heart of one of North America's finest hunting and fishing areas, a town of some 8,000 has grown up near Gander International Airport. The British Air Ministry chose Gander as a transatlantic base in the mid-1930s and the airport opened in 1938.
□ In the modern terminal are *Flight and Its Allegories*, a striking 22-metre mural by Kenneth Lochhead. An aviation museum exhibits a four-bladed wooden propeller from the twin-engine Vickers Vimy biplane that was used by British aviators Capt. J. W. Alcock and Lt. A. W. Brown on the first nonstop transatlantic flight, from St. John's, Nfld., to Clifden, Ireland, in June 1919.
□ Outside the terminal is the Atlantic Ferry Pilot Memorial, a huge cairn surmounted by a Lockheed Hudson bomber in wartime camouflage. It is identical to one that on Nov. 10-11, 1940, made the first transatlantic crossing from Gander. That flight was the first of thousands by pilots of the Atlantic Ferry.

GANDER BAY

In long, narrow Gander Bay boats, guides lead hunters and fishermen upstream on the Gander River in search of moose, salmon and arctic char. Descended from Old Town canoes imported from Maine, the boats are made of spruce, larch and fir and equipped with light outboard motors.

A Stately Parade of Towering Icebergs

The highlight of a visit to Twillingate is often the sight of icebergs drifting south with the Labrador Current until midsummer. Huge masses of curiously eroded ice, as high as 45 metres, are frequently seen off nearby Long Point. A few are islands of ice almost two kilometres long. Others are smaller—about the size of a cathedral or a castle and shaped somewhat the same, with soaring towers, turrets, buttresses and battlements. The bergs' colors range from deep blue to pale green.

Atlantic Ferry Pilot Memorial, Gander

GAMBO

Nearby Square Pond is the habitat of the largest landlocked arctic char in Newfoundland. Canoe routes from Gambo lead to Indian Bay, 64 kilometres northeast, and to Gander Bay, 137 kilometres northwest. Lakes and rivers along these routes are fringed by forests of white birch and balsam fir.

Icebergs off the Newfoundland coast

Timeless Terra Nova Park and Rockbound Outports

Central Newfoundland

Terra Nova National Park, overlooking the rugged shores of Bonavista Bay, is a good base for sight-seeing in central Newfoundland. Peace seems to reign here in sheltered bays, numerous lakes and streams and in dense forests.

A trip from Glovertown, near the park's northern boundary, leads to Salvage, at the tip of the Eastport Peninsula. Here, in one of Canada's oldest outports, travelers visit a snug museum containing early artifacts of the Newfoundland fishing industry. Like

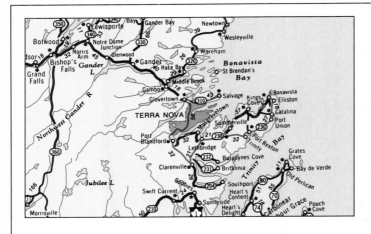

GLOVERTOWN

This town of 2,200 is the main service center for visitors to nearby Terra Nova National Park. Small craft can sail safely here. Glovertown is sheltered by a score of islands which extend almost 30 kilometres into Alexander Bay—one of the many great glacier-carved indentations in the shoreline of Bonavista Bay.

EASTPORT

For five weeks in early summer this village stages a festival of the arts. There are plays, most by local playwrights and about Newfoundland; handicraft areas on the beach, where macramé, embroidery and leatherwork are taught; and concerts featuring semiclassical music.
□ In Happy Adventure (including Lower and Upper Adventure) fishermen sell live lobsters from a lobster pool. Purchasers use an adjoining kitchen to cook the fresh fare. The beach at nearby Sandy Cove is one of the finest in Newfoundland.

Lobster

Terra Nova National Park

TERRA NOVA NATIONAL PARK

Icebergs in the cold Labrador Current drift off Terra Nova's coast in early summer. Atlantic breakers crash against towering headlands, boil along sheltered sounds and roll up long, deserted beaches. Bay and harp seals are occasionally seen offshore; dolphins and killer whales cruise in Bonavista Bay, which is also the habitat of squid up to 15 metres long. Shellfish abound in the park's bays and inlets. Quiet beaches give way to gently rolling hills and dense forests with ponds, streams and bogs, myriad wildflowers and lichens. Among the park's 350 plant species are several rare bog orchids, including dragon's tongue and spotted coralroot. Nature trails lead into marshes and forests inhabited by moose, black bears and red foxes.

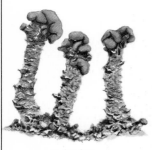

Red jacket

CLARENVILLE

A passenger train which runs from Clarenville to Bonavista in summer is a popular tourist attraction. The old narrow-gauge track is only a metre wide. Like other towns on the western shore of Trinity Bay, Clarenville began as a wood-cutters' camp in the mid-1800s, supplying lumber to fishing settlements on the barren eastern shore.
□ A plaque in nearby Milton commemorates William Epps Cormack, who in 1822 completed a 58-day trek across the unmapped Newfoundland interior to study flora, fauna and geology. Cormack later founded a Beothuk institute and shared his home with Shanawdithit, the last known member of her tribe, before her death in 1829.

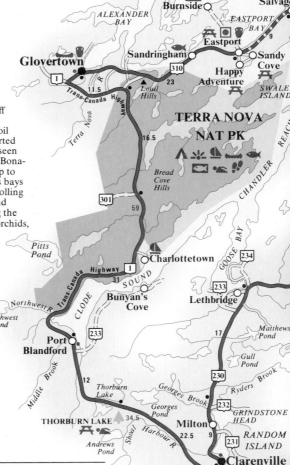

neighboring villages, Salvage provides coastal scenes of dramatic beauty. Locally smoked salmon and capelin are to be had, and in the nearby village of Happy Adventure fresh lobsters can be purchased until late July. Also close by is one of Newfoundland's finest beaches, at Sandy Cove. The farming community of Eastport is another popular stopover.

Clarenville is the starting point for an excursion to Cape Bonavista, possibly the site of John Cabot's landfall in 1497. Along the way is Trinity, where Newfoundland's first Court of Admiralty convened in 1615. Like many early Newfoundland settlements, Trinity was harassed by pirates and seized by the French in the early 1700s. The remains of fortifications and guns dating from 1706 can still be seen. In the graveyard of St. Paul's Church (1734), the oldest tombstone is dated 1744. Farther north lies the busy commercial fishing port of Bonavista, settled in the 1600s. A few kilometres north of the town is a lighthouse whose beacon has guided fishermen around Cape Bonavista for more than a century.

Salvage

SALVAGE
This village at the tip of the Eastport Peninsula is the oldest continuously inhabited settlement in Newfoundland. It was isolated for almost 300 years: until a road was built after the Second World War, its only contact with the outside world was by boat.
□ In a restored century-old frame dwelling, the Salvage Fisherman's Museum displays local artifacts. The floor of a kitchen in the museum is covered with canvas sails—in accordance with an old Newfoundland custom.

BONAVISTA
One of Newfoundland's oldest settlements, Bonavista has a population of 4,200 and has been called the largest all-fishing town in the province. Its important cod industry has a drying plant and cold-storage facilities. Deep-sea fishermen take tuna and swordfish in Bonavista Bay.
□ A stone statue of John Cabot is at Cape Bonavista, which may have been the explorer's landfall in 1497. The lighthouse here began operating in 1842; it is open to the public in summer.
□ At Spillers Cove, near Cape Bonavista, water erosion has formed a double grotto called The Dungeon.

Squid

PORT UNION
Sir William Coaker founded this town as headquarters of his Fishermen's Protective Union in 1914. A bust of the labor leader, who died in 1938, is at the head of his tomb, on a platform with marble railing. Sir William's union organized a political party, and trading, light-and-power, publishing, shipping, shipbuilding and cold-storage companies. But Coaker never realized his dream of political and economic control of Newfoundland.

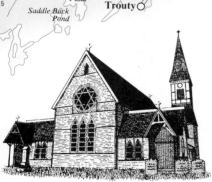

St. Paul's Church, Trinity

TRINITY
Newfoundland's first Court of Admiralty was held at Trinity in June 1615. A plaque honors John Clinch, a medical missionary who administered the first smallpox vaccination in North America here in 1800. Another plaque is near the ruins of a three-story Georgian-style brick house built in 1821 by John Bingley Garland, the first speaker in Newfoundland's House of Assembly.
□ Ship models dating from the 1830s, used for reference and measurement in the building of trawlers and sealers, are displayed at the Trinity Museum along with British bluebacks (19th-century Admiralty charts).

Codfish: Big Business Since the 16th Century

Cod fishing takes place in a narrow belt along the eastern shore of Newfoundland and, to a lesser extent, on the Grand Banks, the rich fishing grounds southeast of the island. The harvest peaks in July and August, when cod swarm to bays and inlets to feed on capelin. (Squid, used as cod bait, appear in Newfoundland waters between mid-July and late October.)

The cod fishery has been a big business since the 16th century when fleets from France, England, Portugal and Spain flocked to Newfoundland's waters. French ships worked the Grand Banks in spring; leather-clad fishermen stood in barrels behind wind barriers, and caught one fish at a time. French catches were dressed on deck and stored in the hold between thick layers of salt. English fishermen, lacking much salt, dried cod on shore, using open-air flakes—wooden racks like those still found in Newfoundland outports.

Where Dories and Long-Liners Brave a Wave-Battered Shore

Avalon Peninsula

A narrow arm of lichen-crusted rock and stunted spruce and fir links the Avalon Peninsula with the rest of Newfoundland. Dense fogs are frequent here, and the weather is often "mausey" (a Newfoundland word describing misty rain); but when the sun shines there are fine views of both Placentia and Trinity bays.

Scorning the life of the "angishore" (mainlander), fishermen along the Avalon's west coast brave the rough coastal waters in dories, skiffs and five-man long-liners,

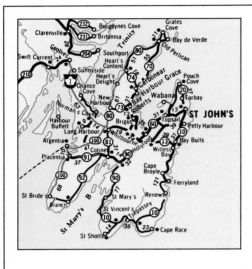

Cod Tongues, Jiggs Dinner and Figged Duff

Many ingredients in Newfoundland cooking—hardtack biscuits, dried peas, salt beef and fish—were staple foods of the English and Irish seamen who fished here four centuries ago.

When Newfoundlanders speak of fish, they mean only one kind: cod. Boiled and baked, in soups and pies, cod appears in hundreds of island recipes. "Fish and brewis" consists of boiled salt cod and hardtack softened in water, garnished with "scrunchions" of crisped salt pork. Cod tongues are a delicacy: sliced and fried, they taste like scallops. Though the ocean's yield is abundant, other food must be imported, either canned, salted, dried or smoked. "Jiggs dinner" is a stew of salt beef, salt pork, potatoes, carrots, turnips and cabbage. Side dishes include pease pudding (mashed split peas) and figged duff (raisin and molasses pudding).

COME BY CHANCE
In recent years a huge oil refinery has brought supertankers to this quiet village at the head of Placentia Bay. On clear days, a lookout in the neighboring fishing settlement of Sunnyside provides a view of Trinity Bay to the east and Placentia Bay to the west—two of Newfoundland's most productive inshore fishing grounds.
□ South of Come By Chance, at Jacks Pond Provincial Park, a stream meanders between grassy banks, then tumbles over a small falls into Jacks Pond. Activities in the park include canoeing and fishing for brook trout.

Atlantic pilot whale

PLACENTIA
In Castle Hill National Historic Park are the ruins of fortifications from which the French directed forays against the first British settlements in Newfoundland. The French built Fort Royal here in 1692 and attacked the British in St. John's and elsewhere until the 1713 Treaty of Utrecht ceded the fortress to England. In the inner fort are the remains of guardrooms, barracks, a powder magazine and the foundations of a British blockhouse. An interpretation center documents the history of Placentia.
□ A car ferry connects nearby Argentia with North Sydney, N.S., during the summer.
□ A plaque at Argentia commemorates the Atlantic Charter, signed by Churchill and Roosevelt aboard a British warship anchored offshore in August 1941.

Gannet colony, Cape St. Mary's Sea Bird Sanctuary

CAPE ST. MARY'S
A sanctuary here shelters a vast seabird colony. Thousands of gannets crowd cliffs on Bird Island, a 150-metre-high sea stack. The streamlined, snow-white birds have wingspans up to two metres. Common and thick-billed murres and black-legged kittiwakes also nest here in densely populated colonies.

hand-jigging for cod or hauling gill and trap nets from many fathoms down. Heavy trawlers with crews of 10 to 15 scour the stormy Grand Banks. The coast is almost a continuous chain of fishing villages—many settled by people of Irish descent. These Newfoundlanders have the lilting accents of Galway and County Clare. They are great talkers and the yarns they spin are laced with the supernatural.

Placentia, the old French capital of Newfoundland, is in a superb setting flanked by two fjords that reach inland for 10 kilometres. Behind it, atop steep hills, brood the ruins of old forts that once made Placentia a formidable stronghold.

Off the tip of Cape St. Mary's looms Bird Island, a vast half-dome awash with nesting gannets, murres and kittiwakes. The birds cling to every ledge and cranny, bowing and cackling, stealing pieces of each others' nests, performing elaborate courtship rituals and—as is the way of life here—ceaselessly commuting between land and sea.

Heart's Content

Black-legged kittiwakes

BELLEVUE BEACH PROVINCIAL PARK
Blue mussels can be picked in a saltwater pond here, protected from pounding waves by a barachois, a natural sand and gravel breakwater. Other shellfish found along the shore include barnacles, periwinkles and tortoise-shell limpets. Black-legged kittiwakes and pigeon guillemots are among the seabirds spotted here.

Tortoise-shell limpet

HEART'S CONTENT
North America's first cable relay station is now a branch of the Newfoundland Museum. The cable ship *Great Eastern* landed the first successful transatlantic telegraph cable here in July 1866, linking Newfoundland with Ireland. A series of stations across Nova Scotia relayed messages from here throughout North America.
□ The Heart's Content station, closed in 1965 after 92 years' service, was reopened in 1972 as a museum. It contains early equipment used for receiving and relaying telegraph messages. The oldest section of the building is furnished as it was when erected in 1873.

CHAPEL ARM
The whaling industry once flourished here and in the neighboring villages of New Harbour and Dildo. Dorymen would "herd" large schools of Atlantic pilot whales into shallow water where they were slaughtered for their valuable oil and meat, which found a ready market in Europe. (The meat was also used as food for mink farms.) The Canadian government imposed a moratorium on pilot whaling in 1973.

Over a Great Cable, at Last: 'All Right'

The ship was the largest in the world; in her hold lay coiled the longest cable ever made, 4,447 kilometres of insulated copper. The 1866 excursion of the *Great Eastern* was the fifth attempt to lay a telegraph cable from Ireland to Newfoundland. The transatlantic cable had cost American businessman Cyrus Field 13 years of effort. Three earlier cables had broken en route; a fourth operated briefly, then failed. The fifth attempt proved successful. For two weeks the *Great Eastern* had steamed across the Atlantic, lowering cable more than three kilometres to the ocean floor. After the ship arrived at Heart's Content (depicted here by Rex Woods), a message sent to Ireland on July 26, 1866, read simply, "All right."

Memories of an 'Iron Isle' and a Thousand Tall Ships

Avalon Peninsula

Storm petrel

Cod-fishing boats at Port de Grave, near Hibbs Cove

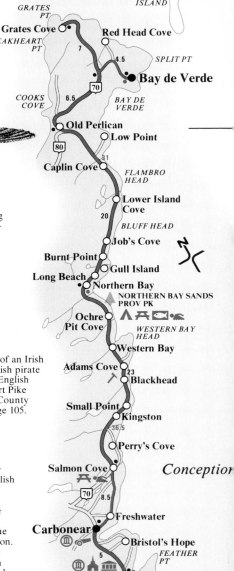

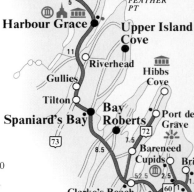

BAY DE VERDE
This large fishing community has an artificial harbor created by blasting down a hill of solid rock and dumping it into the Atlantic to form a breakwater.
□ Boats may be chartered to Baccalieu Island, a nesting site for puffins, storm petrels, gannets, gulls, black guillemots, kittiwakes, murres and razorbacks. In the early 1900s, two kegs of Spanish gold—believed to be pirate booty—were dredged up from a small cove here by local fishermen.
□ John Cabot may have inscribed his name on a rock at nearby Grates Cove in 1497. At one time, the name IO CABOTO and other words were legible; nothing now remains of the inscription.

CARBONEAR
In a private garden here is the gravestone of an Irish princess who wed (and reformed) an English pirate after being kidnapped from a ship in the English Channel. "Sheila Na Geira, wife of Gilbert Pike and daughter of John Na Geira, King of County Down," reads the stone, died in 1753 at age 105. She lived much of her life in Carbonear.

HARBOUR GRACE
This historic town overlooking Conception Bay was settled about 1550 and fortified by the English pirate Peter Easton around 1610.
□ The Conception Bay Museum, a century-old brick and stone former customhouse on the site of Easton's fort, has an exhibit chronicling the history of transatlantic flight. Outside is a plaque commemorating Harbour Grace's role in aviation. Wiley Post began a round-the-world flight here in 1931, and Amelia Earhart took off in 1932 on a solo flight to Londonderry in Northern Ireland.
□ Other plaques honor the Rev. Laurence Coughlan, who established North America's first Wesleyan mission here in 1765; and Sir Thomas Roddick, a Harbour Grace native who was deputy surgeon-general in the expeditionary force that suppressed the Northwest Rebellion in 1885, president of the British Medical Association, a Canadian MP, and dean of medicine at McGill University in Montreal.

HIBBS COVE
Artists and photographers are attracted to the west shore of Conception Bay by picturesque fishing villages and by some of the most striking coastal scenery in Newfoundland.
□ Large, square wooden houses crowd the tiny, rock-ringed harbor of Hibbs Cove, the embodiment of the Newfoundland outport. The Fishermen's Museum here displays handmade furniture, tools and artifacts used by the peninsula's early settlers. The museum's art center, in an old two-story frame house, exhibits works produced in a children's art school.

CUPIDS
John Guy led 39 English colonists here in 1610 and established Sea Forest Plantation, Newfoundland's first official settlement. They built a fort and a battery of three guns but disbanded the colony after 18 years of pirate raids and the opposition of fishermen.
□ Nearby Brigus, a great cod-fishing and sealing center in the 1800s, is the birthplace of Arctic explorer Capt. Robert Abram "Bob" Bartlett. He commanded ships in the polar expeditions of Lt. Robert Edwin Peary and Vilhjalmur Stefansson in the early 1900s.

0 1 2 3 4 5 Miles

0 2 4 6 8 Kilometres

Brooding cliffs and bright fishing ports give the road around Conception Bay its special character. At Pouch Cove, where impressive surf piles up along the shore, fishing dories are winched out of the water on skids. The stages and flakes (fish-drying racks) perched on stilts above the rocks here, once a familiar sight along Newfoundland's coast, are now rare.

Cape St. Francis is a dark headland surrounded by treacherous shoals and white-ringed islands. Topping this crest, the road makes a breathtaking plunge into the surf-battered cove at Bauline. Atop a hill overlooking the town stands a huge iron "barking" kettle still used to cure fishing nets for use in salt water.

Between Portugal Cove and St. Phillips, the bay is dominated by the frowning bulk of Bell Island—the "Iron Isle" as it was called for generations. The precipitous chunk of rock. nine kilometres long and three kilometres wide, had for half a century the largest iron mine in the world.

North and west of Holyrood, the harborless cliffs of the east bay are replaced by a continuous series of deep, fjordlike inlets. A thousand tall ships once plied these waters—and made Newfoundland one of the world's great seafaring centers in the last century. Along the coast, pastures, hayfields and vegetable gardens climb the slopes to the forest, but the houses face the sea, for fish and seals and foreign trade gave all these towns their birth.

POUCH COVE
Settlers first arrived here about 1611. The newcomers chose this site because of its dangerous harbor—permanent settlement in Newfoundland was forbidden in the 17th century, and the rocky harbor entrance discouraged ships from coming close in search of illegal settlers.
□ A rough, five-kilometre dirt road leads to a lighthouse at the tip of Cape St. Francis—for centuries the scene of disastrous shipwrecks.
□ The hardy Newfoundland dog, believed to have originated in this part of the province, is credited with rescuing hundreds of victims of offshore shipwrecks.

Newfoundland dog

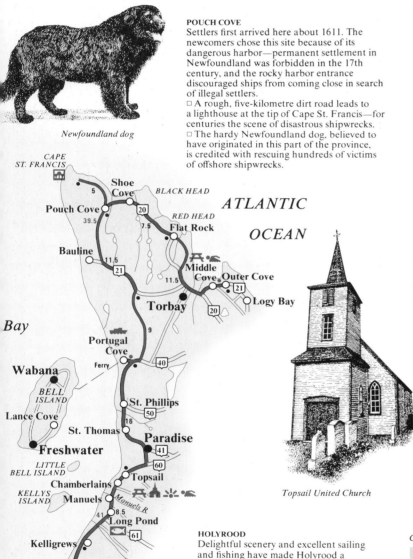

The Hellion of Harbour Grace

For three years, Peter Easton—the "Pirate Admiral"—terrorized Canada's east coast. A veteran of the English navy, he turned to piracy in 1604 and arrived in Conception Bay around 1610. From an embattled fort in Harbour Grace (*above*), with ships manned by fishermen he recruited or pressed into his service, Easton soon controlled the western North Atlantic.

Easton plundered coastal villages, looted French and Portuguese fishing boats off the Grand Banks, and raided English vessels in St. John's Harbour. In 1612 he sailed from Ferryland (south of St. John's) to attack what was then the Spanish colony of Puerto Rico. His ships returned laden with gold.

In 1613 Easton left for the Mediterranean. He bought a palace in France, became a marquis, and ended his days as one of the world's richest men.

Topsail United Church

TOPSAIL
The village offers fine views of Conception Bay and Bell, Little Bell and Kellys islands. Huge iron-ore deposits were mined at Bell Island from 1893 to 1966. Kellys Island is named after a pirate who is said to have made his headquarters there some three centuries ago.
□ At the mouth of the Manuels River are the fossil remains of countless trilobites. The prehistoric marine creatures lived on the floor of a shallow sea approximately 320 million years ago.
□ The Topsail United Church (1870)—"The Church by the Side of the Road"—has a churchyard dating from 1837.

Conception Bay between Topsail and Kelligrews

HOLYROOD
Delightful scenery and excellent sailing and fishing have made Holyrood a popular summer resort. Area streams yield Atlantic salmon and brook trout, and Conception Bay is famous for giant bluefin tuna. Close by are jigging grounds where fishermen use jiggers (grouped hooks with radiating points) to catch squid—used as bait in cod fishing.
□ Off the Trans-Canada Highway near Holyrood is Butter Pot Provincial Park. A lookout atop 305-metre Butter Pot Hill provides scenic views of Conception Bay.

A Storied Harbor, Silent Cannon and a Rock Called Signal Hill

Snug in its harbor below the majestic rock and silent guns of Signal Hill is the capital of Newfoundland, once Britain's oldest colony, now the youngest Canadian province. St. John's, with its stunning natural setting and its clutter of bright wooden houses clinging to hills behind the waterfront, suggests that all its stirring history took place the day before yesterday.

John Cabot anchored here on St. John's Day in 1497, but it was nearly a century later that the first settlers perched houses around Newfoundland's rocky bays. In 1583 Sir Humphrey Gilbert formally claimed the island for Queen Elizabeth. A Dutch squadron plundered the town in 1665 and French forces from Placentia raided and burned it three times. The British regained possession in 1762.

The old town has changed little since it was rebuilt after a disastrous fire in 1892. The modern city spreads back behind some of the oldest streets in North America. As in the days of both world wars—when St. John's was a vital North Atlantic link—ships from many nations appear in port. Waterfront shops and bars are alive with foreign tongues, mingled with the expressive and friendly accent of Newfoundlanders.

Alcock and Brown (18)
A plaque marks where Capt. J. W. Alcock and Lt. A. W. Brown took off June 14, 1919, on the first nonstop transatlantic flight. They safely landed their Vickers Vimy biplane at Clifden, Ireland, less than 16½ hours later.

Anglican Cathedral (10)
This Gothic cathedral, designed by British architect Sir Gilbert Scott in the early 19th century and rebuilt after the fire of 1892, has a small museum of religious artifacts.

Arts and Culture Center (4)
Newfoundland's main 1967 Centennial project has a 1,000-seat theater, libraries, archives, arts and handicrafts studios, an art gallery and a maritime museum.

Basilica of St. John the Baptist (8)
The twin spires of Newfoundland's largest church have dominated the city skyline for 125 years. In a small museum in the Presentation Sisters convent, adjoining the basilica, is *The Veiled Virgin*, a fine marble sculpture by Italian master Giovanni Strazzo (1818-75).

Dories, skiffs and long-liners set out each spring and summer morning from St. John's Harbour in search of fat-flanked cod.

Bowring Park (3)
Three statues grace the park: a caribou in memory of Newfoundlanders killed in the Battle of the Somme; the *Fighting Newfoundlander*; and a replica of the Peter Pan statue in Kensington Gardens.

Cape Spear (5)
This barren and beautiful promontory, 10 kilometres southeast of St. John's, is North America's most easterly point.

Commissariat House

Commissariat House (13)
Between 1821 and 1870 this three-story wooden building served as living and working quarters for the senior officer in charge of pay, food and supplies for the British garrison in St. John's.

Confederation Building (7)
This is Newfoundland government headquarters and the meeting place of the legis-

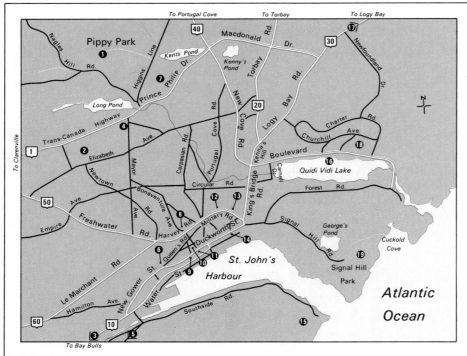

St. John's

1 Pippy Park
2 Memorial University of Newfoundland
3 Bowring Park
4 Arts and Culture Center

5 Cape Spear
6 Tourist Information
7 Confederation Building
8 Basilica of St. John the Baptist
9 CAA
10 Anglican Cathedral

11 Newfoundland Museum
12 Government House
13 Commissariat House
14 Newfoundland War Memorial
15 Fort Amherst
16 St. John's Regatta

17 Logy Bay
18 Alcock and Brown
19 Signal Hill Park

Old Garrison Church (above). Cuckold Cove (below), viewed from Quidi Vidi Battery.

Newfoundland's capital embraces a bustling harbor, an extensive business district, and a university, making it the island's cultural and commercial center. The modern city spreads back behind some of North America's oldest streets (right).

lative assembly. In the building's 11th-floor observation tower is a museum of Newfoundland naval and military history.

Fort Amherst (15)

A footpath leads to the ruins of this fort, built on the south side of the harbor entrance in 1763. A modern lighthouse replaces one that was erected in 1812. Nearby are the remains of a Second World War fortification.

Government House (12)

This Georgian-style stone mansion, built in 1830, is the official residence of the lieutenant governor.

Logy Bay (17)

The Marine Sciences Research Laboratory, operated by Memorial University, overlooks Logy Bay, five kilometres northeast of St. John's.

Memorial University of Newfoundland (2)

Founded in 1925 as a memorial to Newfoundland's First World War dead, Memorial College became a university in 1949.

Newfoundland Museum (11)

An important Beothuk Indian collection includes a caribou-skin coat worn by Shanawdithit, the last of the Newfoundland tribe that was gradually exterminated by white fishermen and settlers. (She died in St. John's in 1829.) Other exhibits deal with settlement, sailing, whaling, sealing and cod fishing, the pulp and paper industry, and Newfoundland archaeology.

Newfoundland War Memorial (14)

Here on King's Beach is where Sir Humphrey Gilbert claimed Newfoundland for England in 1583. The granite memorial, 7.6 metres high and flanked by marble steps, is topped by a statue of Freedom.

Pippy Park (1)

This expanse of woods, meadows and ponds has hiking and bicycle trails, playgrounds, a children's farm, camping and picnic areas, and an 18-hole golf course.

St. John's Regatta (16)

A rowing match highlights what may be North America's oldest annual sporting event, held in August on Quidi Vidi Lake. Six oarsmen, in fixed-seat shells 16 metres long, race over a 2.6-kilometre course. The race is believed to date from 1828.

'Fort Impregnable' Guards St. John's

The Queen's Battery, Signal Hill

The Battle of Signal Hill, the last meeting of French and English troops in North America (Sept. 15-18, 1762), is partly reenacted once each summer on Signal Hill (19). This rocky, windswept headland, once known as "Fort Impregnable," rises 152 metres from the sea at the narrow entrance to St. John's Harbour, and is now a national historic park. The Queen's Battery, commanding the entrance to the Narrows, was built after the 1762 battle. In the Narrows below the Queen's Battery is Chain Rock. As far back as the 1690s, chain and log booms were stretched across the Narrows to keep out enemy ships. Atop the hill is Cabot Tower (*left*), built to commemorate Cabot's discovery of Newfoundland in 1497. It was here, on Dec. 12, 1901, that Guglielmo Marconi received the first transatlantic wireless message, from Cornwall, England.

An Enduring Seafaring Life at Canada's Eastern Tip

Avalon Peninsula

The wrecks of thousands of ships—dashed onto rocky headlands or ripped by hidden shoals—dot the shore between St. John's and Cape Race. In many coves rotting beams and rusted iron hulls can be seen at low tide. The fogs, storms and tides that doomed these ships are a point of pride to Newfoundlanders, who boast about their erratic weather. Despite the dangers fishermen endure, few choose to exchange their way of life for city jobs, preferring the traditional isolation of the outports.

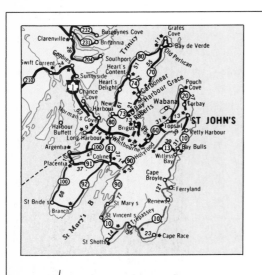

SALMONIER WILDLIFE PARK
A three-kilometre nature trail winds through forests of balsam fir and birch, along boardwalks, over bogs thick with pitcher plants, round-leaved sundews and sphagnum moss, and past marshes where orchids and wild roses bloom. Mammals typical of Newfoundland—moose, arctic hares and foxes, beavers and caribou—roam fenced enclosures. Blackpoll and myrtle warblers, owls, ospreys and bald eagles can also be seen.

Fox sparrow

TREPASSEY
The first plane to cross the Atlantic Ocean from west to east left here in 1919. Three U.S. Navy seaplanes attempted the trip. Two were forced down at sea, but the third touched down in the Azores and flew on to Portugal.
□ In 1928 aviatrix Amelia Earhart left Trepassey on her first transatlantic flight—as a passenger. The thrill of that crossing convinced her to make aviation her career.
□ Holyrood Pond near St. Vincent's provides a saltwater home for a wide variety of marine species. A beach separates the 23-kilometre-long lake from the sea, and ocean perch, sculpines, haddock and thorny skates inhabit its depths.

On the High Seas, a Floating Museum of the Atlantic

"We must keep our sea alive," reads a warning in Newfoundland's floating museum, *Norma & Gladys*. Built in 1945, the 28-metre ship (named for her first captain's two daughters) worked the Labrador fishery until 1951. In the mid-1970s, one of the last coastal schooners afloat, *Norma & Gladys* was chosen to explain Canada's use of the sea.

An exhibit in the ship's hold tells the history of the Newfoundland fishing trade, and the dangers it faces. For centuries, the Grand Banks (a vast undersea plateau southeast of the Avalon Peninsula) teemed with millions of cod. But overfishing and pollution are depleting this resource—and may one day destroy the livelihood of thousands of Newfoundlanders.

Norma & Gladys berths in St. John's, and each summer brings her message to ports throughout the Maritimes.

CAPE RACE
An arm of the ocean cuts between ancient cliffs near Cape Race. The world's richest find of Precambrian fossils—a record of animals that flourished some 500 million years ago—was made at nearby Mistaken Point in 1968. Among the fossils still imprinted in a sloping rock face is one of a metre-long shellfish.
□ Bay seals often congregate in the shallow waters off nearby Chance Cove Provincial Park.

St. Catherine's
Salmonier River
Mount Carmel
Salmonier
Mitchells Brook
Salmonier Arm 12.5
Forest Field
New Bridge
St. Joseph's

Gull Pond
Frank Pon...

Riverhead 33 58.5

AVALON WILDERNESS AREA

Crossing Place River

ST. MARY'S HAR
Point La Haye
Gaskiers
Path End
St. Mary's
HOLYROOD POND PROV PK
FALSE CAPE
13
90
Holyrood Pond
St. Vincent's
St. Stephens
Peter's River
10
Peter's River

Thorny skate

Northeast Brook
Northwest Brook
Daniel's Point 51.5
St. Shotts River 35.5
Back River
Biscay Bay
Cove Brook
Trepassey 16
Biscay Bay
Portugal
22
10
CHANCE COVE PROV PK
POWLES HEAD
BISCAY BAY
Portugal Cove
Portugal Cove South
Frenchmar Cove

TREPASSEY BAY

ATLANTIC OCEAN

19.5
Long Beach
Cape Race
CAPE RACE
MISTAKEN PT

0	2	4	6	8	10 Miles
0	4	8	12		16 Kilometres

Change comes slowly to these villages. Fishermen in such towns as Petty Harbour and Renews set out each morning in wooden dories to jig for cod with hooks and lines. Some preserve their catch as their forefathers did, spreading the salted fish on flakes (wooden racks) to dry in the sun. Many villagers still speak with an Irish brogue.

Newfoundland's east coast is rich in history. Here were pirates' lairs, great sea battles and some of the first permanent settlements in Canada. The Avalon Peninsula was named by the first Lord Baltimore, who in 1621 founded a colony at Ferryland. But colonists found farming hard—the interior mountains, forests, bogs and barrens discouraged a pastoral life.

Most who live here turn to the sea—and the sea rewards their labor. Each day fishermen brave chill waters and stiff ocean breezes, and return at sundown in boats laden with fish.

Petty Harbour

PETTY HARBOUR
Wooden houses in this fishing community cling precariously to a steep hill that rises from the sea. Skiffs, dories and longliners (fishing boats with four- or five-man crews) set out from Petty Harbour's busy wharves each morning during spring and summer. The fishermen jig for cod by hand, or haul up heavy gill nets set in deep water the day before.

BAY BULLS
One of Newfoundland's oldest settlements, Bay Bulls was repeatedly attacked by the French and the Dutch, and several times was destroyed by fire. A hint of the village's stormy history is in the four old cannon used as gateposts at the Roman Catholic church. Bronze statues of saints Patrick, Paul, Joseph and Theresa stand atop the upright cannon.
□ Enormous flocks of seabirds nest on three small islands in nearby Witless Bay. Parts of Gull Island are honeycombed with the burrows of some 1,250,000 Leach's petrels. Black-legged kittiwakes, herring gulls and some 200,000 common puffins also nest here. Green Island supports gulls, black guillemots and Atlantic murres; puffins and Leach's petrels inhabit Great Island. Charter boats circle the islands, which teem with birds during nesting season, from mid-June through early July.

AVALON WILDERNESS AREA
A herd of woodland caribou feeds on lichens that thrive in this protected region. Dwarf spruce and balsam fir grow here. The preserve attracts hikers, canoeists, wilderness campers, and anglers casting for brook trout. Visitors must obtain permits from the Department of Tourism in St. John's before entering the area.

Ferryland

Bronze statues atop cannon, Bay Bulls

FERRYLAND
In 1621, a colony was established at Ferryland by Sir George Calvert, the first Lord Baltimore. Because of repeated French attacks and the harsh climate, he quit Newfoundland in 1629 and transferred his colony to Virginia. A later settlement under Sir David Kirke also failed, and cod fishermen, formerly ousted by colonists, returned to Ferryland.
□ In the 18th century, Ferrylanders built fortifications on Bois Island at the mouth of the harbor and repulsed several attacks by French naval squadrons. Earthworks can still be seen on the island.

Sir George Calvert's coat of arms preserved in an old stone church at Ferryland

North to the Arctic
on a Road of the Future

Yukon Territory/Northwest Territories

From Dawson the Dempster Highway winds through dark forests, past lakes and sloughs and across vast expanses of spongy tundra. Canada's most northern road is named for Inspector W. J. D. Dempster of the North West Mounted Police. An outstanding dog musher, he is famous for a grueling drive of 640 kilometres from Dawson through the Ogilvie Mountains to Fort McPherson to determine the fate of a lost police patrol led by Inspector F. J. Fitzgerald. The four members of the Fitz-

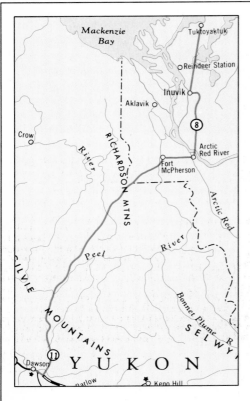

Midnight sun (time-exposure photograph)

ARCTIC CIRCLE
North of Kilometre 406 on the Dempster Highway—the Arctic Circle—the summer sun does not set but appears to circle the top of the world. During the long winter, midday is only a pastel streak on the southern horizon.
□ Across the night sky the ghostly light of the aurora borealis flickers and dances. The northern lights that have mystified man for centuries are now known to be induced in the upper atmosphere by streams of charged particles from eruptions on the sun.

Ogilvie Mountains

OGILVIE MOUNTAINS
Stream beds here are bedrock, not glacial till or gravel, and there is no evidence of glaciers. Like most of the northern Yukon, these mountains survived the ice age relatively unscathed.
□ At Kilometre 196.3, close to the Ogilvie River, is the most northerly campsite in the Yukon.

Arctic fox

ROCK CREEK
Here, where prospectors once scrabbled for gold nuggets, fishermen cast for arctic grayling. A favorite habitat of the brightly colored gamefish is the cold, clear water of the Upper Klondike River a few hundred metres north of the junction of the Dempster and Klondike highways.

RICHARDSON MOUNTAINS
Composed mainly of dull-colored rock, the Richardson Mountains include the White Mountains, whose dolomite and limestone peaks are unusually light-colored. The range's name honors Sir John Richardson, surgeon and naturalist of the Franklin expeditions (1819-22, 1825-27) that first explored the Yukon.

0 10 20 30 40 50 Miles
0 20 40 60 80 Kilometres

gerald party perished on the trail during the winter of 1910-11.

Construction of the highway to link remote northern settlements was begun in 1959. Along much of its length the route is elevated on gravel "berms" to insulate the road from its permafrost bed and prevent excess thawing. The surface is graveled and completed to about Kilometre 450, north of the Arctic Circle. It will eventually reach the Arctic Ocean via a winter road between Inuvik and Tuktoyaktuk, with ferry crossings near Fort McPherson and Arctic Red River.

Although the highway is kept open year round, services are spotty beyond the junction of the Dempster and Klondike highways east of Dawson. Motorists on the Dempster should be well outfitted for emergencies, since traffic is light and there are no telephones.

When completed, the Dempster will stretch across the Far North, linking muskeg and mountain, forest and barren, Inuit villages and frontier towns, and end at the Beaufort Sea, where offshore oil rigs are tapping vast oil reserves in the Arctic.

Pingo, Tuktoyaktuk

A Deep Freezer in a Permafrost Pingo

Volcano-shaped pingos, huge mounds of solid ice pushed out of the flat tundra by permafrost pressure, are common in the Mackenzie Delta. A thin covering of moss and turf insulates the clear, blue ice from the summer sun.

Two pingos, about 30 metres across and 12 metres high, are in the town of Tuktoyaktuk. One has been hollowed by residents to form a natural deep freezer. A food supply of caribou, geese, ducks and fish lies stiffly frozen inside a glistening ice chamber lit by electric light.

FORT McPHERSON

Prior to the establishment of a Hudson's Bay Company post here in 1848, local Indians traded at Good Hope, 320 kilometres distant. In 1852 an Indian village on the banks of the Peel River was moved here to escape flooding. Today, the community is an important trapping center for mink and muskrat.

TUKTOYAKTUK

Visitors to the Nauk Cooperative workshop see Eskimo women fashioning parkas from muskrat, seal and wolf. The skins are tanned commercially but the parkas are finished by hand. The co-op also makes rugs, cushions and mukluks.
□ *Our Lady of Lourdes*, a 15-metre schooner that served in 1931-57 as a supply ship for a Catholic mission here, has been converted into a hostel accommodating 12 people.
□ Milk-white beluga whales summer in the waters of the Beaufort Sea and are sometimes sighted in Kugmallit Bay.

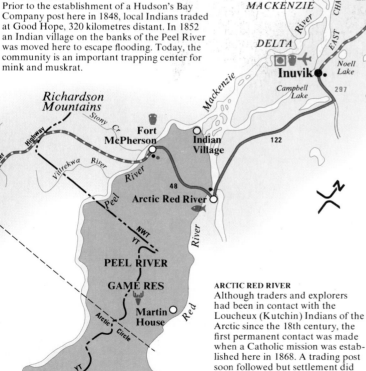

Beluga whale

INUVIK

Buildings in this bustling community 200 kilometres north of the Arctic Circle are on pilings embedded in permafrost. To prevent freezing, sewer and water pipes are housed in aboveground conduits called "utilidors."
□ Our Lady of Victory Church, shaped like an igloo, is built of wood blocks painted white.
□ Canadian and American curlers meet here in March for the International Bonspiel, and cross-country skiers compete in the Top of the World Ski Meet. Delta Daze in September features a parade, street dances and a truck raffle.

ARCTIC RED RIVER

Although traders and explorers had been in contact with the Loucheux (Kutchin) Indians of the Arctic since the 18th century, the first permanent contact was made when a Catholic mission was established here in 1868. A trading post soon followed but settlement did not take place until recently.

BEAUFORT SEA

MACKENZIE BAY

ELLICE ISLAND

RICHARDS ISLAND

KUGMALLIT BAY

TOKER PT

LANGLEY ISLAND

Tuktoyaktuk

Parsons Lake

127

Eskimo Lakes

MACKENZIE

EAST CHANNEL

(winter travel only)

DELTA

Noell Lake

Inuvik

Campbell Lake

297

Richardson Mountains

Stony Cr

Fort McPherson

Indian Village

122

Dempster Highway

Vittrekwa River

Peel River

48

Arctic Red River

NWT

YT

PEEL RIVER GAME RES

Martin House

Arctic Red River

Arctic Circle

YT

NWT

Arctic

Inuvik

A 'City of Gold'
Whose Gaudy Ghosts Live On

Yukon Territory

Battered by fate and slowed by age, Dawson wears the proud marks of its flaming youth as the Yukon's "City of Gold." The fewer than a thousand permanent residents live nostalgically among the ghosts of 25,000 who flocked to Dawson in 1897-98. Here, along creaking boardwalks, once strolled the gaudy characters of the Klondike Gold Rush—Silent Sam Bonifield, Swiftwater Bill Gates, Glass-Eyed Annie and Overflowing Flora—past rowdy dance halls, swinging-door saloons and gambling

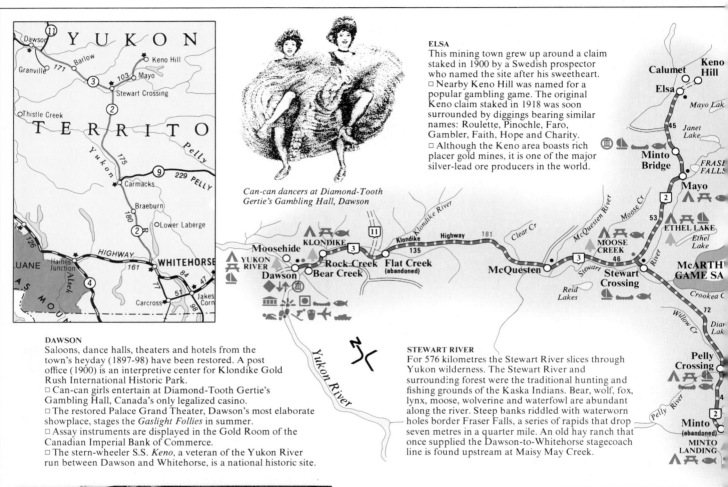

Can-can dancers at Diamond-Tooth
Gertie's Gambling Hall, Dawson

ELSA
This mining town grew up around a claim staked in 1900 by a Swedish prospector who named the site after his sweetheart.
□ Nearby Keno Hill was named for a popular gambling game. The original Keno claim staked in 1918 was soon surrounded by diggings bearing similar names: Roulette, Pinochle, Faro, Gambler, Faith, Hope and Charity.
□ Although the Keno area boasts rich placer gold mines, it is one of the major silver-lead ore producers in the world.

DAWSON
Saloons, dance halls, theaters and hotels from the town's heyday (1897-98) have been restored. A post office (1900) is an interpretive center for Klondike Gold Rush International Historic Park.
□ Can-can girls entertain at Diamond-Tooth Gertie's Gambling Hall, Canada's only legalized casino.
□ The restored Palace Grand Theater, Dawson's most elaborate showplace, stages the *Gaslight Follies* in summer.
□ Assay instruments are displayed in the Gold Room of the Canadian Imperial Bank of Commerce.
□ The stern-wheeler S.S. *Keno*, a veteran of the Yukon River run between Dawson and Whitehorse, is a national historic site.

STEWART RIVER
For 576 kilometres the Stewart River slices through Yukon wilderness. The Stewart River and surrounding forest were the traditional hunting and fishing grounds of the Kaska Indians. Bear, wolf, fox, lynx, moose, wolverine and waterfowl are abundant along the river. Steep banks riddled with waterworn holes border Fraser Falls, a series of rapids that drop seven metres in a quarter mile. An old hay ranch that once supplied the Dawson-to-Whitehorse stagecoach line is found upstream at Maisy May Creek.

Main street of Dawson

Robert Service—
Poet of the Gold Rush

Robert Service's poems immortalized the Klondike Gold Rush even though he took no part in it. "The Yukon was the source of my first real inspiration," he said, "I bubbled verse like an artesian well."
In 1904 Service, a young bank teller, arrived in Whitehorse. Three years later he published *Songs of a Sourdough*, which was an immediate success. It contained his best known poem, *The Shooting of Dan McGrew*—suggested one Saturday night by sounds of barroom revelry. *Ballads of a Cheechako* appeared two years later, after Service had moved to Dawson. Now a successful writer and financially independent, he resigned from the bank and wrote a novel, *The Trail of '98*, in a log cabin on a Dawson hillside. The cabin is a national historic site.

casinos where the motto was "never refuse a drink or kick a dog."

Gold was discovered southeast of Dawson on Bonanza Creek, a tributary of the Klondike River, in 1896. Word of the strike reached the outside world in 1897, touching off the Klondike Gold Rush—three years of hardship and greed, starvation and lavish spending. Dawson and other boom towns along the Yukon River system sprang up almost overnight. Between 1896 and 1904, the creeks yielded more than $100 million in gold. But as the more accessible gold was removed, the population dwindled. Cabins, claims, even whole towns were deserted. Huge dredges became part of the landscape they had furrowed and scarred.

Upriver, Whitehorse not only survived, but has prospered since the 1890s. The city lies at a bend in the Yukon River, north of the wild rapids that were once the most hazardous stretch of the Trail of '98. Modern Whitehorse is a capital city and busy commercial center. Where eager cheechakos (greenhorns) once boarded sternwheelers headed north, river barges now unload washing machines, television sets and other trappings of modern living.

Dawson on the Yukon River

YUKON RIVER
North of Lake Laberge, the Yukon River surges through a winding channel bordered by sand-and-gravel cliffs up to 90 metres high. At Five Finger Rapids four 15-metre-high sandstone columns divide the river into five streams. Near Carmacks is 210-metre-high Eagle's Nest Bluff and north of Minto are black basalt cliffs towering 135 metres. Abandoned cabins—many built during the Klondike Gold Rush—and beaches, sandbars and wooded islands provide excellent campsites for canoeists paddling the 960-kilometre stretch from Lake Bennett, B.C., to Dawson.

McARTHUR GAME SANCTUARY
This preserve was created to protect the Fannin (saddle-backed) sheep, once considered on the verge of extinction, but now known to be a product of interbreeding. Golden eagles, blue grouse, kingfishers and loons are also found in the sanctuary.

PELLY CROSSING
The 400-kilometre Pelly River canoe route from Ross River to Fort Selkirk crosses the Klondike Highway here. Northwest of the Faro Bridge the river meanders past 1,800-metre Rose Mountain; some 60 kilometres downstream are 2,000-metre Mount Hodder and Tay Mountain. The river races through three sets of rapids in Granite Canyon, six kilometres long and up to 75 metres deep.

Kingfisher

WHITEHORSE
Whitehorse, the Yukon's capital and largest city (pop. 14,000), came into being in 1898 as a stopping place for thousands of prospectors who traveled the trail leading to the Klondike goldfields.
□ The last stern-wheeler to operate on the Yukon River, the SS *Klondike* houses a river-transport museum.
□ In February Whitehorse celebrates a three-day Sourdough Rendezvous. Residents dressed in period costumes hold dogsled and snowshoe races, and an ice sculpture contest.
□ The MV *Schwatka* makes daily cruises through Miles Canyon, whose rapids have been tamed by a hydroelectric project.
□ At the Indian Burial Ground, many graves are covered with small houses believed by Tlingit Indians to protect the spirits of the dead.

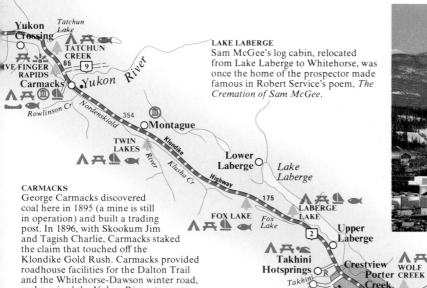

LAKE LABERGE
Sam McGee's log cabin, relocated from Lake Laberge to Whitehorse, was once the home of the prospector made famous in Robert Service's poem, *The Cremation of Sam McGee.*

CARMACKS
George Carmacks discovered coal here in 1895 (a mine is still in operation) and built a trading post. In 1896, with Skookum Jim and Tagish Charlie, Carmacks staked the claim that touched off the Klondike Gold Rush. Carmacks provided roadhouse facilities for the Dalton Trail and the Whitehorse-Dawson winter road, and serviced the Yukon River steamers.

Whitehorse

Where Canada's Highest Peak Looms Above a Lofty Mountain Range

Yukon Territory

In almost every way this corner of the Yukon is a place of superlatives. Kluane National Park preserves a vast tract of northern wilderness (almost four Prince Edward Islands) and is second in size among Canada's national parks. All but an eighth of the park is a rugged landscape of rock and ice. Canada's highest peak, Mount Logan, looms here, in the country's loftiest range, the St. Elias Mountains.

Off the main roads, hikers find stunning mountain vistas. The awesome Kaskawulsh

DESTRUCTION BAY
This tourist center was named during construction of the Alaska Highway when a sudden storm blew down the tents of an army crew camped here.
□ The Kluane Historical Society Museum has displays of Indian and pioneer life and northern flora and fauna.

KLUANE LAKE
The 60-kilometre-long lake is hemmed in by the Kluane Range of the St. Elias Mountains. Dall sheep, grizzly bears, moose and wolves inhabit the mixed spruce-aspen forests surrounding the lake. Canada geese, loons, ducks, and trumpeter and whistling swans summer here.

Arctic loon, Kluane Lake

BEAVER CREEK
For eight months road-builders had labored on the Alaska Highway. Work continued seven days a week, in temperatures which ranged from subtropical heat to well below freezing. On Oct. 20, 1942, the construction crews working south from Alaska and north from Whitehorse met at Beaver Creek. Two bulldozer operators heard the drone of each other's machine in the distance. They bulldozed through the forest separating them, and clasped hands. Formal ribbon-cutting ceremonies opening the highway took place a month later on Soldier's Summit.

HAINES JUNCTION
This community at the junction of the Alaska and Haines highways is the headquarters of Kluane National Park and a center for trail-riding, photographic and mountain-climbing expeditions.
□ Nearby Silver City (Kluane), now a ghost town, is the site of a trading post, roadhouse and North West Mounted Police barracks on the old wagon road from Whitehorse to Kluane Lake.

Dall sheep, Kluane National Park

KLUANE NATIONAL PARK
Towering above Kluane National Park and the rest of the St. Elias Mountains (eight of the peaks are over 4,500 metres) is 5,951-metre Mount Logan, Canada's highest peak. More than half of Kluane is under ice and snow. The Steele Glacier, one of more than 2,000 glaciers in the park, can move as much as 800 metres a month. A layer of white ash spewed from a volcano 1,400 years ago blankets the Klutlan Glacier, whose ice is a kilometre thick in some places. An old packhorse trail from the Slims River bridge passes sand dunes and mud flats, and ends at the foot of the Kaskawulsh Glacier. The glacier's mouth, eight kilometres across, is the widest on the Canadian mainland.

Dall sheep, caribou, mountain goats and grizzly bears inhabit Kluane—a combination of animals found in no other national park. Spruce grouse, bald eagles, rock ptarmigans and whistling swans are among 170 bird species here.
□ Only experienced hikers should venture into the park's vast interior—even in July fierce blizzards are common in the mountains. Climbers and overnight hikers must register with park officials.

St. Elias Mountains

0	10	20	30	40	50 Miles
0	20	40	60		80 Kilometres

Glacier is a five-hour hike from the Slims River bridge at Kilometre 1688 of the Alaska Highway; two rivers that begin at the glacier end hundreds of kilometres apart. Other hiking trails lead to the King's Throne, a grassy expanse adorned with wildflowers, and to Silver City, a ghost town of rotting sluice boxes and sod-and-log cabins.

Wildlife is abundant in and around the park. Along willow-edged rivers visitors may sight some of the largest moose on the continent. The giant mountain caribou is less plentiful, although one band of 125 is often sighted near Burwash Flats, outside the park but near the Alaska Highway. Forests and meadows shelter mountain goats, grizzlies, and black bears.

The landscape constantly astonishes. The grasslands of the Slims River delta could have been borrowed from the Canadian Prairies. Million Dollar Falls cascades 60 metres into the frothing Takhanne River a kilometre west of the Haines Highway.

Snow blankets the higher peaks year round.

Soldier's Summit, overlooking Kluane Lake, commemorates a man-made feature of the northern landscape. On Nov. 20, 1942, the Alaska Highway was officially opened here. Military and civilian workers had pushed a highway through 2,200 kilometres of wilderness, completing in eight months an engineering feat which would normally have taken five years. Today the highway is an artery of northern commerce and a magnet for sportsmen and campers.

Bannock, Hardtack and Jerky

The traditional fare of old-time woodsmen and prospectors is still popular with campers. Fresh bread—sourdough, bannock and hardtack—can be baked easily over an open fire; jerky and pemmican are practical ways to preserve meat.

Sourdough, a spongy mixture of flour, water and yeast, is used as a "starter" to ferment dough for bread or flapjacks. Klondike prospectors became known as "sourdoughs" for this staple food. On winter nights they kept their starter next to their bodies so that it wouldn't freeze.

Bannock, made from flour, water, baking powder and lard, is baked to a golden brown in a greased skillet. Hardtack is simplest of all: a flat cake of flour and water baked until dry and hard.

Jerky is lean meat—moose, deer or caribou—cut into strips and dried in the sun. For pemmican, an Indian specialty, jerky is shredded and mixed with hot animal fat. Jerky and pemmican will keep for months without refrigeration.

Teslin Lake

TESLIN
Rolling, forested hills and the peaks of the Big Salmon Range form a backdrop to the clear, deep waters of Teslin Lake. The Nisutlin Bridge, longest water span of the Alaska Highway (575 metres), crosses an arm of the lake here.

CHAMPAGNE
Now almost deserted, Champagne was a North West Mounted Police post on the Dalton Trail. The town was named by its founder, Jack Dalton, who transported a case of French champagne over the rugged trail and drank it here with friends.

WATSON LAKE
Here are some 1,300 signs with the names of faraway places. The first were erected by homesick soldiers building the road in 1942; tourists have kept up the tradition.

CARCROSS
George Carmack, Skookum Jim and Tagish Charlie set out from here on the prospecting trip that touched off the Klondike Gold Rush. In the Carcross cemetery are the graves of Carmack's wife, Kate, Tagish Charlie (whose headstone is marked "Dawson Charlie") and Skookum Jim ("James Mason"). All were Tagish Indians, all became wealthy, all lived out their days in Carcross.
□ Grouped near the Carcross railway depot are a White Pass and Yukon stagecoach; *Duchess*, a wood-burning locomotive which once hauled supplies on a three-kilometre rail line; and the old stern-wheeler *Tutshi*, beached since 1955.

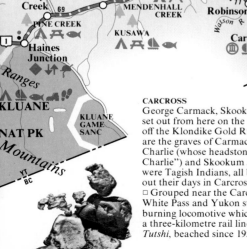
Gold nuggets from the Yukon

Signposts, Watson Lake

A 'Golden Triangle' Gilded by Wheat and Water Power

Northeastern British Columbia

Northeastern British Columbia is a rough triangle bordered by the Yukon and Northwest Territories, Alberta, and the high spine of the Rocky Mountains.

The "Golden Triangle"—an area larger than Great Britain—is unique in western Canada. Although much of the landscape is rolling and often mountainous, several thousand square kilometres are an exten-

LOWER POST
A Roman Catholic mission and an Indian residential school are located in this former Hudson's Bay Company trading post.
□ In 1898 a North West Mounted Police party labored northward through Lower Post, blazing an overland route from Edmonton to Dawson City and the Klondike goldfields. More than a year later the trip was completed, but the scheme proved impractical and the "Yukon Trail" was abandoned.

LIARD RIVER
With the Peace and Athabasca rivers, the Liard was a major trade route of the North West Company. The river drains the eastern slopes of the Rockies and flows across British Columbia's northern plain to empty into the Mackenzie River.
□ Liard River Hot Springs are fed by water flowing at the rate of 2,900 litres per minute. (The 49°C water is reputed to be therapeutic for arthritis and rheumatism.) A surprising feature of the immediate vicinity is the variety of luxurious southern plants including lobelia, red monkey flower, ostrich fern, cow parsnip and dogbane.

Heroic Labor on an Epic Road

More than 1,900 kilometres of the 2,436-kilometre Alaska Highway are in Canada. The highway between Dawson Creek and Fairbanks was built by 16,000 U.S. Army and American and Canadian civilian personnel as a supply road to bases in Alaska during World War II.

Work continued seven days a week, day and night, in conditions that ranged from sub-zero cold to stifling heat. No time was wasted on niceties of engineering. The road was looped over hills to save blasting and rammed through the forest with bulldozers. Overhead, aerial reconnaissance planes photographed the next section to be attacked. The highway was completed in November, 1942, only eight months after construction began.

Alaska Highway near Muncho Lake

Red monkey flower

MUNCHO LAKE PROVINCIAL PARK
Thick forests of white spruce and lodgepole pine carpet most of the park's deep valleys. Scrub alpine spruce clings to the slopes near the timberline.
□ Stone sheep, caribou, mountain goat and moose frequent a small area where calcium and magnesium are exposed in loamy soil. (By licking at the minerals, the animals have hollowed out holes in cliffs and pillars.) Photographers can often approach within close range of feeding animals here.
□ A 12-kilometre trail follows Nonda Creek, near the park's eastern boundary, past dwarf alpine plants, mosses, lichens and showy wildflowers.

sion of the Prairies. Grain elevators and the great sweep of farmland near Fort St. John confirm this impression.

Dreams of furs, gold, wheat and oil have ebbed and flowed in this corner of British Columbia since Alexander Mackenzie's search for an overland route to the Pacific. Crossing the region in 1793, the explorer marveled at the abundant resources, which were to remain untapped for 150 years. Simon Fraser followed in Mackenzie's wake in the 1800s, establishing trading posts for the North West Company along the rivers.

Despite the toehold of the fur trade, and later the Klondike Gold Rush, the Golden Triangle remained a sparsely populated expanse of forest, prairie and muskeg until the Alaska Highway was built in 1942. With this link to the south, the region boomed. Grain farms flourished along the Peace River. The first oil well in British Columbia was wildcatted near Fort St. John. At Hudson's Hope, tons of earth were blasted and bulldozed into Canada's largest dam.

Dogsled Races, Fort Nelson

FORT NELSON

A North West Company post built here around 1800 was destroyed and some of the inhabitants were massacred by Indians in 1813. In 1865 the Hudson's Bay Company founded a second post which is still in operation.

□ Once the town center, Old Fort Nelson is now an Indian settlement. Willow, birch and fireweed have swallowed up many of the settlement's abandoned boats and buildings.

□ A Trapper's Rendezvous in March celebrates winter with snowshoe, dog sled and snowmobile races. Rodeo sports highlight a fair in August.

Mission, Fort St. John

FORT ST. JOHN

Explorer Alexander Mackenzie traveled up the Peace River here on his epic journey to the Pacific in 1793. Rocky Mountain Fort, the original post, was built about 1797 and later renamed Fort St. John. The town claims to be the oldest non-Indian settlement in British Columbia.

□ The foundations of a fort that Indians burned in 1823 after massacring three Hudson's Bay Company traders can be seen about 30 kilometres south.

□ Also south of the town, at Kilometre 73 of the Alaska Highway, are the log buildings of a later HBC post, a now-disused Roman Catholic chapel (1890) and a North West Mounted Police barracks and jail.

TAYLOR

The community is set in a scenic, thickly wooded valley. Local refineries "scrub" (refine) billions of cubic feet of natural gas and millions of gallons of gasoline each year.

□ The Peace Island Park Museum displays pioneer furnishings and tools, an Indian dugout and a birchbark canoe.

□ Annual celebrations include snowmobile races (on grass) in May, and a world championship gold-panning competition in September.

Stone sheep, Stone Mountain Provincial Park

STONE MOUNTAIN PROVINCIAL PARK

Eroded pillars of sand and gravel—some are 18 metres high—stand near 1,265-metre-high Summit Pass, the highest point on the Alaska Highway.

□ Glacial sediment in Summit Lake gives the water an iridescent green hue, a striking contrast with the birch and willow trees along the shore.

□ A six-kilometre trail leads from the Alaska Highway along the North Tetsa River to Flower Spring Lake. Stone sheep and migrating caribou are sometimes sighted grazing in the meadows near the lake.

W.A.C. Bennett Dam

Peace River Powerhouse

British Columbia's biggest lake (428 kilometres long) is man-made Williston Lake on the Peace River. It was formed in 1968 with the construction of the W.A.C. Bennett Dam, one of the world's largest earth-fill structures. From a lookout visitors see a panorama of the dam, lake and surrounding mountains. The powerhouse, 150 metres underground, may be toured.

The first white man to portage around the treacherous rapids of the Peace River canyon was explorer Alexander Mackenzie in 1793. The rapids, tamed by the Bennett Dam, will disappear when a second dam is completed 22 kilometres downstream.

HUDSON'S HOPE

Explorer Simon Fraser founded a trading post on the Peace River here in 1805. The foundations of the original settlement, named Rocky Mountain Portage, are in a meadow near the ferry landing.

□ Until the decline of the fur trade, the community was a strategic trading post and head of navigation for steamboats plying the Peace River. With the completion of the W.A.C. Bennett Dam, Hudson's Hope became a boom town once again.

A Joseph's Coat of Crops
on Canada's Northernmost Farmland

Peace River Valley

Rolling foothills, a patchwork of forest and plains and some of the world's richest farmland are found in the Peace River country. Crystal lakes are hidden in groves of aspen, meandering streams nestle in pastoral valleys, and badlands are filled with the strange shapes of erosion.

The landscape is a Joseph's coat of colorful crops—the brown of oats and barley, the green and gold of wheat, the blue of flax, the yellow of rapeseed, the earthy tones of blocks of summer fallow. In late

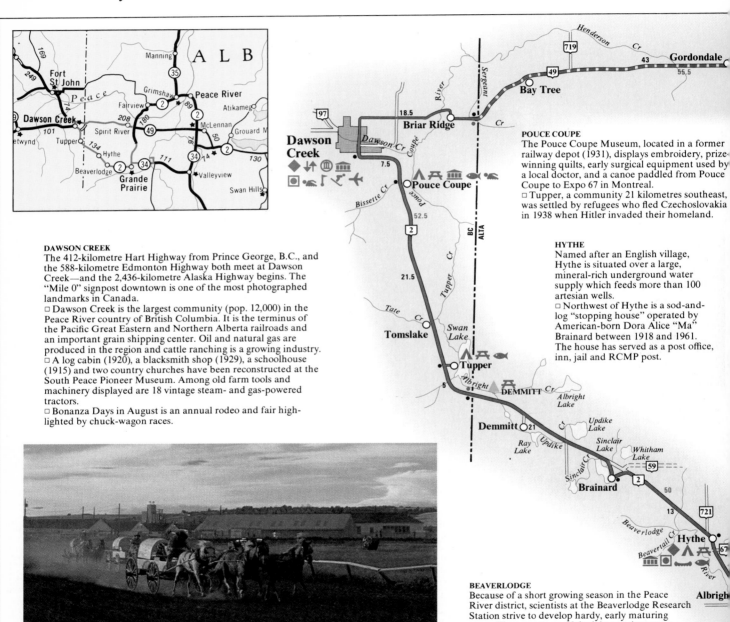

DAWSON CREEK
The 412-kilometre Hart Highway from Prince George, B.C., and the 588-kilometre Edmonton Highway both meet at Dawson Creek—and the 2,436-kilometre Alaska Highway begins. The "Mile 0" signpost downtown is one of the most photographed landmarks in Canada.
□ Dawson Creek is the largest community (pop. 12,000) in the Peace River country of British Columbia. It is the terminus of the Pacific Great Eastern and Northern Alberta railroads and an important grain shipping center. Oil and natural gas are produced in the region and cattle ranching is a growing industry.
□ A log cabin (1920), a blacksmith shop (1929), a schoolhouse (1915) and two country churches have been reconstructed at the South Peace Pioneer Museum. Among old farm tools and machinery displayed are 18 vintage steam- and gas-powered tractors.
□ Bonanza Days in August is an annual rodeo and fair highlighted by chuck-wagon races.

Chuck-wagon races, Dawson Creek, B.C.

POUCE COUPE
The Pouce Coupe Museum, located in a former railway depot (1931), displays embroidery, prize-winning quilts, early surgical equipment used by a local doctor, and a canoe paddled from Pouce Coupe to Expo 67 in Montreal.
□ Tupper, a community 21 kilometres southeast, was settled by refugees who fled Czechoslovakia in 1938 when Hitler invaded their homeland.

HYTHE
Named after an English village, Hythe is situated over a large, mineral-rich underground water supply which feeds more than 100 artesian wells.
□ Northwest of Hythe is a sod-and-log "stopping house" operated by American-born Dora Alice "Ma" Brainard between 1918 and 1961. The house has served as a post office, inn, jail and RCMP post.

BEAVERLODGE
Because of a short growing season in the Peace River district, scientists at the Beaverlodge Research Station strive to develop hardy, early maturing crops. There are tours of the laboratories, greenhouses and experimental fields.
□ Working exhibits at the South Peace Centennial Museum (some of which were used to build the museum) include early gas and steam tractors, plows, a threshing machine and a reconstructed sawmill.
□ A rough, 128-kilometre road into British Columbia leads to the South Pine River and Kinuseo Falls, 90 metres wide and 60 metres high.

summer, columns of harvesters mobilize against the rippling, ripened grain.

Salty inland seas covered this area several times. Farms that checkerboard the countryside are on the bed of prehistoric Lake Agassiz. In the Kleskun Hills, erosion has scoured the glacial till, exposing dinosaur tracks and aquatic fossils.

The human history of the Peace River district is a recent one. Except for a few Indians, trappers and prospectors, the region remained an unpeopled wilderness until the end of the last century.

Since then, homesteaders have carved the most northerly farming belt in Canada. Bush receded to be replaced by sweeping fields of grain and rapeseed. Trails became roads, and roads became highways.

Despite this new prosperity—and the prospect of extensive oil and gas activity, mining and forestry—much of "the Peace" retains a genuine pioneer spirit, original and unspoiled.

Short-eared owl

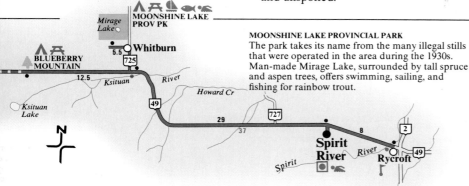

MOONSHINE LAKE PROVINCIAL PARK
The park takes its name from the many illegal stills that were operated in the area during the 1930s. Man-made Mirage Lake, surrounded by tall spruce and aspen trees, offers swimming, sailing, and fishing for rainbow trout.

RYCROFT
Often seen perched on fence posts and tree stumps in Rycroft and throughout the region, the short-eared owl is a crow-sized bird of prey. Unlike most owls, it is active in daylight and inhabits open spaces rather than woodlands. With buoyant wingbeats, the short-eared owl flies over meadow and marsh, pausing to pounce on unwary mice. Like most owls, it is an efficient and valuable destroyer of rodent pests.

Lubricant for Ships From a Little-Known Seed

Ripening rapeseed

One of the most remarkable success stories of the Peace River country is that of the ubiquitous but little-known rapeseed. Introduced during the Second World War to supply lubricating oil for ships, rapeseed also proved useful in products as varied as cooking oil, shortening, margarine, soap, varnish, and printing ink.

A short growing season offset by rich soil and long midsummer days resulted in yields as high as 366 kilograms of seed per hectare, with oil contents of 40 percent. When a major market for rapeseed oil was discovered in Japan in the 1960s, production doubled, then tripled to present levels, assuring that seas of banana-colored rapeseed will continue to wave in the Peace River district.

GRANDE PRAIRIE
Surrounded by rich agricultural land, Grande Prairie is the business and transportation center of Alberta's Peace River country.
□ The Grande Prairie Pioneer Museum's collection of pioneer artifacts includes an antique barber's chair. Among the mounted birds and animals on display are a trumpeter swan and an albino moose.
□ The modern design and earth-colored walls of the Grande Prairie Regional College reflect the rhythm and contours of the surrounding prairie. Five buildings flow into each other without formal passageways, and curving brick walls enclose a central "academic street."
□ Frontier Days and an agricultural fair are held in August. Nearby Bezanson and Teepee Creek have annual rodeos.

SASKATOON ISLAND PROVINCIAL PARK
The park is one of the few nesting areas of the rare trumpeter swan, the largest waterfowl native to North America. The trumpeter has been saved from extinction that threatened in the 1930s, and there are now an estimated 4,500 birds on the continent.
□ About one-third of the park is carpeted with saskatoons, a wild shrub whose sweet, blueberrylike fruit is used in sauces, preserves and pies.

Trumpeter swan

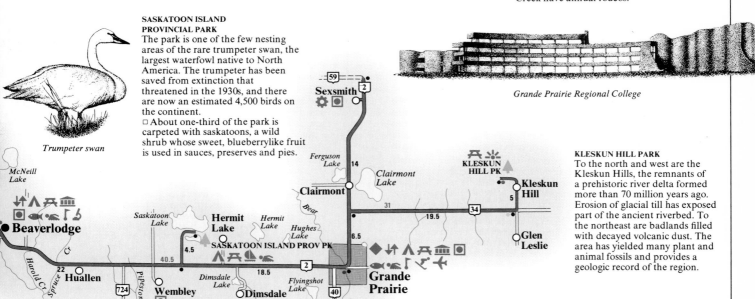

Grande Prairie Regional College

KLESKUN HILL PARK
To the north and west are the Kleskun Hills, the remnants of a prehistoric river delta formed more than 70 million years ago. Erosion of glacial till has exposed part of the ancient riverbed. To the northeast are badlands filled with decayed volcanic dust. The area has yielded many plant and animal fossils and provides a geologic record of the region.

An Ancient River Valley
Where 'Twelve-Foot' Davis Settled

Peace River Valley

The Peace River, together with its connecting rivers and lakes, forms one of the largest river systems in the world. Rising in the Rocky Mountains of British Columbia, the Peace flows east through the plains of northern Alberta, winding more than 1,600 kilometres to its junction with the Athabasca River. Together they form the Slave River, ultimately joining the Mackenzie and flowing north to the Beaufort Sea.

The broad Peace River cuts the Alberta prairie to a depth of 300 metres in places

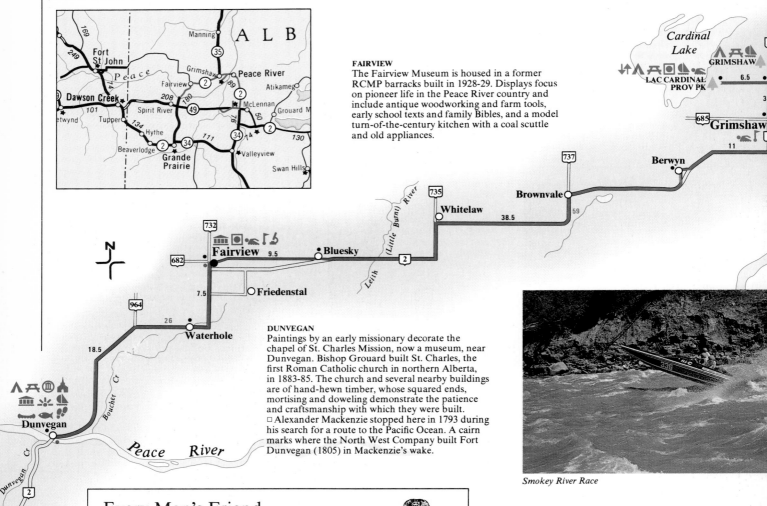

FAIRVIEW
The Fairview Museum is housed in a former RCMP barracks built in 1928-29. Displays focus on pioneer life in the Peace River country and include antique woodworking and farm tools, early school texts and family Bibles, and a model turn-of-the-century kitchen with a coal scuttle and old appliances.

DUNVEGAN
Paintings by an early missionary decorate the chapel of St. Charles Mission, now a museum, near Dunvegan. Bishop Grouard built St. Charles, the first Roman Catholic church in northern Alberta, in 1883-85. The church and several nearby buildings are of hand-hewn timber, whose squared ends, mortising and doweling demonstrate the patience and craftsmanship with which they were built.
□ Alexander Mackenzie stopped here in 1793 during his search for a route to the Pacific Ocean. A cairn marks where the North West Company built Fort Dunvegan (1805) in Mackenzie's wake.

Smokey River Race

Every Man's Friend
Who Never Locked His Door

The tombstone of Henry Fuller "Twelve-Foot" Davis, on a hill overlooking the junction of the Peace and Smokey rivers, records that "he was every man's friend and never locked his cabin door." A statue in Peace River represents Davis as a towering giant. He was really a little man, an American who joined the Cariboo Gold Rush in 1858.

Davis discovered two claims that exceeded regulation width, claimed the 12-foot space between them for his own and mined over $15,000 in gold. Later, in the Peace River country, he was a trader and explorer whose kindness was legendary. As he lay near death in 1900, he was asked whether he was afraid. Said Davis: "I never kilt nobody, I never stole from nobody, and I kept my house open for travelers all my life. No, I ain't afraid to die."

SMOKEY RIVER
Competitors in boats ranging from rubber rafts to 1,100-horsepower twin-engine jet boats brave rapids, rocks and gravel bars during the Smokey River Race between Grande Cache and Peace River. Teams from as far away as New Zealand compete in the five-day, 608-kilometre event each July.
□ The 80-kilometre Smokey River canoe route from Watino to Peace River meanders past 180-metre-high sandstone cliffs and striking hoodoo formations. Spruce, birch and poplar cover the high banks. Tracks of bears, coyotes and deer are seen on the numerous sandbars, and waterfowl are abundant.

0 1 2 3 4 5 Miles

0 2 4 6 8 Kilometres

and forms a valley 3 to 11 kilometres wide. It is an ancient river—one of the few to survive the ravages of the last ice age. Dinosaur tracks millions of years old have been unearthed along the river's course.

In 1793, Alexander Mackenzie wintered in the Peace River valley on his journey to the Pacific. In Mackenzie's wake came fur traders, trappers, prospectors, missionaries and homesteaders. Abundant wildlife and rich, black earth have attracted pioneers as diverse as 19th-century trapper-trader-prospector "Twelve-Foot" Davis and a 1974 wagon train of would-be homesteaders from Toronto.

Most settlers found the country an uncompromising, rough-hewn wilderness, but a few of these persevered and prospered here. Despite a short growing season, the 230,000-square-kilometre region on both sides of the Peace has become famous for its fine barley, wheat, oilseed, and oversize fruits and vegetables.

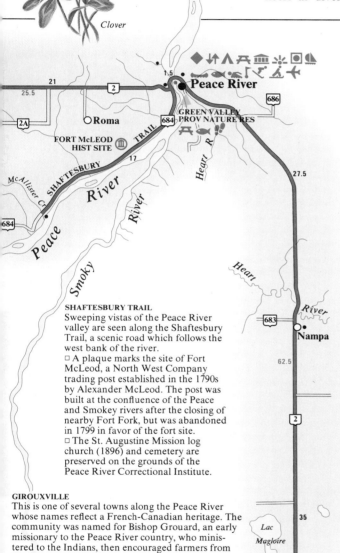

Clover

PEACE RIVER

In the Peace River Centennial Museum is a model of Fort Fork, the trading post where Alexander Mackenzie wintered in 1792-93 on his journey to the Pacific Ocean. The fort's fireplace has been reconstructed with stones from the original. Also displayed is a rare Hudson's Bay Company fur press, used to compact raw furs into bales for shipment.
□ A natural gas fire burns day and night on the Peace River downstream from the town. When an old well was capped in the 1950s, gas was forced up through the riverbed 11 kilometres away, where it ignited and has burned ever since.
□ A 12-passenger boat plies the Peace River on two-day, 60-kilometre sightseeing cruises.
□ The Green Valley Provincial Nature Preserve offers self-guiding nature trails and fishing for northern pike, walleye and goldeye.

The junction of the Peace and Smoky rivers

SHAFTESBURY TRAIL

Sweeping vistas of the Peace River valley are seen along the Shaftesbury Trail, a scenic road which follows the west bank of the river.
□ A plaque marks the site of Fort McLeod, a North West Company trading post established in the 1790s by Alexander McLeod. The post was built at the confluence of the Peace and Smokey rivers after the closing of nearby Fort Fork, but was abandoned in 1799 in favor of the fort site.
□ The St. Augustine Mission log church (1896) and cemetery are preserved on the grounds of the Peace River Correctional Institute.

GIROUXVILLE

This is one of several towns along the Peace River whose names reflect a French-Canadian heritage. The community was named for Bishop Grouard, an early missionary to the Peace River country, who ministered to the Indians, then encouraged farmers from Quebec to settle in northern Alberta.
□ The Girouxville Museum, operated by the Oblate Fathers, displays more than 2,000 artifacts, including fossils, wood carvings, two millstones from an 1895 flour mill, and personal effects of Bishop Grouard. A replica of a trapper's log cabin contains pioneer furniture, clothing and tools.

FALHER

This town claims to be the "Honey Capital of Canada." Some 35,000 beehives in the region produce more than two million kilograms of honey per year. Along the highway are vast fields of fragrant clover.
□ St. Jean Baptiste Mission (1914) is a hand-hewn log building covered with cedar shingles. Two stories high, it combines both church and priest's residence.

Honey bee, Falher

Through Forest and Flying Gravel to the World's Largest Park

Alberta/Northwest Territories

Louise Falls, Hay River

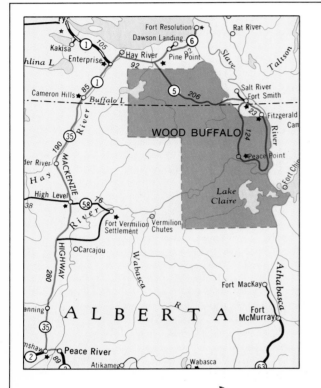

HAY RIVER

With a population of 4,000, Hay River is one of the largest communities in the Northwest Territories. The town is also the center of the Great Slave Lake fishing industry. Annual catches of whitefish and trout in this fifth largest North American lake exceed 270 tonnes.
□ Near Hay River, the Mackenzie Highway passes scenic Alexandra Falls, a 90-metre-wide cataract that plummets 30 metres. Three kilometres away a trail leads to 14-metre-high Louise Falls and, below it, a steep-walled gorge and five kilometres of rapids. To the northwest is 75-metre-wide Lady Evelyn Falls.

HIGH LEVEL

Once little more than a rural bus stop, High Level is now an oil-boom town. The community is the jumping-off point for oil fields at Rainbow and Zama. Over 50 oil rigs are serviced by the town.
□ The Great Slave Lake Railway was completed to High Level in 1963. The GSLR, called the "Eskimo Line" because it employs many of the skilled Inuit trained during construction of the DEW line, was the first railway into the Northwest Territories.
□ Nearby Fort Vermillion, once accessible only by boat or plane, is now linked to High Level by road. The former fur-trade post is surrounded by one of the oldest farming areas in Alberta.

NORTH STAR

The Charles Plavin Homestead (1918), one of the oldest remaining farms in northern Alberta, is being restored as a historical site by the provincial government. The hand-hewn log buildings, sauna and barns reflect the craftsmanship and ingenuity of the early Latvian settler. On display are handmade tools and farm implements.

GRIMSHAW

This is Kilometre Zero of the Mackenzie Highway, a system of northern roads through dense forests, across spongy muskeg, past duck-filled sloughs and lakes, over and alongside swift rivers. It has opened vast tracts of northern wilderness and, when completed, will stretch more than 2,000 kilometres to Tuktoyaktuk on the Beaufort Sea. Road conditions are generally good during the summer, although dust and flying gravel are a constant annoyance. Campsites, food, fuel and supplies are available along the route.

A Northern Sanctuary for a Rare Bird

The magnificent whooping crane, North America's rarest bird, probably has never existed in great numbers. About a century ago there were an estimated 1,500 birds but by 1941, because of man's encroachment, only 15 remained. Now, with protecting legislation, and a Canadian-American breeding program, approximately 100 whooping cranes survive.

Standing erect, the whooping crane is about 150 centimetres tall. Its black beak, wing tips and legs contrast with its glistening white plumage and brilliant red crown. It has a loud, clear buglelike call.

Whooping cranes are thought to mate for life. The eggs are laid after the spring migration to Wood Buffalo National Park from the birds' winter range in the Aransas National Wildlife Refuge on the Texas coast.

0 10 20 30 40 50 Miles
0 20 40 60 80 Kilometres

From Grimshaw, Alta., the Mackenzie Highway reaches north across 940 kilometres of prairie and forest to Fort Simpson, N.W.T. North of Grimshaw the hills and ridges level off to flat alluvial forest land—a dense bush of spruce, poplar, jack pine and tamarack. Occasionally the long stretches of forest, gravel and dust are interrupted by roadside towns. Farming, forestry, mining (and now tourism) are the mainstays of the communities; many residents are descendants of the original British, Mennonite, Ukrainian and Métis settlers of a century ago.

At Hay River, N.W.T., a key northern port and railhead, a secondary highway turns east along Great Slave Lake to Wood Buffalo National Park. The world's largest national park—only slightly smaller than Nova Scotia—was established in 1922 to protect North America's last herd of wood bison. Four migratory flyways overlap in the park and there is an abundance of birdlife. Some 100 whooping cranes—more than half the world population of that rare bird—nest in Wood Buffalo National Park each summer.

The plains near the Slave River are crisscrossed by saline streams. Evaporation has formed salt mounds up to 20 metres across and a metre high. Throughout the park are huge sinkholes where runoff has eroded underlying soft rock. One sinkhole measures 36 metres across and 24 metres deep. Dominating the landscape is the vast expanse of the Peace-Athabasca Delta.

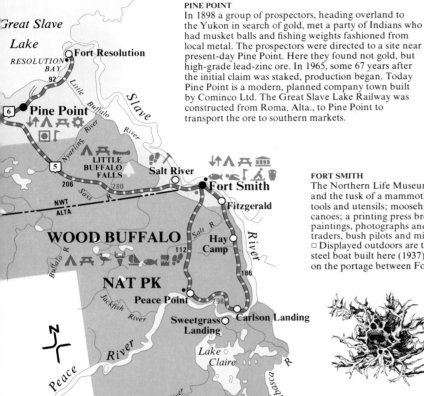

PINE POINT
In 1898 a group of prospectors, heading overland to the Yukon in search of gold, met a party of Indians who had musket balls and fishing weights fashioned from local metal. The prospectors were directed to a site near present-day Pine Point. Here they found not gold, but high-grade lead-zinc ore. In 1965, some 67 years after the initial claim was staked, production began. Today Pine Point is a modern, planned company town built by Cominco Ltd. The Great Slave Lake Railway was constructed from Roma, Alta., to Pine Point to transport the ore to southern markets.

FITZGERALD
Riverboats on the Mackenzie River had a clear, 2,440-kilometre run to the Beaufort Sea except for rapids on the Slave River—the most formidable named the Rapids of the Drowned—which extends 22 kilometres from Fitzgerald, Alta., to Fort Smith, N.W.T. At Fitzgerald the freight for the north country was unloaded from the Athabasca-Slave River barges and hauled, originally by ox- and horse-drawn wagons, later by truck and tractor, to Fort Smith. There it was reloaded onto a second fleet of barges bound for Aklavik on the Mackenzie Delta.

FORT SMITH
The Northern Life Museum displays dinosaur bones and the tusk of a mammoth; early Indian and Eskimo tools and utensils; moosehide and spruce-bark canoes; a printing press brought north in 1873, and paintings, photographs and mementos of trappers, traders, bush pilots and missionaries.
□ Displayed outdoors are the *Radium King*, the first steel boat built here (1937), and an old tractor used on the portage between Fort Smith and Fitzgerald.

Closed gentian

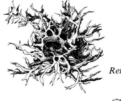

Reindeer moss

Salt plains, Wood Buffalo National Park

Wood bison

Sink hole, Wood Buffalo National Park

WOOD BUFFALO NATIONAL PARK
The park, which straddles the Alberta–N.W.T. border, was established in 1922 to protect the last remaining herd of 1,500 wood bison in North America. Some 6,000 plains bison were later shipped from Wainwright, Alta., and the combined herd now numbers about 12,000.
□ More than a million ducks and geese populate the Peace-Athabasca Delta in summer. Other wildlife in the park includes caribou, moose, bear, fox, and mink.
□ Prairie grasses and wildflowers carpet Wood Buffalo's plains. Shooting stars, closed gentians, asters and bluebells are found in the lush valleys of the Peace and Slave rivers.

Modernity in the 'Land of the Midnight Sun'

Northwest Territories

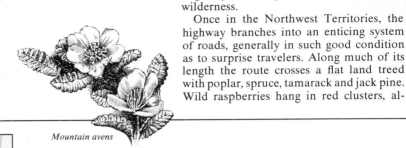

Winding through lush forests, past duck-filled sloughs and lakes, and alongside swift rivers, the Mackenzie Highway is a delight to the visitor craving wilderness.

Once in the Northwest Territories, the highway branches into an enticing system of roads, generally in such good condition as to surprise travelers. Along much of its length the route crosses a flat land treed with poplar, spruce, tamarack and jack pine. Wild raspberries hang in red clusters, al-

Mountain avens

Kildeer

FORT SIMPSON

The great Liard River fights for survival here after joining the mightier Mackenzie. Downstream from the confluence the Mackenzie River is often dark and laden with debris that the Liard has carried from the mountains of the Yukon and British Columbia. Gradually the Mackenzie swallows all trace of the tributary.
□ Fort Simpson is on an island with a commanding view of Gros Cap, a 67-metre-high promontory where the rivers meet. The first fort here was the North West Company's Fort of the Forks (1804). The post was renamed by the Hudson's Bay Company in 1821 for George (later Sir George) Simpson, a HBC governor.
□ The South Nahanni River plunges over 88-metre Virginia Falls and crashes through three immense canyons in Nahanni National Park. The park, accessible by plane from Fort Simpson, preserves a vast riverine wilderness once visited only by a few Indians, trappers and prospectors.

FORT PROVIDENCE

In 1860, when beaver and marten dwindled, this trapping community was moved from Yellowknife Bay to its present site along the Mackenzie River.
□ The National and Historic Sites Service searched for three months for a suitable monument to Alexander Mackenzie, and found it in the bed of the Mackenzie River: a 25-tonne boulder two metres high.

Mackenzie River

Beads, Quills and Tufted Moose Hair

Most Inuit and northern Indians once hunted, fished or trapped for a living—and often went hungry. Today many are self-employed in thriving co-ops, producing traditional crafts for sale in other parts of Canada.

Handmade parkas, gloves, mittens and mukluks are prized for their warmth and decoration. Skilled seamstresses embroider garments in bright cottons; some sew on beads (*right*) or dyed porcupine quills. Footwear made by Fort Providence Indians is ornamented with intricate designs in tufted moose hair.

As the demand for northern prints and soapstone carvings has increased, many co-ops have stepped up production. Their crafts—far more than souvenirs of the North—are now a recognized art form.

MACKENZIE RIVER

Spanning three time zones and draining one-fifth of Canada, the Mackenzie and its tributaries rank as one of the world's largest river systems.

The Mackenzie rises in the British Columbia Rockies 4,200 kilometres from its outlet at the Beaufort Sea. One by one the Parsnip, Peace, Athabasca and Slave pour into the system. In the northwest corner of Great Slave Lake, the Mackenzie proper begins. From here, fed by innumerable streams, the Mackenzie snakes northward to the Arctic Ocean.

Canada lynx

most as thick as the persistent clouds of mosquitoes and black flies. Trophy-size walleye, northern pike and Arctic grayling ply roadside lakes, rivers and streams.

During July and August, when the daytime temperatures are pleasantly mild, the southern part of the Northwest Territories receives 20 hours of sunshine. Throughout the short summer this "Land of the Midnight Sun" bustles with activity. The Mackenzie River and Great Slave Lake are busy with supply barges bound for remote settlements and oil camps. Adventurous visitors sail these waters in canoes and motorboats.

Like the varied scenery, the former fur-trade posts linked by the Mackenzie Highway take southerners by surprise. Most visitors to Yellowknife, the capital of the Northwest Territories, expect a primitive mining town. (Yellowknife owes its existence to a 1934 gold strike.) What they are not prepared for is the modernity of this northern city, with its high-rise buildings and its vital way of life.

Drying arctic char, Rae

RAE

The original Fort Rae, built in 1852 and named after explorer Dr. John Rae, was a seasonal hunting and fishing camp of the Dogrib Indians. In 1902-06 the camp became a permanent settlement; the twin community of Edzo was founded in 1965.

Today the towns are a blend of traditional and modern life-styles. Older women still dry and smoke fish, tan moose hides, scrape caribou skins and do decorative handiwork. Men continue to run traplines, hunt and fish.

Eskimo dogs

Last of the Hardy Husky?

At one time every northern household owned at least half a dozen sled and work dogs. The four common breeds are the Eskimo, Malamute, Samoyed and Siberian husky. These sturdy, hardy dogs are referred to as "huskies" by southerners.

Northern dogs were indispensable. Hunters, forced to travel for days to find caribou, piled sleds with gear and hitched up the dogs in sealskin traces. The teams could reach speeds of 30 kilometres an hour, but averaged a steady trot that covered eight kilometres an hour. Snowmobiles are now replacing the huskies. But there is a disadvantage to this modern form of transport: "You can eat your dog if you're hungry," say the old-timers.

Great Slave Lake

GREAT SLAVE LAKE

This vast lake, the fifth largest in North America (eleventh in the world), is in a transition zone between the boreal forest of the Canadian Shield and the grasses of the Arctic tundra.
□ The Lockhart River drops a total of 200 metres, through rapids and over falls—including 40-metre Parry Falls—in the last 400 kilometres of its descent to the lake.
□ The challenging 480-kilometre Camsell River canoe route winds from Great Slave Lake to Great Bear Lake.

YELLOWKNIFE

Only 500 kilometres south of the Arctic Circle, Yellowknife is the capital of the Northwest Territories and its largest city (pop. 10,000).
□ An annual Caribou Carnival in March features igloo-building, log-sawing, snowshoeing and skiing competitions, and a three-day, 240-kilometre dog sled race on Great Slave Lake.
□ During the Country Fair North of Sixty in September, judges rate flowers and vegetables grown during the long hours of summer daylight.
□ Ravens with a propensity for collecting golf balls from sand "greens" are one of the hazards of the Midnight Golf Tournament, held each June.
□ The Ingraham Trail is a scenic secondary road leading into the bush east of Yellowknife.

Yellowknife

Index

Road unit numbers are given with all references. Numbers in **boldface** signify major references to specific sites and subjects; those in regular typeface indicate incidental references. A number followed by the letter P means a site or subject is pictured in the road unit. A number in *italics* is a map reference.

Picture Credits

The abbreviations used here are these:

AH   Allan Harvey
BD   Barbara K. Deans
BS   Brian Stablyk
DB   Dunkin Bancroft
DW   Daniel Wiener
FP   Freeman Patterson
JdV   John de Visser
MF   Menno Fieguth

NS   Nova Scotia Communications and Informataon Centre
PG   Pierre Gaudard
PK   Peter M. Keane
PM   Patrick Morrow
PvB   Paul von Baich
RV   Richard Vroom

The picture credits are arranged according to the road unit numbers, unless otherwise indicated. Credits are given from left to right, top to bottom, across the two-page unit, with additional information as needed. Four city units—Vancouver (11), Toronto (93), Ottawa (101), and Montreal (108)—have four pages each. In these instances, the first two pages are marked A, and the second two pages, B.

Title page: Bryce Flynn; Hans-L. Blohm; Foreword: © Bedford Ottawa; Road Unit Atlas: BD; Northern Adventure Roads (preceding Map VII in the Road Unit Atlas): PvB. Road Units: 1 Clifford A. Fenner; PvB; 2 Robert Herger; JdV; (top left) Nina Raginski; Bert Hoferichter; Canadian Postal Museum; BK; 3 Clifford A. Fenner; Anna Neilson; AH; 4 MF; PvB (2); 5 British Columbia Government; MF; David Tasker; 6 PvB; Fred Bruemmer; Mildred McPhee; 7 PvB (3); 8 British Columbia Government; Gerry Deiter; J. David Dennings (2); 9 Ted Spiegel; BS; MF; 10 David Clark; Alan Zenuk; 11A Gar Lunney (2); © Joe Munroe/Photo Researchers; 11B AH; (bottom left) Don McPhee; JdV; AH; BS; (top right) AH; 12 Robert Herger; Image Finders/Bill Collins; JdV; 13 Henry Kalen; Valerie J. May; Don McPhee; 14 PvB; Jim Babchuk; BS; 15 Image Finders/Fred Chapman; Nancy Anderson; Alan Zenuk; 16 BS; MF; Dennis Schmidt; 17 Clifford A. Fenner; Creston Valley Wildlife Centre; 18 Valerie J. May; PvB; Nancy Anderson; 19 British Columbia Government; PvB; British Columbia Government; JdV; British Columbia Government/photo by Ross, Best and Co.; PvB (2); 21 Parks Canada; John G. Woods; 22 Valerie J. May; (top) Parks Canada; Tom W. Hall; 23 UBC Museum of Anthropology. From Indian Masterpieces (The Walter and Marianne Koerner Collection) published by UBC Press, 1975; Neil G. Carey; PM; AH; 24 PvB; Richard Wright; 25 British Columbia Government; BS (2); 26 British Columbia Government; David Tasker; PvB; 27 PvB; JdV; Vancouver City Archives; 28 PvB; Native Sons of British Columbia, post no. 2; BS; 29 Richard Wright; David Tasker; Jack Fields/Photo Researchers; 30 Gerald Dumont; MF; BD; 31 Egon Bork (2); 32 Hälle Flygare (2); © J. A. Kraulis/The Image Bank of Canada; 33 J. A. Kraulis; Peter Tasker; Karvonen Films Ltd.; 34 Peter Tasker (2); Donald R. Gunn; 35 Don Beers; © Paolo Koch/Photo Researchers; Colin Michie; The McMichael (2); (top) Peter Tasker; 36 PM (2); (top) George Hunter; Glenbow-Alberta Institute; © Toby Rankin/The Image Bank of Canada; 37 R. B. Walter Kerber; Anne Soicher; Hazel Hudson; 38 Colin Michie; Nicholas Morant; 39 Donald R. Gunn; Stock Photos Unlimited; Kay McGregor; Prairie Farm Rehabilitation Administration; 40 RV; Mary Hampson; Mary M. Smith; Hälle Flygare; 41 Peter Benison; JdV; 42 Wilbur S. Tripp; Jim Martin (2); 43 Edgar T. Jones; Wilhelm Schmidt; Anne Soicher; 44 George Tingle; 45 © Lowell J. Georgia/Photo Researchers; Anne Soicher; 46 JdV; Reynolds Museum (3); 47 PM; PG; PM; 48 Robert N. Smith; © Paolo Koch/Photo Researchers; 49 PM; 50 BS; Stony Plain Farmers' Market; 51 © Lowell J. Georgia/Photo Researchers (2); Alberta Culture Productions/photo by John Sutton; Alberta Culture, The Provincial Museum of Alberta, Edmonton/photo by John Sutton; © Lowell J. Georgia/Photo Researchers (2); 52 BS; BD; S. R. Cannings; 53 Collection of the Ukrainian Women's Association of Canada; PM (2); 54 Egon Bork; Hans-L. Blohm; 55 Department of Indian and Northern Affairs; PM; 56 Saskatchewan Historic Parks; MF; Bob Hewitt; Saskatchewan Government Photograph; 57 Ken Patterson; Robert Baillargeon (2); courtesy of Cominco Ltd.; Parks Canada, Battleford National Historic Park (2); PvB; Richard Knelsen; MF (2); Saskatchewan Government Photograph; 59 MF; Manitoba Government Travel (2); 60 Gar Lunney; Parks Canada; Richard Knelsen; 61 RCMP; Sheila Naiman Photograph; Ken Patterson; 62 RV; MF (2); 63 Lorne Scott; Bryce Flynn; 64 Ken Patterson; Gordon Knight; MF; 65 Government of Saskatchewan (2); Gar Lunney; 66 MF; RV; 67 Douglas C. Harvey; Freshwater Institute, Fisheries and Environment Canada; Manitoba Government Travel (2); 68 Fred Waines; Manitoba Government Travel; Dr. L. Syms (2); Provincial Archives, Victoria, B.C.; 69 Department of National Defence; Fred Clark; Henry Kalen; Manitoba Government Travel; 70 Jack McKinnon; L. B. Shilson; Henry Kalen, Manitoba Government Travel; 71 Henry Kalen; JdV; Bryce Flynn; Manitoba Government Travel; 72 (top) JdV; Manitoba Government Travel (2); Parks Canada, Lower Fort Garry National Historic Park; 73 Colin Hay; JdV (2); 74 MF (2); 75 Bert Hoferichter; Kryn Taconis/Magnun; JdV; 76 JdV (2); Elaine Edwards; Victor C. Last; 77 Sheila Naiman; Algoma Central Railway; JdV; 78 CH; Parks Canada; 79 Sheila Naiman; © JdV/The Image Bank of Canada; Rudi Christl; 80 George Hunter; Victor C. Last; Wm. Lowry; 81 C.P.S. Film Productions; Victor C. Last; 82 Texasgulf; Richard J. Urysz; Canada Wide; 83 John R. Hunt; J. D. Taylor; Quints Museum, Pinewood Park Motor Inn; Sheila Naiman; 84 Parks Canada; CH; Atomic Energy of Canada Ltd.; 85 Oliver J. Dell; JdV; 86 JdV; Marjorie Dezell; Harvey Medland; 87 Courtesy of the city of London; The Stratford Shakespearean Festival Foundation of Canada/photo by Robert C. Ragsdale; 88 C.P.S. Film Productions; Robert Baillargeon; 89 J. D. Taylor; K. M. Guerreiro, Cambridge Community Services Department; JdV; 90 E. Otto/Miller Services; Tom Bochsler; C. W. Perkins; 91 Ontario Ministry of Industry and Tourism; George F. Long; 92 Photo Librarium; Courtesy of the McMichael Canadian Collection, Kleinberg; 93A RV; Randy Bulmer; Bert Hoferichter; 93B © Bill Brooks/The Image Bank of Canada; AH; © Bill Brooks/Bruce Coleman; JdV; AH; © Farrell Grehan/Photo Researchers; Victor C. Last; 94 Courtesy of the McGill Daily; Courtesy Dr. J. Wendell MacLeod, Bethune Memorial Foundation; Mary Ferguson; 95 JdV; Art Gallery of Ontario, gift of the Canadian Unit of Toronto, 1926; Ontario Ministry of Industry and Tourism; 96 JdV; Peterborough Centennial Museum & Archive; Public Archives of Canada © 20121; Kryn Taconis; BD; William R. Wilkins; 99 Hellmut W. Schade; JdV; Sheila Naiman; 100 R. Tait McKenzie Memorial Museum and Mill of Kintail; Ontario Ministry of Industry and Tourism; 101A Rudi Haas; Harold Clark; AH; 101B AH (4); Ted Maginn; JdV (2); 102 Hans-L. Blohm; Crombie McNeil; Alex Onoszko; 103 C.P.S. Film Productions; Oliver J. Dell; JdV; 104 © Roland Weber/The Image Bank of Canada; JdV; Hans-L. Blohm; 105 Courtesy of the Department of Rare Books and Special Collections, McGill University Libraries/photo by Mike Haimes; Ontario Ministry of Industry and Tourism; RV; Osprey Publishing Ltd.; 106 Peter Benison; PvB; Public Archives of Canada © 4899; 107 DW; Peter Benison; PG; 108A CH; Cadel Ettore; 108B JdV; DB; Bernard Martin/Alpha Diffusion; DW; Cadel Ettore; Commission de transports de la Communauté urbaine de Montréal; Photo Librarium; 109 Michel Bleau; © Impart/The Image Bank of Canada; DW; 110 PG; Cynthia Chalk; 111 Claude Lavigne; Parc Safari Africain, Hemmingford; 112 Serge Laurin; CH; Surveys and Mapping Branch, Department of Energy, Mines and Resources; PvB; 113 Photo Librarium; Mia and Klaus; CH; 114 Pedro Rodrigues (2); 115 Jean Côté; Denis Plain; National Museum of Man, National Museums of Canada; DW; 116 PG; DW; Conseil de Développement de la Chaudière; 117 PG; Pierre Kandalaft; Fred Bruemmer; 118 Robert Tessier; Montreal Municipal Library, Gagnon Collection; 119 Paul Gélinas; Yves Tessier; PG; 120 © Paolo Koch/Photo Researchers; Mia and Klaus; Denise Beha; (bottom right) JdV/The Image Bank of Canada; (top right) DB; 121 Adelaide Leitch; Paul E. Lambert; Pierre Kandalaft; 122 Art Gallery of Ontario, gift of the family of Sir Edmund Walker, 1926; Jules Rochon; Paul E. Lambert; 123 Denise Beha; Photo Librarium; Paul E. Lambert; 124 (bottom left) BD; DB; Photo Librarium; 125 JdV; CH; C.P.S. Film Productions; JdV; 126 Société Zoologique de St-Félicien Inc.; Photo Librarium; 127 Roland Weber; Ivan Boulerice; DB; 128 Sheila Naiman; Fred Bruemmer; PG; 129 CH; JdV; Karl Sommerer; 130 Roland Weber; Karl Sommerer; 131 Fred Bruemmer; Sheila Naiman; JdV; 132 FP; JdV; 133 Misho; L. J. Michaud; (top right) Misho; 134 T. Clifford Hodgson; Malak, Ottawa; The Public Archives of Canada PA-26647; New Brunswick Tourism; 135 New Brunswick Tourism (2); Military Compound Board; 137 JdV; (top) Harold Clark; 138 Théâtre du Rideau Vert; Rod Stears; RV; 139 Wamboldt-Waterfield; Michael Saunders; T. Clifford Hodgson; Charles Steinhacker/Black Star; 140 Doris Mowry; Elmer N. Wilcox; 141 New Brunswick Tourism; JdV; © Bill Brooks/Bruce Coleman; JdV; Rod Stears; 142 FP (2); 143 Robert Baillargeon; Charles Steinhacker/Black Star; 144 Department of Tourism, Parks and Conservation, P.E.I.; RV (2); 145 RV; Jean-Claude Hurni; Department of Tourism, Parks and Conservation, P.E.I.; 146 Canadian Government Office of Tourism; Department of Tourism, Parks and Conservation, P.E.I.; Courtesy Dr. Stuart MacDonald; © JdV/The Image Bank of Canada; 147 CH; Canadian Government Office of Tourism (2); 148 RV (2); 149 Department of Tourism, Parks and Conservation, P.E.I.; Canadian Government Office of Tourism; PK; 150 DW; Tim Randall; PK; JdV; 151 Parks Canada, Kejimukujik National Park; DW; FP; DW; 152 Tim Randall; C.W. Condon; Tim Randall; 153 NS; Tim Randall; Nova Scotia Public Archives; Parks Canada, Grand Pré National Historic Park; 154 John Pohl; PK; 155 NS; Gar Lunney; Charles Steinhacker/Black Star; 156 DW; NS; DW; (top right) Sherman Hines; 157 FP; PK; Dan Guravich; 158 NS; PK; 159 PK (3); 160 Bob Brooks; Tim Randall; NS; 161 NS; Bob Brooks; 162 DB; NS; Jill Baillargeon; 163 DB; Stephen Homer; DB; 164 Mary Primrose; PK; Bob Brooks; Jean-Claude Hurni; 165 Mary Primrose; PK (2); 166 Rick Filler; PK; 167 CH; © Nicholas Devore III/Bruce Coleman; Parks Canada; 168 JdV (2); 169 JdV; Dan Guravich; Confederation Life Collection; 170 © Nicholas Devore III/Bruce Coleman; Conception Bay Museum; Rick Filler; 171 Eric Woolgar; JdV; DW; (centre) CH; Dan Guravich; 172 JdV; Dan Guravich, Robert Baillargeon; 173 NFB Photothèque/photo by C. Bruun; Hans-L. Blohm; Department of Information, Government of the Northwest Territories; Richard Fyfe; 174 PvB; Yukon Archives; Wilfried D. Schurig; Yukon Government; 175 J. D. Taylor; PvB (3); 176 PvB (2); 177 Kenneth H. Seto; Anne Soicher; 178 Charles E. McManis, Las Vegas; Anne Soicher; 179 René Fumoleau; Parks Canada (2); 180 Richard Fyfe; Department of Information, Government of the Northwest Territories; Bryce Flynn; William J. Carpenter/Eskimo Dog Research Foundation. This page: Hans-L. Blohm.

Front cover Ontario Ministry of Industry and Tourism (top); Edward Jones/Miller Services (middle left); Doris Mowry (middle right); Victor C. Last (bottom); Back cover Richard Vroom (top); C.P.S. Film Productions (middle left); Ken Patterson (middle right); C.P.S. Film Productions (bottom).

ILLUSTRATORS: Lea Daniel, Louise Delorme, Jean-Claude Gagnon, André Pierzchala

COLOR ILLUSTRATIONS: Jim Bruce (166), Diane Desrosiers, Anker Odum (41, 94)

DIAGRAMS: Réal Lefebvre (22, 60, 79)

CUTAWAYS: Georges Buctel (10, 30, 32, 91)

Illustration source for 79: Courtesy of The Mining Association of Canada

Illustration sources for 12 and 81: Elaine Sears

A special thanks is expressed to Philippe Faucher, Louise Lafrance, Paulin Paquette, and Serge Tremblay, all of Aero Photo Inc., Quebec City

Color separation: Herzig Somerville Limited
Typesetting: The Graphic Group of Canada Limited
Printing: Montreal Lithographing Limited
Binding: Harpell's Press Co-operative
Binding material: Columbia Finishing Mills Limited
Paper: S.D. Warren (A Division of Scott Paper Company)

Away we go . . .